INTERPRETATION IN IN

Interpretation in International Law

Edited by
ANDREA BIANCHI
DANIEL PEAT
MATTHEW WINDSOR

OXFORD
UNIVERSITY PRESS

OXFORD
UNIVERSITY PRESS

Great Clarendon Street, Oxford, OX2 6DP,
United Kingdom

Oxford University Press is a department of the University of Oxford.
It furthers the University's objective of excellence in research, scholarship,
and education by publishing worldwide. Oxford is a registered trade mark of
Oxford University Press in the UK and in certain other countries

Published in the United States of America by Oxford University Press
198 Madison Avenue, New York, NY 10016, United States of America

British Library Cataloguing in Publication Data
Data available

Library of Congress Cataloging in Publication Data
Data available

ISBN 978–0–19–872574–9 (Hbk.)
ISBN 978–0–19–882871–6 (Pbk.)

Cover image: Detail from 'Horses Running Endlessly' by Gabriel Orozco, 1995.
Courtesy of Gabriel Orozco and Marian Goodman Gallery. © Gabriel Orozco

Foreword

Philip Allott has defined a treaty as a disagreement reduced to writing.[1] But some treaties reflect at least some measure of agreement some of the time, a point Allott himself does not deny. The task of the interpreter is to reflect that agreement in the case envisaged, but often it goes further: to resolve what may not have been agreed in a manner as far as possible consistent with the text and any underlying intent. For it may well not be the case that the disagreement which faces the interpreter was one the drafters envisaged. In such a case there is an irreducible element of originality in the act of interpretation. Always, the interpreter is taking a form of words and applying it to a given situation; sometimes she is doing so alone.

For reasons such as this, interpretation has been a perennial topic in international legal theory and practice. This collection of essays teeters intriguingly between interpretation in the way international lawyers normally think about it and interpretation as everything they think about. Legal scholarship has tended to tackle the issue of interpretation either from an abstract, quasi-philosophical perspective, or by focusing on the Vienna Convention on the Law of Treaties and its application. The attempt is made here to bring these divergent approaches into some better relationship with each other, while examining the VCLT rules and processes of interpretation in international law more generally. In their introductory chapter, Daniel Peat and Matthew Windsor (both advanced doctoral students at Cambridge) helpfully remind us that interpretation in international law is not an island, despite contemporary appeals to disciplinary autonomy.

The book is centred on the metaphor of the game. There are players, rules, and strategies, deployed with the object of victory. Bellicose the metaphor may sound, but it cannot be denied that, at least in the heat of battle, international lawyers think that their interpretations are right, and they play the game by trying to convince others of this. Moreover, the metaphor provides a more-or-less illuminating framework in which to situate the practice and process of interpretation. It helps reveal the contingency of current interpretive practices, and demonstrates a refusal to reify the status quo for its own sake. But I do not take the contributors to this volume to resile from the proposition that interpretation in international law is a game that works most of the time and is worth playing. After all, if there is nothing in interpretation beyond the preferences of the interpreter, then apparent agreement is simply a postponement of disagreement, at best a delegation to unascertained others.

There is much to commend here: the creativity on display, the eclectic range of topics canvassed, the way in which the volume brings together established and emerging scholars from a range of interpretive traditions. This thoughtful

---

[1] Philip Allott, 'The Concept of International Law' (1999) 10 EJIL 31, 43.

collection of essays is a valuable companion for those who face problems of interpretation in international law.

James Crawford
Whewell Professor of International Law
University of Cambridge
December 2014

Preface

The genesis of this collection of essays was a conference on interpretation in international law, which we convened at the Lauterpacht Centre for International Law and the Faculty of Law at the University of Cambridge in August 2013. We were delighted to receive over 200 abstracts from around the world in response to our call for papers, a testament to the enduring importance of the conference theme for international law scholars and practitioners. As the conference took shape, we were drawn towards selecting papers that approached the practice and process of interpretation in a cross-cutting way, rather than those that operated according to the conventional mores of international law as a professional discipline. In choosing keynote speakers and assembling panels, we deliberately strove to foster methodological pluralism, highlighting fresh and innovative approaches to a classical topic.

We sincerely thank the contributors to this volume for their impressive scholarly efforts, as well as the many other speakers at the conference who offered important insights on the conference theme. We are very grateful to the panel chairs, including James Crawford, Sir Michael Wood, Douglas Guilfoyle, John Tasioulas, David Feldman, Kate Miles, Surabhi Ranganathan, and Lorand Bartels. We would not have been able to get the event off the ground without the generous support of our sponsors, including the University of Cambridge Faculty of Law's Researcher Development Fund, Gonville and Caius College, Cambridge University Press, Hart Publishing, Ashgate, and Oxford University Press. Professor Marc Weller and Dr Roger O'Keefe of the Lauterpacht Centre provided generous support and advice, and Tara Grant, Karen Fachechi, Naomi Hart, Odette Murray, and Alexia Solomou ably assisted us on the day of the conference.

We thank the *Cambridge Journal of International and Comparative Law* for publishing a symposium of further papers from the conference in 2014, which offers a variety of practical perspectives on the phenomenon of interpretation in international adjudication. Contributors to this symposium included Judge Sir David Baragwanath, Isabelle Van Damme, Andreas Sennekamp, Shai Dothan, Jure Vidmar, Diane Desierto, and Colin Gillespie.

Although they did not present papers at the conference, we extend a special thanks to Iain Scobbie and Michael Waibel, who prepared commissioned chapters for this volume on rhetoric and interpretive communities respectively under considerable time pressures.

Above all, we thank Andrea Bianchi for agreeing to join us as the co-editor of this volume. Andrea delivered a wonderfully entertaining keynote address on the 'game' of interpretation in international law, characterized by insight and levity, which directly informed the structural framework of this volume. At the outset of our academic careers, our collaboration with Andrea confirms that navigating the legal academy need not always be an exercise in hierarchy. As his prefatory remarks below confirm, this has been a thoroughly enjoyable and genuinely egalitarian working relationship, where we have learnt much from Andrea's creative scholarship and his refreshing willingness to think outside the box.

It has been a pleasure to work with Merel Alstein, Anthony Hinton, and Emma Endean at Oxford University Press, who have demonstrated unwavering enthusiasm for our project. We also thank the four anonymous reviewers for the Press, who offered incisive and illuminating feedback on our book proposal.

Daniel would like to thank, first and foremost, the co-editors, who have been a source of inspiration, reliability, and good humour in equal measure. Although we were warned about commencing such a voyage, the friendships formed—as well as the final product that you hold in your hands—mean that I would embark again upon such a journey without a moment's hesitation. My thanks also goes to all those that have made it possible for me to reach this juncture in my career: the opportunities presented, counsel provided, and trust shown to a young academic will not be forgotten. In particular, thanks must go to Michael Waibel, Pierre-Marie Dupuy, Aaron Cosbey, James Crawford, Gonville and Caius College, and The Graduate Institute Geneva. Finally, it rests for me to thank my parents, Gerald and Yvonne Peat, without whom none of this would have been possible.

Matthew would like to thank his PhD supervisors, David Feldman and James Crawford, for their understanding in indulging this detour during doctoral studies; Gonville and Caius College, for their generous provision of the WM Tapp Studentship in Law; Peta Mitchell, Fleur Johns, and other participants at the Melbourne Doctoral Forum on Legal Theory in December 2013, for inspiring discussions about the game metaphor's power and potential; the participants in the Max Planck Masterclass in International Law with Martti Koskenniemi in Heidelberg in April 2014; his brother, Joshua Windsor, for his philosophical prowess; his parents, John and Christine Windsor, for their constant support and for tolerating recurrent book proposal diversions during a long-awaited holiday in St Petersburg; and Charlotte Leslie, for her boundless love, encouragement, and wisdom.

In Gabriel Orozco's *Horses Running Endlessly* (1995), the sculpture on the cover of this book, the game of chess is reimagined. The board is altered, with four times more squares than usual, in four different colours. Knights alone occupy Orozco's board, the sole piece in chess that is able to move vertically and horizontally in a single turn. Common to Orozco's artistic oeuvre is the 'altered design of traditional forms',[1] revealing a playful approach to rules, an awareness of the cultural contingency of games, and a desire to transform their traditional grammar. An early critic of *Horses Running Endlessly* described the work as a 'machine to produce diversity'.[2] Another observed that the absence of familiar rules invites the viewer to consider

[1] Jessica Morgan, *Gabriel Orozco* (Tate Publishing 2011) 117. Orozco has also reconfigured billiard tables (*Carambole with Pendulum* (1996)), ping pong (*Ping-Pond Table* (1998)), Go (*Go 4 No Borders* (2005)), and cricket (*Atomists* (1996)).
[2] Jean-Pierre Criqui, 'Like a Rolling Stone' (1996) Artforum 88, 91.

'what potential remains for playing this new configuration of "wild horses" and what other goals could be identified'.[3] Orozco himself described his motive to 'disturb or to rearrange readymade games' as a deliberate attempt to 'reorient the perception of space in that particular game'.[4]

Orozco's artistic agenda aptly reflects one of the central themes of this book. We have used the metaphor of the game as a structural framework for interrogating interpretation in international law, a field that is traditionally understood as having fairly well-delineated rules. We sincerely hope that this book will be of interest and utility to all international lawyers whose work touches upon the theoretical or practical aspects of interpretation, and that the insights contained in this collection will stimulate further research on interpretation that does not shy away from methodological innovation and creativity.

MRW and DCP, Cambridge, August 2014

Interpreting means attributing meaning to something. Not just to a text, but more broadly, also to whatever happens in life. To interpret what happened to me since I accepted to embark on this editorial adventure with Dan and Matt is no easy task. The outcome of our cooperation being this book, the answer should be simple and straightforward: I worked together with two colleagues on an edited volume with a view to contributing some fresh insights on interpretation in international law. Yet this answer would not account for the experience. It is the process, rather than the outcome, which has contributed to giving meaning to what I have lived and to what we have done. At least, this is how I interpret it.

The process has consisted of sharing tasks and working smoothly together. We have invariably agreed on all the difficult choices we had to make. More than anything else, we had fun doing this together. We waited for the next Skype conversation as one would wait for talking to friends. We exchanged hundreds of email messages and grew accustomed to our regular communication. In the cacophonic medley of messages pouring daily into the mailbox we were just happy to hear from one another: it always sounded like fine and friendly tunes. If—as rarely as this occurred—one would lag behind on something, the other two would happily make up for it. Nobody ever complained about anything and I trust it was not just a matter of politeness. The spirit of camaraderie and the friendship that has developed over this intense period of working together attests to the opportunity for making the profession and its practices more humane and enjoyable.

The only thing that bothers me is that Dan and Matt think that this is normal. I maintain instead that this remains exceptional in the profession, and I am grateful to both of them for what has been to me an extraordinary intellectual and human experience. As for the book, only the reader will tell whether our efforts were worthwhile.

AB, Geneva, August 2014

---

[3] Morgan, *Gabriel Orozco*, 41.
[4] Morgan, *Gabriel Orozco*, 98.

Contents

Table of Cases   xvii
List of Abbreviations   xxiii
List of Contributors   xxix

I. INTRODUCTION

**1. Playing the Game of Interpretation: On Meaning and
Metaphor in International Law**   3
Daniel Peat and Matthew Windsor

Introduction   3
    I. Interpretation in International Law—The State of Play   4
    II. In Search of Meaning   9
    III. What's in a Game?   16
    IV. The Game Plan   28
Conclusion   33

**2. The Game of Interpretation in International Law: The Players,
the Cards, and Why the Game is Worth the Candle**   34
Andrea Bianchi

    I. The Game   34
    II. The Object   36
    III. The Players   39
    IV. The Cards   43
    V. Strategies   49
    VI. Playing the Game of Game Playing   52
    VII. Why is the Game Worth the Candle?   54
    VIII. Conclusion   57

II. THE OBJECT

3. Rhetoric, Persuasion, and Interpretation in International Law   61
Iain Scobbie

    I. The Art of Rhetoric   61
    II. Rhetoric—Legal Argumentation as an Interpretative
    Mechanism   62
    III. Blame it all on the Ancient Greeks   65

IV. Rediscovering the Past—The Resurgence of Rhetoric in the
Twentieth Century 66
V. The Elements of Effective Rhetoric—Audience, Topics, Choice 68
VI. Rhetoric, Interpretation, and Law 73
VII. The Value of Rhetoric 77

4. **The Existential Function of Interpretation in International Law** 78
Duncan B Hollis

Introduction 78
I. The Expository Function of (Treaty) Interpretation in
International Law 80
II. The Existential Function of Interpretation in International Law 84
III. The Consequences of Interpretation's Existential Function 101
Conclusion 108

5. **The Multidimensional Process of Interpretation:
Content-Determination and Law-Ascertainment Distinguished** 111
Jean d'Aspremont

Introduction 111
I. Committed Interpretation and the Necessary Feeling
of 'Out-There-Ness' 113
II. A Dichotomic View on the Game of Interpretation 116
III. Conclusion: Salvaging the Game of Interpretation? 128

III. THE PLAYERS

6. **Interpretation and the International Legal Profession:
Between Duty and Aspiration** 133
Andraž Zidar

Introduction 133
I. Interpretation of International Law as a Complex Process 134
II. International Legal Professions and the Interpretive Process 135
Conclusion: The Duty and Aspiration of Interpretation 144

7. **Interpretive Communities in International Law** 147
Michael Waibel

Introduction 147
I. The Role of Interpretive Communities in Interpretation 148
II. Diverse Interpretive Communities and Fragmentation 154
III. Interpretive Communities as Advocates of Distinct
Normative Visions of International Law 160
Conclusion 164

8. **Interpretative Authority and the International Judiciary**   166
   Gleider Hernández

   Introduction   166
   I.   Interpretative Theory   168
   II. The Fallacy in the Interpretation and Application
        Distinction   175
   Conclusion: Judicial Interpretation and the Claim to
        Normative Authority   181

IV. THE RULES

9. **The Vienna Rules, Evolutionary Interpretation, and the
   Intentions of the Parties**   189
   Eirik Bjorge

   Introduction   189
   I.   Vienna Rules and the Search for Intention   192
   II. A Re-reading of the Vienna Rules   198
   Conclusion   203

10. **Accounting for Difference in Treaty Interpretation Over Time**   205
    Julian Arato

    Introduction   205
    I.   Old and New Explanations of Difference   209
    II. The Nature of the Obligation   217
    Conclusion   226

11. **Interpreting Transplanted Treaty Rules**   229
    Anne-Marie Carstens

    Introduction   229
    I.   An Overview of Transplanted Treaty Rules   231
    II. The Framework for Interpreting Transplanted Treaty Rules   235
    Conclusion   247

V. THE STRATEGIES

12. **A Genealogy of Textualism in Treaty Interpretation**   251
    Fuad Zarbiyev

    Introduction: Taking Historicity Seriously   251
    I.   Textualism: The Dominant Interpretive Paradigm in Modern
         International Law   255
    II. The Official Victory of Textualism: Situating a Success Story   257
    Conclusion   266

13. **Theorizing Precedent in International Law**   268
Harlan Grant Cohen

Introduction   268
   I. Precedent's Purpose   271
  II. Precedent as Practice   275
 III. Telling Precedent's Story   281
Conclusion   288

14. **Interpretation in International Law as a Transcultural Project**   290
René Provost

Introduction   290
   I. Interpretation in International Law   292
  II. The Transcultural Nature of Interpretation in International Law   303
Conclusion   308

VI. PLAYING THE GAME OF GAME-PLAYING

15. **Towards a Politics of Hermeneutics**   311
Jens Olesen

Introduction   311
   I. Against a Politics of Interpretation   313
  II. Nietzsche and the Interpretive 'Will to Power'   315
 III. Enter Language Conventions   322
Conclusion: On Decoding Ideology   327

16. **Cognitive Frames of Interpretation in International Law**   331
Martin Wählisch

Introduction   331
   I. Cognitive Frame Theory and the Sociology of Law   332
  II. Case Studies and Examples   339
Conclusion   347

17. **Is Interpretation in International Law a Game?**   352
Ingo Venzke

Introduction   352
   I. Like a Game of Chess   354
  II. The Grammar of the Game   356
 III. The Nature of the Game Reconsidered   359
 IV. International Law as a Practice   365
  V. And if There Was No Language to Play With?   367

VII. CONCLUSION

18. Interpretation—An Exact Art 373
Philip Allott

Introduction 373
  I. What is Interpretation? 373
 II. The Illusion of Meaning 375
III. Legal Interpretation 376
IV. The Moments of Interpretation 380
 V. Deontology of Interpretation 382
Summary 392

Index 393

Table of Cases

I. INTERNATIONAL TRIBUNALS

European Court of Human Rights

Al-Adsani v United Kingdom (2002) 34 EHRR 273.....................................46
Al-Jedda v United Kingdom (2011) 53 EHRR 23.......................................50
Behrami v France & Saramati v France, Germany and Norway (2007) 45 EHRR 10..........50
Demir & Baykara v Turkey (2009) 48 EHRR 54.......................................223
Golder v United Kingdom (1975) 1 EHRR 524 46
Goodwin v United Kingdom (2002) 35 EHRR 18 .... 50, 51, 137, 251
Loizidou v Turkey (Preliminary Objections) (1995) 20 EHRR 99....................206, 224
Mamatkulov and Askarov v Turkey (2005) 41 EHRR 494...............................45
National Union of Belgian Police v Belgium (1979–80) 1 EHRR 578 198
Soering v UK (1989) 11 EHRR 439..205, 210
Tyrer v United Kingdom (1978) 2 EHRR 1 50

European Court of Justice

Joined Cases G402/05 P and C-415/05 P, *Kadi and Al Barakaat International Foundation
   v Council and Commission* (2009) 46 CMLR 213 97
Case C-584/10 P, *European Commission and Others v Kadi*, Judgment of 18 July 2013 50

ICSID, NAFTA and other arbitral tribunals

ADF Group Inc v USA (NAFTA Ch 11 Arbitration Tribunal, 9 Jan 2003)
   (2003) 18 ICSID Rev 195 90
Affaire de l' ile de Timor (Pays-Bas c Portugal) (1914) 11 RIAA 481.....................195
*Aguas Argentinas, SA, Suez, Sociedad General de Aguas de Barcelona SA and Vivendi
   Universal SA v Argentine Republic*, ICSID Case No ARB/03/19, Order in response
   to a petition for transparency and participation as amicus curiae, 19 May 2005.........139
Aguas del Tunari SA v Bolivia, ICSID Case No ARB/02/3, Decision on Jurisdiction,
   21 October 2005 253
Air Service Agreement of 27 March 1946 between the United States of America and France
   (1978) 18 RIAA 417...260
Award in the Arbitration regarding the Iron Rhine ('Ijzeren Rijn') (Belgium v Netherlands)
   (2005) 27 RIAA 35 .... 190, 214–15, 252
*Case Concerning a Dispute between Argentina and Chile concerning the Beagle
   Channel* (1977) 21 RIAA 53 252
Case concerning the Audit of Accounts *between the Netherlands and France in application of
   the Protocol of 25 September 1991 Additional to the Convention for the Protection of the
   Rhine from Pollution by Chlorides of 3 December 1976 (France/The Netherlands)*
   (2004) 25 RIAA 267 ....199, 202
*Case Concerning the Delimitation of the Maritime Boundary between Guinea-Bissau
   and Senegal (Guinea-Bissau v Senegal)* (1989) 10 RIAA 119....................190, 252
Case concerning the re-evaluation of the German Mark (1980) 19 RIAA 67 ....253, 257
Decision regarding delimitation of the border between Eritrea and Ethiopia
   (2002) 25 RIAA 83 ....195, 202, 225, 226
*Dispute concerning Filleting within the Gulf of St Lawrence ('La Bretagne') (Canada/
   France)* (1986) 82 ILR 591..190, 202
*First Award under the Convention between Costa Rica and Nicaragua of 8 April 1896 for
   the Demarcation of the Boundary between the two Republics* (1897) 28 RIAA 215 252

Int'l Thunderbird Gaming Corp v United Mexican States (Final Award) (26 January 2006)
    2006 WL 247692. 269
*Interpretation of the Air Transport Services Agreement between the United States of America
    and France* (1963) 38 ILR 182 195
Island of Palmas Case (Netherlands v USA) (1928) 2 RIAA 845. 210
Lake Lanoux Arbitration (1957) 12 RIAA 28 . . . . .260, 261
*Methanex v United States, Decision of the NAFTA Tribunal on Petitions of Third
    Persons to Intervene as Amici Curiae* (NAFTA Ch 11 Arbitration Tribunal,
    15 January 2001) 139
*Partial Award on the Lawfulness of the Recall of the Privately Held Shares on 8 January 2001
    and the Applicable Standards for Valuation of Those Shares* (2002) 23 RIAA 183 252
Pope & Talbot Inc v Canada, Damages (NAFTA Ch 11 Arbitration Tribunal,
    31 May 2002) [2002] 41 ILM 1347. 90
RosInvest Co v Russian Federation (SCC Case No V 079/2005) Award on Jurisdiction
    (October 2007) 206, 208, 211, 224, 225
RSM Production Corporation v Grenada, ICSID Case No ARB/05/14, Award,
    13 March 2009 257
Société Générale de Surveillance SA v Islamic Republic of Pakistan, ICSID Case No
    ARB/01/13, Decision on Jurisdiction, 6 August 2003 (2003) 18 ICSID Rev 301. 96
Société Générale de Surveillance SA v Republic of the Philippines, ICSID Case No
    ARB/02/6, Decision on Jurisdiction, 29 January 2004 (2004) 8 ICSID Rev 515. 96
Teinver SA Transportes de Cercanias SA Autobuses Urbanos del Sur SA v Argentine Republic
    (Decision on Jurisdiction and Separate Opinion of Arbitrator Kamal Hossain), ICSID
    Case No ARB/09/1 270
Territorial Sovereignty and Scope of the Dispute (Eritrea/Yemen)
    (1998) 22 RIAA 209 . . . . .206, 210
*Texaco Overseas Petroleum Company (TOPCO)/California Asiatic Oil Company (CAOC) and
    the Government of the Libyan Arab Republic, Award on the Merits* [1978] 17 ILM 1. 92
*USA-UK Arbitration concerning Heathrow Airport User Charges (US-UK): Award on the
    First Question* (revised 18 June 1993) 24 RIAA 3. 96

Inter-American Court of Human Rights

*Effect of Reservations on the Entry into Force of the American Convention on Human Rights
    (Arts 74 and 75)*, Advisory Opinion OC-2/82, Inter-American Court of Human
    Rights Series A No 2 (24 September 1982) 206, 208, 224
*The Right to Information on Consular Assistance in the Framework of the Guarantees of the
    Due Process of Law*, Advisory Opinion OC-16/99, Inter-American Court of Human
    Rights Series A No 16 (1 October 1999) 206, 209, 210, 211, 224

International Court of Justice

*Accordance with International Law of the Unilateral Declaration of Independence in Respect
    of Kosovo* (Advisory Opinion) [2010] ICJ Rep 403. 108
Admission of a State to the United Nations (Advisory Opinion) [1947-48] ICJ Rep 57. . . . .263, 301
Aegean Sea Continental Shelf (Greece v Turkey) [1978] ICJ Rep 3. . . . . 97, 190, 193, 251
Ahmadou Sadio Diallo (Republic of Guinea v Democratic Republic of the Congo)
    (Judgment on Compensation) [2012] ICJ Rep 391 148
Anglo-Iranian Oil Co (UK v Iran) (Judgment) [1952] ICJ Rep 93. 261
*Application of the Convention on the Prevention and Punishment of the Crime of Genocide
    (Bosnia and Herzegovina v Serbia and Montenegro)*, Judgment
    [2007] ICJ Rep 43 . . . . .49, 276
*Application of the Convention on the Prevention and Punishment of the Crime of Genocide
    (Bosnia and Herzegovina v Serbia and Montenegro)* (Order of 13 September 1993)
    [1993] ICJ Rep 407 293

*Application of the International Convention on the Elimination of All Forms of Racial
Discrimination (Georgia v Russian Federation)* (Preliminary Objections)
[2011] ICJ Rep 70 173
Arbitral Award of 31 July 1989 (Guinea Bissau v Senegal) (Judgment) [1991] ICJ Rep 70 235
*Case concerning application of the Convention on the Prevention and Punishment of the
Crime of Genocide (Bosnia and Herzegovina v Serbia and Montenegro)* (Judgment)
[1997] ICJ Rep 43 . . . . .95, 254
*Case concerning Armed Activities on the Territory of the Congo (Democratic Republic of the
Congo v Uganda)* (Judgment) [2005] ICJ Rep 168 287
Case concerning East Timor (Portugal v Australia) (Judgment) [1995] ICJ Rep 90 261
Case concerning Elettronica Sicula S.p.A. (ELSI) (USA v Italy) (Judgment) [1989] ICJ Rep 15 96
Case concerning the Frontier Dispute (Burkina Faso v Republic of Mali) (Judgment)
[1986] ICJ Rep 554 98
Case concerning the Gabčíkovo-Nagymaros Project (Hungary/Slovakia) (Judgment)
[1997] ICJ Rep 7 . . . . .94, 190, 193, 206
Case concerning Kasikili/Sedudu Island (Botswana/Namibia) (Judgment)
[1999] ICJ Rep 1045 . . . . .252, 253, 257
Case Concerning Legality of Use of Force (Serbia and Montenegro v UK) [2004] ICJ Rep 1307 88
*Case concerning Military and Paramilitary Activities in and against Nicaragua (Nicaragua
v USA)* (Merits, Judgment) [1986] ICJ Rep 14 . . . . .95, 287
*Case concerning Military and Paramilitary Activities in and against Nicaragua (Nicaragua
v USA)* (Jurisdiction and Admissibility) [1984] ICJ Rep 392 .88, 103
*Case Concerning the Arrest Warrant of 11 April 2000 (Democratic Republic of Congo
v Belgium)* (Judgment) [2002] ICJ Rep 3 285
Case concerning the Right of Passage over Indian Territories (Portugal v India) (Judgment)
[1960] ICJ Rep 6 96
Case Concerning the Temple of Preah Vihear (Cambodia v Thailand) [1962] ICJ Rep 6 212
Competence of the General Assembly regarding Admission to the United Nations (Advisory
Opinion) [1950] ICJ Rep 4 . . . . .237, 263
Case of Certain Norwegian Loans (France v Norway) [1957] ICJ Rep 9 . . . . .88, 93, 103, 195
*Constitution of the Maritime Safety Committee of the Inter-Governmental Maritime
Consultative Organization* (Advisory Opinion) [1960] ICJ Rep 150 242
Continental Shelf (Libya/Malta) [1985] ICJ Rep 13 . . . . .193, 261
Corfu Channel (UK v Albania) (Judgment) [1948] ICJ Rep 15 261
Delimitation of the Maritime Boundary in the Gulf of Maine Area (Canada/USA)
(Judgment) [1984] ICJ Rep 246 261
Frontier Dispute (Burkina Faso/Mali) [1986] ICJ Rep 554 193
Interpretation of the Agreement of 25 March 1951 between the WHO and Egypt
(Advisory Opinion) [1980] ICJ Rep 73 . . . . 230, 240–3, 245–7
Jurisdictional Immunities of the State (Germany v Italy; Greece Intervening) (Judgment)
[2012] ICJ Rep 99 . . . . .37, 38, 51, 92, 277
LaGrand Case (Germany v USA) [2001] ICJ Rep 466 . . . . .44, 105
*Land and Maritime Boundary between Cameroon and Nigeria (Cameroon v Nigeria:
Equatorial Guinea intervening)* (Judgment) [2002] ICJ Rep 303 .190
*Land, Island and Maritime Frontier Dispute (El Salvador/Honduras, Nicaragua
intervening)* (Judgment) [1990] ICJ Rep 92 261
Legal Consequences of the Construction of a Wall in the Occupied Palestinian Territories
(Advisory Opinion) [2004] ICJ Reports 136 . . . . .51, 287, 340, 341, 342
*Legal Consequences for States of the Continued Presence of South Africa in Namibia
(South West Africa) Notwithstanding Security Council Resolution 276 (1970)*
(Advisory Opinion) [1971] ICJ Rep 16 . . . . .163, 190, 193, 195, 209–10, 253
Legality of the Threat or Use of Nuclear Weapons (Advisory Opinion)
[1996] ICJ Rep 226 . . . . .51, 83, 95, 100, 140, 295

Maritime Delimitation and Territorial Questions (Qatar v Bahrain)
(Judgment) [1995] ICJ Rep 6...93
Maritime Delimitation and Territorial Questions (Qatar v Bahrain)
(Jurisdiction and Admissibility) [1994] ICJ Rep 112.....................88, 92, 96, 255
Monetary Gold Removed from Rome in 1943 (Italy v France, UK, USA) (Judgment)
[1954] ICJ Rep 19 261
Navigational and Related Rights (Costa Rica v Nicaragua) (Judgment)
[2009] ICJ Rep 213 ....190, 191, 192, 193, 195, 201, 210, 251
North Sea Continental Shelf Cases (FRG v Den) [1969] ICJ Rep 3 ....92, 94
Nuclear Tests (Australia/New Zealand v France) [1974] ICJ Rep 267 98
Oil Platforms (Iran v United States) (Merits) [2003] ICJ Rep 161 .... 235–6, 238, 257
Pulp Mills on the River Uruguay (Argentina v Uruguay) (Judgment)
[2010] ICJ Rep 14 ....190, 206, 210
Reparations for Injuries Suffered in the Service of the United Nations (Advisory Opinion)
[1949] ICJ Rep 174...94, 296
Reservations to the Convention on Genocide (Advisory Opinion) [1951] ICJ Rep 15...........195
South West Africa (Liberia v South Africa) (Second Phase) [1966] ICJ Rep 294, ...210
Territorial Dispute (Libya/Chad) [1994] ICJ Rep 6 ....212, 235, 252, 257

International Criminal Court
Prosecutor v Thomas Lubanga Dyilo ICC-01/04-01/06 (14 March 2012)....................88

International Criminal Tribunal for Rwanda (ICTR)
Prosecutor v Kayishema and Ruzindana (Judgment) ICTR-95-I-T (21 May
1999) 298

International Criminal Tribunal on Former Yugoslavia (ICTY)
Prosecutor v Aleksovski, (Appeal Judgment) IT-95-14/1-A (24 March 2000) 49, 50
Prosecutor v Dusko Tadić aka 'Dule' (Appeal Judgment) IT-94-1-A (15 July 1999) 95, 175
Prosecutor v Dusko Tadić aka 'Dule' (Sentencing Judgment) IT-94-1-A (11 November 1999) ...270
Prosecutor v Dusko Tadić aka 'Dule' (Decision on the Defence Motion on Jurisdiction)
IT-94-1-T (10 August 1995)..87–8
Prosecutor v Dusko Tadić aka 'Dule' (Decision on the Motion for Interlocutory Appeal on
Jurisdiction) IT-94-1-A (2 October 1995) 268, 301
Prosecutor v Erdemović ('Pilica Farm') IT-96-22-A (7 October 1997) 96
Prosecutor v Kupreškić et al (Judgment) IT-95-16-T (14 January 2000)...........206, 208, 210
Prosecutor v Simić (Decision on the Prosecution Motion under Rule 73 for a Ruling
Concerning the Testimony of a Witness) IT-95-9 (27 July 1999) 296
Prosecutor v Stanislav Galić (Judgment) ICTY-98-29-A (30 November 2006) 257

International Tribunal for the Law of the Sea
The M/V 'Louisa' Case (Saint Vincent and the Grenadines v Kingdom of Spain) (No 18)
(28 May 2013) 88

Iran-US Claims Tribunal
Esphahanian v Bank Tejarat (1983) 2 Iran-US CTR 157 45
*Interlocutory Award in Case Concerning SEDCO, Inc v National Iranian Oil Company
and the Islamic Republic of Iran* (1986) 10 Iran-US CTR 180 91
Iran v United States (Case No A/18) (1984) 5 Iran-US CTR 251 252

Miscellaneous
United States v Max Schmid, US General Military Court at Dachau, Case no 82,
19 May 1947 294

Permanent Court of International Justice

Access to German Minority Schools in Upper Silesia (Advisory Opinion) PCIJ Rep Series
 A/B No 40 254
Case of the SS Lotus (France v Turkey) (Judgment) PCIJ Rep Series A No 10. . . . . .261, 263
Case of the SS 'Wimbledon' PCIJ Rep Series A No 1. . . . . .195, 237
Certain German Interests in Polish Upper Silesia (Merits) PCIJ Rep Series A No 7 262
Delimitation of the Polish-Czechoslovakian Frontier (Question of Jaworzina) (Advisory
 Opinion) PCIJ Rep Series B No 8 174
Interpretation of the Treaty of Lausanne, Article 3, Paragraph 2
 PCIJ Rep Series B No 12 190
*Interpretation of the Convention of 1919 Concerning Employment of Women During the
 Night* PCIJ Rep Series A/B No 50 213
Lighthouses Case between France and Greece PCIJ Rep Series A/B No 62 195
Mavrommatis Jerusalem Concessions (Greece v UK) (Judgment) PCIJ Rep Series A 176
Rights of Minorities in Upper Silesia (Minority Schools) (Germany v Poland) (Judgment)
 PCIJ Rep Series A No 15 261
Status of Eastern Carelia (Advisory Opinion) PCIJ Rep Series B No 5 261

Special Court for Sierra Leone

Prosecutor v Brima, Kamara, Kanu (AFRC Trial) (Judgment) SCSL-04-16-T (20 June 2007) . . .303
Prosecutor v Charles Ghankay Taylor SCSL-03-1-T (27 October 2008). 290
Prosecutor v Moinina Fofana and Allieu Kondewa SCSL-04-14-T (25 February 2005) 290

United Nations Human Rights Committee

Kindler v Canada (1993) UN Doc CCPR/C/48/D/470/1991 276

WTO Panels and Appellate Body

Brazil: Measures Affecting Desiccated Coconut—Report of the Appellate Body (21 February
 1997) WT/DS22/AB/R 88
China: Audiovisual Entertainment Products—Report of the Appellate Body (21 December
 2009) WT/DS363/AB/R 195
*European Communities: Customs Classification of Certain Computer Equipment—Report of
 the Appellate Body* (5 June 1998) WT/DS62/AB/R, WT/DS67/AB/R, WT/DS68/
 AB/R 256
*European Communities: Measures Affecting the Approval and Marketing of Biotech Products –
 Panel Report* (29 September 2006) WT/DS291-293/R 45, 236, 238, 239, 253
*European Communities and Certain Member States: Measures Affecting Trade in Large
 Civil Aircraft—Report of the Appellate Body* (18 May 2011) WT/DS316/AB/R 238, 240
*European Communities: Measures Concerning Meat and Meat Products—Report of the
 Appellate Body* (13 February 1998) WT/DS48/AB/R. 95
*European Communities: Regime for the Importation, Sale and Distribution of Bananas—Second
 Recourse to Article 21,5 of the OSV by Ecuador and First Recourse by USA—Report of the
 Appellate Body* ('EC—Bananas III') (26 November 2008) WT/DS27/AB/RW2/ECU
 and WT/DS27/AB/RW/USA. 93
Japan: Alcoholic Beverages—Report of the Appellate Body (4 October 1996) WT/DS8/AB/R
 and WT/DS10/AB/R, WT/DS11/AB/R 283
Mexico: Tax Measures on Soft Drinks—Report of the Appellate Body (6 March 2006)
 WT/DS308/AB/R 88
*United States: Definitive Anti-Dumping and Countervailing Duties on Certain Products from
 China—Report of the Appellate Body* (11 March 2011) WT/DS379/AB/R. 238
*United States: Final Anti-Dumping Measures on Stainless Steel From Mexico—Report of the Appellate
 Body* (30 April 2008) WT/DS344/AB/R. 49, 50
United States: Import Prohibition of Certain Shrimp and Shrimp Products—Panel Report
 WT/DS58/R (6 November 1998) modified by Appellate Body Report,
 WT/DS58/AB/R 163, 206, 213–14, 257

II. MUNICIPAL COURTS

Canada

Re Secession of Quebec [1996] 161 DLR (4th) 385 170

Israel

The Public Committee against Torture in Israel v The Government of Israel (14 December 2006)
 HCJ 769/02 277

Italy

Ferrini v Federal Republic of Germany, Decision No 5044/2004, 128 ILR 658. 175

United Kingdom

Investors Compensation Scheme Ltd v West Bromwich Building Society [1998] 1 WLR 896
 (HL). 258
Jones v Ministry of Interior Al-Mamlaka Al-Arabiya As Saudiya (Kingdom of Saudi Arabia)
 [2007] 1 AC 270 51
Liversidge v Anderson [1941] UKHL 1 374
Pratt v Attorney General for Jamaica [1994] 2 AC 1 276
R v Bow Street Metropolitan Stipendiary Magistrate, ex parte Pinochet Ugarte (No 3)
 [2000] 1 AC 147 . . . . .170, 175

United States

Bustillo v Johnson [2006] 271823 WL 30 269
Comfort Women case, *Hwang Geum Joo v Japan* 413 F 3d 45, 51–52 (DC Cir 2006) 89
Filartiga v Peña Irala, 630 F 2d 876 (2nd Cir, 1980). 98
Habyarimana v Kagame, 2012 WL 1572460 (10th Cir 30 April 2012) .286
Hamdan v Rumsfeld 548 US 557 (2006) 157
NML Capital Ltd v Republic of Argentina, Nos 08 Civ. 6978 (TPG), 09 Civ. 1707 (TPG),
 09 Civ. 1708 (TPG) (SDNY 11 November 2012), affirmed *Republic of Argentina v*
 NML Capital Ltd, 695 F 3d 201, *Republic of Argentina v NML Capital Ltd*,
 134 S Ct 2250 (2014). 154
Presbyterian Church of Sudan v Talisman Energy Inc 244 F Supp 2d 289 (SDNY 2003). 298
Presbyterian Church of Sudan v Talisman Energy Inc 582 F 3d 244 (2d Cir 2009) 270, 298
Sarei v Rio Tinto PLC 671 F 3d 736 (9th Cir 2011). 270
Saudi Arabia v Nelson 507 US 349 (1993). 51
Sosa v Alvarez-Machain 542 US 692 (2004) 98
The Paquette Habana 175 US 677 (1900) 9
Yousuf v Samantar, 2011 WL 5040507 (4th Cir 24 October 2011) (No 11-1479). 286

List of Abbreviations

AC	Appeal Cases
AJIL	American Journal of International Law
Alta L Rev	Alta Law Review
Am J Comp L	American Journal of Comparative Law
Am Soc'y Int'l L Proc	American Society of International Law Proceedings
Am U Int'l L Rev	American University International Law Review
Ann Rev L & Soc Sci	Annual Review of Law and Social Science
ARIEL	A Review of International English Literature
ASIL	American Society of International Law
Aust J Int'l Aff	Australian Journal of International Affairs
Aust YBIL	Australian Yearbook of International Law
B J Pol S	British Journal of Political Science
Berk J Int'l L	Berkeley Journal of International Law
BIT	Bilateral Investment Treaty
BJ Middle East Stud	British Journal of Middle East Studies
BUL Rev	Boston University Law Review
BYBIL	British Yearbook of International Law
Cal L Rev	California Law Review
Cal W L Rev	California Western Law Review
Cam Rev Int'l Aff	Cambridge Review of International Affairs
Cardozo L Rev	Cardozo Law Review
Case W Res J Int'l L	Case Western Reserve Journal of International Law
CERD	Convention on the Elimination of Racial Discrimination
Chi J Int'l L	Chicago Journal of International Law
Chinese JIL	Chinese Journal of International Law
CJICL	Cambridge Journal of International and Comparative Law
Colum Hum Rts L Rev	Columbia Human Rights Law Review
Colum L Rev	Columbia Law Review
Comp Pol	Comparative Politics
Conn J Int'l L	Connecticut Journal of International Law
Const Comment	Constitutional Commentary
Cornell L Rev	Cornell Law Review
Cult Anthropol	Cultural Anthropology
DDP	Digesto delle discipline pubblicistiche
Denv J Int'l L & Pol'y	Denver Journal of International Law and Policy
DOJ	Department of Justice
DSB	Dispute Settlement Body
Duke J Comp & Int'l L	Duke Journal of Comparative and International Law
ECHR	European Convention on Human Rights
ECJ	European Court of Justice
ECtHR	European Court of Human Rights

EHRLR	European Human Rights Law Reports
EHRR	European Human Rights Reports
EJHET	European Journal of the History of Economic Thought
EJIL	European Journal of International Law
EJLR	European Journal of Law Reform
Emory L J	Emory Law Journal
Erasmus L Rev	Erasmus Law Review
Ethics & Int'l Aff	Ethics and International Affairs
Eur J Intl Relations	European Journal of International Relations
Eur J Philos	European Journal of Philosophy
FYBIL	Finnish Yearbook of International Law
Ga J Int'l & Comp L	Georgia Journal of International and Comparative Law
Ga L Rev	Georgia Law Review
GATT	General Agreement on Tariffs and Trade
Geo J Int' l L	Georgetown Journal of International Law
Geo L J	Georgetown Law Journal
German LJ	German Law Journal
Go JIL	Goettingen Journal of International Law
GYIL	German Yearbook of International Law
Hague Ybk Intl L	Hague Yearbook of International Law
Harv Hum Rts J	Harvard Human Rights Law Journal
Harv J L & Pub Pol'y	Harvard Journal of Law and Public Policy
Harv J L & Tech	Harvard Journal of Law and Technology
Harv L Rev	Harvard Law Review
Hastings L J	Hastings Law Review
Heidelberg J Int'l L	Heidelberg Journal of International Law
HILJ	Harvard International Law Journal
Hous L R	Houston Law Review
How L J	Howard Law Journal
HRC	UN Human Rights Committee
HRLJ	Human Rights Law Journal
IACtHR	Inter-American Court of Human Rights
ICC	International Criminal Court
ICCPR	International Covenant on Civil and Political Rights
ICJ	International Court of Justice
ICJ Rep	International Court of Justice Reports
ICLQ	International and Comparative Law Quarterly
ICON	International Journal of Constitutional Law
ICRC	International Committee of the Red Cross
ICSID	International Centre for the Settlement of Investment Disputes
ICTR	International Criminal Tribunal for Rwanda
ICTY	International Criminal Tribunal for the former Yugoslavia
IJHR	International Journal of Human Rights
IJIL	Indian Journal of International Law
IJSL	International Journal for the Semiotics of Law
ILC	International Law Commission
ILC Ybk	Yearbook of the International Law Commission

ILM	International Legal Materials
ILO	International Labour Organization
ILR	International Law Reports
IMF	International Monetary Fund
Ind J Global Legal Stud	Indiana Journal of Global Legal Studies
IND LJ	Indiana Law Journal
Indian YB Int'l Aff	Indian Yearbook of International Affairs
Int Theory	International Theory
Int'l Org	International Organization
Interdiscipl Sci Rev	Interdisciplinary Science Reviews
Intl L Studies	International Studies
IO	International Organization
Iowa L Rev	Iowa Law Review
IRRC	International Review of the Red Cross
Israel YB Hum Rts	Israel Yearbook of Human Rights
J Conflict Resol	Journal of Conflict Resolution
J Intl Econ L	Journal of International Economic Law
J L & Courts	Journal of Law and Courts
J Manag Stud	Journal of Management Studies
J of Law & Soc	Journal of Law and Society
J Phil Logic	Journal of Philosophical Logic
J Pragmat	Journal of Pragmatics
J Theor Polit	Journal of Theoretical Politics
JDI	Journal du droit international
JEFCA	Joint Food and Agricultural Organization/ World Health Organization Expert Committee on Food Additives
JEPP	Journal of European Public Policy
Jerusalem Rev Leg Stud	Jerusalem Review of Legal Studies
JICJ	Journal of International Criminal Justice
JIDS	Journal of International Dispute Settlement
JIEL	Journal of International Economic Law
JILIR	Journal of International Law and International Relations
JWIT	Journal of World Investment and Trade
Law & Crit	Law and Critique
Law & Phil	Law and Philosophy
Law & Prac Intl Cts And Tribunals	Law and Practice of International Courts and Tribunals
Law & Soc Inq	Law and Social Inquiry
LCP	Law and Contemporary Problems
Leg Stud	Legal Studies
LJIL	Leiden Journal of International Law
LQR	Law Quarterly Review
LT	Legal Theory
Melb J Int'l L	Melbourne Journal of International Law
Mich J Int'l L	Michigan Journal of International Law

Mich L Rev	Michigan Law Review
Minn L Rev	Minnesota Law Review
MLR	Modern Law Review
NAFTA	North American Free Trade Agreement
NILQ	Northern Ireland Legal Quarterly
NILR	Netherlands International Law Review
Nordic J Intl L	Nordic Journal of International Law
North U L Rev	Northwestern University Law Review
Notre Dame L Rev	Notre Dame Law Review
NYIL	Netherlands Yearbook of International Law
NYU J Int'l L & Pol	NYU Journal of International Law and Politics
OJLS	Oxford Journal of Legal Studies
Org Sci	Organization Science
PAS	Proceedings of the Aristotelian Society
PCIJ	Permanent Court of International Justice
PCIJ Rep	Permanent Court of International Justice Reports
Phil Inv	Philosophical Investigations
Phil & Pub Aff	Philosophy and Public Affairs
Phil Rev	Philosophical Review
PKU Trans L R	Peking University Transnational Law Review
Pol Sci	Policy Sciences
Pol Theory	Political Theory
RBDI	Revue Belge de Droit International
RECIEL	Review of European, Comparative and International Environmental Law
Recueil des Cours	Recueil des Cours de l'Académie de Droit International
RGDIP	Revue Générale de Droit International Public
RIAA	Reports of International Arbitral Awards
Rutgers L Rev	Rutgers Law Review
S Cal L Rev	Southern California Law Review
San Diego L Rev	San Diego Law Review
Santa Clara J Int'l L	Santa Clara Journal of International Law
Scand Stud L	Scandinavian Studies in Law
SCSL	Special Court for Sierra Leone
SJP	Southern Journal of Philosophy
Stan L Rev	Stanford Law Review
STL	Special Tribunal for Lebanon
Syd L R	Sydney Law Review
Temp Int'l & Comp LJ	Temple International and Comparative Law Journal
Tex Int'l L J	Texas International Law Journal
Tex Law Rev	Texas Law Review
Theo Inq L	Theoretical Inquiries in Law
Trans L T	Transnational Legal Theory
U Chi L Rev	University of Chicago Law Review
UDHR	Universal Declaration of Human Rights

U Kan L Rev	University of Kansas Law Review
UNGA	UN General Assembly
Va J Int'l L	Virginia Journal of International Law
Va L Rev	Virginia Law Review
Vand J Transnat'l L	Vanderbilt Journal of Transnational Law
VCDR	Vienna Convention on Diplomatic Relations
VCLT	Vienna Convention on the Law of Treaties
Wash Q	The Washington Quarterly
Wash UJL & Pol'y	Washington University Journal of Law and Policy
Wayne L Rev	Wayne Law Review
World Trade Rev	World Trade Review
WTO	World Trade Organization
Yale J Int'l L	Yale Journal of International Law
Yale J L & Human	Yale Journal of Law and the Humanities
Yale L J	Yale Law Journal

List of Contributors

Philip Allott is Emeritus Professor of International Public Law at the University of Cambridge and a Fellow of Trinity College.

Julian Arato is an Associate in Law at Columbia Law School.

Andrea Bianchi is Professor of International Law at the Graduate Institute of International and Development Studies, Geneva.

Eirik Bjorge is the Shaw Foundation Junior Research Fellow in Law at the University of Oxford and a Fellow of Jesus College.

Anne-Marie Carstens is a Visiting Professor of Law at Georgetown University.

Harlan Grant Cohen is Associate Professor of Law at the University of Georgia.

Jean d'Aspremont is Professor of Public International Law at the University of Manchester and Professor of International Legal Theory at the University of Amsterdam.

Gleider Hernández is Senior Lecturer in Law at Durham University and Deputy Director of the Durham Global Policy Institute.

Duncan B Hollis is the James E Beasley Professor of Law and the Associate Dean for Academic Affairs at Temple University.

Jens Olesen is a Fellow in Government at the London School of Economics and Political Science.

Daniel Peat is an Associate Legal Officer at the International Court of Justice.

René Provost is Associate Professor of Law at McGill University.

Iain Scobbie is Professor of Public International Law at the University of Manchester and Visiting Professor of International Law at SOAS, University of London.

Ingo Venzke is Associate Professor of Law at the University of Amsterdam.

Martin Wählisch is a Fellow at the Issam Fares Institute for Public Policy and International Affairs at the American University of Beirut.

Michael Waibel is University Lecturer at the University of Cambridge Faculty of Law, and a Fellow of Jesus College and the Lauterpacht Centre for International Law.

Matthew Windsor is a Junior Research Fellow in International Law at the University of Oxford.

Fuad Zarbiyev is an associate at Curtis, Mallet-Prevost, Colt & Mosle LLP, New York City.

Andraž Zidar is the Dorset Senior Research Fellow in Public International Law at the British Institute of International and Comparative Law.

PART I

INTRODUCTION

1

Playing the Game of Interpretation

On Meaning and Metaphor in International Law

Daniel Peat and Matthew Windsor

Introduction

The significance of interpretation to the professional practice and academic study of international law is inescapable. Interpretation in international law has traditionally been understood as a process of assigning meaning to texts with the objective of establishing rights and obligations.[1] This has led to a near exclusive focus on one type of international legal instrument (treaties), and one particular interpretive methodology (the Vienna Convention on the Law of Treaties, or VCLT).[2] Outside the auspices of the VCLT rules, interpretation in international law has rarely been regarded as a distinct field of inquiry. As new insights on the practice and process of interpretation have proliferated in other fields, international law and international lawyers have continued to grant an imprimatur to rule-based formalism. However, given that interpretation is a pervasive phenomenon in international law that is irreducible to analysis of the VCLT rules, a greater methodological awareness of interpretive theory and practice in international law is imperative.

The rules contained in the VCLT, and the cluster of concepts therein—including 'ordinary meaning', 'context', and 'object and purpose'—have long provided a focal point for interpretation in international law, and a source of constancy for the international legal profession. Scholars and international courts and tribunals have meticulously elaborated on the meaning of, and practice relating to, the VCLT since it was concluded in 1969. Unquestionably, this project is invaluable: it provides states and other actors in the international arena with a guide to the conventionally accepted norms of interpretation in the community within which they operate. It provides a veneer of stability, of certainty. But the project of doctrinal exegesis, predicated on faith in the objective meaning of interpretive

[1] Matthias Herdegen, 'Interpretation in International Law' in Rüdiger Wolfrum (ed), *Max Planck Encyclopedia of Public International Law* (OUP 2013).
[2] Vienna Convention on the Law of Treaties (adopted 23 May 1969, entered into force 27 January 1980) (1980) 1155 UNTS 331.

rules, does not tell the whole story. For instance, it does not interrogate the larger
purpose of interpretation in the international legal system, whether and why the
VCLT rules act as a constraint on interpretation in practice, whether actors' interpretations differ according to their professional identities, or if strategy motivates
interpretive choice. It does not examine how international law might gain insights
from disciplines dealing with analogous issues, such as literary theory, the philosophy of language and philosophical hermeneutics, not to mention other legal
fields, such as domestic constitutional and statutory interpretation.

The objective of this book is to provoke a reappraisal of interpretation in international law, both inside and outside the VCLT framework. The contributions
reveal that the uncritical incantation of the VCLT as a 'recipe for correct interpretation' fails to acknowledge that interpretation in international law is a more complex and nuanced phenomenon than is often recognized.[3] Accordingly, the book
aims to provide readers with materials to enhance their awareness of the 'nature
of interpretation, and the diverse reasons for engaging in it' in international law.[4]

This introductory chapter is divided into four sections. The chapter starts by
providing a short précis of the 'state of play' in international legal scholarship
and practice on interpretation (Part I). The following section explores different
conceptions of interpretation outside the international legal context, elucidating
how interpretation is understood as the act of assigning meaning in other fields
(Part II). The next section introduces the metaphor of the game, which serves
as a structural framework for the book, and which captures and illuminates the
constituent elements of interpretive activity (Part III). The final section provides
an overview of the chapters in this collection (Part IV). While we do not claim to
have conclusively 'unlocked the secret of interpretation',[5] this book provides a set
of tools for deeper reflection on interpretation in international law, a classical topic
that has too often been shoehorned by conceptual constraints.

I. Interpretation in International Law—
The State of Play

This section provides an inevitably cursory examination of the current treatment of
interpretation in international legal scholarship and practice. The 'state of play' is
characterized by a myopic focus on the rules of treaty interpretation in Articles 31–33
of the VCLT,[6] and an aversion to the more theoretical dimensions of the subject.
The general rule of interpretation, codified in Article 31 of the VCLT, provides that
treaties 'shall be interpreted in good faith in accordance with the ordinary meaning

---

[3] Joseph Raz, *Between Authority and Interpretation* (OUP 2009) 322.
[4] Raz, *Between Authority and Interpretation*, 322.
[5] Francis Mootz III, 'Interpretation' in Austin Sarat, Matthew Anderson, and Catherine O
Frank (eds), *Law and the Humanities: An Introduction* (CUP 2009) 339, 376.
[6] Undoubtedly, interpretation pertains to sources of international law other than treaties.
However, these have been given comparatively scant attention in the literature: see eg Charles de
Visscher, *Problèmes d'interpretation judiciaire en droit international public* (Pedone 1963); Robert

to be given to the terms of the treaty in their context and in the light of its object and purpose'.[7] The International Court of Justice (ICJ) has treated the methodology embodied in the VCLT as declaratory of the customary international law of treaty interpretation, and its application of the VCLT rules has been described as 'virtually axiomatic'.[8] The mission creep of the VCLT was exemplified by its prominence in the fragmentation of international law debate, where it was regarded as the 'elixir for virtually all fragmentation issues',[9] and as crucial to the prospects of systemic integration.[10] While the dangers of VCLT fundamentalism have been observed,[11] often by describing interpretation as ultimately an 'art' not a 'science',[12] the current position appears to be that 'in all matters international, always interpret in accordance with the rules' of the VCLT.[13]

Articles 31–33 of the VCLT have typically been treated as a 'one stop shop' as far as interpretive methodology is concerned; they have been described as a 'self-contained, complete analytical frame that has attempted to systematize and to structure the various possible methods for discerning the meaning of a legal text'.[14] Accordingly, the careful exposition of the meaning of, and practice relating to, the VCLT rules is an extremely instructive undertaking. A range of issues pertaining to the meaning of the VCLT rules continues to be debated, which is hardly surprising given that the rules on interpretation themselves require interpretation. These include the relative weight to be given to the intention of the parties to the treaty, subsequent practice, preparatory documents (*travaux préparatoires*), and the appropriateness of teleological or purposive approaches to interpretation.

The existence of the VCLT rules lends the practice of interpretation in international law an aura of formalism, compelling the international legal profession to 'play by the rules'.[15] Although the attainment of objective meaning through textualist

Kolb, *Interprétation et création du droit international* (Bruylant 2006); Alexander Orakhelashvili, *The Interpretation of Acts and Rules in Public International Law* (OUP 2008) 440–510; Michael Wood, 'The Interpretation of Security Council Resolutions' (1998) 2 Max Planck Yearbook of United Nations Law 73; Anthea Roberts, 'Traditional and Modern Approaches to Customary International Law: A Reconciliation' (2001) 95 AJIL 757.

[7] Article 32 deals with supplementary means of interpretation, and Article 33 deals with the interpretation of treaties authenticated in two or more languages.

[8] Richard Gardiner, *Treaty Interpretation* (OUP 2008) 15.

[9] Tomer Broude, 'Keep Calm and Carry On: Martti Koskenniemi and the Fragmentation of International Law' (2013) 27(2) Temp Int'l & Comp LJ 279, 290.

[10] Campbell McLachlan, 'The Principle of Systemic Integration and Article 31(3)(c) of the Vienna Convention' (2005) 54 ICLQ 279.

[11] See eg James Crawford, *Brownlie's Principles of Public International Law* (8th edn, OUP 2012) 380: 'Care must be taken to ensure that such "rules" do not become rigid and unwieldy instruments that might force a preliminary choice of meaning rather than acting as a flexible guide.'

[12] Robert Jennings, 'General Course on Principles of International Law' (1967) 121 Recueil des Cours 323, 544.

[13] Jan Klabbers, 'Virtuous Interpretation' in Malgosia Fitzmaurice, Olufemi Elias, and Panos Merkouris (eds), *Treaty Interpretation and the Vienna Convention on the Law of Treaties: 30 Years On* (Martinus Nijhoff 2010) 17, 24.

[14] Gleider Hernández, 'Interpretation' in Jörg Kammerhofer and Jean d'Aspremont (eds), *International Legal Positivism in a Post-Modern World* (CUP 2014) 317, 326.

[15] See generally Frederick Schauer, *Playing By the Rules: A Philosophical Examination of Rule-Based Decision-Making in Law and in Life* (Clarendon Press 1991).

technique proves elusive, the VCLT rules retain a stranglehold on interpretation in international dispute settlement, perhaps for the following reasons:

They have, in the first place, served as captions under which the tribunal could marshal existing precedents, so as to afford a general indication of relevant factors. They have, in the second place, given to tribunals a sense of continuity of tradition, relieving the psychological loneliness inseparable from the responsibility of policy-making. They have, in the third place, given some support (though often quite illusory support) to the claim of tribunals that their reasoning and the decisions arrived at had an objective validity even before they reached them, and have thus lightened the felt burden of responsibility.[16]

Notwithstanding the famous admonition that 'there is no part of the law of treaties which the text-writer approaches with more trepidation' than interpretation,[17] the literature on treaty interpretation is voluminous.[18] The scholarship ranges from learned treatises and handbooks on the VCLT,[19] to the interpretive approach in particular subfields of international law, such as international economic law,[20] human rights,[21] and international investment law and arbitration.[22] The VCLT looms large here, and even scholarship that purports to go 'beyond' the VCLT still largely abides by its strictures.[23] With some exceptions,[24] the scholarship on treaty

---

[16] Jan Klabbers, *International Law* (CUP 2013) 364.

[17] Arnold McNair, *The Law of Treaties* (Clarendon Press 1961) 364.

[18] See eg Duncan Hollis (ed), *The Oxford Guide to Treaties* (OUP 2012); Gardiner, *Treaty Interpretation*; Alexander Orakhelashvili, *The Interpretation of Acts and Rules*; Jan Klabbers, *The Concept of Treaty in International Law* (Kluwer Law International 1996); Ulf Linderfalk, *On the Interpretation of Treaties: The Modern International Law as Expressed in the 1969 Vienna Convention on the Law of Treaties* (Springer 2007); Anthony Aust, *Modern Treaty Law and Practice* (3rd edn, CUP 2014); Kolb, *Interprétation et création du droit international*; Christian Tams, Antonios Tzanakopoulos, and Andreas Zimmermann (eds), *Research Handbook on the Law of Treaties* (Edward Elgar 2014); and 'Symposium—*Les techniques interprétatives de la norme internationale*' (2011) 115 RGDIP 289.

[19] See eg Oliver Corten and Pierre Klein (eds), *The Vienna Convention on the Law of Treaties* (OUP 2011); Fitzmaurice, *Treaty Interpretation*; Mark Villiger, *Commentary on the 1969 Vienna Convention on the Law of Treaties* (Martinus Nijhoff 2009); Oliver Dörr and Kristen Schmalenbach (eds), *Vienna Convention on the Law of Treaties: A Commentary* (Springer 2012).

[20] See eg Isabelle Van Damme, *Treaty Interpretation by the WTO Appellate Body* (OUP 2009); Asif Qureshi, *Interpreting WTO Agreements: Problems and Perspectives* (CUP 2006); Marion Panizzon, *Good Faith in the Jurisprudence of the WTO: The Protection of Legitimate Expectations, Good Faith Interpretation and Fair Dispute Settlement* (Hart 2006).

[21] See eg George Letsas, *A Theory of Interpretation of the European Convention of Human Rights* (OUP 2007); Malgosia Fitzmaurice and Panos Merkouris (eds), *The Interpretation and Application of the European Convention of Human Rights: Legal and Practical Implications* (Martinus Nijhoff 2012).

[22] See Todd Weiler, *The Interpretation of International Investment Law: Equality, Discrimination and Minimum Standards of Treatment in Historical Context* (Martinus Nijhoff 2013); J Romesh Weeramanatry, *Treaty Interpretation in Investment Arbitration* (OUP 2012); Joanna Jemielniak, *Legal Interpretation in International Commercial Arbitration* (Ashgate 2014); Anthea Roberts, 'Power and Persuasion in Investment Treaty Interpretation: The Dual Role of States' (2010) 104 AJIL 179.

[23] In Enzo Cannizzaro (ed), *The Law of Treaties Beyond the Vienna Convention* (OUP 2011), despite the title, the major focus is on interpreting the provisions of the VCLT in light of subsequent developments.

[24] See eg Ingo Venzke, *How Interpretation Makes International Law* (OUP 2012); Andrea Bianchi, 'Textual Interpretation and (International) Law Reading: The Myth of (In)Determinacy and the Genealogy of Meaning' in Pieter Bekker, Rudolf Dolzer, and Michael Waibel (eds), *Making*

interpretation is descriptive and practical, rather than theoretical.[25] Joseph Weiler has described this literature on interpretation as one 'which simply reports how interpretation takes place in various courts and simply assumes that what is done is how it should be done'.[26] The 'implicit over-valuation of jurisprudence and the under-valuation of scholarly opinion' is another characteristic feature.[27] Indeed, for many international legal scholars, the matter of interpretation is settled and no longer open to debate. As one leading monograph recounts, 'the text of the Vienna Convention, the process of its drafting, and the practice of its application are all unanimous in affirming that the rules on treaty interpretation are fixed rules and do not permit the interpreter a free choice among interpretive methods'.[28]

Yet the circumstances of the VCLT's passage, notably the extensive involvement of British special rapporteurs in the drafting, reveals a distinct intellectual heritage of pragmatism that has left an indelible mark on the way in which interpretation in international law has been understood since. In the preparatory debates on treaty interpretation in the International Law Commission (ILC), Sir Humphrey Waldock, the Principal Reporter, opined that some rules of a practical nature could be usefully summarized, but that he would view with apprehension any attempt to delve too deeply into theoretical issues.[29] Accordingly, the post-VCLT thinking on interpretation in international law has been described as 'captive...to the conceptual world of [Waldock], himself captive to intuitive common law pragmatism'.[30] Waldock's attitude is indicative of a more general posture by public international lawyers to 'remainder or denigrate theory'.[31] Yet, as Patrick Atiyah has observed, 'the pure pragmatist who professes to scorn all theory is himself usually proceeding on the basis of some theory, seeking (albeit

---

Transnational Law Work in the Global Economy: Essays in Honour of Detlev Vagts (CUP 2010) 34; Denis Alland, 'L'interprétation du droit international public' (2014) 362 Recueil des Cours 47.

[25] See eg Gardiner, *Treaty Interpretation*, 8: 'This book is not about theory. It is about the practical use of the Vienna rules.'

[26] Joseph HH Weiler, 'Prolegomena to a Meso-Theory of Treaty Interpretation at the Turn of the Century', NYU Institute for International Law and Justice Legal Theory Colloquium: Interpretation and Judgment in International Law (NYU Law School, 14 February 2008) 3.

[27] Jörg Kammerhofer, 'Review—A Orakhelashvili, *The Interpretation of Acts and Rules in Public International Law*' (2009) 20 EJIL 1283, 1283.

[28] Orakhelashvili, *The Interpretation of Acts and Rules*, 309.

[29] Humphrey Waldock, 'Third Report on the Law of Treaties' (1964) II ILC Ybk 53–4.

[30] Weiler, 'Prolegomena to a Meso-Theory of Treaty Interpretation', 7. On the difference between the European and American approaches to treaty interpretation prior to adoption of the VCLT, see Christian Djeffal, 'Establishing the Argumentative DNA of International Law: A Cubistic View on the Rule of Treaty Interpretation and its Underlying Culture(s)' (2014) 5(1) Trans L T 128. On the American approach, see Harold D Lasswell, James C Miller, and Myres S McDougal, *The Interpretation of International Agreements and World Public Order: Principles of Content and Procedure* (Martinus Nijhoff 1994); Detlev Vagts, 'Treaty Interpretation and the New American Ways of Law Reading' (1993) 4 EJIL 472. Michael Waibel has criticized the authors of recent monographs on treaty interpretation in international law for failing to make a 'sustained attempt to build bridges to American legal thinking on interpretation': 'Demystifying the Art of Interpretation' (2011) 22(2) EJIL 571, 586.

[31] Colin Warbrick, 'The Theory of International Law: Is There an English Contribution?' in *Theory and International Law: An Introduction* (British Institute of International and Comparative Law 1991) 49, 49.

perhaps unconsciously) some rational objective; and his pragmatism may simply amount to an unwillingness to discuss his objectives, to examine his premises, to open himself to accountability'.[32]

In their mantra-like recital of the VCLT as a formal methodology for the interpretation of international legal rules,[33] international lawyers till a bounded field, largely insulated from interdisciplinary influence or insight.[34] The focus on rule-based approaches to interpretation, exemplified by the VCLT, means that international law lags behind other fields in which interpretive issues are examined in a more nuanced and theoretically informed fashion.[35] Yet a greater awareness of these broader debates helps shed light on both the underlying premises and shortcomings of the rule-based orthodoxy. Interpretation in international law is not an island,[36] and many 'new' interpretive controversies in international law have taxed minds in other fields for a considerable period of time (for example, the debate regarding originalism in constitutional interpretation).[37]

Rather than focusing exclusively on doctrinal exposition of interpretive techniques, this book highlights the practice and process of interpretation as well as the professional identity of those involved in the interpretation of international law.[38] Rather than

---

[32] Patrick Atiyah, *Pragmatism and Theory in English Law* (Sweet and Maxwell 1987) 3.

[33] Jean d'Aspremont 'Formalism versus Flexibility in the Law of Treaties' in Christian Tams, Antonios Tzanakopoulos, and Andreas Zimmermann (eds), *Research Handbook on the Law of Treaties* (Edward Elgar 2014) 257.

[34] There has been some scholarship on interpretation in international law that has been informed by an interdisciplinary outlook, but this is the exception rather than the rule. In international relations, see Shirley Scott, *The Political Interpretation of Multilateral Treaties* (Martinus Nijhoff 2004); Joost Pauwelyn and Manfred Elsig, 'The Politics of Treaty Interpretation: Variations and Explanations across International Tribunals' in Jeffrey Dunoff and Mark Pollack (eds), *Interdisciplinary Perspectives on International Law and International Relations* (CUP 2012) 445. In semiotics, see Evandro de Carvalho, *Semiotics of International Law: Trade and Translation* (Springer 2011). For an approach informed by literary theory, see Ian Johnstone, 'Treaty Interpretation: The Authority of Interpretive Communities' (1991) 12 Mich J Int'l L 371.

[35] Bianchi, 'Textual Interpretation and (International) Law Reading', 35. There are no chapters addressed specifically to the topic of interpretation in Samantha Besson and John Tasioulas (eds), *The Philosophy of International Law* (OUP 2010). There is plenty of general jurisprudential literature on interpretation: see eg Andrei Marmor (ed), *Law and Interpretation: Essays in Legal Philosophy* (Clarendon Press 1995); Raz, *Between Authority and Interpretation*; Kent Greenawalt, *Legal Interpretation: Perspectives from other Disciplines and Private Texts* (OUP 2010); Ronald Dworkin, *Law's Empire* (Hart 1986); Fernando Atria and Neil MacCormick (eds), *Law and Legal Interpretation* (Ashgate 2003).

[36] The plurilingual dimension of interpretation in international law is a unique facet: Article 33 VCLT. See Jean Hardy, 'The Interpretation of Plurilingual Treaties by International Courts and Tribunals' (1961) 37 BYBIL 72.

[37] David Kennedy has observed the perpetual reappearance of classic debates, tensions, and ambivalences in international law: 'When Renewal Repeats: Thinking Against the Box' (2000) 32 NYU J Int'l L & Pol 335. For literature on statutory interpretation, see Kent Greenawalt, *Statutory and Common Law Interpretation* (OUP 2012); Neil MacCormick and Robert Summers (eds), *Interpreting Statutes: A Comparative Study* (Aldershot 1991); Adrian Vermeule, *Judging Under Uncertainty: An Institutional Theory of Legal Interpretation* (Harvard University Press 2006); Lawrence Solan, *The Language of Statutes: Laws and their Interpretation* (University of Chicago Press 2010).

[38] Scholarship on interpretation has typically failed to examine the important role of interpreters themselves, and the focus has invariably been on judicial behaviour, if interpreters are discussed: Jeffrey Dunoff and Mark Pollack, 'Reviewing Two Decades of IL/IR Scholarship: What We've

focusing exclusively on how to interpret, the book asks why we interpret and who has, or claims to have, the authority to interpret. Rather than approaching issues of interpretation in a disciplinary vacuum, the book considers interpretation in a cross-cutting way, enabling authors to break free from the conceptual 'straitjacket' of the VCLT.[39]

II. In Search of Meaning

Interpretation is a multifarious concept that is defined and appropriated by those using the term to serve different functions.[40] Across the divergent conceptions of interpretation, one commonality is manifest: the notion that interpretation is concerned with discerning or clarifying *meaning*.[41] A 'retrieval' view of interpretation, whereby the subject matter has an established meaning which the interpreter must discover 'as in a hunt for buried treasure',[42] can be contrasted with views which regard the interpretive process as involving creativity and the construction of meaning.[43] This section considers how meaning is sought in fields other than those traditionally examined by international lawyers. While it does not purport to be exhaustive or conclusive in its analysis, a brief review of alternative approaches highlights the contingent bases upon which any theory of interpretation rests. By acknowledging this, we are forced to reflect critically upon the presuppositions that we hold when approaching the interpretive inquiry.

There are, broadly speaking, four sources of meaning identified in the interpretation literature: the author of the object of interpretation, the object of interpretation itself, the interpreter, and the society in which the interpretation occurs.[44] 'Ordinary meaning', in Article 31 of the VCLT, is regarded as emerging in the context of the treaty as a whole and in the light of its object and purpose.[45] Although Article 31 does not employ the language of intention, the orthodoxy amongst positivist international lawyers is that the 'aim of treaty interpretation is to give effect to the intentions of the parties'.[46] This view accords with a state-centric,

---

Learned, What's Next' in Dunoff and Pollack (eds), *Interdisciplinary Perspectives*, 626, 637. An important recent exception is Venzke, *How Interpretation Makes International Law.*

[39] Weiler, 'Prolegomena to a Meso-Theory of Treaty Interpretation', 5.

[40] Pierre Brunet, 'Aspects théoriques et philosophiques de l'interprétation normative' (2011) 115 RGDIP 311; Kolb, *Interprétation et création du droit international*, 11. Cf Lawrence Solum, 'The Unity of Interpretation' (2010) 90 BUL Rev 551, 560–1.

[41] See eg Dennis Patterson, 'Poverty of Interpretive Universalism: Toward the Reconstruction of Legal Theory' (1993) 72 Tex Law Rev 1, 1; William Twining and David Meirs, *How to Do Things With Rules: A Primer of Interpretation* (CUP 2010) 10; Hernández, 'Interpretation'; Neil Duxbury, *Elements of Legislation* (CUP 2013) 123–4.

[42] Raz, *Between Authority and Interpretation*, 241–64.

[43] See Venzke, *How Interpretation Makes International Law.*

[44] Stanley Fish, 'Intention is All There Is: A Critical Analysis of Aharon Barak's Purposive Interpretation in Law' (2008) 29(3) Cardozo L Rev 1109, 1116.

[45] See eg Crawford, *Brownlie's Principles of Public International Law*, 381 (on the principle of integration); Andrew Clapham, *Brierly's Law of Nations* (7th edn, OUP 2012) 349.

[46] Gerald Fitzmaurice, 'The Law and Procedure of the International Court of Justice: Treaty Interpretation' (1951) 28 BYBIL 1, 3–4. Cf the view that the VCLT 'put paid' to the notion of

consensualist conception of international law in which it is those that are subject to the law who determine the substance and limits of their obligations.[47]

The view that legal meaning is co-extensive with authorial intent is vociferously supported by Stanley Fish.[48] Fish claims that interpretation is inherent in the communicative process through which an author conveys meaning to an interpreter. Because words have no inherent meaning, they can mean anything that the author wishes.[49] Whilst it is convention to call a receptacle for waste a 'bin' or 'garbage can', Fish believes that it would be just as tenable to call the receptacle a 'penguin'. A dictionary, Fish proclaims, is 'a statistical report, not a normative one; it tell[s] you about the usage most people employ (in ordinary situations), not the usage demanded by some linguistic essence'.[50] The success of an interpretation is to be judged by the transmission of the author's intended meaning to the interpreter, which can then serve as the basis for a critical analysis on the part of the interpreter.[51] For Fish, the latter is something quite different from interpretation, as is any act that does not aim to understand the intention that the author aims to communicate via the utterance.[52] Fish uses authorial intent to act as a limit on the interpreter, arresting the arbitrariness of teleological or purposive interpretation and separating the technical task of interpretation from the more charged questions of the appropriateness of, and desirable amendments to, the law.[53]

The position that meaning is determined by authorial intent has attracted critics. The notion that words are simply endowed with meaning by the author—albeit normally in line with their conventionally accepted usage, for communicative efficacy—does not account for the existence of natural language.[54] Unlike Fish, Andrei Marmor claims that the meaning of some utterances is semantically determined, that is to say determined by the rules and conventions of natural language.[55] In the case of such utterances, interpretation is not required to facilitate successful communication. For Marmor, interpretation is limited to the ascertainment of the meaning of utterances that are not semantically determined. The goal of interpretation is either to ascertain the communicative intent of the author, or of

interpretation according to the intention of the parties: Jean-Marc Sorel and Valérie Boré Eveno, 'Article 31' in Corten and Klein (eds), *The Vienna Convention on the Law of Treaties*, 804–37.

[47] The move towards a 'communitarian' paradigm in international law might cause us to question the centrality of the intention of states to the interpretive process. See Bruno Simma, 'From Bilateralism to Community Interest in International Law' (1994) 250 Recueil des Cours 217; Joseph HH Weiler, 'The Geology of International Law—Governance, Democracy and Legitimacy' (2004) 64 Heidelberg J Int'l L 547.

[48] Cf Stanley Fish, *Is There a Text in This Class? The Authority of Interpretive Communities* (Harvard University Press 1980) where, in the context of literary theory, Fish argues that it is interpretive communities that produce meaning, not the text or reader. See Michael Robertson, *Stanley Fish on Philosophy, Politics and Law: How Fish Works* (CUP 2014).

[49] Stanley Fish, 'There is No Textualist Position' (2005) 42 San Diego L Rev 629, 632–3, 647.

[50] Fish, 'Intention is All There Is', 1123.

[51] Fish, 'There is No Textualist Position', 634.

[52] Fish, 'Intention is All There Is', 1129.   [53] Fish, 'Intention is All There Is', 1145.

[54] For a discussion of the interpretive constraints resulting from the literal meaning of lexical terms, see Umberto Eco, *The Limits of Interpretation* (University of Indiana Press 1994) 5–6.

[55] Marmor, *Law and Interpretation*, 64.

a 'stipulated hypothetical speaker, whose identity and nature are either explicitly defined or, as is more often the case, presupposed by the particular interpretation offered'.[56] The postulated intention of a hypothetical speaker brings a teleological or purposive dimension within Marmor's conception of interpretation.

In international law, this teleological or purposive dimension is particularly visible in the context of evolutionary interpretation.[57] For example, in *Goodwin v UK*, the European Court of Human Rights determined that the United Kingdom had a positive obligation to recognize the post-operative gender of transsexuals under Article 8 of the European Convention on Human Rights (ECHR).[58] Although consensus within the Council of Europe states had not changed since previous decisions denying the existence of such an obligation,[59] international consensus regarding the recognition of post-operative transsexuals had increased.[60] The Court's interpretation of Article 8 in *Goodwin* was not based on the attempted retrieval of the ECHR drafters' intention—far from it. Instead, characterized in a Marmorian fashion, the Court interpreted the provision according to the intent of a hypothetical speaker: that of the international community.[61]

While Marmor considers interpretation to be all that occurs when semantic meaning is indeterminate, some constitutional scholars in the United States draw a distinction between legal interpretation and legal construction:[62] the realm of interpretation is limited to the elucidation of the semantic meaning of the legal text, whereas construction entails 'putting [the semantic meaning] into effect by applying it in particular cases and controversies'.[63] The aim of this distinction is to separate the 'neutral (or thinly normative) linguistic facts' from the correctness of the normative legal doctrine that they give rise to.[64] Sometimes the legal construction exactly mirrors the semantic meaning of the law. Take, for example, the application of the provision of the UN Charter providing that each 'member of the Security Council shall have one representative'.[65] But where the semantic meaning of a text is vague, interpretation is of no use.[66] This zone of indeterminacy has been described as the 'construction zone', in which the interpreter must have recourse to extra-textual material to apply the provision at hand.[67]

---

[56] Marmor, *Law and Interpretation*, 3–28. Cf Dworkin, *Law's Empire*, 58–9.

[57] See Eirik Bjorge, *The Evolutionary Interpretation of Treaties* (OUP 2014).

[58] *Christine Goodwin v UK* (2002) 35 EHRR 447, [56], [90].

[59] See *Rees v United Kingdom* (1987) 9 EHRR 56, [37]; *Cossey v UK* (1991) 13 EHRR 622, [40]; *Sheffield and Horsham v UK*, Reports of Judgments and Decisions 1998-V, [57].

[60] *Goodwin*, [56].   [61] *Goodwin*, [90], [93].

[62] See eg Lawrence Solum, 'Communicative Content and Legal Content' (2013) 89(2) Notre Dame L Rev 479; Randy Barnett, 'Interpretation and Construction' (2011) 34 Harv J L & Pub Pol'y 65; Lawrence Solum, 'The Interpretation-Construction Distinction' (2010) 27 Const Comment 95.

[63] Barnett, 'Interpretation and Construction', 65.

[64] Solum, 'The Interpretation-Construction Distinction', 100–6.

[65] Article 23(3) Charter of the United Nations (adopted 26 June 1945, entered into force 24 October 1945), 1 UNTS XVI.

[66] Cf Timothy Endicott, 'Interpretation and Indeterminacy' (2015) Jerusalem Rev Leg Stud (forthcoming). On the distinction between vagueness and ambiguity, and lawyers' inbuilt propensity to act a certain way in cases of ambiguity, see Jill C Anderson, 'Misreading like a Lawyer: Cognitive Bias in Statutory Interpretation' (2014) 127(6) Harv L Rev 1521, 1535.

[67] Solum, 'The Interpretation-Construction Distinction', 108.

Legal construction has been described as creating a 'double bind', both because it seems inevitable and because it shifts the full burden of legitimation to whoever is tasked with construction.[68] This constitutive function challenges the orthodoxy that interpretation in international law is grounded on an 'inherent objective intelligibility' and is in the business of 'textual mining—that is, extracting an idea or rule from the text which exists objectively'.[69]

The migration of concerns about linguistic indeterminacy from the philosophy of language to philosophy of law challenges the premise that legal meaning can ever be semantically determined à la Marmor. Michael Rosenfeld argued that the practice of legal interpretation is 'mired in a deep and persistent crisis', due to a 'loss of faith concerning the availability of objective criteria permitting the ascription of distinct and transparent meanings to legal texts'.[70] The advent of critical legal studies shed new light on the shortcomings of formalist interpretive techniques, centred on adherence to objectivity and textualism.[71] For instance, HLA Hart's interpretive conception of a 'core of certainty' and 'penumbra of doubt' has been critiqued for 'presuppos[ing] the schema according to which every case is located either in the area of determinacy or in the penumbra'.[72] Duncan Kennedy has described such presuppositions as an example of strategic behaviour in interpretation, where interpreters strive to 'generate a particular rhetorical effect: that of the legal necessity of their solutions without regard to ideology'.[73] The legal interpreter frequently '"brackets" whether the resistance of a given rule to reinterpretation is a result of what the meaning "really" is or is merely an effect of time, strategy and skill'.[74]

Concerns about the ineradicability of ideology and politics in international legal interpretation have been well ventilated, most notably in the work of Martti Koskenniemi. Koskenniemi argues that attempts to argue on the basis of a 'natural code are … camouflaged attempts to impose the speaker's subjective, political opinion on others'.[75] On this account, VCLT maxims such as ordinary meaning, context, and purpose emerge as 'constructive justifications for an interpretation rather than something which existed by themselves and could be looked at when

---

[68] Ralf Poscher, 'Hermeneutics, Jurisprudence and Law' in Jeff Malpas and Hans-Helmuth Gander (eds), *Routledge Companion to Hermeneutics* (Routledge 2015).

[69] d'Aspremont, 'Formalism versus Flexibility', 277.

[70] Michael Rosenfeld, *Just Interpretations: Law Between Ethics and Politics* (University of California Press 1998) 13.

[71] See eg David Kennedy, 'The Turn to Interpretation' (1985) 58 S Cal L Rev 251; Peter Goodrich, 'Rhetoric as Jurisprudence: An Introduction to the Politics of Legal Language' (1984) 4(1) OJLS 88.

[72] Duncan Kennedy, 'A Left Phenomenological Alternative to the Hart/Kelsen Theory of Legal Interpretation' in Duncan Kennedy, *Legal Reasoning: Collected Essays* (Davies Book Publishers 2008) 154, 157.

[73] Duncan Kennedy, *A Critique of Adjudication* (Harvard University Press 1997) 1–2.

[74] Kennedy, *A Critique of Adjudication*, 161.

[75] Martti Koskenniemi, *From Apology to Utopia: The Structure of International Legal Argument* (CUP 2005) 18.

concepts proved ambiguous'.[76] In short, for Koskenniemi, 'interpretation creates meaning rather than discovers it'.[77]

An attempt to achieve a *via media* between determinacy and indeterminacy, focusing on the communitarian dimension of meaning, has been articulated by Andrea Bianchi, the co-editor of this book.[78] For Bianchi, '[t]he shackles of both formalism and radical critical approaches have scleroticised the debate by focusing on opposite, yet equally sterile, stances that refuse to take duly into account the more sociological aspects of interpretive processes'.[79] Bianchi argues that the interpretive process, 'far from being merely the produce of linguistic analysis, is deeply embedded in a societal context where different actors interact with one another'.[80] This necessitates a shift in focus from the 'alleged inherent properties of the text to the interpretive communities whose strategies ultimately determine what a text means'.[81] On this approach, meaning is the product of a complex web of social relations, including the context in which an utterance occurred, the conventional meaning of a word within society, and the cognitive frames that condition interpretive activity. Accordingly, the determination of meaning by reference solely to the author or object of interpretation is overly reductive.

If insights from the philosophy of language, critical legal studies, and literary theory are the 'devil' troubling the straightforward ascertainment of meaning in international law, then philosophical hermeneutics is the 'deep blue sea'. Common to both the 'linguistic turn' and philosophical hermeneutics is a decisive turn away from authorial intent. Yet philosophical hermeneutics in particular necessitates a shift in focus from 'the object of interpretation—the text and its sense—to the activity of interpreting—the process of sense-making'.[82] It emphasizes what the interpreter contributes to interpretation and the creation of meaning, rather than what the text offers the interpreter. In the context of legal interpretation, this leads to a corresponding shift from analysis conducted in a positivist framework to an approach that treats law itself as an interpretive discipline. Robert Cover observed that an interest in interpretation and hermeneutics in this latter sense is 'quite a different phenomenon from the traditional set of questions about how a particular word, phrase or instrument should be given effect in some particular context'.[83]

---

[76] Koskenniemi, *From Apology to Utopia*, 530. This concern far pre-dates the critical legal studies movement. See Hersch Lauterpacht, 'Restrictive Interpretation and the Principle of Effectiveness in the Interpretation of Treaties' (1949) 26 BYBIL 48, 53: rules are 'not the determining cause of judicial decision, but the form in which the judge cloaks a result arrived at by other means'.

[77] Koskenniemi, *From Apology to Utopia*, 531.

[78] Bianchi, 'Textual Interpretation and (International) Law Reading'.

[79] Bianchi, 'Textual Interpretation and (International) Law Reading', 53.

[80] Bianchi, 'Textual Interpretation and (International) Law Reading', 35.

[81] Bianchi, 'Textual Interpretation and (International) Law Reading', 36 (referring to Stanley Fish, *Is There a Text in this Class?*, and Ludwig Wittgenstein's notion of 'forms of life').

[82] Steven Mailloux, 'Interpretation' in Frank Lentricchia and Thomas McLaughlin (eds), *Critical Terms for Literary Study* (University of Chicago Press 1995) 121, 124.

[83] Robert Cover, 'Violence and the Word' (1986) 95 Yale L J 1601, 1602.

A core premise of the hermeneutical ontology is that there is no text that can be interpreted objectively so as to provide a fixed meaning available for later use.[84] This is because texts cannot insulate meaning from historical contingency and the interpreter's presuppositions or prejudices.[85] For Hans-Georg Gadamer, the 'effective history' of a text and the interpreter's 'fore-understandings' gives rise to an expectation of meaning that 'determines in advance both what seems to us worth inquiring about and what will appear as an object of investigation'.[86] Meaning is thus not something that can be extracted from a text, but something that takes place in the process of interpretation. Gadamer rejected the idea that interpretation should seek to reconstruct authorial intent because this does not take account of the situatedness of the interpreter. For Gadamer, the case in point for showing that understanding always involves presuppositions, fore-understandings, and situatedness is legal interpretation, where the central task is the application of a (historical) text to a present case. Although interpretive activity in law regards itself as wholly bound by textual meaning, that meaning is concretized and realized only in the act of interpretation. Put another way, Gadamer contends that we ground the rule of law on a commitment to meaning, but this fidelity does not presuppose that meaning is static.[87]

On Gadamer's account, interpretation occurs through a 'fusion of horizons' of the interpreter and the text, where the effective history of the text and the interpreter's fore-understandings are constantly challenged and transformed.[88] Just as in conversation where the horizons of the participants must merge in order for understanding to be possible, likewise in interpretation, the horizon of the interpreter has to merge with that of the text in order for interpretation to succeed. The provocative implication is that the notion of an 'ordinary meaning' is illusory.

Notwithstanding Gadamer's discussion of legal interpretation,[89] philosophical hermeneutics has been largely ignored in international law circles.[90] A notable exception is Outi Korhonen's Gadamerian account of international legal interpretation, which argues that international law 'norms complete with meaning and

---

[84] Francis Mootz III, 'Hermeneutics and Law' in Niall Keane and Chris Lawn (eds), *Blackwell Companion to Hermeneutics* (Wiley-Blackwell 2015) (forthcoming).

[85] Mootz, 'Hermeneutics and Law'.

[86] Hans-Georg Gadamer, *Truth and Method* (2nd edn, Continuum 1989) 299–300. Jürgen Habermas endorsed Gadamer's conception of 'effective history', on the basis that we cannot 'leap over' our relation to tradition. However, he criticized Gadamer's hermeneutic account because it does not allow for the rational criticism of tradition, and forecloses the possibility that tradition can be changed through reflection: 'A Review of Gadamer's *Truth and Method*' in Fred Dallmayr and Thomas McCarthy (eds), *Understanding and Social Inquiry* (Notre Dame University Press 1977) 335. For further discussion of Habermas' critique of Gadamer, see Paul Gorner, *Twentieth Century German Philosophy* (OUP 2000) 172–80.

[87] Mootz, 'Hermeneutics and Law'.   [88] Mootz, 'Hermeneutics and Law'.

[89] Gadamer, *Truth and Method*, 321–36.

[90] See eg Fuad Zarbiyev, 'Review—R Kolb, *Interprétation et création du droit international*' (2009) 22(1) LJIL 211, 212: it is 'difficult to understand how a work expressly bearing on legal hermeneutics can, without any justification whatsoever, neglect to use modern philosophical hermeneutics'; Kammerhofer, 'Review—A Orakhelashvili, *The Interpretation of Acts and Rules*', 1284: 'theories of hermeneutics or language theory have not even been mentioned, much less discussed...the unquestioned adoption of the plain meaning doctrine in the face of all those who have ventured further into the theoretical realm is perhaps too problematic to be upheld'.

significance do not exist *a priori* as independent objectives which could be picked up by whomever, whenever'.[91] Yet the situationality of interpreters and the constitution of meaning inherent in international legal interpretation are obscured by the VCLT, which purports to 'uncover the meaning in a process which totally determines the encounter of the interpreter and interpreted'.[92] Instead of repressing hermeneutic insights in international legal interpretation, Korhonen suggests that 'only a reflected understanding of one's situation is a fruitful basis for finding solutions—meaningful interpretations—in normative practice'.[93]

Arguably the legal theorist most closely associated with a Gadamerian style of hermeneutics is Ronald Dworkin.[94] Dworkin's oeuvre is best understood as advancing an interpretive ethic that he regards as preferable to positivist rule-based practice, rather than necessarily embracing the more far-reaching ontological premises underlying philosophical hermeneutics.[95] In *Law's Empire*, Dworkin explicitly endorsed Gadamer's view 'that interpretation must *apply* an intention',[96] reflecting the view that interpretation is inevitably constructive, even if it merely aims at the retrieval of authorial intent.[97] In his famous theory of 'law as integrity', the best interpretation is one that *fits* the text and provides the strongest *justification* of the principles of political morality underpinning the system.[98]

Dworkin developed a general value-based theory of interpretation in his last major work, *Justice for Hedgehogs*.[99] For Dworkin, interpretation can be understood to involve three analytically distinct stages. First, interpreters must 'individuate' social practices, so they can take themselves to be engaged in legal rather than, say, literary interpretation.[100] Interpretation cannot begin until a genre is specified or assumed: 'Interpreting light flashes as a message has a dramatically different point from interpreting them as artistic expression.'[101] At this stage, interpreters seek the rules and standards recognized by social consensus to provide the 'tentative content of the practice' in their genre.[102] Second, interpreters are required to attribute a 'justifying purpose' to the genre, which signals 'the value that it does and ought to provide'.[103] Third, interpreters are required to identify the best realization of the justifying purpose on a particular occasion.[104]

---

[91] O Korhonen, 'New International Law: Silence, Defence or Deliverance?' (1996) 7 EJIL 1, 1.
[92] Korhonen, 'New International Law', 7.   [93] Korhonen, 'New International Law', 9.
[94] Dworkin, *Law's Empire*, 55, 62.   [95] Mootz, 'Hermeneutics and Law'.
[96] Dworkin, *Law's Empire*, 55.   [97] Poscher, 'Hermeneutics, Jurisprudence and Law'.
[98] Dworkin, *Law's Empire*, 255.
[99] Ronald Dworkin, *Justice for Hedgehogs* (Belknap Press of Harvard University Press 2011).
[100] Dworkin, *Justice for Hedgehogs*, 131.   [101] Dworkin, *Justice for Hedgehogs*, 149.
[102] Dworkin, *Law's Empire*, 65–6.
[103] Dworkin, *Justice for Hedgehogs*, 131. In a posthumously published article, Dworkin discussed the 'justifying purpose' of international law as follows: 'The correct interpretation of an international document, like the UN Charter, is the interpretation that makes the best sense of the text given the underlying aim of international law, which is taken to be the creation of an international order that protects political communities from external aggression, protects citizens of those communities from domestic barbarism, facilitates coordination when this is essential, and provides some measure of participation by people in their own governance across the world': 'A New Philosophy for International Law' (2013) 41(1) Phil & Pub Aff 2, 22.
[104] Dworkin, *Justice for Hedgehogs*, 131.

One implication of the foregoing account of interpretation is that Dworkin rejects the view that retrieving authorial intention is the presumptive aim of interpretation.[105] Instead, his general theory of interpretation helps explain when and why that goal is appropriate.[106] Authors' states of mind are relevant only to the extent they are made so by the best account of the value served by interpreting in the genre in question.[107]

The extent to which the insights from alternative theoretical approaches to interpretation might be brought to bear on the specific dictates of international law as a professional tradition is severely under-examined. The illustration of alternative approaches to the ascertainment of meaning in this section demonstrates that any approach to interpretation rests upon pre-existing views regarding meaning, language, and the importance of societal context and norms that must be called into question. The search for 'ordinary meaning', traditionally understood as coextensive with the search for authorial intent, demands to be understood as a contingent and contestable conception of interpretation in international law. We agree with Rosenfeld that a professional commitment to the 'interchangeability of interpretation with particular techniques leads to an arid state of inquiry'.[108] Indeed, the view that the interpretive inquiry is reducible to, and exhausted by, a set of rules such as the VCLT is naive. The various interpretive approaches canvassed in this section have not been discussed to endorse their stance in the context of international law,[109] but to urge the expansion of the repertoire of available interpretive postures, and to foster reflexivity in those who interpret international law. Such approaches function as a salutary reminder to international law scholars to 'pursue a more robust description of the hermeneutical situation in which interpreters find themselves'.[110]

III. What's in a Game?

In an effort to pursue a 'more robust description of the hermeneutical situation' in international law, this book uses the metaphor of the game as a heuristic framework. The metaphor helps explain the operation of interpretation in international law, and captures its constituent elements in novel ways. Given our use of a metaphor as a structural device, this section discusses the figurative resonance of the game, the insights the metaphor is capable of generating in international law, and some of the challenges attendant on the use of the metaphor.

---

[105] Dworkin, *Justice for Hedgehogs*, 7.   [106] Dworkin, *Justice for Hedgehogs*, 130.
[107] Dworkin, *Justice for Hedgehogs*, 149.   [108] Rosenfeld, *Just Interpretations*, 1.
[109] For example, there are limits to the use of Gadamer's theory of hermeneutical play in the context of international law. While Gadamer emphasized the 'primacy of play over the consciousness of the player', contributors to this book tend to subscribe to the view that interpreters have agency in a way that Gadamer was at pains to avoid: *Truth and Method*, 105. Yet the ambition of the contributions here do not extend to overarching ontological explanation in a Gadamerian vein.
[110] Mootz, 'Interpretation', 374–5.

A. The game metaphor

One of the most ubiquitous metaphors across a wide range of disciplines is the reference to games as 'prototypes for other forms of interdependent behaviour'.[111] The game metaphor has appeared in a bewildering range of settings, and has been used to describe everything from the art of seduction to life itself.[112] In his seminal book *Homo Ludens*, Dutch historian Johan Huizinga argued that games and play are basic human activities that help constitute culture. Huizinga investigated the relationship between play and a wide variety of human activities, from poetry and art to law and war.[113] He understood play as a 'free activity standing quite consciously outside "ordinary" life...but at the same time absorbing the player intensely and utterly'.[114] For Huizinga, a chief characteristic of play is an order conferred by rules which 'determine what "holds" in the temporary world circumscribed by play'.[115] Particular significance is attached to the demarcation of play according to time and space:

The arena, the card-table, the magic circle, the temple, the stage, the screen, the tennis court, the court of justice, etc. are all in form and function play-grounds, i.e. forbidden spots, isolated, hedged round, hallowed, within which special rules obtain.[116]

Of particular importance for present purposes is the way in which play 'interposes itself benignly into the most serious activities', including the administration of justice and the conduct of war.[117] While the domains of law and play initially appear to be antithetical, Huizinga identifies an affinity between lawsuits and contests. He suggests that the 'style and language in which the juristic wranglings of a modern lawsuit are couched often betray a sportsmanlike passion for indulging in argument and counter-argument'.[118] Yet the judicial contest is always subject to rules that bring semblance and structure to the legal playground. Huizinga goes on to maintain that the community of states bound by international law also constitute a play-community:

Its principle of reciprocal rights, its diplomatic forms, its mutual obligations in the matter of honouring treaties and, in the event of war, officially abrogating peace, all bear a formal resemblance to play rules inasmuch as they are only binding while the game itself—i.e. the need for order in human affairs—is recognised.[119]

---

[111] Francis Beer, 'Games and Metaphors' (1986) 30 J Conflict Resol 171, 175. See generally Michael Oriard, *Sporting with the Gods: The Rhetoric of Play and Game in American Literature* (CUP 2008).

[112] Neil Strauss, *The Game: Undercover in the Secret Society of Pickup Artists* (Canongate 2007); Bernard Suits, 'Is Life a Game We Are Playing?' (1967) Ethics 209.

[113] Johan Huizinga, *Homo Ludens: A Study of the Play-Element in Culture* (Routledge 1938). See also Roger Caillois, *Man, Play and Games* (University of Illinois Press 2001); Brian Sutton-Smith, *The Ambiguity of Play* (Harvard University Press 2001).

[114] Huizinga, *Homo Ludens*, 13.   [115] Huizinga, *Homo Ludens*, 11.

[116] Huizinga, *Homo Ludens*, 8.

[117] John Tasioulas, 'Games and the Good' (2006) 80(1) PAS 237, 244.

[118] Huizinga, *Homo Ludens*, 77.   [119] Huizinga, *Homo Ludens*, 100.

Homo Ludens concludes by acknowledging that the observance of play-rules in the relations between states is of paramount importance.[120] In not abiding by international agreements, states 'break the play-rules inherent in any system of international law'.[121] The ambitious claim advanced here is that the 'immemorial play-spirit' and claims to civilization and the maintenance of an international community run in parallel.[122]

In international relations and political science, figurative references to the game are a discursive mainstay. In *Politics Among Nations*, Hans Morgenthau referred to foreign policy as the 'sport of kings, not to be taken more seriously than games and gambles played for strictly limited stakes'.[123] A non-exhaustive list of other frequently cited tropes include: the likening of the world to a billiard table, with states imagined as billiard balls;[124] the reference to 'two-level games' between the domestic and international levels of policy analysis;[125] references to the 'Great Game' in geopolitical discussion;[126] the discussion of 'sovereignty games' as a mode of analysing the role of language and intersubjective rules in the constitution of international social reality;[127] and the application of the game metaphor to particular controversies, such as the Israel–Palestine conflict and Operation Desert Storm.[128] A particularly prevalent treatment of the game metaphor in international relations scholarship draws on game theory and rational choice articulations of the Prisoner's Dilemma as a model for strategic decision-making.[129]

[120] Huizinga, *Homo Ludens*, 210.   [121] Huizinga, *Homo Ludens*, 210.

[122] Huizinga, *Homo Ludens*, 101.

[123] Hans Morgenthau, *Politics Among Nations: The Struggle for Power and Peace* (5th edn, Alfred A Knopf 1973) 190.

[124] John Burton, *World Society* (CUP 1972) 28–32.

[125] Robert Putnam, 'Diplomacy and Domestic Politics: The Logic of Two Level Games' (1988) 42 Int'l Org 427. For a discussion of how this metaphor reinforces the divide it was designed to bridge, see Michael Marks, *Metaphors in International Relations Theory* (Palgrave 2011) 151; Christopher Hill, *The Changing Politics of Foreign Policy* (Palgrave 2002) 221.

[126] See Diane Desierto, 'Rewriting the New "Great Game": China, the United States and their International Public Lawyers' (2013) 1(2) PKU Trans L R 351.

[127] See Rebecca Adler-Nissen and Thomas Gammeltoft-Hansen (eds), *Sovereignty Games: Instrumentalizing State Sovereignty in Europe and Beyond* (Palgrave 2008); Robert H Jackson, *Quasi-States: Sovereignty, International Relations and the Third World* (CUP 1993); Charles Anthony Woodward Manning, *The Nature of International Society* (Bell and Sons 1962); Tanja Aalberts, 'Playing the Game of Sovereign States: Charles Manning's constructivism *avant-la-lettre*' (2010) 16 Eur J Intl Relations 247.

[128] Cathleen Bridgeman, 'Playing at Peace: Game Metaphors in Discussions of the Israeli-Palestinian Conflict' (2002) 29(2) BJ Middle East Stud 165; Dale Herbeck, 'Sports Metaphor and Public Policy: The Football Theme in Desert Storm Discourse' in Francis Beer and Christ'l De Landtsheer (eds), *Metaphorical World Politics* (Michigan State University Press 2004) 121.

[129] See eg T Schelling, *The Strategy of Conflict* (Harvard University Press 1990); Robert Leonard, 'Value, Sign and Social Structure: The "Game" Metaphor and Modern Social Science' (1997) 4(2) EJHET 299. For an attempt to transpose game theory to demarcate the 'limits of international law', see Jack L Goldsmith and Eric A Posner, *The Limits of International Law* (OUP 2006). For a critique, see Jens D Ohlin, 'Nash Equilibrium and International Law' (2012) 23(4) EJIL 915; Jens D Ohlin, *The Assault on International Law* (OUP 2014); Friedrich Kratochwil, *The Status of Law in World Society* (CUP 2014) 35–7.

As with international relations, the metaphor of the game is ubiquitous both in mainstream and critical strands of international legal scholarship. A few examples will suffice. Shabtai Rosenne described international law as the 'product of the co-ordinated wills of its own subjects, what we might call the agreed rules of the game'.[130] In the context of sovereign equality, James Crawford observed that 'every recognised state and its government has a full ticket to the game'.[131] Jeffrey Dunoff argued that the international lawyer's decisions are largely regulated by 'rules of the game: who can even be a player in the first place; what moves are available to these players; what tactics can the players utilise; and what ends are permissible to pursue'.[132] And Martti Koskenniemi's *From Apology to Utopia* is bookended by references to games: the book commences with an epigraph on Snakes and Ladders from Salman Rushdie's *Midnight's Children*,[133] and ends by urging international lawyers to 're-imagine the game':

Instead of impartial umpires or spectators, we were cast as players in a game, members in somebody's team. It is not that we need to play the game better, or more self-consciously. We need to re-imagine the game, reconstruct its rules, redistribute the prizes.[134]

B. Why the game metaphor?

The close linkages drawn between game-playing and culture has no doubt given rise to the prevalence of game metaphors across a large range of disciplines, including international law and relations. Indeed, it has been argued that any social situation, given appropriate conditions, may be analogized to a strategic game.[135] Given the dizzying and divergent array of usages to which it has been put, it would be tempting to conclude that the game metaphor is little more than a 'rhetorical flourish' that could not add significantly to our cognition of interpretation in international law.[136] Although there are challenges associated with the use of the metaphor in this context, the game metaphor effectively illuminates the constituent elements of the practice and process of interpretation in international law for the following three reasons.

---

[130] Shabtai Rosenne, 'The Perplexities of Modern International Law: General Course on Public International Law' (2001) 291 Recueil des Cours 39.

[131] James Crawford, *Chance, Order, Change: The Course of International Law* (Brill 2014) 365.

[132] Jeffrey Dunoff, 'From Interdisciplinarity to Counterdisciplinarity: Is There Madness in Martti's Method?' (2013) 27(2) Temp Int'l & Comp LJ 309, 335.

[133] Salman Rushdie, *Midnight's Children* (Picador 1981) 141: 'All games have morals; and the game of Snakes and Ladders captures, as no other activity can hope to do, the eternal truth that for every ladder you climb, a snake is waiting just around the corner; and for every snake, a ladder will compensate.'

[134] Koskenniemi, *From Apology to Utopia*, 561.

[135] See John von Neuman and Oskar Morgenstern, *The Theory of Games and Economic Behaviour* (Princeton University Press 1947).

[136] George Lakoff and Mark Johnson, *Metaphors We Live By* (University of Chicago Press 1980) 3. For a discussion of the lexicalization of metaphor, see Paul Ricoeur, *The Rule of Metaphor: Multi-Disciplinary Studies of the Creation of Meaning in Language* (Routledge 1978).

1. The game metaphor as heuristic framework

First, the game metaphor posits a general *heuristic framework*, which foregrounds topics of crucial importance in order to foster innovative thinking on interpretation in international law. Although the specific analytic categories used to structure this book are detailed in the next chapter by Andrea Bianchi,[137] a few remarks about the power and potential of metaphor are in order. Metaphor has been variously understood to mean 'understanding and experiencing one kind of thing in terms of another',[138] a 'carrying over of a word from its normal use to a new use',[139] a 'fusion between two disparate notions',[140] and 'understanding one conceptual domain in terms of another conceptual domain'.[141] Metaphors can play an essential role in framing discourse, defining problems, generating assumptions and delineating the scope of consideration.[142]

Opinions differ as to whether metaphor serves an ornamental or more generative purpose. Some argue that if a metaphorical term is synonymous with its referent and imparts no new information, then the metaphor has only 'decorative value'.[143] Others regard metaphor as having a constitutive function, given that language not only mirrors social reality but contributes to the formation of it.[144] On this view, metaphor functions as a 'peremptory invitation to discovery'.[145] Rather than describing and mediating between pre-existing similarities, metaphor can contribute to the establishment of such similarities.[146] Accordingly, a recent monograph on metaphor described its essential characteristic as prophetic,[147] arguing that the 'value of a metaphor seems to consist in the audacity of the transfer, the determination on the part of the writer to set new possibilities astir'.[148]

In their pioneering scholarship on cognitive linguistics, George Lakoff and Mark Johnson argued that metaphors suffuse our everyday language and

---

[137] See Chapter 2 (Andrea Bianchi).

[138] Lakoff and Johnson, *Metaphors We Live By*, 5.

[139] Ivor Armstrong Richards, *Practical Criticism: A Study of Literary Judgment* (Harcourt, Brace and World 1929) 221.

[140] Gustaf Stern, *Meaning and Change of Meaning with Special Reference to the English Language* (Indiana University Press 1965) 298.

[141] Zoltan Kövescses, *Metaphor: A Practical Introduction* (OUP 2002) 4.

[142] Beer and De Landtsheer (eds), *Metaphorical World Politics*, 6. See also Marks, *Metaphors in International Relations Theory*, 188.

[143] Ricouer, *The Rule of Metaphor*, 21.

[144] See James Geary, *I is an Other: The Secret Life of Metaphor and How It Shapes the Way We See the World* (Harper Perennial 2012); Nicholas Onuf, 'Fitting Metaphors' in *Making Sense, Making Worlds: Constructivism in Social Theory and International Relations* (Routledge 2013).

[145] Don R Swanson, 'Toward a Psychology of Metaphor' in Sheldon Sacks (ed), *On Metaphor* (University of Chicago Press 1978) 163.

[146] Petr Drulák, 'Motion, Container and Equilibrium: Metaphors in the Discourse about European Integration' (2006) 12(4) Eur J Intl Relations 499, 503.

[147] Denis Donoghue, *Metaphor* (Harvard University Press 2014) 51.

[148] Donoghue, *Metaphor*, 170. Clifford Geertz has argued that the power of metaphor derives from 'the interplay between the discordant meanings it symbolically coerces into a unitary conceptual framework...while the success of the metaphor is determined by its ability to overcome the psychic resistance such semantic tension inevitably generates': 'Ideology as a Cultural System' in *The Interpretation of Cultures: Selected Essays* (Fontana Press 1993) 211.

communication; their central claim is that our 'ordinary conceptual system, in terms of which we both think and act, is fundamentally metaphorical in nature'.[149] They use a well-known metaphor—'argument is war'—to explain what it means for a concept to be metaphorical and to structure an everyday activity:

It is important to see that we don't just *talk* about arguments in terms of war. We can actually win or lose arguments. We see the person we are arguing with as an opponent. We attack his positions and we defend our own. We gain and lose ground. We plan and use strategies. If we find one position indefensible, we can abandon it and take a new line of attack. Many of the things we *do* in arguing are partially structured by the concept of war.[150]

Like the 'argument is war' metaphor, we claim that interpretation in international law can be 'partially structured, understood, performed and talked about' in terms of a game.[151] The structural framework of this book 'selects, emphasises, suppresses and organises' features of interpretation by implying things about it that normally apply to games.[152] Our contributors consider whether the game metaphor has more than an ornamental value by placing interpretation in a 'net of new complex relations, through which it is brought into a new light...and is comprehended more vividly and completely than before'.[153]

The use of the game metaphor as a structural framework for evaluating interpretation in international law may not strike everyone as useful or appropriate.[154] Even though metaphor is pervasive in international law,[155] the conceptual fusion dictated by metaphor might be regarded as something of a fox in the interpretive henhouse, given the discipline's definitional fixation with 'ordinary meaning'. An initial objection to the use of the game metaphor might draw on Ludwig Wittgenstein's rejection of the viability of defining games.[156] Wittgenstein discussed the game as an example of a 'family resemblance' concept, for which necessary and sufficient conditions could not be given.[157] He warned against assuming the existence of such conditions: 'Don't say: "There *must* be something common,

---

[149] Lakoff and Johnson, *Metaphors We Live By*, 3.

[150] Lakoff and Johnson, *Metaphors We Live By*, 4.

[151] Lakoff and Johnson, *Metaphors We Live By*, 5.

[152] Max Black, *Models and Metaphors: Studies in Language and Philosophy* (Cornell University Press 1962) 44.

[153] Stern, *Meaning and Change of Meaning*, 308.

[154] The functional utility of metaphor has been the subject of divergent critical appraisal. While Aristotle extolled the 'command of metaphor' as a 'mark of genius', Thomas Hobbes suggested that the use of metaphor gave rise to 'innumerable absurdities' and that the 'settled signification' of words should be preferred. See Aristotle *Poetics* (Hill and Wang 1966) 104 and Thomas Hobbes *Leviathan* (Oxford Paperbacks 2008) 30, 32.

[155] Euan MacDonald has argued that the metaphor of the legal system 'continues to drive our search for closure, for completion, for a unified mode of functioning that would render all contradictions merely apparent': *International Law and Ethics After the Critical Challenge: Framing the Legal within the Post-Foundational* (Martinus Nijhoff 2011) 396. See also Nikolas Rajkovic, 'On Fragments and Geometry: The International Legal Order as Metaphor and How It Matters' (2013) Erasmus L Rev 6.

[156] Ludwig Wittgenstein, *Philosophical Investigations* (Wiley-Blackwell 2009) [65]–[71].

[157] See Heather Gert, 'Alternative Analyses' (1995) 33(1) SJP 31.

or they would not be called 'games'"—but *look and see* whether there is anything common to all'.[158] In the game context, instead of necessary and sufficient conditions, Wittgenstein found only family resemblances, a 'complicated network of similarities overlapping and criss-crossing':

Look for example at board-games, with their multifarious relationships. Now pass to card-games; here you find many correspondences with the first group, but many common features drop out, and others appear. When we pass next to ball-games, much that is common is retained, but much is lost.[159]

The implications of Wittgenstein's 'family resemblance' analysis is that concepts such as games 'apply in virtue of multiple features which not all their instances share and which defy capture in a definition'.[160] Disputes about the ability to define games speak to a larger tension between those who expect to be able to define the necessary and sufficient conditions of philosophical words and concepts and those who do not.[161] However, the purpose of the current project is not to define what all games have in common, but to interrogate the utility of the game metaphor as a heuristic framework in a demarcated context: interpretation in international law.

Ultimately, the book is more interested in testing the metes and bounds of the metaphor in this domain, rather than uncritically accepting and transposing it. The argument is not that interpretation *is* a game, but that particular facets of the comparison are illuminating and capable of capturing both routine interpretive operations as well as those advances that transform the law.[162] Indeed, contributors have been given free rein to evaluate critically the utility of the metaphor, with several rejecting aspects of its use.[163]

For that reason, we have deliberately not committed to a specific game—for example, chess, football, or cards—as the metaphoric referent for interpretation in international law, so as not to impose a conceptual straitjacket on our contributors. However, in the context of an argument against general jurisprudence, Jeremy Waldron has argued that it is more productive to speak about specific incarnations of football, rather than proffer a general theory of football.[164] One problem with failing to specify a particular game as the metaphoric referent is that it is ambivalent to the question of where the players are situated and their levels of

---

[158] Wittgenstein, *Philosophical Investigations*, [66].

[159] Wittgenstein, *Philosophical Investigations*, [66].

[160] Michael Forster, 'Wittgenstein on Family Resemblance Concepts' in Arif Ahmed (ed), *Wittgenstein's Philosophical Investigations: A Critical Guide* (CUP 2010) 66, 67.

[161] Jonathan Ellis, 'On the Concept of a Game' (2011) 34(4) Phil Inv 381, 382. Sutton-Smith argued that 'when it comes to making theoretical statements about what play is, we fall into silliness': *The Ambiguity of Play*, 1. The most extensive effort to refute Wittgenstein's analysis of games and establish an underlying definitional structure was set out by Bernard Suits, *The Grasshopper: Games, Life and Utopia* (3rd edn, Broadview Press 2014) (describing the prelusory goal, the constitutive rules, and the lusory attitude as the three necessary and sufficient conditions of games). See also Mary Midgley, 'The Game Game' (1974) 49 Philosophy 231, 232.

[162] Allan Hutchinson, *It's All in the Game: A Nonfoundationalist Account of Law and Adjudication* (Duke University Press 2000) 12. See also Scott Hershovitz, 'The End of Jurisprudence' (2015) 124 Yale LJ (forthcoming).

[163] See Chapter 9 (Eirik Bjorge) and Chapter 17 (Ingo Venzke).

[164] Jeremy Waldron, 'Can There Be a Democratic Jurisprudence?' (2009) 58 Emory L J 675, 677.

agency. In cricket and football, the players are inside the game and their action is defined by the role they play within it, whereas the players are 'above' the field in chess.[165] Accordingly, there are two levels of playing:

> Those of the pieces who are 'in' the game, and whose identity and room for manoeuvre are defined (constituted) by the rules of the game; and those of the players, who sit behind the board and merely 'do' the game and are themselves exogeneous to it.[166]

In the international relations literature, states have typically been regarded as players behind the board. However, in the legal context, this use of the metaphor has the potential to impair the ability to evaluate legal practice from an internal as well as an external perspective.[167] We prefer François Ost's account of the epistemological perspective underlying the game paradigm as an outside viewpoint that is nonetheless respectful of the internal viewpoint.[168]

2. *The game as social practice*

Secondly, the game metaphor helps 'blow away the juristic fog' perpetuated by adherence to VCLT maxims to reveal interpretation in international law as, first and foremost, a complex *social practice*.[169] Alasdair MacIntyre defined 'practice' as:

> [A]ny coherent and complex form of socially established cooperative human activity through which goods internal to that form of activity are realized in the course of trying to achieve those standards of excellence which are appropriate to, and partially definitive of, that form of activity.[170]

MacIntyre used the games of football and chess as examples of practices with such 'internal goods'. For MacIntyre, 'internal goods' for football or chess would be the 'analytical skill, strategic imagination and competitive intensity' that enables one to excel at the game,[171] as opposed to the pursuit of prestige or wealth, which could be pursued in other ways and are extrinsic to the game.[172] If assigning meaning is understood as one of the 'internal goods' in interpretation in international law, then the game metaphor helps us perceive that the production of meaning:

> results less from a unilateral intentional awareness...than from an uninterrupted, multi-directional collective process of circulation of meaning: 'meaning of the game',

---

[165] Manning, *The Nature of International Society,* 207.

[166] Aalberts, 'Playing the Game of Sovereign States', 257.

[167] David Pozen, 'Self-Help and the Separation of Powers' (2014) 124 Yale L J 2, 74.

[168] François Ost, 'Between Order and Disorder: The Game of Law' in Gunther Teubner, *Autopoietic Law: A New Approach to Law and Society* (de Gruyter 1988) 70, 94, citing Vittorio Villa, 'Legal Science between Natural and Human Sciences' (1984) 3 Leg Stud 264.

[169] Hutchinson, *It's All in the Game,* 61; Bianchi, 'Textual Interpretation and (International) Law Reading', 53.

[170] Alasdair MacIntyre, *After Virtue: A Study in Moral Theory* (Bloomsbury 1981) 218.

[171] MacIntyre, *After Virtue,* 219.

[172] For critical discussion, see James Laidlaw, *The Subject of Virtue: An Anthropology of Ethics and Freedom* (CUP 2014) 61.

'spirit of the system', not as the will of some sort of hypostatised legal order, but as a 'practical faith' shared by the players.[173]

The use of the game metaphor to shed light on law as a social practice has a distinguished pedigree in legal theory. Hart's inaugural lecture as Professor of Jurisprudence at Oxford University centred on the game, with a key argument being that the rules of law are akin to rules of a game.[174] In a Hartian vein, Marmor argued that legal rules and the rules of chess rise to the level of obligation by becoming conventions that are followed by a particular community on the basis of shared understandings.[175] In these examples, the game metaphor illuminates the way in which legal practice might be conceived as a bounded exercise in rule application, predicated on the view that it is feasible to define the range of available moves with sufficient determinacy, such that there are correct and incorrect ways of playing the game.[176]

Against that positivist orthodoxy, Alan Hutchinson developed a theory of adjudication as an 'engaged game of rhetorical justification', and as a 'game of infinite dimensions'.[177] Rather than seeking to trivialize adjudication, Hutchinson believes that the game metaphor helps one grasp the 'practical operation, the political determinants and the transformative possibilities' of adjudication.[178] For Hutchinson, the game of adjudication is a social practice that is as much about 'playing with the rules as it is about playing within the rules'.[179] One implication of Hutchinson's account is that there is nothing sacrosanct about present conceptions of adjudicatory practice because they merely amount to a 'melange of historical accident, human design, political affiliation and economic interest'.[180] Because social practices like football, chess, adjudication, and interpretation are a socio-historical product, their 'internal goods' are not inherently immutable but a product of history.[181] Through the use of the game metaphor, this book aims to advance understanding of what the 'internal goods' pertaining to interpretation in international law are, albeit recognizing their socio-historical contingency and capacity for reinvention.

3. *Reimagining the game*

Thirdly, if the game metaphor demonstrates that the current way of playing the interpretive game in international law is a contingent understanding, then perceiving interpretation in terms of a game has distinct *emancipatory implications* for international law as a discipline and profession. The game metaphor helps

---

[173] Ost, 'Between Order and Disorder', 91, citing Pierre Bourdieu, *Le Sens Pratique* (Seuil 1980).
[174] HLA Hart, 'Definition and Theory in Jurisprudence' (1954) 70 LQR 37.
[175] Andrei Marmor, 'How Law is Like Chess' (2006) 12(4) LT 347. See HLA Hart, *The Concept of Law* (Clarendon Press 1961) 55.
[176] Schauer, *Playing By the Rules*.
[177] Hutchinson, *It's All in the Game*, ix, 2. Hutchinson's account is extensively influenced by David Fraser, *Cricket and the Law: The Man in White is Always Right* (2nd edn, Routledge 2005).
[178] Hutchinson, *It's All in the Game*, 2.   [179] Hutchinson, *It's All in the Game*, 11.
[180] Hutchinson, *It's All in the Game*, 12.   [181] MacIntyre, *After Virtue*, 226.

comprehend the delicate balance between freedom and constraint in the interpretive process; a 'playful account of law…takes seriously both the rules' restrictive pull and their interpretation's liberating push'.[182] A variety of critical thinkers have oriented their use of the game metaphor in just this way,[183] including Michel Foucault, Hannah Arendt, and Gilles Deleuze and Félix Guattari.

Mainstream political theory has the tendency to 'universalise a state of play and so obscure rather than illuminate how we constitute and are constituted by the games and practices in which we think and act'.[184] Michel Foucault argued that the 'games' or governance structures in which individuals participate are not closed by a frontier,[185] and affirmed the latitude to adopt 'strategies of freedom' and to negotiate the rules of the game.[186] In her discussion of political freedom, Hannah Arendt similarly used a game metaphor:[187] 'like players in most games, humans take on their identities *as* citizens and peoples due to participation in this intersubjective activity and…bring into being and sustain the "field of action" of the game'.[188] In the game of political freedom, players can bring something 'new, contingent, singular and unpredictable into the world, breaking with routine and changing the game to some extent'.[189] Arendt's conception of play—the freedom of speaking and acting differently during the course of the game—has the potential to modify the rules and transform the game itself.

Perhaps the most extensive account of the emancipatory possibilities attendant on the game metaphor was developed by Deleuze and Guattari.[190] They developed the concepts of smooth and striated assemblages as a 'language in which to describe micropolitical movements and infrapolitical processes that give rise to new forms of constitutional and legal order'.[191] While striated assemblages are

---

[182] Hutchinson, *It's All in the Game*, 321. See Ost, 'Between Order and Disorder', 83: 'we have to develop concepts that enable us to think simultaneously of constraint, regularity, reproduction *and* freedom, inventiveness, openness'.

[183] The OULIPO (or Workshop for Potential Literature), which included Italo Calvino and Marcel Duchamp, was devoted to illustrating how all literature is a combination of creative latitude and constraint, and to exploring the generative potential of formal constraints. For example, the structure of Georges Perec's *Life: A User's Manual* (Vintage Classics 1996) mimics the 'knight's tour' problem in chess. See generally Daniel Levin-Becker, *Many Subtle Channels: In Praise of Potential Literature* (Harvard University Press 2012).

[184] James Tully, *Public Philosophy in a New Key—Volume I: Democracy and Civic Freedom* (CUP 2008) 141.

[185] Michel Foucault, 'Truth, Power, Self: An Interview with Michel Foucault' in Luther H Martin, Huck Gutman, and Patrick H Hutton (eds), *Technologies of the Self: A Seminar with Michel Foucault* (University of Massachusetts Press 1988) 15.

[186] Michel Foucault, 'The Ethics of the Concern for Self as a Practice of Freedom' in Paul Rabinow (ed), *The Essential Works of Foucault Vol 1: Ethics: Subjectivity and Truth* (New Press 1997) 291–3.

[187] Hannah Arendt, 'What is Freedom?' in *Between Past and Future: Eight Exercises in Political Thought* (Penguin 1977) 142.

[188] Tully, *Public Philosophy in a New Key*, 136.

[189] Tully, *Public Philosophy in a New Key*, 136.

[190] Gilles Deleuze and Félix Guattari, *A Thousand Plateaus* (University of Minnesota Press 1987).

[191] Paul Patton, 'Deleuze's Political Philosophy' in Daniel W Smith and Henry Somers-Hall (eds), *The Cambridge Companion to Deleuze* (CUP 2012) 198, 206.

defined by general, universalizable rules that direct energy towards instrumental ends, smooth assemblages are characterized by rulelessness.[192]

To illustrate the distinction between smooth and striated assemblages, Deleuze and Guattari contrasted the smooth spaces of Go, a Japanese tile game, with the striated spaces of chess. While Go pieces are pellets which have an 'anonymous, collective or third person function', the pieces in chess have an 'internal nature and intrinsic properties from which their movements, situations and confrontations derive'.[193] The differences between the pieces is borne out by game-play:

> Chess is indeed a war, but an institutionalized, regulated, coded war, with a front, a rear, battles. But what is proper to Go is war without battle lines, with neither confrontation nor retreat, without battles even.[194]

Tauel Harper has considered this distinction between smooth and striated assemblages in relation to game-playing spaces where special rules obtain (the 'magic circle').[195] He argues that it is reductive to conclude that games are predicated on flight or capture (or freedom or constraint), solely depending on their ability to transcend the magic circle. Instead, it is possible to conceive of the magic circle as having both smooth and striated elements. In regarding the magic circle as striated, we see that the game-playing space is instrumentally constructed in order to achieve the successful playing of the game. On the other hand, the magic circle can be seen as a smooth space, which allows players to distribute themselves in transgressive ways 'in the course of one's crossing'.[196] This corresponds with Deleuze and Guattari's ontological interest in the interplay between smooth and striated elements:

> What interests us in operations of striation and smoothing are precisely the passages or combinations: how the forces at work within space continually striate it, and how in the course of its striation it develops other forces and emits new smooth spaces.[197]

For Harper, conceiving the game-playing space in terms of the interaction between smoothing and striation, between flight and capture, promotes 'deep reflection on the meaning of the magic circle and the reason why we play'.[198] In like manner, we hope that the use of the game metaphor fosters such reflection in relation to interpretation in international law. As 'players in a game, members in somebody's team',[199] international lawyers all too frequently 'act like highly serious cogs when we might be free people'.[200] This is not to suggest that smoothing the striations

---

[192] Tauel Harper 'The Smooth Spaces of Play: Deleuze and the Emancipative Potential of Games' (2009) 17 symplokē 129, 136.

[193] Deleuze and Guattari, *A Thousand Plateaus*, 352.

[194] Deleuze and Guattari, *A Thousand Plateaus*, 353.

[195] Harper, 'The Smooth Spaces of Play', 134. See also Stewart Woods, '(Play) Ground Rules: The Social Contract and the Magic Circle' (2009) 8 Observatorio 205.

[196] Harper, 'The Smooth Spaces of Play', 137.

[197] Deleuze and Guattari, *A Thousand Plateaus*, 500.

[198] Harper, 'The Smooth Spaces of Play', 139.

[199] Koskenniemi, *From Apology to Utopia*, 561.

[200] Midgley, 'The Game Game', 247.

embodied by the VCLT should be a regulative ideal. Rather, the challenge is to examine the dynamic interplay between freedom and constraint in the game of interpretation in international law.[201]

The way in which the game metaphor is deployed by Foucault, Arendt, and Deleuze and Guattari offers a conceptual apparatus for re-imagining the game of interpretation in international law. It is inevitable that changes in the way the game of interpretation in international law is played would have an impact on the structure of legal and political authority, which might in turn affect the 'epistemic core' of interpretation.[202] For example, what might be the implications of playing the interpretive game in a cooperative rather than adversarial or agonistic manner, with so-called global public goods firmly in view?[203] After all, besides their adversarial dimensions, play and games can also be regarded as generative of communal capacities and engagement based on shared understandings.[204] Yet, recalling the 'argument is war' metaphor discussed earlier, if we are 'preoccupied with the battle aspects, we often lose sight of the cooperative aspects'.[205] The challenge in re-imagining the game of interpretation is that cooperative concern for the communal goods of a practice are always vulnerable to the competitiveness of the institutions that house the practice,[206] with the significant risk of regress to an adversarial posture, even in the context of auto-interpretation. For that reason, those who play the game of interpretation in international law should remember that one of the chief goals of the game is to 'secure peace between all the players'.[207]

Ultimately, the use of a game metaphor, connoting playfulness, should not be regarded as trivializing or undermining the significance of the interpretive process.[208] To say that interpretation in international law is akin to playing a game does not imply that the process is frivolous or that the parties involved in interpretation are not seriously engaged in it.[209] Rather, in its attention to interpretation as a complex social practice, and in its focus on socio-historical contingency and the relationship between freedom and constraint, the game metaphor helps reinsert some vitality in a discipline that has too often become bogged down in

---

[201] Ost, 'Between Order and Disorder', 85: 'However regulated it may be, the game would no longer be a game if it did not have a proportion of uncertainty, risk and arbitrariness that no pre-established rule can totally control.'

[202] Cf Rebecca Adler-Nissen and Thomas Gammeltoft-Hansen, 'Epilogue: Three Layers of a Contested Concept' in Adler-Nissen and Gammeltoft-Hansen, *Sovereignty Games*, 197, 205.

[203] Nico Krisch, 'The Decay of Consent: International Law in an Age of Global Public Goods' (2014) 108(1) AJIL 1.

[204] In *The Balance of Powers in International Relations: Metaphors, Myths and Models* (CUP 2007) 20, Richard Little discusses the way in which the 'balance of powers' metaphor transforms the understanding of power in international relations discourse, from one based on agency to a structural concept, and the residual ambivalence due to the divergent conceptions of balance as an adversarial or associational phenomenon.

[205] Lakoff and Johnson, *Metaphors We Live By*, 10. See also Richard Sennett, *Together: The Rituals, Pleasures and Politics of Cooperation* (Penguin 2012) 5.

[206] MacIntyre, *After Virtue*, 226.

[207] David Dyzenhaus, 'Hobbes on the International Rule of Law' (2014) 28(1) Ethics & Int'l Aff 53, 63.

[208] Hutchinson, *It's All in the Game*, 28.

[209] Eric Berne, *Games People Play* (Penguin 1969) 17.

formalist interpretive technique. If the VCLT has something of a sacred aura for international lawyers, perhaps what is needed (and what the game metaphor provides) is a healthy jolt of profanation.[210]

IV. The Game Plan

In the following chapter, consistently with what we have argued above, Andrea Bianchi provides a detailed exposition of how the game metaphor enhances understanding of interpretation in international law (Chapter 2). The analytic categories in Bianchi's chapter—the object of the game, the players, the rules, the strategies, and what it means to 'play the game of game playing'—provide the structural framework for the book.[211] He argues that the *object* of the game of interpretation is to secure adherence with one's preferred interpretation of the law. There are *players* who are engaged in the game, namely functionally specialized interpretive communities who deploy international law as a professional vocabulary. The VCLT *rules* of play are known and complied with by the players, even though much is left to their *strategies*. After examining the practice of 'how to do interpretation' against the backdrop of the game metaphor, Bianchi's focus shifts to the meta-discourse of '*playing the game of game playing*', which involves reflection upon the nature of the game and why the players think the game is 'worth the candle'.

Part II of the book comprises three chapters that deal with the object of the game of interpretation in international law. Following Bianchi's conception of the object of interpretation, Iain Scobbie unpacks how the players of the game of interpretation can deploy rhetorical strategies in order to secure adherence to their preferred interpretation (Chapter 3). After tracing the history of rhetoric as an object of study, Scobbie draws on the work of the legal philosopher, Chaïm Perelman, to lay out the 'ground rules' for successful legal argumentation. Although rhetoric may help guide the strategies adopted, it cannot—Scobbie points out—ensure success *a priori*; instead, the effectiveness of rhetorical strategies is determined by the skill of the interpreter and the choices he or she makes in deploying an argument in a given situation.

The following two chapters explore the object of the game, in terms of the overarching purpose or function of interpretation in international law. In exploring the existential function of interpretation in international law, Duncan Hollis argues that the object of interpretation is not simply the act of ascribing meaning to a particular rule (Chapter 4). For Hollis, the meaning arrived at by an

---

[210] Giorgio Agamben described the profanation in play as 'freeing a behavior from its genetic inscription within a given sphere…it opens them and makes them available for a new use': *Profanations* (Zone Books 2007) 85–6.

[211] Lakoff and Johnson give the example of the metaphor 'life is a gambling game' to reveal how a set of lexical items can be 'coherently structured' by a single metaphorical concept: *Metaphors We Live By*, 51.

interpreter is not simply a function of the method or technique employed, but rests on an array of earlier interpretive choices about the existence of the object of interpretation in the first place. Hollis explores how all interpretations have existential effects as they create, confirm, or deny the existence of the object of interpretation. In this respect, according to Hollis, one of the objects of the game of interpretation is to constitute the legal reality to be interpreted.

The chapter by Jean d'Aspremont argues, along similar lines, that the object of the game of interpretation should be regarded as multidimensional (Chapter 5). d'Aspremont suggests that the game of interpretation consists not only of attributing meaning to the rules (content-determination), but also of ascertaining what is and what is not law in the identification of rules (law-ascertainment). While constraints on content-determination have usually been envisaged as 'rules', constraints on law-ascertainment are better regarded as indicative of a professional community's practices and traditions.

Part III of the book deals with the players in the game of interpretation in international law. In keeping with a growing scholarly focus on international law as a profession,[212] the three chapters in this section reveal that the relationship between latitude and constraint in interpretation depends in part on the interpreter's conception of his or her professional role.[213]

The chapter by Andraž Zidar provides a typology of the roles and activities of the following players in international legal interpretation: legal advisers, NGO activists, judges, academics, and litigators (Chapter 6). Zidar considers the pertinence of Lon Fuller's distinction between the morality of duty and morality of aspiration for the ethical conduct of the international legal profession and the strengthening of the international legal system.

Michael Waibel's chapter discusses the nature of interpretive and epistemic communities in international law, and how interpretation may be influenced by practices and shared understandings within those communities (Chapter 7). He considers whether interpretive debates in international law are frequently, in reality, a fight by various actors to advance particular normative visions of international law in their various subfields.

Gleider Hernández's chapter seeks to identify how international courts work within the system of international law to construct interpretive authority, and the limits within which such a claim is constructed (Chapter 8). Hernández claims that an essential function of the international judiciary's engagement with international law is to safeguard the coherence of the international legal order, and he offers some reflections about the responsibility that ought to be assumed by judicial institutions when exercising normative authority within the international legal order.

---

[212] See eg James Crawford, 'International Law as Discipline and Profession' (2012) 106 Am Soc'y Int'l L Proc 471; Martti Koskenniemi, 'Between Commitment and Cynicism: Outline for a Theory of International Law as Practice' in *The Politics of International Law* (Hart 2011).
[213] Twining and Miers, *How to Do Things With Rules*, 122.

Part IV of the book focuses on the rules of the game of interpretation in international law, exploring different facets of the VCLT rules of interpretation. The three chapters in this section function as an instructive reminder that many interpretive controversies occur under the umbrella of the VCLT, and that 'to participate in the system is necessarily to participate in its idea of itself; to play a game is to play the rules of the game'.[214]

Eirik Bjorge's chapter provides an analysis of the common denominator of the VCLT rules (Chapter 9). The received wisdom about the approach to treaty interpretation in the VCLT was that it lay to rest the notion of interpreting according to the 'intention of the parties'. However, Bjorge argues that the aim of treaty interpretation, according to the VCLT rules, is the establishment of an objectivized intention of the parties. He explores this thesis through an assessment of the premium put upon the intention of the parties in cases involving evolutionary interpretation.

Julian Arato's chapter confronts the paradox that, despite the unity and universality of the VCLT rules, there is a practice of affording some treaties special treatment in the process of interpretation (Chapter 10). Arato considers and rejects the usual explanations for differential treatment, based on generalizations about a treaty's subject matter, or based on its particular object and purpose. He argues that the crucial consideration is the nature of the obligations incorporated by the parties in order to achieve their goals. The critical question is whether a treaty provision entails a merely reciprocal exchange of rights and duties, or rather incorporates a more absolute commitment by the parties to take on an obligation insulated from their changing intentions, and over which their subsequent mastery might prove limited.

While the chapters by Bjorge and Arato deal with diachronic issues—the evolution or change in the interpretation of rules over time—Anne-Marie Carstens focuses on the under-explored phenomenon of transplanted treaty rules and their interpretation (Chapter 11). Transplantation occurs when pre-existing treaty rules ('source rules') are incorporated into a subsequent treaty between different parties, in a different context or legal regime. Despite repeated references to source rules, interpreters often fail to indicate how they factor into the VCLT framework governing treaty interpretation. Although source rules might be regarded as a supplemental means of interpretation under Article 32 of the VCLT, the treatment that interpreters afford to source rules elevate them to a higher relevance. Carstens concludes her analysis by suggesting that the VCLT is sufficiently flexible to allow more predictable and consistent consideration of source rules.

Part V of the book concerns some of the strategies available to those who play the game of interpretation in international law. A recent analysis of 'sovereignty games' sought to transcend descriptions of sovereignty to emphasize how sovereignty is deployed strategically in legal and political practice.[215] This section adopts a similar mandate in the context of interpretation in international law.

---

[214] Philip Allott, 'International Law and the Idea of History' in *The Health of Nations: Society and Law Beyond the State* (CUP 2002) 316, 318.
[215] Adler-Nissen and Gammeltoft-Hansen, *Sovereignty Games*, 7.

Fuad Zarbiyev's chapter characterizes the interpretive method of textualism in strategic terms, revealing the historical contingencies that led to it being regarded as sacrosanct in international law (Chapter 12). In his genealogy of textualism, Zarbiyev identifies a series of factors pertaining to the intellectual history of international law and the historical circumstances prevailing at the time of the adoption of the VCLT that explain textualism's superior status. He concludes by arguing that textualism cannot claim any trans-historical validity and that its contingency needs to be acknowledged and investigated.

Harlan Grant Cohen's chapter seeks to explain the strategic use of the doctrine of precedent in international law (Chapter 13). While judicial decisions interpreting international law are not binding on future parties in future cases, international precedent is ubiquitous; prior decisions are invoked, argued over, and applied by practitioners and tribunals. Cohen focuses on three sets of factors relevant to a prior interpretation's precedential weight: (1) the varied potential sources of precedent, (2) the factors that might imbue a source with authority, and (3) the actors and audiences who might invoke a precedent or respond to it. He goes on to describe three overlapping accounts of how these factors may interact—rationalist, jurisprudential, and sociological accounts—before arguing that these factors and accounts help explain the patterns of precedent we observe in international law today.

The chapter by René Provost explores how international law creates narratives of (il)legality, in the context of international criminal law, and how the strategic deployment of culture may function as a justification for particular interpretive postures (Chapter 14). If a practice, considered to amount to an international crime, holds deep cultural meaning in a given circumstance, must legal interpretation yield to a significant extent to the interpretation of that practice from a standpoint internal to the community concerned? Provost argues that the interpretation of international law and of local culture emerge as ineluctably interwoven, with international law acting as a tool and justification to reinterpret local culture through the prism of legal norms devoid of any local rootedness. For Provost, the danger is an outcome whereby international law fails to be perceived as legitimate by the agents whose behaviour it seeks to regulate, and fails to trigger the kind of normative engagement required to make law real.

Part VI of the book comprises three chapters on 'playing the game of game playing'. As Susan Sontag has argued, interpretation is not 'an absolute value' but 'must itself be evaluated'.[216] After all, what it means to play the game of interpretation in international law is not fixed, but a 'shifting ideal that [is] part and parcel of [a] contingent practice'.[217]

Jens Olesen examines the question of whether there is such as thing as a 'politics of interpretation' (Chapter 15). He seeks to elucidate the relationship between interpretation and politics by examining the extent to which an act of interpretation embodies the 'will to power' of the interpreter, and the performative

---

[216] Susan Sontag, *Against Interpretation and Other Essays* (Penguin 2009) 7.
[217] Hutchinson, *It's All in the Game*, 8–9.

dimension and political consequences of interpretive speech acts. Olesen suggests that philosophical theories of language underestimate the constraints under which the interpreter is placed by neglecting the role of conventions in the process of interpretation, and concludes by identifying how the ideological underpinnings of interpretations might be decoded.

The chapter by Martin Wählisch explores cognitive frames in interpretation in international law (Chapter 16). Wählisch details how cognitive frames can help to build coalitions and mobilize international consensus; at the same time, they can hinder the development of generally accepted principles and relativize the application of norms. He describes how individual and institutional frames shape the interpretation of international law, demonstrating how strategic interpretations accord not just with interpretive norms but take advantage of pre-held biases that indelibly affect our subconscious. The objectivity of law, Wählisch argues, is not diminished by the existence of cognitive biases. Rather, it reflects the fact that international law is a forum of competing ideas, conflicting interpretations, and evolving practices.

Ingo Venzke's chapter examines the metaphor of the language of international law in light of the metaphor that structures this book: the game (Chapter 17). Established approaches picture interpretation as a rule-governed activity, instructed by a given language, ordered by a pervasive grammar, and based on a set of constitutive background rules. However, Venzke argues, in law, as in language, we make the rules as we go along, and suggests that there are a variety of good methodological, political, and strategic reasons for rejecting the dualism between a background scheme and its execution. Can we still see interpretation as an ordered activity? Venzke first fleshes out a view of interpretation as a creative practice in which actors struggle for the law, a practice that is constrained and stabilized by tradition. A more radical alternative suggests that there is no language to play with. On this view, interpretation aims at better understanding the speaker, rather than any language of international law.

It is entirely appropriate to conclude this book with a chapter by Philip Allott, whose own scholarship has effectively deployed metaphor in order to reimagine the international law game (Chapter 18).[218] Allott's chapter addresses the following questions: What is interpretation? What is the place of language in interpretation? When are the moments in which the act of interpretation is undertaken and how do interpretations alter according to their temporal setting and context? How and why are interpretations constrained? Allott's chapter highlights issues that the reader of this book will have undoubtedly asked him- or herself while surveying the preceding chapters. In many ways, it is emblematic of the aim of the book—to promote critical and open-minded reflection on interpretive practices and processes in international law.

---

[218] See Philip Allott, *Eunomia: New Order for a New World* (OUP 2001). For a discussion of the use of metaphor in *Eunomia*, see MacDonald, *International Law and Ethics After the Critical Challenge*, 351–9.

Conclusion

In Andrei Makine's novel *Human Love*, the protagonist, Elias, reflects on the revolutionary tactics he has been taught as follows:

At the end of all these sessions on insurrection techniques, so ingenious and ruthless were the tricks designed to outwit one's fellow human beings that Elias found himself asking, What's the point? In the mouths of the instructors, these tactics for fighting and subversion became art for art's sake, glorious goals in their own right, which eclipsed the goal of the revolution itself. They would spend their whole lives, Elias told himself, perfecting their methods, like chess players hypnotised by the marquetry of their own chessboards. What's the point?...He hurriedly silenced this question, unworthy of a professional.[219]

Elias' musings are not dissimilar to the conviction that prompted this collection of essays on interpretation in international law. International lawyers who reify the methods in the VCLT as 'glorious goals in their own right' and who spend their professional lives perfecting these interpretive techniques 'like chess players hypnotised by the marquetry of their own chessboards' frequently pay scant attention to the 'point' of interpretation in international law. Rather than denigrate the latter enquiry as 'unworthy of a professional', this collection seeks to provide what has been termed an 'interpretation of interpretation', an examination of 'the place and function of interpretation in the international legal system'.[220]

In an attempt to understand interpretation as the search for meaning in international law, the book is creatively structured around the metaphor of the game, which captures and illuminates the constituent elements of interpretive activity. The book aims to break free from the myopic focus on the VCLT that pervades international legal scholarship to reveal interpretation as a phenomenon that permeates all areas of international law as a discipline and professional practice. We hope to convince the reader that the game metaphor is not a frivolous conceit but one that helps 'set new possibilities astir',[221] and crystallizes a set of concerns that are too often neglected in a formalist rule-based paradigm. The contributions in this collection constitute a 'critical cartography' of the practice and process of interpretation in international law.[222] Ultimately, the book should be read as a plea for methodological self-reflexivity by those who play the game of interpretation in international law.

---

[219] Andrei Makine, *Human Love* (Arcade Publishing 2004) 107.
[220] Weiler, 'Prolegomena to a Meso-Theory of Treaty Interpretation', 6.
[221] Donoghue, *Metaphor*, 170.
[222] David Koller, '...and New York and the Hague and Tokyo and Geneva and Nuremberg and...: The Geographies of International Law' (2012) 23(1) EJIL 97, 118.

2

The Game of Interpretation in International Law

The Players, the Cards, and Why the Game is Worth the Candle

*Andrea Bianchi**

I. The Game

When Stanley Fish famously stated that 'interpretation is the only game in town',[1] most legal commentators focused on the consequences of conceiving of 'law as interpretation'.[2] The term 'game' was completely overlooked. This chapter examines interpretation as a 'game', while leaving in the background the issue of whether law as such is only about interpretation.

From a socio-historical perspective, the importance of games generally, and board games in particular, can hardly be overestimated.[3] Games reflect people's habits and culture. They thrive on deeply rooted ideas and beliefs and stimulate reflexes attuned to the prevailing culture of the social group to which the players belong. Board games, just like music, dance, and literature, are part and parcel of the life that human beings experience within a social group or community. They help constitute a common collective identity and change over time alongside culture and *mores*. Everyone in the group can play them, although individual skills

* I am grateful to Thomas Schultz and Fuad Zarbiyev for their comments on earlier drafts.

[1] Stanley Fish, *Is There a Text in This Class? The Authority of Interpretive Communities* (Harvard University Press 1980) 355.

[2] See Peter Schanck, 'The Only Game in Town: Contemporary Interpretive Theory, Statutory Construction and Legislative Histories' (1990) 38 U Kan L Rev 815; Judith Schelly, 'Interpretation in Law: the Dworkin-Fish Debate (or, Soccer Amongst the Gahuku-Gama)' (1985) 73 Cal L Rev 158.

[3] See Elliott Avedon and Brian Sutton-Smith, *The Study of Games* (Wiley & Sons 1971), examining games from a variety of different disciplinary perspectives and providing an extensive bibliography. See also Harold JR Murray, *A History of Board Games Other Than Chess* (OUP 1952); Frederic Grunfeld, *Games of the World* (Holt, Rinehart and Winston 1975); RC Bell, *Board and Table Games from Many Civilizations* (Dover Publications 1979); Peter Arnold, *The Book of Games* (Exeter Books 1985); David Parlett, *The Oxford History of Board Games* (OUP 1999).

vary remarkably from one player to another. Everyone knows the rules and abides by them. Strategies are deployed to be successful at the game. Individual skills are definitely important, but chance also plays a role.

Certainly, the game is a metaphor.[4] As such, it helps to capture the essential traits of a concept or activity, the contours of which might be difficult to define with any accuracy otherwise. Metaphors are powerful tools of mediated knowledge that may help us to understand reality better, particularly when they provide mental links and associations to objects and situations that we experience in our daily life.[5] The metaphor of the game is an apt one, as it contains *mutatis mutandis* all the elements that an act of interpretation requires. There are players who are engaged in the game and who are supposed to interpret the law. The 'rules of play' are known and complied with by the players, even though which cards to play and when is left to the skills and strategies of the individual players. And—quite obviously—the game has an object. In order to win the game, one must secure adherence with his or her own interpretation of the law.

The chapter will start by expounding the object of the game and will then set out to explore who the players are and how they play the game. Attention will be paid not only to the rules and practices but also to the tricks and stratagems that can be used to score points and be successful at the game. In other words, the practice of 'how to do interpretation' will be analysed against the backdrop of the game metaphor. Afterwards, the focus will be shifted to the meta-discourse of 'playing the game of game playing', where fundamental questions such as the nature of the game and who gets to decide by what rules one should play will be cursorily addressed. Finally, some considerations on the reasons why everyone seems to be convinced that the game is worth the candle will be advanced.

Short of any major epistemological ambition, the chapter simply aims to disclose the modalities by which the game of interpretation takes place in international law. Although practically all the actors agree on the rules of play, the historically contingent nature of the rules of interpretation is often overlooked. Just as board games have evolved and changed over time, so has the game of interpretation in international law. This should caution against any posture that considers the rules of the game or the players entitled to participate in it as immutable data or realities not subject to change. Furthermore, the purposeful nature of any interpretive act and the strategies pursued by the players in order to accomplish their goals can be conveniently framed in terms of 'game playing'. The rule-based approach that characterizes almost all recent scholarly contributions to interpretation in international law fails to shed light on how the interpretive process actually

---

[4] The game metaphor is frequently used in relation to law: see Michel Van De Kerchove and François Ost, *Le droit ou les paradoxes du jeu* (Presses Universitaires de France 1992); Michel Van De Kerchove and François Ost, *Le jeu, un paradigme pour le droit?* (LGDJ 1992).

[5] See George Lakoff and Mark Johnson (eds), *Metaphors We Live By* (2nd edn, University of Chicago Press 2003); Mark Johnson (ed), *Philosophical Perspectives on Metaphor* (University of Minnesota Press 1981); George Lakoff, *Women, Fire, and Dangerous Things: What Categories Reveal about the Mind* (University of Chicago Press 1990).

works, as well as on its underlying stakes.[6] To realize that the game of interpretation is an ongoing, partly self-constitutive process, in which players and rules change over time, and where the stakes are generated by the game itself, is a sound approach to understanding the nature and functioning of the interpretation process in international law.

Let's now have a look at the game's instructions sheet!

II. The Object

The ultimate object of the game of interpretation is to persuade one's audience that his or her own interpretation of the law is the correct one. In other words, the winner is he or she who succeeds in securing adherence to his or her own interpretation. The recreational character of the game of interpretation should not be overstated. In fact, most of the time this is a highly competitive contest, in which the stakes are high and the battle to impose one's interpretation is fiercely and ruthlessly fought.

How to gain acceptance of one's views and interpretations more properly pertains to the 'strategies' section of the 'instructions sheet', which will be discussed further below.[7] It suffices to say here that rhetorical tools and argumentation techniques that resonate deeply with international lawyers and other social agents engaged in the game are likely to be a very important component of a successful strategy. The way in which a player is capable of effectively addressing his or her audience, by capturing its attention and by leading it through his or her line of argumentation, will depend on a variety of different factors, ranging from the authority of the player and his or her rhetorical skills to the receptivity and disposition of the audience. Chaïm Perelman has discussed this in the context of rhetoric to mean the set of techniques geared towards securing the audience's adherence to the speaker's argumentation.[8] The more the discourse is attuned to what the audience needs or wants to hear, the greater the player's impact on the audience will be.

By audience, I refer in this context to those individuals who participate, watch, or have stakes in the game. The notion is fundamental insofar as this is the ambit in which the game takes place. Individual human beings with distinct cognitive faculties, in a given professional setting, form the audience addressed by the players/speakers. Whoever speaks (or writes) usually does so to an audience.

---

[6] See eg Richard Gardiner, *Treaty Interpretation* (OUP 2008); Alexander Orakhelashvili, *The Interpretation of Acts and Rules in Public International Law* (OUP 2008); Ulf Linderfalk, *On the Interpretation of Treaties* (Springer 2007); Robert Kolb, *Interprétation et création du droit international: esquisse d'une herméneutique juridique moderne pour le droit international public* (Bruylant 2006). For an exception to this approach, see Ingo Venzke, *How Interpretation Makes International Law. On Semantic Change and Normative Twists* (OUP 2012).

[7] See nn 66–87 and accompanying text.

[8] Chaïm Perelman and Lucie Olbrechts-Tyteca, *The New Rhetoric: A Treatise on Argumentation* (University of Notre Dame Press 1969).

The audience may be constituted by only one person or by a group of persons. Whether wide or limited, the audience can be addressed in a variety of different ways and by different means and modes of communication. What matters is that there is always somebody at the receiving end of the communication process, who listens and to whom the oral or written expression is addressed. Perelman defines the audience as 'the ensemble of those whom the speaker wishes to influence by his argumentation'.[9] This definition epitomizes the interrelational dimension of the relationship between 'audience' and 'speaker'.

The *Jurisdictional Immunities of the State* case, decided by the International Court of Justice (ICJ) in 2012, provides a good example of this point.[10] It will be recalled that the case concerned the alleged conflict between serious human rights violations and the jurisdictional immunities that foreign states enjoy before the domestic courts of another state. As I have argued elsewhere,[11] the judgment sounds so persuasive to the skilled reader because it is perfectly adjusted to its audience, which is already predisposed to accept certain types of argument, particularly if the latter emanate from a judicial body that is already perceived in and of itself as being particularly authoritative. The close relationship between the ICJ and its audience, the shared cultural and professional identity, and the common *habitus* of the participants in the game cause certain arguments and rhetorical devices to play out better and, eventually, to be more effective than others that are simply not suitable for the audience which they are meant to address.[12] I surmised that the coupling of the authority that the ICJ possesses vis-à-vis the other players and the rhetorical skills it showed in drafting the judgment would bear heavily on the interpretation of the legal issues underlying the case. This is why I predicted with some degree of confidence that the interpretation of the law of state immunity given by the ICJ would impose itself and mark the end of the interpretive game, at least for the time being.[13]

For the very same reason, some of the judges who attached dissenting opinions to the majority's judgment had clearly lost the game of interpretation and stood no chance of influencing their audience.[14] By founding their conflicting views about state immunity on the quest for justice in international law, on the rights of victims to have access to justice in order to seek redress, and on the alleged pre-eminence of such values over the jurisdictional immunities of states, the views of the dissenting judges were unlikely to be well received by states, the primary audience of the ICJ.

[9] Perelman and Olbrechts-Tyteca, *The New Rhetoric*, 19.
[10] *Jurisdictional Immunities of the State (Germany v Italy: Greece Intervening)* (Judgment) [2012] ICJ Rep 99.
[11] Andrea Bianchi, 'Gazing at the Crystal Ball (Again): State Immunity and *Jus Cogens* beyond *Germany v Italy*' (2013) 4(3) JIDS 457.
[12] On the concept of *habitus*, see Pierre Bourdieu, *The Logic of Practice* (CUP 1990) 53.
[13] Andrea Bianchi, 'On Certainty' (*EJIL: Talk!*, 16 February 2012) <http://www.ejiltalk.org/on-certainty/> accessed 15 May 2013. My prediction seems to have been confirmed by recent case law. See, for instance, the judgment of the Fourth Section of the European Court of Human Rights in *Jones v United Kingdom* App no 34356/06 and 40528/06 (ECtHR, 14 January 2014).
[14] *Jurisdictional Immunities*, Dissenting Opinions of Judge Cançado Trindade and Judge Yusuf.

The privileging of the protection of individuals, with the fundamental principles of human rights as a normative background, was always unlikely to make
inroads amongst those who view the state as the main hinge upon which the
whole international legal system pivots. It would be naive to think that this way
of thinking would be adopted by the ICJ, where the overwhelming majority of
judges acted as legal advisers to states or international organizations in their prior
professional experience.[15] By the same token, to hold that the international legal
regime of state immunity is 'as a matter of fact, as full of holes as Swiss cheese',[16]
is a metaphor that is unlikely to appeal to those who have been trained to believe
that international law is made by states for states only. Paradoxically, the simple suggestion to strike a balance between the conflicting needs of jurisdictional
immunities and human rights protection[17]—in and of itself a moderate and reasonable proposal—ended up irritating the majority of the judges,[18] who remain
fundamentally opposed to this way of thinking. To appeal to values other than
those traditionally upheld in the state-centred view of international law, such as
the principle of sovereign equality, can be counter-productive in a context such
as the ICJ.

Given the utter inadequacy of the rhetorical and argumentative structure of
their discourse for their audience, some of the dissenting opinions risk going
unnoticed by that audience. Here lies the dissenting judges' fundamental mistake. By neglecting the characteristics and the predispositions of the audience,
and by refusing to call into question the self-proclaimed primacy of their own values over other conflicting values, they end up paying insufficient attention both
to the efficacy of their argumentative strategies and to the need to adjust them
to the audience. The securing of the audience's adherence to one's arguments is
fundamental if one is to have a real-world impact and win the interpretive game.[19]
This is not to say that the dissenting judges are wrong or that their arguments
are flawed. It may be that in another context, or with another composition of the
Court, their language and reasoning would resonate better.

Another apt illustration of failure in securing adherence to one's own view
on matters of interpretation is Sir Gerald Fitzmaurice's experience as a judge
at the European Court of Human Rights (ECtHR) in Strasbourg. As recently
illustrated by Ed Bates, Fitzmaurice's strong aversion to the way in which the

---

[15] It suffices to browse the *curricula vitae* of the judges currently sitting at the ICJ: <http://www.
icj-cij.org/court/index.php?p1=1&p2=2&p3=1> accessed 24 July 2014.

[16] *Jurisdictional Immunities*, Dissenting Opinion of Judge Yusuf, [26].

[17] *Jurisdictional Immunities*, Dissenting Opinion of Judge Yusuf, [28]–[29], referring to the Joint
Separate Opinion of Judges Higgins, Kooijmans, and Buergenthal in *Arrest Warrant of 11 April
2000 (Democratic Republic of Congo v Belgium)* [2002] ICJ Rep 3, [75].

[18] *Jurisdictional Immunities*, [106]: '[A]ccording to international law, State immunity, where it
exists, is a right of the foreign State...Immunity cannot, therefore, be made dependent upon the
outcome of a balancing exercise of the specific circumstances of each case to be conducted by the
national court before which immunity is claimed.'

[19] Perelman and Olbrechts-Tyteca, *The New Rhetoric*, 23: 'The great orator, the one with a hold
on his listeners, seems animated by the very mind of his audience. This is not the case for the ardent
enthusiast whose sole concern is with what he himself considers important.'

European Convention had been interpreted throughout the 1970s by the Court as if it were some sort of European Bill of Rights—with the Court acting in a quasi-constitutional capacity—led to a long series of dissenting opinions and, eventually, to an early resignation before the end of his term.[20] The story is quite telling of the sharp contrast that divided Fitzmaurice from his fellow judges at the Court. While the majority looked at the text of the Convention as a 'living instrument', Fitzmaurice saw the Convention as an international treaty to protect fundamental human rights rather than an instrument to promote social policies by way of legal interpretation.[21] It does not matter whether Fitzmaurice's view was correct. What counts is that he did not win the game of interpretation, in which he participated for six years as the British judge.

III. The Players

The game in question is, at least at first sight, a fairly liberal one. By that I mean that almost everyone who has a place in the profession—broadly understood—can participate in it. On closer scrutiny, however, the superficially egalitarian character of the game is quickly unveiled. The truth is that everyone's views do not carry the same weight and not everyone's voice is listened to, or even heard for that matter, by the audience.

It should be clear that when I talk about 'players' in the game of interpretation, I am not referring to the so-called 'subjects' or 'actors' of international law. In other words, I am not concerned here with the issue of who has rights and obligations under international law, which entities enjoy a full-fledged or limited personality or who has standing before international courts and institutions. More pragmatically, the focus is on who—regardless of status or qualification—plays the game and is recognized as a player having a stake in the game.

The notion of a group of individuals and entities playing the game of interpreting the law is reminiscent of the concept of the 'interpretive community' that shapes the common understanding of legal rules in the different areas of international law.[22]

---

[20] Ed Bates, *The Evolution of the European Convention on Human Rights: From its Inception to the Creation of a Permanent Court of Human Rights* (OUP 2010) 361.

[21] Interestingly, Fitzmaurice distinguished between 'genuine human rights', meaning those rights 'so fundamental, so founded in nature and *la condition humaine*, as to constitute a different order of right', and 'ordinary everyday…rights deriving from man-made laws': Gerald Fitzmaurice, 'Some Reflections on the ECHR—and on Human Rights' in Rudolf Bernhardt (ed), *Völkerrecht als Rechtsordnung Internationale Gerichtsbarkeit Menschenrechte: Festschrift für Herman Mosler* (Springer Verlag 1983) 209, as cited in Bates, *The Evolution of the European Convention on Human Rights*, 363.

[22] On the concept of 'interpretive community', see Stanley Fish, *Is There a Text in This Class? The Authority of Interpretive Communities* (Harvard University Press 1980); Stanley Fish, *Doing What Comes Naturally: Change, Rhetoric, and the Practice of Theory in Literary and Legal Studies* (Duke University Press 1989). Fish developed the 'interpretive community' concept in connection with literary studies, to explain the source of interpretive authority. Fish describes an interpretive community as 'not so much a group of individuals who shared a point of view, but a point of view or way of organizing experience that shared individuals in the sense that its assumed distinctions, categories of understanding, and stipulations of relevance and irrelevance were the content of the

A few years ago, I inquired into the extent to which the content and scope of application of the international legal rules on the use of force are affected by the disagreement existing within the interpretive community on the method that must be used for interpreting the law.[23] In that context, I identified the interpretive community concerned with the use of force, consisting not only of national governments and their legal advisers or the judges of the ICJ. I argued that the interpretive community 'includes also the handful of academics that have made the use of force their specialty or occasionally write about it, non-governmental organizations, lobbies, and pressure groups that may have an interest in particular instances, and intellectuals and opinion-makers who influence public opinion by publicly voicing their position on any given matter'.[24]

Along the same lines, I submit that there is a community of players engaged in the game of interpretation that play their cards and contribute to the understanding of the game and the development of strategies to be used to win it. They also determine how the game is to be played, but I will revert to this particular aspect at a later stage when examining the issue of 'playing the game of game playing'.[25] If one were to expressly mention the players that take part in the interpretive game, one would certainly include states and international organizations, or more accurately the individuals who work for them; courts, both international and domestic; non-governmental organizations and professional associations, including international law ones such as the International Law Association and the *Institut de droit international*; practitioners working as counsel, advocates, or experts in international law cases; and academics working on matters of interpretation and general theory or touching on interpretive issues while working on substantive areas of the law. With a little malice, but with practically no risk of being proven wrong, one could add to the list clerks and assistants who 'help' judges and arbitrators draft their judicial opinions and arbitral awards, and research assistants who 'help' academics write their books and articles.

No accreditation procedure is demanded of players, except for the need to be associated more or less formally with the profession. As I said at the outset, however, not everybody's voice is equally important. For instance, international lawyers attribute an enormous importance to judicial interpretation. Admittedly, this is not a distinctly 'international law' feature, as in the domestic law arena judges

---

consciousness of community members who were therefore no longer individuals, but, insofar as they were embedded in the community's enterprise, community property. It followed that such community-constituted interpreters would, in their turn, constitute, more or less in agreement, the same text, although the sameness would not be attributable to the self-identity of the text, but to the communal nature of the interpretive act': *Doing What Comes Naturally*, 141.

[23] Andrea Bianchi, 'The International Legal Regulation of the Use of Force: the Politics of Interpretive Method' (2009) 22(4) LJIL 651.

[24] Bianchi, 'The International Legal Regulation of the Use of Force', 653–4: 'The concept of interpretive community is key to understanding that the discourse about the legal aspects of the use of force is a single one, in which different societal forces are at work and several actors interact at different levels and with varying degrees of influence and responsibility with a view to imposing their own way of interpreting legal rules.'

[25] See nn 88–93 and accompanying text.

are also revered, and their interpretive activity is considered as particularly valuable when determining the meaning of the law.[26] International lawyers, however, do tend to look at law and at legal interpretation from the perspective of the judicial function. Most of the time, the interpretive questions that are posed in the profession are related to the way in which a judge would interpret a certain legal provision and apply it to any given case. This is in conformity with the utter deference that international lawyers show towards international courts. It suffices to think of how we analyse judicial decisions, particularly those rendered by particularly authoritative judicial bodies such as the ICJ. Robert Jennings aptly noticed that the judgments of the Court tend to be considered by international lawyers as 'holy writs'.[27] Single lines and often single words are dissected, analysed, and often used completely out of context as evidence of any given interpretation of the law.

The central role still played by the ICJ in what one could term the 'official' or the 'traditional' discourse of international law can hardly be denied. Reference is often made to it as 'the Court' and whoever can get a precedent of the Court or even a small *dictum* on their side will have a considerable comparative advantage over the other party in terms of persuasive force. This means that the ICJ's authority in the field is deeply rooted and still solidly grounded. Thirty years ago, Ian Brownlie wrote that the ICJ 'stands at the centre of the world of the professional international lawyer',[28] which reveals much about the charm exercised by the Court on the members of the profession! What remains striking is that the pre-eminence of the judicial function as well as the 'glorification' of the international judge that goes hand in hand with it are attitudes that are not limited to those who practise law. Rather, they are shared also by academics, whom—one would expect—should keep some distance from the object of their intellectual inquiry.[29]

The reasons for this deferential attitude towards the ICJ in international law circles and, more generally, towards judicial determinations across different areas of specialization can be explained against the backdrop of tradition. Tradition plays a major role in determining the attitudes of a social group towards 'authority'. Surely, the fact that international law has been constantly benchmarked against domestic law may also constitute a plausible explanation. The inferiority complex long suffered by international lawyers due to the widespread perception amongst domestic lawyers that international law is not really law could also explain why the profession has emphasized the existence and the good functioning of judicial

---

[26] See Pierre Schlag, *The Enchantment of Reason* (Duke University Press 1998).

[27] Robert Jennings, 'The Role of the International Court of Justice' (1997) 68 BYBIL 1, 41–2; Robert Jennings, 'The Judicial Function and the Rule of Law in International Relations' in *International Law at the Time of its Codification: Essays in Honour of Roberto Ago* (Giuffrè 1987) Vol 3, 139, 142–3.

[28] Ian Brownlie, 'The Calling of the International Lawyer: Sir Humphrey Waldock and His Work' (1983) 54 BYBIL 7, 68.

[29] René Girard, *Deceit, Desire and the Novel: Self and Other in Literary Structure* (Johns Hopkins University Press 1966). Girard's elaboration of the theory of 'mimetic desire' helps explain the emulation effect that leads international lawyers incessantly to refer to judicial determinations.

bodies in international law 'just like' in domestic law.[30] Yet another plausible explanation lies in the structural flaw of international law lacking a general law-making mechanism other than the one producing custom. Judicial pronouncements could thus be seen as an indirect modality of general law-making, given the inadequacy of the system to produce generally applicable rules. In other words, the international judge would make up, at least in part, for the lack of an international legislature.[31]

To reason always from the perspective of the judge is not without consequences. To look at law from the perspective of the judge is fairly simplistic if one regards law as a social phenomenon and interpretation as a choice amongst different options. The judge—as aptly put by Pierre Schlag—has a practical task, which consists of providing satisfactory judicial solutions.[32] This self-identification with the perspective of the judge entails a myopia of sorts as regards the problematic aspects of (international) law and legal interpretation, and makes one believe that law has a ready-made answer to any question, thus leaving little room for interpretation. Such an attitude, curiously also metabolized and interiorized by legal scholarship, provides an explanation for many a professional reflex and also for the predisposition by many international lawyers to emphasize the phase of the judicial ascertainment of the 'rule' by way of judicial interpretation.

The current pre-eminence accorded to judicial interpretation and to judges as players in the game of interpretation would appear to be set in stone. However, players change over time. There is nothing immutable in the game's rules of play. Players who used to have an important role in the game may have seen their importance diminished. Others may have gained prominence over time. Finally, some players are relatively new to the game and have brought into it new strategies and unprecedented modalities of action. What is important to realize is the contingent character of the game. As we shall see shortly,[33] the fact that the rules, principles, and criteria of interpretation seem now to be uncontroversial and almost universally accepted by the players is a relatively new development, which is in and of itself subject to change. Societal consensus may direct interpretation towards other criteria and the very composition of the societal body may vary, by including other players or by diminishing or increasing the importance of extant ones. What matters most is that the game will continue to be played.

It should be stressed once again that the game is far from being peaceful. It may be worth recalling that etymologically *ludus* refers to both the game as well as the enclosure or school where gladiators were trained to fight. Indeed, players may get aggressive and misbehave. They certainly are unruly most of the time. They wear

---

[30] See Gerry Simpson, 'On the Magic Mountain: Teaching Public International Law' (1999) 10 EJIL 70.

[31] See Luigi Condorelli, 'L'autorité de la décision des juridictions internationales permanentes' in Société Française de Droit International, *La juridiction internationale permanente, Colloque de Lyon* (Pedone 1987) 277. See also Volker Röben, 'Le précédent dans la jurisprudence de la Cour Internationale' (1989) 32 GYIL 405.

[32] Pierre Schlag, 'Anti-intellectualism' (1995) 16 Cardozo L Rev 1111.

[33] See nn 37–65 and accompanying text.

different 'hats' in their professional career, sometimes at the same time, and by performing different roles they hope to increase their capacity to have impact on the game. It is notorious that academics often act as advocates and counsel before tribunals or give their opinions in other non-contentious settings or are appointed as judges and arbitrators. The contrary is also true. Practitioners are often the beneficiaries of academic appointments or they serve in capacities that once were exclusively the prerogative of academics, such as membership on law journal editorial boards or academic search committees. In a recently published study on the functioning of the investment arbitration world, researchers have demonstrated the existence of these 'revolving doors' amongst various professional roles, as well as the increasing influence of practitioners on academia.[34]

Even though interpretive communities shape the content and meaning of rules in the different areas of international law,[35] the players of the interpretive game are entrusted with the most important task of all: that of determining the rules of play! In other words, the fight for determining by what means legal prescriptions should be interpreted has very high stakes, insofar as it permits control of the whole of the discipline of international law by fixing the criteria and the modalities that everyone should follow to interpret the law. Against this backdrop, it is easy to understand why 'generalists' and 'specialists' often quarrel about who has the authority to speak for international law.[36] The claim often laid down by so-called 'generalists'—that they are the ones that should be listened to as far as general international law is concerned—appears in a different light when one realizes that the rules of interpretation are traditionally thought to be part and parcel of general international law. The fight is about controlling the discursive policies of the discipline.

IV. The Cards

It is inconceivable to play a board game without cards. In order to keep the metaphor under control, I would rather have cards on the table, although it could just as well be tokens or characters. The interpretive game in international law is no exception and it has got its own cards. This is perhaps the easiest part of the 'rules of play' to go through, as what the cards are is a relatively uncontroversial issue. The cards are mostly those contained in the Vienna Convention on the Law of

---

[34] Pia Eberhardt and Cecilia Olivet, *Profiting from Injustice: How Law Firms, Arbitrators and Financiers are Fuelling an Investment Arbitration Boom* (Corporate Europe Observatory and Transnational Institute 2012) 64.

[35] On the importance of interpretive communities for forming and shaping meaning within social (and professional) groups, see Andrea Bianchi, 'Textual Interpretation and (International) Law Reading: The Myth of (In)Determinacy and the Genealogy of Meaning' in Pieter Bekker, Rudolf Dolzer, and Michael Waibel (eds), *Making Transnational Law Work in the Global Economy: Essays in Honour of Detlev Vagts* (CUP 2010) 34.

[36] Ronnie RF Yearwood, *The Interaction between World Trade Organisation (WTO) Law and External International Law* (Routledge 2012) 93.

Treaties (VCLT). There are some slight variations to the game, whereby one can draw additional cards from the general principles of law, or justify departures from the VCLT on the basis of the peculiarity of the treaty in question,[37] or in light of the subject matter covered by the treaty in such areas as human rights,[38] or investment arbitration.[39] By and large, however, the most well-known version of the game relies on the VCLT cards.

Such unconditional success is hardly surprising, as the flexibility of the system is such that recourse to the VCLT accommodates practically all approaches to interpretation. The principles and rules of the VCLT can be twisted and bent, turned upside down and the criteria codified in it can be prioritized to one's liking. The VCLT almost invariably appears in any argument concerning the interpretation of a text in international law.[40] We teach students, assistants, and clerks that anything to do with interpretation has to be grounded in the VCLT, as any judge, whether in a moot court or presiding at the ICJ, is unlikely to be persuaded by an argument on interpretation that is not strongly rooted in the VCLT. Since its rules are manipulable at will, the VCLT rules are invoked by anyone in any context in which interpretation is relevant.

The potential for interpretation under the VCLT to impact strongly on the state of the law is huge. An apt illustration is international tribunals using the VCLT in the context of the determination of the obligatory character of interim measures. Regardless of strong textual indications to the contrary,[41] the ICJ found in the *LaGrand* case that the interim measures it had issued were binding on the United States.[42] The Court's reasoning hinged entirely upon Articles 31 and 33(4) of the VCLT, both deemed declaratory of customary international law. After a cursory look at the text, the ICJ emphasized the 'object and purpose' of the ICJ Statute to conclude, at the end of a fairly convoluted passage, that '[t]he contention that provisional measures indicated under Article 41 might not be binding would be

---

[37] See eg the case law of the European Court of Justice and the ECtHR justifying the special character of their respective constitutive treaties. For references to the relevant case law, see Fuad Zarbiyev, 'Judicial Activism in International Law—A Conceptual Framework for Analysis' (2012) 3(2) JIDS 247, 273–4.

[38] See eg Alexander Orakhelashvili, 'Restrictive Interpretation of Human Rights Treaties in the Recent Jurisprudence of the European Court of Human Rights' (2003) 14(3) EJIL 529; Gerard Cohen-Jonathan, 'La territorialisation de la juridiction de la Cour européenne des droits de l'homme' (2002) *Revue trimestrielle des droits de l'homme* 1079–80; Francis Jacobs and Robin White, *The European Convention on Human Rights* (Clarendon Press 1996) 33; and David Harris, Michael O'Boyle, Colin Warbrick, Edward Bates, and Carla Buckley, *The Law of the European Convention on Human Rights* (2nd edn, OUP 2009) 17.

[39] See J Romesh Weeramantry, *Treaty Interpretation in Investment Arbitration* (OUP 2012); Mahnoush H Arsanjani and W Michael Reisman, 'Interpreting Treaties for the Benefit of Third Parties: The "Salvors' Doctrine" and the Use of Legislative History in Investment Treaties' (2010) 104 AJIL 597.

[40] Interestingly, invocation of the VCLT is not limited to treaties. The VCLT may also be of guidance with regards to the interpretation of Security Council resolutions. In this respect, see *Accordance with International Law of the Unilateral Declaration of Independence in Respect of Kosovo (Advisory Opinion)* [2010] ICJ Rep 403, [94].

[41] See Article 41 of the ICJ Statute in both its English and French versions.

[42] *LaGrand Case (Germany v USA)* [2001] ICJ Rep 466, [99].

contrary to the object and purpose of that Article'.[43] In an equally convoluted passage and always in the negative form, the ICJ subsequently found that 'the preparatory work of the Statute does not preclude the conclusion that orders under Article 41 have binding force'.[44]

By the same token, in the *Mamatkulov* case,[45] the ECtHR held that non-compliance by a contracting state with its interim measures would amount to a violation of the right of individual application under Article 34 of the European Convention. The ECtHR attributed a prominent role to the VCLT in the presentation of the law and practice relevant to the case at the outset.[46] It then went on to argue that, on the basis of the object and purpose test, Article 34 'requires the Contracting States to refrain not only from exerting pressure on applicants, but also from any act or omission which, by destroying or removing the subject matter of an application, would make it pointless or otherwise prevent the Court from considering it under its normal procedure'.[47]

To further reinforce its reasoning, the ECtHR quoted the similar decisions already taken by other international tribunals and human rights supervisory bodies on the compulsory nature of interim or provisional measures. Once again, interpretive legitimacy is drawn from the VCLT. In particular, the ECtHR quoted Article 31(3)(c) to argue that the Convention must be interpreted in light of 'any relevant rules of international law applicable in the relations between the parties'. Although the appropriateness of invoking Article 31(3)(c) in this context could aptly be called into question, the Court makes this reference in introducing the case law and jurisprudence of other international judicial bodies. It would be an exercise in fantasy to hold that a decision of the UN Human Rights Committee or a judgment of the Inter-American Court of Human Rights is a 'rule of international law applicable in the relations between the parties' of the European Convention. Short of any scientific or methodological rigour, the reference creates in the reader the sense that the interpretive operation is justified under the applicable canons of interpretation, and the mere reference to the VCLT regime provides the argument with legitimacy.

Incidentally, Article 31(3)(c) of the VCLT is a multi-functional card that allows disparate objectives to be reached in divergent contexts. It has been used to determine the range of claimants before the Iran–United States Claims Tribunal,[48] and to exclude the applicability of the precautionary principle in the World Trade Organization (WTO).[49] The ECtHR has played the same Article 31(3)(c) card to expand and restrict the scope of application of Article 6 respectively, by holding that

[43] *LaGrand Case (Germany v USA)*, [102].
[44] *LaGrand Case (Germany v USA)*, [104]. It will be recalled that under Article 32 VCLT, preparatory works can be used as a supplementary means of interpretation 'to confirm the meaning resulting from the application of Article 31'.
[45] *Mamatkulov and Askarov v Turkey* (2005) 41 EHRR 494.
[46] *Mamatkulov and Askarov v Turkey*, [39].
[47] *Mamatkulov and Askarov v Turkey*, [102].
[48] *Esphahanian v Bank Tejarat* (1983) 2 Iran-US CTR 157.
[49] WTO, *European Communities: Measures Affecting the Approval and Marketing of Biotech Products—Panel Report* WT/DS291-293/R, [7.65]–[7.68].

the right of access to a court is an implicit requirement of Article 6,[50] and, subsequently, by upholding the limitation of state immunity to the same right of access under Article 6.[51] It has been submitted that Article 31(3)(c) 'serves a function analogous to that of a master-key in a large building'.[52] Faithful to the metaphor of the game, I would rather qualify it as a joker and would play it as sparingly as I could, particularly when the stakes are high and other avenues of interpretation of no avail.

The customary character of the rules of treaty interpretation, codified in the VCLT and repeatedly asserted by international tribunals, as well as the absence of controversy within the profession that issues of interpretation should be addressed on the basis of the VCLT, might cause one to think that such rules have become so solidly entrenched in the professional mindset of international lawyers that they could now be considered as unalterable and almost immutable. Certainly, this is the attitude of my own generation (and I suppose also of later generations of international lawyers) who have come to believe that the consensus surrounding the VCLT's rules on treaty interpretation has been there from time immemorial.

In fact, such consensus on the cards is a relatively new phenomenon. Before the VCLT, both within the International Law Commission (ILC) and at the *Institut de droit international*, a heated debate had taken place on whether or not it was a good idea to codify the rules of interpretation and, if so, which criteria should be chosen and given priority over others. To account for this debate goes beyond the scope of this chapter and other scholars have already inquired into this.[53] For the limited purpose of our analysis in this context, let me briefly refer to the conflicting visions on the codification of rules of treaty interpretation of Hersch Lauterpacht and Gerald Fitzmaurice, who acted as rapporteurs on the topic for the *Institut de droit international* in the 1950s. Lauterpacht submitted a draft resolution at the *Institut*'s session in Bath in 1950. The resolution stated that the main aim of interpretation is to seek the real intention of the parties and that the obvious starting point of any interpretive exercise is the 'natural meaning' (*sens naturel*) of the words. The burden of proving that the words that appear in the treaty carry a meaning different from their natural one lies with the party invoking such different meaning. Preparatory works are a legitimate and even desirable means to establish what the intention of the parties was, if there is controversy about the meaning of a treaty. While restrictive interpretation has no standing in international practice, the principle of effective interpretation (or *effet utile*) is a legitimate and solid means of interpretation, unless the parties clearly intended to exclude its application. With very minor adjustments, the draft was submitted as final in the Siena and Aix-en-Provence sessions in 1952 and 1953.[54]

---

[50] *Golder v United Kingdom* (1975) 1 EHRR 524, [35]–[36].
[51] *Al-Adsani v United Kingdom* (2002) 34 EHRR 273, [55]–[56].
[52] Campbell McLachlan, 'The Principle of Systemic Integration and Article 31(3)(c) of the Vienna Convention' (2005) 54 ICLQ 279, 281, attributing the analogy to Xue Hanquin, the then Ambassador of China to the Netherlands and member of the ILC.
[53] See Chapter 12 (Fuad Zarbiyev).
[54] See *Annuaire de l'Institut de Droit International* (1952) Vol 44-II, 361; *Annuaire de l'Institut de Droit International* (1953) Vol 45-I, 225–6. For the reports submitted by Lauterpacht as Special

The draft resolution spurred a heated debate in which different positions emerged on how a treaty should be interpreted. A wide range of methodological postures were put forward, with the constant swing of the pendulum between ardent supporters of 'textualism', and those who—like Lauterpacht—favoured looking at the 'real intention' of the parties. Be that as it may, consensus existed on the need to codify only the broad fundamental principles and not the highly technical and specific rules, which would have been *'inutile, voire dangéreux'.*[55] This is interesting, insofar as it shows the unwillingness to codify the plethora of principles (often expressed in latin *maximae*), of an often contradictory character, occasionally resorted to in international practice.

As is often the case, a change in material circumstances and happenstance played a role in the subsequent shift of focus in the *Institut*'s project, and in determining who the winner was. With the election of Lauterpacht to the ICJ, Fitzmaurice—one of the staunchest opponents to Lauterpacht's project focusing on the intention of the parties—took over as rapporteur.[56] This event carried with it important consequences, as Fitzmaurice's final submission and proposal, adopted by the *Institut* by a Resolution on the interpretation of treaties at its 1956 Grenada session,[57] was dramatically different from Lauterpacht's. The Grenada Resolution had only two articles.[58] The first focuses on the importance of the text, whose natural and ordinary meaning must be the starting point, as the text sanctions the agreement of the parties. Only if it were established that the words were meant to convey another meaning could such natural and ordinary meaning be set aside. Second, the Resolution conferred to international tribunals to which disputes are submitted the task of determining, having taken into account the rule of interpretation on the natural and ordinary meaning of the words, whether and if so the extent to which other interpretive means should be used. Amongst such means, Article 2 lists recourse to the preparatory works, the practice in the effective implementation of the agreement, as well as a consideration of the purposes of the treaty.

The debate within the *Institut* is significant in many different ways. Not only did it mark the pre-eminence of the textual approach, it also showed how divergent the views were on the existence of rules of treaty interpretation at international law. When Sir Humphrey Waldock introduced the topic of treaty interpretation in his third report to the ILC as Special Rapporteur on the law of treaties,[59] he was bound to acknowledge that, amongst those who were sceptical

---

Rapporteur, see *Annuaire de l'Institut de Droit International* (1950) Vol 43-I, Session de Bath, 366–460; and *Annuaire de l'Institut de Droit International* (1952) Vol 44-I, Session de Sienne, 197–221.

[55] *Annuaire de l'Institut de Droit International* (1952) Vol 44-II, 360.

[56] In fact, Lauterpacht's function as rapporteur on the topic of the interpretation of treaties should have been taken over by Sir Arnold McNair, who was unable to participate in the Grenada session and was thus replaced by Sir Gerald Fitzmaurice.

[57] *Annuaire de l'Institut de Droit International* (1956) 317.

[58] *Annuaire de l'Institut de Droit International* (1956) 358–9. The Resolution was adopted with 35 votes for, 0 against, and 6 abstentions.

[59] See Third Report on the Law of Treaties by Sir Humphrey Waldock, Special Rapporteur, A/CN.4/167 and Add.1-3, reproduced in (1964) II ILC Ybk 52.

about the existence of technical rules on treaty interpretation in international law, one should also include the first two rapporteurs on the topic to the ILC, James Brierly and Lauterpacht.[60]

In the debates within the ILC, the British tradition of textualism—personified at this time by Waldock—ended up prevailing over conflicting views.[61] Waldock comfortably straddled the ambiguity between the primacy of textualism,[62] and the idea that, far from establishing a hierarchy, the provision that would later become Article 31 of the VCLT had to be looked at as a 'crucible in which all the elements of interpretation would be mixed'.[63] Eventually, at the Vienna Conference, there were very few dissonant voices on the matter of interpretation of treaties. A notable exception was the American delegation, led by Myres McDougal, who insisted until the end on the importance of the intention of the parties in the interpretive process and openly criticized the rigid system embodied by the VCLT.[64] Not without merit, at some point McDougal criticized textualism on the grounds that the very presence at the Conference of Waldock (former Special Rapporteur to the ILC) as Expert Consultant whose views were so often solicited—despite the availability of the preparatory works of the ILC—was in and of itself evidence that the textual approach had serious limits.[65] Be that as it may, the ambiguity of the VCLT codification accommodated most needs and paved the way for what has become, in a fairly short time span, one of the most established regimes in the whole of international law, at least in terms of social agreement on the applicable principles and rules (if not on how to apply them!).

---

[60] JL Brierly, *The Law of Nations* (6th edn, OUP 1963) 325; *Annuaire de l'Institut de Droit International* (1950) Vol I, 336–74. Waldock also makes reference to McNair's similar views in *The Law of Treaties* (OUP 1961) 366.

[61] The textual approach that ended up prevailing in the *Institut* and the ILC and later in the VCLT was the expression of the British tradition in the field of interpretation, as well epitomized by Sir Robert Jennings: 'In short, the process of interpretation must begin and end with the actual text to be interpreted.' See 'General Course on Principles of International Law' (1967) 121 Recueil des Cours 323, 545.

[62] Sir Humphrey Waldock noted that '[t]hroughout, the Commission had shown a strong predilection for textual interpretation in the interests of stability and certainty of treaty relations': *Yearbook of the International Law Commission*, Vol II (1964) 314, [71].

[63] *Yearbook of the International Law Commission*, Vol I (1966) 267, [96].

[64] United Nations Conference on the Law of Treaties, First Session, Vienna 26 March–24 May 1968, Official Records. Summary records of the plenary meetings and the meetings of the Committee of the Whole (New York 1969) 167.

[65] United Nations Conference on the Law of Treaties, First Session, Vienna 26 March–24 May 1968, 167–8: 'The fact that the textual approach to interpretation was impossible to apply was demonstrated by the very presence at the Conference of the Expert Consultant and by the frequent appeals to him for enlightenment on the "ordinary" meaning of the wording of the draft articles—necessary despite the full availability of the International Law Commission's preparatory work; the unquestioned authority exercised by him when clarifying that meaning was based not on his linguistic ability or his skill as a logician, but rather on his very special knowledge, as the Commission's Special Rapporteur on the law of treaties, of all the circumstances attending the framing of the draft.' I learnt of this most interesting (and witty) observation from Fuad Zarbiyev, *Le discours interprétatif en droit international: une approche critique et généalogique* PhD thesis submitted at The Graduate Institute of International and Development Studies (Thèse No. 848) (Geneva 2010) 131, to be published as *Le discours interprétatif en droit international contemporain: Un essai critique* (Bruylant 2015) (forthcoming).

The gist of this short story is that what we take nowadays as uncontroversial and as something that goes without saying was far from being considered as such until recently. To highlight the contingency of the cards is not meant to lead to any relativism or indeterminacy of sorts. There is no denying that these are the rules, criteria, and practices that are followed by the profession in the interpretation of treaties and even of other relevant legal texts. In other words, there is social consensus amongst the players that these are the instruments by which one plays the game of interpretation. Their historicity and contingent character, however, need to be stressed in order to avoid attributing to them an ineluctability that they do not possess and that they were never meant to possess. The history of games demonstrates that the rules of play may change (even substantially) over time.

V. Strategies

Individual players that one could represent and visualize around a table with piles of tokens of different colours will try to strengthen their position by adopting conservative or bold strategies, by making unexpected moves or thriving on the perception of the audience they address, or by discrediting other players in order to enhance their own credibility and strategic power.[66] One could mention in this context, by way of example, the remarks made by the ICJ in the *Genocide* case, critiquing the International Criminal Tribunal for the Former Yugoslavia's (ICTY) interpretation of the rules of attribution under the law of state responsibility.[67] The ICJ emphasized the fact that issues of general international law 'do not lie within the specific purview' of the ICTY, implying that it is primarily for the ICJ to pass judgment on issues of general international law and to interpret the rules of international responsibility.[68] Along similar lines, the Appellate Body of the WTO and the Appeals Chamber of the ICTY have imposed their hierarchical superiority and interpretive primacy on the WTO panels and the trial chambers of the ICTY respectively.[69] Incidentally, the language used to justify their supremacy is adjusted to their different audiences. Whereas the ICTY Appeals Chamber relies, among other things, on human rights considerations related to

---

[66] The image of the players and the tokens is taken from Pierre Bourdieu and Loïc JD Wacquant, *An Invitation to Reflexive Sociology* (University of Chicago Press 1992) 98: 'We can picture each player as having in front of her a pile of tokens of different colors, each color corresponding to a given species of capital she holds, so that her *relative force in the game*, her *position* in the space of play, and also her *strategic orientation toward the game*, what we call in French her "game", the moves she makes, more or less risky or cautious, subversive or conservative, depend both on the total number of tokens and on the composition of the piles of tokens she retains, that is on the volume and structure of the capital' (emphasis in the original).

[67] *Application of the Convention on the Prevention and Punishment of the Crime of Genocide (Bosnia and Herzegovina v Serbia and Montenegro)* [2007] ICJ Rep 43, [403].

[68] *Application of the Convention on the Prevention and Punishment of the Crime of Genocide (Bosnia and Herzegovina v Serbia and Montenegro)*.

[69] See WTO, *United States: Final Anti-Dumping Measures on Stainless Steel From Mexico—Report of the Appellate Body* (30 April 2008) WT/DS344/AB/R, [158]–[162]; *Prosecutor v Aleksovski* (Judgment) ICTY-95-14/1-A, ICTY Appeals Chamber (24 March 2000), [112]–[113].

the right to a fair trial,[70] the WTO Appellate Body emphasizes the importance of the legitimate expectations of the parties to the WTO as well as the need to promote 'security and predictability' in the dispute settlement mechanism.[71]

The above examples are evidence that strategies are more likely to be effective if they are adjusted to the audiences that the players want or need to address. There is no doubt that the 'living instrument' or 'evolutive interpretation' doctrines resonate better in human rights circles, when it comes to interpreting broadly states' human rights obligations.[72] It is unlikely that they would carry with it the same persuasive force if they were to be invoked for the interpretation of the UN Charter. By the same token, the doctrine of implied powers—in many ways an enhanced version of the 'object and purpose' test—has originated and thrived in the context of international organizations and it has been pushed forward primarily by judicial bodies acting from within the very organizations whose powers were to be expanded by way of interpretation.[73] Tactics may vary, of course, and are heavily dependent on context and contingencies. The fairly surprising turn that the ECtHR had taken in *Behrami and Saramati*[74]—with regards to the effects of UN Security Council anti-terror resolutions on the human rights protected by the European Convention—was later reconsidered,[75] most likely due to the different attitude taken by the European Court of Justice on similar issues.[76]

Consistency and predictability are important rhetorical mantras that play out very well in the context of interpretation. Nonetheless, as Lauterpacht once put it,[77] there is nothing one can do if a court has decided to change its jurisprudence or interpretation of the law on any legal issue. One should look carefully at adverbs—such as 'however' and 'nonetheless'—as it is by this linguistic means that sudden *révirements* of jurisprudence are usually introduced in a judgment. In *Goodwin v UK*,[78] for example, the ECtHR changed its interpretation of Article 8 in relation to the rights of transsexuals in the United Kingdom. After highlighting

---

[70] *Prosecutor v Aleksovski*, [113].

[71] *United States—Final Anti-Dumping Measures*, [158] and [161].

[72] For an early formulation of the doctrine, see *Tyrer v United Kingdom* (1978) 2 EHRR 1, [31]: 'The Court must also recall that the Convention is a living instrument which, as the Commission rightly stressed, must be interpreted in the light of present-day conditions.' On the interpretive techniques elaborated by the ECtHR, see George Letsas, *A Theory of Interpretation of the European Convention on Human Rights* (OUP 2007).

[73] Viljam Engström, *Constructing the Powers of International Institutions* (Martinus Nijhoff 2012).

[74] *Behrami v France & Saramati v France, Germany and Norway* (2007) 45 EHRR 10. The priority accorded to the UN Security Council's Chapter VII resolutions over the European Convention took many by surprise, particularly because the finding was largely unnecessary in reaching a decision in the case at hand.

[75] *Al-Jedda v United Kingdom* (2011) 53 EHRR 23. At this time, the ECtHR took the view that unless the contrary is expressly stated, Security Council resolutions should be interpreted in a manner consistent with the European Convention.

[76] Case C-402/05 P *Yassin Abdullah Kadi v Council and Commission* (2009) 46 CMLR 213. This judgment was recently confirmed by the ECJ Grand Chamber in *European Commission et al v Kadi*, Judgment of 18 July 2013.

[77] Hersch Lauterpacht, *The Development of International Law by the International Court* (Grotius Publications Ltd 1982) 14.

[78] *Goodwin v United Kingdom* (2002) 35 EHRR 18.

the importance of sticking to its previous judgments for reasons of legal certainty, stability, and equality before the law, it suddenly distinguished the need to depart from them for good reason! By using the adverb 'however', the Court introduced a radical change in the interpretation of Article 8 as it applied to the rights of transsexuals in the UK.[79] Incidentally, the Court backed up its novel approach by quoting the practice of extra-European states.[80] As a matter of treaty interpretation, surely this is not a particularly persuasive argument, as Australia and New Zealand are not parties to the European Convention. However, the demonstration of similar state conduct in other parts of the world is a good rhetorical strategy to secure the reader's adherence to the necessity of changing human rights policies as well as interpreting the Convention differently.

The importance of rhetorical tools and techniques in establishing interpretive strategies ought not to be underestimated. Tricks or interpretive devices, well accepted in the profession, can be used to channel interpretation in one direction rather than another. An apt illustration is the general rule/exception paradigm. In a situation in which the state of the law is uncertain, to decide to adopt a certain rule as a general rule may have dire consequences. Most of all, this causes a shift in the burden of proof for whomever is to argue that an exception to a general rule has emerged. This technique has been widely used by international and domestic courts to preserve or to expand (as the case may be) the scope of the allegedly general rule of state immunity to the detriment of an alleged exception for serious human rights violations.[81] At the time of the early domestic codifications of the law of state immunity, it was regarded as a rather arbitrary choice as a matter of international law to regard immunity as a general rule.[82] Be that as it may, this technique has allowed the rule of state immunity to be interpreted broadly with obvious systemic consequences.

Another extraordinary example of how interpretive criteria can be turned upside down and used to reach opposite outcomes is given by the use of the *lex specialis* rule in determining the relationship between international humanitarian law and human rights law in times of armed conflict. As is well known, the criterion—originally introduced by the ICJ in the *Nuclear Weapons* advisory opinion in relation to the right to life,[83] and later expanded without much reflection in a convoluted passage in the *Israeli Wall* advisory opinion[84]—has been interpreted,

---

[79] *Goodwin v United Kingdom*, [74].   [80] *Goodwin v United Kingdom*, [84].

[81] See eg *Jurisdictional Immunities; Jones v Ministry of Interior Al-Mamlaka Al-Arabiya AS Saudiya (Kingdom of Saudi Arabia)* [2007] 1 AC 270; *Al-Adsani v United Kingdom; Saudi Arabia v Nelson* 507 US 349 (1993).

[82] See Sompong Sucharitkul, 'Developments and Prospects of the Doctrine of State Immunity: Some Aspects of the Law of Codification and Progressive Development' (1982) 29 NILR 252; Rosalyn Higgins, 'Certain Unresolved Aspects of the Law of State Immunity' (1982) 29 NILR 265. The opposite approach of adopting an international treaty that retained jurisdiction rather than immunity as the general residual rule had been proposed by Lauterpacht in the 1950s: see Hersch Lauterpacht, 'The Problem of Jurisdictional Immunities of Foreign States' (1951) 28 BYBIL 220.

[83] *Legality of the Threat or Use of Nuclear Weapons* (Advisory Opinion) [1996] ICJ Rep 226, [25].

[84] *Legal Consequences of the Construction of a Wall in the Occupied Palestinian Territories* (Advisory Opinion) [2004] ICJ Rep 136, [106].

on the one hand, as excluding the applicability of human rights law altogether in a situation of armed conflict;[85] and, on the other hand, as giving priority to the more protective human rights standards in the same circumstances of armed conflict.[86] Ultimately, it all depends on the goal one wants to pursue, interpretive strategies being adaptable and flexible enough to serve different purposes.

Finally, one may well wonder why the players are (or, at least, give the impression of being) so little aware of the strategies they use, and act as if they were not playing a game or implementing a strategy. The reason for this most likely lies in the constant process of socialization among players that cause certain moves or reflexes to consolidate over time and to become a *habitus* of sorts, which is interiorized by the players and then becomes a natural attitude for the players participating in the game.[87]

VI. Playing the Game of Game Playing

So far the discussion has focused on how one plays the game of interpretation. If you like, I have just laid down the board on the table, unfolded the sheet containing the 'rules of play', and explained what the game is about, who wins it, what cards are available, and how one can play with them and develop strategies to be successful at the game. In other words, we have been concerned with the 'to do' part of the game of interpretation, with the issue of how to interpret. We all know how to play. However, one may well come to know how to play the game—fairly easily one must admit!—but have no clue or, simply, no interest in knowing why the game is being played at all. Furthermore, one may wonder whether or not the players think that this is a game that is worth their time and their energy, for its underlying stakes.

What is it then that is not written in the 'rules of play', and that does not concern the 'set up', the 'equipment', and the 'cards' or 'tokens' that are used to play the game? Is there anything else to the game? After all, board games have been invented and are still used for various purposes including: the amusement of the players; fostering socialization amongst individuals; allowing parents to keep their children busy while they attend to other things; securing profits to their manufacturers, and so on and so forth. Undoubtedly some of the games are highly competitive and have different types of stakes.

---

[85] See the Second and Third Periodic Report submitted by the United States to the Human Rights Committee under the ICCPR in 2005: UN Doc CCPR/C/USA/3 (28 November 2005). For a comment see Colette Connor, 'Recent Development: the United States Second and Third Periodic Report to the United Nations Human Rights Committee' (2008) 49 HILJ 509.

[86] See the human rights-friendly reading of the *lex specialis* rule in this context made by the Office of the High Commissioner for Human Rights: *International Legal Protection of Human Rights in Armed Conflict* (United Nations 2011) 58.

[87] Once the *habitus* is internalized, it becomes a sort of second nature to the players and as such is 'forgotten as history': Bourdieu, *The Logic of Practice*, 53.

Is asking this sort of question still part of the game? This is a more difficult query to answer. On the one hand, one could safely say 'no', as players can play the game independently of these issues. On the other hand, it is undeniable that there is also a 'meta-discourse' about the game, which can be the object of intellectual inquiry and *must* be the object of analysis, at least by those who lay claim to be engaged in an intellectual analysis of legal processes. Regrettably, most of the current scholarship on interpretation is limited to describing the 'rules of play' and there is hardly any interest in the meta-discourse of interpretation.[88]

To inquire into these issues means to engage in a different kind of activity than simply playing the game. To paraphrase Laurence Tribe's appraisal of Bruce Ackerman's contribution to US constitutional law scholarship, one could say that this is about 'talking the talk' of interpretation.[89] Or, to draw inspiration from JM Coetzee's *Diary of a Bad Year*, one could call it 'playing the game of game playing', as in the title of this section.[90] To me, 'playing the game of game playing' means to reflect above all on the nature of the game and its underlying stakes. This is a game of its own, where the players are concerned more about determining eligibility to participate in the game as well as with all the other aspects of the 'rules of play', including by what cards one should play. By discussing those issues, one constantly influences the game and tries to affect its rules and practices.

As regards the nature of the game, I believe that interpretation is primarily a purposeful activity.[91] In other words, anyone who engages in an act of interpretation does so with a more or less conscious intent to achieve a desired outcome. The desired outcome may or may not be shared by the other participants in the game, but the challenge is to persuade or impose, as the case may be, the interpretation that best serves the pursued purpose. 'Cards' and 'strategies' are but tools that are

---

[88] In legal philosophy, the issue of interpretation has been thoroughly analysed. See eg Joseph Raz, *Between Authority and Interpretation: On the Theory of Law and Practical Reason* (OUP 2009); Matthew Kramer, *Objectivity and the Rule of Law* (CUP 2007); Andrei Marmor, *Interpretation and Legal Theory* (2nd edn, Hart 2005); Andrei Marmor (ed), *Law and Interpretation: Essays in Legal Philosophy* (Clarendon Press 1997); Paul Amselek (ed), *Interprétation et droit* (Bruylant 1995); Neil MacCormick and Robert Summers, 'Interpretation and Justification' in Neil MacCormick and Robert Summers (eds), *Interpreting Statutes: A Comparative Study* (Aldershot 1991) 511; Ronald Dworkin, *Law's Empire* (Harvard University Press 1986); Ronald Dworkin, *A Matter of Principle* (Harvard University Press 1985).

[89] Laurence Tribe, 'Taking Text and Structure Seriously: Reflections on Free-Form Method in Constitutional Interpretation' (1995) 108 Harv L Rev 1221, 1225.

[90] JM Coetzee, *Diary of a Bad Year* (Penguin 2007) 69. I am grateful to my colleague and friend Fuad Zarbiyev for referring me to this.

[91] There is an interesting analogy with some strands of linguistics and semiotics. See eg Claire Kramsch, 'Social Discursive Constructions of Self in L2 Learning' in James P Lantolf (ed), *Sociocultural Theory and Second Language Learning* (OUP 2000) 133–4: 'Linguistic signs are never arbitrary. They are created, used, borrowed, and interpreted by the individual for the purposeful action in which he/she is engaged'; TL Short, *Pierce's Theory of Signs* (CUP 2007). This concept of purposeful interpretation is distinct from what has become known as the 'purposive interpretation' theory or method, which aims to establish the ultimate purpose and meaning of a legal text by considering the simultaneous interaction between subjective elements (such as subjective purpose, author's intent, and subjective teleology) and objective elements (such as objective intent, the intent of a reasonable author, and the legal system's values) at the time of interpretation of the text. See Aharon Barak, *Purposive Interpretation in Law* (Princeton University Press 2005) 88.

put at the service of the player who aims at achieving a certain goal. This thesis holds true also for formalists who believe that the rules of interpretation are there and must be applied in order to achieve stability and certainty in the law. There is always a purpose behind interpretation and the way one carries out the process of interpreting the law is determined more or less consciously by the need to achieve that particular purpose.[92] The fact that lawyers are sometimes not aware of this simply attests to the fact that this reflex has become so entrenched that it is no longer visible.[93]

The nature of the stakes of the game is also worthy of inquiry. The stakes are individual and collective and vary depending on players and settings. They could consist of acquiring, enhancing, or consolidating an individual's or a group's authority to speak legitimately for the profession or the discipline. Or, rather, they could concern the preservation or subversion of a certain social ordering; the keeping of the legal status quo or the promotion of an agenda for legal reform; or a call for stability or for change. This, in turn, may reflect beliefs and intimately held convictions or, rather, be the expression of vested interests and corporate attitudes. To explore the dynamic between individual and collective dimensions in the shaping and development of the game stakes and to unveil the players' bias and presuppositions may be an interesting exercise, and one that would enhance understanding of what the game is about and how the rules of play are formulated, and by whom and how game practices and strategies develop over time. Admittedly, this is not the way in which international legal scholarship usually looks at the game of interpretation, which is in itself a purposeful act that sheds light on the desired outcome of the players—amongst whom we as academics stand out—who play the game of game playing.

VII. Why is the Game Worth the Candle?

Finally, one may wonder whether the players think that the game is worth the candle and, if so, why. The fact that the game is deeply embedded in the professional (and social) structure of international law makes playing it an obvious choice for anyone who is involved in the field. Players are allowed to pursue their goals by resorting to the interpretive tools we described above—the cards—and they feel empowered by playing the game. They feel free insofar as they can play the different cards in a myriad different ways in order to pursue the goals they set for themselves, and to attempt to secure the adherence of the other players to their own interpretive postures. In a way, the game is a blend of freedom and

---

[92] I expressly advocated recourse to purposeful interpretation in the context of state immunity and *jus cogens*: see Andrea Bianchi, 'Human Rights and the Magic of *jus cogens*' (2008) 19(3) EJIL 491, 504.

[93] On the need for reflexivity in the profession, see Andrea Bianchi, 'Reflexive Butterfly Catching: Insights from a Situated Catcher' in Joost Pauwelyn, Ramses Wessel, and Jan Wouters (eds), *Informal International Lawmaking* (OUP 2012) 200.

constraint. While one is free to lay different cards on the table, the adopted strategies and interactions with the other players are situated within the boundaries of the game and the rules that the players recognize collectively as the 'rules of play'. The empowerment inherent in the very act of game playing is a forceful incentive to believe that the game is worth playing. Furthermore, the prospect of winning the game makes the players believe that they can one day be 'lawmakers'.

Social consensus exists nowadays amongst the players on some fundamental aspects of the game of interpretation in international law. First and foremost, this consensus bears on the 'rule-based' approach to interpretation. The idea that interpretation is an activity that is rule-dependent ends up empowering the players even more, as they feel and look at themselves as the repositories of the 'rules of play'. Second, there is consensus also on the criteria, principles, and specific rules that must be applied. For the most part these are codified in the VCLT. Recognition of and identification with this core of beliefs and parlance on matters of interpretation produces a sense of shared identity. So deeply rooted is the collective belief that interpretation in international law must be carried out in light of the rules codified in the VCLT that the latter instrument has lost its historical and contingent character to become an almost eternal and immutable truth. The paradox lies in the fact that the extant social consensus on how to do interpretation in international law is probably due to the open-ended character of what is perceived to be the applicable regime. Even if the cards one plays and the way one lays them on the table can produce an almost infinite series of interpretive outcomes, nobody seriously calls into question the type of cards chosen for playing the game.

This probably explains a number of peculiarities, including the negligible inclination by international legal scholarship to pay attention to the (paucity of) historical or genealogical studies that highlight the contingent character of the rules of treaty interpretation.[94] I suspect that the unconditional allegiance to a rule-based process of interpretation presupposes some sort of *horror vacui* argument, whereby anarchy would follow if one were to abandon the current rule-based approach to interpretation.[95] The absence of criticism, and historical analysis, of the regime of interpretation in the official discourse of international law hardly hides the stakes of preserving the current structure of power in the interpretation game. The fact that before the codification of the law of treaties such an approach was far from being the object of widespread social acceptance in international legal scholarship seems to have been forgotten,[96] although less than 50 years have passed since the adoption of the VCLT. International life before then was no more unruly and anarchical than it is nowadays and interpretation would take place on a daily basis. The only difference is that the 'rules of play' as well as some of the players were slightly different.

---

[94] See Chapter 12 (Fuad Zarbiyev).

[95] On the use of the *horror vacui* argument in this context, see Jan Klabbers, 'Reluctant Grundnormen: Articles 31(3)(c) and 42 of the Vienna Convention on the Law of Treaties and the Fragmentation of International Law' in Matthew Craven, Malgosia Fitzmaurice, and Maria Vogiatzi (eds), *Time, History and International Law* (Brill 2007) 141, 160.

[96] See nn 37–65 and accompanying text.

To be able to rely on a set of uncontroversial and neutral rules of interpretation, which enjoy almost universal acceptance, also allows players to identify as members of a highly cohesive community where—despite the occasional uncertainty in the content of some particular rules—coherence and stability are guaranteed by sharing an objective code of interpretation. If not a panacea, it is a safe and effective remedy against some of the major flaws of the system. It ensures stability and coherence where there is no general lawgiver and no centralized law-making system. It soothes the anxiety of fragmentation and conflict and nurtures the illusion that harmony, stability, and unity can be brought about by the magic wand of the technical rules of treaty interpretation. It suffices to think of all the expectations raised by the concept of 'systemic integration' codified in Article 31(3)(c) of the VCLT,[97] particularly amongst the community of so-called 'generalists', to understand the power of the interpretation game. Resort to what is largely perceived as 'technicism' or 'technical rule' is also very much in conformity with contemporary societal culture at large. Whatever is perceived as technical or scientific enjoys respect and is highly valued, given the shift that has occurred in our societies from normative to cognitive expectations.[98]

Most of all, however, the players are convinced that the game is worth the candle simply because they are fully taken up with what Bourdieu used to call the *illusio* of the game. According to Bourdieu, every social or scientific field requires such an *illusio* (from *ludus*, the game): that is 'the fact of being caught up in and by the game, of believing the game is "worth the candle", or, more simply, that playing is worth the effort'.[99] Players 'concur in their belief (*doxa*) in the game and its stakes; they grant these a recognition that escapes questioning. Players agree, by the mere fact of playing, and not by way of a "contract", that the game is worth playing...and this *collusion* is the very basis of their competition'.[100] In fact, if one is deeply enmeshed in the game and entrenched in its professional power structures and mindset, it is unlikely that one will ask the question of whether the game is worth the candle. As is often the case with social games, for one to play the game is something that goes without saying; it is part of the socialization process that unites the players and makes them feel like they belong to the same community, whose identity they share. This is also the reason why there is hardly any meta-discourse about game playing in international legal scholarship. You

---

[97] McLachlan, 'The Principle of Systemic Integration and Article 31(3)(c)'. See also *Conclusions of the Work of the Study Group on the Fragmentation of International Law: Difficulties arising from the Diversification and Expansion of International Law*, UN Doc A/61/10 (2006).

[98] See Niklas Luhmann, *Social Systems, Writing Science* (Stanford University Press 1995); Andreas Fischer-Lescano and Gunther Teubner, 'Regime-Collisions: The Vain Search for Legal Unity in the Fragmentation of Global Law' (2003) 25 Mich J Int'l L 999, 1000: 'In 1971, while theorizing on the concept of world society, Luhmann allowed himself the "speculative hypothesis" that global law would experience a radical fragmentation, not along territorial, but along social sectoral lines. The reason for this would be a transformation from normative (politics, morality, law) to cognitive expectations (economy, science, technology); a transformation that would be effected during the transition from nationally organized societies to a global society.'

[99] See Pierre Bourdieu, *Practical Reason: On the Theory of Action* (Stanford University Press 1998), 76–7.

[100] Bourdieu and Wacquant, *An Invitation to Reflexive Sociology*, 98.

just play the game you have been trained to play and in which you believe just as much as the others do. There is no questioning about much else. You simply have the feel for the game.[101]

VIII. Conclusion

Come this way, ladies and gentlemen: today there is a free session one can attend. There is no entrance fee, and everyone is welcome. International attractions are present and fun is guaranteed. You can come and play the game of interpretation for free and for as long as you like. Like in the Land of Toys in *The Adventures of Pinocchio*, '[d]ays are spent in play and enjoyment from morn till night. At night one goes to bed, and next morning the good times begin all over again'.[102] This is a direct quote of Lampwick speaking to Pinocchio and I should not be tempting you like Lampwick did with Pinocchio. But the metaphor holds true, at least to some extent, with the additional advantage that international lawyers run no risk of being turned into donkeys. 'But is it really true that in that country boys never have to study?', Pinocchio asks Lampwick. 'Never, never, never', responds Lampwick. 'What a wonderful, beautiful, marvellous country!', Pinocchio exclaims. Oh boy, here is Lampwick speaking again. Come on, hurry up the wagon is approaching. Let's get on board. We don't need to study there. We can just play (the game).

---

[101] Bourdieu, *Practical Reason*, 77: 'If…your mind is structured according to the structures of the world in which you play, everything will seem obvious and the question of knowing if the game is "worth the candle" will not even be asked. In other words, social games are games that are forgotten *qua* games, and the *illusio* is the enchanted relation to a game that is the product of a relation of ontological complicity between mental structures and the objective structures of social space…[g]ames which matter to you are important and interesting because they have been imposed and introduced in your mind, in your body, in a form called the feel for the game.'

[102] Carlo Collodi, *The Adventures of Pinocchio* (Harper Press 2012) ch 30.

PART II
THE OBJECT

3

Rhetoric, Persuasion, and Interpretation in International Law

*Iain Scobbie**

I. The Art of Rhetoric

All games have rules, and all games have strategies for effective play. Ultimately, the aim is to win the game. Legal argumentation inevitably calls upon players to interpret the facts, rules, and concepts upon which their argument rests. The art of rhetoric sets out ground rules for successful argumentative, and thus interpretative, practice, and provides tactics and strategies by which this may be achieved—although, as in all games, success is never guaranteed for any specific player. All lies in the knowledge and skill of the player and the choices he makes.

Rhetoric has ancient roots, and for centuries its study was a standard component of a university education in the humanities. For example, Adam Smith, the eighteenth-century economist and moral philosopher, also lectured on rhetoric at the University of Glasgow. A student's notes of the lecture series Smith delivered in 1762–63 survives, and records Smith as saying:

[It is] however from the consideration of these [tropes and figures of speech], and the divisions and subdivisions of them, that so many systems of retorick both ancient and modern have been formed. They are generally a very silly set of books and not at all instructive.[1]

Smith's antipathy to other rhetorical works flowed from his view that rhetoric should be a form of plain speaking—'Perspicuity of stile requires not only that the expressions we use should be free from all ambiguity proceeding from

* My interest in legal reasoning was first stimulated when I was an undergraduate by the late Neil MacCormick, then Regius Professor of Public Law and the Law of Nature and Nations at the University of Edinburgh, who taught me jurisprudence. I first came across a reference to Chaïm Perelman in one of his essays, in whose work I became very interested during my doctoral studies at the University of Cambridge under the tutelage of Philip Allott and Eli Lauterpacht. To all three, I owe thanks for their support and indulgence. For their indulgence and patience, I should also thank the editors, and, for his support, my colleague Jean d'Aspremont.

[1] Adam Smith, *Lectures on Rhetoric and Belles Lettres* (Clarendon Press 1983: ed JC Bryce) 26, [i.v.59]. For 'retorick', read 'rhetoric': the student's spelling is inconsistent and, at times, archaic throughout his notes.

synonimous words but that the words should be natives if I may say so of the language we speak in'.[2] He abhorred ornamentation in argument which he thought masked and obscured meaning:

What are generally called ornaments or flowers in language, as allegoricall, metaphoricall and such like expressions are very apt to make ones stile dark and perplex'd. Studying much to vary the expression leads one also frequently into a dungeon of metaphorical obscurity.[3]

Smith's injunction that rhetorical style books are 'not at all instructive' is an over-statement. Yet rhetoric is often viewed warily, perceived as a perversity of true argument, and as the conscious presentation of false and florid argument which seeks to distort or mask the truth of a situation rather than examine it dispassionately. There is no doubt that there is some degree of truth in this. The orations of, for instance, politicians and their spokesmen can often be slick, self-serving, and emotive,[4] attempting to justify the unjustifiable and unpalatable, but there is a more serious aspect to the art of rhetoric upon which we shall focus. As Chaïm Perelman, without doubt the leading theorist of rhetoric in the twentieth century, argued:

Rhétorique...n'est pas l'art de bien parler, dans un style fleuri et ampoulé: c'est l'art de persuader et de convaincre, qui peut se manifester par un discours ou par un écrit et qui, pour les juristes, consiste essentiellement dans l'usage de l'argumentation.[5]

II. Rhetoric—Legal Argumentation as an Interpretative Mechanism

From the early twentieth century onwards, there was a resurgence of philosophical interest in the art of rhetoric. In 1936, the literary critic Ivor A Richards was pessimistic about the contemporary status of rhetoric in academic circles:

So low has Rhetoric sunk that we would do better just to dismiss it to Limbo than to trouble ourselves with it—unless we can find reason for believing that it can become a study that will minister successfully to important needs.[6]

---

[2] Smith, *Lectures on Rhetoric and Belles Lettres*, 3, [i.i.1] (textual apparatus suppressed).
[3] Smith, *Lectures on Rhetoric and Belles Lettres*, 8, [i.i.14] (textual apparatus suppressed). For Smith's views on plain style, see generally Lecture 2: 3–8.
[4] For an incisive introduction to political rhetorical technique, see Max Atkinson, *Our Masters' Voices: The Language and Body Language of Politics* (Routledge 1984).
[5] Chaïm Perelman, *Le Champ de l'argumentation* (Presses Universitaires de Bruxelles 1970) 139: 'rhetoric...is not the art of speaking well in a high-flown flowery style: it is the art of persuading and convincing, whether in speech or in writing, and which for lawyers lies essentially in the use of argumentation'. See also Chaïm Perelman and Lucie Olbrechts-Tyteca, *The New Rhetoric: A Treatise on Argumentation* (University of Notre Dame Press 1969) 6–9, and [96], 450–9.
[6] Ivor A Richards, *The Philosophy of Rhetoric* (OUP 1936) 3.

Richards was influential in redeeming the reputation of rhetoric in literary and philosophical circles, and from the 1950s there was also an upsurge in interest of the role that rhetoric could play in practical reason generally, and in law in particular, by theorists such as Perelman and Lucie Olbrechts-Tyteca, Stephen Toulmin,[7] and Theodor Viehweg.[8] The most prolific and significant author in this discipline, which he termed 'la nouvelle rhétorique', or 'the new rhetoric', was Perelman.[9]

A central and common theme in modern rhetorical theory is the ambiguity and malleability of the meaning of natural language, as opposed to the absolute referents of the formal languages of logic and mathematics.[10] This might have been influenced, at least in early twentieth-century literary circles, by the serious playfulness of the desire to disrupt readers' confidence in the apparent certainties of language by modernist authors such as TS Eliot, James Joyce, and Gertrude Stein. Joyce, particularly in *Finnegans Wake* (1939), and Stein, especially in her work preceding the fame, and income, which accrued to her with the publication of *The Autobiography of Alice B Toklas* (1933), trashed conventional expectations about the stability of language and the accessibility of its meaning:

Stein's true radical legacy lay in her insistence on showing how words and their meanings could be undone; she took it as her right that she had the freedom to use words exactly as she pleased, and in doing so she undermined the relation between words and the world.[11]

---

[7] See Stephen Toulmin, *The Uses of Argument* (CUP 1958).

[8] Theodor Viehweg, *Topics and the Law: A Contribution to Basic Research in Law* (Peter Lang 1993: tr WC Durham). The first German edition of Viehweg's *Topik und Jurisprudenz* was published in 1953. Durham's translation is of the fifth edition which was published in 1973.

[9] Chaïm Perelman and Lucie Olbrechts-Tyteca collaborated to produce the foundational work and most extensive statement of Perelman's 'new rhetoric': *La Nouvelle Rhétorique: Traité de l'argumentation* (Presses Universitaires de France 1958); *The New Rhetoric: A Treatise on Argumentation* (University of Notre Dame Press 1969: tr John Wilkinson and Purcell Weaver). Perelman subsequently published a condensed version of *The New Rhetoric: L'empire Rhétorique: Rhétorique et Argumentation* (Vrin 1977); *The Realm of Rhetoric* (University of Notre Dame Press 1982: tr William Kluback). Other important works by Perelman include: *Le Champ de l'argumentation; Justice et Raison* (2nd edn, Editions de l'Université de Bruxelles 1972); *Logique juridique: Nouvelle Rhétorique* (Dalloz 1976); *The New Rhetoric and the Humanities: Essays on Rhetoric and its Applications* (Reidel 1979); *Justice, Law, and Argument: Essays on Moral and Legal Reasoning* (Reidel 1980). There are numerous commentaries on Perelman's work. See eg Ray Dearin (ed), *The New Rhetoric of Chaïm Perelman: Statement and Response* (University Press of America 1989); Benoît Frydman and Michel Meyer (eds), *Chaïm Perelman (1912–2012): de la Nouvelle Rhétorique à la Logique juridique* (Presses Universitaires de France 2012); Alan Gross and Ray Dearin, *Chaïm Perelman* (SUNY Press 2003); Guy Haarscher and León Ingber, *Justice et Argumentation: Essais à le Mémoire de Chaïm Perelman* (Editions de l'Université de Bruxelles 1986); William Kluback, 'The Implications of Rhetorical Philosophy' (1986) 5 Law & Phil 315; and Roland Schmetz, *L'argumentation selon Perelman* (Presses Universitaires de Namur 2000). A good brief critical account of Perelman's theory is Robert Alexy, *A Theory of Legal Argumentation* (Clarendon Press 1989: tr Ruth Adler and Neil MacCormick) 155–76.

[10] See Charles K Ogden and Ivor A Richards, *The Meaning of Meaning* (Kegan Paul 1946).

[11] Lucy Daniel, *Gertrude Stein* (Reaktion Books 2009) 190. A forensic examination of Stein's conscious effacement of 'meaning' is Ulla Dydo, *Gertrude Stein: The Language that Rises 1923–1934* (Northwestern University Press 2003) 12:

she challenges our capacity to read and our expectations of what written words and sentences are, what they do and how they do it. Her writing calls for radical redefinition of genre, representation, language, reading, and writing.

Language, and especially the manipulation of language and its meaning, reference, and extension—in other words, the interpretation of terms—is fundamental to rhetoric because rhetoric examines the techniques of argumentation which aim to persuade someone, or some people or group, to take some action or make some decision. These attempted acts of persuasion are constructed from natural language:

Pour communiquer avec son auditoire, l'orateur considérera le langage comme un vaste arsenal dans lequel il choisira les moyens qui lui semblent les plus favorables à sa thèse.[12]

Not all theorists consider that persuasion is the sole aim of rhetoric—for instance, Richards argues that rhetoric also has an expository function 'which is concerned to state a view, not to persuade people to agree or to do anything more than examine it'.[13] White sees three elements in rhetoric—the Aristotelian enthymeme which tries to establish probabilities, 'the ignoble art of persuasion', and his notion of constitutive rhetoric.[14] We are not concerned here with these variants, but with rhetoric as a form of practical reasoning, particularly as this is employed in international legal argumentation and interpretation.

Legal argumentation is a specialized form of rhetoric which is principally concerned with interpretation—the interpretation of facts, of legal terms and concepts, of meaning and value, of what the law is meant to achieve, of what the parties to a case want the law to 'mean', or of what the parties to a transaction aim to achieve. Legal argument is essentially instrumental because it aims to have a practical effect, but by its nature it aims at securing the assent or adhesion of those to whom the argument is addressed rather than demonstrating the truth of the proposition or interpretation advanced. This is because rhetoric comprises non-compelling argumentation which argues from probabilities and possibilities rather than from certainties.

Perelman claims that to say that a text is clear in a given case is only to indicate that its interpretative possibilities were not discussed. Such an impression of clarity may be less the expression of good understanding than a failure of imagination.[15] He sees litigation as an eristic dialogue, which occurs when there is a third party who decides between the arguments presented, in which counsel present their arguments with a complete indifference to the truth. Their function is to perplex their adversary and win the argument.[16] This view is too schematic: while litigation might well be seen as the central case of legal oratory, legal rhetoric is employed in many other interpretative situations—for example, in advising clients, arguing

---

[12] Perelman, *Logique juridique*, [60], 119: 'To communicate with his audience, the orator will see language as a vast arsenal from which he will choose the means which seem to him the most favourable to his proposition.'

[13] Richards, *The Philosophy of Rhetoric*, 24.

[14] James Boyd White, 'Law as Rhetoric, Rhetoric as Law: The Arts of Cultural and Communal Life' (1985) 52 U Chi L Rev 684.

[15] Perelman, *Logique juridique*, [25], 36.

[16] Perelman and Olbrechts-Tyteca, *The New Rhetoric*, [8], 38; Perelman, *The Idea of Justice and the Problem of Argument* (Kegan Paul 1963) 101, 161–7; Perelman, *Justice et Raison*, 221; and Perelman, *Logique juridique*, [7], 7, [50], 101–2, [71], 135.

whether proposed legislation or agreements are consonant with existing law, or in constructing academic commentaries.

III. Blame it all on the Ancient Greeks

The art of rhetoric has deep historic and functional roots. Hand in hand with the emergence of democracy in Athens and other Greek cities in the fifth century bce came the study of rhetoric: participation in government by adult male citizens required that they must be able to speak effectively in public. Similarly, as there were no professional lawyers, if a citizen were involved in legal proceedings, he was expected to be able to speak for himself. The approaches to the practice of rhetoric adopted were, however, divisive. On the one hand were the Sophists, professional teachers of rhetoric who taught their students how to marshal arguments, divide speeches into sections, and choose and combine words and phrases.[17] Socrates and Plato were hostile to this approach. In *Gorgias*,[18] Plato attacked Sophist rhetoric as immoral and dangerous, being more a manipulative form of flattery than the pursuit of truth. He later moderated his views in *Phaedrus*,[19] arguing that it could be a useful tool of persuasion in the hands of a true philosopher.

Aristotle, on the other hand, took the view that rhetoric was a morally neutral form of communication, with its persuasive value being dependent on:

the truth and logical validity of what is being argued; the speaker's success in conveying to the audience the perception that he or she can be trusted; and the emotions that a speaker is able to awaken in an audience to accept the views advanced and act in accordance with them.[20]

Aristotle drew a clear line between logic and rhetoric. He saw logic as the technique of arguing from truths or certainties to render an answer which is equally true, while rhetoric comprises the techniques of persuasion which may be used to structure argument over a range of subjects where the issue under discussion is debatable—'we debate about things that seem to be capable of admitting two possibilities; for no one debates things incapable of being different either in past or future or present, at least not if they suppose that to be the case; for there is nothing more [to say]'.[21] Thus rhetoric deals with arguing from possibilities and probabilities, rather than the demonstration of the certainties of logic. Nonetheless, for Aristotle, a rhetorical argument should be logical in structure, proceeding by way of enthymemes, that is by employing rhetorical syllogisms which use probabilities rather than truths as premises:

---

[17] For selective examples of Sophists' work, see Michael Gagarin and Paul Woodruff (eds), *Early Greek Political Thought from Homer to the Sophists* (CUP 1995) 173–311.

[18] Various modern translations and editions are available. See eg Plato *Gorgias* (OUP 2008: ed and tr Robin Waterfield).

[19] See eg Plato, *Phaedrus* (OUP 2002: ed and tr Robin Waterfield).

[20] Aristotle, *On Rhetoric: A Theory of Civic Discourse* (OUP 1991: ed and tr George Kennedy) ix.

[21] Aristotle, *On Rhetoric*, 41 (Book I, Chapter 2.12).

few of the premises from which rhetorical syllogisms are formed are necessarily true (most of the matters with which judgment and examination are concerned can be other than they are; for people deliberate and examine what they are doing, and [human] actions are all of this kind, and none of them [are], so to speak, necessary)…it is evident that [the premises] from which enthymemes are spoken are sometimes necessarily true but mostly true [only] for the most part…enthymemes are derived from probabilities.[22]

The aim of rhetoric is persuasion, and a rhetorical argument principally takes the form of an exercise in practical reason. Aristotle argued that there are three types of rhetoric: the deliberative, the judicial, and the epideictic. The first concerns what should be done, while the second examines what happened in the past; both are aimed at making decisions and thus are forms of practical reason. Epideictic rhetoric is a speech of praise or blame but which does not call for any immediate action by the audience.[23]

In constructing an argument, the main resource the speaker should draw upon is the *topos* (topic), which 'literally means "place", metaphorically that location or space in an art where a speaker can look for "available means of persuasion"'.[24] *Topoi* (topics) can be of two forms: those that are general or common to a wide range of substantive issues, and those which are specific to a given field.[25] In deliberative and judicial rhetoric, the aim of the speaker is to persuade his audience:

Persuasion occurs through the arguments [*logoi*] when we show the truth or apparent truth from whatever is persuasive in each case.[26]

Accordingly, the Aristotelian concept of rhetoric was practical, and differed from the fine speeches of the Sophists which were often aimed at simply arousing the emotions of the audience.

IV. Rediscovering the Past—The Resurgence of Rhetoric in the Twentieth Century

Perelman and Olbrechts-Tyteca, Toulmin, and Viehweg were all firmly rooted in the Aristotelian notion of rhetoric,[27] rather than that of the Sophists, but they also reacted against a Cartesian world-view of systematization and logical deduction:

When agreement can easily be reached by means of calculation, measuring, or weighing, when a result can be either demonstrated or verified, nobody would think of resorting to

---

[22] Aristotle, *On Rhetoric*, 42–43 (Book I, Chapter 2.14).
[23] Aristotle, *On Rhetoric*, 47–50 (Book I, Chapter 3). On this genre of rhetoric, see Perelman and Olbrechts-Tyteca, *The New Rhetoric*, [11], 47–51; Perelman, *Realm of Rhetoric*, 19–20.
[24] Aristotle, *On Rhetoric*, 45 (translator's note).
[25] Aristotle, *On Rhetoric*, 46–47 (Book I, Chapters 21–22).
[26] Aristotle, *On Rhetoric*, 39 (Book I, Chapter 2.6).
[27] See eg Perelman and Olbrechts-Tyteca, *The New Rhetoric*, 4–9; Perelman, *The Idea of Justice and the Problem of Argument*, 161–7; Viehweg, *Topics and the Law*, 7–12; and Giovanni Damele, 'Aristotle et Perelman: L'Ancienne et la Nouvelle Rhétorique' (28 October 2009) <http://papers.ssrn.com/sol3/papers.cfm?abstract_id=2167799> accessed 7 August 2014.

dialectical discussion. The latter concerns only what cannot be so decided and, especially, disagreements about values. In fact, in matters of opinion, it is often the case that neither rhetoric nor dialectic can reconcile all the positions that are taken.[28]

Perelman's fundamental critique regarding the role of logic in practical decision-making revolves around the notion that formal logical systems are isolated from any context—'un système purement formel, et un jeu avec ses règles, n'étant pas des moyens visant à réaliser une fin sociale'.[29] This is a point reinforced graphically by Toulmin.[30]

Perelman argues that only formal logical arguments can compel a conclusion, but that outside mathematics, the conditions required in order that such an argument may be asserted are absent. A formal logical argument may only take place within a system which is complete, contains no internal contradictions, and where the terms are univocal and unambiguous.[31] He argues that these requirements are not met in any legal system—in particular, natural language cannot fulfil the requirement of univocity and is inherently ambiguous.[32] Conversely, because the terms employed in a logic calculus are determinate, univocal, and unambiguous, there can be no room for their interpretation in a formal system. Simply because law is expressed in natural language, propositions are open to interpretation and thus law is not amenable to systematization as a formal logical system:

That language combines within itself an almost incomprehensible abundance of continuously varying horizons of understanding becomes increasingly clear to us today... [N]atural language constantly takes up inventive new viewpoints. In this way it proves its fertility and pliability, but at the same time unremittingly jeopardizes the deductive system. Concepts or propositions which turn up in the natural language are unreliable for purposes of system building. If one is dependent upon natural language, as one presumably always is in the realm of law, then one hovers as a systematizer in constant danger of being unconsciously led with gentle force by its interpretations and reinterpretations. One has already lost the game if one refers in case of need to ordinary language, an occurrence which takes place continuously in legal practice and, reasonably enough, must frequently occur.[33]

---

[28] Perelman, *The New Rhetoric and the Humanities*, 13; Perelman, *Justice, Law, and Argument*, 143–4.

[29] Perelman, *Logique juridique*, [34], 59: 'a purely formal system, and games with its rules, are not ways which are aimed at achieving a social purpose'; Perelman and Olbrechts-Tyteca, *The New Rhetoric*, [1], 13–14.

[30] Toulmin, *The Uses of Argument*, 146–210.

[31] Perelman, *Justice, Law, and Argument*, 137. Perelman, however, immediately qualifies the requirement of completeness, claiming that this can only be fulfilled in very simple systems: 'There is a general tendency to say that every system having a certain richness of expression is necessarily incomplete. This means that we can show that sufficiently rich systems necessarily contain undecidable propositions which can be neither affirmatively nor negatively demonstrated' (138). See also Perelman, *The Idea of Justice and the Problem of Argument*, 99–100.

[32] This is a recurring theme throughout Perelman's work. See eg Perelman and Olbrechts-Tyteca, *The New Rhetoric*, [1], 13–14, [30], 120–3, [33], 130–3; Perelman, *The Idea of Justice and the Problem of Argument*, 89–90, 95 *et seq*, 99–100, 114–15, 143–50; Perelman, *Justice et Raison*, 81 *et seq*; Perelman, *Logique juridique*, [24], 34–6, [56], 114–15; Perelman, *Justice, Law, and Argument*, 95–106, 126, 137–8.

[33] Viehweg, *Topics and the Law*, 77–8. See 69–82 generally.

Perelman repeatedly illustrates the non-univocity of natural language using the notion of apparent tautology such as 'boys will be boys' or 'business is business'. To give these propositions meaning, different interpretations must be given to the repeated terms whereas in formal systems they would be meaningless because of the systemic requirement of the principle of identity which mandates that terms must be univocal.[34]

Accordingly, because the determinative nature of a formal logical system is lacking, rhetoric is the study of non-compelling argumentation. It analyses methods of argument in which the conclusion is not simply a syllogistically valid deduction from given premises. Rather the conclusion depends on the appreciation of the relative strengths of the arguments adduced and, ultimately, requires a non-arbitrary power of decision being vested in someone to determine which argument is to succeed. The outcome reached thus depends on choice, and not simply on logical proof.[35]

V. The Elements of Effective Rhetoric—Audience, Topics, Choice

In modern rhetorical theory, the function of argument is to persuade an audience to take action or make a decision. The concept of the audience is most developed in Perelmanien theory. He claims that the worth of an argument is dependent on the audience (or auditor) to which it is presented. A successful argument is simply one that persuades the relevant audience. There is an infinite variety of audiences which may be addressed by a rhetor,[36] but Perelman's main dichotomy is drawn between particular and general audiences. Particular audiences represent essentially sectional interests, whereas Perelman sees the universal audience as objective.[37] The new rhetoric aims to describe argumentative techniques which are valid for all audiences, or at least all audiences composed of rational and competent people. Objective argument aims at transcending the contingencies inherent in sectional interests, thus gaining the adherence of the universal audience.[38]

---

[34] See eg Perelman and Olbrechts-Tyteca, *The New Rhetoric*, [51], 216–18, 442–3; Perelman, *Logique juridique*, [56], 114–16; Perelman, *Justice, Law, and Argument*, 97, 126.

[35] See eg Perelman and Olbrechts-Tyteca, *The New Rhetoric*, [13], 59–62; Perelman, *The Idea of Justice and the Problem of Argument*, 101; Perelman, *Justice et Raison*, 220; Perelman, *Justice, Law, and Argument*, 129, 150.

[36] Perelman, *Logique juridique*, [52], 107. Following Lyndel Prott, 'rhetor', a now generally obsolete term, shall be used to refer to someone who engages in rhetoric, whether spoken or written, with the aim of persuading an audience: *The Latent Power of Culture and the International Judge* (Professional Books 1979) 125. The most obvious alternative, 'rhetorician', tends now to have pejorative overtones which are best avoided.

[37] Perelman and Olbrechts-Tyteca, *The New Rhetoric*, [7], 31–5, [15], 65–6.

[38] Perelman and Olbrechts-Tyteca, *The New Rhetoric*, [6]–[7], 26–35; Perelman, *Logique juridique*, [52], 107.

Nonetheless, Perelman argues that the universal audience can only be a construct of the rhetor.[39] It is a conceptual category, rather than a material entity, but it is nonetheless useful because:

By thus generalising the idea of the audience, we can ward off Plato's attack against the rhetoricians for showing greater concern for success than for the truth. To this criticism we can reply... that the worth of an argument is not measured solely by its efficacy but also by the quality of audience at which it is aimed. Consequently, the idea of a rational argumentation cannot be defined *in abstracto*, since it depends on the historically grounded conception of the universal audience.[40]

Perelman's notion of the universal audience has been criticized as philosophically problematic, requiring the rhetor to construct an objective model on the basis of his own subjective understanding.[41]

This controversy need not detain us, as Perelman acknowledges that a rhetor may substitute an elite or, more importantly, a specialist audience for the universal. The latter is one whose members have specialist knowledge of a given area and which therefore may be assimilated to the universal in that field—for instance, the scientist addressing other scientists.[42] Specialized disciplines, such as law, contain recognized modes of argument, techniques, predispositions, as well as substantive content which can act as the foundations for an argument.[43] Perelman, however, cautions:

Reasons considered good at one period of time and one milieu are not in another; they are socially and culturally conditioned as are the convictions and aspirations of the audience they must convince.[44]

Following Aristotle, central to modern theories of rhetoric is the notion of topics—'Topics is a technique of problem oriented thought that was developed by rhetoric'.[45] For Aristotle, a topic was a metaphor for the place where a speaker can look for materials or arguments which are persuasive to his thesis. Durham illustrates this metaphor with specific reference to the use of topical argument in legal research:

The standard approach to researching a legal problem in common law settings is to identify relevant cases. A good lawyer has a sense for the topography of case law. To use terminology reminiscent of Aristotle, he or she knows the 'region' where relevant arguments (the reasoning of specific cases) can be found... The instinctive common law approach is

---

[39] Perelman and Olbrechts-Tyteca, *The New Rhetoric*, [4], 19–23, [7], 32–3; Perelman, *Logique juridique*, [52]–[53], 107–9.

[40] Perelman, *The New Rhetoric and the Humanities*, 14. See also Perelman and Olbrechts-Tyteca, *The New Rhetoric*, [6]–[7], 30–6; Perelman, *Justice et Raison*, 100–3.

[41] For discussions of this criticism, see Alexy Aarnio, 'Argumentation Theory and Beyond: Some Remarks on the Rationality of Legal Justification' (1983) 14 Rechtstheorie 385, 391–2; Gross and Dearin, *Chaïm Perelman*, 32–9; Allen Scult, 'Perelman's Universal Audience: One Perspective' in Dearin, *The New Rhetoric of Chaïm Perelman*, 153; Schmetz, *L'argumentation selon Perelman*, 47–88.

[42] Perelman and Olbrechts-Tyteca, *The New Rhetoric*, [7], 33–4.

[43] Perelman and Olbrechts-Tyteca, *The New Rhetoric*, [26], 99–104.

[44] Perelman, *Justice, Law, and Argument*, 131.   [45] Viehweg, *Topics and the Law*, 1.

to start with a problem, and then identify cases that involve maximally similar problems in order to identify arguments and insights that bear on the problem at hand.[46]

International law, to borrow Tammelo's terminology, is a rhetorically oriented rather than an axiom-oriented system because it is neither codified nor based on precisely formulated basic principles which can operate as major premises in deductive syllogistic reasoning.[47] Topics, however, aid in the consolidation of this system where legal materials and opinion consolidate around settled points—'a topical approach is our principal technique of logically managing opinions and, especially, of turning a mass of opinions into an ordered system'.[48] In this light, it has been argued that commonly used, or established, interpretative methods and canons are essentially 'rival meta–*topoi* we invoke in the process of determining how various other rhetorical constructs (statutes, prior judicial opinions, etc) should be interpreted'.[49]

The rhetor's aim is to persuade his audience to adhere to his conclusions. To be effective, he must build on propositions or premises to which the audience already agrees.[50] This provides a general premise for the development of the rhetor's argument. Perelman refers to these, fairly indiscriminately, as *loci*, commonplaces (*lieux communs*) or topics,[51] and argues that the audience and the discourse interact. The rhetor adapts his discourse to the audience by hooking his argument onto a proposition the audience already accepts in order to show that his conclusion is a development from that initial position. The audience is not a *tabula rasa*, but already accepts certain facts and presumptions, and has beliefs and opinions, including views on legitimate argumentative techniques. The aim is to transfer to the conclusion the audience's existing adhesion or agreement to the premise.[52] Thus topics, as starting points for argument, play a role which is

---

[46] Viehweg, *Topics and the Law*, xxiii–xxiv (translator's foreword).

[47] See Ilmar Tammelo, 'On the Logical Openness of Legal Orders' (1959) 8 Am J Comp L 187, 187–8; Ilmar Tammelo, 'The Law of Nations and the Rhetorical Tradition of Legal Reasoning' (1964) 13 Indian YB Int'l Aff 227, 252–4; Samuel Stoljar, 'System and Topoi' (1981) 12 Rechtstheorie 385; Samuel Stoljar, 'Paradigms and borderlines' (1982) 13 Rechtstheorie 133. The rhetorical nature of all legal systems is, of course, a key issue emphasized by Perelman and Olbrechts-Tyteca, and Viehweg.

[48] Stoljar, 'System and Topoi', 389.

[49] Viehweg, *Topics and the Law*, xxii, xxiv–xxv (translator's foreword), 30.

[50] Perelman terms this an 'object of agreement', which fall into two categories: those relating to the real (facts, truths, and presumptions), and those relating to the preferable (values, hierarchies, and lines of agreement on the preferable). See Perelman and Olbrechts-Tyteca, *The New Rhetoric*, [15]–[28], 66–114, and Part Two, Chapter One in general.

[51] 'Topics' is the term adopted throughout this chapter. Perelman breaks with classical rhetorical tradition by using the term *loci* only in relation to general premises which can serve as the basis for values or hierarchies. These may be general or special: a general *locus* is an affirmation regarding a value which is presumed to be relevant in all circumstances whatsoever, whereas a special *locus* concerns what is preferable in a given situation. As *loci* become more specific in character, there is a gradual shift from *loci* which may serve as general argumentative premises, to *loci* which Perelman sees as agreements on actual values or value hierarchies: Perelman and Olbrechts-Tyteca, *The New Rhetoric*, [21], 83–5, [24]–[25], 95–6.

[52] See Perelman and Olbrechts-Tyteca, *The New Rhetoric*, [10]–[11], 45–51, [15], 65–6, [25], 96, [27], 104–10, [44], 189; Perelman, *Logique juridique*, [53]–[54], 109–11. Perhaps the best exposition of the 'audience is not a *tabula rasa*' notion is in Perelman, *Justice, Law, and Argument*, 169–70.

analogous to that of axioms in formal logical systems. They differ from axioms in that the adhesion which topics attract is not based on evidence but often on their ambiguity and the possibility that they might be interpreted and applied in different ways. Rhetorical arguments, starting from the same premises, can end in different, or even opposed, conclusions. There is often more agreement on the initial starting topic of an argument than on its ultimate outcome.[53]

A clear illustration of this point may be made by reference to Perelman's concept of abstract (or universal) values. Certain values are thought to be universal—such as the good, the true, the beautiful—but they can only claim to be universal values because they are abstract. The universal audience can only adhere to such values as long as their content is relatively vague: as specific content is attributed to an abstract value, only the adherence of particular audiences is possible because disagreements can reasonably arise regarding the specific implications of, for instance, beauty.[54]

However, universal values have a persuasive function: they may be used to justify a choice or decision by operating as an empty frame of reference. For instance, Perelman argues that the adoption of the Universal Declaration of Human Rights proceeded on this basis. By inserting abstract values as empty frames within the text, states with different ideological affiliations could interpret the Universal Declaration in different ways, because its content was free from specific reference. Perelman sees this as useful. Although agreement on the text was only possible using empty frames and abstract values, a single text was produced which could serve as the basis for further action. Use of this methodology also ensured the continuity of dialogue.[55]

This also illustrates the point that an audience may be composite because its members adhere to diverse opinions. The rhetor must seek to persuade each subset of the audience, and thus cumulation of argument is a characteristic of rhetorical reasoning. This can lead to the adduction of apparently inconsistent arguments, because each is aimed at a different sector of the audience. Perelman sees this strategy not as inconsistent, but as the use of redundancy, because the acceptance of one argument makes the others unnecessary. This type of redundancy is fully justified in Perelman's conception of rhetoric.[56]

The predispositions of the audience also account for the doctrine of inertia, which is considered to be one of Perelman's major contributions to general argumentation theory because it provides a foundation for the ascription of the burden of proof in practical discourse.[57] Inertia simply refers to the presumption that, failing contrary proof, an attitude—or a particular interpretation of the law for that matter—adopted in the past will subsist, either for a desire for coherence

---

[53] Perelman, *Logique juridique*, [58], 118, [64], 125.

[54] See eg Perelman and Olbrechts-Tyteca, *The New Rhetoric*, [18]–[19], 74–9, [34], 133–8; Perelman, 'L'usage at l'abus des notions confuses' (1978) 7 Études de logique juridique 3; Perelman, *Justice, Law, and Argument*, 95–106; Perelman, *Realm of Rhetoric*, 27–8.

[55] Perelman, *Justice, Law, and Argument*, 98–9; Perelman, 'Peut-on fonder les droits de homme?', translated as 'Can the Rights of Man Be Founded?' in Alan Rosenbaum (ed), *The Philosophy of Human Rights: International Perspectives* (Aldwych Press 1981) 45.

[56] On cumulation, see Perelman and Olbrechts-Tyteca, *The New Rhetoric*, Ch 5.

[57] Alexy, *A Theory of Legal Argumentation*, 171–3.

or from force of habit, and thus may be relied upon in subsequent argument. Change, on the other hand, requires justification. Perelman argues that inertia underlies the rule of formal justice, namely that what has been considered as valid in one situation will be considered valid in all similar situations.[58]

Because natural language is ambiguous, and because topics may be applied and interpreted in diverse ways, Perelman sees specific argumentative figures as techniques which the rhetor may exploit in the presentation of his thesis. The decision regarding which techniques to use, or manipulate, in an argument is not pre-determined. These are not automatically selected without consideration of the end in view. On the contrary, the techniques employed will be consciously chosen with the hope of maximizing the persuasive force of the argument with the audience. The bulk of *The New Rhetoric* and *Logique juridique*, as well as numerous essays, comprise the exposition of various types of argumentative techniques, structures, and figures.[59] These discussions bear on such matters as pragmatic arguments,[60] analogy and metaphor,[61] quasi-logical arguments,[62] arguments from authority,[63] and so on.

Along with the choice of topic and technique, each rhetor may choose to give presence to different aspects of the argument. Presence is simply the argumentative concentration on particular factors in order to stress their importance to the audience while discounting or de-emphasizing other factors.[64] The selection of data, topics, and modes of argument is inevitable in rhetoric:

> choice is...a dominant factor in scientific debates: choice of the facts deemed relevant, choice of hypotheses, choice of the theories that should be confronted with the facts, choice of the actual elements that constitute facts. The method of each science implies such a choice, which is relatively stable in the natural sciences, but is much more variable in the social sciences.

By the very fact of selecting certain elements and presenting them to the audience, their importance and pertinency to the discussion are implied. Indeed, such a choice endows those elements with a presence, which is an essential factor in argumentation.[65]

---

[58] Perelman and Olbrechts-Tyteca, *The New Rhetoric*, [27], 104–10, [52], 218–20; Perelman, *Justice, Law, and Argument*, 27–8, 169–71. Perelman sees inertia as allowing the transition from normal to norm by way of argumentative justification, although he concedes the validity of David Hume's view that this is a logically illicit transition: see *Justice, Law, and Argument*, 28. Hume's argument is in David Hume, *A Treatise on Human Nature* (OUP 1978: ed LA Selby-Bigg and PH Nidditch) [III.i.1], 455–70. On Hume's argument, see JL Mackie, *Hume's Moral Theory* (Routledge 1980) Ch 4; Perelman, *Logique juridique*, [49], 99–101.

[59] See eg Perelman and Olbrechts-Tyteca, *The New Rhetoric*, [41]–[42], 167–79, [44]–[96], 185–458; Perelman, *The Idea of Justice and the Problem of Argument*, 196–207; Perelman, *Logique juridique*, [33], 54–9, [64]–[65], 125–7, [67]–[69], 129–32; Perelman, *Realm of Rhetoric*, 53–137.

[60] See eg Perelman and Olbrechts-Tyteca, *The New Rhetoric*, [62], 266–70; Perelman, *The Idea of Justice and the Problem of Argument*, 196–207; Perelman, *Logique juridique*, [65], 126–7.

[61] See eg Perelman and Olbrechts-Tyteca, *The New Rhetoric*, [82]–[88], 371–410; Perelman, *Logique juridique*, [68], 129–30; Perelman, *Realm of Rhetoric*, 114–25.

[62] See eg Perelman and Olbrechts-Tyteca, *The New Rhetoric*, [45]–[59], 193–260; Perelman, *Logique juridique*, [64], 126; Perelman, *Realm of Rhetoric*, 53–80.

[63] See eg Perelman and Olbrechts-Tyteca, *The New Rhetoric*, [70], 305–10.

[64] See eg Perelman and Olbrechts-Tyteca, *The New Rhetoric*, [29], 115–20, [36], 142; Perelman, *Logique juridique*, [59], 118–19; Perelman, *Realm of Rhetoric*, 35–6.

[65] Perelman and Olbrechts-Tyteca, *The New Rhetoric*, [29], 116.

Argumentation is always selective and thus dependent on choice, but this necessary act of selection may be self-defeating. The emphasis inherent in presence could distract the audience, or lead the argument in an unintended or unwanted direction—for example, a rhetor may give presence to his opponent's argument by concentrating on its refutation and thus add weight to it, especially if his counter-argument is weak.[66]

Choice of the elements of an argument is unavoidable because all argumentation is subject to limitation one way or another—for example by constraints of time or length. Even if this is not institutionally regulated, the audience's attention cannot be prolonged indefinitely. The fullness of a discourse is thus a question of choice, and that choice ascribes presence to specific arguments.[67] However, temporal limitations cut both ways: a practical obligation is not only imposed on the rhetor(s) to compress the debate, but also the audience is required to make a decision even if none of the arguments presented seem convincing.[68]

VI. Rhetoric, Interpretation, and Law

Perelman's theory of legal reasoning, 'la logique juridique', is essentially an extension of his general theory of rhetoric. Like general rhetoric, legal reasoning is centred on attaining the adhesion of the audience, rather than establishing an objective truth, and for this purpose proceeds from topics. Further, it is generally the case that the audience being addressed is a specialist audience of lawyers which has its own predispositions regarding legitimate or accepted modes of legal reasoning. Also, as the categorization of facts is dependent on the rule under which they are alleged to be subsumed, each party may stress different laws and precedents as decisive.[69] A consequence of the concentration on adhesion is that the interpretation of a given text might not be disputed. At most this can only lead to the conclusion that possible alternative interpretations of the text did not interest either party because these offered neither any advantage.

Perelman's 'logique juridique', however, also has a normative component, and is geared towards domestic litigation within a legal system which observes a tripartite separation of powers. The core of his argument is that judicial decisions must be both just and in conformity with the law in force:[70]

The judge's mission is to speak the law but in a way that conforms to the sensibilities of society. Why? Because his role is to establish legal peace and this peace comes about only when he can convince the parties, the public and his superiors that he has adjudicated in an equitable way.[71]

---

[66] Perelman and Olbrechts-Tyteca, *The New Rhetoric*, [98], 470, [101], 481; Perelman, *Realm of Rhetoric*, 141–2.

[67] Perelman and Olbrechts-Tyteca, *The New Rhetoric*, [37], 143.

[68] Perelman, *Le Champ de l'argumentation*, 46.

[69] See Perelman and Olbrechts-Tyteca, *The New Rhetoric*, [8], 38; Perelman, *Logique juridique*, [39], 72–4, [44], 83, [84]–[85], 158–9, [95], 174; Perelman, *Justice, Law, and Argument*, 129.

[70] This is constantly reiterated in Perelman's work: see eg Perelman, *Logique juridique*, [38]–[39], 70–2, [46], 87, [50], 102, [71], 136–7, [87], 162, [96]–[97], 175; Perelman, *Justice, Law, and Argument*, 121–2, 124, 129, 143.

[71] Perelman, *Justice, Law, and Argument*, 143.

This aspect of his theory, because it is intrinsically tied to domestic constitutional structures,[72] is less germane to questions of interpretation in international law than his exposition of techniques of argumentation and rhetorical theory in general, but his application of rhetoric to legal reasoning does contain some useful additional points.

In constructing his analysis of legal reasoning, Perelman focused on the judiciary. Although he saw the judicial process as involving the dialectical opposition of the parties' claims, he restricted his field of analysis to the judicial decision, thus rejecting the view that judgments should be seen as the outcome of a process:

Pour préciser la notion de raisonnement juridique, nous entendons par cette expression le raisonnement du juge, tel qu'il se manifeste dans un jugement ou arrêt qui motive une décision. Les analyses doctrinales d'un juriste, les plaidoiries des avocats, l'acte d'accusation du ministère public, fournissent des raisons qui peuvent exercer une influence sur la décision du juge: seul le jugement motivé nous fournit l'ensemble des éléments qui nous permettent de dégager les caractéristiques du raisonnement juridique.[73]

There is more to legal rhetoric as a mechanism for interpretation than the judicial decision, and the context for interpretative argument in international law is not, principally, in the field of litigation. This is also the case in domestic law: few disputes end up in court. Both internationally and domestically most acts of interpretative argument will lie in activities such as advising clients, engaging in negotiations, research and the construction of academic arguments, or the presentation of a proposed text or its interpretation to non-judicial bodies. On the other hand, to a greater or lesser extent, these non-judicial uses are instrumental and may be partial, aimed at advancing a particular agenda, while one would hope that the judiciary is more disinterested in its endeavours and focused on the legal merits of the case in hand. Accordingly, Perelman's field of analysis is justifiable in order to discern 'l'ensemble des éléments', but his conclusions are capable of generalization to legal argumentation as a whole.

Perelman sees cumulation of argument as a specific characteristic of legal reasoning. If several distinct arguments lead to the same conclusion, the value the audience attributes to it, and to each argument individually, will be increased. There is little likelihood that several entirely wrong arguments could lead to the same conclusion.[74] Cumulation arises simply because law is value-dependent,

---

[72] See Perelman, *Logique juridique*, 'Première Partie', [15]–[48], 21–96.

[73] Perelman, *Droit, morale et philosophie* (2nd edn, LGDJ/Pichon et Durand-Auzias 1976) 93: 'To define legal reasoning, by this term we mean judicial reasoning as disclosed in a judgment or order which justifies a decision. The doctrinal analysis of a legal commentator, the lawyers' pleadings and the indictment of the prosecutor provide reasons which might influence the judge's decision: only the reasoned judgment contains all the elements which allow us to extricate the characteristics of legal reasoning.' See also Perelman, *Logique juridique*, [81], 153–4, [98], 177, noting that he concentrated particularly on the reasoning of Cours de cassation. This focus on judicial reasoning was one of the tenets of the 'Brussels School' of legal theorists which was associated with the Belgian Centre National de Recherches de Logique. Its legal section was headed by Perelman. For an account of the Brussels School, see Paul Foriers, 'L'état des recherches de logique juridique en Belgique' (1967) 2 Études de logique juridique 23, 34–40.

[74] Perelman and Olbrechts-Tyteca, *The New Rhetoric*, [99]–[100], 471–9; Perelman, *The Idea of Justice and the Problem of Argument*, 161.

and values cannot be captured in a formal system. The application of law lies not in defining each word, but requires recourse to the values underlying the norms. This aspect is ignored if the process is assimilated to a syllogistic operation.[75] Cumulation is thus required because legal argumentation is not logically compelling.

Perelman is barely prescriptive on how his theory should be applied in legal reasoning and interpretative argument. This is true of rhetorical theories generally, but is probably inevitable as all argumentation is intimately dependent on context and subject, as well as the aims of the rhetor. What rhetoric does provide is a strategy or broad structure for argumentation which has the potential to be effective, or in short, to be persuasive. Fundamental to this argumentative process is choice. Choice permeates the whole process, from the choice of the initial topic, the object of agreement the audience already accepts which the rhetor thinks is most suitable to achieve his end or is most supportive to the interpretation he proposes, through the elaboration of the argument, and the decision of what points to emphasize, and which points to refute. These choices are not free: the rhetor must exercise judgement in the identification of the audience's predispositions and decide how to adapt his argument accordingly.

Established canons of interpretation can act as topics—an obvious example is the interpretative rules set out in the VCLT. Even then, however, the opening gambit is instrumental, and thus subject to choice: should one argue that the text is clear in the light of the treaty's object and purpose; or should it be read in the light of the parties' subsequent practice; or that recourse should be made to the *travaux préparatoires* to clarify matters? This can only be a matter of choice—the decision of what is the best and most effective way to try to persuade. General propositions such as the VCLT interpretative rules might perhaps, as Durham suggests, best be seen as meta-*topoi*, as over-arching argumentative structures which only gain substance once more specific topics are adduced, such as the adverse party's prior practice, its interpretative views expressed in official statements to international organizations or conferences, or in diplomatic *démarches*, or even in statements to the press.

Rhetorical theory, however, offers no certainties in interpretation—by definition, it seeks to explicate non-constraining argument. It offers ideas of topics, tropes, and types of argumentation, but no sure solutions. All depends on context and the audience. It offers little guidance on the inherent strength of interpretative arguments, and how strong arguments may be differentiated from the weak. The strength of an argument is ultimately centred on the intensity of the audience's initial adhesion and its subsequent persuasion. All that Perelman says is that if the audience adheres to ascertained presuppositions and methodological rules, then the inadequacy of some arguments can be identified. Even then, there is no certainty that an argument can be persuasive in its totality: the audience retains its

---

[75] Perelman, *Logique juridique*, [24], 34–6, [31], 52, [34], 59, [37], 67–70, [49], 99–100; Perelman, *Justice, Law, and Argument*, 140–1, 143–4, 150, 154, 160.

power of appraisal and decision.[76] One can only conclude that a 'strong' argument is one that the audience accepts, but this is only trivially true. Successful arguments can only be determined situationally, and *ex post facto*. Given the recounting of specific argumentative figures which constitutes a great part of Perelman's work, one is left with the impression that he was intent on providing something akin to an array of styles and samples while failing to provide detailed instructions for their use. Alexy has argued that there is a measure of truth in the view that a topic is a reasonable or generally accepted proposition used as an argumentative premise. He comments, however, that this is too general because it fails to differentiate between the different types of legal material which might be used, and the role they play in the construction of an argument.[77]

Perelman's topical approach is also open to the objection that it presents law as asystemic. It concentrates on dealing with legal disputes and questions of interpretation episodically and instrumentally, and fails to systematize legal material. Any systematizing function that topics possess becomes subservient to situational acts of persuasion, and Perelman pays no attention to the role topics play in the justification of the decision. In Perelmanien theory, topics can only be persuasive. They cannot be binding because this would make the theory self-contradictory because Perelman denies that legal reasoning can ever be deductive. In particular, when he considers international law, he thinks that discussion is open-ended:

The recourse to confused notions which is sometimes indispensable in internal law proves to be completely inevitable in public international law when the confusion of notions is an indispensable condition for achieving agreement on a text between States having different, if not incompatible, ideologies.[78]

This goes too far. Instruments may be entered into between states which share a world-view and, to be honest, states also have different bargaining strengths and one (or some) may effectively impose a text on others—either because it has the whiphand on an issue, or because the others are willing to compromise their interests in order to establish a text which they hope will ensure the participation of another. We might term this the 'League of Nations syndrome', the fear that some institution or convention will fail to be effective unless state X is part of it.

Further, every act of interpretation precludes others. In terms of Perelman's own theory, once an interpretation is made, it takes on inertia and that interpretation needs no further justification in the future. It becomes a topic itself for future arguments, and only a changed interpretation will require justification. Through interpretation, abstract values thus become concrete, and as interpretations and practice coalesce around an issue, the point will be reached when 'a mass of opinions [become] an ordered system'.[79] This does not mean that the legal

[76] Perelman, *Champ de l'argumentation*, 114–15, 126; Perelman, *Logique juridique*, [95], 174; Perelman, *Justice, Law, and Argument*, 129; Perelman, *Realm of Rhetoric*, 139–40.
[77] Alexy, *A Theory of Legal Argumentation*, 20–4.
[78] Perelman, *Justice, Law, and Argument*, 98–9.   [79] Stoljar, 'System and Topoi', 389.

system is transformed into an axiomatically oriented Cartesian system where logic is substituted for rhetoric. There is still room for argument:

Often...what one finds in the '*topoi* catalogues' are divergent strands of reasoning and factual settings more or less analogous to the case to be resolved. Great lawyering at this point requires ingenuity and insight. The process of weaving persuasive arguments, either as an advocate or a judge, is a creative and constitutive exercise, even if ultimately the objective is to exhibit fidelity to statutes and precedents.[80]

VII. The Value of Rhetoric

In playing the interpretation game, much depends on the skill of the rhetor and the rhetorical choices he makes. Rhetoric can provide the method and the technique by which interpreters achieve the object of securing the audience's adherence to their argumentative stance, but even a skilled rhetor cannot guarantee a successful outcome. Rhetoric is an art, not a science. Although rhetorical theory contains ground rules for persuasive argument—start from a topic which is an object of agreement, pay attention to the audience's pre-conceptions, including its understanding of legitimate or proper argumentative methods, adapt the argument to the audience—how the array of cards rhetoric provides is played depends on choice. Aristotelian rhetoric, and the theories it has inspired, aims to set out and explain guidelines for persuasive and reasoned argument. Nevertheless, the pejorative impressions associated with the Sophists have always remained attached to rhetoric. There has always been the lingering suspicion that it is merely a technique for the manipulation of societies, groups, or individuals by rabble-rousers, by demagogues, or by those who can simply speak well:

Thanks in no small part to Platonic critique of the Sophists and rhetoricians of ancient Greece, rhetoric...has enjoyed a less than stellar reputation in the history of philosophy. In some respects, rhetoric has contributed to its own demise by paying excessive attention to surface issues of ornamentation and eloquence to the detriment of issues of substance. Moreover, its reputation, like that of lawyers, has suffered from a meretricious tendency toward promiscuous service of all causes.[81]

Like lawyers in popular consciousness, the art of rhetoric seems to be in need of some rehabilitation.

---

[80] Viehweg, *Topics and the Law*, xxiv (translator's note).
[81] Viehweg, *Topics and the Law*, xiii–xiv (translator's foreword).

4

The Existential Function of
Interpretation in International Law

Duncan B Hollis

Introduction

International law does not exist without interpretation. Consider the Syrian crisis.[1] It has spawned much debate on whether the 'Responsibility to Protect' (R2P) authorizes the use of force in Syria to prevent mass atrocities.[2] For some, the answer turns on standard interpretative inquiries—asking what R2P means (ie does it require Security Council authorization) and how does that meaning apply to Syria?[3] Interpreters can use different methods and techniques to respond to such inquiries, which may, in turn, generate different answers on whether R2P justifies foreign use of force there.[4]

[1] Since protestors sought to oust Syrian President Bashar Al-Assad in March 2011, thousands have died and more than a million people have fled Syria amid accusations of grave human rights violations by both sides, including the use of chemical weapons. See eg Press Release, The White House, 'Government Assessment of the Syrian Government's Use of Chemical Weapons on August 21, 2013' (30 August 2013); 'Russia claims Syria rebels used sarin at Khan al-Assal' *BBC News*, 9 July 2013 <http://www.bbc.co.uk/news/world-middle-east-23249104> accessed 28 July 2014.
[2] On the grounds that a state has a 'responsibility to protect' its population from mass atrocities, R2P provides other states a right to intervene when that state manifestly fails to do so, including the proportionate use of force as a last resort. See eg International Commission on Intervention and State Sovereignty, 'The Responsibility to Protect' (IDRC, 2001) vii; UN Secretary General, 'Implementing the Responsibility to Protect' (12 January 2009) UN Doc A/63/677; UNGA, '2005 World Summit Outcome Document' UNGA Res 60/1 (24 October 2005) UN Doc A/RES/60/1, [138]–[139]; UN Secretary General, 'The Secretary-General's High-level Panel on Threats, Challenges, and Change, A More Secure World: Our Shared Responsibility' (2 December 2004) UN Doc A/59/565, [207].
[3] R2P proponents differ on whether R2P is a justification for the UN Security Council to authorize uses of force or a new, stand-alone legal doctrine. Compare Dapo Akande, 'The Legality of Military Action in Syria: Humanitarian Intervention and Responsibility to Protect' (*EJIL: Talk!*, 28 August 2013) <http://www.ejiltalk.org/humanitarian-intervention-responsibility-to-protect-and-the-legality-of-military-action-in-syria/> accessed 28 July 2014 (Security Council authorization required) with Paul R Williams, J Trevor Ulbrick, and Jonathan Worboys, 'Preventing Mass Atrocity Crimes: The Responsibility to Protect and the Syria Crisis' (2012) 45 Case W Res J Int'l L 473, 489 (R2P works '[i]n the face of Security Council inaction').
[4] Compare Williams, Ulbrick, and Worboys, 'Preventing Mass Atrocity Crimes', 492–502 (arguing Syria satisfies R2P's criteria) with Gareth Evans, 'Saving the Syrians' (*Project Syndicate*,

Many others, however, never make it to this interpretative stage. For them, the R2P question is existential—does R2P exist within the corpus of international law at all?[5] For those who deny it such a status, R2P affords no legal basis for justifying intervention generally, let alone in Syria specifically.

Conventional wisdom conceives of international legal interpretation as an exercise in exposition—a process of assigning meaning to international law. But the R2P debates reveal interpretation is not just an expository process, but an existential one. Simply put, *all interpretations of international law have an existential function.* The very act of interpreting validates the existence of that which is being interpreted. Interpretations of R2P with respect to the legality of a Syrian intervention necessarily accept the existence of R2P within international law. International law's interpretative processes can thus be likened to an iceberg—a rule's meaning arrived at by an interpreter is not simply a function of the method and technique employed (the visible tip), but rests on an array of earlier choices about whether the rule 'exists' to be interpreted in the first place (the iceberg's hidden, critical mass).

At the same time, deciding whether or not R2P exists in international law comprises a distinctive type of interpretation, what I call *existential interpretation.* Existential interpretations are binary—a process of deciding whether or not the subject of interpretation exists or has validity. Existential interpretations are most visible in the context of assertions (or denials) of 'new' rules of international law like R2P. But existential interpretations can arise at all levels of international legal discourse, from evidentiary questions to ontological ones. Existential interpretations are central to debates over what 'counts' for purposes of state practice under customary international law. Interpreters who only recognize what states 'do' as state practice may generate different content for a rule than those who also consider what states 'say' about it, even holding constant the interpretative method and technique employed. More broadly, existential interpretations suffuse questions about whether sources of international law exist beyond the troika of treaties, custom, and general principles listed in Article 38(1) of the Statute of the International Court of Justice.

To date, international law's interpretative theories and practices have given little attention to the phenomenon of existential interpretation. This chapter seeks to

---

23 March 2012) <http://www.project-syndicate.org/commentary/saving-the-syrians> accessed 28 July 2014 (finding R2P's criteria not satisfied). Evans—who is widely credited with first elaborating R2P—later agreed Syria triggered R2P. Gareth Evans, 'A Talking Cure for Syria' (*Project Syndicate*, 29 May 2013) <http://www.project-syndicate.org/commentary/why-diplomacy-is-the-only-option-in-syria-by-gareth-evans> accessed 28 July 2014.

[5] See eg Neomi Rao, 'The Choice to Protect: Rethinking Responsibility for Humanitarian Intervention' (2013) 44 Colum Hum Rts L Rev 697, 718–19 (R2P not yet international law); Rachel VanLandingham, 'Politics or Law? The Dual Nature of the Responsibility to Protect' (2012) 41 Denv J Int'l L & Pol'y 63 (denying any legal right to intervene if states fail in their duty to protect their citizens); Mehrdad Payandeh, 'With Great Power Comes Great Responsibility? The Concept of the Responsibility to Protect Within the Process of International Lawmaking' (2010) 35 Yale J Int'l L 469, 491; Carsten Stahn, 'Responsibility to Protect: Political Rhetoric or Emerging Legal Norm?' (2007) 101 AJIL 99, 120.

remedy that oversight. Part I briefly surveys the existing field of interpretation in international law to demonstrate its emphasis on exposition. Part II distinguishes interpretation's existential function, introduces the concept of existential interpretation, and identifies examples from practice with respect to authority, evidence, rules and sources of international law. Part III examines how existential interpretations impact international legal (i) *discourse*, by broadening or limiting discursive boundaries; (ii) *doctrine*, by directly or indirectly generating international law; and (iii) *theory*, by operating as a proxy for theoretical disagreement about the nature and source(s) of international law (ie positivists may insist interpreters exclude from their toolbox the same soft law sources that naturalists insist require effectiveness as a matter of right).

The chapter concludes with a call for international actors to pay more attention to interpretation's existential functions. If, as this volume suggests, international legal interpretation operates like a game, then those who play it may wish to consider the costs and benefits of employing existential interpretations in their international legal discourse and in delegating interpretative authority. Moreover, by studying when states and others deploy existential interpretations, we may gain a new lens for evaluating the unity and fragmentation of international law itself.

I. The Expository Function of (Treaty) Interpretation in International Law

International law is all about language. Words are used to describe facts, laws, and their sources, not to mention the larger values and interests at stake in international coordination and conflict. As a result, one might expect studies of international legal interpretation to have a wide ambit, examining, for example, how interpretation processes real-world facts or remedies for agreed violations. At a minimum, one would think that the objective of the interpretation game would be clear—to ascribe meaning to international law in all its forms.

To date, however, interpretative scholarship has treated the interpretation game as occupying a much smaller field. Conventional wisdom focuses almost entirely on one form of international legal obligation—treaties—and a single interpretative method—Articles 31 and 32 of the VCLT.[6] The attraction is not

---

[6] Vienna Convention on the Law of Treaties (opened for signature 23 May 1969, entered into force 27 January 1980) 1155 UNTS 331. Recent, major works on international legal interpretation focus on treaty interpretation specifically or avoid analysis of non-written norms. See eg Ingo Venzke, *How Interpretation Makes International Law—On Semantic Change and Normative Twists* (OUP 2012); Malgosia Fitzmaurice, Olufemi Elias, and Panos Merkouris (eds), *Treaty Interpretation and the Vienna Convention on the Law of Treaties: 30 Years On* (Martinus Nijhoff 2010); Isabelle Van Damme, *Treaty Interpretation by the WTO Appellate Body* (OUP 2009); Richard Gardiner, *Treaty Interpretation* (OUP 2008); Ulf Linderfalk, *On the Interpretation of Treaties: The Modern International Law as Expressed in the 1969 Vienna Convention on the Law of Treaties* (Springer 2007). Cf Alexander Orakhelashvili, *The Interpretation of Acts and Rules in Public International Law* (OUP 2008) (examining interpretation in international law generally).

hard to fathom. Unlike other international legal norms, treaties usually present a text from which to launch the interpretative inquiry. And Articles 31 and 32 are widely accepted, emerging after years of negotiation in the International Law Commission and the Vienna Convention Conference.[7]

The treaty's centrality to existing interpretative inquiries has not, however, translated into certainty or consensus on treaty interpretation itself. Whatever appearance of unity the VCLT articles offer, debate continues over (i) their legal status, (ii) the interpretative method(s) and techniques they privilege, and (iii) the boundaries they set in defining what constitutes interpretation. First, it is not clear whether the VCLT provisions are 'rules' that mandate certain interpretative behavior *ex ante*, akin to Owen Fiss' disciplining rules.[8] Some assert they are only 'principles', guiding rather than dictating behaviour.[9] For others, the VCLT provisions are non-normative, methodological devices; Jan Klabbers compares them to recipes—'different ways to engage in many activities, without it being possible to specify which one would be the best'.[10]

Second, proponents of different interpretative methods claim that the VCLT accommodates, or privileges, their method. Textualists ascribe to treaty interpretation an *objective* purpose; a process for 'finding' an existing meaning in the choice and arrangement of words (in contrast to acts 'creating' law).[11] The textual method holds pride of place in VCLT Article 31's direction that a 'treaty shall be interpreted in good faith in accordance with the ordinary meaning to be given to the terms of the treaty in their context and in light of its object and purpose'.[12] But the VCLT also continues to give succour to those who adopt a *subjective* method, ascribing meaning based on what the original authors (in this case, negotiators) intended. Although Article 32 suggests an examination of preparatory work may only confirm textual efforts or supply meaning when those efforts fail, such caveats have done little to bar treaty interpretations on subjective terms.[13] Nor have they proven fatal to those who view interpretation as a *teleological* exercise, designed

---

[7] For more on the negotiating history, see Gardiner, *Treaty Interpretation*, 69–73.

[8] See eg Orakhelashvili, *The Interpretation of Acts and Rules in Public International Law*, 285–6; Gardiner, *Treaty Interpretation*, 36–8; see also Owen Fiss, 'Objectivity and Interpretation' (1982) 34 Stan L Rev 739, 744 et seq (discussing disciplining rules for interpreters).

[9] See eg Van Damme, *Treaty Interpretation by the WTO Appellate Body*, 35.

[10] Jan Klabbers, 'The Invisible College', *Opinio Juris On-Line Symposium: Richard Gardiner's Treaty Interpretation* (*Opinio Juris*, 3 March 2009) <http://opiniojuris.org/2009/03/03/the-invisible-college/> accessed 28 July 2014.

[11] Orakhelashvili, *The Interpretation of Acts and Rules in Public International Law*, 288; see also Andrea Bianchi, 'Textual Interpretation and (International) Law Reading; The Myth of (In)Determinacy and the Genealogy of Meaning' in Pieter HF Bekker, Rudolf Dolzer, and Michael Waibel (eds), *Making Transnational Law Work in the Global Economy—Essays in Honour of Detlev Vagts* (CUP 2010) 34, 36 (describing the linguistic paradigm of legal interpretation and its emphasis on determinacy).

[12] Article 31(1) VCLT; see also Bianchi, 'Textual Interpretation and (International) Law Reading', 34 (describing the theory of textual determinacy as 'still the prevailing paradigm').

[13] See Gardiner, *Treaty Interpretation*, 303, 324. Nor is it clear that the ILC meant to limit reliance on subsidiary work: Julian Mortenson, 'The Travaux of Travaux: Is the Vienna Convention Hostile to Drafting History?' (2014) 107(4) AJIL 780.

to support values instead of negotiators or their dictionaries.[14] The VCLT's references to 'object and purpose' and 'any relevant rules of international law' afford ample opportunities to interpret instrumentally in favour of some over-arching goal, whether defined in moral or political terms.[15] The ILC itself suggested that the VCLT articles would operate holistically, where '[a]ll the various elements as they were present in any given case, would be thrown into the crucible and their interaction would give the legally relevant interpretation'.[16] And even where interpreters agree on the appropriate method, further differences can arise over particular interpretative techniques.[17]

Third, alongside methodological and technical debates, treaty scholarship and practice often wrestles with boundaries. In some cases, the boundaries are literal—eg duelling interpretations of whether a treaty's territorial application extends beyond the party's territory.[18] Other boundaries are conceptual, such as the line between a treaty's interpretation and its application.[19] Disciplinary boundary issues exist as well, with various academics pushing to bring 'outside' perspectives—eg semantic linguistics, international relations—into international law's interpretative process.[20] Most boundary questions though are doctrinal, such

---

[14] Gardiner, *Treaty Interpretation*, 189. Although Myres McDougal suggested that the VCLT would require an 'insistent emphasis upon an impossible, conformity-imposing textuality', Gardiner has shown that such fears were misplaced: *Treaty Interpretation*, 303–50.

[15] See eg Article 31(1) and (3)(c) VCLT. Although still occasionally invoked, a fourth, *restrictive* method—favouring interpretations with the least imposition on state sovereignty—has less support in the VCLT. See Luigi Crema, 'Disappearance and New Sightings of Restrictive Interpretation(s)' (2010) 21 EJIL 681–700.

[16] [1966] YBILC, vol II, 219 [8].

[17] For example, should a word retain the meaning it had at a treaty's conclusion or shift over time, a move known as dynamic or evolutive interpretation? The issue is technical since the objective method's reference to 'ordinary' meaning offers no fixed position and, subjectively speaking, negotiators may not have considered the issue. See eg Orakhelashvili, *The Interpretation of Acts and Rules in Public International Law*, 291; Georg Nolte (ed), *Treaties and Subsequent Practice* (OUP 2013); Julian Arato, 'Subsequent Practice and Evolutive Interpretation: Techniques of Treaty Interpretation over Time and Their Diverse Consequences' (2010) 9 LPICT 443; Malgosia Fitzmaurice, 'Dynamic (Evolutive) Interpretation of Treaties (Part I)' (2008) 21 Hague Ybk Intl L 101; Malgosia Fitzmaurice, 'Dynamic (Evolutive) Interpretation of Treaties (Part II)' (2009) 22 Hague Ybk Intl L 3.

[18] See eg Syméon Karagiannis, 'The Territorial Application of Treaties' in Duncan B Hollis (ed), *The Oxford Guide to Treaties* (OUP 2012) 305–27.

[19] For some, application is a distinct process that post-dates the interpretative one: Orakhelashvili, *The Interpretation of Acts and Rules in Public International Law*, 285; Marko Milanovic, 'The ICJ and Evolutionary Treaty Interpretation' (*EJIL: Talk!*, 14 July 2009) <http://www.ejiltalk.org/the-icj-and-evolutionary-treaty-interpretation/> accessed 28 July 2014; Lawrence B Solum, 'The Interpretation/Construction Distinction' (2010) 27 Constitutional Commentary 95, 95–118. Others dispute the ability of interpreters to separate out meaning from the context of its application. See eg Separate Opinion of Judge Shahabuddeen, *Applicability of the Obligation to Arbitrate under Section 21 of the United Nations Headquarters Agreement of 26 June 1947* (Advisory Opinion) [1988] ICJ Rep 57, 59; Gardiner, *Treaty Interpretation*, 27–9.

[20] See eg Joost Pauwelyn and Manfred Elsig, 'The Politics of Treaty Interpretation: Variations and Explanations Across International Tribunals' in Jeffrey L Dunoff and Mark A Pollack (eds), *Interdisciplinary Perspectives on International Law and International Relations; The State of the Art* (CUP 2013) (integrating international law and international relations theories of interpretation); Bianchi, 'Textual Interpretation and (International) Law Reading' (applying linguistics to international legal interpretation); Venzke, *How Interpretation Makes International Law* (applying linguistics as well).

as debates over whether particular types of treaties—eg those on human rights or international institutions—lie beyond the VCLT articles' ambit.[21] Meanwhile, debates on how to navigate treaty conflicts have gained attention as part of the larger inquiry into the fragmentation of international law.[22]

The fragmentation phenomenon has, however, provided new opportunities to consider issues beyond treaty interpretation. New methodological and technical questions have arisen from questions of how to navigate treaty conflicts, not just with each other, but with other international legal (and non-legal) norms.[23] For example, as international tribunals proliferate—and compete—the role of precedent in interpretation has begun to garner attention.[24] Larger conceptual puzzles over the supposed unity of the international legal order also persist. Cases like *Nuclear Weapons*—which refused to say international law absolutely prohibits nuclear weapons—suggest the possibility of *non liquet* (gaps) in international law's coverage.[25] Whether such gaps exist has important interpretative implications; interpreters who believe international law must provide answers to each inquiry necessarily pursue a different process from those who conclude that meaning may be inconclusive in some—or many—cases.

A survey of existing interpretative thinking in international law would be incomplete without mentioning those who challenge the very idea of fixed meanings. Martti Koskenniemi famously described international legal discourse in terms of formal determinacy *and* substantive indeterminacy. Formal determinacy refers to international lawyers' shared language—a fixed and highly determined set of discursive techniques. In contrast, international law's substantive indeterminacy suggests that all arguments deconstruct into one of two opposing—and mutually exclusive—positions, apology or utopia.[26] Koskenniemi opposed efforts

---

[21] See eg Basak Çali, 'Specialized Rules of Treaty Interpretation: Human Rights' in Duncan B Hollis (ed), *The Oxford Guide to Treaties* (OUP 2012) 526–33; Catherine Brölmann, 'Specialized Rules of Treaty Interpretation: International Organizations' in Duncan B Hollis (ed), *The Oxford Guide to Treaties* (OUP 2012) 507–24.

[22] See eg International Law Commission, *Fragmentation of International Law: Difficulties Arising from the Diversification and Expansion of International Law—Report of the Study Group of the International Law Commission* (13 April 2006) UN Doc A/CN.4/L.682, as corrected (11 August 2006) UN Doc A/CN.4/L.682/Corr.1 (finalized by Martti Koskenniemi) 10–11 ('ILC Study Group') (defining international law's fragmentation as 'the emergence of specialized and (relatively) autonomous rules or rule-complexes, legal institutions and spheres of legal practice').

[23] Fragmentation may even extend to the sources of international law themselves. See eg Harlan Grant Cohen, 'Finding International Law, Part II: Our Fragmenting Legal Community' (2012) 44 NYU J Int'l L & Pol 1049, 1052–3.

[24] Cohen, 'Finding International Law', 1078–80; Anthea Roberts, 'Power and Persuasion in Investment Treaty Interpretation: The Dual Role of States' (2010) 104 AJIL 179, 188–91.

[25] *Legality of the Threat or Use of Nuclear Weapons* (Advisory Opinion) [1996] ICJ Rep 226, [105(2)(E)]; see also Daniel Bodansky, '*Non liquet* and the incompleteness of international law' in Laurence Boisson de Chazournes and Philippe Sands (eds), *International Law, the International Court of Justice and Nuclear Weapons* (CUP 1999) 153–70.

[26] See eg Martti Koskenniemi, *From Apology to Utopia: The Structure of International Legal Argument* (CUP 2005). Apology arguments define international law as a product of concrete state behaviour; utopian arguments do so on moral grounds anterior or superior to such behaviour. Given the mutually exclusive nature of these arguments, Koskenniemi claimed any attempt at reconciling them becomes self-contradicting or simply adopts a new version of apology or utopian arguments. Any

to divine a 'more determinate' system, embracing international legal discourse as a structure for 'open political conflict and constant institutional revision'.[27] Agreed outcomes within this structure ultimately depend upon (and reveal) *extra-legal* agreement (on political or moral grounds).[28]

In sum, international law's current interpretative discipline implicates a rich and maturing set of issues. But the focus generally remains fixed on a single role for interpretation—its *expository* function.[29] The interpretative process is envisioned as an effort to ascribe a treaty text (or some other international legal norm) with meaning. Debates over the nature of the VCLT articles and their boundaries are, at bottom, debates about whether and how rules should discipline interpreters in this search for meaning. And the various methods—eg text, intent, purpose, or a crucible approach—offer different (and competing) vehicles for arriving at meaning, while critical scholarship questions interpretation's capacity to do so in substantive terms.

II. The Existential Function of Interpretation in International Law

As debates over R2P's legal status suggest, interpretation need not function exclusively in expository terms. International legal interpretations may have one or more additional functions, be they *inventive, relational*, or—as this chapter suggests—*existential*.[30] In ascertaining meaning, interpretation operates to confirm—or even establish—the existence of the subject interpreted within (or outside) the corpus of international law. This existential function operates through a distinct interpretative process—existential interpretation—that is visible at all levels of international legal discourse, including which particular authorities, evidence, rules, or sources exist for purposes of international law.

A. Beyond exposition—other functions of the interpretative process

International lawyers recognize that interpretation is a creative process. The ILC famously conceded that treaty interpretation 'is to some extent an art, rather than

---

proposed legal solution can thus be contested as too utopian (disconnected from the concrete reality of law based on state consent) or too apologetic (excusing state behaviour regardless of objective norms). And if apology arguments can always contest utopian arguments—or vice versa—Koskenniemi concluded international law must oscillate between poles of state consent and universal normativity, leaving any middle ground as a 'terrain of irreducible adversity'. Koskenniemi, *From Apology to Utopia*, 597; see also 59–69.

[27] Koskenniemi, *From Apology to Utopia*, 556, 597. As Bianchi summarized it, '[t]he fundamental idea behind indeterminacy theories is that one can never stop interpreting': 'Textual Interpretation and (International) Law Reading', 48.

[28] Koskenniemi, *From Apology to Utopia*, 23, 515, 548–61.

[29] See eg Orakhelashvili, *The Interpretation of Acts and Rules in Public International Law*, 2: 'The classical concept of interpretation relates to the clarification of meaning of legal rules and instruments'.

[30] This is not an exhaustive list. Interpretation may have other functions as well, such as empowering certain actors in international law.

an exact science'.[31] Maurice Mendelson similarly emphasized that, since practice creates custom, it is 'misleading...to suggest the formation and application of customary law are two distinct stages'.[32] Nonetheless, interpreters continue to debate if they can simply 'apply' pre-existing rules or if all interpretation requires some invention (or, in legal terms, legislation).[33] Hence contested claims that judges must never 'make' law, but should only 'apply' it.[34]

This *inventive* potential of interpretation should not, however, be confused with its *existential* function. Certainly, if an interpreter 'invents' a new rule via an act of interpretation, that interpretation also serves to establish (or at least claim to establish) the rule's existence. But existential interpretations are also in play when an interpreter adopts a more destructive stance; denying, for example, that the subject of interpretation exists for the purposes of international law. And even if an interpreter focuses on explaining the meaning of some purportedly pre-existing norm—eg a treaty—the resulting interpretation still does existential work by confirming the treaty's existence in explaining what it means. Interpretation's existential function thus operates whether or not one views invention as an inherent part of the interpretative enterprise.

Nor should the existential function be confused with interpretation's *relational* potential, situating the interpreted subject vis-à-vis other subjects of interpretation. This may be done hierarchically, as when interpreters ascribe a norm the status of *jus cogens*, making it non-derogable by treaty or otherwise.[35] But the relational function also situates a norm among other norms with the same hierarchical status. Article 31(c) of the VCLT makes this function explicit, requiring treaty interpretation to take account of 'any relevant rules of international law applicable in relations between the parties'. Of course, interpreters may take account of such rules in different ways. They may pursue what Çali calls 'an accumulation of interpretation' where other interpretative precedents generate a coherent or overlapping meaning for the interpreted subject.[36] Or, interpreters may identify conflicts between the subject of interpretation and other rules. In both cases, though, the question is not whether the subject of interpretation exists in international law, but what it exists *as* (eg *jus cogens*, *lex specialis*).

Distinguishing interpretation's *existential* function from other *expository*, *inventive*, and *relational* features serves two purposes. First, it reveals the existential

---

[31] 'Report of the Int'l Law Comm on the Work of Its 16th Session' UN GAOR, 19th Session, Supp at 200, UN Doc A/CN.4/173 (11 July 1964) (R Ago).

[32] Maurice H Mendelson, 'The Formation of Customary International Law' (1998) 272 Recueil des Cours 159, 174–5.

[33] See eg Joseph Raz, *Between Authority and Interpretation* (OUP 2009) 224 (noting interpretation straddles a divide between identification of existing laws and creation of new ones); HLA Hart, *The Concept of Law* (2nd edn, Clarendon Press 1994) 204 (noting 'the open texture of law leaves a vast field for creative activity, which some call legislative').

[34] See eg Roberts, 'Power and Persuasion in Investment Treaty Interpretation', 188; Richard A Posner, 'The Incoherence of Antonin Scalia' *The New Republic* (24 August 2012) ('Judges like to say that all they do when they interpret...is apply, to the facts of the particular case, law that has been given to them. They do not make law').

[35] Article 53 VCLT.

[36] Çali, 'Specialized Rules of Treaty Interpretation: Human Rights', 542.

function as an essential aspect of all international legal interpretation. Interpreters cannot ascertain what the subject of their interpretation means, who bears responsibility for creating it, or what relationship it has to other subjects of interpretation, unless they first acknowledge the subject's existence.

Second, and more importantly, the existential function addresses the difficulty of separating the ideas of ascertaining 'law' from ascertaining 'meaning'. In many quarters, the two processes are treated as categorically distinct, or mutually exclusive. In his interpretative theory of law, Ronald Dworkin distinguished (i) a 'pre-interpretative stage', where an interpretative community identifies a shared set of assumptions or convictions about 'what counts as part of the practice in order to define the raw data' from (ii) a separate 'interpretative stage'.[37] But as Dworkin himself acknowledged, interpretation is necessary even in the pre-interpretative stage.[38] Indeed, there is a specific 'existential' interpretative process that accompanies efforts to ascertain what subjects (eg data, rules, standards) exist for purposes of further interpretation. At the same time, traditional, expository interpretative processes incorporate existential aspects by confirming (or denying) the subject's legal status or validity. In other words, all existential inquiries involve interpretations just as all interpretative inquiries have existential effects. The concept of existential interpretation accommodates such synergies.

B. Existential interpretations

How are existential interpretations identified? In many cases, they are hidden, lying in background assumptions or convictions, revealed only by implication. For example, few—if any—interpreters include in interpretations of Article 2(4) of the UN Charter an analysis of the Charter's status as a treaty, let alone explain why treaties are sources of international law. But, even without explicitly acknowledging its legal existence, the very process of ascertaining what Article 2(4) means claims for the Charter a status as a valid or 'existing' subject for international legal interpretation.

In other cases, existential interpretations come out of hiding into the foreground. This may occur, as Dworkin assumed, when the question of the subject's existence constitutes the entire interpretative inquiry. Alternatively, existential interpretations may form part of a larger interpretative project. For example, in recent R2P debates, interpreters might seek to establish or confirm R2P's international legal status in the course of delineating what that doctrine means.

Whether they are in the background or foreground, existential interpretations are still interpretative acts. As such, they may employ the various methods and techniques that occupy the expository context. And, just like the expository context, interpreters may disagree about which interpretative methods or processes are

---

[37] Ronald Dworkin, *Law's Empire* (Harvard University Press 1986) 65–7. Dworkin also identified a third 'postinterpretative or reforming stage' where interpreters adjust their sense of what 'practice "really" requires' to better serve justifications from the interpretative stage: 66.
[38] Dworkin, *Law's Empire*, 66.

permitted (or required) when it comes to existential questions (ie objective, subjective, teleological, holistic). To make things even more complicated, where interpreters pursue both existential and expository functions in the same process, it is possible to envision interpreters selecting the same *or* different methods. For example, an interpreter might employ one interpretative method (eg subjective) in discerning whether states consented to a particular treaty to determine its existence, but adopt a different method (eg objective, teleological) to ascertain the parties' obligations under that treaty.[39]

If neither form nor method distinguishes existential interpretations, what separates them from other interpretative processes? Two elements appear key. The first—their function—has already been elaborated in contrast to other potential interpretative purposes. The second element is structural. Existential interpretations are inherently a binary—as opposed to a relative—inquiry. They assume a structure in which there are only two possible answers: 'yes' (the subject exists or is otherwise valid for further interpretative processes) or 'no' (the subject is excluded from any further legal interpretation). In the evidentiary context of custom, for example, the existential inquiry asks if a particular act (ie an extradition, a minister's speech, an industry's code of conduct) constitutes 'state practice' or not. The answer 'yes' legitimizes the evidence for purposes of further exposition (what does a particular example of state practice mean?) or relational analysis (what's the probative value of the evidence; how strong or weak is the evidence given other examples?). A 'no' answer means the evidence does not exist—it cannot be given any weight at all—with respect to international law. In short, if the question is whether something does (or does not) exist for purposes of international law, that's existential interpretation.

C. Existential interpretations in practice

Existential interpretations are everywhere. Although often hidden in the background, these interpretations have become visible at every stage of international legal discourse. Four areas of particular importance—legal authority, evidence, rules, and sources—illustrate this phenomenon.[40]

1. *The existence of authority to interpret*

Interpreters often assume authority to interpret. But, on occasion, they may be required or otherwise feel a need to explain why their interpretative authority exists. The most visible examples arise in the judicial context. Jurisdictional

---

[39] Jean d'Aspremont makes a similar point in distinguishing law ascertainment from interpretation: *Formalism and the Sources of International Law* (OUP 2011) 157. See also Chapter 5 (Jean d'Aspremont).

[40] Other areas where existential questions may arise include questions on whether (a) an international actor legally 'exists'; (b) whether an international organization has authority to bind member states; or (c) whether a remedy exists for specific violations of international law. See eg *Prosecutor v Dusko Tadic aka 'Dule'* (Decision on the Defence Motion on Jurisdiction) ICTY-94-1 (10 August 1995), [32]–[48] (tribunal interprets the lawfulness of its own existence).

questions are almost always existential—the Court either has jurisdiction to hear the claim before it, or it doesn't.[41] In some cases, a court's interpretative process will answer the inquiry in the affirmative; notable ICJ examples include the *Nicaragua* and *Qatar v Bahrain* cases.[42] In other cases, the Court's inquiry denies the existence of jurisdiction à la *Norwegian Loans*.[43] The case law of other international courts and tribunals provides similar examples.[44]

Of course, jurisdictional issues are not the only vehicle for existential questions on interpretative authority. They get the most attention because courts can (usually) proffer an authoritative or 'binding' resolution as to their authority. Other actors may, however, claim similar authority; some treaties (eg NAFTA) contemplate the parties collectively issuing subsequent binding interpretations of the treaty.[45] Several international organizations (IOs) claim similar authority under their constituent treaties.[46] Sometimes, interpretative authority may be claimed without an express grant. In a well-known example, the UN Human Rights Committee (HRC) issued General Comment 24, claiming for itself binding authority to interpret the admissibility of reservations to the International Covenant on Civil and Political Rights (ICCPR).[47]

---

[41] Sometimes, jurisdictional issues persist even after jurisdiction is established. See eg WTO, *Mexico: Tax Measures on Soft Drinks—Report of the Appellate Body* (6 March 2006) WT/DS308/AB/R, [44]–[57] (examining discretion not to exercise existing jurisdiction).

[42] *Case concerning Military and Paramilitary Activities in and against Nicaragua (Nicaragua v USA)* (Jurisdiction and Admissibility) [1984] ICJ Rep 392, [65]; *Maritime Delimitation and Territorial Questions (Qatar v Bahrain)* (Jurisdiction and Admissibility) [1994] ICJ Rep 112, [27].

[43] *Case of Certain Norwegian Loans (France v Norway)* [1957] ICJ Rep 9, 27; see also *Case Concerning Legality of Use of Force (Serbia and Montenegro v UK)* [2004] ICJ Rep 1307. Of course, courts may interpret jurisdiction to exist (or not) in various ways. In many cases, a court's existential interpretation involves exposition—deciding what the basis of jurisdiction (eg a dispute settlement clause) *means* given the facts before it. The ICJ majority in *Norwegian Loans* adopted such reasoning, finding no jurisdiction existed because of how it interpreted France's declaration accepting the Court's compulsory jurisdiction: *Norwegian Loans*, 23–4. In other cases, a court may find jurisdiction exists (or not) based on a separate, underlying existential inquiry with respect to the evidence or rules involved. In *Nicaragua*, for example, the ICJ held US efforts to revoke jurisdiction, via a letter, were unavailing, because it found the letter was not valid given the earlier US acceptance of compulsory jurisdiction: *Nicaragua*, [59]–[61].

[44] See eg *The M/V 'Louisa' Case (Saint Vincent and the Grenadines v Kingdom of Spain)* (No 18) (28 May 2013) (ITLOS); *Prosecutor v Thomas Lubanga Dyilo* ICC-01/04-01/06 (14 March 2012) (ICC); *Brazil: Measures Affecting Desiccated Coconut—Report of the Appellate Body* (21 February 1997) WT/DS22/AB/R, [7] (WTO); *Tadic*, [32]–[48] (ICTY).

[45] North American Free Trade Agreement, 17 December 1992 [1993] 32 ILM 289, Article 1131(2) ('An interpretation by the Commission of a provision of this Agreement shall be binding on a Tribunal established under this Section'); Gabrielle Kaufmann-Kohler, 'Interpretive Powers of the Free Trade Commission and the Rule of Law' in Emmanuel Gaillard and Frédéric Bachand (eds), *Fifteen Years of NAFTA Chapter 11 Arbitration* (Juris 2011) 175, 176–8 (identifying treaties granting interpretative authority).

[46] See eg General Agreement on Tariffs and Trade 1994, Marrakesh Agreement Establishing the World Trade Organization (adopted 15 April 1994, entered into force 1 January 1995) Annex 1A, 1867 UNTS 187, Article IX(2) (WTO 'Ministerial Conference and the General Council shall have the exclusive authority to adopt interpretations of this Agreement and of the Multilateral Trade Agreements').

[47] Human Rights Committee, 'General Comment No 24: General comment on issues relating to reservations made upon ratification or accession to the Covenant or the Optional Protocols thereto, or in relation to declarations under article 41 of the Covenant' (4 November 1994) CCPR/C/21/Rev.1/Add.6.

The existence of interpretative authority does not always revolve around questions of bindingness. Beyond 'authoritative' interpretations, interpretative authority may be interrogated at a more basic level in terms of 'voice'—ie asking whether an actor has (or lacks) the ability to offer a view on what international law (or some portion of it) means. States are the most obvious candidates for such authority. Notwithstanding the now-robust literature on constitutionalization, the international legal order continues to lack universal legislative and adjudicatory bodies to dictate what constitutes the law and who has interpretative authority over it. As Leo Gross noted 60 years ago, we are left in a situation where 'each state has a right to interpret the law, the right of autointerpretation, as it might be called'.[48] Thus, states regularly presume that they have authority to opine on what international law means by virtue of their status as states. On occasion, states explicitly justify their interpretative authority. In the context of the Antarctic Treaty, several states insisted they had (or should have) authority to participate in regulating that continent even without territorial claims there. These arguments matured into treaty provisions giving these states voting rights as 'Consultative Parties'.[49] In a few cases, states have even denied their interpretative authority. Thus, in the *Comfort Women* case, the United States declaimed authority for its courts to interpret the scope of claims waiver agreements in Japan's peace treaties with China (Taiwan), South Korea, and the Philippines.[50]

Like states, non-state actors—eg IOs, treaty bodies, non-governmental organizations (NGOs), publicists—may also opine on the existence of their interpretative authority. Recent examples of regime interaction involve IOs asserting rights to participate in interpretations of international law outside the treaty regime in which they normally operate.[51] One might also think of NGO petitions for observer status (or more) in multilateral treaty regimes in interpretative terms. NGOs invoke various rationales (eg technical expertise, democratic legitimacy) for why they should have a voice in particular regimes.[52]

Nor are existential interpretations of authority solely self-judging. States and non-state actors may just as easily endorse (or reject) claims of interpretative authority by other actors. With respect to HRC General Comment 24, for example,

[48] Leo Gross, 'States as Organs of International Law and the Problem of Autointerpretation' (1953), reprinted in Alfred P Rubin (ed), *Essays on International Law and Organization* (Transnat'l Pub 1984) 386–8.

[49] See eg Scott Barrett, *Environment & Statecraft: The Strategy of Environmental Treaty-Making* (OUP 2003) 156–7; see also Bruno Simma and Christian Tams, 'Reacting against Treaty Breaches' in Duncan B Hollis (ed), *The Oxford Guide to Treaties* (OUP 2012) 576, 589–90 (describing instances where states claim to be 'specially effected' by a treaty breach so as to have authority to opine on the existence of that breach).

[50] See *Hwang Geum Joo v Japan* 413 F 3d 45, 51–52 (DC Cir 2006).

[51] See Jeffrey L Dunoff, 'A New Approach to Regime Interaction' in Margaret E Young (ed), *Regime Interaction in International Law: Facing Fragmentation* (CUP 2012) 136, 156–73. Of course, regime interaction includes assertions of a right to interpret non-legal norms as well, particularly where regime complexes now encompass international law, soft law, and purely political commitments.

[52] See Kal Raustiala, 'NGOs in International Treaty-Making' in Duncan B Hollis (ed), *The Oxford Guide to Treaties* (OUP 2012) 150; Steve Charnovitz, 'Nongovernmental Organizations and International Law' (2006) 100 AJIL 348.

France, the United Kingdom, and the United States rejected the HRC's interpretation of its authority when it came to the admissibility of ICCPR reservations.[53]

None of this should suggest that all questions of international legal authority are existential. Even where interpreters agree an actor has authority to interpret, questions may arise as to what such authority means more precisely. A notable example occurred when the NAFTA parties—through their Free Trade Commission—responded to perceived excesses in interpretative authority in several NAFTA tribunal opinions by issuing a joint interpretative statement.[54] The question for later NAFTA tribunals was whether the 'binding' interpretative authority accorded the parties by NAFTA itself (specifically, Article 1131) meant the parties could override a tribunal's interpretative authority. NAFTA tribunals have since provided conflicting responses to that question.[55] Of course, the line between existential and expository interpretations of authority may not always be clear-cut; many interpretative projects about the 'scope' of authority can be recast as existential ones about whether authority exists (or not) for purposes of the proposed interpretation.

2. The existence of evidence

Evidentiary questions are prevalent in international law. Often, they involve factual inquiries of the 'what happened' variety. When it comes to interpreting international law itself, the evidentiary question may be one of probative value—how should interpreters weigh the evidence they have?[56] Not surprisingly, different interpreters assign different weight to particular pieces of evidence. For example, the US Department of State recently contested the conclusions of a study identifying customary international humanitarian law (IHL) sponsored by the International Committee of the Red Cross (ICRC).[57] The US complaints were

---

[53] 'Observation by the United States of America on General Comment No 24(52)' (28 March 1995) CCPR A/50/40/Annex VI, 126–134 ('the Committee lacks the authority to render binding interpretations or judgments'); see also 'Observation by France on GC No 24 on Reservations to the ICCPR' (8 September 1995) CCPR A/51/40 104–6; 'Observations by the United Kingdom on GC No 24' (21 July 1995) CCPR A/50/40/Annex VI, 126–34.

[54] NAFTA Free Trade Commission, Notes of Interpretation of Certain Chapter 11 Provisions (31 July 2001) <http://www.sice.oas.org/tpd/nafta/Commission/CH11understanding_e.asp> accessed 28 July 2014.

[55] Compare *ADF Group Inc v USA* (NAFTA Ch 11 Arbitration Tribunal, 9 January 2003) [2003] 18 ICSID Rev 195, [177] ('we have the Parties themselves—all the Parties—speaking to the Tribunal') with *Pope & Talbot Inc v Canada, Damages* (NAFTA Ch 11 Arbitration Tribunal, 31 May 2002) [2002] 41 ILM 1347, [47] (finding FTC interpretation was an illegitimate attempt to amend the treaty retroactively to interfere with an ongoing case where the panel had already issued an interpretation contrary to that adopted by the NAFTA Parties).

[56] For example, ICJ Statute Article 38 establishes judicial opinions are valid evidence in international legal disputes, but questions of how much precedential weight to accord them remain given their 'subsidiary' status. See eg Harlan Grant Cohen, 'Finding International Law: Rethinking the Doctrine of Sources' (2007) 93 Iowa L Rev 67, 88.

[57] See Jean-Marie Henckaerts and Louise Doswald-Beck, *Customary International Humanitarian Law* (ICRC 2005); John B Bellinger and William J Haynes, 'A US government response to the International Committee of the Red Cross study *Customary International Humanitarian Law*'

almost entirely evidentiary—the ICRC had 'insufficiently dense' evidence of state practice; it gave 'too much emphasis' or 'undue weight' to certain evidence; and offered 'inadequate' attention to others.[58] As formulated, the complaints all targeted matters of exposition—the meaning ascribed to various pieces of evidence of customary IHL.

Existential interpretations of evidence, in contrast, are not about probative value or balancing. Instead, they examine whether the subject of interpretation 'counts' as evidence at all. If it does, then it can be employed in further interpretative processes (the aforementioned weighing and other expository efforts). But if it does not, interpreters leave the material outside the international legal interpretative process entirely.

The most notable examples of evidentiary existential interpretation come from customary international law. Broadly speaking, customary international law requires state practice done out of a sense of legal obligation (*opinio juris*).[59] What counts as evidence of state practice and *opinio juris*? Some interpretations are relatively uncontested—few interpreters count individual or corporate practice as 'state' practice absent some attribution of that practice to a state.[60] Similarly, although lump sum settlements may constitute evidence of state practice, the US–Iran Claims Tribunal noted that they cannot constitute evidence of *opinio juris* where payment occurs on an *ex gratia* basis.[61]

Other existential evidentiary issues have generated more discussion, particularly how to deal with what states 'say' about custom. For some, state statements are exclusively evidence of *opinio juris*; they are not evidence of state practice, which involves conduct (or lack thereof) by states.[62] Others accept what states say as evidence of both state practice and *opinio juris*.[63] A third group accepts it as evidence

---

(2007) 89 IRRC 443; Jean-Marie Henckaerts and Louise Doswald-Beck, 'Customary International Humanitarian Law: A Response to US Comments' (2007) 89 IRRC 473, 477–8.

[58] See eg Bellinger and Haynes, 'A US Government Response', 444–5 ('The Study places too much emphasis on written materials, such as military manuals and other guidelines published by States, as opposed to actual operational practice by States during armed conflict. Although manuals may provide important indications of State behavior and *opinio juris*, they cannot be a replacement for a meaningful assessment of operational State practice in connection with actual military operations').

[59] The relationship between these two elements remains in dispute particularly between adherents to the 'traditional' approach (who favour inductive techniques looking for evidence of state practice of sufficient duration, generality, and uniformity) and the 'modern' approach (who emphasize the search for *opinio juris* evidenced in written statements or declarations). See eg Anthea Roberts, 'Traditional and Modern Approaches to Customary International Law: A Reconciliation' (2001) 95 AJIL 757, 757; Jörg Kammerhofer, 'Uncertainty in the Formal Sources of International Law: Customary International Law and Some of its Problems' (2004) 15 EJIL 523, 525.

[60] Christiana Ochoa, 'The Individual and Customary International Law Formation' (2007) 48(1) Va J Int'l L 119 (advocating for a change in this view).

[61] *Interlocutory Award in Case Concerning SEDCO, Inc v National Iranian Oil Company and the Islamic Republic of Iran* (1986) 10 Iran-USCTR 180, 185.

[62] See eg Anthony D'Amato, *The Concept of Custom in International Law* (Cornell University Press 1971) 89–90, 160; Roberts, 'Traditional and Modern Approaches to Customary International Law', 757–8; J Patrick Kelly, 'The Twilight of Customary International Law' (2000) 40 Va J Int'l L 449, 485–7; Anthony D'Amato, 'Trashing Customary International Law' (1987) 81 AJIL 101, 102.

[63] See eg Arthur A Weisburd, 'Customary International Law: The Problem of Treaties' (1988) 21 Vand J Transnat'l L 1; Michael Akehurst, 'Custom as a Source of International Law' (1974–75)

of one or the other, but not both.[64] Over time, more inclusive interpretations have become predominant, exemplified by the acceptance of Oscar Schachter's proposition that law-declaring resolutions of the UN General Assembly (UNGA) constitute evidence for purposes of identifying custom to be weighed alongside other evidence of state practice and *opinio juris*.[65] Thus, in the TOPCO arbitration, René-Jean Dupuy accepted UNGA Resolutions as evidence of customary international law, comparing voting patterns for various resolutions to identify the international law on compensation due for an expropriation.[66] Controversies over whether national court opinions constitute evidence of custom appear to be following a similar course, with the ICJ accepting them as evidence in *Jurisdictional Immunities of the State*.[67]

In other instances, interpreters deny evidentiary status to certain things states do.[68] For example, although reports of states practising torture remain (unfortunately) prevalent, human rights interpreters regularly refuse to regard this as evidence of state practice that might compromise customary international law's existing prohibition on torture.[69] Incidents of torture are interpreted as violations of international law, rather than evidence of its contents.

Evidentiary existential interpretations similarly arise in the treaty context. In *Qatar v Bahrain*, for example, the ICJ's jurisdiction turned on whether Bahrain and Qatar had concluded an international agreement.[70] As part of that inquiry, Bahrain submitted a statement by its Foreign Minister indicating that he had not intended to create an international agreement in signing certain Minutes with his Qatari

---

BYBIL 1, 2, 36; Andrew Guzman, 'Saving Customary International Law' (2005) 27 Mich J Int'l L 115, 149–57. Frederic Kirgis advocates for analysing the requirements of practice and *opinio juris* on a sliding scale: 'Custom on a Sliding Scale' (1987) 81 AJIL 146.

[64] See eg Mendelson, 'The Formation of Customary International Law', 206–7.

[65] Oscar Schachter, *International Law in Theory and Practice* (Martinus Nijhoff 1991) 88–9 (UNGA Resolutions on law 'are official expressions of the governments concerned and consequently are relevant and entitled to be given weight in determinations of the law in question. By characterizing them as "evidentiary" we invite an assessment of the pertinent data'); Cohen, 'Finding International Law', 20.

[66] *Award on the Merits in Dispute Between Texaco Overseas Petroleum Company (TOPCO)/ California Asiatic Oil Company (CAOC) and the Government of the Libyan Arab Republic* [1978] 17 ILM 1, [85]–[87]. In the SEDCO Arbitration, the US–Iran Claims Tribunal acknowledged that UNGA 'Resolutions are not directly binding upon States and generally are not evidence of customary law. Nevertheless, it is generally accepted that such resolutions in certain specified circumstances may be regarded as evidence of customary international law ': *SEDCO*, 186.

[67] *Jurisdictional Immunities of the State (Germany v Italy: Greece Intervening)* Judgment [2012] ICJ Rep 99, [55], [77], [83]–[85]; see also Ingrid Wuerth, 'National Court Decisions and *Opinio Juris*' <http://law.duke.edu/cicl/pdf/opiniojuris/panel_3-wuerth-national_court_decisions_and_ opinio_juris.pdf> accessed 28 July 2014.

[68] See eg *North Sea Continental Shelf Cases (FRG v Den)* [1969] ICJ Rep 3, 43 (declining to consider certain cases as evidence of state practice, including delimitations among disputing parties).

[69] See Cohen, 'Finding International Law', 19; Roberts, 'Traditional and Modern Approaches to Customary International Law', 764; Bruno Simma and Philip Alston, 'The Sources of Human Rights Law: Custom, *Jus Cogens*, and General Principles' (1988–89) Aust YBIL 82, 86, 91–2; see also Daniel Bodansky, 'Customary (and not so Customary) International Environmental Law' (1995–96) 3 Ind J Global Legal Stud 105, 110–12 (discussing disconnect between international law's prohibition on transboundary harm and prevalent contrary state practice).

[70] *Qatar v Bahrain*, [27].

counterpart. The Court refused to accept this statement as evidence, finding an agreement had arisen by the 'terms of the instrument itself and the circumstances of its conclusion, not from what the parties say afterwards was their intention'.[71]

Where a treaty exists, interpreters may interrogate existentially the evidence they use to give it meaning. Interpretation may be required to determine what counts as 'supplementary means of interpretation' under Article 32 of the VCLT.[72] Or, the existence of a 'supplementary agreement' may be called into question.[73] In *EC–Bananas III*, for example, the parties disagreed on whether a waiver adopted at a Ministerial conference constituted a supplementary interpretative agreement; the Appellate Body concluded that it did not since it modified (rather than interpreted or applied) the treaty Schedule to which it related.[74]

Like questions of authority, therefore, evidentiary existential interpretations start off as all or nothing propositions. They focus on whether the subject of interpretation is evidence for purposes of further interpretation (ie deciding what the evidence means or how much weight to give it). In his concurring opinion in *Norwegian Loans*, for example, Judge Lauterpacht questioned whether a critical piece of evidence—France's declaration of acceptance of the Court's compulsory jurisdiction—existed. Lauterpacht concluded that it did not. He found the exclusion in France's declaration of 'differences relating to matters which are essentially within the national jurisdiction as understood by the Government of the French Republic' inconsistent with the Court's plenary jurisdictional authority under Article 36(6) of its Statute. Thus, Lauterpacht denied the French declaration's existence—declaring it 'invalid *ab initio*'—and, absent such a declaration, there was no basis for the Court's compulsory jurisdiction.[75] In contrast, a majority of the Court accepted France's declaration as evidence, focusing instead on what the declaration meant, and reasoning that if it meant France could exclude 'national jurisdiction' matters from the Court's compulsory jurisdiction, so could Norway.[76] Thus, Lauterpacht and the majority reached the same result—no

---

[71] *Qatar v Bahrain*, [27]; see also *Maritime Delimitation and Territorial Questions (Qatar v Bahrain)* (Judgment) [1995] ICJ Rep 6.

[72] Article 32 VCLT ('Recourse may be had to supplementary means of interpretation, including the preparatory work of the treaty and the circumstances of its conclusion'); WTO, *Chile: Price Band System and Safeguard Measures Relating to Certain Agricultural Products—Report of the Appellate Body* (23 September 2002) WT/DS207/AB/R, [230] (Appellate Body disputes Panel's determination that documents pre-dating the treaty's conclusion fell within the 'circumstances of its conclusion'). But see Gardiner, *Treaty Interpretation*, 316 (noting the willingness of judges and arbitrators in practice to consider whatever the parties proffer as preparatory work 'even if it does not clearly form part of the preparatory work').

[73] Article 31(3) VCLT ('There shall be taken into account, together with the context: (a) any subsequent agreement between the parties regarding the interpretation of the treaty or the application of its provisions').

[74] WTO, *European Communities: Regime for the Importation, Sale and Distribution of Bananas—Second Recourse to Article 21.5 of the OSV by Ecuador and First Recourse by USA—Report of the Appellate Body* ('EC–Bananas III') (26 November 2008) WT/DS27/AB/RW2/ECU and WT/DS27/AB/RW/USA, [388]–[392]. The ILC has devoted significant attention to defining the existence and meaning of subsequent agreements (and practice) in recent years. See Nolte, *Treaties and Subsequent Practice*, Part 5 (reproducing ILC Study Group reports).

[75] *Norwegian Loans*, 61, 66 (Lauterpacht J, concurring).   [76] *Norwegian Loans*, 27.

jurisdiction—but one did so by denying there was evidence of a commitment to jurisdiction while the other accepted the existence of such evidence, but read it to mean no jurisdiction existed in the case at hand.

3. *The existence of international law*

How do interpreters decide whether international law exists? From the foregoing sections it seems at least three steps are involved. First, interpreters must decide they have authority to interpret international law whether generally or specifically with respect to the particular subject. Second, interpreters must decide what evidence exists with respect to that subject. Third, interpreters 'interpret' that evidence to decide whether or not the claimed rule (or principle) of international law exists. As with interpretations of authority and evidence, interpreters may adopt different (and divergent) interpretative methods and techniques to discern the existence of international law.[77] Whatever reasoning they adopt, the process involves an existential inquiry, asking if the subject of interpretation falls within (or outside) the corpus of international law.

Judge Baxter once famously described the 'infinite variety' of international law.[78] So, it should come as no surprise that existential interpretations of international law come in various shapes and sizes. Broadly speaking, interpreters may establish the law's existence by induction (eg the *Paquette Habana*[79]) or deduction (eg the implied powers doctrine[80]). They may also deny the existence of the claimed law—in the *North Sea Continental Shelf* cases, for example, the ICJ denied that a principle of equidistance governed maritime boundary delimitations.[81]

With respect to custom, interpreters may discern the existence of customary international law at varying levels of precision, including rules, standards, and principles.[82]

---

[77] How they do so may vary. Sometimes interpreters adopt the step-by-step, linear logic suggested here, but it is certainly not required. One or more steps may be presumed. Other times, interpreters may adopt a holistic approach where it is difficult to identify the steps, methods, or techniques employed.

[78] Richard R Baxter, 'International Law in "Her Infinite Variety"' (1980) 29 ICLQ 549.

[79] *The Paquette Habana* 175 US 677, 686–714 (1900) (US Supreme Court reviews extensive state practice to identify a customary rule that exempts fresh fish fishing vessels from capture during wartime).

[80] *Reparations for Injuries Suffered in the Service of the United Nations* (Advisory Opinion) [1949] ICJ Rep 174, 182 (ICJ reasons that international law allows the implication of certain powers for IOs that are necessary for their functions).

[81] *North Sea Continental Shelf Cases*, 44–5 (interpreting the existing state practice to lack the requisite *opinio juris*). In some cases, the denial may be emphatic. See Separate Opinion of Judge Bedjaoui, *Case concerning the Gabčíkovo-Nagymaros Project (Hungary/Slovakia)* (Judgment) [1997] ICJ Rep 7, 127–8 (rejecting the existence of 'approximate application' or 'close approximation' principles in international law and suggesting the very idea deserved 'wholehearted censure').

[82] Rules seek to bind parties to respond in specific, determinate ways when certain facts exist; once the facts are clear, so too is the expected behaviour. Standards afford decision-makers discretion to decide (often *ex post*) what behaviour satisfies an obligation by either widening the range of relevant facts or authorizing direct application of some background policy or principle. Principles, in contrast, set forth broad considerations for evaluating future behaviour without providing any particular norm for the behaviour itself. See eg Daniel Bodansky, 'Rules vs. Standards in International

Some principles, like R2P, have a contested existence.[83] For decades, competing interpretations have examined whether international law includes a principle of compensation in the event of expropriation.[84] In the environmental arena, the United States and the European Union advance conflicting interpretations on whether customary international law contains a 'precautionary principle' or if, instead, a 'precautionary approach' operates without legal force.[85] Sometimes though, existential interpretation of a principle will generate consensus, even if further expository questions remain. For example, no one disputes the existence of a prohibition on perfidy in international armed conflicts, even as interpreters struggle with what that concept means in the context of modern warfare.[86]

Existential interpretations also arise with respect to more precisely formulated rules.[87] In *Nuclear Weapons*, for example, the ICJ concluded that it could not interpret international law to contain an absolute prohibition on the use of nuclear weapons.[88] In contrast, in *Nicaragua*, the ICJ interpreted international law to contain a rule imposing responsibility on a state for acts of non-state actors over which it has 'effective control'.[89] Of course, simply because one interpreter finds a rule to exist, does not mean other interpreters will agree; thus, the ICTY notably interpreted the existence of a different rule—one of 'overall control'—in assessing legal responsibility for non-state actors than states.[90]

Environmental Law' (2004) 98 Am Soc'y Int'l L Proc 275; Kathleen M Sullivan, 'The Justices of Rules and Standards' (1992) 106 Harv L Rev 22, 57–9; Ronald Dworkin, *Taking Rights Seriously* (Harvard University Press 1977) 22–8.

[83] See n 5 and accompanying text.

[84] See eg 'Official Documents' (1938) 32 AJIL Supp 181, 193 (United States interprets international law to include a compensation standard of 'prompt, adequate, and effective compensation'); 'Permanent Sovereignty over Natural Resources' UNGA Res 1803 (14 December 1962) 17 UN GAOR Supp (No 17), 15 (contemplating 'appropriate compensation in accordance with the states' rules...in accordance with international law'); UNGA Res 3171 (5 February 1974) UN Doc A/Res/3171 (XXVIII) (only state law governs expropriations); 'Charter of Economic Rights and Duties of States' UNGA Res 3281 (12 December 1974) UN Doc A/9946 (same).

[85] See eg Daniel Bodansky, 'Deconstructing the Precautionary Principle' in David Caron and HN Scheiber (eds), *Bringing New Law to Ocean Waters* (Martinus Nijhoff 2004) 382; see also WTO, *EC: Measures Concerning Meat and Meat Products Report of the Appellate Body (EC–Hormones)* (13 February 1998) WT/DS48/AB/R, [123] (noting that 'at least outside the field of international environmental law', the precautionary principle has not received 'authoritative formulation as a customary principle of international law').

[86] See eg Protocol Additional to the Geneva Conventions of 12 August 1949, and Relating to the Protection of Victims of Armed Conflict, 8 June 1977, 1125 UNTS 3 (Protocol I) Article 37 (defining and prohibiting perfidy); Michael N Schmitt (ed), *Tallinn Manual on the International Law Applicable to Cyber Warfare* (CUP 2013) 180–5 (discussing what perfidy means, including areas of interpretative disagreement among international experts with respect to cyberwarfare).

[87] Witness recent debates over whether a 'duty to capture' exists under the laws of war. See eg Ryan Goodman, 'The Power to Kill or Capture Enemy Combatants' (2013) 24 EJIL 819, 820–1; Geoffrey S Corn, Laurie R Blank, Chris Jenks, and Eric Talbot Jensen, 'Belligerent Targeting and the Invalidity of a Least Harmful Means Rule' (2013) 89 Intl L Studies 536; Jens David Ohlin, 'Duty to Capture' (2013) 97 Minn L Rev 1268, 1270.

[88] *Nuclear Weapons*, 266, [105(2)(E)].

[89] *Case concerning Military and Paramilitary Activities in and against Nicaragua (Nicaragua v USA)* (Merits, Judgment) [1986] ICJ Rep 14, 64–5, [115]; *Case concerning application of the Convention on the Prevention and Punishment of the Crime of Genocide (Bosnia and Herzegovina v Serbia and Montenegro)* (Judgment) [1997] ICJ Rep 43, 208–9, [399]–[401].

[90] *Prosecutor v Dusko Tadic aka 'Dule'* (Judgment) ICTY-94-1-A (15 July 1999) [131], [145].

Like custom, interpreters may arrive at the existence of 'general principles of law' by induction or deduction. The existential process is inductive for those who view this category as an analogic vehicle for bringing principles common to national legal systems into international law. Sometimes this interpretative process confirms the principle's existence (eg laches,[91] exhaustion of local remedies[92]) while denying it in others (eg easements,[93] duress[94]). Where interpreters view general principles as a vehicle for natural law, they may deduce the general principle's existence based on its 'necessity' to the international legal order (eg *pacta sunt servanda*).[95] For some, therefore, international human rights laws should exist as general principles of law in lieu of the customary status to which they traditionally aspire.[96]

Nor are existential interpretations limited to unwritten international law. Treaty interpreters who adopt a teleological method may identify the existence of new rights—such as the right to water—even where the treaty is silent.[97] Even textualists wrestle with existential issues: witness disagreements on whether or not certain private contracts exist as treaty commitments in light of 'umbrella clauses' in various bilateral investment treaties.[98]

As in *Qatar v Bahrain*, interpreters may have to discern the treaty's existence before ascribing meaning to one or more of its provisions.[99] In the Heathrow Airport User Charges Arbitration, the panel interpreted a MOU to have international legal effect, a status the British Government had disputed.[100] Sometimes,

---

[91] See eg Ashraf Ray Ibrahim, 'The Doctrine of Laches in International Law' (1997) 83 Va L Rev 647, 650.

[92] See eg Chittharanjan Felix Amerasinghe, *Local Remedies in International Law* (2nd edn, CUP 2003) 3; Draft Articles on the Responsibility of States for Internationally Wrongful Acts, *Report of the ILC on the Work of its Fifty-third Session*, UN GAOR, 56th Session Supp No 10, p 43, UN Doc A/56/10 (2001), art 44(b). For its part, the ICJ interprets exhaustion of local remedies to exist as customary international law. See eg *Case Concerning Elettronica Sicula S.p.A. (ELSI) (USA v Italy)* (Judgment) [1989] ICJ Rep 15, 42.

[93] *Case concerning the Right of Passage over Indian Territories (Portugal v India)* (Judgment) [1960] ICJ Rep 6, [39]–[40] (declining to recognize easements generally under international law).

[94] *Prosecutor v Erdemović ('Pilica Farm')* ICTY-96-22-A (7 October 1997) 16, [19].

[95] Schachter, *International Law in Theory and Practice*, 50–5.

[96] Simma and Alston, 'The Sources of Human Rights Law', 107.

[97] See eg Committee on Economic, Social, and Cultural Rights (CESCR), *General Comment 15* E/C.12/2002/11 (CESCR infers a right to water from teleological interpretation of Articles 11 and 12 of the International Covenant on Economic Social and Cultural Rights); see also Monica Hakimi, 'Secondary Human Rights Law' (2009) 34 Yale J Int'l L 596 (describing competing interpretations of the ICCPR by the HRC and the United States on whether that treaty contains a rule on *refoulement*).

[98] Compare the contrary interpretations in *Société Générale de Surveillance SA v Islamic Republic of Pakistan*, ICSID Case No ARB/01/13, Decision on Jurisdiction, 6 August 2003 (2003) 18 ICSID Rev 301, with *Société Générale de Surveillance SA v Republic of the Philippines*, ICSID Case No ARB/02/6, Decision on Jurisdiction, 29 January 2004 (2004) 8 ICSID Rev 515; see also Christoph Schreuer, 'Traveling the BIT Route: of Waiting Periods, Umbrella Clauses and Forks in the Road' (2004) 5 JWIT 231; Thomas Wälde, 'The Umbrella Clause in Investment Arbitration—A Comment on Original Intentions and Recent Cases' (2005) 6 JWIT 183.

[99] *Qatar v Bahrain (Jurisdiction and Admissibility)*, [27]. Not all international agreements constitute treaties; other possibilities include contracts (governed by a state's domestic law), and political commitments (governed by morality or political forces).

[100] *USA-UK Arbitration concerning Heathrow Airport User Charges (US-UK): Award on the First Question* (revised 18 June 1993) 24 RIAA 3, 131.

the question of a treaty's existence and its meaning may be difficult to untangle. In the *Aegean Sea Continental Shelf* case, for example, the Court found that there was no intent to submit a dispute to the Court under the commitment in question.[101] Scholars disagree whether this was because the commitment was not intended to be legally binding (ie it did not exist as a treaty) or because its scope did not trigger ICJ jurisdiction on the facts presented.[102]

Existential interpretations of international law do not, of course, occupy the entire field. Even after an interpreter determines a principle like exhaustion of local remedies exists, questions remain with respect to what that principle means (eg what the criteria for 'exhaustion' are). In other contexts, interpreters have to decide how multiple rules of international law interact—ie questions of conflict or hierarchy, such as those before the European Court of Justice in the *Kadi* case or between international trade law and other international legal regimes.[103]

4. *The existence of secondary rules and other 'sources' of international law*

HLA Hart famously divided his concept of law into two distinct categories: *primary rules* that regulate the subjects of law directly and *secondary rules* that delineate how primary rules form and operate.[104] The foregoing sections have considered existential interpretation in the context of primary rules. But in international law, existential interpretations also arise with respect to secondary rules via sources doctrine.[105] The existence of three standard sources for forming international law—treaties, custom, and general principles of law—is rarely challenged, especially given its location in Article 38 of the ICJ Statute.[106] Many (but not all) international lawyers do question, however, whether Article 38 constitutes an exhaustive list of ways to create international law's primary rules.[107] As a result, various

---

[101] *Aegean Sea Continental Shelf (Greece v Turkey)* [1978] ICJ Rep 3, 43.

[102] Compare Anthony Aust, *Modern Treaty Law & Practice* (2nd edn, CUP 2007) 20 (reading the opinion to find 'no intention to conclude an international agreement'), with Christine Chinkin, 'A Mirage in the Sand? Distinguishing Binding and Non-Binding Relations Between States' (1997) 10 LJIL 223, 234 (reading the opinion not to 'dismiss the [joint communiqué] as being without any legal effect but only as insufficient to support a unilateral application of the dispute to the Court').

[103] See eg Joined Cases G402/05 P and C-415/05 P, *Kadi and Al Barakaat International Foundation v Council and Commission* (2009) 46 CMLR 213, [316] (non-derogable right to fair trial has priority over UN Security Council resolutions); Joost Pauwelyn, *Conflict of Norms in Public International Law: How the WTO Law Relates to other Rules of International Law* (CUP 2003) (discussing how trade law relates to other international legal regimes such as international environmental law).

[104] See generally Hart, *The Concept of Law*, 94–9. Of course, Hart denied that international law had a single 'rule of recognition' for delineating what constitutes law. He viewed international law as merely a set of rules, not a legal system: 236.

[105] Cohen, 'Finding International Law', 1057 (noting various roles claimed for sources doctrine including as a '"rule of recognition" or international law's "secondary rules" more generally').

[106] Sir Gerald Fitzmaurice did famously emphasize the difficulty of referring to treaties as a source of law where they only bind treaty parties: 'Some Problems Regarding the Formal Sources of International Law' (1958) Symbolae Verzijl 153, 157.

[107] See eg Robert Y Jennings, 'What is International Law and How Do We Tell It When We See It' (1981) Schweitzerisches Jahrbuch Für Internationales Recht 37, 60 (declaring it 'an open question whether [Article 38] is now itself a sufficient guide to the content of modern international law' and proposing additional candidates).

existential interpretations have proffered other candidates as secondary rules of international law.

In 1973, for example, the ICJ interpreted into existence a new category of international legal obligation—unilateral declarations. In *Nuclear Tests*, the Court found France was bound under international law by public statements of its President and Foreign and Defence Ministers to cease nuclear tests in the South Pacific.[108] A WTO Panel gave a US declaration similar preclusive effect in 1999.[109] And in 2006, the ILC elaborated on how and why 'Declarations publicly made and manifesting the will to be bound may have the effect of creating legal obligations' under international law.[110]

Although its drafters denied it was intended to constitute a source of international law, some interpreters have assigned the Universal Declaration of Human Rights (UDHR) that status. In the seminal human rights case, *Filártiga v Peña-Irala*, the US court cited the UDHR as a source for the customary international law prohibition of torture.[111] Several years later, however, the US Supreme Court interpreted the UDHR *not* to constitute a source of law unto itself.[112] Many interpreters chart a middle path, accepting the UDHR's existence as *evidence* of customary international law rather than suggesting that the Declaration itself has become international law.[113]

The General Assembly's adoption of the UDHR highlights another candidate for a source of international law—IO decisions. IOs interpret their authority based on delegations from Member States in their constituent instruments. That authority is primarily limited to non-legal functions (serving as a fora for discussion, expertise, information gathering, monitoring, negotiations, etc). However, some IOs (eg ICAO) have authority to take decisions binding the organization or its member states.[114] Interpreters differ as to why such IO decisions are legally

---

[108] *Nuclear Tests (Australia/New Zealand v France)* [1974] ICJ Rep 267, [43]–[50]. Today, unilateral declarations are widely accepted as binding under international law. See eg *Case concerning the Frontier Dispute (Burkina Faso v Republic of Mali)* (Judgment) [1986] ICJ Rep 554, 573–74, [39]–[40]; Antonio Cassese, *International Law* (2nd edn, OUP 2005) 184.

[109] WTO, *United States-Sections 301–310 of the Trade Act of 1974—Report of the Panel* (22 December 1999) WT/DS152/R, [7.118]–[7.123].

[110] ILC, 'Guiding Principles applicable to unilateral declarations of States capable of creating legal obligations, with commentaries thereto' (2006) 58th Session UN Doc A/61/10, Guiding Principle 1. Several states questioned the utility of the ILC's project given the wide range of unilateral acts. See ILC, 'Unilateral Acts of States, Replies of Governments to the Questionnaire' (6 July 2000) UN Doc A/CN.4/51, 2–5.

[111] 630 F 2d 876, 883 (2nd Cir 1980).

[112] *Sosa v Alvarez-Machain* 542 US 692, 734 (2004) (Plaintiff 'says that his abduction by Sosa was an "arbitrary arrest" within the meaning of the Universal Declaration of Human Rights...But the Declaration does not of its own force impose obligations as a matter of international law', referencing the views of its US negotiator, Eleanor Roosevelt, who viewed it as '"a statement of principles" and "not a treaty or international agreement...impos[ing] legal obligations"').

[113] See n 65, and accompanying text.

[114] Convention on International Civil Aviation (signed at Chicago 7 December 1944, entered into force 4 April 1947) 15 UNTS 295, Articles 37, 54(1), 90. Other UN Specialized Agencies, like the World Health Organization (WHO), have similar powers to generate 'regulatory acts'. See eg WHO Constitution (opened for signature 22 July 1946, entered into force 7 April 1948) 14 UNTS 185, Articles 21–22.

binding. For some, their legal force derives from the law of treaties; IO decisions bind where member states agreed in the treaty constituting the IO that they would be so bound.[115] Others interpret these decisions to exist as stand-alone sources of international law—legislative acts binding directly on member states.[116] Both views have been advanced with respect to the TRIPS Doha Declaration.[117] Meanwhile, EU Regulations are widely interpreted as having an independent legislative character independent of treaty law and practice.[118] A similar legislative status is claimed for the WHO's Code on Marketing of Breast-Milk Substitutes.[119]

Finally, questions persist about the existence of 'soft law' as a source of international law. Soft law recasts the binary distinction between law and non-law into a continuum reflecting degrees of bindingness, ranging from soft to hard.[120] The label 'soft law' is given to describe 'legally non-binding norms' produced by state and non-state actors (eg G8 Declarations, industry codes of conduct) that may generate compliance.[121]

The soft law thesis has several potential impacts on existential interpretations of international law. On the one hand, its emphasis on compliance and effectiveness with respect to 'norms' de-privileges the importance of sources of international

---

[115] See eg Malgosia Fitzmaurice, 'Modifications to the Principles of Consent in Relation to Certain Treaty Obligations' (1997) ARIEL 275, 316–17; GM Danilenko, *Law-Making in the International Community* (Martinus Nijhoff 1993) 192.

[116] See eg Brölmann, 'Specialized Rules of Treaty Interpretation', 518–19 (discussing both views); Vladimir D Degan, *Sources of International Law* (Martinus Nijhoff 1997) 6 (considering 'non-obligatory' rules as a possible newly emerging source of international law); see also Christian Tomuschat, 'Obligations Arising for States Without or Against Their Will' (1993) 241 Recueil des Cours 195, 328; Charles Henry Alexandrowicz, *The Law-Making Functions of the Specialised Agencies of the United Nations* (Angus and Robertson 1973) 152.

[117] Compare James Thuo Gathii, 'The Legal Status of the Doha Declaration on TRIPS and Public Health under the Vienna Convention on the Law of Treaties' (2002) 15 Harv J L & Tech 291, 299–313 (examining the declaration through a VCLT lens) with Steve Charnovitz, 'The Legal Status of the Doha Declaration' (2002) 5 J Intl Econ L 207, 211 (suggesting declaration is possibly the first instance of a 'legislative body' creating world trade law). A third view denies the Declaration has any status under international law. See Gathii at 314–16 (describing the US view).

[118] See eg Brölmann, 'Specialized Rules of Treaty Interpretation', 519; PJ Kuijper, 'The European Courts and the Law of Treaties: The Continuing Story' in Enzo Canizzaro (ed), *The Law of Treaties Beyond the Vienna Convention* (OUP 2011) 268–70 (surveying recent CJEU practice); Peter L Lindseth, 'Constitutionalism Beyond the State? The Administrative Character of European Governance Revisited' (2012) 33 Cardozo L Rev 1875, 1879.

[119] José E Alvarez, *International Organizations as Law-makers* (OUP 2005) 234–5.

[120] See eg Alan Boyle, 'Some Reflections on the Relationship of Treaties and Soft Law' (1999) 48 ICLQ 901, 913; Gregory C Shaffer and Mark A Pollack, 'Hard vs. Soft Law: Alternatives, Complements, and Antagonists in International Governance' (2010) 95 Minn L Rev 706, 712–17; Pierre-Marie Dupuy, 'Soft Law and the International Law of the Environment' (1991) 12 Mich J Int'l L 420, 434–5; Christine M Chinkin, 'The Challenges of Soft Law: Development and Change in International Law' (1989) 38 ICLQ 850, 865–6.

[121] See Dinah Shelton, 'Law, Non-Law and the Problem of "Soft Law"' in Dinah Shelton (ed), *Commitment and Compliance: The Role of Non-Binding Norms in the International Legal System* (OUP 2000) 1. Other definitions of soft law persist, however, including one that defines 'soft law' as norms incapable of enforcement, whether because of ambiguity, intention or lack of sanctions. See Prosper Weil, 'Towards Relative Normativity in International Law' (1983) 77 AJIL 413, 417–18; W Michael Reisman, 'The Supervisory Jurisdiction of the International Court of Justice: International Arbitration and International Adjudication' (1996) 258 Recueil des Cours 1, 180–1.

'law' and, with them, questions of international legal interpretation. Instead of asking what generates international law, soft law proponents evaluate norms in terms of effectiveness, asking how much a particular norm generates compliance by states and other actors. Global Administrative Law makes this move away from sources doctrine overtly. Instead of interpreting the rules of 'international law', it focuses on a new category—'global law'—that includes norms from traditional international legal sources (eg the WTO) and avowedly non-legal regimes (eg the Basel Committee, the International Organization for Standardization).[122]

Alternatively, to the extent states do comply with soft law instruments, then, as Dinah Shelton notes, 'perhaps the concept of international law, or the list of sources of international law, requires expansion'.[123] In other words, soft law may actually exist as a new source of international law. Other scholars like Klabbers deny 'soft law' such a separate existence, labelling it a redundant concept.[124] Not surprisingly, therefore, existential interpretations of soft law generate both affirmative and negative outcomes on the sources question. In some cases, soft law is interpreted as part of the sources family, whether as a stepping stone to treaties or custom,[125] a way to fill in gaps in existing legal regimes,[126] or even as the purportedly final word on some legal question.[127] In other instances, the non-legal nature of soft law is emphasized to deny it the status of a source.[128] Like the UDHR, moreover, a middle ground exists where soft law instruments are treated as evidence of international law.[129]

---

[122] See Benedict Kingsbury, Nico Krisch, and Richard B Stewart, 'The Emergence of Global Administrative Law' (2005) 68 LCP 15, 22; Benedict Kingsbury, Nico Krisch, Richard B Stewart, and Jonathan B Wiener, 'Foreword: Global Governance as Administration—National and Transnational Approaches to Global Administrative Law' (2005) 68 LCP 1, 5 ('This field of law is described as "global" rather than "international" to reflect both the inclusion in it of a large array of informal institutional arrangements...and normative sources, that are not encompassed within standard conceptions of "international law"').

[123] Shelton, 'Law, Non-Law and the Problem of "Soft Law"', 11.

[124] See Jan Klabbers, 'The Redundancy of Soft Law' (1996) 65 Nordic J Intl L 167, 181 (arguing that soft law must either exist as part of 'hard' law or non-law, and suggesting that much of soft law can exist within the binary mode of international law); see also Kal Raustiala, 'Form and Substance in International Agreements' (2005) 99 AJIL 581, 592 (rejecting soft law thesis).

[125] International law's 'prior informed consent procedure' originated in non-binding standards issued by the UN Food and Agriculture Organization and the UN Environment Program before maturing into a multilateral treaty—the Rotterdam Convention. See eg Mohamed Ali Mekouar, 'Pesticides and Chemicals: The Requirement of Prior Informed Consent' in Shelton, *Commitment and Compliance*, 146–55.

[126] The Recommendations of the OECD's Financial Action Task Force (FATF) address gaps and holes 'in a complex web of binding agreements'. David Wirth, 'Compliance with Non-Binding Norms of Trade and Finance' in Shelton, *Commitment and Compliance*, 330, 333.

[127] See Christine Chinkin, 'Normative Development in the International Legal System' in Shelton, *Commitment and Compliance*, 30–1 (describing how soft law can elaborate hard law, serve as a pre-cursor for it, co-regulate hard law, or itself operate directly as a source of law, 'perhaps against the original intentions of the parties'); see also Dinah Shelton, 'Commentary and Conclusions' in Shelton, *Commitment and Compliance*, 461.

[128] See eg *Nuclear Weapons*, 241 (noting states questioned the binding legal quality of the Stockholm and Rio Declarations with respect to establishing a prohibition on transboundary environmental harm under international law).

[129] Chinkin, 'Normative Development in the International Legal System', 30–1 (describing how soft law can serve 'as evidence of the existence of hard obligations').

Taken together, the foregoing examples reveal a layered and interconnected process of interpretation. Whether an interpreter is inquiring as to authority, evidence, international law, or its sources, existential interpretations may operate in the foreground, prior to or alongside the expository project of deciding what the existing authority (or evidence, or law, etc) means. In other cases, existential interpretations remain hidden as a background presumption while interpreters focus only on giving meaning. But existential and expository interpretative processes are clearly interrelated. Existential interpretations may lead to expository interpretations which may lead to more existential interpretations. For example, the existence of evidence in international law is a function of the sources of international law—one has to understand what sources exist (eg custom) and what they mean (ie custom requires state practice and *opinio juris*) to undertake the existential interpretation of evidence (ie deciding that practice by states counts for custom, but the acts of individuals do not). Expository analyses of existing evidence are, in turn, interpretative vehicles for determining the existence of international law. To decide whether a particular international legal obligation exists, for example, treaty interpreters weigh the existing evidence (the treaty text, the context, any subsequent agreements, other rules of international law, etc) and, if necessary, reconcile that evidence with competing evidence (the text of earlier or later treaties, a peremptory norm, etc). Thus, existential interpretations are distinct but not autonomous from other interpretative processes. They are a necessary, but not determinative, aspect of giving international law meaning.

III. The Consequences of Interpretation's Existential Function

So far, this chapter has sought to identify and explain the existential function of international legal interpretation. In doing so, it highlights a particular structure of interpretative argument—existential interpretation—that can occupy the foreground of interpretative processes. But just because we can conceptualize interpretation in existential terms does not explain why international lawyers should do so. If all interpretative processes have an existential function, does it matter that in some cases the existential interpretation remains hidden in background presumptions, but in others it occupies the foreground? What can the existential aspects of interpretation tell us that we do not already know from existing inquiries into interpretative method, techniques, and larger projects exploring the (in)determinacy of international law?

Existential interpretations matter because they clearly impact both the theory and practice of international law. Classifying interpretation's existential function is not merely taxonomic; identifying interpretative functions just to categorize them. Rather, existential interpretation has important implications for international legal (i) discourse, (ii) doctrine, and (iii) theories of international law itself.

A. Existential interpretations as fences: setting boundaries for international legal discourse

Existential interpretations implicate how states and others talk about international law. An interpreter's existential interpretation tells the audience (whether states, IOs, domestic courts, international tribunals, etc) what the interpreter believes are the appropriate boundaries for interpretation. Where the existential function lies hidden in the background, the interpreter signals a belief that the interpreted subject's existence is not open to question. To use the language coined by Robert Cover, hidden existential interpretations are *jurispathic*.[130] An interpreter who presumes a particular subject exists—whether it is authority, evidence, international law, or its source—signals that existential questions have been asked and answered; they are not subject to further dialogue. The interpreter may pursue additional interpretative acts (eg explaining what the evidence means or determining priority among competing rules), but such acts presume the existence of the evidence or rules in question.

Conversely, when interpreters foreground existential interpretations, it signals an appreciation that the subject's existence is open to interpretation. In Cover's language, explicit existential interpretations of authority, evidence, law, and sources are potentially *jurisgenerative*—a process of creating or confirming the existence of the interpreted subject.[131] Of course, interpreters may also employ existential interpretations to destroy, denying claims that some piece of evidence (eg lump sum payments), principle (eg precaution), or source (eg the UDHR) exists within international law. But whether they answer their inquiry positively or not, interpreters who employ existential interpretations suggest to their audience that their project incorporates existential questions, whether prior to—or in concert with—issues of meaning.

Taken together, the *jurispathic* and *jurisgenerative* potential of existential interpretations may set the boundaries for international legal discourse. States and others proffer interpretations of international law (or evidence, or sources, etc) in the course of disputes or discussions about creating or changing international law. If none of the interpretations of a rule (eg UN Charter Article 2(4)) foreground the existential question, that fences in the discussion. It suggests a consensus on the rule's international legal existence and lays the boundaries for any dispute along expository or relational lines.[132] But if interpreters explain why they believe

---

[130] Robert M Cover, 'The Supreme Court, 1982 Term—Foreword: Nomos and Narrative' (1983) 97 Harv L Rev 4. For an earlier example extending Cover's work to international law, see Dunoff, 'A New Approach to Regime Interaction', 144–56.

[131] This will not always be the case. Courts that justify the existence of jurisdiction usually act jurispathically, pronouncing finally on the matter.

[132] It would be a mistake to assume that interpreters only background existential interpretations in cases of consensus and foreground them where controversy is expected. Interpreters may assume a consensus that does not exist or offer an existential interpretation that the audience considers unnecessary. Still, international lawyers should expect more contestation where existential interpretations occupy the foreground rather than the background.

the rule exists *and* what it means (eg R2P), the discursive fence is broadened quite a bit. These interpreters concede—whether explicitly or by implication—that a consensus may be absent on the existential issue and it needs to be discussed more. Similarly, where an interpreter offers a meaning for a rule (eg right to water) on the assumption that the rule exists, another interpreter may challenge this proposed boundary, and broaden the discussion by challenging whether there is any such right alongside (or in lieu of) an examination of what the right actually means.

Thus, existential interpretations may expand discursive boundaries.[133] To the extent existential interpretations are evident at various levels of discourse, the possibilities for expansion are quite significant. An interpreter inclined to be contrarian might contest an interpretation's conclusions on the existence of authority, evidence, law, *and* sources while simultaneously contesting the meaning of each if they do exist. Presumably, the more interpretative inquiries facing parties in dispute or discussion, the more difficult it is for the sides to reach a positive outcome (ie there are more possibilities for the parties to fail to reach consensus). Interpreters may even introduce existential questions to shift the boundaries of discussion away from the content of some evidence or rule to more abstract questions about international law's categories and procedures.

On the other hand, where interpretations background existential issues, the nature of the dispute or discourse is narrowed. Questions of meaning may still reflect deep disagreements, but the nature of that disagreement is less fundamental than where the very existence of the interpreted subjects are contested. As a result, the presence or absence of explicit existential interpretations may impact not just international legal discourse, but dispute outcomes by broadening (or narrowing) opportunities for contestation.

B. Existential interpretations and doctrine: direct and indirect effects

Just as existential interpretations impact discourse, they also impact the content of the international legal doctrine on which that discourse often centres. These impacts occur even where the interpretation goes to the existence of something other than international law per se (eg authority to interpret, evidence, secondary rules). When courts interpret jurisdictional questions, their answers directly impact the tribunal's jurisdictional doctrine. For example, in finding no jurisdiction existed given France's unilateral declaration in *Norwegian Loans*, the ICJ established (contra Lauterpacht) its acceptance of self-judging declarations, a doctrine against which later cases (eg *Nicaragua*) were measured.[134] Existential claims of authority may also impact doctrine indirectly, as when a new actor claims a voice—binding or not—to interpret international law. For example, interpreters who accept the HRC's authority to interpret ICCPR reservations view the law

---

[133] In the case of jurisdiction, the existential inquiry may actually determine whether a dispute can be resolved authoritatively or not.

[134] See nn 43, 75–6, and accompanying text.

of reservations quite differently from those (eg the United States) who reject the existence of such authority.

Doctrinal impacts follow the existential interpretation of evidence as well. The choice to allow (or deny) evidence for interpretative purposes impacts the existence and content of international law itself. Denying that the practice of torture is evidence of state practice preserves the prohibition on torture more absolutely than if interpreters allowed such evidence in giving meaning to that doctrine. Similar consequences follow existential interpretations of international law's sources. For example, international human rights law may contain an individual right to asylum if the UDHR is interpreted as a source of international law,[135] but not if interpreters only look to treaties and custom.[136]

Not surprisingly, existential interpretations of international law also have doctrinal consequences as well. Every time an interpreter identifies an implied power for an IO, it elaborates the implied powers doctrine.[137] Other doctrinal impacts are more indirect. For example, when interpreters consider 'other rules' in giving a treaty provision meaning pursuant to Article 31(3)(c) of the VCLT, they are necessarily affirming the international legal status of those rules.[138] And if there's widespread acceptance of the treaty interpretation that follows, it may imply widespread acceptance of the doctrinal status of the rules used to generate that interpretation as well.[139]

Existential interpretations thus impact the content of international law. Interpretations of international law's existence may attract adherents, whose subsequent interpretations accumulate support for that rule's existence in international law. Eventually, interpreters may stop explaining why the rule exists (eg diplomatic immunity) and move straight to expository analysis, pushing the existential function of such interpretations into the background. Alternatively, existential interpretations may generate detractors whose interpretations contest or deny a claimed rule's international legal status. But even in such cases, the existential contestation still impacts international law. The fact that there are *some* reasoned interpretations that a doctrine (eg R2P) exists, establishes a claim that other interpreters have to engage with doctrinally, even if only to deny it. Moreover, where an interpretative resolution *is* possible—whether by consensus or some authoritative interpretation (eg by a court)—the resulting international law doctrine remains a function of the underlying existential choices made.

---

[135] Universal Declaration of Human Rights (adopted 10 December 1948) UNGA Res 217 A(III) (UDHR) UN Doc A/810 at 7, Article 14 (listing a right to asylum for refugees).

[136] The ICCPR does not contain such a right. See International Covenant on Civil and Political Rights (adopted 16 December 1966, entered into force 23 March 1976) 999 UNTS 171, [1967] 6 ILM 368 (ICCPR). Nor is there a general and uniform state practice of doing so. See Hurst Hannum, 'The Status of the Universal Declaration of Human Rights in National and International Law' (1996) 25 Ga J Int'l & Comp L 287, 346; Roman Boed, 'The State of the Right of Asylum in International Law' (1994) 5 Duke J Comp & Int'l L 1, 4–6, 8 n 35, 16.

[137] See n 80.

[138] Not to mention the status of the VCLT interpretive rules themselves.

[139] But see n 148 below, and accompanying text.

C. Existential interpretations and theory: proxies for conceptual disagreements

The discursive and doctrinal potential of existential interpretations helps explain why interpreters assert—and contest—the existence of authority, evidence, international law and its sources. But these are not the only motivations for existential interpretations. Differences in method or technique may also account for existential disagreements. In the *LaGrand* case, for example, the United States and Germany disagreed on whether an individual right to consular notification existed under the Vienna Convention on Consular Relations. Germany read the *travaux préparatoires* to support such a right, while the United States suggested they did not.[140] The ICJ agreed with Germany on the individual right's existence but did so without referring to the *travaux*, relying only on the text's ordinary meaning and the surrounding context.[141] Such variations suggest differences over technique (ie Germany and the United States read the *travaux* differently) and interpretative method (the Court and the United States differed on when to use *travaux*). But all involved appeared to share a conception of international law in which treaties bind parties and the VCLT rules direct the interpretative process through the use of text, context, and *travaux*.

Beyond methodological or technical differences, existential disagreements may also serve as proxies for very different conceptions of international law. This is perhaps most obvious in debates over sources. Those who deny sources status to the UDHR, for example, almost invariably do so based on the original intention of the state representatives who voted for it, implying a positivist theory of international law in which the general consent of states creates rules of general application.[142] In contrast, those who invoke the UDHR as a direct source appear to disavow the positivist's reification of state consent; instead, they may credit the UDHR with sources status because it articulates a common agenda for the world community, whether based on morals (ie naturalist) or a policy-orientation (ie the New Haven School).[143] Others might emphasize the UDHR as a source by ascribing to it a constitutional status for human rights or because of the *process* by which international actors invoke it (ie international legal process).[144] In other words, interpreters may differ over the UDHR's status because they hold fundamentally different theories of the international legal order.

---

[140] *LaGrand Case (Germany v USA)* [2001] ICJ Rep 466, [75]–[76].

[141] *LaGrand Case*, [77].

[142] Duncan B Hollis, 'Why State Consent Still Matters—Non-State Actors, Treaties, and the Changing Sources of International Law' (2005) 23 Berkley J Int'l L 137, 140–2. Positivism isn't the only theory that might deny the UDHR source status. Some might object based on its inattention to the equal rights of men and women or its adoption during the colonial era, arguments that implicate feminist and third world approaches to international law ('TWAIL') respectively.

[143] Hollis, 'Why State Consent Still Matters', 140 n 10; see also Hannum, 'The Status of the Universal Declaration of Human Rights', 317–40 (reviewing various views of UDHR's status).

[144] Although not comprehensive, a very useful discussion of various methods and theories of international law is Steven R Ratner and Anne-Marie Slaughter (eds), *The Methods of International Law* (ASIL 2004).

Conceptual differences may similarly lie beneath existential disagreements over evidentiary questions or the content of international law itself. Positivist theories of international law motivate various interpretations: for example denying UNGA resolutions are evidence of state practice or *opinio juris*; allowing states to self-judge the scope of the ICJ's compulsory jurisdiction; or accepting a *non liquet* when it comes to nuclear weapons. Naturalist theories, in contrast, justify denying the label of 'state practice' to morally repugnant acts like torture, or finding rules to exist as 'general principles'. And international legal process approaches may justify new international law doctrines like R2P or precaution that other conceptual approaches would not support (and might even oppose).

Nor are existential interpretations of authority immune from a proxy role. Those who object to the HRC's authority to assess the validity of ICCPR reservations invariably favour a positivist vision of international institutions owing complete fealty to the states that create them, or what international relations scholars dub principal-agent (PA) theory.[145] In contrast, those who favour the existence of HRC authority do so with different theories in mind, envisioning a world in which the importance of states is diminished or where they accept a 'trusteeship' theory of international delegation.[146]

Such conceptual underpinnings of existential interpretations have at least three significant implications. For starters, they allow interpreters to advance their theory of international law *implicitly*; an existential claim about evidence or authority may not immediately be evident as a claim about theory.[147] This does not mean the implicit theory must be adopted expressly by others to reach a consensus on how to answer the existential inquiry. There can be agreement that some particular authority, evidence, rule, or source exists without agreement on *why* it exists. Indeed, Cass Sunstein's theory of incompletely theorized agreements suggests that we should expect such outcomes in a world of diverse actors and interests.[148] Thus,

---

[145] PA theory suggests that we can understand how international institutions behave if we think of their relationship with the states who create them as that of agent to principal. The principal (ie the states acting collectively) delegates certain functions to an agent (eg an IO, a treaty-body), which the agent is charged to perform on the principal's behalf. When agents do not comport with their delegations—what's called agency slippage—the theory anticipates principals will react to bring the agent back within the realm of delegated authority. See Alvarez, *International Organizations as Law-makers*, 633–4; Daniel L Nielson and Michael J Tierney, 'Delegations to International Organizations: Agency Theory and World Bank Environmental Reform' (2003) 57 Int'l Org 214.

[146] Originated by Karen Alter, the trusteeship theory suggests that international institutions have independent sources of authority beyond the delegation they receive from states (eg expertise, reputation) *and* that they should act autonomously from the principals who create them to enhance the credibility of their actions. Thus, for trustees, slippage is not only expected, but encouraged. See Karen J Alter, 'Agents or Trustees? International Courts in their Political Context' (2008) 14 Eur J Intl Relations 33; Karen J Alter, 'Delegation to International Courts and the Limits of Recontracting Political Power' in Darren G Hawkins, David A Lake, Daniel L Nielson, and Michael J Tierney (eds), *Delegation and Agency in International Organizations* (CUP 2006) 312, 316.

[147] Although sophisticated interpreters may recall Oscar Schachter's point that interpretative difficulties over treaties, custom, general principles cannot set aside issues of obligation or a 'grand theory' of international law: Oscar Schachter, 'Towards a Theory of International Obligation' in Stephen Schwebel (ed), *The Effectiveness of International Decisions* (Sijthoff 1971) 9–31.

[148] Cass R Sunstein, 'Incompletely Theorized Agreements in Constitutional Law' (2007) 74 Social Research 1. In an example from the US context, Sunstein noted that '[p]eople may believe

interpreters adopting a positivist or TWAIL perspective might both deny the existence of R2P, even if they have antithetical reasons for doing so. Nonetheless, interpreters may still cite any subsequent consensus as a practice or precedent in support of their particular theory of international law.

Second, where existential differences do emerge, their conceptual underpinnings may make reaching a resolution difficult. Inconsistent or conflicting first principles may preclude interpreters from subjugating their theory to a competing one or otherwise conceding the existential point. In such cases, any resolution may turn on some third party having authority to resolve the competing existential claims.

The need for some authority to definitively resolve existential questions suggests a third—and quite important—point about the conceptual significance of existential interpretations: delegations of interpretative authority may not only resolve competing existential questions, but, in doing so, advance or undermine the theories on which they rest. Where a court accepts a party's self-judging declaration on jurisdiction it advances the positivist conception on which that declaration rests, just as a Court endorsing the UDHR as a source of international law undercuts the positivist vision of state consent as the quintessential source of international law.

This conceptual dimension of existential interpretations challenges the traditional account of interpretative theory with which this chapter began. States may believe that when they create international institutions and invest them with interpretative authority, the scope of that authority is limited to exposition (eg the ICJ may only interpret and apply the sources listed in Article 38; the WTO's Dispute Settlement System may only interpret and apply the WTO Agreements).[149] But, if all interpretations have existential functions, then *any* delegation of interpretative authority necessarily involves a delegation of existential authority. And to the extent such existential authority may have conceptual consequences, any decision on existential matters may implicitly favour or falsify particular theories of international law. Courts or IOs might make existential choices that endorse the positivist vision of the states from whom the delegation comes. But it should be apparent at this point how difficult it may be to ensure such outcomes. Absent some explicit limitations on what authority, evidence, law, *and* sources a court or other interpretative body may use, existential decisions may favour other, competing theories of international law. As a result, those who would delegate interpretative authority should appreciate that such delegations include authority to pursue expository, existential, *and* conceptual functions.

---

that it is important to protect religious liberty while having quite diverse theories about why this is so. Some people may stress what they see as the need for social peace; others may think that religious liberty reflects a principle of equality and a recognition of human dignity; others may invoke utilitarian considerations; still others may think that religious liberty is itself a theological command'. Ibid.

[149] ICJ Statute, Article 38(1); Understanding on Rules and Procedures Governing the Settlement of Disputes, Marrakesh Agreement establishing the WTO (adopted 15 April 1994, entered into force 1 January 1995) 1869 UNTS 299, Article 1.1 (delegating authority for consultation and dispute settlement for specifically covered WTO agreements).

Conclusion

This chapter highlights the existential function of interpretation in international law. To date, this function has received little attention as interpretative theory has primarily wrestled with questions of method and technique. But the existential function *is* important; every interpretation involves the creation, confirmation, or denial of the existence of that which is interpreted. Existential interpretations are the vehicle by which interpreters decide whether a particular subject exists or not, in contrast to other forms of interpretation that look to weigh or balance existing subjects or relate them to each other. Interpreters may foreground their existential interpretations or let them rest in hidden interpretative presumptions. But make no mistake—existential interpretations manifest themselves throughout international legal discourse. As such, they form an important, if as yet unheralded, aspect of the game of interpretation.

This chapter has provided examples of existential interpretations with respect to the existence of authority, evidence, international law and its sources. The phenomenon arises in other areas as well, such as existential interpretations of legal personality (does Kosovo exist as a state?) and remedies (do individuals have a remedy to VCCR violations?).[150] In all these cases, existential interpretations and the functions they serve have significant consequences. They delineate the boundaries for interpretative discourse, narrowing it in cases of consensus on the existence of the interpreted subject, and broadening it in cases of dispute. Where interpretative resolutions of existential questions are possible, they may impact the content of international law doctrine, either directly or indirectly. And, where resolution is not possible, existential interpretations may operate as proxies for theoretical disagreement about the nature or purpose of international law.

Given the implications of existential interpretations for international legal discourse, doctrine, and theory, international lawyers need to pay closer attention to this particular type of argument. Studying existential interpretations could have important lessons for international practice and our understanding of the current international legal order(s).

First, practically speaking, it would be useful to know more about when and how states and non-state actors actually foreground existential interpretations. Obviously, there may be cases where an interpreter does so in good faith, ie where there is an open question about the interpreted subject's existence. But existential interpretations might also be deployed instrumentally. In some cases, the existential interpretation may be employed constructively—to advocate for the existence of some authority or rule because of the interests or values that would be served by

[150] See *Accordance with International Law of the Unilateral Declaration of Independence in Respect of Kosovo* (Advisory Opinion) [2010] ICJ Rep 403, [49]–[51] (declining to answer whether Kosovo exists as a state); *Case Concerning Avena and Other Mexican Nationals (Mexico v USA)* (Judgment) [2004] ICJ Rep 12, [115]–[123] (discussing what remedies exist for violation of consular notification requirements of the Vienna Convention on Consular Relations). For additional examples, see n 40.

doing so. Thus, IOs may interpret themselves to have implied powers or a human rights NGO might interpret international law to contain additional human rights.

In other cases, existential interpretations might be employed precisely because they can obscure or obstruct interpretative claims. Consider the possibilities when a state (or other actor) objects to an interpreter X claiming that rule Y means Z. Of course, the state might simply disagree that Z is the correct meaning of rule Y. But a state could expand the scope of the interpretative dispute by also questioning whether X has authority to interpret the evidence on which rule Y rests as well as the source of international law it is derived from. The objecting state may thus complicate the dispute by expanding its scope.

Introducing existential issues may also change the nature of a dispute, shifting discussions away from the original issue to issues of authority or procedure. For example, debating what R2P *means* in Syria requires interpreters to face and weigh the extent of the humanitarian crisis there. But by challenging the status of R2P as a binding legal rule, interpreters shift attention from humanitarian questions to (more abstract) issues of authority to use force generally and the procedures for doing so. Studying existential interpretations, therefore, would allow international lawyers to gain a better sense of how they are used in practice, as well as their efficacy in constructing or deconstructing other interpretative arguments.

Second, studying existential interpretations may also have theoretical significance, particularly for pervasive questions about unity and fragmentation in international law. Fragmentation[151] has revived Hart's controversial suggestion that international law constitutes not a system, but a simple set of rules.[152] The ensuing debates have tended to take one of two guises: either an emphasis on 'normative' fragmentation where specialized regimes of international law regulate the same conduct with inconsistent or conflicting rules; or 'institutional' fragmentation where different institutions interpret the same rule differently.[153]

By studying existential interpretations, international lawyers obtain a new lens for examining fragmentation. Instead of examining fragmentation along a single axis (eg norms), mapping existential arguments offers a way to gauge the extent of unity versus fragmentation along multiple axes. Since existential interpretations are manifest throughout international legal discourse, questions of unity or fragmentation can be examined in terms of authority, the sources of international law, the rules of international law and the evidence on which they are based, the actors who may participate, or the remedies international law affords. In each area, the number and depth of existential debates offer a rough gauge for mapping unity versus fragmentation. Where existential inquiries are absent or where a consensus exists on the answers, unity may be presumed. Conversely, where there are existential disputes, they indicate fragmentation.

[151] See n 22.   [152] Hart, *The Concept of Law*, 236.
[153] On normative fragmentation, see eg ILC Study Group; Pauwelyn, *Conflict of Norms in Public International Law*. For a discussion of institutional fragmentation, see eg Philippa Webb, *International Judicial Integration and Fragmentation* (OUP 2013).

We might even use the number and types of existential disagreements to map international law's interpretative communities.[154] One could envision some areas of universal agreement—core areas of consensus on the existence of certain aspects of international law (eg *pacta sunt servanda*, states as subjects of that law). And where existential disagreements do arise, we might be able to map different interpretative communities based on adherents or opponents to different existential interpretations. All told, studying existential interpretations could provide a more nuanced view of unity and fragmentation than existing efforts.

Ronald Dworkin once suggested that 'Law cannot flourish as an interpretive enterprise in any community unless there is enough initial agreement about what practices are legal practices'.[155] He assumed, moreover, that lawyers 'have no difficulty identifying the practices that count as legal practices in our own culture'.[156] In its current form(s), international law tests both propositions. At every level—from authority to the sources of law—international lawyers contest what 'counts' for purposes of international law. But contrary to Dworkin's assertions, these existential debates do not demonstrate that international law is failing to flourish. On the contrary, existential interpretations evidence a legal order that is maturing in both depth and breadth. Even if there is fragmentation of views on the distribution of authority, law, and its sources, this does not necessarily signal a lack of unity in other respects. International lawyers may, as Mario Prost noted, still share a commitment to a common language or culture.[157] Indeed, whatever else the existential function of interpretation in international law may say, one thing is clear: international law exists as something worthy of our ongoing efforts to give it meaning.

---

[154] See Bianchi, 'Textual Interpretation and (International) Law Reading', 52 (describing Stanley Fish's theory of interpretive communities and its application to international law).

[155] Dworkin, *Law's Empire*, 90–1.   [156] Dworkin, *Law's Empire*, 90–1.

[157] Mario Prost, 'All Shouting the Same Slogans: International Law's Unities and the Politics of Fragmentation' (2006) 17 FYBIL 131 (suggesting cultural unity/fragmentation as an alternative narrative from one focused on substantive unity/fragmentation in international law or axiological unity/fragmentation (in terms of the values that the international legal order should serve)).

5

The Multidimensional Process of Interpretation

Content-Determination and Law-Ascertainment Distinguished

Jean d'Aspremont

Introduction

The world any human or corporate person operates in is an aggregation of normative universes which are all individually structured around the possibility of right or wrong, of permissible or impermissible, of valid or invalid.[1] International law constitutes one of these normative universes. Like other normative universes, international law is a vehicle for methods and narratives that construct a certain reality and validate or invalidate certain practices. This particular universe is inhabited by international lawyers, whose membership of the universe is not only institutional or professional.[2] It is also the result of a commitment, namely a commitment to the field's rhetoric and traditions,[3] and to the system of knowledge and argumentation that comes with it. Such a commitment is the primary cement and the main constitutive element of the universe of international law. Indeed, it is by virtue of this commitment that interpretation of international law is not totally unbridled and operates within the framework of pre-existing social constraints.

---

[1] Cf Robert Cover, 'The Supreme Court 1982 Term—Foreword: Nomos and Narrative' (1983) 97 Harv L Rev 4, 4–5 (for whom there is only one single normative universe which we all inhabit and where the dichotomies of 'right and wrong, of lawful and unlawful, of valid and void' are constantly at play).

[2] On membership of the international law profession, see Jean d'Aspremont, 'Wording in International Law' (2012) 25 LJIL 575.

[3] Martti Koskenniemi argues that such a commitment necessarily comes with a countervailing professional doubt about the identity of international law and that of the profession organized around it. See Martti Koskenniemi, 'Between Commitment and Cynicism: Outline for a Theory of International Law as Practice' in *Collection of Essays by Legal Advisers of States, Legal Advisers of International Organizations and Practitioners in the Field of International Law* (United Nations 1999) 495.

This commitment by international lawyers to the normative universe of international law manifests itself in very different ways. This chapter grapples specifically with two of the main expressions of international lawyers' commitment towards international law: their embrace of (i) the methods to determine the content of legal rules, and (ii) the methods to identify legal rules that are made available by the normative universe of international law. This chapter is premised on the idea that international lawyers, while trying to give meaning to legal rules (content-determination) or while engaging in the identification of rules (law-ascertainment), necessarily commit themselves to certain techniques, rhetoric, and traditions that are provided by the normative universe of international law. In doing so, this chapter draws on the insightful metaphor at the heart of this volume and argues that the object of the game of interpretation should be seen as multidimensional. Playing the game of interpretation consists not only of attributing meaning to the rules (content-determination), but also of ascertaining what is and what is not law (law-ascertainment).

It is true that the two interpretive processes referred to here can be easily indistinguishable, as they both manifest a commitment to the techniques, rhetoric, and traditions of the normative universe of international law. Practice often makes them part of the same intellectual operation, illustrated by the way in which the mainstream theory of customary international law is applied by international courts and tribunals.[4] Yet the gist of the argument here is that, although the processes are both committal and interpretive in nature, law-ascertainment and content-determination must be clearly distinguished. Each of them engages different questions of law, power, and authority. Moreover, each of them also comes with a distinct approach to controlling indeterminacy and arbitrariness in adjudication.

This chapter is structured as follows. Part I discloses the understanding of interpretation on which the subsequent argument is premised. Part II sets out the central distinction between content-determination and law-ascertainment as interpretive processes. Both the common and distinctive features of law-ascertainment and content-determination processes are discussed here, with a focus on the type of constraints that have been put in place to domesticate them. While constraints on content-determination processes have most of the time been envisaged as 'rules' in mainstream international legal scholarship, constraints on law-ascertainment processes, although often referred to as 'secondary rules', are better seen as indicative of a professional community's practices and traditions. Part III concludes with a few epistemological remarks on the place and the state of the debate on interpretation in contemporary international legal scholarship.

In seeking to analyse the relationship between these two interpretive processes, this chapter neither purports to vindicate any particular method of interpretation,

---

[4] For a classical account, see Hugh Thirlway, *International Customary Law and Codification* (Sijthoff 1972). See also the literature cited and discussed in Jean d'Aspremont, *Formalism and the Sources of International Law* (OUP 2011) 161–74.

nor seeks to offer a general theory of interpretation.[5] Rather, it aims to raise awareness of the multidimensional object(s) of the game of interpretation, and to shed light on the theoretical and practical implications of distinguishing content-determination and law-ascertainment interpretive processes when playing the game of interpretation in international law.

I. Committed Interpretation and the Necessary Feeling of 'Out-There-Ness'

For the purposes of this chapter, interpretation is a performative and constitutive activity in that it contributes to the making of what it purports to find.[6] This means that interpretation is constitutive of international law and the world which international law is supposed to apply to. In the specific context of adjudication, for instance,[7] this understanding implies that interpretation produces both law and fact and the relation between them. The constitutive and performative character of interpretation is uncontroversial,[8] and it is therefore not necessary to dwell upon it. More noteworthy is the contention that, by being constitutive of both the law itself and the world to which the law is meant to apply, interpretation can be either broad or restrictive. Indeed, interpretation can expand the realm of international law by qualifying norms that were previously considered alien to the international legal order as rules of international law. Interpretation can also broaden the ambit of international law by fleshing out the content of existing rules.[9] Conversely, interpretation can be restrictive in that it can strip a rule of law of any meaningful content. Interpretation can also go as far as to deprive a rule of any legal pedigree. Understanding interpretation this way presupposes that international law ought to be construed not only as a set of rules,[10] but also as an argumentative practice aimed at persuading target audiences.[11] Seen in this way,

---

[5] Indeed, it is not clear that such a theorization is possible from the vantage point of international legal theory. However, see Gleider Hernández, 'Interpretation' in Jorg Kammerhofer and Jean d'Aspremont (eds), *International Legal Positivism in a Postmodern World* (CUP 2014) 317.

[6] See Ingo Venzke, 'Post-modern Perspectives on Orthodox Positivism' in Kammerhofer and d'Aspremont (eds), *International Legal Positivism in a Postmodern World*, 182; Nicholas Onuf 'Constructivism: A User's Manual' in Vendulka Kublakova, Nicholas Onuf, and Paul Kowert (eds), *International Relations in a Constructed World* (Sharpe 1998) 59: 'saying is doing; talking is undoubtedly the most important way that we go about making the world what it is'.

[7] For some critical remarks on the tendency of international lawyers to reflect on interpretation solely from the perspective of the judge, see Chapter 2 (Andrea Bianchi).

[8] See HLA Hart, *The Concept of Law* (2nd edn, OUP 1994) 144–50; Hans Kelsen, *Pure Theory of Law* (University of California Press 1967) 348–56.

[9] On the possible agenda behind the expansionist use of interpretation, see Jean d'Aspremont, 'The Politics of Deformalization in International Law' (2011) 3 Go JIL 503.

[10] d'Aspremont, *Formalism and the Sources of International Law*.

[11] Martti Koskenniemi, 'Methodology of International Law' (2007) *Max Planck Encyclopedia of Public International Law*, [1].

interpretation is a ubiquitous phenomenon,[12] with all practices and discourses about international law having an interpretive dimension.[13]

The ubiquitous nature of interpretation explains the confrontational character of the discipline of international law. First, this is because there is no independent meta-criterion allowing the interpreter to choose between methods of interpretation and to validate one as being superior to the other.[14] Whether the question is one of content-determination, law-ascertainment, or establishment of the facts to which these rules are meant to apply, 'it is the consensus in the profession—the invisible college of international lawyers—that determines, at any moment, whether a particular argument is or is not persuasive'.[15] Indeed, there is no validating standard other than the assent of the relevant community.[16] Some choices are held in higher esteem than others in the specific community where they are made,[17] depending on the constant fluctuation of accepted aesthetics and institutional and political dynamics.[18] This is why interpretation should be seen as an act of authority dependent on its ability to induce acceptance by way of argument or persuasion.[19]

Second, the confrontational character of interpretation stems from the fact that each method of interpretation remains unstable and can produce a variety of rules, meanings, or discourses. Indeed, it is a truism that none of the traditional methods of interpretation, whether textualism, intentionalism, or purposivism,[20] can mechanically produce one single stable meaning. Nor can the theory of sources provide full stability in the process of law-ascertainment.[21] In this sense, there seems to be a wide agreement that meaning is constructed and not extracted through interpretation. In other words, interpretation should be seen as evaluative and normative rather than empirical.[22]

---

[12] Cover, 'Nomos and Narrative', 4–5.

[13] Interpretation, in that sense, is said to permeate all of legal life. See Hernández, 'Interpretation'. However, some claim that legal reasoning and interpretation cannot be conflated and that not all legal reasoning involves interpretation: Timothy Endicott, 'Legal Interpretation' in Andrei Marmor (ed), *Routledge Companion to Philosophy of Law* (Routledge 2012) 109.

[14] It has been argued that a purely perspectivist attitude is impossible. See Alasdair MacIntyre, *Whose Justice? Which Rationality?* (Duckworth 1988) 351–2.

[15] Koskenniemi, 'Methodology of International Law'.

[16] See Thomas Kuhn, *The Structure of Scientific Revolutions* (50th anniversary edn, University of Chicago Press 2012).

[17] Martti Koskenniemi, 'Letter to the Editors of the Symposium' (1999) 93 AJIL 351, 353.

[18] Kuhn, *The Structure of Scientific Revolutions*, 155. See also d'Aspremont, 'Wording in International Law'.

[19] Hernández, 'Interpretation'.

[20] Textualism resorts heavily to inductive technique, allowing the interpreter to infer the command from the text itself. According to intentionalism, the interpreter strives to reconstruct the actual intention of the lawmaker. In adopting a purposivist approach, the interpreter purports to continue the legislative task based on the purpose pursued by an idealized legislator in order to give effect to the policy goals pursued in the specific case concerned. See Andrei Marmor, 'Textualism in Context' *USC Gould School of Law Legal Studies Research Paper Series* No 12–13 (18 July 2012).

[21] d'Aspremont, *Formalism and the Sources of International Law*.

[22] George Letsas, 'Strasbourg's Interpretive Ethic: Lessons for the International Lawyer' (2010) 21 EJIL 535.

A third source of confrontation is the absence of any authority in a position to produce a single authoritative interpretation and impose it on all professionals. Indeed, since international law emerged as an academic discipline more than a century ago, no interpretative authority has been able to empower itself as a monopolistic interpretive standard setter for international legal rules. Neither the establishment of a world court nor the *Institut de Droit international*, intended to mirror 'the legal conscience of the civilized world',[23] came to offset the absence of a supreme guardian of interpretation in the epistemic community of international lawyers. Interpretative power in international law has accordingly remained extremely diffuse. It is nowadays scattered between influential and prolific minds affiliated with prestigious research institutions, domestic and international courts, international and regional law-codifying bodies, and, more occasionally, non-governmental organizations (NGOs), which compete with one another for interpretative authority and persuasiveness.[24] As a result, all the interpreters are involved in a difficult and sometimes ruthless struggle,[25] each of them trying to bar the interpretative superiority of the other.[26] The fragmented state of the interpretive space in the argumentative arena of international law inevitably fuels the confrontational nature of the discipline.

For these reasons, one can argue that interpretative disagreements are inherent in the normative universe of international law and that the normative universe of international law is bound to be confrontational.[27] Put shortly, interpretation necessarily yields confrontation in the whole discipline. It makes the profession of, and the production of knowledge in, international law very confrontational at the level of normative and substantive values and at the level of form and procedure.[28]

What is particularly noteworthy is that this confrontation unfolds behind the veil of a quest for what could be termed '*out-there-ness*'. Indeed, there seems to be consensus on the necessity of perpetuating an intuitive, empiricist, and inductive understanding of interpretation as an activity geared towards unearthing what is already *out there*. Accordingly, observers of, and stakeholders in, international adjudicatory processes feel bound to perpetuate the Montesquieuan

---

[23] The authoritative French text reads as follows: 'Il a pour but de favoriser le progrès du droit international. En travaillant à formuler les principes généraux de la science de manière à répondre à la conscience juridique du monde civilisé.' For some critical insights, see Martti Koskenniemi, *The Gentle Civilizer of Nations: The Rise and Fall of International Law 1870–1960* (CUP 2001) 39.

[24] See Chapter 6 (Andraž Zidar), Chapter 7 (Michael Waibel), and Chapter 8 (Gleider Hernández).

[25] See Chapter 2 (Andrea Bianchi).

[26] On the role of legal science and checks and balances, see Alexander Somek, 'The Indelible Science of Law' (2009) 7(3) ICON 424.

[27] For some remarks on the confrontational nature of the discipline, see Sahib Singh, 'International Law as a Technical Discipline: Critical Perspectives on the Narrative Structure of a Theory' in d'Aspremont, *Formalism and the Sources of International Law*, 236–61.

[28] See Gerry Simpson, 'On the Magic Mountain: Teaching Public International Law' (1999) 10 EJIL 70, 78: 'At one time, when societies were relatively homogenous, law could secure agreement through appeal to fundamental shared values or cultural practices or comprehensive moralities. Now the appeal to procedural values or decision-making processes as legitimating devices has replaced the search for substantive agreement on higher order goals.'

or Blackstonian myth of the mechanical extraction of pre-ordained meaning. In other words, everyone repeats that courts do not fight for semantic authority but simply unearth the semantics that are already in the text.[29] The rules of interpretation in the VCLT—the cards of the game that enjoy almost universal social consensus[30]—further buoy this fiction.[31] At least as far as adjudicatory processes are concerned, the above-mentioned confrontation is presented in mechanical and inductive terms, probably because this is a necessary twist to preserve the authority and legitimacy of such processes.[32] Yet it remains that, for the purposes of this chapter, the confrontation at stake in the whole discipline, including in adjudicatory processes, is better understood as an argumentative battle for semantic authority.[33]

Interpretation is thus discussed in this chapter in its multifaceted manifestations: as a commitment; as being constitutive of the world to which it purports to apply; as being omnipresent in the practice of international law; as breeding a pervasive confrontation between professionals; and as an activity geared toward the extraction of the meaning *out there*. The central argument, however, remains that interpretation is not a homogenous and one-dimensional phenomenon. Tearing off the veil of unicity in which interpretation is too often shrouded constitutes a necessary prerequisite to grasp the most fascinating and challenging theoretical, doctrinal, and normative issues which the game of interpretation in international law raises.

II. A Dichotomic View on the Game of Interpretation

This section puts forward a conceptual dichotomy that helps foster a multidimensional understanding of interpretation. This dichotomy calls for a move away from a monolithic concept of interpretation in international law and reveals—as much as it creates—a whole new range of questions and issues of law, power, and authority, as well as indeterminacy-mitigating techniques. This means that the dichotomy put forward here simultaneously carries the epistemological project of redefining the agenda of studies on interpretation in international law, as is explained in the last section of this chapter.[34]

---

[29] For a compelling contemporary challenge of this mainstream view, see Ingo Venzke, *How Interpretation Makes International Law: On Semantic Change and Normative Twists* (OUP 2012).

[30] See Part III below.

[31] For some critical remarks in this respect, see Hernández, 'Interpretation'.

[32] That does not mean that the formalist position is necessarily an easy or convenient one. It 'is not merely a linguistic doctrine, but a doctrine that implies, in addition to a theory of language, a theory of the self, of community, of rationality, of practice, of politics': Stanley Fish, *Doing What Comes Naturally: Change, Rhetoric, and the Practice of Theory in Literary and Legal Studies* (Duke University Press 1989) 6 (referring to Roberto Unger).

[33] See d'Aspremont, 'Wording in International Law'; Venzke, *How Interpretation Makes International Law*.

[34] It should be noted that the multidimensional approach to interpretation advocated here is not fundamentally groundbreaking. Ronald Dworkin famously identified several interpretative stages: *Law's Empire* (Harvard University Press 1986), 65–7. See Chapter 4 (Duncan Hollis).

As argued in the previous section, interpretation is a ubiquitous, performative, and constitutive activity conducive to the confrontational nature of the discipline. It produces the law as well as the facts, and the relation (and potential conflicts) between them. Yet even if it is taken as a ubiquitous activity constitutive of the whole discipline, it does not mean that interpretation is a homogenous and unitary phenomenon. Rather, the central argument of this chapter is that two specific types of interpretive processes must be distinguished: interpretive processes geared towards the determination of the content of rules and interpretive processes aimed at the ascertainment of the rules themselves.

According to the first of these interpretive processes, a judge interprets the law which she is empowered to apply, with a view to determining—or creating according to a Kelsenian account—the applicable standard of behaviour or the normative guideline for the case of which she is seized. This is interpretation for content-determination purposes, which is certainly not an activity reserved to the judge. Any professional dealing with international law will engage in content-determination.[35] Yet it is within the context of adjudication that content-determination interpretation is the most visible.

There is a distinct interpretive process whereby any professional is also called upon to interpret the pedigree of rules in order to ascertain whether a given rule can claim to be part of the international legal order. This will usually involve the interpretation of a doctrine of sources of law. Significantly, this interpretive process of rule-ascertainment cannot be conflated with that of content-determination. The main point to be made here is that our understanding of interpretation should not be limited to content-determination.

This particular distinction between content-determination processes and law-ascertainment processes is crucial to understand the concept and the practice of interpretation as well as international law as a whole. Mainstream studies of interpretation in international law look almost exclusively at the content-determination interpretation process. However, interpretation should not be understood as a content-determination technique only. What qualifies as law itself involves an act of interpretation. When ascertaining the law, the judge, counsel, academic, activist, adviser, or even the remote observer necessarily interprets some pre-existing—and sometimes unconsciously inherited—standards of identification of law.

Readers may find that the above-mentioned dichotomy is reminiscent of another distinction, namely that the interpretation of primary norms must be distinguished from the interpretation of the rules of recognition.[36] The resemblance

[35] On some of the cross-cutting professional dynamics affecting all those who are involved in the business of argumentation about international law, see d'Aspremont, 'Wording in International Law'.
[36] On the traditional use of this classical distinction made by HLA Hart in international law, see Jean Combacau and Denis Alland, 'Primary and Secondary Rules in the Law of State Responsibility Categorizing International Obligations' (1985) 16 NYIL 81. For some critical remarks on Hart and international law, see Jean d'Aspremont, 'Herbert Hart in Today's International Legal Scholarship' in Jörg Kammerhofer and Jean d'Aspremont (eds), *International Legal Positivism in a Post-Modern World* (CUP 2014) 114.

to the distinction between primary and secondary rules further confirms—rather than contradicts—the possibility and necessity of distinguishing between the interpretation of primary standards (content-determination) and those standards that determine what constitutes valid law to interpret (law-ascertainment).

It must again be highlighted that singling out these two specific interpretive processes is not meant to exhaust and capture the whole phenomenon of interpretation. For example, facts are also the object of several types of interpretive processes.[37] The facts falling within the scope of the exercise of authority of a judge must be apprehended and given a meaning in relation to the rule that is invoked and for which the judge concerned has authority. The exclusion of factual interpretation is probably what distinguishes the argument made here from that made by Duncan Hollis in this volume.[38] This chapter excludes interpretation of facts, even if such interpretation of facts sometimes comes with an existential dimension, as is the case with the determination of state practice in relation to customary international law. When this chapter refers to law-ascertainment interpretation, it means interpretation of the formal or non-formal law-ascertainment yardsticks according to which international legal rules are identified, to the exclusion of the interpretation of facts having a law-ascertaining value.

Although not groundbreaking, the dichotomy presented here is far from being self-evident. It often remains tempting to conflate content-determination and law-ascertainment, or at least to approach them as being part of exactly the same interpretive phenomenon. This is not surprising, for these two interpretive processes have much in common. Part II(A) sketches out some of the elements of resemblance between the two interpretive processes. However, these elements of resemblance do not at all put into question the overarching dichotomy. Part II(B) goes on to review the main distinguishing factors between content-determination and law-ascertainment.

A. Elements of resemblance: behaviour, authority, power, formalization, instability of meaning

Content-determination and law-ascertainment interpretations share many similar features. These common characteristics explain why they cannot always be easily distinguished. The difficulty in distinguishing them is exacerbated by the fact that they may operate simultaneously in practice. This is true with respect to application of the mainstream doctrine of customary international law, whereby the ascertainment of customary law and the determination of its content are simultaneous operations. It could even be argued that when the ascertainment of law is a matter of ascertainment of facts, like in the mainstream doctrine of customary international law, the distinction loses its explanatory force.

---

[37] See Jean d'Aspremont and Makane Mbengue, 'Strategies of Engagement with Scientific Fact-Finding in International Adjudication' (2014) 5(2) JIDS 240.
[38] See Chapter 4 (Duncan Hollis).

The main areas of resemblance between content-determination and law-ascertainment interpretation processes are the following. First, both content-determination and law-ascertainment processes are interpretive activities of a delineating and definitional nature with respect to the type of behaviour allowed in the international legal order. In other words, these two interpretive processes seek to define the lawful and the non-lawful, reflecting what Fleur Johns describes as 'the tendency to try to confer upon international law some delimited time, space and subject matter for its "proper" (albeit not autonomous) operation'.[39] They are part of the 'practices of references, spatialisation and temporalisation through which international lawyers convey a sense of what may be opposed to international legal compliance'.[40]

Second, both content-determination and law-ascertainment processes are instrumental in the constitution of the authority of both international law and international legal arguments. Indeed, the theories and techniques that are used in a content-determination or law-ascertainment operation—that is usually a theory of interpretation for the former and a theory of sources for the latter—are conducive to determining the authority of legal argumentation in general, and that of scholarly studies and judicial decisions in particular. In that sense, exactly like methods, style, and aesthetics, they are constitutive elements of the 'machine for the production of statements' in international law.[41] They both provide 'rules of discourse-production'[42] that will locate and validate an argument in the discipline's order of truth, within the normative universe of international law.

Third, both processes are the theatre of a power struggle as much as they are manifestations of power. Both content-determination and law-ascertainment processes are constituted by and constitutive of power. This Foucauldian and Marxist understanding of content-determination and law-ascertainment interpretive processes is probably not controversial.[43] It has long been recognized that it is in formal categories that real power resides despite them seeming 'simply descriptive of independent realities'.[44] This means that there is an inherent hegemonic dimension in each of these interpretive processes. Each of them seeks the universalization of meaning in relation to the specific context in which interpretation occurs.[45] The winner of the interpretive confrontation succeeds in establishing her own rule-of-use for the specific community where the interpretation takes place.[46]

---

[39] Fleur Johns, *Non-Legality in International Law—Unruly Law* (CUP 2013) 8.

[40] Johns, *Non-Legality in International Law*, 22.

[41] Mario Prost, *The Concept of Unity in Public International Law* (Hart 2012) 149.

[42] Prost, *The Concept of Unity in Public International Law*, 149.

[43] Wendy Brown, 'Power After Foucault' in John Dryzek Bonnie Honig, and Anne Phillips (eds), *Oxford Handbook of Political Theory* (OUP 2008) 65.

[44] Fish, *Doing What Comes Naturally*, 23–4.

[45] See Martti Koskenniemi, 'Hegemonic Regimes' in Margaret Young (ed), *Regime Interaction in International Law* (CUP 2012) 305.

[46] See Dietrich Busse, 'Semantic Strategies as a Means of Politics' in Pertti Ahonen (ed), *Tracing the Semiotic Boundaries of Politics* (de Gruyter 1993) 122–3. See the discussion by Venzke, 'Postmodern Perspectives on Orthodox Positivism'.

Fourth, both processes fail to create stable meaning and knowledge about what law prescribes and to rein in indeterminacy. This is not to say that they leave the indeterminacy of the law unaffected.[47] It is more that both content-determination and law-ascertainment contribute to creating indeterminacy itself. Indeed, indeterminacy is not determinable in the abstract.[48] There is no such thing as context-less indeterminacy that is the simple corollary of the absence of an a priori meaning of language. Indeterminacy is itself a product of interpretation and as such it is derived from the individual and collective context as well as the predispositions of the interpreter.[49]

Fifth, since they fail to produce stable meaning, both content-determination and law-ascertainment processes have been the objects of formalization by international lawyers. International legal scholars have long tried to offset the instability of the meaning of rules by a sometimes naive formalization of the techniques and methods attendant on the interpretive process. It is noteworthy that this attempted formalization has not been the same for content-determination and law-ascertainment, demonstrating the extent to which the two processes are distinct. As far as content-determination is concerned, attempts to formalize such a process have manifested themselves in theories of interpretation hinging upon a subtle balance between textualist, intentionalist, and purposivist methods. The VCLT can be seen as the embodiment of such an attempt to formalize the methods and techniques of content-determination. In the case of law-ascertainment, formalization has materialized in the doctrine of sources being portrayed as a formal enunciation of the pedigree of rules despite the contradictory but uncontested resort to intent or state practice as law-ascertainment yardsticks.[50] None of the attempts to formalize the methods or techniques of content-determination or law-ascertainment have been very successful.[51]

While there are important elements of resemblance, the endeavour to formalize the constraints on these two interpretive processes point to structural and systemic differences between content-determination and law-ascertainment interpretive processes. Indeed, irrespective of their practical impact, the nature of the constraints envisaged by international lawyers for each of these interpretive processes varies fundamentally. This is the subject of the next subsection.

---

[47] For a taxonomy of different types of indeterminacy, see the distinction made between ordinary vagueness, transparent vagueness, and extravagant vagueness: Andrei Marmor, 'Varieties of Vagueness in the Law' *USC Legal Studies Research Paper* No 12-8, 18 July 2013.

[48] Singh, 'International Law as a Technical Discipline'.

[49] Andrea Bianchi argues that the interpretive process is 'deeply embedded in a societal context where different actors interact with one another': 'Textual Interpretation and (International) Law Reading: The Myth of (In)Determinancy and the Genealogy of Meaning' in Pieter Bekker, Rudolf Dolzer, and Michael Waibel (eds), *Making Transnational Law Work in the Global Economy—Essays in Honour of Detlev Vagts* (CUP 2010) 35.

[50] d'Aspremont, *Formalism and the Sources of International Law* (arguing that in the mainstream theory of sources, ascertainment is not properly formal as, for both custom-identification and treaty-identification, it rests on non-formal criteria like intent or state practice).

[51] I have argued that the formalization attempted by the mainstream theory of sources was a sham: d'Aspremont, *Formalism and the Sources of International Law*.

B. Elements of dissimilarity: functions and constraints

It goes without saying that the semantics of the proposed dichotomy already indicates a functional divergence between content-determination and law-ascertainment. Even though both content-determination and law-ascertainment processes are interpretive activities of a delineating and definitional nature, each process performs a different function. The former purports to elucidate the content of rules with a view to determining the standard of behaviour or normative guidance provided by them. The latter seeks to determine whether a given norm qualifies as a legal rule and can claim to be part of the international legal order. In other words, the former is intended to produce meaning and a standard of conduct, while the latter is intended to produce a binary structure of ascertainment that distinguishes between law and non-law. This functional criterion is the one that Duncan Hollis' chapter in this volume uses to ground the distinction between the two interpretive processes.[52]

The distinction between content-determination and law-ascertainment need not only be upheld in functional terms. The varying argumentative authority among international law professionals may also be explained in terms of this distinction. In particular, the authority that one may enjoy with respect to content-determination may not necessarily be the same as far as law-ascertainment is concerned. For instance, the voice of the activist might be heard when it comes to the content of international legal rules while her interpretive influence in terms of ascertaining international legal rules may be very thin. The international legal scholar may find herself in exactly the opposite situation. The international judge, in turn, may enjoy distinct clout with respect to both interpretive processes, not to mention the interpretation of facts. The same probably holds true for the International Law Commission. This should suffice to show that each interpretive process comes with a different distribution of authority among professionals involved in the interpretation of international law.

However, the main structural difference between content-determination and law-ascertainment lies in the very nature of the constraints curtailing the interpreter's interpretive freedom. More specifically, it is submitted that the constraints on content-determination interpretation have usually been construed as disciplining rules in mainstream legal scholarship, whereas those restricting law-ascertainment interpretation proceed from practice and tradition.

This structural tension between disciplining rules and social practices and traditions is certainly not new. It is reminiscent of a debate that goes well beyond the study of interpretation in international law, epitomized by the famous disagreement between Owen Fiss[53] and Stanley Fish,[54] which Ronald Dworkin[55] and

---

[52] See Chapter 4 (Duncan Hollis).

[53] Owen Fiss, 'Objectivity and Interpretation' (1982) 34 Stan L Rev 739; Owen Fiss, 'The Jurisprudence (!) of Stanley Fish' (1985) 80 ADE Bulletin 1.

[54] Stanley Fish, 'Fish v. Fiss' (1984) 36 Stan L Rev 1325.

[55] Ronald Dworkin, 'My Reply to Stanley Fish (and Walter Benn Michaels): Please Don't Talk About Objectivity Any More' in WJT Mitchell (ed), *The Politics of Interpretation* (University of Chicago Press 1983) 287.

Pierre Schlag[56] later contributed to. Needless to say, it would be of no avail to rehash those classic arguments here. This chapter only seeks to make the point that the structural differences between content-determination and law-ascertainment hinges upon the same contours of that debate. As a result, references to this traditional confrontation are inevitable.

One last remark must be made before the constraints on content-determination and law-ascertainment are spelt out. Although the constraints imposed upon each process diverge, there seems to be some consensus as to the origin of those constraints. Subject to some notable exceptions that are discussed in Ingo Venzke's chapter in this volume,[57] the constraints on each interpretive process are largely the product of a community. Yet despite ample support for the idea that constraints on each interpretive process originate in the professional community of international law, there is much disagreement as to the form that such constraints should take.

1. *The disciplining rules constraining content-determination interpretation*

As noted above, mainstream international legal scholarship has always promoted a predominantly rule-based approach to interpretation, in the sense that the interpretive process of content-determination must be based on formal rules. This is the overall model provided by the VCLT, which purports to provide formal rules for the interpretation of treaties. Although other international legal acts are subject to different and specific regimes of content-determination interpretation,[58] a rule-based approach has also prevailed when it comes to the content-determination of non-treaty legal acts. These rules are meant to operate as formal constraints on interpretive freedom. As Andrea Bianchi puts it, the 'current reflection of mainstream international legal scholarship remains imbued with traditional rule-based approaches to legal interpretation'.[59]

Formal constraints on content-determination interpretation can be of several types. In mainstream international legal scholarship, these formal constraints can be either textualist, intentionalist, purposivist, or a combination of the three,

---

[56] Pierre Schlag, 'Fish v. Zapp, The Case of the Relatively Autonomous Self' (1987) 76 Geo L J 36.

[57] See Donald Davidson, 'A Nice Derangement of Epitaphs' in AP Martinich (ed), *The Philosophy of Language* (3rd edn, OUP 1996) 465. Davidson rejects the idea that language and meaning are governed by conventions, arguing that conventions are not necessary for communication to be successful and that communication can do without conventions.

[58] *Accordance with International Law of the Unilateral Declaration of Independence in Respect of Kosovo* (Advisory Opinion) [2010] ICJ Rep 403, [94]. See Efthymois Papstavridis, 'Interpretation of Security Council Resolutions under Chapter VII in the Aftermath of the Iraqi Crisis' (2007) 56 ICLQ 83.

[59] Bianchi, 'Textual Interpretation and (International) Law Reading'. This presupposes a *horror vacui* argument according to Jan Klabbers: 'Reluctant Grundnormen: Article 31(3)(c) and 42 of the Vienna Convention on the Law of Treaties and the Fragmentation of International Law' in Matthew Craven, Malgosia Fitzmaurice, and Maria Vogiatzi (eds), *Time, History and International Law* (Brill 2007) 141, 160.

as put forward by the VCLT. It is of no avail to dwell on the substance of the constraints that these rules seek to impose on the interpreter. Likewise, for the purposes of our analysis, it does not matter whether they are *legal* rules properly so-called, or merely guiding principles or directives,[60] as their legal force is unlikely to affect their potential for yielding constraints. The doubts expressed by some of the drafters of the VCLT are worth recalling in this respect. For instance, Alfred Verdross raised the question of the nature of the rules of interpretation which the International Law Commission intended to codify, arguing that 'the Commission ought first to decide whether it recognised the existence of such rules'.[61] In his view, 'it was highly controversial whether the rules established by the case-law of arbitral tribunals and international courts were general rules of international law or merely technical rules'.[62] In the same vein, Sir Humphrey Waldock conceded that he 'was decidedly lukewarm on rules on interpretation, including them more because he thought this was expected of him than out of genuine expectation that rules on interpretation would be of much use'.[63]

Rather than the substance or binding character of such rules, what matters for the sake of the argument made here is the *form* of the constraints on content-determination interpretation. They are largely thought of as rules by mainstream international law scholarship. This is precisely where one is bound to revive the debate between Owen Fiss and Stanley Fish mentioned above. Indeed, if construed as rules by the mainstream international legal scholarship, such constraints on content-determination interpretation correspond to what Fiss calls 'disciplining rules'.[64]

Yet, if they are thought of as 'disciplining rules', irrespective of their substance and binding character, such constraints on content-determination meet the fundamental objection of an infinite regress made by Fish, according to which such rules themselves need interpretive constraints which in turn also need another set of interpretive constraints.[65] The objection against disciplining rules of interpretation is that the criteria to which rules of interpretation refer cannot themselves be exempted from interpretation.[66] For Fish, such rules 'are in need of interpretation and cannot themselves serve as constraints on interpretation'.[67] This objection led Fish to understand constraints on interpretation not as rules but as practices of an interpretive community. This is also what allows us to differentiate constraints

---

[60] Isabelle Van Damme, *Treaty Interpretation by the WTO Appellate Body* (OUP 2009) 35.

[61] ILC, 726th Meeting, A/CN.4/167 reproduced in (1964) I ILC Ybk 20–21, [15].

[62] ILC, 726th Meeting, A/CN.4/167 reproduced in (1964) I ILC Ybk 20–21, [15].

[63] Jan Klabbers, 'Virtuous Interpretation' in Malgosia Fitzmaurice, Olufemi Elias, and Panos Merkouris (eds), *Treaty Interpretation and the Vienna Convention on the Law of Treaties: 30 Years On* (Martinus Nijhoff, 2010) 17, 18.

[64] Fiss, 'Objectivity and Interpretation'.

[65] See Chapter 17 (Ingo Venzke); Venzke, 'Post-modern Perspectives on Orthodox Positivism'. See also Letsas, 'Strasbourg's Interpretive Ethic', 534.

[66] Bianchi, 'Textual Interpretation and (International) Law Reading', 48. This is a criticism made by HLA Hart, *The Concept of Law* (2nd edn, OUP 1994) 126. For some mitigating factors, see Hernández, 'Interpretation'.

[67] Fish, 'Fish v. Fiss'.

on content-determination interpretation from constraints on law-ascertainment interpretation, as explained below.

2. The social practice and tradition constraining law-ascertainment interpretation

In contrast to the rule-based approach to binding constraints on content-determination interpretation, questions about the nature of constraints on law-ascertainment have been almost ignored by mainstream international legal scholarship.[68] It is as if international legal scholarship had decided to restrict interpretation to content-determination processes.[69] Constraints on law-ascertainment processes have only been the object of attention in relation to the argument that they cannot be distinguished from content-determination interpretation.[70]

In the absence of any studies to rely on, one could be tempted to construe constraints on law-ascertainment interpretation similarly to the mainstream understanding of constraints placed on content-determination interpretation. This rule-based understanding of constraints on law-ascertainment interpretation would correspond to the common wisdom that the theory of sources constitute a set of 'secondary rules' of international law, which, at face value, seems to equate these systemic principles to rules properly so-called. This is also the impression generated by Article 38 of the Statute of the International Court of Justice, which is often regarded as the gospel in terms of law-ascertainment.[71] This type of constraint would engender the infinite regress objection, given the need for rules on the interpretation of secondary rules in international law.[72] The argument offered here is that constraints on law-ascertainment interpretation should rather be construed as a community practice.

I have argued elsewhere that the pedigree requirements prescribed by the doctrine of sources, which provides the criteria by which law-ascertainment interpretation is carried out, originates in social practice.[73] Law-ascertainment is a practice whereby the community of law-applying authorities shares some linguistic signs to determine its object of study, and its objects of agreement and disagreement. The social practice of law-applying authorities is thus embedded in a larger community sharing common signs of communication. I would like to extend this argument by submitting that this specific social understanding of the sources of international law allows one to move away from a rule-based understanding of constraints

---

[68] See Chapter 4 (Duncan Hollis).

[69] I have not engaged with interpretation in my study of law-ascertainment: d'Aspremont, *Formalism and the Sources of International Law.*

[70] See eg Olivier Corten, *Méthodologie du droit international public* (Université Libre de Bruxelles 2009) 213–15.

[71] See Alain Pellet, 'Article 38' in Andreas Zimmermann, Christian Tomuschat, Karin Oellers-Frahm, and Christian Tams (eds), *The Statute of the International Court of Justice: A Commentary* (OUP 2006) 731.

[72] Venzke, 'Post-modern Perspectives on Orthodox Positivism'.

[73] d'Aspremont, *Formalism and the Sources of International Law.*

on law-ascertainment interpretation (and hence a rule-based understanding of the sources themselves).

This notion of a community in which the social practice of law-applying authorities takes place is where the objections raised by Fish against Fiss have real purchase. Fish famously contended that rules are not necessary to constrain interpretation processes.[74] For him, it is a mistake 'to think of interpretation as an activity in need of constraints, when in fact interpretation is a structure of constraints'.[75] Fish considered that 'practice is already principled, since at every moment it is ordered by an understanding of what is practice (the law, basketball), an understanding that can always be put into the form of rules—rules that will be opaque to the outsider—but is not produced by them'.[76] He suggests that meanings 'do not proceed from an isolated individual but from a public and conventional point of view'.[77] This public and conventional point of view is what Fish has famously identified with the 'interpretive community'.[78]

The concept of interpretive community does not need to be addressed at great length here. What is worth mentioning is that the idea of interpretive communities makes constraints on interpretation a question of 'knowledge', rather than being referable to a 'list' of rules.[79] At the same time, the concept of interpretive community allows one to understand the social practice in which constraints on law-ascertainment interpretation originate as being principled, without falling into the indeterminacy and infinite regress of rules argument.[80] In other words, it makes it possible to reject rule-based constraints on law-ascertainment interpretation while avoiding complete sceptical or relativist positions concerning interpretation.[81]

---

[74] Stanley Fish objects to disciplining rules on the basis that they are not necessary because the reader and texts are not in need of the constraints that disciplining rules would provide: 'The trainee is not only possessed of but possessed by a knowledge of the ropes, by a tacit knowledge that tells him not so much what to do, but already has him doing it as a condition of perception and even of thought'. See Fish, 'Fish v. Fiss', 1333.

[75] Stanley Fish, *Is There A Text in This Class? The Authority of Interpretive Communities* (Harvard University Press 1980) 356.

[76] Fish, 'Fish v. Fiss', 1331–2.   [77] Fish, *Is There A Text in This Class?*, 14.

[78] Fish, *Is There A Text in This Class?*, 14: 'The relationship between interpretation and text is thus reversed: interpretive strategies are not put into execution after reading; they are the shape of reading, and because they are the shape of reading, they give texts their shape, making them rather than, as is usually assumed, arising from them' (13). According to Fish, these 'interpretive strategies' do not make the reader an independent agent. They 'proceed not from him but from the interpretive community of which he is a member'.

[79] Fish, 'Fish v. Fiss', 1329. Cf Judith Schelly, 'Interpretation in Law: The Dworkin-Fish Debate (or Soccer amongst the Gahuku-Gama)' (1985) 73 Cal L Rev 158, 163–4. According to Schelly, Fish and Dworkin both agree that authority for interpretation derives from a process that is complex, communal, and political. The ultimate difference between them is that, for Dworkin, morality ultimately constrains interpretation, whereas for Fish, epistemic communities are subject to political rather than moral constraints.

[80] Dworkin famously conceived of interpretation as a social and communitarian practice, likening the role of the interpreter to a chain novelist. See Ronald Dworkin, 'Law as Interpretation' (1982) 9 Critical Inquiry 179. However, Fish argues that the interpreter is not constrained by the past but recreates it. See Stanley Fish, 'Working on the Chain Gang: Interpretation in the Law and in Literary Criticism' (1982) 9 Critical Inquiry 201.

[81] See MacIntyre, *Whose Justice?*, 352.

It is true that the community and the constraints it produces are 'not fixed and finite',[82] thereby making constraints on law-ascertainment rather unstable. Fish writes that 'interpretive communities are no more stable than texts because interpretive strategies are not natural or universal, but learned'.[83] However, this community-constraining practice is not fully indeterminate and inevitably comes with an element of continuity. Indeed, communitarian practice, as Alasdair MacIntyre taught us, comes with an element of tradition which involves the practice of the past and its constant re-writing. According to that view, each actor 'contributes to the content of the tradition that develops' and continuously adjusts it to the needs of the time.[84] Interpretation is accordingly anchored in a pattern inherited from the past which is then reconstructed.[85]

This relative instability of social constraints on interpretation could be seen as conferring a welcome flexibility that 'allows for [a] significant degree of conflict and dissent'.[86] As Mark Mitchell contends when commenting on MacIntyre's and Michael Polanyi's concept of tradition, 'entering into a tradition requires an act of submission to an authority'.[87] One's submission to authority, however, does not need to be absolute or completely unquestioning. According to that view, tradition leaves intact the possibility of dissent.[88] Understanding the origin of constraints on law-ascertainment interpretation thus allows such constraints to accommodate uncertainty without putting communication between professionals in peril. What is more, it is this lack of complete certainty about the maxims of conversation that enables the success of communication in spite of certain divergences in communicative expectations or intentions. The lack of certainty 'leaves certain content hanging in the air, as it were, leaving each party to the conversation with an option of understanding the full communicated content somewhat differently'.[89]

The social approach to constraints on law-ascertainment interpretation advocated here, grounded in practice and tradition, is neither conceptually watertight nor a theoretical panacea. This account, like the rule-based approach to content-determination, has not been spared from controversy. For instance, Fiss has famously objected that '[j]ust as one cannot understand or formulate

[82] Fish, 'Fish v. Fiss', 1329.   [83] Fish, *Is There A Text in This Class?*, 172.

[84] Mark Mitchell, 'Michael Polanyi, Alasdair MacIntyre, and the Role of Tradition' (2006) 19 Humanitas 97, 104–5 (referring to Michael Polanyi, *Personal Knowledge: Towards a Post Critical Philosophy* (Routledge 1958) 160).

[85] Martti Koskenniemi, 'Constitutionalism as Mindset: Reflections on Kantian Themes about International Law and Globalization' (2006) 8 Theo Inq L 9, 22: 'This is what traditions do: they try to accommodate new phenomena in patterned, familiar understandings, seeking to balance reverence for the past with openness to the future, with innovators sometimes rejected as degraders, sometimes celebrated as regenerators.'

[86] Polanyi as described by Mitchell, 'Michael Polanyi', 106.

[87] Mitchell, 'Michael Polanyi', 106.   [88] Mitchell, 'Michael Polanyi', 106.

[89] Andrei Marmor, 'Can the Law Imply More than it Says? On Some Pragmatic Aspects of Strategic Speech' in Andrei Marmor and Scott Soames (eds), *Philosophical Foundations of Language in the Law* (OUP 2011) 83.

rules unless one is a participant in the practice, so one cannot participate successfully within the practice known as law...unless one is able to understand or formulate the rules governing the practice'.[90] This alludes to the impossibility of standardizing the constraints. Fiss goes on to suggest that, since Fish 'rejects the disciplining rules—or any general normative standards—he is left without any basis for resolving conflicting interpretations in any principled way'.[91] Schlag has also denounced the failure by Fish to define the set of constraints generated by the interpretive community. According to Schlag, Fish shies away from such a definition because such a descriptive exercise would condemn Fish to produce a text which would give a contradictory spin to his argument. For Schlag, Fish's notion of interpretive community is a pure convenience as it allows him to resist deconstruction.[92] Others have also seen an element of circularity in the concept of interpretive community.[93]

This is certainly not the place to resolve such controversies or salvage either Fiss' or Fish's accounts of constraints on interpretation. For present purposes, the point is that the non-rule-based conception of constraints on law-ascertainment seems the only viable direction in which law-ascertainment can possibly operate. If constraints on law-ascertainment were to be construed as rules, that would condemn the identification of international law (and, in my view, the discipline as a whole) to remain in a state of flux, thereby precluding the possibility of communication between professionals.[94]

As indicated above, besides promoting a distinction between content-determination and law-ascertainment, this chapter makes a normative claim about how law-ascertainment ought to be understood. It invites international legal scholars and practitioners to apprehend and understand constraints on law-ascertainment interpretation as the social practice of an interpretive community rather than a set of rules, in contrast to the mainstream rule-based approach to constraints on content-determination interpretation. Such a normative agenda lends itself to the criticisms of those who believe that the resort to tradition (like any social practice) makes international lawyers more indulgent when it comes to the deficiencies of international law.[95] This is certainly true, but is only problematic to the extent that the international lawyer thinks of herself as a reformer.

In the end, the way in which constraints on content-determination and law-ascertainment interpretation are understood and operate does not matter much for the purposes of the dichotomy put forward in this chapter. The mere fact that constraints on content-determination and law-ascertainment can be construed

---

[90] Fiss, 'Objectivity and Interpretation', 2.
[91] Fiss, 'Objectivity and Interpretation', 2.   [92] Schlag, 'Fish v. Zapp', 42–9.
[93] For both Polanyi and MacIntyre, 'belief must necessarily precede knowing'. This necessarily brings about circularity because one must commit oneself to certain premises and the conclusions one reaches are necessarily entailed by the premises embraced. See Mitchell, 'Michael Polanyi', 109–11.
[94] See d'Aspremont, *Formalism and the Sources of International Law*.
[95] Frédéric Megret, 'International Law as Law' in James Crawford and Martti Koskenniemi (eds), *Cambridge Companion to International Law* (CUP 2012) 64, 77.

differently, at least from a theoretical perspective, suffices to show that the object of the game of interpretation must be regarded as multidimensional.

III. Conclusion: Salvaging the Game of Interpretation?

Dichotomies, like the one described in this chapter, are by their very nature exclusive and constitutive. They rest on a binary construction of the world and reject a more all-inclusive approach to the phenomenon of interpretation. Moreover, the embrace of such a dichotomy is not neutral but it is informed by conceptual and methodological choices, which, in turn, are determined by some normative agenda and by intellectual preferences. Some of these preferences have been disclosed in the previous sections. In particular, it should now be clear to the reader that the reason for inviting international legal theorists to distinguish between content-determination and law-ascertainment interpretive processes is derived from an overarching normative desire to preserve the possibility of communication between professionals involved in argumentation about international law. It is a desire to make the game of interpretation possible in the first place.

As this chapter draws to a close, another dimension of the distinction between content-determination and law-ascertainment interpretive processes is worth addressing, namely its particular epistemological agenda. The dichotomy advocated here has the ambition to bring a new dimension to the debate about interpretation in international law. As was repeatedly indicated above, international legal scholarship has long restricted its study of interpretation to content-determination, thereby failing to pay any attention to the interpretive processes at play in law-ascertainment. This restrictive focus on content-determination interpretation in international legal studies—and thus on only one aspect of the object of the game of interpretation—is what prompts the following final observations.

Content-determination interpretation continues to occupy a prominent place in the research agenda of international lawyers. Half a dozen monographs have been produced on interpretation in international law in recent years.[96] This is not to mention scholarly articles and book chapters. Unsurprisingly, most of them continue to be prejudiced by the rule-based approach fostered by the VCLT, discussed above. These studies on the content-determination interpretive process continue to be caught in the infinite regress affecting the rule-based approach. Interestingly, such an objection does not seem to suffice to prompt a paradigmatic change in international legal studies. International legal scholars continue, generation after generation, to study content-determination interpretation from a rule-based perspective, thereby repeating the same inconclusive paradigmatic move made by previous generations. In my view, broadening the scope of international legal studies on interpretation by including law-ascertainment interpretive processes would help international

---

[96] See Michael Waibel, 'Demystifying the Art of Interpretation' (2011) 22 EJIL 571.

lawyers emancipate themselves from the prison of a rule-based approach to constraints on interpretation, and could help them both realize the limits of their current conceptual framework and engage in a critical reflection about the paradigms they use.

Refusal to engage with this broader view of interpretive processes risks relegating international legal scholarship to the hamster wheel of studies on content-determination interpretation, where the rules, rather than the practice of, interpretation is the perpetual focus.[97] It must be acknowledged that training and exercising skills has self-educational virtue in itself. By running indefinitely in the hamster wheel of content-determination interpretation, the techniques to secure persuasiveness and argumentative authority within the professional community of international law may be enhanced. Furthermore, this may provide international lawyers with thoughts, insights, and self-reflections on foundational questions in the social sciences like the relationship between fact and norm, the performativity of language, the tensions between textualism and arbitrariness, and some aspects of a theory of knowledge.

Irrespective of the undisputed virtues of exercising in the hamster wheel, however, one may wonder whether it is worth continuing to write articles, research papers, monographs, and edited collections on the theme of interpretation if the only resulting virtue is self-education. It only makes sense for studies on interpretation in international law to remain on the research agenda if international lawyers are prepared to open their eyes to other interpretive processes at work in international law, thereby seizing a chance to emancipate themselves from the circularity of rule-based approaches to interpretation. This is a necessary step if one wants to salvage studies about interpretation in international law. This is also one of the lofty goals of this volume, which is, in my view, an enterprise that is worth undertaking.

---

[97] See David Kennedy, 'When Renewal Repeats: Thinking Against the Box' (2000) 32 NYU J Int'l L & Pol 335.

PART III
THE PLAYERS

6

Interpretation and the International Legal Profession

Between Duty and Aspiration

Andraž Zidar*

Introduction

The aim of this chapter is to provide an overview of the contributions of the major players in the game of interpretation in international law. These players have a role in the process of generating the meaning of international legal texts, which is emphasized by the pluralistic and fluid nature of international law in its present form.[1]

Part I of the chapter characterizes interpretation in international law as an open-textured and dynamic process. Central to this process are various categories of legal professionals that form an interpretive community. Part II surveys the role and contribution of these players in the interpretation of international norms. It focuses on the following professional communities: legal advisers, NGO lawyers, judges, academics, and litigators. A survey of all these professions points to some obvious differences, but also reveals surprising similarities in their approach to legal interpretation. Drawing inspiration from the work of Lon Fuller, the contribution concludes by highlighting the dialectic between the duty to fulfil a professional role and a commitment to the international legal system that shapes the interpretive approach of actors within the system.

* The author wishes to thank Robert McCorquodale, Hadrian Tulk, Catherine Gibson, and the editors of this book for useful suggestions in preparing this contribution.

[1] Kazuko Kawaguchi, *A Social Theory of International Law* (Martinus Nijhoff 2003) 113. On the pluralist nature of international law, see Nico Krisch, *Beyond Constitutionalism: The Pluralist Structure of Postnational Law* (OUP 2010) and Paul Schiff Berman, *Global Legal Pluralism: A Jurisprudence of Law beyond Borders* (CUP 2012).

I. Interpretation of International
Law as a Complex Process

Traditionally, jurisprudence makes a clear distinction between interpretation by legal professionals who are in a position of legal authority, and those who are not. Judges, in particular, enjoy a privileged position when it comes to the interpretation of legal texts. According to Hans Kelsen, only interpretation by law-applying organs creates law and is therefore authentic; other interpretations do not create law and are considered 'non-authentic'.[2] A popular contemporary approach to legal interpretation, which transcends Kelsen's rigid dichotomy, focuses on the notion of interpretive communities. In the context of the international legal system, these communities emerge from discursive interaction between participants in a particular field or enterprise. Interpretive communities help to define the rules and norms that become embedded in institutions. At the same time, they set parameters of acceptable argumentation, that is, the terms in which positions are explained, defended, and justified to others.[3] The contemporary process of interpretation in international law is 'instrumental in shaping legal outcomes at all levels, from the decision-making process to adjudication and enforcement'.[4]

The interpretive process in international law comprises a broad group of relevant interpreters, including judges at international courts and tribunals, academics, legal advisers of states and international organizations, NGO lawyers and international litigators.[5] Frequently, participants in this process look to the courts as authoritative determiners of meaning.[6] However, one cannot deny the fact that other protagonists—directly or indirectly—bear some influence upon the way in which legal rules are interpreted in the international legal community.[7] The process of creating meaning through interpretation in international law should therefore be understood as an enormously complex process to which a variety of actors contribute.[8]

---

[2] Hans Kelsen, *Pure Theory of Law* (University of California Press 1967) 354–5.

[3] Ian Johnstone, 'The Power of Interpretive Communities' in Michael Barnett and Raymond Duvall (eds), *Power in Global Governance* (CUP 2004) 186.

[4] Andrea Bianchi, 'Textual Interpretation and (International) Law Reading: The Myth of (In)Determinacy and the Genealogy of Meaning' in Pieter Bekker, Rudolf Dolzer, and Michael Waibel (eds), *Making International Law Work in the Global Economy: Essays in Honour of Detlev Vagts* (CUP 2010) 54.

[5] Cf Matthias Herdegen, 'Interpretation in International Law' in Rüdiger Wolfrum (ed), *Max Planck Encyclopedia of Public International Law* (OUP 2012) 261 and David Caron, 'Towards a Political Theory of International Courts and Tribunals' (2006) 24 Berk J Intl L 401, 414.

[6] Detlev Vagts, 'Treaty Interpretation and the New American Ways of Law Reading' (1993) 4 EJIL 472, 481.

[7] Kawaguchi, *A Social Theory of International Law*, 114; Vagts, 'Treaty Interpretation', 480.

II. International Legal Professions and the Interpretive Process

Competence or craftsmanship in interpreting international law is a necessary part of various professional roles in international law, including legal advisers of states and international organizations, NGO lawyers, judges, academics, and litigators before international courts. These roles represent the five most common types of international legal professionals.[9] What follows is a more thorough analysis of their role in the complex and dynamic interpretive process in international law.

A. Legal advisers

Among all international law professions, the role of the legal adviser is one of the most complex. Legal advisers find themselves in a position of defending the interests of their institution (a foreign ministry or an international organization) while shielding the values and integrity of the system of international law.[10] They also exert decisive influence on the formation of the practice of their states and are a driving force behind the formation of customary international law.[11] Therefore, advisers are in reality custodians and exponents of international law at their institutions. In general terms, the position of the legal adviser comprises two roles: the role of counsellor and the role of acting as the conscience of the institution where he or she works.

The task of a *counsellor* is to provide legal opinions in the course of making decisions,[12] functioning as an interpreter of the existing body of international legal principles, rules, and obligations. Generally, there are two approaches as to when legal advisers should provide legal advice on the interpretation of international obligations.

The first is the American approach that rose to prominence during the Cuban missile crisis, requiring that a legal adviser must be 'in at the take-off' of a new foreign policy episode and participate in the policy-making process.[13] Under this

---

[9] I draw this classification from Martti Koskenniemi, 'Between Commitment and Cynicism: Outline for a Theory of International Law as Practice' in *Collection of Essays by Legal Advisers of States, Legal Advisers of International Organizations and Practitioners in the Field of International Law* (United Nations 1992) 512. See also Wilfred Jenks, 'Craftsmanship in International Law' (1956) 50 AJIL 32 and Chanaka Wickremasinghe (ed), *The International Lawyer as Practitioner* (BIICL 2000). This group can be slightly larger, including actors such as lobbyists, pressure groups, engaged intellectuals, and opinion makers. Cf Andrea Bianchi, 'The International Regulation of the Use of Force: The Politics of Interpretive Method' (2009) 22 LJIL 651, 653–4.

[10] Ronald St John MacDonald, 'The Role of the Legal Adviser of Ministries of Foreign Affairs' (1977) Recueil des Cours 385.

[11] Arthur Watts, 'International Law and International Relations: United Kingdom Practice' (1991) 2 EJIL 163.

[12] Robbie Sabel, 'The Role of the Legal Advisor in Diplomacy' (1997) 8 Diplomacy & Statecraft 1.

[13] Harold Koh, 'The State Department Legal Adviser's Office: Eight Decades in Peace and War' (2012) 100 Geo L J 1756 and Steven Schwebel, 'Remarks on the Role of the Legal Advisor of the US State Department' (1991) 2 EJIL 132.

approach, law constitutes one of a complex set of inputs during the consideration of available policy choices.[14] Interpretation of legal documents is situated at the centre of the policy making. This approach, which acknowledges an important role for international law in the policy decision-making process, is also gaining importance in other countries.[15]

The second is a more traditional approach according to which the legal adviser provides advice only when he or she is requested to do so. Here, the legal adviser is not part of the broader policy process and is perceived more as a technician.[16] Other departments are responsible for the policy and have to ensure that legal advice is taken where appropriate.[17] Thus, when policy is being formulated it is important that departments take into account the interpretation of specific legal instruments and norms and give them due weight. In this context, the legal advice needs to take an objective view on strengths and weaknesses of various possible courses of action and how best to adapt the proposals to secure their conformity with the law.[18]

In contemporary practice, however, the distinction between playing a role in policy formation and dispensing legal advice has become increasingly blurred.[19] This is especially the case with certain issues in multilateral forums—such as the UN Security Council—where pressing events demand fast responses.[20] Consequently, interpretations provided by legal advisers may become part of the policy process at the introductory stage or after the completion of the policy stage.

On the other hand, the legal adviser also serves as *conscience* at the institution for which he or she works. This role derives from the aspiration of the adviser to remain sensitive to the needs and interests of the international community and to the integrity of the international system itself.[21] This is especially so in foreign ministries, where the legal adviser is in a unique position to offer opinions on the wisdom and morality of proposed actions.[22] In doing so, the legal adviser speaks law to power.[23] Acting as a conscience obliges legal advisers to argue against policies that are 'lawful, but awful' and policies that, although strictly legal, may not be in the best long-term interests of a country or an institution.[24]

[14] Abram Chayes, *The Cuban Missile Crisis: International Crises and the Role of Law* (OUP 1974) 102.

[15] For example, in British foreign policy, see Franklin Berman, 'The Role of the International Lawyer in the Making of Foreign Policy', in Wickremasinghe, *The International Lawyer as Practitioner*, 4 and 9; and Daniel Bethlehem, 'The Secret Life of International Law' (2012) 1 CJICL 1, 26 and 29.

[16] HCL Merillat, 'Summary Report' in HCL Merillat (ed), *Legal Advisers and Foreign Affairs* (Oceana Publications 1964) 19.

[17] Watts, 'International Law and International Relations', 160.

[18] Watts, 'International Law and International Relations', 163.

[19] Berman, 'The Role of the International Lawyer', 13; Jenks, 'Craftsmanship in International Law', 51; and Merillat, 'Summary Report', 16–17.

[20] See Michael Wood, 'The Role of Legal Advisers at Permanent Missions to the United Nations' in Wickremasinghe, *The International Lawyer as Practitioner*, 73 and 81–4.

[21] MacDonald, 'Role of Legal Advisers of Ministries of Foreign Affairs', 387.

[22] Harold Koh and Aaron Zelinsky, 'Practicing International Law in the Obama Administration' (2009) 35 Yale J Int'l L Online 9.

[23] Richard Bilder, 'The Office of the Legal Adviser' (1962) 56 AJIL 141, 142.

[24] Koh and Zelinsky, 'Practicing International Law in the Obama Administration', 10.

In international organizations, in particular, the legal adviser does not function as a 'handmaiden' of the policy-making organs, but rather as an active participant in the development of law and practice.[25] Therefore, besides being a technician, the legal adviser is also a guardian of international law.[26] The adviser has a role in the interpretive and creative process leading towards the further development of international law.[27] Although legal decisions and opinions are scattered through records of meetings, secretariat memoranda, press releases, and other miscellaneous documents, it is clear that these decisions add, bit by bit, to the body of international law.[28] Thus, although the process of authoritative decision-making in political organs consists of a multiplicity of factors, influences, and uncertainties, legal prescriptions have an important place in that process.[29]

B. NGO lawyers

NGOs are 'formal (professionalized) independent societal organizations whose primary aim is to promote common goals at the national or the international level'.[30] Under the traditional scheme of international law, NGOs do not enjoy recognition as a subject of international law.[31] Gradually, however, NGOs have obtained importance in international law as an actor that may influence policy and legal decisions.[32] A study presented by the NGO Liberty, for example, influenced the interpretive approach of the European Court of Human Rights regarding Article 8 of the European Convention on Human Rights.[33] Because they represent international civil society, international NGOs provide the potential to democratize international relations and institutions.[34] Driving factors behind

---

[25] See Oscar Schachter, 'Development of International Law through Legal Opinions of the United Nations Secretariat' (1948) 25 BYBIL 91.

[26] See Treasa Dunworth, 'The Legal Adviser in International Organizations: Technician or Guardian?' (2009) 46 Alta L Rev 869.

[27] Ralph Zacklin, 'The Role of the International Lawyer in an International Organisation' in Wickremasinghe, *The International Lawyer as Practitioner*, 63–4.

[28] Schachter, 'Development of International Law', 91 and Zacklin, 'The Role of the International Lawyer', 64.

[29] Oscar Schachter, 'The Place of Policy in International Law' (1972) 2 Ga J Int'l & Comp L 176.

[30] Kerstin Martens, 'Mission Impossible? Defining Nongovernmental Organizations' (2002) 13 Voluntas 282. There is also a problem of definition since the term itself (non-governmental organizations) is marked with the negative prefix 'non-'.

[31] Philippe Sands, 'The Environment, Community and International Law' 1989 (30) HILJ 412.

[32] See Jean d'Aspremont, 'Wording in International Law' (2012) 25 LJIL 575, 577–8; Jan Klabbers, Anne Peters, and Geir Ulfstein, *The Constitutionalization of International Law* (OUP 2009) 219; Sergey Ripinsky and Peter van den Bossche, *NGO Involvement in International Organizations* (BIICL 2007) 1.

[33] *Goodwin v UK* (2002) 35 EHRR 18, [103].

[34] Kenneth Anderson, 'The Ottawa Convention Banning Landmines, the Role of International Non-governmental Organizations and the Idea of International Civil Society' (2000) 11 EJIL 111. See also Klabbers, Peters, and Ulfstein, *The Constitutionalization of International Law*, in this context, expert knowledge is a basis and prerequisite for the professional practice of NGOs. For expert knowledge, see Holly Cullen and Karen Morrow, 'International Civil Society in International Law' (2001) 1 Non-State Actors in International Law 7, 32–4, and Farhana Yamin, 'NGOs and International Environmental Law: A Critical Evaluation of their Roles and Responsibilities' (2001) 10 RECIEL 149, 156–7.

NGO activists are therefore twofold: idealism directed towards promotion of what they perceive as 'common goals', and professionalism, which is based on their accumulated expert knowledge.

The NGO activists as international lawyers thus oscillate between their commitment to the political objectives that underlie their activism and adherence to the international legal profession.[35] NGOs are increasingly keen to promote their interests by reference to, and interpretation of, international legal arguments.[36] The main difference between, for example, the NGO lawyer and the legal adviser is not in the degree of their competence but in their focus. The interests of the NGO lawyer will be more narrowly focused on the use of law and legal argument to promote the specific interests of the NGO,[37] while the working agenda of the state's or the international organization's legal adviser will usually cover a broader area of issues.

The NGO lawyer participates in the process of interpretation of international law in different capacities. The first role is that of *counselling* in bringing forward and shaping international litigation. Many of the larger NGOs have in-house lawyers who specialize in international law. Other smaller NGOs will seek advice or assistance on public international law from outside counsel, be it from private practice or from the academy.[38] However, in doing so, external counsel steps into the shoes of NGOs and act as representatives of their interests. The two perspectives merge in the process of counselling which is, in turn, a process of interpretation along the lines of the NGO's objectives.

In international litigation, the submission of *amicus curiae* briefs is particularly important since it can have a significant influence on the judicial interpretation of international law.[39] In this way, interpretation by NGOs serves as an impetus for judicial interpretation. NGOs act as *amici* with the permission of the court and provide input on matters of fact and law within their knowledge.[40] More specifically, they often submit detailed analysis of points of law, legislative or jurisprudential history, scholarly exposition of the law and arguments not contained in the submissions of the parties.[41] Submission of *amicus* briefs is a common practice before international human rights courts and international criminal tribunals,

---

[35] Koskenniemi, 'Between Commitment and Cynicism', 519 and 521.

[36] Cf Philippe Sands, 'International Law, the Practitioner and Non-State Actors' in Wickremasinghe, *The International Lawyer as Practitioner*, 105.

[37] Sands, 'International Law, the Practitioner and Non-State Actors', 118.

[38] Sands, 'International Law, the Practitioner and Non-State Actors', 111 and Sands, 'The Environment, Community and International Law', 416.

[39] See eg Dean Zagorac, 'International Courts and Compliance Bodies: The Experience of Amnesty International' in Tullio Treves, Marco Frigessi di Rattalma, Attila Tanzi, Alessandro Fodella, Cesare Pitea, and Chiara Ragni (eds), *Civil Society, International Courts and Compliance Bodies* (TMC Asser 2005) 11. In general terms, see Klabbers, Peters, and Ulstein, *The Constitutionalization of International Law*, 229–33.

[40] Dinah Shelton, 'The Participation of Nongovernmental Organizations in International Judicial Proceedings' (1994) 88 AJIL 611, 640.

[41] Shelton, 'The Participation of Nongovernmental Organizations in International Judicial Proceedings', 618.

and its importance in trade and investment arbitration is growing.[42] In addition, even though the International Court of Justice (ICJ) does not allow for the formal participation of NGOs in judicial proceedings, it has adopted a solution according to which NGO material is submitted to a designated place in the Peace Palace for further consultation and reference in a case.[43] *Amicus* briefs have shaped decisions in more cases than is commonly realized, which is a unique contribution of NGO lawyers to the interpretation and development of principles and rules of international law.[44]

Last but not least, NGO lawyers have an impact on the enforcement process of international treaties. This role also gives them a unique position of influence when it comes to the interpretation of international commitments accepted by states. NGOs interpret how these commitments should be translated into the domestic legal system and how they should work in practice. The interpretation of particular treaty provisions is important because it will not only affect the implementation of a particular convention, but will also influence the shape of future related agreements.[45]

C. Judges

In contrast to other international legal professionals, judges are arguably more focused on the international legal system as a whole.[46] Judges are supposed to 'rise above' and 'put aside' their personal interests, sympathies, group affiliations, and ideological commitments. They are supposed to submit to something 'bigger' and 'higher' than 'themselves'.[47] They rise above specific interests that might motivate the work of legal advisers and NGO lawyers and other participants in

---

[42] See eg *Methanex v United States*, Decision of the NAFTA Tribunal on Petitions of Third Persons to Intervene as *Amici Curiae*, 15 January 2001; *Aguas Argentinas, SA, Suez, Sociedad General de Aguas de Barcelona SA and Vivendi Universal SA v Argentine Republic*, ICSID Case No ARB/03/19, Order in response to a petition for transparency and participation as *amicus curiae*, 19 May 2005.

[43] Steve Charnovitz, 'Nongovernmental Organizations and International Law' (2006) 100 AJIL 348, 353–4; Ruth Mackenzie, 'The *Amicus Curiae* in International Courts: Towards Common Procedural Approaches?' in Treves, di Rattalma, Tanzi, Fodella, Pitea, and Ragni (eds), *Civil Society, International Courts and Compliance Bodies*, 297, 309–10.

[44] Cf Shelton, 'The Participation of Nongovernmental Organizations in International Judicial Proceedings', 619; Treves, di Rattalma, Tanzi, Fodella, Pitea, and Ragni (eds), *Civil Society, International Courts and Compliance Bodies*, 6.

[45] Cf Thomas Nash, 'The Role of NGO Activism in the Implementation of the Convention on Cluster Munitions' (2010) 1 Disarmament Forum 53.

[46] For the purpose of this chapter, I consider arbitrators as judges since they essentially perform an adjudicative function in the international community. Naturally, there is a difference between arbitrators, who sit in ad hoc cases, and judges in permanent international courts. However, there is little difference between the commitment of arbitrators and judges in relation to the integrity of the international legal system. The difference is rather one of an adjudicative focus than of a commitment to the same epistemic (legal) postulates. One has to take into account, for example, the intellectual effort of Sir Hersch Lauterpacht who managed to defend and develop the integrity of the international legal system mainly on the basis of arbitral judicial decisions. See Hersch Lauterpacht, *Private Law Sources and Analogies of International Law* (Longmans, Green and Co 1927); Hersch Lauterpacht, *The Function of Law in the International Community* (Clarendon Press 1933).

[47] Duncan Kennedy, *A Critique of Adjudication {fin de siècle}* (Harvard University Press 1997) 3.

the adjudicatory process. Decisions of judges must be objective and free from bias: they must withhold judgment until all evidence has been examined and all arguments have been heard.[48] On the other hand, they are concerned with whether adopted legal solutions work in a broader social context and political reality. Thus, adjudicators in an institution created by a particular community will consider the significance of an individual decision in the overall framework of the institution's jurisprudence and how it relates to the community that created the judicial institution.[49] Their adjudicative process therefore oscillates between routine problem solving (*per substitutionem*) and insights that address profounder dimensions of the case (*per profundationem*). In that sense judges represent a bridge between legal practice and theory.[50]

From a broader perspective, courts serve the following functions: (i) conflict resolution, (ii) social control or regime enforcement, and (iii) law-making.[51] Although there are some reservations about law-making in international law, there is no doubt that judicial law-making is a corollary of judicial activity.[52] Law-making activity takes place in the context of a structure of legal rules when judges face a particular gap, conflict, or ambiguity in that structure. Interpretation is a process through which judges restate some part of this structure and deploy a set of arguments to justify their solutions.[53] Andrew Clapham explains this in the following way:

We speak of the process of interpretation because we do not care to admit that the court puts something into the document which was not there before . . . The act of the court is a creative act, in spite of our conspiracy to represent it as something less.[54]

However, international judges often deny that they embark on a task of legislation and see their task as 'something less'.[55] They understand the enunciation of a new rule to be no more than the application of an existing legal principle or an interpretation of an existing text.[56] However, there is a marked difference between creating international rules *de novo* and developing them through interpretation. Any judicial activity that would lead to creating entirely new rules of international law, in deliberate disregard of the existing law, would amount to usurpation

---

[48] Lon Fuller, 'The Adversary System' in Harold Berman (ed), *Talks on American Law* (Vintage Books 1971) 42.

[49] Caron, 'Towards a Political Theory of International Courts and Tribunals', 415.

[50] Boštjan M Zupančič, *The Owlets of Minerva: Human Rights in the Practice of the European Court of Human Rights* (Eleven International Publishing 2012) vii. See also Robert Jennings, 'Introduction', in Wickremasinghe, *The International Lawyer as Practitioner*, xxii.

[51] Martin Shapiro, *Courts: A Comparative and Political Analysis* (University of Chicago Press 1981) 63.

[52] Fuad Zarbiyev, 'Judicial Activism in International Law—A Conceptual Framework for Analysis' (2012) 3 JIDS 253.

[53] Kennedy, *A Critique of Adjudication*, 1.

[54] Andrew Clapham, *Brierly's Law of Nations: An Introduction to the Role of International Law in International Relations* (OUP 2012) 349–50.

[55] See *Legality of the Threat or Use of Nuclear Weapons* (Advisory Opinion) [1996] ICJ Rep 226, [18].

[56] Hersch Lauterpacht, *The Development of International Law by the International Court* (Stevens & Sons Limited 1958) 155.

of judicial powers.[57] Nevertheless, as Lauterpacht puts it, the act of interpretation is unescapably judicial legislation or judicial law-making:

[I]n interpreting and applying concrete legal rules the Court... exercises in each case a creative activity, having as its background the entirety of international law and the necessities of international community. [58]

When the law is clear and non-controversial, judicial discretion is confined within narrow limits. On the other hand, when the law is not clear or undisputed, judicial freedom is increased.[59] For example, when interpreting a treaty, the judge will not seek to give it a meaning that the actual parties to the agreement clearly did not intend.[60] On the other hand, judicial law-making activity may result from the strategies of states to leave treaty provisions vague on purpose, leaving it to the judge to further interpret the agreed provisions.[61]

The role of judges in the process of international law interpretation thus suggests a commitment to the integrity and values of the judicial system. Precisely because of this function, it is of the utmost importance to underline ethical prerequisites for judicial activity. [62] For example, Article 2 of the Statute of the ICJ requires judges to be 'persons of high moral character'.[63]

D. Academics

Academics are those who are engaged in research and teaching in the higher education system.[64] It could be argued that academics are torn between two extremes. On the one hand, academics in international law seem to suffer from an inferiority complex, especially with regard to their fellow domestic lawyers.[65] This leads to worries that their views might not be taken seriously in the context of legal practice and theory.[66] On the other hand, academics have an enduring fear that they might be taken too seriously, namely, that their views would be abused as a justification for governmental policies.[67] Despite the contradiction between these

[57] Lauterpacht, *The Development of International Law*, 156.

[58] Lauterpacht, *The Function of Law*, 319. Lauterpacht used 'judicial legislation' to mean judicial law-making—or judicial interpretation—which is also the way I use the expression. See Lauterpacht (n 56) 155–7.

[59] Lauterpacht, *The Development of International Law*, 394.

[60] Robert Jennings, 'The Role of the International Court of Justice' (1997) 68 BYBIL 41.

[61] Tom Ginsburg, 'Bounded Discretion in International Judicial Lawmaking' (2005) 45 Va J Int'l L 42.

[62] Ruth Mackenzie and Philippe Sands, 'International Courts and Tribunals and the Independence of the International Judge' (2003) 44 HILJ 271.

[63] United Nations, Statute of the International Court of Justice, as an integral part of the Charter of the United Nations, 24 October 1945, 1 UNTS XVI.

[64] Aoife O'Donoghue, 'Agents of Change: Academics and the Spirit of Debate at International Conferences' (2012) 1 CJICL 279.

[65] Jennings, 'The Role of the International Court of Justice', 41–2.

[66] Gerry Simpson, 'On the Magic Mountain: Teaching Public International Law' (1999) 10 EJIL 70, 73–4, and 83–4.

[67] Manfred Lachs, *The Teacher in International Law: Teachings and Teaching* (Martinus Nijhoff Publishers 1987) 203; Koskenniemi, 'Between Commitment and Cynicism', 522.

two poles, the true importance of the teacher of international law is in strengthening 'the moral commitment of the internationalist to shaping a more humane
world'.[68]

There is probably no other system of law in existence where scholars enjoy such
an overt influence over the content and evolution of rules and principles of law.[69]
Indeed, in recognition of their deemed objectivity and the importance of their
work, Article 38(1)(d) of the Statute of the ICJ stipulates that the Court accepts
'the teachings of the most highly qualified publicists of the various nations' as
subsidiary means for the determination of international law. Academic commentary is influential and adds value to contemporary international law when
it combines critical analysis with the exploration of new ideas.[70] The academic
interpretive process is, in this sense, not only mechanical but also an imaginative
process, which nevertheless should reflect contemporary realities to the fullest
extent possible.[71] The potential for innovative interpretation opens the possibility
to exert influence on law-making, decision-making, and the application of the law
in novel ways.[72]

Jennings gives a useful account of the original and innovative contribution
of academics to the process of interpretation. He situates their contribution in
the area between the law as it is (positivist *de lege lata*) and the law is it should
be (aspirational *de lega ferenda*). Jennings suggests that academics may bridge
this division by asserting 'that a proposal *de lege ferenda*, if not already law,
is near-law, or law in the process of being made; and also of suggesting that
the *lege lata* is corresponding[ly] weakened, or obsolescent'.[73] However, the
unique position of academics in the interpretative landscape of international
law puts them in a privileged position where their influence can proliferate
through their teaching, writings, and advice to governments.[74] On the basis
of his or her scholarly work, propelled by imagination, reason, and humanism,
the academic enjoys a privileged position—and a mission—to move across new
frontiers, to help and inspire, and to make the study of international law more
humane.[75]

---

[68] Lachs, *The Teacher in International Law*, 228.

[69] Robert Jennings, 'International Lawyers and the Progressive Development of International
Law' in Jerzy Makarczyk (ed), *Theory of International Law at the Threshold of the 21st Century: Essays
in Honour of Krzystof Skubiszewski* (Kluwer 1996) 413.

[70] Gillian Triggs, 'The Public International Lawyer and the Practice of International Law'
(2005) 24 Aust YBIL 205.

[71] Peter Hilpold, 'What Role for Academic Writers in Interpreting International Law?' (2009)
8 Chinese JIL 297–8.

[72] Lachs, *The Teacher in International Law*, 8.

[73] Robert Jennings, 'Teachings and Teaching in International Law' in Makarczyk, *Theory of
International Law*, 127.

[74] Lachs, *The Teacher in International Law*, 228; O'Donoghue, 'Agents of Change', 296.

[75] Lachs, *The Teacher in International Law*, 229.

E. Litigators

Litigators are those lawyers that are engaged in contentious proceedings before international courts and tribunals.[76] As members of the 'International Bar', these lawyers also take part in the interpretive process before various international courts. Traditionally, litigation has been understood to be 'a contest between two individuals or at least two unitary interests, diametrically opposed, to be decided on a winner-takes-all basis'.[77] In principle, the role of counsel in international litigation does not differ much from the role of attorneys in domestic legal proceedings. Their main function is to represent one party to the conflict and defend his or her side of the story and contingent interests before the court.[78] A quintessential part of a litigator's role is the interpretation of international principles, norms, and rules to substantiate the legal claims of his or her client. In short, litigators take part in what can be called a battle for 'semantic authority' before the court.[79]

By taking part in litigation, counsel performs various roles that can be in opposition to each other. Their primary role is, as we have seen, that of representation of clients and their best interests before international courts. In doing so, the main task of counsel is to proffer persuasive legal interpretations that would influence the outcome of the case and the court's judgment. But they also act as 'officers of the court' or 'ministers of justice' (custodians of justice) who work for the broader public interest, with the integrity of the judicial system in mind.[80] In this sense, litigators interpret international norms to contribute to the more efficient, fair, and comprehensive conduct of proceedings.

The role of representing clients is largely self-explanatory and derives from the vocation of being a legal counsel. The second role of being a custodian of justice consists in attempting to forestall and prevent conflicts, and ensuring that conflicts—if they arise—are resolved on the basis of the rule of law.[81] Thus, in

---

[76] This category includes government-lawyers who act as representatives of the government in litigation. Koh and Zelinsky call them defenders of the government's interest: 'Practicing International Law in the Obama Administration', 10–11. For an in-depth treatment of this role, see Catherine Gibson, 'Representing the United States Abroad: Proper Conduct of U.S. Government Attorneys in International Tribunals' (2013) 44 Geo J Int'l L 1167–216.

[77] Abram Chayes, 'The Role of the Judge in Public Law Litigation' (1976) 89 Harv L Rev 1282. This is monocentric as opposed to polycentric decision-making. See Lon Fuller, 'Adjudication and the Rule of Law' (1960) 54 ASIL Proceedings 1.

[78] A precondition of the adjudicative process is a conflict that parties have decided to resolve through peaceful means. In it, the two parties try to influence the judicial outcome with opposing accounts of the controversy at stake. See Boštjan M Zupančič, *The Owl of Minerva: Essays on Human Rights* (Eleven 2008) 43; Fuller, 'The Adversary System', 31; Chayes, 'The Role of the Judge in Public Law Litigation', 1282.

[79] On semantic authority, see Ingo Venzke, *How Interpretation Makes International Law: On Semantic Change and Normative Twists* (OUP 2012) 57–64.

[80] Gibson, 'Representing the United States Abroad', 1167, 1186, 1196; *Charter of Core Principles of the European Legal Profession and Code of Conduct for European Lawyers* (CCBE 2013) 10.

[81] *Charter of Core Principles*, 7–8; International Bar Association, *International Legal Principles on Conduct for the Legal Profession*, adopted on 28 May 2011, 10.

their practical work, counsel must always seek a balance between their duties to the client and their role in the fair administration of justice.[82]

Conclusion: The Duty and Aspiration of Interpretation

The purpose of this contribution is to portray the interpretive process in international law as a complex, pluralistic, and nuanced enterprise in which a variety of actors exercise their professional roles. This understanding of interpretation is hardly surprising since all professionals in international law form what Schachter called an 'invisible college'.[83] The invisible college is a professional community engaged in a common and continuous intellectual process of communication, elaboration, and exchange of ideas.[84] This includes legal interpretation as one of the most essential professional tasks.

However, participation in the interpretive process is not determined solely by the participant's professional position in the international legal system. It is also determined by the individual international lawyer's ethical stance.[85] In surveying the contributions of various legal professionals to the process of interpretation, the argument was made that the work of all professionals in international law—legal advisers, NGO lawyers, judges, academics, and litigators—is underpinned by a dichotomy between observing specific interests linked to the mandate of the professional and his or her duty to further principles of justice and the legitimacy of the international legal system.[86]

---

[82] Gibson, 'Representing the United States Abroad', 1204–7. Both roles have a strong ethical underpinning that is a central subject of some recent studies. See Arman Sarvarian, *Professional Ethics at the International Bar* (OUP 2013); Frédéric Mégret, 'Accountability and Ethics' in Luc Reydams, Jan Wouters, and Cedric Ryngaert (eds), *International Prosecutors* (OUP 2012) 416. For an earlier contribution see Detlev Vagts, 'The International Legal Profession: A Need for More Governance?' (1996) 90 AJIL 250. Admittedly, this is not always the case: see W Michael Reisman and Christina Skinner, *Fraudulent Evidence Before Public International Tribunals: The Dirty Stories of International Law* (CUP 2014).

[83] Oscar Schachter, 'The Invisible College of International Lawyers' (1977) 72 North U L Rev 217.

[84] Schachter, 'The Invisible College of International Lawyers', 225.

[85] Cf Macdonald, 'Role of Legal Advisers of Ministries of Foreign Affairs', 386, 388; Berman, 'The Role of the International Lawyer', 7–9, 13–14; Bilder, 'The Office of the Legal Adviser', 145–6; Harold Koh, 'An Uncommon Lawyer' (2001) 42 HILJ 9.

[86] This professional dichotomy is nothing new in the legal profession: see eg Leonard Niehoff, 'In the Shadow of the Shrine: Regulation and Aspiration in the ABA Model Rules of Professional Conduct' (2008) 54 Wayne L Rev 3; Koskenniemi, 'Between Commitment and Cynicism'. Cf Lon Fuller, 'The Forms and Limits of Adjudication' (1978) 92 Harv L Rev 384 (citing a report co-authored with JD Randall): 'The lawyer's highest loyalty is at the same time the most intangible. It is a loyalty that runs, not to persons, but to procedures and institutions. The lawyer's role imposes on him a trusteeship for the integrity of those fundamental processes of government and self-government upon which the successful functioning of our society depends...He has an affirmative duty to help shape the growth and development of public attitudes toward fair procedures and due process.'

The professional tension faced by international lawyers bears a resemblance to the dual tenets of Lon Fuller's 'inner morality of law'.[87] The inner morality of law embraces two aspects of morality: the morality of duty and the morality of aspiration. The former encompasses the most obvious and essential moral duties without which a legal system, and law creation, is impossible.[88] This is the morality that must be maintained for law to fulfil its purpose: for Fuller, it provides the minimum requirements of legality.[89] The morality of aspiration, on the other hand, pertains to the highest achievements open to man. It is the morality of striving for excellence.[90]

On a moral scale, the morality of duty stands at the bottom, whereas the morality of aspiration occupies the upper end. Fuller referred to an invisible pointer on the moral scale that divides the two moralities, 'where the pressure of duty leaves off and the challenge of excellence begins'.[91] However, there is no clear dividing line between the two moralities. Therefore, rather than being a pointer on a scale, the meeting ground between the two moralities represents a continuum.[92] What is more important is that in this process the morality of aspiration serves as guidance.

These two moralities are analogous to the considerations that, it has been argued, shape international legal professionals' interpretive practice. On the one hand, the morality of duty is akin to the professional duties and constraints that shape interpretation. They are those that must be adhered to in order for the actor to fulfil their professional role. The morality of aspiration is similar to the legal professionals' commitment to the promotion of the international legal system as a whole. Interpretation occurs within this dialectic, which imposes limits and provides guidance as to the appropriate interpretation.

Whilst it is clear that an interpretation that does not meet the minimum standards of competency for one's professional role serves as a limit to feasible interpretations, interpretation in overt promotion of the values and ideals of the international legal system should be cautioned. If one's interpretation is too idealistic, this may lead to the violation of the minimum standards of professional competency.[93] For example, judges may not be receptive to an untenably idealistic argument, and counsel that advances such an argument will not be presenting the case of their client in its best light.

The inner morality of law, and practical legal work in furtherance of it, is a useful construct because it fosters professional awareness that the morality of duty is an ethical floor rather than a ceiling. At the same time, the inner morality of

---

[87] Lon Fuller, *The Morality of Law* (Yale University Press 1964) 42, 96–7.

[88] Fuller, *The Morality of Law*, 5.

[89] See David Luban, *Legal Ethics and Human Dignity* (CUP 2007) 101, 112.

[90] Fuller, 'The Forms and Limits of Adjudication', 9–10, 41–2; Luban, *Legal Ethics and Human Dignity*, 106.

[91] Fuller, 'The Forms and Limits of Adjudication', 10.

[92] Wibren van der Burg, 'The Morality of Aspiration: A Neglected Dimension of Law and Morality' in Willem Witteveen and Wibren van der Burg (eds), *Rediscovering Fuller: Essays on Implicit Law and Institutional Design* (Amsterdam University Press 1999) 173, 175.

[93] Cf van der Burg, 'The Morality of Aspiration', 173.

law reminds us that the morality of aspiration is one of the central features of professional ethics.[94] In terms of the interpretive process, a legal professional at the highest moral stage creatively contributes to the progressive development of the legal system as a whole.[95] It is also worth emphasizing that within a particular group of international legal professionals its members are able to exert moral influence on the social structure and other members of the group.[96] Every international legal professional is therefore functioning in the ambit of two moralities: he or she should master professional work in the domain of the morality of duty and, at the same time, keep evolving to the stage of the morality of aspiration. Interpretation by legal professionals on the basis of the inner morality of law—in both of its spheres—thus significantly contributes to the development and strengthening of international law.

---

[94] Luban, *Legal Ethics and Human Dignity*, 107.

[95] Boštjan Zupančič, 'From Combat to Contract: "What Does the Constitution Constitute?"' (1998) 1 EJLR 77, 92–3. For more on stages of moral development, see Lawrence Kohlberg, 'The Claim to Moral Adequacy of a Highest Stage of Moral Development' (1973) 70 J Phil Logic 630; Robert Kegan, *The Evolving Self* (Harvard University Press 1983). For an application of Kohlberg's theory to international law, see Roger Alford and James Fallows Tierney, 'Moral Reasoning in International Law' in Donald Childress III (ed), *The Role of Ethics in International Law* (CUP 2012) 11.

[96] Alford and Tierney, 'Moral Reasoning in International Law', 30.

7

Interpretive Communities
in International Law

Michael Waibel

'[T]he problem is the fragmentation into interpretive communities!'[1]

Introduction

This chapter explores how the wide range of interpreters that populate international law, forming part of interpretive communities, affects interpretation in international law.[2] To understand how interpretation in international law works in practice, we need to appreciate the role of interpretive communities in the interpretive process—an influence that is routinely overlooked.[3]

To look only at interpretive directions, such as the principles of interpretation found in the Vienna Convention on the Law of Treaties (VCLT), is insufficient.[4] Any account of interpretation is incomplete without the sociological dimension of interpretive communities. The meaning of international law norms hinges on background principles shared by interpreters who form part of one or several interpretive communities. The focus is not on individual interpreters, but rather on the relationship among interpreters.

Individual and group identity, the background and the shared understandings of interpreters are key ingredients in the interpretive process. 'Objective' interpretation is impossible. According to James Crawford, international law's 'central problem is that the *interpreters* of international law are necessarily partial and

---

[1] Andrea Bianchi, 'Looking Ahead: International Law's Main Challenges' in David Armstrong (ed), *Routledge Handbook of International Law* (Routledge 2009) 392, 404.

[2] Ingo Venzke, *How Interpretation Makes International Law: On Semantic Change and Normative Twists* (OUP 2012) 54; Michael Waibel, 'Uniformity versus Specialisation (2): A Uniform Regime of Treaty Interpretation?' in Christian Tams, Antonios Tzanakopoulos, and Andreas Zimmermann (eds), *Research Handbook on the Law of Treaties* (Edward Elgar 2014) 375.

[3] Michael Waibel, 'Demystifying the Art of Interpretation' (2011) 22 EJIL 571, 586.

[4] Frank Easterbrook, 'Abstraction and Authority' (1992) 59 U Chi L Rev 349, 359 ('the meaning of a text lies in its interpretation by an interpretive community').

selective in their reading of the sources of international law, since no-one commands the material sources, let alone the vast literature now available'.[5]

Yet even if, by a stroke of magic, an interpreter could command the panoply of sources and the entirety of the literature, individual interpreters, even if they wanted to, cannot simply leave behind their membership of an interpretive community, or cast aside their educational and professional background. Each interpreter looks at the interpretive task through her own glasses. As Andrea Bianchi's quote above highlights, the emergence of distinct interpretive communities in international law is potentially a serious risk for international law as a field.

This chapter first discusses the character of interpretive communities (Part I), before showing how practices and shared understandings within those interpretive communities shape interpretation (Part II). Part III contends that interpretive debates in international law are a contest between various actors over which normative vision of international law to advance in various issue areas.

I. The Role of Interpretive Communities in Interpretation

The multiplicity of international courts and tribunals, rising specialization, and the diversification of international law's scope is often seen as a threat to international law as a unified system.[6] In recent decades, international law has arguably fragmented into 'regimes', existing in various degrees of separation from general international law. Imported from regime theory in international relations, the term 'regime' refers to a specialized issue area of international law that is characterized by common institutions (eg the WTO), common framework treaties (eg the UN Framework Convention on Climate Change), or a shared ethos (eg human dignity in human rights law).

The formation of regimes often goes hand in hand with the emergence of distinct epistemic and interpretive communities.[7] Interpreters in international law often form part of functionally specialized interpretive communities (in trade, human rights, or arbitration), or of geographical interpretive communities (national versus international). These communities sometimes overlap and their members routinely interact.

---

[5] James Crawford, *Chance, Order, Change: The Course of International Law* (Brill 2014) 153 (emphasis in original).

[6] Philippa Webb, *International Judicial Integration and Fragmentation* (OUP 2013); *Ahmadou Sadio Diallo (Republic of Guinea v Democratic Republic of the Congo)* (Judgment on Compensation) [2012] ICJ Rep 391 (Declaration of Judge Sir Christopher Greenwood).

[7] On epistemic communities as a reason for divergent approaches to interpretation, see Part III below.

A. The notion of epistemic and interpretive communities

The notion of epistemic community originates in constructivist international relations theory. Its central insight is that the various actors that populate a regime exert an important influence on its operation, including through interpretation. Interpretation is dependent upon the social and interpretive context – the background against which the members of an institution or adjudicative body decide. International legal rules acquire meaning only in the light of background norms common to particular interpretive communities.

According to Peter Haas, an epistemic community is 'a network of professionals with recognized expertise and competence in a particular domain and an authoritative claim to policy-relevant knowledge within that domain or issue area'.[8] Such a community is characterized by:

(1) a shared set of normative and principled beliefs, which provide a value-based rationale for the social action of community members; (2) shared causal beliefs, which are derived from their analysis of practices leading or contributing to a central set of problems in their domain and which then serve as the basis for elucidating the multiple linkages between possible policy actions and desired outcomes; (3) shared notions of validity—that is, intersubjective, internally defined criteria for weighing and validating knowledge in the domain of their expertise; and (4) a common policy enterprise—that is, a set of common practices associated with a set of problems to which their professional competence is directed, presumably out of the conviction that human welfare will be enhanced as a consequence.[9]

John Ruggie defines an epistemic community as a 'dominant way of looking at social reality, a set of shared symbols and references, mutual expectations and a mutual predictability of intention. Epistemic communities may be said to consist of interrelated roles which grow up around an *episteme*; they delimit, for their members, *the* proper construction of social reality'.[10]

Over time, the epistemic community associated with a particular regime develops its own views of what constitutes 'reasonable' conduct in respect of that regime. Acculturation and learning among the actors within a regime leads to shared background understandings, shared preferences, and a common worldview.[11] As Dirk Pulkowski observes, in each international regime, 'a variety of states, non-governmental organizations, lobbyists, and pressure groups appropriate the regime's legal discourse to garner support for their preferred policy goals'.[12]

---

[8] Peter Haas, 'Introduction: Epistemic Communities and International Policy Coordination' (1992) 46 Int'l Org 1, 3.

[9] Haas, 'Introduction', 3.

[10] John Ruggie, 'International Responses to Technology' (1975) 29 Int'l Org 557, 569–70.

[11] Alexander Wendt, *Social Theory of International Politics* (CUP 1999) 215–20.

[12] Dirk Pulkowski, *Law and Politics of Regime Conflicts: Trade in Cultural Products* (OUP 2014) 16. See also Harold Koh, 'The 1998 Frankel Lecture: Bringing International Law Home' (1998) 35 Hous L R 622.

Epistemic communities often use a specialized, common vocabulary that sets them apart from other communities.[13] They share certain historical, political, and social contexts that provide the background for interpretation.[14] The individuals who constitute epistemic communities often see the world through distinct glasses.[15] All these factors, consciously or unconsciously, potentially affect the interpretive process.[16]

By contrast, the concept of interpretive community originated in literary studies. It is a notion that remains deliberately vague. Stanley Fish, the creator of the concept, explains it as follows:

[An interpretive community] is not so much a group of individuals who share... a point of view, but a point of view or way of organizing experience that share[s] individuals in the sense that its assumed distinctions, categories of understanding, and stipulations of relevance and irrelevance [are] the content of the consciousness of community members who [are] therefore no longer individuals, but, insofar as they [are] embedded in the community's enterprise, community property.[17]

Interpretive communities discipline and channel interpretation. What is central is that the interpretive community involves 'implicitly shared ideas which become part of the "professional sensibility" of participants... and produce a characteristic way of categorising the world and orienting their response to it'.[18] As professional norms, and as a standard to judge the correctness of interpretation, they constrain legal interpretation.[19] 'Disciplining rules' also define the interpretive community itself.[20] By that token, anyone who routinely applies the VCLT could be regarded as forming part of the interpretive community of international lawyers.[21] As Oscar Schachter writes:

The 'construct' of interpretive community has been invoked as an alternative to the 'invisible college of international law'... Interpretive communities have also been identified as

---

[13] Owen Fiss, 'Objectivity and Interpretation' (1982) 34 Stan L Rev 739; Detlev Vagts, 'Treaty Interpretation and the New American Ways of Law Reading' (1993) 4 EJIL 472, 480; Bianchi, 'Looking Ahead', 404.

[14] Gregory Shaffer and Joel Trachtman, 'Interpretation and Institutional Choice at the WTO' (2011) 52 Va J Int'l L 103, 131.

[15] In the context of constitutional adjudication, see John Hart Ely, *Democracy and Distrust: A Theory of Judicial Review* (Harvard University Press 180) 67.

[16] Ian Johnstone, 'Treaty Interpretation: The Authority of Interpretive Communities' (1990–91) 12 Mich J Int'l L 371, 371–2; Shaffer and Trachtman, 'Interpretation and Institutional Choice at the WTO', 119.

[17] Stanley Fish, *Doing What Comes Naturally: Change, Rhetoric, and the Practice of Theory in Literary and Legal Studies* (Duke University Press 1990) 141. Cf Pierre Schlag, 'Fish v. Zapp: The Case of the Relatively Autonomous Self' (1987) 76 Geo L J 42 (interpretive communities as a 'black box', providing a 'safe sense of closure').

[18] Andrew Lang, *World Trade Law After Neoliberalism: Reimagining the Global Economic Order* (OUP 2011) 133.

[19] Fiss, 'Objectivity and Interpretation', 746.

[20] Owen Fiss, 'Conventionalism' (1985) 58 S Cal L Rev 177, 184; Fiss, 'Objectivity and Interpretation', 745 ('the disciplining rules that govern an interpretive activity must be seen as defining or demarcating an interpretive community consisting of those who recognize the rules as authoritative').

[21] Michael Waibel, 'Uniformity versus Specialisation (2): A Uniform Regime of Treaty Interpretation?' in Christian Tams, Antonios Tzanakopoulos, and Andreas Zimmermann (eds), *Research Handbook on the Law of Treaties* (Edward Elgar 2014), 375, 382.

a significant element in specialized areas. Historically, the leading maritime powers have left their imprint on the law of the sea. Even more visible today is the 'community' of the permanent members of the UN Security Council, who collectively are continuously engaged in construing the UN Charter on issues of security.[22]

Eben Moglen and Richard Pierce define 'interpretive community' as 'the social group whose shared comprehension of a context makes possible the common interpretation of socially relevant texts. The group element is absolutely necessary to the interpretive process. If the context in which each reader functions is too idiosyncratic—devoid of shorthand reductions of experience portable enough to be shared—"meaning" is threatened'.[23] In international affairs, the shared context is likely much more limited than is typically the case in a domestic legal setting. No single interpretive community exists in international law, if it ever did.[24]

As we have seen, an 'interpretive community' differs from an 'epistemic community' in its emphasis.[25] Interpretive community concerns interpretation specifically. By contrast, epistemic community is a more generic term that centres on networks of experts and their role in creating a regime, or in applying the regime on an ongoing basis.[26] Epistemic communities emphasize the character of consensual, technocratic knowledge.[27] The *episteme* is a group of transnational experts who share specific ideas about a particular substantive issue area. By contrast, the term interpretive community refers to those who share a common approach to interpretation.

[22] Oscar Schachter, 'Metaphors and Realism in International Law' (2002) 96 ASIL Proceedings 268, 269.

[23] Eben Moglen and Richard Pierce, 'Sunstein's New Canons: Choosing the Fictions of Statutory Interpretation' (1990) 57 U Chi L Rev 1203, 1207.

[24] Andrea Bianchi, 'On Certainty' (*EJIL: Talk!*, 16 February 2012) <http://www.ejiltalk.org/on-certainty/> accessed 20 July 2014; Ruti Teitel and Robert Howse, 'Cross-Judging: Tribunalization in a Fragmented but Interconnected Global Order' (2009) 41 NYU J Int'l L & Pol 959, 960, 966 (referring to international lawyers and judges as separate epistemic communities, or alternatively, as sharing an epistemic community with domestic lawyers, as one of several competing channels that could militate against fragmentation in international law). One influential view regards all judges and legal scholars (in a national legal system) as a single interpretive community: James Boyd White, *When Words Lose Their Meaning* (University of Chicago Press 1984); Ronald Dworkin, 'Law as Interpretation' (1982) 60 Tex L Rev 527; Sanford Levinson, 'Law as Literature' (1982) 60 Tex L Rev 373. That judges and legal scholars 'define the law as an interpretive community necessarily depends upon a close cultural link between them, and their ability to understand each other': Edward Rubin, 'Law and The Methodology of the Law' in Steve Sheppard (ed), *The History of Legal Education in the United States: Commentaries and Primary Sources* (Lawbook Exchange 1997) 1027, 1032.

[25] Fish, *Is There a Text in this Class?*, 167–73; Fish, *Doing What Comes Naturally: Change, Rhetoric and the Practice of Theory in Literary and Legal Studies*; Andrew Goldsmith, 'Is There Any Backbone in This Fish? Interpretive Communities, Social Criticism, and Transgressive Legal Practice' (1998) 23 L & Soc Inq 373; Bianchi, 'Looking Ahead', 404; Waibel, 'Demystifying the Art of Interpretation' (uses 'epistemic community' and 'interpretive community' as equivalents).

[26] Stephen D Krasner, 'Structural Causes and Regime Consequences: Regimes as Intervening Variables' (1982) 36 Int'l Org 185. On the distinction between the creation and day-to-day operation of a regime, see Pulkowski, *Law and Politics of Regime Conflicts*, 103 (the latter refers to the 'resolution of concrete problems in accordance with the regime's principles, norms, rules and decision-making procedures').

[27] Easterbrook, 'Abstraction and Authority', 362 (a consensus answer rather than the interpreter's subjective answer).

B. Identifying epistemic/interpretive communities

Identifying interpretive communities is not straightforward as the boundaries are fluid and intersecting.[28] Its members increasingly interact and overlap. One approach is to equate the interpretive community with the parties to a multilateral or even bilateral treaty.[29] Regimes, and with them interpretive communities, evolve over time.[30]

A good example is the interpretive community of European judges. The desire for uniform interpretation of EU law led the drafters of the EU treaties to vest exclusive jurisdiction in the European Court of Justice (ECJ), enabling it to ensure the consistent and uniform interpretation of EU law on the basis of overseeing a decentralized network of national courts. Against the background of diverse national interpretive communities to begin with, the ECJ's interpretive monopoly was designed to prevent national varieties of interpretation of EU law. Over time, it arguably led to the emergence of an interpretive community of European judges with ultimate responsibility for ensuring the coherence of EU law.[31]

Interpretive communities exist both nationally and internationally, and interact with one another. An interpretive community of actors with relevant expertise can be limited to one country, or extend regionally or across the globe. For example, Matthew Conaglen refers to the interpretive community in (English) land law as comprised of 'judges, practitioners and academic commentators, rather than the general populace'.[32] Judge Frank Easterbrook identifies a historic interpretive community in 1791 with respect to the US Constitution when the Eighth Amendment was adopted.[33] For Owen Fiss, there is a single interpretive community in the United States:

In law the interpretive community is a reality. It has authority to confer because membership does not depend on agreement. Judges do not belong to an interpretive community as a result of shared views about particular issues or interpretations, but belong by virtue of a commitment to uphold and advance the rule of law itself.[34]

Yet Judge Easterbrook, focusing solely on judges, rejects the idea of a unified judicial interpretive community:

In the United States judges are selected from such divergent parts of the profession that it is a mistake to speak even of a judicial interpretive community. A judge devoted to selecting a modern interpretive community external to his own preferences may play the field.[35]

---

[28] Easterbrook, 'Abstraction and Authority', 364 (identifying the interpretive community is a stumbling block).
[29] Johnstone, 'Treaty Interpretation', 371–2.
[30] Fish, *Doing What Comes Naturally*, 141, 150.
[31] Karen Alter, *Establishing the Supremacy of European Law: The Making of an International Rule of Law in Europe* (OUP 2001).
[32] Matthew Conaglen, 'Mortgagee Powers Rhetoric' (2006) 69 MLR 583, 585.
[33] Easterbrook, 'Abstraction and Authority', 360.
[34] Fiss, 'Objectivity and Interpretation', 746.
[35] Easterbrook, 'Abstraction and Authority', 364.

Similarly, Cass Sunstein underscores that the US legal system (or any other legal system) lacks a single interpretive community. To him, the main interpretive community are the 800 or so US federal judges,[36] though he recognized that other actors are part of the penumbra of the same community, such as agency administrators.[37] Sunstein explains, in terms that apply analogously to international law, that:

> ... in hard cases and over time, the community will be badly divided. Different people will bring disparate background norms to bear on the question of meaning, and these norms will produce disagreements over the construction of statutes.[38]

Adopting this reasoning, international judges and arbitrators are *a fortiori* members of diverse interpretive communities. For example, an ICJ judge may simultaneously be a member of four interpretive communities: (1) the interpretive community of international judges, (2) the interpretive community of investment treaty arbitrators, (3) the interpretive community associated with his or her professional background (eg government legal advisers or academics focused on human rights), and (4) the interpretive community of lawyers in the jurisdiction where the judge received her legal education, was socialized or practised.

The complex interpretive community that produces the official discourse on the use of force is one example of an interpretive community in international law that is often divided.[39] A second example drawn from environmental protection is the network of environmental experts who produce environmental impact assessments. They are not necessarily lawyers, let alone international lawyers. This interpretive community has its own journals, professional organizations, conferences, and research facilities.[40] A third example is the interpretive community in trade law, which extends beyond lawyers despite the existence of the Dispute Settlement Body (DSB). This community includes individuals within government bureaucracies, elite law firms, business associations, the law, economics and political science academy, think tanks, and civil society organizations.[41] One can identify much narrower interpretive communities within the interpretive community of general international trade. A good example is the interpretive community centred around the Joint Food and Agricultural Organization/World Health

---

[36] Cass Sunstein, 'Interpreting Statutes in the Regulatory State' (1989) 103 Harv L Rev 405.

[37] Sunstein, 'Interpreting Statutes in the Regulatory State', 413.

[38] Cass Sunstein, *After the Rights Revolution: Reconceiving the Regulatory State* (Harvard University Press 1993) 189.

[39] Andrea Bianchi, 'The International Regulation of the Use of Force: The Politics of Interpretive Method' (2009) 22 LJIL 651.

[40] Neil Craik, *The International Law of Environmental Impact Assessment: Process, Substance and Integration* (CUP 2008) 220.

[41] See Thomas Cottier and Markus Krajewski, 'What Role for Non-Discrimination and Prudential Standards in International Financial Law?' (2010) 13 JIEL 817, 818; William Drake and Kalypso Nicolaïdis, 'Ideas, Interests and Institutionalization: "Trade in Services" and the Uruguay Round' (1992) 46 Int'l Org 37; A Claire Cutler, 'Toward a Radical Political Economy Critique of Transnational Economic Law' in Susan Marks (ed), *International Law on the Left: Re-examining Marxist Legacies* (CUP 2008) 199, 217.

Organization Expert Committee on Food Additives (JEFCA).[42] Thus, there is no single, coherent epistemic community in international trade. National epistemic communities exist side by side with the international trade community, even if they are transnationally linked.[43] The same applies in other issue areas.

In 2012, Judge Griesa of the US Federal District Court in Southern Manhattan adopted a 'rateable payment' interpretation of the *pari passu* clause contained in defaulted Argentine sovereign bonds. He thereby departed from the shared background understanding of the participants of the epistemic community on sovereign debt. His interpretation raised the spectre of financial instability.[44] Other examples of interpretive communities include: security experts and arms control specialists;[45] the Delors Committee which devised European Monetary Union;[46] and, more broadly, the epistemic community of European policy entrepreneurs who pushed European integration.[47]

II. Diverse Interpretive Communities and Fragmentation

The growing diversity of actors who interpret international law catalyses the fragmentation into interpretive communities. It is also a source of divergent approaches to interpretation, which in turn can lead to divergent substantive outcomes.[48] A second, linked factor is the increasingly narrow legal education and subject matter specialization of the heterogeneous set of actors interpreting international law.[49] As historian Robert Darnton contended, the 'history of books

---

[42] Jacqueline Peel, *Science and Risk Regulation in International Law* (CUP 2010) 214–15.

[43] Gregory Shaffer and Michelle Ratton Sanchez, 'Winning at the WTO: The Development of a Trade Policy Community within Brazil' in Gregory Shaffer and Ricardo Meléndez-Ortiz (eds), *Dispute Settlement at the WTO: The Developing Country Experience* (CUP 2010) 21, 24.

[44] *NML Capital Ltd et al v Republic of Argentina*, Nos 08 Civ 6978 (TPG), 09 Civ 1707 (TPG), 09 Civ 1708 (TPG) (SDNY 11 November 2012); *NML Capital Ltd v Republic of Argentina*, Nos 08 Civ 6978 (TPG), 09 Civ 1707 (TPG), 09 Civ 1708 (TPG) (SDNY 11 November 2012), affirmed *Republic of Argentina v NML Capital*, 695 F 3d 201, *Republic of Argentina v NML Capital, Ltd*, 134 S Ct 2250 (2014). On the *pari passu* clause and the sovereign debt community's understanding of the clause, see Lee Buchheit and Jeremiah Pam, 'The Pari Passu Clause in Sovereign Debt Instruments' (2004) 53 Emory LJ 869.

[45] Emanuel Adler, 'The Emergence of Cooperation: National Epistemic Communities and the International Evolution of the Idea of Nuclear Arms Control' (1992) 46 Int'l Org 101 (Soviet and US experts creating a regime to regulate dangerous arms competition).

[46] Amy Verdun, 'The Role of the Delors Committee in the Creation of EMU: An Epistemic Community?' (1999) 6(2) JEPP 308.

[47] Barry Eichengreen, 'European Integration' in Barry Weingast and Donald Wittman (eds), *The Oxford Handbook of Political Economy* (OUP 2006) 799, 803–13.

[48] Waibel, 'Uniformity versus Specialisation'.

[49] Letter from Felix Frankfurter, Professor, Harvard Law School, to Mr Rosenwald, 13 May 1927, quoted in Hany T Edwards, 'The Growing Disjunction Between Legal Education and the Legal Profession' (1992) 91 Mich L Rev 34, 34: 'In the last analysis, the law is what lawyers are. And the law and the lawyers are what the law schools make them'; Theodor Mayer-Maly, 'Der Jurist: Enzyklopädist oder Spezialist' in Detlef Merten (ed), *Probleme der Juristenausbildung* (Duncker & Humblot 1980) 15–28; Anthony Kronman, *The Lost Lawyer: Failing Ideals of the Legal Profession* (Harvard University Press 1995).

has become so crowded with ancillary disciplines, that one can no longer see its general contours'.[50] The same risk exists in international law.

How does the emergence of distinct interpretive communities affect interpretation? Is more fragmentation the inevitable consequence?[51] The degree to which interpretive communities heighten fragmentation hinges on how sealed off they are from the broader community of international lawyers, and how much exchange occurs between international and domestic lawyers.[52] For example, it is likely that the close-knit epistemic communities in human rights law and international trade law are more influential, as compared to the more diffuse epistemic community in general international law.[53] Cohesive epistemic communities find it easier to engage in collective action to pursue their shared goals, whereas divided epistemic communities will struggle to enlist others in their project.

A. A diverse universe of interpretive actors in international law

The universe of interpreters in international law is more diverse than those interpreting statutes or contracts in domestic legal systems. In domestic law, the shared background of interpreters is more alike. By contrast, international law has many different interpreters and associated perspectives, such as judges and arbitrators on international courts and tribunals, national courts, government legal advisers, the staff of international organizations, and a wide range of non-state actors.[54] National courts or international tribunals have historically played only a subordinated role.[55]

While only a tiny percentage of interpretive disputes reach international or national courts, the role of national courts as interpreters of international law has grown in the last three decades.[56] Together with government legal advisers,

---

[50] Robert Darnton, 'What is the History of Books?' (1982) 111(3) Daedalus 65, 67.

[51] Fish, *Is There a Text in this Class?*; Johnstone, 'Treaty Interpretation'; Ian Johnstone, 'Security Council Deliberations: The Power of the Better Argument' (2003) 14 EJIL 437, 443–7; Vagts, 'Treaty Interpretation and the New American Ways of Law Reading', 480.

[52] Pulkowski, *Law and Politics of Regime Conflicts*, 80 (voicing concern about 'closed epistemic communities').

[53] Joost Pauwelyn and Manfred Elsig, 'The Politics of Treaty Interpretation' in Jeffrey Dunoff and Mark Pollack (eds), *Interdisciplinary Perspectives on International Law and International Relations* (CUP 2012) 445, 467.

[54] Maarten Bos, 'Legal Archetypes and the Normative Concept of Law as Main Factors in the Defining and Development of International Law' (1976) 23 NILR 72, 74 (distinguishing three 'archetypes' of law appliers, namely the lawmaker, the judge, and the scholar). He builds on the interpretation *authentica, usualis et doctrinalis* developed by Bartolus: Stefan Vogenauer, 'History of Interpretation of Statutes' in Jürgen Basedow, Klaus J Hopt, Reinhard Zimmermann, and Andreas Stier (eds), *Max Planck Encyclopaedia of European Private Law* (OUP 2012) 979, 989.

[55] RP Schaffer, 'Current Trends in Treaty Interpretation and the South African Approach' (1976) Aust YBIL 129, 148.

[56] William Burke-White and Anne-Marie Slaughter, 'The Future of International Law is Domestic (or, The European Way of Law)' (2006) 47(2) HILJ 327; William Burke-White, 'A Community of Courts: Toward a System of International Criminal Law Enforcement' (2002) 24 Mich J Int'l L 1; Anne-Marie Slaughter, 'A Global Community of Courts' (2003) 44 HILJ 191.

international judges, and arbitrators, national courts in a small number of typically Western jurisdictions form the dominant interpretive communities in international law. Their interpretations of international law are much more likely to prevail than those of national courts in less influential states and most non-state actors, including legal academics.

The pathways to become a member of the various interpretive communities dealing with international law differ by issue area and at times by country. For example, the career trajectories of national judges differ widely across countries. Some interpretive communities generally—governmental legal advisers, international judges, and international arbitrators—and some communities depending on the subject matter—international peace and security or investment—will be more difficult to join than others such as human rights and environmental law.

Joining the most selective and influential of interpretive communities—judges on the ICJ, governmental legal advisers, and senior national court judges—often requires decades-long career commitments. Others require a lesser investment of intellectual and social capital, and are more open to those without a narrower set of credentials. The influence of interpretive communities is inversely related to their openness: the more accessible an interpretive community, the less influential it is. The higher the barriers to entry, the more weight the members of an interpretive community carry. The interpretive community of investment arbitrators is in an intermediate position. Conversely, it is comparatively easier to join the interpretive community of legal academics or human rights activists.

Given the diversity of interpreters and epistemic communities, interpretive methodologies in international law vary considerably.[57] The VCLT does not significantly constrain interpretation. The great majority of interpretive disputes are settled in non-judicial or arbitral fora, including international organizations. States and, to a lesser extent, international organizations play a crucial role in determining the meaning of rules of international law.[58] Government legal advisers have traditionally been the primary actors in interpretation. They continue to be an influential interpretive community, for example with regard to the collective system for maintaining international peace and security under the UN Charter.[59] A lot of interpretation in international law is auto-interpretation by governments of their own obligations. As the role of formal and informal international organizations in global governance has increased, their contribution to interpretation has grown. However, they often remain beholden to their member states, with significant consequences for interpretation.[60]

---

[57] David Sloss, *The Role of Domestic Courts in Treaty Enforcement: A Comparative Study* (CUP 2009); Michael Waibel, 'International Rules of Interpretation: Developed for and Applied by National Courts?' in Helmut P Aust and Georg Nolte (eds), *Interpretation of International Law by Domestic Courts: Converging Approaches?* (OUP 2015) (forthcoming).

[58] Michael Barnett and Martha Finnemore, 'The Politics, Power, and Pathologies of International Organizations' (1999) 53 Int'l Org 699, 712.

[59] Bianchi, 'The International Regulation of the Use of Force', 651.

[60] Pulkowski, *Law and Politics of Regime Conflicts*, 40.

Different branches of government can diverge on the interpretation of international legal norms, as the executive and judicial branch did in *Hamdan v Rumsfeld*.[61] Similar cleavages appear in other issue areas. For example, Julia Black distinguishes between regulatory interpretive communities and legal interpretive communities (ie the courts) in the area of financial regulation. She emphasizes that 'regulatory practices, understandings and reasoning may be very different from those of the legal interpretive community'.[62]

1. National judges

National judges in a select number of jurisdictions constitute another influential interpretive community in international law. They are increasingly influential in interpreting international law. They are typically part of an interpretive community of other lawyers steeped in a particular national legal tradition or legal family. Depending on their specialization within national law, they may form part of other functional epistemic communities at the national or international level (for example, tax, labour, or administrative law). At the same time, they are likely part of diverse, state-based interpretive communities rather than transnational ones, heightening the risk of fragmentation. Their allegiance to their home jurisdiction might lead them to approach the task of interpretation from the perspective of their national epistemic community, even if they formally apply the framework for treaty interpretation set out in Articles 31–32 of the VCLT.[63] National courts may be particularly prone to interpreting treaties through a national lens, and as a result of their growing role could constitute a major source of interpretive fragmentation.

One of the aims of the VCLT is precisely to 'bridge the "gulfs in language, culture and values that separate nations" by providing a set of "conventions of description, argument, judgment and persuasion" to facilitate interjudicial dialogue'.[64] One aspiration of Articles 31–32 is to help overcome interpretive divergence between diverse interpretive communities of national judges. The question is whether the VCLT provides a strong enough 'glue' to counterbalance the centrifugal tendencies due to the rise of interpretive communities that participate in the interpretation of international law, including at the national level.

---

[61] *Hamdan v Rumsfeld* 548 US 557 (2006).

[62] Julia Black, 'Regulatory Conversations' (2002) 29 J of Law & Soc 163, 177.

[63] Eyal Benvenisti, 'Judicial Misgivings Regarding the Application of International Law: An Analysis of the Attitudes of National Courts' (1993) 4 EJIL 159, 161; Anthea Roberts, 'Comparative International Law? The Role of National Courts in Creating and Enforcing International Law' (2011) 60 ICLQ 57, 75; James Crawford and Penelope Nevill, 'Relations between International Courts and Tribunals' in Margaret Young (ed), *Regime Interaction in International Law: Facing Fragmentation* (CUP 2012) 249; Waibel, 'Uniformity versus Specialisation' (on 'interpretive home bias').

[64] *Trans World Airlines, Inc. v Franklin Mint Corp.* 66 US 243, 262 (1984) (Stevens, J, dissenting); Fish, *Is There a Text in this Class?*, 116; Johnstone, 'Treaty Interpretation', 378; Antonios Tzanakopoulos, 'Judicial Dialogue as a Means of Interpretation' in Helmut P Aust and Georg Nolte, *Interpretation of International Law by Domestic Courts: Converging Approaches?* (OUP 2015) (forthcoming).

As for other interpretive communities, a pertinent question is who the national judges are, and of which epistemic community or communities they form a part. Their exposure to international law may be one factor determining their openness towards international law, including its methods of interpretation. Moreover, the teaching of international law varies significantly across jurisdictions.[65] Training national judges could go a long way to ensure that they apply the VCLT's interpretive methodology.[66]

2. *International lawyers*

To a considerable degree, international lawyers are a product of their own culture and legal system. Frederick Dunn's remarks dating back to the 1930s continue to resonate today: the international lawyer 'carries with him the whole collection of habitual ways of acting, of fixed ideas and value judgments of his own community, which he is prone to expand into ideas of universal validity'.[67] As James Crawford lucidly observes:

> [International lawyers] are commonly municipal lawyers first, and bring to the international sphere a collection of presumptions and perceptions as part of our training. Each legal tradition may carry with it a rather different concept of international law and its possibilities... Divisions of opinion are, moreover, amplified by a lack of a shared language; while the builders of the Tower of Babel speak mutually incomprehensible languages, there is no guarantee that they are building the same Tower.[68]

The counter-argument is that contemporary international lawyers are exposed to many different types of law, and are more cosmopolitan in outlook than their predecessors were.[69] Even if the increased internationalistion of legal education acts as a counterbalance, the generalist international lawyer is an endangered species. Specialization in international law has fuelled the rise of interpretive communities.

B. Specialization and the entrenchment of interpretive communities

Educational background and professional experience is likely to shape approaches to interpretation in international law. Both are likely to vary by country and by field of specialization, in national or international law. The approach to interpretation could differ depending on the interpreter's specialism and legal education. The emergence of specialized international lawyers who eclipse generalist international lawyers has heightened the fragmentation into a plurality of interpretive communities, and risks entrenching these interpretive communities.

---

[65] Anthea Roberts, *Is International Law International?* (OUP 2015) (forthcoming).

[66] See eg David Bederman, Christopher J Borgen, and David A Martin, *International Law: A Handbook For Judges* (ASIL 2003).

[67] Frederick Dunn, *The Protection of Nationals: A Study in the Application of International Law* (Johns Hopkins Press 1932) 105–7.

[68] Crawford, *Chance, Order, Change*, 152–3.

[69] Adam Smith, '"Judicial Nationalism" in International Law: National Identity and Judicial Autonomy at the ICJ' (2005) 40 Tex Int'l LJ 197, 224 n 157.

The generalist international lawyer who forms part of Schachter's famed 'invisible college' of international lawyers with broadly shared background norms is today an endangered species,[70] if there ever was one. Harold Laswell anticipated this danger in the early 1970s, when he observed that 'those who contribute to the knowledge process lose their vision of the whole and concern themselves almost exclusively with their specialty'.[71] The increased specialization among international lawyers has been accompanied by growing 'tunnel vision'.[72] Bianchi has identified two channels that lead epistemic communities to operate in isolation from one another:

What all these epistemic communities that shape the discipline's discourse in their respective areas of specialization have in common is: (i) to ignore for the most part what is going on in other unrelated areas of international law, (ii) to believe that the only meaningful practice or the very core business of international law is their own specialization...[73]

Investment arbitral tribunals adopt different interpretive paradigms depending on who the arbitrators are.[74] Commercial lawyers are part of one interpretive community, public international lawyers are part of another, international trade lawyers form part of a third, and public lawyers part of a fourth interpretive community. Anthea Roberts argues that 'epistemic communities of lawyers...come to the investment treaty system with distinct conceptual frameworks', and that 'the analogies and paradigms invoked by arbitrators, academics, and (to some extent) advocates are influenced by their backgrounds, training, and interests'.[75] While it is likely that the background of adjudicators affects interpretation, precisely how it does so is an open empirical question. Investment arbitrators form a 'small and closely-knit epistemic community',[76] which shares a common ethos and background norms.[77] As Alex Mills notes, a distinct epistemic community of investment lawyers has emerged:

Investment arbitrators also have a professional interest in perceptions of [International Investment Law or IIL] and dispute resolution as a functional system. An important part

[70] Oscar Schachter, 'The Invisible College of International Lawyers' (1977) 72 North U L Rev 217; David Kennedy, 'The Politics of the Invisible College: International Governance and the Politics of Expertise' (2001) 5 EHRLR 463.

[71] Harold Lasswell, 'From Fragmentation to Configuration' (1971) 2 Pol Sci 439, 440.

[72] Horatia Muir Watt, 'Private International Law Beyond the Schism' (2011) 2(3) Trans L T 347.

[73] Andrea Bianchi, 'Gazing at the Crystal Ball (again): State Immunity and *Jus Cogens* Beyond *Germany v Italy*' (2013) 4(3) JIDS 457.

[74] Anthea Roberts, 'Clash of Paradigms: Actors and Analogies Shaping the Investment Treaty System' (2013) 107 AJIL 45 (Roberts herself does not use the term 'interpretive community').

[75] Roberts, 'Clash of Paradigms', 54.

[76] Stephan W Schill, 'Ordering Paradigms in International Investment Law: Bilateralism-Multilateralism-Multilateralization' in Zachary Douglas, Joost Pauwelyn, and Jorge E Viñuales (eds), *The Foundations of International Investment Law: Bringing Theory Into Practice* (OUP 2014) 109, 123.

[77] Daphna Kapeliuk, 'The Repeat Appointment Factor: Exploring Decision Patterns of Elite Investment Arbitrators' (2010) 96 Cornell L Rev 47; Jason Yackee, 'Controlling the International Investment Law Agency' (2010) 53 HILJ 391, 401–6; Roberts, 'Clash of Paradigms'; Jeswald Salacuse, 'The Emerging Global Regime for Investment' (2010) 51(2) HILJ 427, 465–6; Santiago Montt, *State Liability in Investment Treaty Arbitration: Global Constitutional and Administrative Law in the BIT Generation* (Hart 2009) 19.

of the history of IIL is the technical and sociological process of its establishment as its own distinct professional specialization, a new 'field' of study and work. It has emerged in recent years as not merely a particular application of general rules of public international law or procedures for commercial dispute settlement, but as a new discipline requiring specialist (and expensive) knowledge and expertise, provided and supported by an 'epistemic community' with its own networks, conferences, and journals. An interest in promoting this sense of progress in professional development may lead an arbitrator not only to seek to make 'balanced' (or 'rebalanced') decisions in individual cases, but to strive for coherence and consistency across different investment disputes.[78]

Consequently, a shared outlook is often absent among the members of ad hoc investment arbitration tribunals, whose members are recruited from more diverse backgrounds than the typical international judge on a standing international court such as the ICJ or the International Tribunal for the Law of the Sea. A first group of investment arbitrators are specialists in particular areas of international law, a second are public international law generalists, and a third are commercial lawyers with limited previous exposure to public international law (including its methods of interpretation). These diverse actors are unlikely to be part of the same 'invisible college' of international lawyers. Similarly, WTO panel members and judges on human rights tribunals may no longer share the same ethos. As part of two distinct interpretive communities, they may increasingly speak different languages, base their interpretive task on different priors and be animated by a different ethos.

III. Interpretive Communities as Advocates of Distinct Normative Visions of International Law

International law is 'colonized' by an ever-increasing number of issue areas that are often in a relationship of conflict with one another.[79] Each regime, with its own language, background norms, and shared understandings promotes varied policy goals. Each is primarily concerned with the pursuit of its own goals, be it the protection of the environment, human rights, or cross-border investment. The epistemic community associated with each regime has strong incentives to work towards the achievements of their regime's goals, as the effectiveness of the regime is likely to contribute to its own prestige and the influence of its members.

Interpretive communities accompany specialization and may encourage 'group think' and 'tunnel vision' through the circulation of narrow technical expertise. The risk of the expertise-based model of interpretive communities is that

---

[78] Alex Mills, 'The Balancing (and Unbalancing?) of Interests in International Investment Law and Arbitration' in Zachary Douglas, Joost Pauwelyn, and Jorge E Viñuales (eds), *The Foundations of International Investment Law: Bringing Theory into Practice* (OUP 2014) 437, 454.

[79] Pulkowski, *Law and Politics of Regime Conflicts*, 36; C Wilfred Jenks, 'The Conflict of Law-making Treaties' (1953) 30 BYBIL 401.

it privileges technocrats over all those whose interests are affected by interpretation more broadly.[80] Technocrats have the incentives and the ability to advance their own normative vision of a given substantive issue area. Those affected by the interpretation, such as indigenous populations in the area of intellectual property rights protection, people in conflict zones when the UN Security Council adopts measures under Chapter VII to maintain international peace and security, and consumers benefiting from trade, often lack voice and the tools to articulate their interests in interpretive terms.

A crucial difference between law and literary studies, where the concept of interpretive community originated, is that the consequences of interpretation in law are more serious. Some interpretive communities in the international legal arena have the power to issue binding decisions (eg ICJ judges and WTO Appellate Body members), and the power to insist on compliance; other interpreters lack that formal, binding adjudicatory authority.[81] In law, the choice of an interpretive method is the continuation of the politics of international law by other means.[82]

Which interpretation ultimately prevails hinges in no small part on which is the '[d]ominant legal interpretive community',[83] the one with the formal authority to interpret the law with binding effect. As Paul Brest notes in the context of the US legal system, the dominant interpretive community in the United States is 'mostly white, male, professional, and relatively wealthy. However humble their backgrounds, they are members of a ruling elite'.[84] The same applies to international law.

Members of the epistemic communities in international law are involved in 'promoting, resisting or reshaping the incorporation of different kinds of knowledge'.[85] For instance, 'WTO lawyers may intuitively feel that their rules are the most "serious" ones'.[86] The WTO as an institution, in tandem with trade experts from influential member states, filled the concept of a 'trade barrier' with meaning.[87] Regime participants moved the trade regime away from the embedded liberalism that had prevailed during the three decades after World War II,[88] toward the Washington Consensus that lasted from 1990–2008.[89]

Interpretive communities use various strategies to enhance their prestige and influence over competing communities. A first strategy involves careful screening

---

[80] Robert Howse, *The WTO System: Law, Politics and Legitimacy* (Cameron May 2007) 233.

[81] Paul Brest, 'Interpretation and Interest' (1982) 34 Stan L Rev 765.

[82] Ian Johnstone, 'The Shifting Sands of Treaty Interpretation: Introduction' (2008) 102 ASIL Proceedings 411, 411 ('a proxy for a larger debate about international law's relation to politics').

[83] Brest, 'Interpretation and Interest', 771.

[84] Brest, 'Interpretation and Interest', 771.

[85] Andrew Lang, 'Legal Regimes and Professional Knowledges: The Internal Politics of Regime Definition' in Margaret Young (ed), *Regime Interaction in International Law: Facing Fragmentation* (CUP 2012) 113, 132.

[86] Pulkowski, *Law and Politics of Regime Conflicts*, 15.

[87] Lang, *World Trade Law After Neoliberalism*.

[88] John Ruggie, 'International Regimes, Transactions, and Change: Embedded Liberalism in the Postwar Economic Order' (1982) 36 Int'l Org 379.

[89] Lang, *World Trade Law After Neoliberalism*; Eric Helleiner and Stefano Pagliari, 'The End of an Era in International Financial Regulation? A Postcrisis Research Agenda' (2011) 65 Int'l Org 169.

in the admission of new members, particularly into a dominant interpretive community, to ensure that their specialized expertise and normative orientation remains the dominant paradigm in a particular issue area. Such screening of international judges and arbitrators can focus on their political philosophy (for example a demonstrated commitment to human rights or free markets), their career trajectory, and publication record.

A second strategy involves cooperating with other actors to build support for their particular normative visions. This strategy can involve regular exchange of views with governments, academics, and practising lawyers; teaching to mould the thinking of the next generation of policymakers and lawyers; giving speeches setting out their broad normative visions, in the hope of inspiring other lawyers and the population at large; and publishing books and articles with a view to shaping the academic and policy debate.

Third, 'scientific' interpretation and supposedly neutral technical expertise in international law can cloak the exercise of power and the pursuit of interests. In particular, interpretive communities that are supposed to interpret international law in a detached manner, such as national judges and international judges and arbitrators (in contrast to auto-interpretation by governments), can increase their legitimacy by employing widely accepted principles of interpretation, even if only as a cover for advancing their own normative vision of international law.

Articles 31–32 of the VCLT arguably 'swept away...all the supposed special tenets of interpretation that had enveloped the subject like cobwebs'.[90] Even if we accept that the VCLT thereby managed to introduce a uniform regime of treaty interpretation, the emergence of competing interpretive communities undercuts this uniformity. These communities advance diverse normative projects of international law. They use international law as a professional vocabulary to achieve the outcomes they desire. In the words of Martti Koskenniemi, international law is 'sliced up in institutional projects that cater for special audiences with special interests and special ethos'.[91]

Robert Jennings famously referred to the 'tendency of particular tribunals to regard themselves as different, as separate little empires which must as far as possible be augmented'.[92] More broadly, regimes are 'frameworks of thinking and "regimes of truth"...[that create] mini-sovereignties out of themselves'.[93] It is not the tribunals themselves that exhibit this tendency, but the people that populate them: judges, arbitrators, and other decision-makers. They can acquire or

---

[90] Franklin Berman, 'Community Law and International Law: How Far Does Either Belong to the Other?' in Basil S Markesinis (ed), *The Clifford Chance Lectures Volume I: Bridging the Channel* (OUP 1996) 250.

[91] Martti Koskenniemi, 'The Politics of International Law—20 Years On' (2009) 20 EJIL 7, 9.

[92] Robert Jennings, 'The Proliferation of Adjudicatory Bodies: Dangers and Possible Answers' in *Implications of the Proliferation of International Adjudicatory Bodies for Dispute Resolution* (1995) 9 ASIL Bulletin 2; Robert Jennings, 'The Judiciary, International and National, and the Development of International Law' (1996) 45 ICLQ 1, 5–6.

[93] Martti Koskenniemi, 'Hegemonic Regimes' in Margaret Young (ed), *Regime Interaction in International Law: Facing Fragmentation* (CUP 2011) 305, 317.

augment their own prestige and that of their tribunal in various ways, for instance by developing a distinctive normative orientation that responds to the demands of stakeholders, by engaging in legal innovation, or by establishing legal certainty.

Creating differentiated regimes can be a strategy by hegemonic states to further their political influence.[94] States can only fully achieve the strategic goals they pursue in creating distinct regimes if interpretation preserves at least some differences between regimes. Interpretation can play a centripetal or a centrifugal role, depending on the interpreter's decision to construe the relevant legal system narrowly or broadly.[95] As Pulkowski notes, '[i]nstead of espousing the United States' *lex specialis* argument, the Appellate Body in *US-Shrimp* chose to interpret the law of one regime "in the light of" the law of another regime'.[96]

From the perspective of advancing particular normative projects, interpretive communities play a crucial role in interpretation. They can ensure goal attainment in line with the philosophy animating a particular regime, and ensure that 'extraneous' interests that are not central to the regime at issue are kept largely at bay (eg environmental protection in investment law and economic efficiency in human rights law). In addition to the three strategies mentioned above, a time-tested strategy of avoiding overreach on the part of a regime focused on a particular issue area is to refrain from creating an institution or a dispute settlement body independent of states in the first place, giving states virtually unfettered control over the evolution of the regime (eg the maintenance of international peace and security, and the international monetary regime).

The ICJ lacks the power to authoritatively interpret the UN Charter, shifting power to the Members of the Security Council, in particular the permanent five members. Which interpretive community has the authority to interpret constitutive documents of international organizations matters. Another illustration is the International Monetary Fund (IMF). References to the VCLT abound in trade and investment law,[97] yet are less common in tax law, and virtually absent in international monetary law. Why does interpretation follow such a different path in the four areas of international economic law?

---

[94] Eyal Benvenisti and George W Downs, 'The Empire's New Clothes: Political Economy and the Fragmentation of International Law' (2007) 60 Stan L Rev 595; Surabhi Ranganathan, *Strategically Created Treaty Conflicts and the Politics of International Law* (CUP 2014).

[95] *Legal Consequences for States of the Continued Presence of South Africa in Namibia (South West Africa) Notwithstanding Security Council Resolution 276 (1970)*, Advisory Opinion, ICJ Rep 1971, 16, 31 ('an international instrument has to be interpreted and applied within the framework of the entire legal system prevailing at the time of the interpretation').

[96] Pulkowski, *Law and Politics of Regime Conflicts*, 38; *United States—Import Prohibition of Certain Shrimp and Shrimp Products,* Panel Report, WT/DS58/R, adopted 6 November 1998, modified by Appellate Body Report, WT/DS58/AB/R, DSR 1998:VII, 2821, [3.105].

[97] Christoph Schreuer, 'Diversity and Harmonization of Treaty Interpretation in Investment Arbitration' in Malgosia Fitzmaurice, Olufemis Elias, and Panos Merkouris (eds), *Treaty Interpretation and the Vienna Convention on the Law of Treaties: 30 Years On* (Brill 2010) 129; J Romesh Weeramantry, *Treaty Interpretation in Investment Arbitration* (OUP 2012); Michael Waibel, 'International Investment Law and Treaty Interpretation' in Rainer Hofmann and Christian Tams (eds), *International Investment Law and General International Law: From Clinical Isolation to Systemic Integration?* (Nomos 2011) 29.

The make-up of the relevant interpretive communities furnishes a ready answer. At the apex of the trade regime sits the WTO Appellate Body, a standing dispute settlement body composed of individuals that consider themselves to be part of the 'international judiciary'. In the case of investment law, ad hoc arbitral tribunals drawn from a diverse pool of commercial and international lawyers are united by a common ethos of investor protection. In international tax law, it is primarily national courts and other national administrative agencies that interpret tax treaties. Finally, in international monetary law, the IMF is dominated by executive decision-making by financial experts rather than lawyers.[98] The drafters of the IMF Articles sought to ensure that control over the meaning of the IMF's constitutive treaty rested with these subject experts, rather than with lawyers. They were adamant that no lawyers sitting on a judicial tribunal external to the organization with no specific expertise in international monetary affairs should have any significant influence over the regime's operation.[99]

The extensive discourse on fragmentation in international law oscillates between the two extreme poles: the view that fragmentation poses a mortal threat to the international legal order, or that it is a natural outgrowth of international law's advanced state of development, mirroring earlier developments in national law.[100] The entrenchment of various interpretive communities in particular has fuelled centrifugal tendencies in international law, and raises systemic concerns about international law's unity as a system, its sources, and its methods (including a unified interpretive method).

Conclusion

This chapter showed that interpretive communities are a major factor behind the observed variation in interpretation across different issues areas of international law. Beneath the veneer of uniformity of the VCLT's interpretive principles, distinct interpretive communities have contributed to diverse interpretive approaches in international law. The choice of an interpretive method is the continuation of the decisions of states to create a distinct regime in the first place.[101]

The success of international law—in the sense of the almost infinitely greater scope of its subject matter compared to even just a few decades ago—also sowed the seeds of greatly increased diversity among the actors that populate the international realm. Lawyers, like other experts, are also increasingly specialized. Traditional international lawyers represent just a small, and not necessarily the

---

[98] Gregory Shaffer and Michael Waibel, 'The (Mis)Alignment of the Trade and Monetary Legal Orders' in Gregory Shaffer and Terence Halliday (eds), *Transnational Legal Orders* (CUP 2015) 187.
[99] Ervin Hexner, 'Interpretation by Public International Organizations of their Basic Instruments' (1953) 53 AJIL 341, 344.
[100] Bianchi, 'Looking Ahead', 404.
[101] Johnstone, 'The Shifting Sands of Treaty Interpretation', 411 ('a proxy for a larger debate about international law's relation to politics').

most influential, group among all the participants in global governance. The role of lawyers varies from regime to regime. By design, the role of international lawyers differs in investment and trade law compared to international monetary and financial law.[102]

As a result of these developments, whether international lawyers are all part of a single epistemic community that crosses the boundaries between its diverse regimes is increasingly doubtful. To be sure, professional societies such as the American Society of International Law have played a crucial role in fostering a sense of the 'invisible college'.[103] Yet international law has also seen the emergence of more specialized professional societies, such as the Society of International Economic Law, mirroring professional associations and dedicated journals in specialized fields of law or methodology (eg the American Law and Economics Association or the Law and Society Association). These are emanations of the broader trend towards specialization and technocratic expertise that fuelled the rise of interpretive communities.

The 'invisible college' of international lawyers appears to be crumbling before our eyes. A patchwork quilt of specialized international lawyers is taking their place. Specialization in international law, as well as the accrued role of national judges, has led to divergence on interpretation. Admittedly, numerous links between subject specialists and the interpretive communities exist. Regimes also overlap and interact, but the trend towards much greater specialization is likely here to stay.

It is too early to tell how serious the real-world consequences of fragmentation will be. While there are early signs that international law does not operate as a unified system today, establishing the counterfactual is difficult, as the scope of international law has expanded dramatically. True, international law was more unified a hundred years ago when its scope was much more limited, and most international affairs were left to politics and national law. Yet significant fragmentation occurred simply at another level, between what was within the field of international law, and the large part of international affairs left outside.

With the dramatic expansion of international law over the last century, fragmentation was imported into international law in its almost infinite variety. The entrenchment of distinct interpretive communities could collapse international law as a system. Fragmentation results from the growing tendency of interpreters of international law to slice and dice international law into discrete building blocks with few connections to one another, and is animated by diverse, and sometimes conflicting, normative goals. It is up to the members of international law's diverse interpretive communities to take the common origin of their various regimes seriously. Should international lawyers rise to this collective challenge, they will be able to achieve a reasonable balance between specialization and fragmentation.

---

[102] Shaffer and Waibel, 'The (Mis)Alignment of the Trade and Monetary Legal Orders'.
[103] Schachter, 'The Invisible College of International Lawyers'.

8

Interpretative Authority and the International Judiciary

Gleider Hernández

Introduction

International lawyers have claimed authority for international law through defining it as an objective science: a discipline through which 'truth' about law and legal texts can be found. Yet, as with all legal systems, international law carries with it a degree of indeterminacy that cannot just be overcome through scientific rigour or the application of presumptions. Though all legal orders are prescriptive, in that they seek to set abstract rules, the more complex the system, the more frequently one arrives at an instance where the rules are in apparent conflict, or where they appear unclear. At the point of application, when the rules are determinative of the outcome of a situation, understanding how the claim to legitimacy of the interpreter is constructed becomes crucial.

For all this, the international legal system seems to avoid questions of how interpretative authority is allocated within it. Formally, it knows of no centralized judicial function that can discharge the systemic function presumed to exist in domestic legal orders; the interpretations of international courts and tribunals are in theory no different than an interpretation set down by an individual scholar. In practice, however, this is inaccurate for two reasons. First, judicial interpretation of legal texts and rules are binding on parties before that judicial institution, and thus create subjective legal obligations. Secondly, even if they are not formally law-creative, international judicial decisions possess a *centrifugal* normative force. By this, it is meant that other international legal actors tend to follow judicial reasoning faithfully: in this sense, judicial decisions can be substantively constitutive of international law. That normative effect is exacerbated when dealing with *unwritten* sources of law, in particular customary international law or the nebulous general principles of law: there is no balancing between the text, its authors, and the interpreter in such situations, and the certainty of judicial reasoning holds an intrinsic appeal and is often invoked as evidence for the existence of unwritten law.

Judicial institutions play an outsized role in the processes of interpretation. The very vagueness of the general rules on the interpretation of positive acts in international law has created enormous discretion for judicial institutions, both international and municipal, to participate in the interpretation of acts and rules of international law. This situation was merely codified with the advent of the VCLT: as Sir Hersch Lauterpacht once ventured, 'almost the entire history of the work of the Permanent Court of International Justice could be given in terms of cases arising out of the interpretation of treaties'.[1] So too is it with the International Court of Justice, and indeed with the bulk of investment arbitration awards, the WTO dispute settlement panels and the Appellate Body, the ad hoc international criminal tribunals, ITLOS, and the ICC. The interpretation of acts is thus a quintessential judicial activity, and sometimes is assumed by judicial institutions themselves to be a separate prong of the judicial function in the international legal order. Accordingly, studying the role of judicial institutions, or at least a broader enquiry as to the role of the *interpreter*, can surely advance the understanding of the function of interpretation and its role within a legal system. It is the interpreter who stands in the foreground when a text or rule is interpreted, even when the claim is advanced that there is a 'correct' interpretation which is presupposed to exist independently of the interpreter.[2] This is the key point to be developed here.

To situate the practice of interpretation within the judicial function is not to suggest that judicial institutions are *a fortiori* the best situated to participate in the interpretation of legal rules. Instead, it is to recognize that, in practice, the bulk of the judicial role primarily consists in interpreting the acts and rules placed before it when resolving disputes. What distinguishes the interpretation of acts by judicial institutions is that these work necessarily and formally within the confines of a defined legal system. This is important: the interpretation of international law by 'legal organs', authorized by the legal system itself, can have normative authority.[3] Again, to recall Lauterpacht, 'the work of interpretation is one of discovering the intention of the parties not only by reference to rules of interpretation, but to rules of international law bearing upon the subject-matter of the disputed contractual stipulation. These rules may be ready at hand, or they may have to be developed by the legitimate methods of judicial activity'.[4] In a sense, therefore, the argument favouring the judicial role in the interpretation of rules and norms goes further than merely recognizing the judicial role in interpretation. It suggests that judicial institutions are in fact guardians of the very coherence of these rules

---

[1] Hersch Lauterpacht, *The Function of Law in the International Community* (Clarendon Press 1933) 108.

[2] Stig Jørgensen, 'Lawyers and Hermeneutics' (2000) 40 Scand Stud L 181, 181.

[3] Hans Kelsen, *Pure Theory of Law* (2nd edn, University of California Press 1970) 355: '[t]he interpretation of law by the science of law (jurisprudence) must be sharply distinguished as non-authentic from the interpretation by legal organs. Jurisprudential interpretation is purely cognitive ascertainment of the meaning of legal norms. In contrast to the interpretation by legal organs, jurisprudential interpretation does not create law.'

[4] Kelsen, *Pure Theory of Law*, 355.

themselves: they are, as Andrea Bianchi has suggested here, very much players in the 'game' of interpretation.[5] In an indeterminate system like the international legal system, this claim has heightened relevance, as according to it, the international judiciary would gain an interpretative authority out of proportion with the manner in which it discharges its function in practice, especially in relation to the development of international law.

As such, the present chapter is a starting point for a wider project: it aims to explore whether there can be some form of wider theorizing as to the judicial function in relation to interpretation. Are international judges, when interpreting and applying international law, making a claim to normative (or semantic) authority? Are they more modest 'agents' in the international legal process? More ominously, are they cloaking themselves in the formalism of classical legal positivism so as to abdicate political responsibility for the constitutive role of their interpretations? Based both on the self-perception of international judges themselves, but also on wider theorizing as to the judicial function within a legal order, the argument made here is that international law is ripe for a conceptual re-examination of the international judiciary's place within the interpretative process. The silent claim judges make, through the safeguarding of systemic coherence of the legal system they inhabit, must be better understood and cognized within the international legal order.

The argument will unfold in the following stages. First, it is important to review some tenets of interpretative theory, about the cognition of the law and its application within a system by certain categories of actors. Secondly, this chapter will highlight how the function of interpretation can be distinguished from that of application in relation to the judicial function. The argument made here is that international judges do not merely enjoy persuasive authority by virtue of the quality of their reasoning. It is judges' particular position, *within the legal system*, that distinguishes the judicial function from other forms of interpretative activity. This piece will conclude with some brief thoughts about judicial lawmaking and the claim to authority arrogated by judicial institutions.

I. Interpretative Theory

A. A brief word on indeterminacy

Hans Kelsen's 'theory of legal science', as a project of cognizing the law through the methods of striving for truth,[6] did contain certain categorical assertions relating to the nature of the interpretative process. Chief amongst these is the claim that participants in legal cognition, be they scholars, judges, or practitioners, ought to be limited purely to cognizing positive acts of law and measuring them

---

[5] See Chapter 2 (Andrea Bianchi).

[6] For further discussion, see Jörg Kammerhofer, 'Hans Kelsen in Post-Modern International Legal Scholarship' in Jean d'Aspremont and Jörg Kammerhofer (eds), *International Legal Positivism in a Post-Modern World* (CUP 2014) 81.

according to their positive validity.[7] Yet to do so in international law is to conflate positivism with voluntarism;[8] and Kelsen and other critics of classical legal positivism were sufficiently responsive to difficulties with indeterminacy in legal texts. Kelsen readily conceded the 'intentional indefiniteness' of certain law-applying acts and even the unintended indefiniteness inherent in the linguistic formulation of legal norms.[9] His vision of the legal system was that it formed a 'frame' that admitted of possible applications of norms in concrete cases.[10] The act of individual application helped further to determine and constitute a general legal rule.[11] Kelsen's critique of classical legal positivism questioned the idea that the act of interpretation was nothing but an act of understanding and clarification: he situated it as an act of will or cognition: a *choice*.[12] This characterization renders untenable any categorical distinction, within a given frame, between law-creation and law-application by law-applying actors. To him, these were also law-making acts.[13] His solution was to admit of the constitutive nature of discretion, in the application of such rules, by law-applying authorities in a legal system. Similarly, Herbert Hart conceded a certain place for discretion in a legal system whose rules were sufficiently determinate to supply standards of correct judicial decision,[14] although he also foresaw that hard cases helped to prove a fundamental 'incompleteness' in law, where the law could provide *no* answer.[15] This is in part because Hart's theory was essentially reductionist,[16] insofar as it tried to confine itself to describing how law and a legal system could arrive at the validity of rules, and not on the determinacy of the legal order itself.

It is well known that Ronald Dworkin rejected the idea that the law could be incomplete and contain gaps, choosing instead a view that law is not incomplete and indeterminate, being supplemented by *principles*, principles that can themselves be derived from moral justifications if necessary.[17] This would have been unacceptable to Kelsen: '[i]t is, from a scientific and hence objective point of view, inadmissible to proclaim as solely correct an interpretation that from a subjectively political viewpoint is more desirable than another, logically equally possible, interpretation. For in that case, a purely political value judgment is falsely

---

[7] Kammerhofer, 'Hans Kelsen in Post-Modern International Legal Scholarship', 85.

[8] Kammerhofer, 'Hans Kelsen in Post-Modern International Legal Scholarship', 90; Jean d'Aspremont, 'Herbert Hart in Post-Modern International Legal Scholarship' in d'Aspremont and Kammerhofer (eds), *International Legal Positivism in a Post-Modern World*, 114, who argues that reductionism is indifferent as to the material source of the law, concerning itself only with its formal validity.

[9] Kelsen, *Pure Theory of Law*, 350.   [10] Kelsen, *Pure Theory of Law*, 351.

[11] Kelsen, *Pure Theory of Law*, 349.   [12] Kelsen, *Pure Theory of Law*, 82–3.

[13] Kelsen, *Pure Theory of Law*, 85. See also Ingo Venzke, *How Interpretation Makes International Law: Between Normative Twists and Semantic Authority* (OUP 2012) 31.

[14] HLA Hart, *The Concept of Law* (2nd edn, Clarendon Press 1994) 145. Hart's reliance on specifically *judicial* discretion was premised on his view that judges are law-applying officials within a given legal system; and thus specifically entrusted with safeguarding that system.

[15] Hart, *The Concept of Law*, 252.

[16] d'Aspremont, 'Herbert Hart in Post-Modern International Legal Scholarship', 2.

[17] Cf Hart, *The Concept of Law*, 204–5, denying the legality of recourse to moral justification.

presented as scientific truth.'[18] In any event, what is notable about Dworkin's theory is that the discretion exercised in the interpretative act requires the construction and balancing of the principles underlying legal rules, a 'weak' form of discretion exercised within the 'open texture' of a legal system.[19] Legal interpretation would then become an act of cognizing the possibilities available *within* the frame of the system.[20] In this respect at least, Dworkin's approach may be reconcilable with those of Kelsen and Hart, in that it also situates the interpretative process *within* the frame of a legal system. With respect to international law, such limits are part of its inner logic and the inherent structural biases that are deeply embedded within the international legal system itself.[21]

Read in this light, Hart's suggestion, that certain theorists are 'prepared to ignore any actual decisions of judges which run counter to their own logical calculations',[22] suggests a certain faith in judicial decisions as being the expression of a legal text, and thus establishing the validity of a claim.[23]

B. Limits to indeterminacy

Although the indeterminacy of legal language is in many respects presumed, it does not allow for unlimited choices in how interpretation shapes and constructs the meaning of a text. Within that indeterminacy comes a measure of determinacy; the 'canonical terms' within a legal text provide a limit to the political choices available to the interpreter. He or she cannot arrive at interpretations that clearly offend the actual words used, or that are justified by policies and principles wholly absent from the canonical terms.[24] Certainly the text is the 'first authoritative reference point' through which the interpretation of a norm is constructed;[25] but the

---

[18] Kelsen, *Pure Theory of Law*, 356.

[19] Ronald Dworkin, *Taking Rights Seriously* (Harvard University Press 1978) 31–2. He distinguished his form of 'weak' discretion from the 'strong' discretion that he suggested Kelsen and Hart attributed to judges, which allowed them to reach for principles *outside* a legal system. Dworkin's point is fair. If one examines Kelsen, *Pure Theory of Law*, 352, his refusal to privilege any acceptable meaning within the frame is evident: '[f]rom the point of view of positive law, one method is exactly as good as the other'. Similarly, Hart, *The Concept of Law*, 204–5 admits that the interpretation of legal texts and precedents by judges leaves open a 'vast field' for judicial law-creation, yet gives few indicia as to what standards should guide judges should the legal rules in question be ambiguous.

[20] Kelsen, *Pure Theory of Law*, 351.

[21] Martti Koskenniemi, *From Apology to Utopia: The Structure of International Legal Argument* (CUP 2005) 568.

[22] HLA Hart, *Essays in Philosophy and Jurisprudence* (OUP 1984) 268.

[23] Jason Beckett suggests that the United Kingdom House of Lords' *Pinochet* judgment (*R v Bow Street Metropolitan Stipendiary Magistrate, ex parte Pinochet Ugarte (No 3)* [2000] 1 AC 147), and the Canadian Supreme Court's decision in *Re Secession of Quebec* [1996] 161 DLR (4th) 385, despite the obvious lack of expertise of either of those domestic courts in public international law, are regarded as 'authoritative' determinations on the customary nature of the prohibition on torture. Any teacher of international law is likely to be regarded with similar suspicion in this respect. See 'Fragmentation, Openness, and Hegemony: Adjudication and the WTO' in Meredith Kolsky Lewis and Susie Frankel (eds), *International Economic Law and National Autonomy* (CUP 2010) 65: '[l]awyers, in short, like cases!'.

[24] Venzke, *How Interpretation Makes International Law*, 5.

[25] Venzke, *How Interpretation Makes International Law*, 5.

text is not reducible to a fixed, immutable expression of the rule. What is more, the engagement of actors with a legal text is historically contingent: it is structured by the frame in which it is situated, and it is measured against rules contained within that frame, not to mention the past practices of other actors or disputants.[26] As such, rule understanding is a situated activity.[27] But one should not take this point too far: radical subjectivism has its limits as well, with some such limits rooted in the language of law itself.[28] Although inter-subjective meanings and the exercise of discretion are in some respects the essence of subjectivism, legal materials are neither intrinsically determinate nor indeterminate.[29] Owen Fiss' depiction of 'dynamic interaction between reader and text' comes to mind here.[30]

If the process of legal interpretation and application is a form of practical reasoning, it must take place within the confines of rational legal argument. To claim that an interpretation is correct implies that the legal decision being sought or justified is rationally defensible, and plausible, in the context of the legal system.[31] Through a 'rational reconstruction' of legal materials, an interpreter arrives at a decision and justifies it through consistent reasoning, which must conform to the grammar of legal discourse.[32] It is the essence of the third-party decider's role not that they ask themselves as to the correctness or reasonableness of primary rules, but rather, whether and how such primary rules can be applied to the specific context of a case before them.[33] This suggests that the drive for coherence is a systemic presumption that must also be addressed. To argue the opposite demands a more difficult burden of justification: the interpreter must prove why the norms

---

[26] Venzke, *How Interpretation Makes International Law*, 49.

[27] Outi Korhonen, *International Law Situated: An Analysis of the Lawyer's Stance Towards Culture, History and Community* (Kluwer 2000).

[28] Paul Ricoeur would suggest that whilst 'it is true that there is always more than one way of construing a text, it is not true that all interpretations are equal and may be assimilated to so-called rules of thumb. The text is a limited field of possible constructions': *From Text to Action: Essays in Hermeneutics* (Northwestern University Press 1991) 160. See also William Eskridge and Philip Frickey, 'Statutory Interpretation as Practical Reasoning' (1990) 42 Stan L Rev 321, 382: '[a]lthough interpretation is neither objective nor predictable, it is bounded...The historical text itself constrains, for the interpreter is charged with learning from the text and working from it to the current problem. Moreover, the interpreter's perspective is charged with learning from the text and working from it to the current problem. Moreover, the interpreter's perspective itself is conditioned by tradition—the evolution of the historical text as it has been interpreted, the values of society, and current circumstances. While these constraints certainly do not dictate a result, the interpreter cannot disregard the force of that which envelops and situates her in present society.'

[29] See Duncan Kennedy, 'A Left Phenomenological Critique of the Hart/Kelsen Theory of Legal Interpretation' in Enrique Cáceres Nieto, Imer Flores, Javier Saldaña, and Enrique Villanueva (eds), *Problemas Contemporáneos de la Filosofía de Derecho* (UNAM 2005) 371, 380–1.

[30] Owen Fiss, 'Objectivity and Interpretation' (1982) 34 Stan L Rev 739.

[31] Dirk Pulkowski, *The Law and Politics of International Regime Conflict* (OUP 2014) 252.

[32] Neil MacCormick, 'Risking Constitutional Collision in Europe?' (1998) 18 OJLS 556. See also Jack Balkin, 'Understanding Legal Understanding: The Legal Subject and the Problem of Legal Coherence' (1993) 103 Yale L J 105, 122: '[t]he experience of legal coherence is the result of our attempt to understand law through the process of rational reconstruction...To rationally reconstruct the law is to attempt to understand the substantive rationality emanating from it.'

[33] Jürgen Habermas, *Between Facts and Norms: Contributions to a Discourse Theory of Law and Democracy* (MIT Press 1998) 267.

and rules under competing regimes do not constitute a rational approach to the problem at hand.[34] Or one could go as far as Robert Cover, who suggested that coherent legal meaning is an element in legal interpretation, not as an end in itself, but because the privileging of a certain interpretation displaces other possible alternatives, always with a view to the coherence of the overall legal system.[35]

Therefore, the outer limits that mark the field of possible interpretations may be recognized in an act of scientific legal cognition by capable legal scholars.[36] True to the Kantian inspiration of Kelsen's legal theory, the concrete meaning of a norm in the individually disputed case cannot be *discovered* but only *created*. This is broadly consonant with Hart's social thesis, where the claim to authority of an interpretative act is determined by adherence to the standards of legal argument and interpretation that are *accepted* by officials within that system.[37] Understood thus, interpretation is a relatively open exercise taking place within a confined setting, a setting defined by the four corners of the text itself.[38] Even in classical legal positivism there is a certain openness based in the *language* used in constructing a text: '[b]y virtue of linguistic openness, legal positivism in its purest form is never immune to such changes in meaning and to the consequent informal development of law'.[39] As such, the theoretical possibilities of reasonable meaning—and thus, the contestability of meaning—are constrained by these practical limits, which would confirm the binding force of international law.[40]

The space opened by indeterminacy opens up a powerful normative function for judiciaries. Hart was adamant that 'once the myths which obscure the nature of the judicial processes are dispelled by realistic study, it is patent ... that the open texture of law leaves a vast field for a creative activity which some call legislative'.[41] Judges, as agents of the system, work within that system: they are guided to safeguard the purpose of the rules that they are interpreting; they do not have to make blind and arbitrary judgments, or reduce themselves to 'mechanical' deduction.

Agency within the system distinguishes the judicial function from that of legal scholars, or activists. To Dworkin, 'the interpretive attitude cannot survive unless members of the same interpretive community share at least roughly the same assumptions' about 'what counts as part of the practice'.[42] Dworkin's theories have been taken to be less a theory of *law* than a theory of *adjudication*, but it is in that theory of adjudication that Dworkin situates interpretation—the most powerful weapon in a judge's arsenal—to participate in the development of that legal system. The opposite position is that proposed by Ian Johnstone: 'Interpretive authority ... resides in neither the text nor the reader individually, but with the

---

[34] Pulkowski, *The Law and Politics of International Regime Conflict*, 255.

[35] Robert Cover, 'The Supreme Court 1982 Term—Foreword: Nomos and Narrative' (1983) 97 Harv L Rev 4, 47.

[36] Hans Kelsen, *General Theory of Norms* (Clarendon Press 1991) 44.

[37] Ronald Dworkin, *Law's Empire* (Harvard University Press 1986) 67.

[38] Dworkin, *Taking Rights Seriously*, 108–9.

[39] Ulrich Fastenrath, 'Relative Normativity in International Law' (1993) 4 EJIL 315, 316.

[40] Venzke, *How Interpretation Makes International Law*, 49.

[41] Hart, *The Concept of Law*, 204.   [42] Dworkin, *Law's Empire*, 67.

community of professionals engaged in the enterprise of treaty interpretation and implementation'.[43] Owen Fiss, within the American domestic context, situates the relevant interpretive community as the judiciary, 'by virtue of their office', which carries with it a 'commitment to uphold and advance the rule of law itself'.[44] The claim of authority is therefore extrinsic to the process of interpretation,[45] and in fact somewhat grounded on any meta-law on sources. In short, the claim is not one of intellectual cogency, but *formal* legitimacy: the judicial office automatically confers authority on the interpretation issued therefrom. The same reasoning cannot obtain at the international level, for the international judiciary, formally at least, does not occupy a similar hierarchical position.[46]

C. Authenticity in interpretation and the authority of the interpreter

1. Concept of 'authentic interpretation'

The concept of 'authentic interpretation',[47] as representing an interpretation on which all parties were agreed, was first mentioned in the case law of the PCIJ. Judge Hudson drew a distinction between interpretation and application, and the function of interpretation more generally: he saw it as imperative that 'the definitely entertained and expressed intentions of the parties should be effectuated',[48] thus privileging the natural meaning of terms over consideration of purpose. He also distilled a few practices from the case law of the PCIJ that came to be embodied in Articles 32–33 of the VCLT, notably, its reliance on preparatory works to confirm interpretations over which it had no doubt.[49]

2. Identity of the interpreter in the theory of international law

What became Articles 31–33 of the VCLT prescribed the methods of treaty interpretation but not *who* was to interpret them; a point not lost even within the

---

[43] Ian Johnstone, 'Treaty Interpretation: the Authority of Interpretive Communities' (1990–1991) 12 Mich J Int'l L 371, 372.

[44] Owen Fiss, 'Objectivity and Interpretation' (1982) 34 Stan L Rev 739, 754, criticized as a 'theory of judicial interpretation' by Stanley Fish, 'Fiss v. Fish' (1984) 36 Stan L Rev 1325.

[45] Johnstone, 'Treaty Interpretation', 375.

[46] See Julius Stone, 'Fictional Elements in Treaty Interpretation: A Study in the International Judicial Process' (1954) 1 Syd LR 344, 364; Richard Falk, 'On Treaty Interpretation and the New Haven Approach: Achievements and Prospects' (1967–1968) 8 Va J Intl L 323, 326. On the 'communicative' judicial function, see Johnstone, 'Treaty Interpretation', 375–6.

[47] Manley Hudson, *The Permanent Court of International Justice 1920–1942* (Macmillan 1943), 640–1; Ole Spiermann, *International Legal Argument in the Permanent Court of International Justice: The Rise of the International Judiciary* (CUP 2005) 236–7.

[48] Hudson, *The Permanent Court of International Justice*, 643–4.

[49] Hudson, *The Permanent Court of International Justice*, 653–4. Cf *Application of the International Convention on the Elimination of All Forms of Racial Discrimination (Georgia v Russian Federation)* (Preliminary Objections) [2011] ICJ Rep 70, [142] where the ICJ used the *travaux préparatoires* of CERD to confirm the interpretation that it had already given.

International Law Commission.[50] This is an old question: in *Jaworzina*, the PCIJ indicated that 'it is an established principle that the right of giving an authoritative interpretation of a legal rule belongs solely to the person or body who has the power to modify or suppress it'.[51] It is inherent in the process of interpretation itself, as treaties between states almost invariably provide that questions of interpretation and application of a treaty are to be resolved by a third party.[52]

The real question is not who most often interprets and applies treaties, which invariably concerns the parties to the treaty most. The conceptually interesting question arises when there are diverging views on the interpretation of an obligation, and whether there is a *hierarchy* of *authority*. In other words, whose interpretation can be regarded as authoritative? The judicial (or at the very least, the 'impartial third party') role there comes to be acutely important, as it conditions the practice of states in contracting obligations.[53]

3. 'Authoritative interpretation' formalized

Authoritative interpretation in the classic sense is a relevant consensual undertaking, where consent is given by the parties and the interpreter operating on the basis of delegated authority.[54] But what of situations where that authority is not delegated clearly, for example, with rules of customary international law, or general principles of law? Can one genuinely say that there is authoritative interpretation writ large, or for general international law?

The openness of the interpretative process leads directly to a consideration of the *limits* of legal order in international society; in short, if the interpretative act

---

[50] See intervention by Mr Tsuruoka, (1964) I ILC Ybk 280, [72].

[51] *Delimitation of the Polish-Czechoslovakian Frontier (Question of Jaworzina)* (Advisory Opinion) PCIJ Rep Series B No 8, 37. Ruda raised this in the ILC as well: see 765th meeting (14 July 1964) in (1964) I ILC Ybk 277, [34]: '[i]nterpretation occurred at two different levels. First, as between States, the only legally valid interpretation of a treaty was the authentic interpretation by the parties to the treaty. The other level was that of interpretation by arbitration, for which there were fundamental principles...'.

[52] Although Richard Gardiner, *Treaty Interpretation* (OUP 2007) 109 makes the point, he does not link it conceptually.

[53] See eg *The Restatement of the Law (Third), The Foreign Relations Law of the United States* (American Law Institute 1987) 3: '...this Restatement represents the opinion of The American Law Institute *as to the rules that an impartial tribunal would apply* if charged with deciding a controversy in accordance with international law' (emphasis added).

[54] Georg Schwarzenberger, 'Myths and Realities of Treaties of Treaty Interpretation: Articles 27–29 of the Vienna Draft Convention on the Law of Treaties' (1968) 9 Va J Int'l L 1, 11; Arnold McNair, *The Law of Treaties* (2nd edn, Clarendon Press 1961), 531–2. This has to be distinguished from Kelsen's idea of 'authentic' interpretation (as distinguished from 'scientific' interpretation). As Jörg Kammerhofer, *Uncertainty in International Law: A Kelsenian Perspective* (Routledge 2011) 115 describes Kelsen's concept, authentic interpretation is performed by organs authorized by the law to apply it; the *result* of authentic interpretation is a norm, or a law-creating act; authentic interpretation is an act of *will*, whereas scholarly interpretation is an act of *cognition*; 'one determining what is law, the other finding the law'. He then makes the claim (with which the present author disagrees) that '[b]ecause an act of will is necessary for the creation of positive law, authentic interpretation as law-creation must be an act of will; mere cognition cannot create norms'. In short, one needs an act of *volition*, not merely an act of cognition; and the question is *whose* act of volition is creative of law.

is properly understood, there is no way for an international tribunal to render an authoritative judgment.[55] Yet whatever the (lack of) formal authority, the reality is that some interpretations are simply more authoritative than others: they carry with them the idea of *normativity*. In so doing, the claim to authority provides a target audience with the comfort of precedent, of black robes, of objectivity; legal scholars thus can evade engaging in meaningful and original criticism when they can hide behind these alluring sources. In this respect, despite the fact that the third party interpreter settling a dispute (an 'authorized organ') *decides*, thus on some level applying the law (unlike the scholar, who merely 'cognizes'[56]), one must reject the Kelsenian conceit that this renders nugatory any normative effect any 'non-authorised' interpretation may have.[57] Serge Sur attempted to distinguish between 'doctrinal' and 'juridical' interpretation on the same basis: the former had as its wider aim the understanding of the international legal order, while the latter, by 'qualified legal agents', was only interested in its functioning.[58] But the distinction was not hermetic: 'juridical' interpretation was a combination of 'cognition' and 'will', fusing the doctrinal with the functional to favour one particular solution.[59]

II. The Fallacy in the Interpretation and Application Distinction

The distinction between 'application' and 'interpretation' was first articulated in the Harvard Draft Convention on the Law of Treaties, which provided that:

Interpretation is closely connected with the carrying out of treaties, for before a treaty can be applied in a given set of circumstances it must be determined whether or not it was meant to apply to those circumstances... In any particular case there may be no expressed

---

[55] Falk, 'On Treaty Interpretation', 336.

[56] Kammerhofer, *Uncertainty in International Law*, 106.

[57] Kammerhofer, *Uncertainty in International Law*, citing Hans Kelsen, *The Law of the United Nations: A Critical Analysis of its Fundamental Problems* (London Institute of World Affairs 1950) xvi: 'Non-authentic interpretation of the law, that is interpretation by persons not authorised by the law itself, is legally as irrelevant as the judgment of a private person on the guilt or innocence of an individual accused before a competent court of having committed a crime.' This is emphatically not the case in international law. To give equally simple (and even trite!) examples of when 'non-authorised interpretation' created serious doctrinal controversy and threatened to change the law: when Chile extended its exclusive economic zone to 200 nautical miles; when the ICTY threw down its 'overall control' test in *Prosecutor v Tadić* (1999) 38 ILM 1518; when the House of Lords in *Regina v Bow Street Metropolitan Stipendiary Magistrate And Others, ex parte Pinochet Ugarte (No 3)* [2000] 1 AC 147 constructed a doctrine of implied waiver to extradite General Pinochet to Spain on charges of torture; and when the Italian Court of Cassation in *Ferrini v Federal Republic of Germany*, Decision No 5044/2004, 128 ILR 658 disregarded the jurisdictional immunity of Germany. All of these cases led to serious wrangling and a realignment by states of how they perceived customary international law. In short, whatever the correctness of any of these acts, and even if they failed to change the law in substance, their potential for normativity (actualized in some cases) is manifest. Kelsen was wrong.

[58] Serge Sur, *L'interprétation en droit international public* (LGDJ 1974) 98.

[59] Sur, *L'interprétation en droit international public*, 98–9.

doubt or difference of opinion as to the meaning of the treaty concerned; its purpose and applicability may be regarded as perfectly evident. Yet, even in such a case, the person or persons deciding that the meaning of the treaty is 'clear', and that it is plainly intended to apply to the given circumstances, must do so, consciously or unconsciously, by some process of reasoning based upon evidence.

In short, the 'application' of treaties, it would seem, must almost inevitably involve some measure of 'interpretation'. There is, however, a recognized distinction between the two processes. Interpretation is the process of determining the meaning of a text; application is the process of determining the consequences which, according to the text, should follow in a given situation.[60]

It is arguable that interpretation and application can be easily distinguished through their outcomes: as Georg Schwarzenberger asserted in 1968, '[i]nterpretation is the process of establishing the legal character and effects of a consensus achieved by the parties. In contrast, application is the process of determining the consequences of such an interpretation in a concrete case'.[61] To Schwarzenberger's mind, interpretation is thus 'independent of, and need not be followed by, the application of the treaty',[62] therefore clearly delineating a doctrinal function for interpretation distinct from the judicial function of application. Although he did acknowledge that any application of a treaty, 'including its execution, presupposes, however, a preceding conscious or subconscious interpretation of the treaty'.[63] This view, argues Ulf Linderfalk, would reduce international courts and arbitration tribunals to police, civil servants, and military officials: they are all (in his terms) 'appliers' of international law.[64]

The judicial role in all of this becomes clear: according to the orthodox positivist view, judicial interpretation and application are to be nothing more than to fulfil the Montesquieuian role to 'speak the law' (*jus dicere, dire la loi*). Whatever language was used, 'interpretation was always present as a supplement to the

---

[60] 29 (1935) AJIL Supplement 938 (see also Gardiner, *Treaty Interpretation*, ch 2 for comments on the Harvard Convention generally).

[61] Schwarzenberger, 'Myths and Realities of Treaties of Treaty Interpretation', 7, citing the Dissenting Opinion of Judge Ehrlich in *Case concerning the Factory at Chorzów (Germany v Poland)* (Claim for Indemnity: Jurisdiction) PCIJ Rep Series A No 9, 39.

[62] Schwarzenberger, 'Myths and Realities of Treaties of Treaty Interpretation', 8, citing *Case concerning certain German Interests in Polish Upper Silesia (Germany v Poland)* (Merits) PCIJ Rep Series A No 7, 8–19.

[63] Schwarzenberger, 'Myths and Realities of Treaties of Treaty Interpretation', 8, citing *Mavrommatis Jerusalem Concessions (Greece v UK)* (Judgment) PCIJ Rep Series A No 5, 47–8. This was also the language used by the Harvard Draft on the Law of Treaties, 938; and cited approvingly on this point by Jean d'Aspremont, *Formalism and the Sources of International Law: A Theory on the Ascertainment of Legal Rules* (OUP 2011) 157. Cf Dissenting Opinion of Judge Anzilotti in *Interpretation of the 1919 Convention concerning Employment of Women During the Night* (Advisory Opinion), PCIJ Rep Series A/B No 50, 383: '[i] Article 3, according to the natural meaning of its terms, were really perfectly clear, it would be hardly admissible to endeavour to find an interpretation other than that which flows from the natural meaning of its terms. But I do not see how it is possible to say that an article of a convention is clear until the subject and the aim of the convention have been ascertained, for the article only assumes its true import in this convention and in relation thereto.'

[64] Ulf Linderfalk, *On the Interpretation of Treaties: The Modern International Law as Expressed in the 1969 Vienna Convention on the Law of Treaties* (Springer 2007) 1.

judicial truth-saying role. Power over truth'.[65] And yet, reality has always been quite different:

'Application' of the law... was the repository of power, in service of interpretation as inter-pretation served the law. These relations do divide truth from power and can be seen to deny power. But it is more accurate to think of the discourse as managing a shifting place for power within the liberal order. 'Interpretation' in traditional liberal legal discourse endangered the serenity of truth-disguised power as it reinforced that hegemony by both domesticating and diverting acknowledgment of judicial action.[66]

To fixate on interpretation merely as a 'clarifying operation',[67] one aiming merely at understanding or lending meaning to a text, is a distinctive feature of the orthodox positive view, which presumes there to exist some 'correct' or 'proper' interpretative process. That view does not, for example, take account of the active role of the interpreter within the interpretative act, and reinforces the sense that interpretation as a process serves only to uncover what is objectively true. As Lauterpacht suggests, 'there is nothing easier than to purport to give the appearance of legal respectability and plausibility—by the simple operation of selecting one or more rules of interpretation—to a judicial decision which is lacking in soundness, in impartiality, or in intellectual vigour'.[68] Accordingly, even the *process* of identifying legal norms requires a choice as to which theory of sources one privileges, thus further demonstrating how the claim to objectivity in law-identification can be problematic.[69]

In this respect, it almost does not matter whether one favours an approach to judicial interpretation that serves to constrain or to empower a judge, for example, by invoking overarching principles such as restrictive interpretation or of 'effective-ness'. The real issue is that any such overarching principle temporarily privileges an imaginary displacement of judicial power, be it in favour or against judicial discretion. But each is defined by connection of the judge to the truth, be truth a matter either of text or merely of the effects generated by a judicial decision.[70] The

---

[65] D Kennedy, 'The Turn to Interpretation' (1985) 58 S Cal L Rev 251, 253.

[66] Kennedy, 'The Turn to Interpretation', 253.

[67] McNair, *The Law of Treaties*, 365: '[t]he words "interpret", "interpretation" are often used loosely as if they included "apply, application". Strictly speaking, when the meaning of the treaty is clear, it is "applied", not "interpreted". *Interpretation is a secondary process which only comes into play when it is impossible to make sense of the plain terms of the treaty, or when they are susceptible of different meanings.* The *Concise Oxford Dictionary* says: "Interpret: expound the meaning of (abstruse words, writings, &c.); make out the meaning of"' (emphasis added). Cf Gardiner, *Treaty Interpretation*, 27: 'it is difficult to see how this sustains the distinction... between the circumstances for interpret-ation and for application, and the relation [McNair] attributes to them... This sets on its head the natural sequence that is inherent in the process of reading a treaty: first ascribing meaning to its terms and then applying the outcome to a particular situation.'

[68] Lauterpacht, *The Function of Law in the International Community*, 53.

[69] Jason Beckett, 'Countering Uncertainty and Ending Up/Down Arguments: *Prolegomena* to a Response to NAIL' (2005) 16 EJIL 213.

[70] Kennedy, 'The Turn to Interpretation', 253.

rules of interpretation are 'not the determining cause of judicial decisions, but the *form* in which the judge cloaks a result arrived at by other means'.[71]

Look, then, at the normative move proposed in Lauterpacht's deliberate tie between interpretation and adjudication. Lauterpacht's concept of law upheld the centrality of the judicial function within any legal system, in terms that would suggest that the judicial function served to ensure that the values and priorities embodied within the legal system would be generally respected. It was not to act mechanically:

[t]he judicial function is not that of an automaton which registers a gap, an obscurity, an absurdity, a frustrated purpose, without an attempt to fill the lacunae by reference to the intentions of the parties in the wider context of the agreement as a whole and the circumstances accompanying its adoption, to the needs of the community, and to the requirement of good faith.... But...that quasi-legislative function ought not to be so deliberate or so drastic as to give justifiable ground for the reproach that the tribunal has substituted its own intention for that of the parties.[72]

Defining the judicial function as 'quasi-legislative', even in the absence of an international legislative body or process, goes beyond merely affirming the centrality of the judicial function within the legal system. It is a statement that affirms, in terms redolent of Dworkin, that the judicial function exists not only as a guardian of the coherence of the legal system, but equally as the guardian of the wider interests of the political community, even when these have not necessarily been embodied in specific legal rules. They become, to use Dworkin's terms, a 'deputy legislature' rather than a 'deputy *to* the legislature',[73] in the sense that law-creation, using the methods and techniques of interpretation, becomes regarded as legitimate judicial activity.

Yet, even in the distinction between operative interpretation (those who apply) the law and 'doctrinal' interpretation (those who consider and study the law),[74] the role of the interpreter is often over-simplified. Scholars concerned with interpretation, by examining merely what a judge *has decided* when he or she says the law, but without questioning the process of judicial decision and the methods used to settle a dispute, are engaging in apologetic scholarship. What is meant by apologetic scholarship is that they are in essence domesticating judicial activity and distracting attention from judicial power; this destabilizes the patterns of traditional judicial discourse, as it privileges description rather than critical scrutiny. Julius Stone was correct in decrying the canonist rhetoric as fundamentally apologist, obscuring the judicial function in interpretation through a veneer of objectivity: 'the appearance of an objective decision based on compulsive legal directives, where in reality no legal compulsion does exist'.[75] In so doing, judicial

---

[71] Hersch Lauterpacht, 'Restrictive Interpretation and the Principle of Effectiveness in the Interpretation of Treaties' (1949) 26 BYBIL 48, 53.

[72] Lauterpacht, 'Restrictive Interpretation', 74.

[73] Dworkin, *Taking Rights Seriously*, 83.

[74] Linderfalk, *On the Interpretation of Treaties*, 12.

[75] Stone, 'Fictional Elements in Treaty Interpretation', 334, 347: '[i]t is notorious that...treaty terms may often be intended, not to express the consensus reached, but rather to conceal the failure

interpretation can be imagined as simultaneously more and less constrained than judicial application; the process of interpretation was both prior to and in service of substance.[76] The purpose of this subterfuge was 'to disarm the still prevalent prejudice against judicial law-making',[77] whatever the ambiguity intentionally or accidentally provided by the parties.[78] Indeed, as Jason Beckett cautions, '[w]ho describes and who decides are interrelated, cumulative, problems. The question of expertise gives way to one of epistemic authority, the need to decide, and thus to appropriation by the authoritative discourse'.[79] And as Martti Koskenniemi explains, knowledge of the forum in which a dispute will be decided is tantamount to knowledge of the decision which will be made.[80]

There is a better view: judgments and actions are '*commitments* that are subject to a kind of normative assessment, as correct or incorrect'.[81] They are a commitment to legal rationality and to the view that the legal aspects of issues can be resolved in isolation, if only the application of the 'correct' rules can be made. Judicial interpretation does not carry with it the same weight as that of the military commander, for example; as an exercise, it is a fusion of both operational and doctrinal interpretation, given the claim to heightened authority of judicial interpretations, not to mention its application to a concrete set of facts, and finally enhanced by the normative weight to be given. The so-called 'validity of the interpretation result' is therefore not limited to the factual situation at hand, but carries normative repercussions for the legal order as a whole—whether that judicial interpretation is purely international or on the domestic plane. 'Precision' in this sense merely confuses the result—the reality is that however precise a judicial institution will aim to be, scholars and practitioners will naturally gravitate towards judicial decisions to lend them guidance, especially in a legal order where room is allowed for indeterminacy and a degree of incoherence.

---

to reach one. In multilateral instruments, especially political ones, that agreed content expressed by the terms may be far less important than the non-agreed terms concealed by them. When a case arises involving the non-agreed content of the treaty, interpretation of the terms, even if purporting to find the intention of the parties is not in fact doing so. The imputation of intention in such a case is a fiction concealing the true nature of the activity'.

[76] Kennedy, 'The Turn to Interpretation', 253.

[77] Stone, 'Fictional Elements in Treaty Interpretation', 349. Stone suggests that the exercise of institutional rule-creation is obscured behind assumed intention, with the consequence of 'exercising power without the acceptance of responsibility for it': 358.

[78] The critique proffered by Myres McDougal, Harold Laswell, and James Miller, *The Interpretation of Agreements and World Public Order: Principles of Content and Procedure* (Yale University Press 1967) 264–5, is interesting: '[i]t is highly unlikely that international tribunals will be adequately protected against "premature strains" by "fictions"; neither the participants in processes of decision nor scholarly observers are likely to be tranquilized by attempts to "conceal judicial creativeness" by such evasions, even if skillful.'

[79] Beckett, 'Fragmentation, Openness, and Hegemony', 44, 56.

[80] Martti Koskenniemi, 'The Fate of Public International Law: Between Technique and Politics' (2007) 70 MLR 1, 8.

[81] Robert Brandom, 'Some Pragmatist Themes in Hegel's Idealism: Negotiation and Administration in Hegel's Account of the Structure and Content of Conceptual Norms' (1999) 7 Eur J Philos 164, 165–6 (emphasis added).

The claim of judicial institutions to a heightened role in the interpretation of legal rules, or even to 'authoritative interpretation', remains highly contentious, not least because of the systematic constraints that permeate the work of international courts. Judicial institutions remain accountable to states externally, through their limited jurisdiction (whether optional jurisdiction, or jurisdiction limited *ratione personae* or *ratione materiae*), and internally, through the processes of nomination and selection of judges to the international bench.[82] If one accepts the nature of international law as a law of coexistence at least in part, and one also accepts Robert Kolb's premise that the interpretative act is also capable of developing the international law on the matter, then the role of judicial institutions must be conceptually limited, as states must continue to hold at least a default or first-order role in the interpretation of the obligations which they themselves have entered.[83] Even if one makes the argument that states could have delegated their first-order role in the interpretation of obligations to judicial institutions when they consented to their jurisdiction, the constraints on these adjudicatory bodies has resulted in such judicial institutions hewing, broadly speaking, to the views of states.

Finally, it is important, within the context of the claim to interpretative authority advanced by international courts, to remain cognizant of the targeted audience. The effective authority commanded by a court is reliant on the ability to persuade the wider audience of international society; as Bianchi has explained, the court can only be regarded as persuasive if it calibrates its argument precisely to appeal to its target audience.[84] In international law, that audience is not merely the parties before the judicial institution, but equally, future and potential parties, other international courts, and to an extent, the views of other members of the 'epistemic community' of international lawyers.[85]

In this respect, the idea of a 'syntax' common to international lawyers suggested by Pierre-Marie Dupuy, '*qui autorise la création et la validité des normes*',[86] which would emanate from functionally different specialized regimes in international law, could be very useful. This idea of syntax, of a common grammatical code, would serve to distinguish international law from other legal orders (or, for that matter, from other normative orders). And this idea of commonality also has

---

[82] Gleider Hernández, 'Impartiality, Bias, and the International Court of Justice' (2012) 1(3) CJICL 183.

[83] Robert Kolb, *Interprétation et création du droit international* (Bruylant 2006) 103–15. This is an issue coming to the fore in the realm of international investment law, where the decentralized (and voluminous) resolution of disputes by arbitral awards has led to wider debates as to the role of investment tribunals and their awards as a source of law: see eg Anthea Roberts, 'Power and Persuasion in Investment Treaty Arbitration: The Dual Role of States' (2010) 104 AJIL 179, 188.

[84] See Chapter 2 (Andrea Bianchi).

[85] The concept of 'epistemic communities' is understood in the same sense as in Andrea Bianchi, 'Gazing at the Crystal Ball (again): State Immunity and *Jus Cogens* beyond *Germany v Italy*' (2013) 4 JIDS 1.

[86] Pierre-Marie Dupuy, 'L'unité de l'ordre juridique international' (2002) 297 Recueil des Cours 1. A similar idea of '*discourse rules of international law*—a grammar for communicative interaction' was put forward in Pulkowski, *The Law and Politics of International Regime Conflict*, 238.

a darker side: to privilege systemic unity and coherence over other priorities deigns to presume, or if necessary, construct the existence of norms that resolve normative conflicts, impose a hierarchy of norms, and if necessary, even harkens back to the ultimate rule or *Grundnorm* that will legitimate the entire legal order. It is, in some respects, the conceit of the epistemic community of international lawyers that our international legal system can and necessarily must take this form:

A professionally competent argument is rooted in a *social concept of law*—it claims to emerge from the way international society is, and not from some wishful construction of it. On the other hand, any such doctrine or position must also show that it is not just a reflection of power—that it does not only tell what States do or will but what they *should* do or will.[87]

The final focus of this piece is on how the methods and forms of interpretation constitute a claim to wider normative authority by judicial institutions. The wider question of the identity and function of the interpreter does seem generally to be an area of enquiry which most major recent books on interpretation (Orakhelashvili, Kolb, and Gardiner, with perhaps Linderfalk's linguistic analysis, and excluding of course Venzke) seem to have ignored. Accordingly, the role *judicial* interpreters themselves play in interpretation in law-making will be briefly discussed.

Conclusion: Judicial Interpretation and the Claim to Normative Authority

There is resistance to the idea that judicial institutions possess authority for the development of international law. Such a claim is seen as problematic precisely because the foundation for courts' authority within a legal system usually subordinates them to the law-creating actor: again, to use Dworkin's paradigm, they are *deputy to the legislature* rather than *deputy legislator* (although Dworkin did foresee that when the rules run out, the latter is permissible). Judges cloak their decisions through an outward show of judicial technique, behind which judges shield themselves from the accusation that they are engaging in law-creation rather than merely the interpretation of the law.

It behoves legal scholars to dispense with this fallacy. Interpretation remains primarily a purposeful activity; anyone who engages in the interpretative process does so with a desire to achieve a certain outcome.[88] Whether or not judgments are a *source of law* or merely a means for the *determination of the law*,[89] a court's interpretation nevertheless contributes to the creation of what it finds.[90] This occurs

---

[87] Koskenniemi, *From Apology to Utopia*, 573–4.

[88] See Chapter 2 (Andrea Bianchi), 53.

[89] The classic distinction is well explained in Georg Schwarzenberger, *International Law* (3rd edn, Longmans 1957) 26–8. See also Michael Akehurst, 'The Hierarchy of the Sources of International Law' (1974–5) 47 BYBIL 273, 280.

[90] Venzke, *How Interpretation Makes International Law*, 71.

through a process of 'normative accretion',[91] through which law is not created as with legislative processes, but rather in a more modest, incremental fashion, clarifying ambiguities and resolving perceived gaps in the law. The open texture of law—and especially of international law—gives judicial institutions heightened influence on the internal understanding of legal rules within the system, offering a set of normative expectations that can be relied upon by states. They are, to borrow a phrase from Christian Tams and Antonios Tzanakopoulos, agents in the international law-making process.[92] Once a general statement on a legal principle or rule has been elucidated by a court, and channelled into the judicial form and buttressed by whatever authority that institution claims, both parties and non-parties cannot in good faith contest that general principle.[93]

There is nothing radical about this; for example, one can turn to Kelsen's interpretative theory, which sought to leave the 'legal politics' of trying to divine the 'right' interpretation,[94] and situated interpretation instead as an act of cognition or of will. In this respect, he expressly endorsed the law-constitutive nature of judicial decisions, in so far as these constructed individual norms form the frame of the general norm of the law.[95] This cognitive process may even take into account norms not based on the positive law (morals, natural justice, 'constituting social values'). Due to the systemic role of law-applying organs, these are *transformed* into norms of positive law through the act of will or cognition by these organs: '[t]he interpretation by the law-applying organ is always authentic. It creates law'.[96] In this respect, 'authentic interpretation' must be understood as law-creative. It can possess a general character, in that it creates law not only for a concrete case but for all similar cases before it; but it is also authentic if it creates law only for an individual case, because as soon as the validity of the norm is justified through a final judgment by a law-applying organ, it is seen as an authentic interpretation (and thus to be distinguished from the interpretation of a private actor or a legal scholar).[97] In this respect, Kelsen seems

---

[91] Thomas Buergenthal, 'Lawmaking by the ICJ and Other International Courts' (2009) ASIL Proceedings 403, 403.

[92] Christian Tams and Antonios Tzanakopoulos, 'Barcelona Traction at 40: The ICJ as an Agent of Legal Development' (2010) 23 LJIL 781, 784; Christopher Weeramantry, 'The Function of the International Court of Justice in the Development of International Law' (1997) 10 LJIL 309, 311.

[93] Gerald Fitzmaurice, 'Some Problems Regarding the Formal Sources of International Law' in *Symbolae Verzijl* (Martinus Nijhoff 1958) 153, 172–3, terms judicial decisions 'quasi-formal' sources of international law. Weeramantry, 'The Function of the International Court of Justice', 321 goes further: the Court's 'role and duty must extend beyond the immediate case to the elucidation of relevant principles that have arisen for discussion in the context of the case, thereby helping in the development of the law'.

[94] Kelsen, *Pure Theory of Law*, 353.   [95] Kelsen, *Pure Theory of Law*, 353.

[96] Kelsen, *Pure Theory of Law*, 353–4.

[97] Kelsen, *Pure Theory of Law*, 355–6. Kelsen denies private or scholarly interpretation all law-creative force. Because the filling of gaps in the law can only be performed by law-applying organs, jurisprudential interpretation does nothing more than 'exhibit all possible meanings of a legal norm. Jurisprudence as cognition of law cannot decide between the possibilities exhibited by it, but must leave the decision who, according to the legal order, is authorized to apply the law.' A legal academic propounding an interpretation 'does not render a function of legal science, but of legal politics. He seeks to influence legislation...But he cannot do this in the name of legal science...Jurisprudential interpretation must carefully avoid the fiction that a legal norm admits only of one as the "correct" interpretation'.

to accept the constitutive normative force of judicial decision-making: he even goes so far as to suggest that judicial interpretation is simply a form of legislation, the motives of judges for which being irrelevant for analytical positivists. Interpretation is thus no juristic analysis, but belongs to politics and sociology.[98] This is an important concession: it conceptualizes the frame through which the act of interpretation or application of law by certain organs constitutes the law itself, thus turning the classical legal positivist posture on its head.

Interestingly, the grasp towards coherence embodied by judicial techniques, such as giving reasons, or adhering to previous judicial decisions, is revelatory of the values and norms that are embedded within the legal system.[99] Yet the privileging of coherence as a value is the imposition of one view, not merely its 'identification':

The interpretative techniques lawyers used to proceed from a text or a behaviour to its 'meaning' *create* (and do not 'reflect') those meanings...Hermeneutics, too, is a universalisation project, a set of hegemonic moves that make particular arguments or preferences because they seem, for example 'coherent' with the 'principles' of the legal system...But they offer no...authentic translation of the 'raw' preferences of social actors (into) universal law.[100]

In suggesting that hierarchy, order, and coherence are intrinsic to juristic thought, one arrives at the implied claim that juristic thought is inherently *good*, valuable. Yet as Beckett argues, the attempt to introduce a meta-system to ensure coherence makes a necessarily hegemonic claim. It claims its own absolute truth (or a 'neutrality amongst the other systems'); or 'it internalises conflicts within and between systems into itself'.[101]

As such, in a sense, any study of the rules of interpretation, which indeed is but a secondary topic in the light of the role of interpretation as a hermeneutic tool, necessarily extends further than the rules themselves, and must also study the *practice* of relevant law-applying actors as an equally important locus for the construction of meaning. For it is the claim of law-applying actors to what Venzke calls 'semantic authority', or the 'capacity to influence and shape meanings as authoritative reference points in legal discourse',[102] that is equally important. The focus on interpretative authority opens a discussion on legal normativity, going beyond obligation and very much into the practice of international actors. Any such study might even address the conceptual disagreement as to the *form* of international law itself, a much wider project for all international lawyers.

Yet with power comes responsibility: interpretation cannot just be reduced to the recognition of a norm's meaning, nor by omnipresent and all-pervasive

[98] Lon Fuller, *The Morality of Law* (Yale University Press 1969) 226.
[99] Beckett, 'Fragmentation, Openness, and Hegemony', 59.
[100] Beckett, 'Fragmentation, Openness, and Hegemony', referring to Koskenniemi, *From Apology to Utopia*, 597–8.
[101] Beckett, 'Fragmentation, Openness, and Hegemony', 67.
[102] Venzke, *How Interpretation Makes International Law*, 63.

structures. The interpretative act, when undertaken by certain law-applying actors (and in particular judicial institutions), involves not only a considerable degree of freedom, but amounts to a claim to authority.[103] In this respect, I defer to Julius Stone, who suggested that '[t]he important question is whether the tribunal will choose more wisely if it chooses in consciousness of its responsibility rather than in the belief that it has no choice open'.[104] To reject judicial law-creation may accord nicely with a traditional view on the 'meta-law' on sources: yet so to do eschews judicial *responsibility* for the interpretation given by a court. Concealed behind the 'assumed', 'implied', or 'imputed' intention of the parties, judicial interpretation is given power or authority, but judicial institutions are not tasked with any *responsibility* for the law so created;[105] and, to cite Stone again, 'to conceal creative power by fictions does not prevent its actual exercise'.[106]

Lest we forget that judges are also human beings, not only acting to perpetuate their own power (although in fact, often very concerned with their prestige), but also *normative* actors conditioned by their legal upbringing and the career that brought them to the international bench in the first place,[107] one must be chary of placing undue weight on judicial interpretation as authoritative:

Self-interested interpretation presented as authoritative or objective interpretation has been an essential ingredient of all patterns of domination, veiling oppressive and exploitative relationships in the guise of that which is 'natural' or 'true' or 'necessary'.[108]

Is there another way? Beckett makes an interesting suggestion in the context of his thoughts on fragmentation, and I wonder whether his words have relevance here: 'we must learn to embrace this loss of control, or better still, to re-imagine it as an assumption of responsibility. Coherence, hierarchy, accommodation and other mechanisms of conflict displacement are, perhaps better understood as conflict denial, and thus of a refusal of responsibility'.[109] In this regard, the impulse towards coherence is an attempt to refuse responsibility: by *exercising* semantic authority without claiming the authority to do so, judicial institutions can evade

---

[103] Venzke, *How Interpretation Makes International Law*, 13.

[104] Stone, 'Fictional Elements in Treaty Interpretation', 367: '[t]here is room, therefore, for the view that the fictions which combine to conceal judicial creativeness in international law serve the proper social function of protecting the growing judicial arm against premature strains.'

[105] Stone, 'Fictional Elements in Treaty Interpretation', 349. At 363–4, he again touches upon this theme of the result of a refusal to consider the law-creating judicial role in interpretation.

[106] Stone, 'Fictional Elements in Treaty Interpretation', 364. As he suggests, canons of interpretation have served judicial institutions threefold: first, by creating 'captions' under which precedents and principles could be marshalled; second, they gave tribunals a sense of 'continuity of tradition', situating them in a larger work; third, they gave tribunals support that their reasoning and decisions had 'an objective validity' even before such decisions were reached. At 365, he suggests that canons of interpretation can 'serve as rules of *prudence* reminding the tribunal of the complexity of its task, and the need to embrace the full range of relevant considerations before making a final choice'.

[107] See Falk, 'On Treaty Interpretation', 354 (characterizing these 'biasing impacts' as curiously overlooked by the New Haven School).

[108] Falk, 'On Treaty Interpretation', 324–5.

[109] Beckett, 'Fragmentation, Openness, and Hegemony', 68.

responsibility for the substance of the international legal order, and equally so, the international legal order—the embodiment of rationality and logic—can evade the responsibility for the substantive problems caused within the law itself. It is perhaps a step too far to isolate the judicial function fully from any responsibility for political choice; yet it is all too often the case, insulated in the reassuring positivism of 'objectivity', that judicial institutions exercise that political role described by Dworkin.

PART IV
THE RULES

9
The Vienna Rules, Evolutionary Interpretation, and the Intentions of the Parties

Eirik Bjorge

Introduction

The rules of interpretation, in Andrea Bianchi's metaphor, relate to the process of treaty interpretation in the way that a deck relates to a game of cards.[1] The cards that the players are dealt may, he explains, vary slightly with different types of game; specialized cards may be present in games concerning, for example, human rights law or investment arbitration.[2] Nevertheless, the Vienna Rules (Articles 31–33 of the VCLT)[3] broadly make up the hand dealt to the players in the game of treaty interpretation. The present chapter ventures behind these cards in order to find the common denominator of the Vienna Rules. The view taken in this chapter is that the underlying goal of treaty interpretation is to give effect to the objectivized intention of the parties. This effectively constitutes a limit on how the 'rules', in Bianchi's metaphor, are deployed, and goes against the idea that the rules can be deployed at will for one's strategy.[4]

The received wisdom about the approach to treaty interpretation opted for in the VCLT has been that the general rule of interpretation put paid to the notion of interpreting in accordance with 'the intention of the parties'. With the adoption of Article 31 of the VCLT, it has been stated, the intention of the parties no longer matters in treaty interpretation; what matters instead, leading authors argue, is the ascertainment of the meaning of the text.[5] Such an understanding of treaty interpretation, however, does not sit comfortably with the jurisprudence of

---

[1] See Chapter 2 (Andrea Bianchi).   [2] See Chapter 2 (Andrea Bianchi), 44.
[3] Vienna Convention on the Law of Treaties (concluded on 23 May 1969, entered into force 27 January 1980) 1155 UNTS 331.
[4] See Chapter 2 (Andrea Bianchi).
[5] See Jean-Marc Sorel and Valerie Boré Eveno, 'Article 31' in Olivier Corten and Pierre Klein (eds), *The Vienna Convention on the Law of Treaties: A Commentary* (OUP 2011) 804; Ian Brownlie, *Principles of International Law* (7th edn, OUP 2008) 630.

the International Court of Justice (ICJ), especially in cases where the Court has arrived at what could be termed evolutionary interpretations.[6]

The approach which the ICJ takes to treaty interpretation generally was foreshadowed by the jurisprudence of the Permanent Court, which in *Interpretation of the Treaty of Lausanne* held that a tribunal interpreting a convention clause must:

> in the first place, endeavour to ascertain from the wording of this clause what the intention of the Contracting Parties was; subsequently, it may consider whether—and, if so, to what extent—factors other than the wording of the Treaty must be taken into account for this purpose.[7]

It is important to stress that these rules are a single set of rules;[8] they are in principle to be applied simultaneously.[9] Following this approach, the ICJ in *Namibia* referred to 'the primary necessity of interpreting an instrument in accordance with the intentions of the parties',[10] and used this as a basis on which to make an evolutionary interpretation of the concepts contained in Article 22 of the Covenant of the League of Nations.[11] The same was the case in *Aegean Sea*,[12] *Gabcikovo–Nagymaros*,[13] *Navigational and Related Rights*,[14] and *Pulp Mills*;[15] the Court arrived at an evolutionary interpretation of the instrument at issue specifically by stressing the importance in treaty interpretation of the intentions of the parties. As is clear from the selection of cases (running the gamut, from the *traité-contrat* in *Navigational and Related Rights* to the *traité-loi* in *Namibia*), this approach is taken regardless of the type of treaty at issue.[16] Against this background, the present chapter argues that the search for that intention is the very aim of the process set out in Article 31 of the VCLT, and that evolutionary interpretation thus can be explained by perhaps the most traditional of concepts in the law of treaties—the intention of the parties.

It is clear that some questions of interpretation seem so elusive as to defy resolution—hence Lord McNair's assertion that 'there is no part of the law of

---

[6]　See Eirik Bjorge, *The Evolutionary Interpretation of Treaties* (OUP 2014) 56–141.

[7]　*Interpretation of the Treaty of Lausanne, Article 3, paragraph 2* (1925) PCIJ Rep Series B No 12, 19.

[8]　Richard Gardiner, *Treaty Interpretation* (OUP 2010) 5.

[9]　Paul Reuter, *Introduction to the Law of Treaties* (Paul Kegan International 1995) 96–7.

[10]　*Legal Consequences for States of the Continued Presence of South Africa in Namibia (South West Africa) notwithstanding Security Council Resolution 276* (Advisory Opinion) [1970] ICJ Rep 1971 16, [53]; *Land and Maritime Boundary between Cameroon and Nigeria (Cameroon v Nigeria: Equatorial Guinea intervening)* (Judgment) [2002] ICJ Rep 303, 346.

[11]　Covenant of the League of Nations, 28 June 1919, 225 CTS 195.

[12]　*Aegean Sea Continental Shelf (Greece v Turkey)* [1978] ICJ Rep 3, [77].

[13]　*Gabcikovo-Nagymaros Project (Hungary v Slovakia)* (Judgment) [1997] ICJ Rep 7, [142].

[14]　*Navigational and Related Rights (Costa Rica v Nicaragua)* (Judgment) [2009] ICJ Rep 213, [63].

[15]　*Pulp Mills on the River Uruguay (Argentina v Uruguay)* (Judgment) [2010] ICJ Rep 14, [204].

[16]　See Vera Gowlland-Debbas, 'The Role of the International Court of Justice in the Development of the Contemporary Law of Treaties' in Christian Tams and James Sloan (eds), *The Development of International Law by the International Court of Justice* (OUP 2013) 35–7. See also *Young Loan Arbitration* (1980) 59 ILR 494, [18]–[19]; *Dispute concerning Filleting within the Gulf of St Lawrence ('La Bretagne') (Canada/France)* (1986) 82 ILR 591, 659–60; *Case Concerning the Delimitation of the Maritime Boundary between Guinea-Bissau and Senegal (Guinea-Bissau v Senegal)* (1989) 10 RIAA 119, [85]; *Award in the Arbitration regarding the Iron Rhine ('Ijzeren Rijn') (Belgium v Netherlands)* (2005) 27 RIAA 35, 65, 73.

treaties which the text writer approaches with more trepidation than the question of interpretation'.[17] But we should not be deterred, if for no other reason than that difficult questions, too, need an answer.

In that spirit it is appropriate to begin by giving a working definition of the terms 'evolutionary interpretation' and 'the intention of the parties'. By the words 'evolutionary interpretation', I mean situations in which an international court or tribunal concludes that a treaty term is capable of evolving, that it is not fixed once and for all, so that allowance is made for, among other things, developments in international law. This is, in other words, a situation where account is taken of the meaning acquired by the treaty terms when the treaty is applied.[18]

This chapter relies upon the definition of 'the intention of the parties' set out by the International Law Commission (ILC).[19] The concept of the intention of the parties, according to the ILC, 'refers to the intention of the parties as determined through the application of the various means of interpretation which are recognized in articles 31 and 32';[20] it 'is thus not a separately identifiable original will, and the *travaux préparatoires* are not the primary basis for determining the presumed intention of the parties'.[21] 'Intention' is thus, according to the ILC, a construct to be derived from the articulation of the 'means of interpretation admissible' in the process of interpretation,[22] and not a separately identifiable factor. What is central in the method of treaty interpretation, then, is that a convention, whatever its kind, is interpreted so as to be effective in terms of the intention of the parties. As the ILC's first Special Rapporteur on the law of treaties put it: the object is 'to give effect to the intention of the parties as fully and fairly as possible'.[23] And, as Giorgio Gaja has explained, within the approach set out in Articles 31–33 of the VCLT, the treaty interpreter reconstructs the meaning of an 'objectivized intention of the parties'; the means of interpretation are 'objective elements' which guide the treaty interpreter to the establishment of the intention of the parties.[24]

The body of this chapter is composed of three parts. Part I turns to the pre-VCLT approach to treaty interpretation and shows what in that approach was codified in Article 31 and what was not. Part II makes clear that what the ILC codified in the Vienna Rules were the means admissible in the establishment of the intention of the parties. It is no wonder therefore that the ICJ has been prominent in putting a premium upon the intention of the parties in cases bearing upon

---

[17] Arnold McNair, *The Law of Treaties* (2nd edn, OUP 1962) 392.

[18] *Navigational and Related Rights*, [63].

[19] Report of the International Law Commission on the Work of Its Sixty-Fifth Session A/68/10 27; 1966 ILC Ybk II 218–19.

[20] Report of the International Law Commission on the Work of Its Sixty-Fifth Session A/68/10 27.

[21] Report of the International Law Commission on the Work of Its Sixty-Fifth Session A/68/10 27. See James Crawford, *State Responsibility: The General Part* (CUP 2013) 247.

[22] 1966 ILC Ybk II 218–19.

[23] James Brierly, *The Law of Nations: An Introduction to the International Law of Peace* (OUP 1928) 168.

[24] Giorgio Gaja, 'Trattati internazionali' (1999) 15 DDP 344, 355–6.

evolutionary interpretation. Part III, the conclusion, shows how the pre-VCLT and post-VCLT approaches are really cut from the same cloth. The intention is, on both these approaches, an 'objectivized' or a 'presumed' intention; it is an intention that is determined, in cases bearing upon evolutionary as well as non-evolutionary concepts, through the application of the various means of interpretation now codified in the Vienna Rules.

I. Vienna Rules and the Search for Intention

A. Introduction

This part turns to the pre-VCLT approach to treaty interpretation and shows what in that approach was codified in the Vienna Rules and what was not. I intend to make clear, in this way, that what the ILC codified in the Vienna Rules were the means admissible in the establishment of the intention of the parties. Francesco Capotorti, one of the Italian representatives at the Vienna Conference, made the point in 1969 that although the Vienna Rules take an objective approach, 'the solution adopted in the VCLT provides a keyhole through which to look for the common intention of the parties'.[25] The reason why the approach has to be objective is that the treaty parties were, of course, never 'of one mind' but agreed instead to 'whatever'; *ad quidquid* is closer to the truth than *ad idem*.[26] This is, as Anne-Marie Carstens observes, all the more so in connection with the interpretation of transplanted treaty rules, where negotiations are 'once, twice, thrice (or more) removed'.[27]

As was seen above, the Vienna Rules set out the 'means of interpretation *admissible*' in the process of interpretation.[28] The keyhole view we get is shaped by the admissible means of interpretation; what we see, by definition, is the presumed intention of the parties. It is perfectly in keeping with the ILC approach therefore that the ICJ has been prominent in putting a premium upon the intention of the parties, also in cases bearing on evolutionary interpretation.

The ICJ in *Navigational and Related Rights* made clear that the treaty interpreter may arrive at an evolutionary interpretation in two types of case. On the one hand, the Court said, the subsequent practice of the parties, within the meaning of Article 31(3)(b) of the VCLT, can result in a departure from the original intent on the basis of a tacit agreement between the parties.[29]

On the other hand, continued the Court, there are situations in which the common intention of the parties was, or may be presumed to have been, to give

---

[25] Francesco Capotorti, *Convenzione di Vienna sul diritto dei trattati* (CEDAM 1969) 36.
[26] See Chapter 18 (Philip Allott), 377.   [27] See Chapter 11 (Anne-Marie Carstens), 233.
[28] 1966 ILC Ybk II 218–19 (italics mine).
[29] See Georg Nolte (ed), *Treaties and Subsequent Practice* (OUP 2013); Julian Arato, 'Subsequent Practice and Evolutive Interpretation: Techniques of Treaty Interpretation over Time and their Diverse Consequences' (2010) 9 LPICT 443; Richard Gardiner, 'The Vienna Convention Rules on Treaty Interpretation' in Duncan Hollis (ed), *The Oxford Guide to Treaties* (OUP 2012) 494–5.

some or all of the terms used a meaning or content capable of evolving, not one fixed once and for all, so as to make allowance for, among other things, developments in international law:

> In such instances it is indeed in order to respect the parties' common intention at the time the treaty was concluded, not to depart from it, that account should be taken of the meaning acquired by the terms in question upon each occasion on which the treaty is to be applied.[30]

Thus, in *Navigational and Related Rights*, the ICJ 'impute[d] an intention to be bound by an evolving interpretation of the terms of the treaty'.[31] In that sense, as adumbrated above, the case takes the same approach as both earlier and later cases to have reached the Court. In post-VCLT cases such as *Namibia*,[32] *Aegean Sea*,[33] *Gabcikovo–Nagymaros*,[34] and *Pulp Mills*,[35] the Court arrived at an evolutionary interpretation of the instrument at issue specifically by stressing the importance in treaty interpretation of the intentions of the parties. Catherine Redgwell must be right in saying that it cannot be the case that environmental treaty-making—such as the treaties in issue in cases such as *Gabcikovo–Nagymaros* and *Pulp Mills*— has engendered new rules of treaty interpretation applicable only in that sphere. Rather the development of such treaties and attendant techniques of interpretation should be seen as contributing to the development of the *general* law of treaties.[36]

The ICJ was reluctant in the 1970–80s to have explicit recourse to the VCLT more generally in cases bearing upon treaty interpretation; it was only in the 1990s that the Court began referring to Article 31 in its judgments.[37] Other examples dating from after the VCLT but not specifically dealing with evolutionary interpretation, such as *Continental Shelf (Libya/Malta)*[38] and *Frontier Dispute (Burkina Faso/Mali)*,[39] could also be given of the International Court, or a Chamber of the Court, seemingly going directly to the notion of the intention of the parties without, overtly at any rate, having recourse to Article 31. The tendency is, however, strikingly pronounced in cases bearing upon evolutionary interpretation.

---

[30] *Navigational and Related Rights*, 242–3.

[31] Andrew Clapham, *Brierly's Law of Nations: An Introduction to the Role of International Law in International Relations* (OUP 2012) 356.

[32] *Namibia*, [53].   [33] *Aegean Sea Continental Shelf*, [77].

[34] *Gabcikovo–Nagymaros*, [142].   [35] *Pulp Mills*, [204].

[36] Catherine Redgwell, 'Multilateral Environmental Treaty-Making' in Vera Gowlland-Debbas (ed), *Multilateral Treaty-Making: The Current Status of Challenges to and Reforms Needed in the International Legislative Process* (Martinus Nijhoff 2000) 107. See also Patricia Birnie, Alan Boyle, and Catherine Redgwell (eds), *International Law & the Environment* (3rd edn, OUP 2009) 20–2.

[37] See eg *Arbitral Award of 31 July 1989 (Guinea-Bissau v Senegal)* (Judgment) [1991] ICJ Rep 53, 70; *Territorial Dispute (Libya/Chad)* (Judgment) [1994] ICJ Rep 6, 21–2; *Application of the Convention on the Prevention and Punishment of the Crime of Genocide (Bosnia and Herzegovina v Serbia and Montenegro)* (Judgment) [2007] ICJ Rep 43, 109–10.

[38] *Continental Shelf (Libya/Malta)* [1985] ICJ Rep 13, 23.

[39] *Frontier Dispute (Burkina Faso/Mali)* [1986] ICJ Rep 554, 577.

Lately it is especially the Court's ruling in *Navigational and Related Rights* which has been criticized for the way in which it dealt with the issues of evolution and intent.[40] Commentators have wondered whether, in interpreting the convention at issue evolutionarily, the Court was in fact applying the general rule of interpretation as laid down in Article 31 of the VCLT.

Thus Paolo Palchetti has stated that the ICJ and other international courts and tribunals,[41] in reaching evolutionary interpretations, 'do not refer to the general rule stated in the VCLT in order to justify their solution, preferring, instead, to rely on a argument which is based on the identification of the presumed intentions of the parties at the time of the conclusion of the treaty'.[42]

Against this background, the question arises whether the ICJ does or does not follow the general rule of interpretation when, in interpreting an instrument evolutionarily, it seeks above all to give effect to the intentions of the parties.

Interestingly, Palchetti makes the observation that although, to his mind, searching for the intention of the parties is *not* the approach laid down in Article 31, there is some similarity between the approach taken by the ICJ in such cases and the approach of the general rule of interpretation. As he says: 'The presumed intention is deduced from objective factors which are substantially the same factors on which one should rely when interpreting a treaty according to the general criterion stated in the Vienna Convention'.[43] As will be seen, this way of putting the matter is very apt indeed.

B. The ILC approach and its antecedents

In searching for the intention of the parties in relation to evolutionary interpretation, the ICJ is in fact nothing if not applying the framework of Article 31 of the VCLT. Although the general rule of interpretation does not expressly mention the intention of the parties—or what role, if any, this construction ought to play in treaty interpretation—all the elements of the general rule have one sole aim and that is to provide the basis for establishing the intention of the parties. This is clear not only from the post-VCLT jurisprudence of the ICJ and of arbitral tribunals. It follows, too, from the approach taken by the ILC in its

---

[40] Arato, 'Subsequent Practice and Evolutive Interpretation'; Bruno Simma, 'Miscellaneous Thoughts on Subsequent Agreements and Practice' in Nolte, *Treaties and Subsequent Practice*, 48; Paolo Palchetti, 'Interpreting "Generic Terms": Between Respect for the Parties' Original Intention and the Identification of the Ordinary Meaning' in Nerina Boschiero, Tullio Scovazzi, Chiara Ragni, and Cesare Pitea (eds), *International Courts and the Development of International Law: Essays in Honour of Tullio Treves* (Brill 2013) 103–4.

[41] *Iron Rhine*, 65, 73–4; *La Bretagne*, 659–60; *Young Loan Arbitration* (1980) 59 ILR 494, 531, [18]–[19]; WTO, *United States: Import Prohibition of Certain Shrimp and Shrimp Products—Report of the Appellate Body* (12 October 1998) WB/DS58/AB/R [130]; WTO, *China: Measures Affecting Trading Rights and Distribution Services for Certain Publications and Audiovisual Entertainment Products—Report of the Appellate Body* (21 December 2009) WT/DS363/AB/R, [396].

[42] Palchetti, 'Interpreting "Generic Terms"', 103–4.

[43] Palchetti, 'Interpreting "Generic Terms"', 104.

work—most notably that of Special Rapporteur Waldock—leading up to the adoption of the VCLT.

The approach taken to treaty interpretation before the VCLT was squarely one in which, as the Tribunal in *Air Transport Services Agreement* put it on the eve of the VCLT's adoption, the goal was to 'establish with the maximum possible certainty what the common intention of the Parties was'.[44]

In the early twentieth century, this was even clearer, as tribunals at that time were quite prepared, in the ascertainment of the common intention of the parties, to interpret treaties *contra legem*.[45] Thus the Tribunal composed under the aegis of the Permanent Court of Arbitration in *Island of Timor* expanded, in 1914, on the importance in the law of treaties of establishing that which the Tribunal called 'the actual and mutual intention' of the parties.[46] Treaties bind the parties to loyal and complete execution, the Tribunal said, 'not only of what has been literally promised but of that to which a party has bound itself, and also that which conforms to the essence of any treaty whatsoever as to the harmonious intention of the contracting parties'.[47] Thus, concluded the Tribunal in *Timor*, the interpretation of treaties ought 'to be made in conformity with the real mutual intentions of the parties, and also in conformity with what can be presumed between parties acting loyally and with reason, not that which has been promised by one to the other according to the meaning of the words used'.[48]

The ILC began to concern itself, in 1949, with the law of treaties, and eventually also the interpretation of treaties. In 1966, it adopted 75 draft articles that formed the basis for the VCLT of 22 May 1969, which entered into force on 27 January 1980.[49] The Special Rapporteurs were all British: first James Brierly, then Hersch Lauterpacht, Gerald Fitzmaurice, and in the last and most important stages, Humphrey Waldock.[50]

---

[44] *Interpretation of the Air Transport Services Agreement between the United States of America and France* (1963) 38 ILR 182, 229; *Lighthouses Case between France and Greece* (1934) PCIJ Rep Series A/B No 62 4, 13, 18; *Reservations to the Convention on Genocide* (Advisory Opinion) [1951] ICJ Rep 15, 23; *Case of Certain Norwegian Loans (France v Norway)* (Judgment) [1957] ICJ Rep 9, 23, 27; *Namibia*, [53]; *Navigational and Related Rights*, 237, [48]; *Decision regarding delimitation of the border between Eritrea and Ethiopia* (2002) 25 RIAA 83, 109–10; WTO, *China: Audiovisual Entertainment Products—Report of the Appellate Body* (21 December 2009) WT/DS363/AB/R, [405].

[45] See eg Dissenting Opinion Judges Anzilotti and Huber *Case of the SS 'Wimbledon'* (1923) PCIJ Rep Series A No 1 15, 36; Max Sørensen, *Les sources du droit international: Étude sur la jurisprudence de la Cour permanente* (Einar Munksgaard 1946) 214.

[46] *Affaire de l'île de Timor (Pays-Bas c Portugal)* (1914) 11 RIAA 481, 497.

[47] *Affaire de l'île de Timor*, 496–7.

[48] *Affaire de l'île de Timor*, 496–7. See *Affaire de la Dette publique ottomane (Bulgarie, Irak, Palestine, Transjordanie, Grèce, Italie et Turquie)* (1925) 1 RIAA 529, 548; *Affaire relative à la concession des phares de l'Empire ottoman (Grèce c France)* (1956) 12 RIAA 155, 184; *Affaire Chevreau (France c Royaume-Uni)* (1931) 2 RIAA 1113; *Arbitral Award in the Matter of the Claim of Madame Chevreau against the United Kingdom* (1933) 27 AJIL 153; *Sarropoulos* in (1927–28) *Annual Digest of Public International Law Cases* Case No 291; *Polyxene Plessa v the Turkish Government* in (1929) VIII *Recueil des décisions des tribunaux arbitraux mixtes* 224; *Ottoman Debt Arbitration* in (1925–26) *Annual Digest of Public International Law Cases* No 270; *Lederer v German State* in (1928) III *Recueil des décisions des tribunaux arbitraux mixtes* 762–9. Hersch Lauterpacht, *The Development of International Law by the International Court* (Stevens & Sons 1958) 56.

[49] James Crawford, *Brownlie's Principles of International Law* (8th edn, OUP 2012) 367.

[50] The principal items, with respect to treaty interpretation, are: 1964 ILC Ybk I–II; 1966 ILC Ybk I–II; ILC Final Report and Draft Articles, ILC Ybk 1966 II.

To some extent running in parallel with the work of the ILC was the work on treaty interpretation undertaken by the *Institut de Droit international*, which elected as their Special Rapporteurs first Lauterpacht and then, on his elevation to the ICJ, Fitzmaurice.[51]

Fitzmaurice held, in an important contribution,[52] that any analysis of the jurisprudence of the ICJ, or indeed the pronouncements of any tribunal on treaty interpretation, can only be properly evaluated against the backdrop of the various theories of interpretation that are or recently have been current.[53] He drew up three possible approaches to treaty interpretation: the textual approach, the intention-based approach, and the teleological approach. Fitzmaurice never presented these schools of interpretation as authorities on their own, still less in terms of balancing policies and perceptions. Rather, they were rational attempts on Fitzmaurice's part at explication and taxonomization of the approaches taken in the doctrine.[54]

The tripartite split drawn up by Fitzmaurice became influential and made up the backdrop of the debates in the ILC in its work on the law of treaties.[55] Thus Special Rapporteur Waldock in his 'Third Report on the Law of Treaties' saw the question as a matter of writers differing in their basic approach to the interpretation of treaties according to the relative weight they were willing to 'give to' the text of the treaty, the intentions of the parties, and objects and purposes of the treaty.

This debate was closely linked to the question of what role to consign the *travaux préparatoires* in treaty interpretation. Lauterpacht had been an ardent advocate of giving pride of place to preparatory works.[56] As Special Rapporteur for the *Institut de Droit international*, Lauterpacht drew up 'projets de résolution' on the interpretation of treaties, where he suggested in a text best rendered in the original that:

Le recours aux travaux préparatoires, lorsqu'ils sont accessibles, est notamment un moyen légitime et désirable aux fins d'établir l'intention des parties dans tous les cas où, malgré sa clarté apparente, le sens d'un traité prête à controverse. Il n'y a aucun motif d'exclure l'usage de travaux préparatoires dûment consignés et publiés, à l'encontre d'États ayant adhéré au traité postérieurement à sa signature par les parties originaires.[57]

---

[51] The principal items are (1950) 43 *Annuaire de l'Institut de Droit international*; (1956) 46 *Annuaire de l'Institut de Droit international*.

[52] See 1964 ILC Ybk II 53–4.

[53] Gerald Fitzmaurice, 'The Law and Procedure of the International Court of Justice 1951–54: Treaty Interpretation and Other Treaty Points' (1957) 33 BYBIL 203, 204.

[54] Alexander Orakhelashvili, 'The Recent Practice on the Principles of Treaty Interpretation' in Alexander Orakhelashvili and Sarah Williams (eds), *40 Years of the Vienna Convention on Treaties* (BIICL 2010) 118.

[55] 1964 ILC Ybk II 53–4.

[56] Hersch Lauterpacht, 'De l'interprétation des traités' (1950) 43 *Annuaire de l'Institut de Droit international* 366.

[57] Lauterpacht, 'De l'interprétation des traités', 433.

This approach was criticized. Prominent in criticizing the approach was Eric Beckett, who saw the reliance upon *travaux préparatoires* as a danger to the legal certainty which to his mind could be procured only if one stuck as closely as possible to the text of the treaty, even to the exclusion of other means of interpretation.[58] If too ready an admission of preparatory work was allowed, he considered that the state which had found a clear provision of the treaty inconvenient was likely to be furnished with a *tabula in naufragio*; there would always be something in the preparatory work fit to support their contention.[59]

It is worth mentioning, however, that Beckett made an important concession by taking a large view of what the treaty was; quite a number of the elements which he saw as being part of the treaty and not of the *travaux préparatoires* could very well have been seen as part of the preparatory works.[60] This of course considerably softens the brunt of his claims.

Later, the problem with too ready a reliance upon the *travaux préparatoires* was summarized as being that 'it is beyond question that the records of treaty negotiations are in many cases incomplete or misleading, so that considerable discretion has to be exercised in determining their value as an element of interpretation'.[61] Nonetheless, as explained by Mortenson,[62] the VCLT is not as hostile to *travaux* as is sometimes thought.[63] Waldock also stressed that *travaux*:

are simply evidence to be weighed against any other relevant evidence of the intentions of the parties, and their cogency depends on the extent to which they furnish proof of the *common* understanding of the parties as to the meaning attached to the terms of the treaty.[64]

According to the approach taken by the ILC, and unanimously adopted by the initial parties to the VCLT, in what would become Articles 31–33 of the VCLT, the ILC made clear that to the extent that it was confronted with a choice between the textual approach, the intention-based approach, and the teleological approach, it chose the textual one.[65]

---

[58] Eric Beckett (1950) 43 *Annuaire de l'Institut de Droit international* 435, 435–44.

[59] Beckett (1950), 438–40. See Jiménez de Aréchaga at the First Session of the 26 March–24 May 1968 United Nations Conference on the Law of Treaties: A/CONF.39/C.1/SR.31, 160; Gerald Fitzmaurice and Francis Vallat, 'Sir (William) Eric Beckett, KCMG, QC (1896–1966): An Appreciation' (1968) 17 ICLQ 267, 307.

[60] Beckett (1950), 442. The list is surprisingly long: the 'treaty' will on his admission 'include everything that was signed at the time even though this consists of a main document, called the treaty, together with a whole lot of letters, protocols and even (probably) agreed minutes…In addition to everything which is published and registered, there may exist yet further specially initialled minutes which have been deliberately prepared for the purposes of its interpretation…and further, within the general mass of the *travaux préparatoires* there may be special reports of a Rapporteur with regard to which it may be demonstrated that it falls into a special category, being specially adapted as a guide for interpretation'.

[61] ILC Ybk 1966 II 220.

[62] Julian Mortenson, 'The Travaux of Travaux: Is the Vienna Convention Hostile to Drafting History?' (2014) 107 AJIL 780, 820–1.

[63] See eg Sorel and Boré Eveno, 'Article 31', 817.   [64] ILC Ybk 1964/II, 58.

[65] ILC Ybk 1964/II, 56.

Leading authors have assumed that in choosing this approach the ILC had dismissed, in one fell swoop, the age-old principle according to which the aim of treaty interpretation was to ascertain what was the common intention of the parties.[66] But whilst the ILC did indeed opt for that which it termed the textual approach, it was not the case that the ILC jettisoned the idea that the object of treaty interpretation is the ascertainment of the intention of the parties. It is plain enough that Article 31(1) does not mention in terms the intention or will of the parties. Only in Article 31(4) does the general rule have recourse to the intention of the parties: 'A special meaning shall be given to a term if it is established that the parties so intended.'[67]

Conversely, in Lauterpacht's 1950 'projet de résolution', the intention of the parties enjoyed pride of place in the very terms of the first article:

La recherche de l'intention des parties étant le but principal de l'interprétation, il est légitime et désirable, dans l'intérêt de la bonne foi et de la stabilité des transactions international, de prendre le sens naturel des termes comme point de départ du processus d'interprétation.[68]

As will have become clear, by contrast, 'the intention of the parties' is conspicuous by its absence in Article 31(1) of the VCLT. It is important to make the point, however, that the general rule of interpretation lists the means of interpretation; it does not set out to explicate what the aim of treaty interpretation is.

II. A Re-reading of the Vienna Rules

A. Introduction

Making the point that Article 31 does not mention the intention of the parties, Fitzmaurice, sitting as a judge of the European Court of Human Rights, said that 'though it does not in terms mention it', Article 31 'implicitly recognises the element of intentions'.[69] This must be correct. But whilst it is true that the VCLT 'implicitly recognises the element of intentions', putting the matter in this way runs the risk of confusing the issues.

Article 31(1) does not implicitly recognize intentions as just another (unmentioned) means of interpretation; rather, it recognizes intention as the very *aim* of

---

[66] Gardiner, *Treaty Interpretation*, 6; Rudolf Bernhardt, 'Evolutive Treaty Interpretation—Especially of the European Convention on Human Rights' (1999) 42 GYIL 11, 14; Rudolf Bernhardt, *Die Auslegung völkerrechtlicher Verträge—insbesondere in der Rechtsprechung internationaler Gerichte* (Heymann 1963) 32; Sergio Sur, *L'interprétation en droit international public* (LGDJ 1974) 194.

[67] See Gardiner, *Treaty Interpretation*, 6–7.

[68] Hersch Lauterpacht, 'De l'interprétation des traités' (1950) 43 *Annuaire de l'Institut du Droit international* 366, 433 (until 1957 the resolutions of the Institut were available only in French; as there does not exist an English version, I have not provided an English translation of this authoritative text).

[69] Separate Opinion of Judge Fitzmaurice, *Case of National Union of Belgian Police v Belgium* (1979–80) 1 EHRR 578, [9].

the whole process. Charles de Visscher made this point about the intention of the parties, already before the VCLT was adopted. He stressed the point that the discovery of the intention of the parties is the *object* of interpretation, and must not be thought to be anything else. It is, he said, the very thing to be proven, 'la chose à démontrer', and one cannot regard as a means of interpretation that which can only be the result of the interpretive process itself!.[70]

Apart from the text of Article 31 itself, the safest guide to that to which the ILC wanted to give expression in the general rule of interpretation might be thought to be Special Rapporteur Waldock's comments to the draft articles, later unanimously adopted. Waldock made his approach clear when he stated the reason why he took the text of the treaty as a starting point (in common with Lauterpacht's proposed articles for the *Institut de Droit international* some 15 years earlier):[71]

It takes as the basic rule of treaty interpretation the primacy of the text as evidence of the intentions of the parties. It accepts the view that the text must be presumed to be the authentic expression of the intentions of the parties.[72]

In 1966, Waldock described treaty interpretation as geared towards 'appreciating the meaning which the parties may have intended to attach to the expressions that they employed in a document'.[73] Indeed, one of the main reasons why the ILC felt bound to tackle head on the difficult task of formulating the comparatively few general principles which appear to constitute general rules for the interpretation of treaties was, he said, to set out 'the means of interpretation admissible for ascertaining the intention of the parties'.[74] This was later well summarized by Robert Jennings and Arthur Watts: on the approach of the general rule of interpretation, they explained, 'it is the intention which is being sought'; 'the question is primarily one of determining what elements *may properly be taken into account* as indirect evidence of the parties' intention and what weight is to be given to those elements'.[75]

The ILC made it clear, however, that what it was codifying was an approach to treaty interpretation that relied in the first instance upon the text of the treaty (incidentally a broader concept than the 'terms' of the treaty), as the most important means of ascertaining the common intention of the parties.[76] The relation between text and intention has been well brought out by James Crawford, who

---

[70] Charles de Visscher, *Problèmes d'interprétation judiciaire en droit international public* (Pedone 1963) 50.

[71] Waldock in fact pointed out that his proposed Article 70—which would become Article 31—'corresponds to article 1 of the Institute's resolution': 1964 ILC Ybk 1964 II 56.

[72] 1964 ILC Ybk II 56. Also: 1966 ILC Ybk II 220; Crawford, *Brownlie's Principles of International Law*, 379.

[73] 1966 ILC Ybk II 218.   [74] 1966 ILC Ybk II 218, 218–19.

[75] Robert Jennings and Arthur Watts, *Oppenheim's International Law* (9th edn, Longman 1992) 1271.

[76] Note that 'text' of the treaty is broader than the 'terms' of the treaty: *Case concerning the audit of accounts between the Netherlands and France in application of the Protocol of 25 September 1991 Additional to the Convention for the Protection of the Rhine from Pollution by Chlorides of 3 December 1976 (France/The Netherlands)* (2004) 25 RIAA 267, [63].

describes the unitary process of interpretation in the general rule of interpretation thus: 'Article 31 emphasizes the intention of the parties as expressed in the text, as the best guide to their common intention.'[77]

Mustafa Yasseen, one of the leading members of the ILC during the drafting of the VCLT, made it clear, in his 1976 Hague lectures on the interpretation of treaties, that when the ILC took the text as the starting point for interpretation, that was in no way to minimize the importance of the intention of the parties: 'Going first to the text is inevitable; the text is taken to contain the common intention of the parties.'[78] He continued by saying: 'What is the point of a text if, in order to interpret the treaty, the intention of the parties is to be searched *ab initio*? Taking the text as the point of departure is not to minimize the importance of the intention of the parties; rather, it means proceeding to discover it by examining the instrument by way of that which it is expressed.'[79]

Paul Reuter, another leading member of the ILC in the period leading up to the VCLT, in his writings after 1969, made the same point as Yasseen about the close nexus between textuality and intentionality in the general rule: 'The purpose of interpretation', he said, 'is to ascertain the intention of the parties from a text'; 'interpretation means going backwards from the text to the initial intention'. In the interpretation of treaties, because of what he called the submission to the *expression* of the parties' intention, he argued it was essential to identify exactly how and when that intention was expressed; thus, Reuter said about the means of interpretation enumerated in Article 31, 'it is from these elements, since they primarily incorporate the parties' intention, that the meaning of the treaty should normally be derived'.[80]

Far from minimizing the importance of the intention of the parties, then, the approach taken by Article 31 gives the treaty interpreter the admissible and agreed upon way of ascertaining it. That way begins, as does virtually all interpretation of texts, with the text itself.[81] This gist is conveyed with clarity in Waldock's words, referred to above, to the effect that the task of the ILC was to enumerate '*the means of interpretation admissible* for ascertaining the intention of the parties'.[82] As can be seen from Yasseen's words, too, the only real difference between what, in the run up to the VCLT, had been termed (slightly confusingly, as it turns out) the 'textual' and the 'intentions' method, therefore, is that the textual method

---

[77] Crawford, *Brownlie's Principles of International Law*, 379.

[78] Mustafa Yasseen, 'L'interprétation des traités d'après la convention de Vienne sur le droit des traités' (1976) 151 Recueil des Cours 1, 25: 'C'est au texte que de prime abord il est inévitable de recourir pour interpréter le traité. Ce texte est censé contenir l'intention commune des parties.'

[79] Yasseen, 'L'interprétation des traités d'après la convention de Vienne sur le droit des traités', 25–6: 'A quoi sert un texte, si, pour interpréter le traité, il faut chercher *ab initio* l'intention des parties? Prendre le texte comme point de départ, ce n'est donc pas minimiser l'importance de l'intention des parties, mais procéder à sa découverte, par l'examen de l'instrument par lequel elle s'est exprimée.'

[80] Reuter, *Introduction to the Law of Treaties*, 96–7; Paul Reuter, *La Convention de Vienne du droit des traités* (Armand Colin 1971) 17; Martin Dawidowicz, 'The Effect of the Passage of Time on the Interpretation of Treaties: Some Reflections on *Costa Rica v Nicaragua*' (2011) 24 LJIL 201, 206–7.

[81] *Iron Rhine*, [47]; *Territorial Dispute*, [41].

[82] 1966 ILC Ybk II 218–19 (emphasis added).

takes, in the ascertainment of the intention of the parties, as its starting point the *text*, whereas the intentions approach investigates *ab initio* the intentions of the parties. The one defining difference is, then, that the textual approach is founded upon a presumption that, as Special Rapporteur Waldock put it (quoting Max Huber), 'the signed text is, with very few exceptions, the only and the most recent expression of the common will of the parties'.[83] Even Beckett, who in the debates of the *Institut de Droit international* in 1950 registered probably the most critical view of the category of 'the intention of the parties' to have entered the debate, was of the view that the text of a treaty was so important because 'treaties must be deemed to be drawn up with legal advice and *prima facie* to express completely the intentions of the parties'.[84]

Malgosia Fitzmaurice is right, therefore, to say that whilst the ILC distanced itself from an approach to treaty interpretation which put too large an accent on preparatory works, 'the concept of the intention of the parties, *in a different and more objective sense*, remains, however, a fundamental concept for illuminating the bounds of allowable interpretation within the terms of the VCLT'.[85]

B. Evolutionary interpretation under the Vienna Rules

In light of the above, how do we deal with the problem of interpretation caused by an evolution in the meaning generally attached to a concept embodied in a treaty provision (the problem of evolutionary interpretation)?

In *Navigational and Related Rights*, it was Nicaragua who argued for a contemporaneous interpretation on the basis of the intentions of the parties, not Costa Rica (who argued for an evolutionary interpretation)—though in the event the Court concluded in favour of Costa Rica on the basis of the intention of the parties. This goes a long way to show the difficulty that may be encountered in marrying the concepts of intent and evolution.[86]

At the end of his career in the beginning of the 1980s, Waldock, the then President of the ICJ, returned to this particular issue. In a series of works on evolutionary interpretation, especially of human rights treaties, he stated that the VCLT did not deal specifically with the effect of an evolution in treaty terms: 'The International Law Commission's commentary, however, which I myself wrote', he continued, 'explained that so much depends on ... the intention of the parties in the particular treaty, that it would be difficult to lay down any general rules'.[87]

---

[83] 1966 ILC Ybk 1966 II 220, citing (1950) 43 *Annuaire de l'Institut du Droit international* 199 ('le texte signé est, sauf de rares exceptions, la seule et la plus récente expression de la volonté commune des parties').

[84] Beckett (1950), 442; Fitzmaurice and Vallat, 'Sir (William) Eric Beckett', 307–8.

[85] Malgosia Fitzmaurice, 'Interpretation of Human Rights Treaties' in Dinah Shelton (ed), *Handbook of International Human Rights Law* (OUP 2013) 745; Rolf Einar Fife, 'Les techniques interprétatives non juridictionnelles de la norme internationale' (2011) 115 RGDIP 367, 372.

[86] Dawidowicz, 'The Effect of the Passage of Time on the Interpretation of Treaties', 213.

[87] Humphrey Waldock, 'The Effectiveness of the System Set up by the European Convention on Human Rights' (1980) HRLJ 1, 3–4.

Asking the question of how courts ought to approach the problem of evolutionary interpretation specifically, he stated that:

The problem of interpretation caused by an evolution in the meaning generally attached to a concept embodied in a treaty provision is, of course, neither new nor confined to human rights.... But the problem is a general one which may present itself whenever the original meaning of a concept forming the basis of a treaty provision is found to have evolved. If the International Law Commission's view of the matter is correct, as hardly seems open to doubt, the answer to the problem in any given case must be looked for in the intention of the parties to the particular treaty.[88]

Confronted with the question of how, according to the general rule of interpretation, a tribunal ought to approach treaty terms which may or may not be deemed to be evolving, Yasseen made exactly the same point: 'That depends, to my mind, on what the parties really intended'.[89] This answer is, of course, question-begging, for as Waldock was quick to point out: 'that intention, however, may not always be easily discernible'.[90]

The broader point, however, remains. And that is why, in cases bearing upon evolutionary interpretation, the ICJ and arbitral tribunals alike have proceeded as the Tribunal did in *La Bretagne*, where, in order to find out whether the treaty term 'fishing regulation' ought or ought not to be interpreted in an evolutionary fashion, the Tribunal stressed 'the primary necessity of interpreting an instrument in accordance with the intentions of the parties'.[91] 'This', the Tribunal continued, 'will be done by following the general rule of interpretation'.[92]

International jurisprudence has been consistent in taking this approach. Thus the Eritrea–Ethiopia Boundary Commission in *Border between Eritrea and Ethiopia* followed 'the general rule that a treaty is to be interpreted in good faith in accord-ance with the ordinary meaning to be given to the terms of the treaty in their context and in the light of its object and purpose' because 'each of these elements guide the interpreter in establishing what the Parties actually intended, or their common will'.[93] The Tribunal, in *Protection of the Rhine from Pollution by Chlorides*, stated that the reason international jurisprudence has adhered to Article 31 was, simply, that 'all the elements of the general rule of interpretation provide the basis for establishing the common will and intention of the parties'.[94]

---

[88] Humphrey Waldock, 'The Evolution of Human Rights Concepts and the Application of the ECHR' in *Mélanges Paul Reuter* (Pedone 1981) 536.

[89] Yasseen, 'L'interprétation des traités d'après la convention de Vienne sur le droit des traités', 27: 'Cela dépend à notre avis de ce que les parties ont vraiment voulu.'

[90] Waldock, 'The Evolution of Human Rights Concepts and the Application of the ECHR', 536.

[91] *La Bretagne*, 624.   [92] *La Bretagne*, 659–60; Crawford, *State Responsibility*, 247.

[93] *Eritrea*, 109–10 (inverted commas deleted).   [94] *Audit of Accounts*, [62].

Conclusion

As was adumbrated in the Introduction, the ILC made it clear that it set out in the general rule of interpretation 'the means of interpretation admissible for ascertaining the intention of the parties'.[95] The keyhole view we get when we follow the Vienna Rules is fashioned by the admissible means of interpretation, which enable us to discern the intention of the parties.[96] This explains why the ICJ has put such a premium upon establishing the intention of the parties: the establishment of that intention is the aim of the general rule of interpretation. With the latest work of the ILC on treaty interpretation,[97] it is tempting to say that the issue of the intention of the parties has come full circle. In Draft Conclusion 3, the ILC agreed on the following wording:

Interpretation of Treaty Terms as Capable of Evolving over Time
Subsequent agreements and subsequent practice under article 31 and 32 may assist in determining whether or not the presumed intention of the parties upon the conclusion of the treaty was to give a term used a meaning which is capable of evolving over time.[98]

The ILC Commentary to the Draft Conclusion leaves little to be desired in terms of clarity when it comes to just what its approach to evolutionary interpretation and 'presumed intention' is. Any evolutionary interpretation of the meaning of a treaty term, the ILC observes, must be justifiable as a result of the ordinary process of treaty interpretation.[99] And more specifically: 'The phrase "presumed intention" refers to the intention of the parties as determined through the application of the various means of interpretation which are recognized in articles 31 and 32'.[100] 'Presumed intention', the ILC concluded:

is thus not a separately identifiable original will, and the *travaux préparatoires* are not the primary basis for determining the presumed intention of the parties, but they are only, as article 32 indicates, a supplementary means of interpretation. And although interpretation must seek to identify the intention of the parties, this must be done by the interpreter on the basis of the means of interpretation which are available at the time of the act of interpretation.[101]

It is not necessarily the case that the approach based on the ascertainment of 'the intention of the parties', for which this chapter has argued, is the *only* way of explicating the pedigree of evolutionary interpretation. The question is one

---

[95] 1966 ILC Ybk II 218–19 (emphasized here).
[96] Capotorti, *Convenzione di Vienna sul diritto dei trattati*, 36.
[97] See Report of the International Law Commission on the Work of Its Sixty-Fifth Session A/68/10 9–49; Georg Nolte, 'Introductory Report of the Study Group on Treaties over Time and Second Report of the ILC Study Group on Treaties over Times' in Nolte (ed), *Treaties and Subsequent Practice*.
[98] Report of the International Law Commission on the Work of Its Sixty-Fifth Session A/68/10 12.
[99] Report of the International Law Commission on the Work of Its Sixty-Fifth Session A/68/10 27.
[100] Report of the International Law Commission on the Work of Its Sixty-Fifth Session A/68/10 27.
[101] Report of the International Law Commission on the Work of Its Sixty-Fifth Session A/68/10 27.

of emphasis. To some extent, therefore, the hand which the treaty interpreter is dealt—the 'cards' of treaty interpretation[102]—seems to grant the interpreting authority a measure of flexibility. This chapter has, however, argued that there comes a point at which a particular argument or interpretation becomes untenable. Even as sceptical an observer as Koskenniemi has observed that whatever else international law might be, at least it is how international lawyers argue; acceptable legal arguments are explicable on the basis of 'a limited number of rules that constitute the "grammar"—the system of production of good legal arguments'.[103] From this it is possible to conclude that it is not the case that 'every argument goes'. There is, in the context of treaty interpretation, a grammar that structures which arguments are legitimate and which are not. Whatever view one takes of structural biases in international law, interpreters cannot escape this grammar. As has been seen, this grammar is spelled out, where treaty interpretation is concerned, in the Vienna Rules. Whatever reasons or motivations underlie a suggested interpretation, the interpretation must be couched in the grammar of the rules of interpretation.[104] The point at which an argument becomes untenable is when the cards are used in such a way that they no longer purport to search, or actually search, for the intention of the parties.

---

[102] See Chapter 2 (Andrea Bianchi).
[103] Martti Koskenniemi, *From Apology to Utopia* (CUP 2005) 568.
[104] Ingo Venzke, *How Interpretation Makes International Law* (OUP 2012) 47–50.

10

Accounting for Difference in Treaty Interpretation Over Time

*Julian Arato**

Introduction

The law of treaty interpretation presents a familiar paradox. All students of public international law are at some point taught (perhaps with a wink) that as a matter of doctrine all treaties are subject to the same unified rules of interpretation—those principles codified at Articles 31–33 of the Vienna Convention on the Law of Treaties (VCLT), generally understood as reflecting customary international law.[1] Yet at the same time, everyone knows that some treaties are special. Time and again we hear that some kinds of treaties are different. Courts, tribunals, and scholars often intone that some types of treaties are entitled to special treatment when it comes to interpretation, especially as regards those changes of circumstances and intentions attending the passage of time. The problem is that the explanations offered for such differentiation rarely satisfy.

The most common case involves the special nature of human rights treaties. Perhaps most famously, the European Court of Human Rights (ECtHR) has extolled the special place of the European Convention on Human Rights (ECHR) as an 'instrument for the protection of individual human beings'.[2] As the Court famously stated, in *Soering v UK*, '[i]n interpreting the Convention regard must be had to its special character as a treaty for the collective enforcement of human rights and fundamental freedoms'.[3] According to the Court, such special characteristics call for an outsized reliance on effective interpretation,[4]

* I am grateful to Ryan Goodman, Eyal Benvenisti, Malgosia Fitzmaurice, Eirik Bjorge, Harlan Cohen, Anthea Roberts, and Brandon Ruben for invaluable comments and discussion at various stages.

[1] See eg Ulf Linderfalk, *On the Interpretation of Treaties* (Springer 2007) 3; Vienna Convention on the Law of Treaties (concluded on 23 May 1969, entered into force 27 January 1980) 1155 UNTS 331 (hereinafter VCLT).

[2] *Soering v UK* (1989) 11 EHRR 439, [87].

[3] *Soering v UK* (1989) 11 EHRR 439, [87].

[4] *Soering v UK* (1989) 11 EHRR 439, [87].

and justify viewing the Convention as a 'living instrument'.[5] The Inter-American Court of Human Rights (IACtHR) has similarly emphasized the special nature of human rights treaties in general, and the American Convention on Human Rights in particular, finding that such instruments 'are not multilateral treaties of the traditional type concluded to accomplish the reciprocal exchange of rights for the mutual benefit of the contracting States',[6] and that 'human rights treaties are living instruments whose interpretation must consider the changes over time and present-day conditions'.[7]

Such arguments are not limited to the field of human rights. Similar claims have been raised regarding the 'special' nature of treaties for the protection of the environment,[8] territorial treaties,[9] and treaties for the protection of civilians during armed conflict.[10]

So on the one hand we have the universal Vienna rules, equally applicable to the interpretation of all treaties; on the other hand we have differential treatment. Faced with the familiar paradox of accounting for difference under the sign of equality, the question of the day is how to *explain* such differential treatment within the law of treaties. What justifies weighing some rules of interpretation more strongly than others (ie emphasizing object and purpose over text, or vice versa)? When and to what extent might deviation from the usual rules be justified?

Even in the abstract, the interpretation of treaties over time can lead to doctrinal difficulties.[11] Under what circumstances can a treaty change over time? To what extent can it change on the basis of the parties' subsequent intentions—as

---

[5] *Loizidou v Turkey* (preliminary objections) (1995) 20 EHRR 99, [71].

[6] *Effect of Reservations on the Entry into Force of the American Convention on Human Rights (Arts 74 and 75)*, Advisory Opinion OC-2/82, Inter-American Court of Human Rights Series A No 2 (24 September 1982), [29].

[7] *The Right to Information on Consular Assistance in the Framework of the Guarantees of the Due Process of Law*, Advisory Opinion OC-16/99, Inter-American Court of Human Rights Series A No 16 (1 October 1999), [114]. Such views are not limited to human rights courts. For example, the investor-state arbitral tribunal in *RosInvest* similarly acknowledged that human rights treaties are especially amenable to evolutive interpretation—by contrast to the bilateral investment treaty (BIT) at issue, which was not capable of autonomous evolution. *RosInvest Co v Russian Federation* (SCC Case No V 079/2005) Award on Jurisdiction (October 2007), [40].

[8] See eg *Gabčíkovo-Nagymaros (Hungary v Slovakia)* [1997] ICJ Rep 7, [112]; *Pulp Mills (Argentina v Uruguay)* [2010] ICJ Rep 14, Separate Opinion of Judge Cançado-Trindade, [116], [119]; WTO, *US: Import Prohibition of Certain Shrimp and Shrimp Products—Appellate Body Report* (12 October 1998), WT/DS58/AB/R, [130].

[9] See Malcolm Shaw, 'Title, Control, and Closure? The Experience of the Eritrea-Ethiopia Boundary Commission' (2007) 56 ICLQ 755, 761 (boundary treaties 'constitute a special kind of treaty in that they establish an objective territorial regime valid *erga omnes*'); Marcelo Kohen, 'The Decision on the Delimitation of the Eritrea/Ethiopia Boundary of 13 April 2002: A Singular Approach to International Law Applicable to Territorial Disputes' in Marcelo Kohen (ed), *Promoting Justice, Human Rights and Conflict Resolution through International Law: Liber Amicorum Lucius Caflisch (Brill 2007) 767, 772; Territorial Sovereignty and Scope of the Dispute (Eritrea/Yemen)* (1998) 22 RIAA 209, [153].

[10] See eg *Kupreškić et al* (Judgment) ICTY-95-16-T (14 January 2000), [517]–[519].

[11] While all treaty interpretation is in some sense 'interpretation over time', I employ the expression here as a shorthand for the question of treaty change or development over time through interpretation—specifically on the basis of certain codified (or quasi-codified) techniques of interpretation, ie evolutive (dynamic) interpretation and interpretation on the basis of the subsequent practice of the parties. See further Julian Arato, 'Subsequent Practice and Evolutive

evidenced by their subsequent agreement and practice?[12] To what extent can a treaty evolve over time in the absence of authorization by the parties at the time of interpretation, or even in spite of their intentions to the contrary ('evolutive interpretation')?[13] And where these canons conflict with one another, or with the other components of the Vienna rules, which principles take precedence? These questions go to the core of the law of treaties—the consent of the parties to be bound by mutual agreement and the extent to which they remain the masters of their treaties in the long term.

At the least, if the doctrine of universality is to be believed, the answer to these questions would remain constant, across treaties of all stripes. Yet we see frequent attempts to insulate certain kinds of treaties from the potentially shifting will of the parties, or to classify some 'special' treaties as autonomous from their creators—capable of large-scale evolutionary change more or less beyond the parties' continued control. These intuitions are often valuable—but as yet it remains unclear, beyond broad generalizations, what considerations explain and justify such distinctions in particular cases.

Differential treatment tends to be explained in one of two ways, both of which prove ultimately unsatisfying. On the one hand, many scholars and tribunals appeal to the general subject matter of certain treaties in singling them out for special treatment (eg treaties for the protection of human rights, or the environment).[14] In light of their special subject matter, the argument goes, such treaties should be understood as insulated from the changing will of the parties, and even in some instances capable of autonomous evolution. On the other hand, the second main school of thought rejects such generalizations, calling instead for a more particularized approach to treaty interpretation over time based on the object and purpose of the specific treaty in question.[15] For the latter group, the touchstone must always be the intention of the parties, as reflected in the goals their particular agreement seeks to achieve.

By contrast to the 'subject-matter approach', which I suggest creates an unhelpful typology of treaties, I suggest that the 'object and purpose approach' goes too far toward the position that there is no benefit to be gained from thinking about

Interpretation: Techniques of Treaty Interpretation over Time and their Diverse Consequences' (2010) 9 Law & Prac Intl Cts And Tribunals 443.

[12] See Article 31(3)(b) VCLT; see also Georg Nolte (ed), *Treaties and Subsequent Practice* (OUP 2013); Arato, 'Subsequent Practice and Evolutive Interpretation'.

[13] See ILC, 'Fragmentation of International Law: Difficulties Arising from the Diversification and Expansion of International Law' (finalized by Martti Koskenniemi) (2006), [478] (hereinafter the *'Fragmentation Report'*); Eirik Bjorge, *The Evolutionary Interpretation of Treaties* (OUP 2014); Malgosia Fitzmaurice, 'Dynamic (Evolutive) Interpretation of Treaties, Part I' (2008) Hague YB Intl L 101.

[14] Treaties protecting the human person form a special category, according to one perennial recital, such as those concerning international humanitarian law or human rights. See eg Theodor Meron, *The Humanization of International Law* (Brill 2006); *Fragmentation Report*, [428]. More recently one also hears that treaties protecting the environment have a special place: *Fragmentation Report*, [250].

[15] See Rosalyn Higgins, 'Time and the Law: International Perspectives on an Old Problem' (1997) 46 ICLQ 501, 519.

types of treaties at all (for the purposes of taking a differential approach to interpretation over time). Moreover, the latter approach runs into problems of its own, related to the difficulty of determining the object and purpose of a treaty or treaty provision in a meaningful way. I want to propose a middle ground.

This chapter argues that the crucial consideration lies not in the subject matter of the treaty, nor even purely in its object and purpose, but rather in the *nature of the obligations* incorporated by the parties in order to achieve their goals. The critical question is whether a treaty provision entails a merely reciprocal exchange of rights and duties, or rather incorporates a more absolute commitment by the parties to take on an obligation insulated from their changing intentions, and over which their subsequent mastery might prove relatively limited. The two most important examples of such absolute (non-reciprocal) obligations are: *interdependent* norms, meaning obligations of coordination entirely dependent upon the mutual compliance of all of the parties for their effect; and *integral* norms, which may be understood as absolute obligations *stricto sensu*—norms meant to withstand non-compliance, for which violation requires redress, but never justifies retaliatory breach by the other parties.[16] Whereas a reciprocal obligation entails a bilateral exchange of rights and duties between two treaty parties, absolute obligations are owed to all the states parties as a collective group (*erga omnes partes*) or even to a higher collectivity like the international community as a whole (*erga omnes*).[17] This typology reflects, in other words, the level of commitment by the states parties toward achieving their treaty aims. This chapter argues that the type of obligation is a crucial consideration in the process of treaty interpretation over time.[18]

To be clear, I do not want to suggest that the nature of a norm is *decisive* for the applicability or non-applicability of any particular technique of interpretation. I am not arguing for a typology of treaty norms that would mechanically determine when and how techniques of treaty interpretation should be seen as appropriate. I only mean to suggest that the nature of a norm as reciprocal, integral, or interdependent should be a consideration—an important consideration—in the interpretation of treaties over time. This characteristic should be taken into account alongside the more familiar factors articulated at

---

[16] In the dramatic words of the ICTY, the notion of absolute obligations marks 'the translation into legal norms of the "categorical imperative" formulated by Kant in the field of morals: one ought to fulfill an obligation regardless of whether others comply with it or disregard it': *Kupreškić*, [518].

[17] *Effect of Reservations*, [29].

[18] A handful of the more reflective cases stress the centrality of the distinction. See *Ireland v UK* (Judgment) (1978) 2 EHRR 25, [239] ('[u]nlike international treaties of the classic kind, the Convention comprises more than mere reciprocal engagements between Contracting States. It creates...objective obligations'); *Effect of Reservations*, [29] ('modern human rights treaties...are not multilateral treaties of the traditional type concluded to accomplish the reciprocal exchange of rights'); *Kupreškić*, [517]–[518] (contrasting the 'absolute nature' of most IHL treaties to merely reciprocal commercial treaty norms); *RosInvest*, [40] (contrasting reciprocal BIT provisions to more absolute obligations in human rights treaties).

Articles 31–32 of the VCLT: text, context, object and purpose, subsequent agreement and practice, etc.[19]

In Part I, I canvass several venerable and more recent attempts to explain (or advocate) variations in approach to the interpretation of different kinds of treaties. While some of these views produce valuable insights, they each prove either untenable or ultimately incomplete. In Part II, I present a case for grounding differential treatment on the nature of the obligation under interpretation.

I. Old and New Explanations of Difference

This part canvasses three prominent attempts to explain variations in approach to the interpretation of different kinds of treaties over time, based on: (a) the subject matter of the treaty; (b) object and purpose; and (c) whether the treaty grants rights to non-state actors. I suggest that each proves ultimately insufficient. The first is outright misleading. The object and purpose approach, on the other hand, is valuable but overly abstract if taken on its own. Only the third approaches the matter from the right perspective, but it proves to be perhaps too narrowly confined—its private law focus on third party rights and reliance contains only a kernel of what I take to be the best explanation (and justification) for affording certain kinds of treaty norms special treatment in interpretation: the nature and extent of the obligations undertaken by the parties.

A. Subject matter

The most common justification for taking a differential approach to the interpretation of certain treaties over time has been an appeal to their 'special subject matter', echoing the common refrain that human rights treaties are special *because* they concern fundamental human rights.[20] Judge Tanaka expressed this view in now-classical terms in a dissenting opinion to the 1966 *South West Africa* case. In calling for the evolutive interpretation of the treaty-basis for the mandate system in light of a new rule of customary international law, Tanaka explained:

[T]he protection of the acquired rights of the Respondent is not the issue, but its obligations, because the main purposes of the mandate system are ethical and humanitarian.

---

[19] This chapter seeks to account for differential treatment *within* the voluntaristic structure of the law of treaties. Of course it is possible to reach beyond the confines of party consent. Though beyond the scope of the present exercise, it is also well worth reflecting on the possibility some treaties may be entitled to special treatment for reasons completely external to consent—eg by shifting focus toward the communal or human interests reflected in a particular agreement. See Bruno Simma, 'From Bilateralism to Community Interest in International Law' (1994) 250 Recueil des Cours 6; Robert Kolb, *Interprétation et création du droit international: Esquisse d'une herméneutique juridique moderne pour le droit international public* (Bruylant 2006) 202–3; Eyal Benvenisti, 'Sovereigns as Trustees of Humanity: On the Accountability of States to Foreign Stakeholders' (2013) 107 AJIL 295.

[20] *Information on Consular Assistance.*

The Respondent has no right to behave in an inhuman way today as well as during these 40 years. *Therefore the recognition of the generation of a new customary international law on the matter of non-discrimination is not to be regarded as detrimental to the Mandatory, but as an authentic interpretation of the already existing provisions... of the Mandate and the Covenant*...What ought to have been clear 40 years ago has been revealed by the creation of a new customary law...[21]

At the time it was usually assumed that treaties were static, to be interpreted strictly according to the so-called inter-temporal rule—requiring that in most circumstances they should be interpreted in light of the law extant at the time of promulgation, not at the time of interpretation.[22] However, Tanaka here explained that treaties concerning the rights of the human person must be treated differently. They must be understood as open to the evolution of general international law concerning the human person. In his view, such treaties should be open to progressive change in light of developments in customary international law in the same field. In the intervening decades, various courts and tribunals have confirmed the 'special' nature of human rights treaties—that such treaties may have a more autonomous existence, less in thrall to the mastery of the parties.[23] More recently, similar arguments have arisen in favour of special treatment for treaties concerning other subjects, ranging from the protection of civilians in armed conflict,[24] to the protection of the environment,[25] to territorial boundaries.[26]

Most of the time, such claims that a particular type of treaty is entitled to special treatment rest on a mere assertion about the importance of the treaty's subject matter. The draw of this kind of explanation is at least partially explained by the diversification and specialization of international courts and tribunals (and to some extent specialization in scholarship)—in other words, by asking who is offering the explanation. Increasingly specialized courts have highlighted the special nature of the treaties over which they have jurisdiction.[27] Likewise, not surprisingly, expert scholars tend to emphasize the special nature of the kinds of treaties over which they have expertise. Such explanations arise in other settings

---

[21] *South West Africa (Liberia v South Africa)* (Second Phase) [1966] ICJ Rep 294, Dissenting Opinion of Judge Tanaka (emphasis added); Higgins, 'Time and the Law', 516.

[22] See *Island of Palmas Case (Netherlands v USA)* (1928) 2 RIAA 845. In general the rule has been significantly diluted since *Palmas* in a wide range of contexts. See Higgins, 'Time and the Law', 515–16. But the presumption of contemporaneity nevertheless retains firm adherents. See *Dispute Regarding Navigational and Related Rights (Costa Rica v Nicaragua)* [2009] ICJ Rep 242, Separate Opinion of Judge Skotnikov; ibid, Declaration of Judge ad hoc Guillaume.

[23] See *Soering v UK*, [87]; *Information on Consular Assistance*, [114]–[115].

[24] See *Kupreškić*, [517]–[519].

[25] See *Pulp Mills*, Separate Opinion of Judge Cançado-Trindade, [116], [119]; *Fragmentation Report*, 250.

[26] *Eritrea/Yemen Arbitration*, [153].

[27] The ECtHR and IACtHR, for example, have stressed the special nature of human rights treaties: *Soering*, [87]; *Information on Consular Assistance*, [114]–[115]. Similarly the ICTY has proclaimed the special nature of the Geneva Conventions: *Kupreškić*, [517]–[519]. See Joost Pauwelyn, 'A Typology of Multilateral Treaty Obligations: Are WTO Obligations Bilateral or Collective in Nature' (2003) 14 EJIL 907, 929; Michael Waibel, 'Uniformity versus Specialization (2): A Uniform Regime of Treaty Interpretation?' in Christian Tams, Antoninos Tzanakopoulos, and Andreas Zimmermann (eds), *Research Handbook on the Law of Treaties* (Edward Elgar 2014) 375.

as well, as in the *RosInvest* arbitration where an investor-state tribunal rejected the notion that the underlying bilateral investment treaty (BIT) was entitled to any special treatment. The Tribunal distinguished the BIT from human rights treaties or the constituent instruments of international organizations, which it deemed more appropriate candidates for evolutionary interpretation.[28] Although many of these courts, tribunals, and commentators may be right to adopt a differential approach to the interpretation of their particular treaties over time, it is difficult to see how subject matter per se does any legal work.[29]

The most obvious problem with the subject-matter approach is that it tends to obscure the fact that most treaties, and especially multilateral ones, are package deals, often touching on multiple areas of law. In the example of the *Fragmentation Report*, 'a treaty on, say, maritime transport of chemicals, relates at least to the law of the sea, environmental law, trade law, and the law of maritime transport'.[30] If the question of interpretation over time depends on pigeon-holing legal instruments as 'trade law' instead of 'environmental law', or 'human rights law' instead of 'investment law', then the question of special treatment would be wholly dependent upon the seemingly arbitrary choice of how to label a complex treaty.[31] It would thus be a good first step to avoid asking why some treaties are different from others, and ask instead why some treaty *provisions* are different from others (bearing in mind, of course, that the context of the rest of the treaty remains important evidence for interpretation). Any move away from trying to essentialize a treaty's sole subject matter, toward inquiring into the subject of the particular provision under interpretation, would already represent some progress. However, there is a second, more fatal difficulty with reliance on subject matter as the touchstone for a differential approach.

The deeper problem with the subject-matter approach is that it ultimately cannot capture much of legal significance—even if we limit our analysis to particular norms. Privileging subject matter simply gives rise to a problem of branding. Even a single norm can be described as having different subject matters depending on perspective. For example, a BIT provision could be described as being about protecting foreign investment, about development, or even about human rights (ie the right to property). Beyond the problem of essentializing complex instruments, Martti Koskenniemi rightly suggests that 'characterizations ("trade law", "environmental law") have no normative value per se...The characteristics have less to do with the "nature" of the treaty than the interests from which it is described'.[32] To return to the example of investment disputes, an advocate for investors' interests might try to argue that a treaty provision obliging the state to provide investors with fair and equitable treatment (FET) concerns the

---

[28] See *RosInvest*, [39].
[29] I am only criticizing the tendency in these cases to appeal to subject matter in accounting for treating some treaties differently. These cases are not always devoid of other, better, reasons. A few also hit upon the crux of the issue: *Effect of Reservations*, [29]; *RosInvest*, [40].
[30] *Fragmentation Report*, [21].   [31] *Fragmentation Report*, [22].
[32] *Fragmentation Report*, [21].

human right to property, and thus justifies an evolutionary approach (expanding investor rights). Conversely a state-friendly advocate could just as convincingly argue that FET represents a concession between states to grant rights to a certain class of individuals to facilitate investment and development—since investors are not party to the treaty at all, there can be no argument that their rights expand over time to the detriment of the host state's sovereignty. Subject matter is inherently contestable, and devolves into a matter of interest or perspective-based branding. It is ultimately an unsuitable, even arbitrary basis on which to ground a differential approach to the interpretation of treaties over time.

I do not want to unfairly impugn the arguments of these specialized courts or scholars in grounding their differential approaches on the basis of subject matter. Often they are absolutely right in identifying these treaties as having a special relationship to the parties and their intentions over time. Without doubt the results of this approach have had an enormous and beneficial effect on international law over the years, especially in the areas of human rights and humanitarian law. However, I want to probe more deeply into *why* certain regimes are considered 'special'. In other words, the foundational question is how to qualify what characteristics of these various treaties give judges and scholars pause in determining whether the usual consent-oriented rules apply in the usual way.

B. Object and purpose

Rosalyn Higgins provides a somewhat more compelling explanation for the differential approach to treaty interpretation over time. According to Higgins, the root criterion for assessing whether and how a treaty may be susceptible to change over time is its specific object and purpose. She explains Judge Tanaka's 1966 opinion in *South West Africa* on the basis of the centrality of protecting the human person as an object of the mandate system.[33] One might likewise explain the supposed special nature of a territorial treaty by reference to its particular object and purpose, which necessarily entails 'the need for the stability of boundaries'.[34] Unlike the subject-matter approach, this object and purpose approach rejects generalizing abstract types of treaties. Instead it analyses the propriety of applying the various techniques of interpretation over time on a case-by-case basis, in light of a particular treaty's goals. And it has the advantage of being the only explanation purely immanent in the Vienna rules themselves. Because object and purpose is recognized in Article 31(1) of the VCLT, this approach explains variations in the

---

[33] Higgins, 'Time and the Law', 519. For Higgins, subject matter cannot explain exempting human rights provisions from a general presumption of static-interpretation: '[H]uman rights provisions are not really random exceptions to a general rule. They are an application of a wider principle—intention of the parties, reflected by reference to the objects and purpose—that guides the law of treaties.'

[34] Shaw, 'Title, Control, and Closure?', 761; Kohen, 'The Decision on the Delimitation of the Eritrea/Ethiopia Boundary', 772; *Territorial Dispute (Libya/Chad)* [1994] ICJ Rep 6, 37; *Case Concerning the Temple of Preah Vihear (Cambodia v Thailand)* [1962] ICJ Rep 6, 34.

weight afforded to the different factors listed at Article 31 by appeal to one of those self-same factors.

There is no doubt that object and purpose is essential to the analysis of interpretation over time. That said, it is not a panacea. On its own, it constitutes an unsatisfying touchstone for determining when and how a treaty should be capable of change over time. The inquiry into object and purpose entails troubling doctrinal and conceptual ambiguities, and seems, moreover, fundamentally incomplete. As a result, reliance on object and purpose alone risks obscuring some of the most important considerations about a treaty germane to the question of change over time.

The first problem concerns the long-standing doctrinal debate as to whether a treaty has just one 'object and purpose' or whether it can have several. And if several, are they all general, or can individual provisions have different objects and purposes? On the one hand, some scholars insist that a treaty has only one object and purpose, properly understood. In the emphatic words of Judge Anzilotti of the Permanent Court of International Justice:

I do not see how it is possible to say that an article of a convention is clear until the subject and aim of the convention have been ascertained, for the article only assumes its true import in this convention and in relations thereto.[35]

Thus, according to Anzilotti, a treaty term cannot be understood except in light of the object and purpose of the treaty as a whole. It simply does not make sense, on this view, to talk about the intent of the provision in isolation from the object and purpose of the whole.[36] Jan Klabbers concurs, adding that 'when the notion of object and purpose of a treaty is used to refer to single provisions of a treaty, or when object and purpose becomes numerous objects and purposes, something valuable is lost'—specifically the idea of an overarching goal of the treaty, against which reservations, modifications, and purported interpretations should be measured.[37]

On the other hand, some commentators insist that treaties can have multiple, and perhaps even divergent objects and purposes. Ian Sinclair states that 'most treaties have no single, undiluted object and purpose but a variety of differing and possibly conflicting objects and purposes'.[38] In this vein, the Appellate Body of the WTO held in *Shrimp–Turtle* that the General Agreement on Tariffs and

---

[35] *Interpretation of the Convention of 1919 Concerning Employment of Women During the Night* [1932] PCIJ Rep Series A/B No 50, Dissenting Opinion of Judge Anzilotti, 383. The older usage 'subject and aim' appears to have been one of several synonyms of 'object and purpose' that have ultimately given way to the latter term. See Isabelle Buffard and Karl Zemanek, 'The "Object and Purpose" of a Treaty: An Enigma?' (1998) 3 ARIEL 311, 317.

[36] Buffard and Zemanek, 'The "Object and Purpose" of a Treaty', 342–3 contend that a treaty has only a general object and purpose, and suggest that some articles may be essential to it while others may not be (eg for purposes of reservations).

[37] Jan Klabbers, 'Treaties, Object and Purpose' in Rüdiger Wolfrum (ed), *Max Planck Encyclopedia of Public International Law* (OUP 2012) [6], [7], [23].

[38] See eg Ian Sinclair, *The Vienna Convention on the Law of Treaties* (2nd edn, Manchester University Press 1984) 130.

Trade (GATT) has multiple objects and purposes in its varied provisions, and in particular that the purposes of the General Exceptions clause at Article XX (here, environmental protection) are separate and must be assessed separately from the Treaty's more general purposes (ie trade liberalization).[39] According to the Appellate Body, different provisions are included for different reasons, and these reasons should not be subsumed into the general goals of the treaty.

The *Shrimp–Turtle* case usefully illustrates why the question of one or several object(s) and purpose(s) matters. Framing the issue in caricatured form, Article XX(g) is a lonely, but important, provision incorporating environmental protection (specifically the protection of 'exhaustible natural resources') in a treaty otherwise mostly dedicated to trade liberalization. Assume, for convenience, that environmental protection would be typical of the kind of object and purpose that could support evolutive interpretation, while the goal of trade liberalization would militate in favour of static interpretation along the principle of contemporaneity—ie sticking to the bargain struck. If the GATT has only one general object and purpose, it would be difficult to say that environmental protection is anything but an ancillary concern. Environmental considerations would thus not legitimately affect the question of how the provision should be interpreted along the steady march of time (even as environmental law and science rapidly outpace understandings contemporaneous with the GATT's promulgation). On the other hand, if Article XX(g) has its own object and purpose, 'environmental protection', and this is taken to be the referent for determining how the treaty should be interpreted over time, the picture looks very different.

The more conceptual problem is the level of abstraction at which to frame object and purpose. Nuance in the framing of even a single object and purpose can be decisive. The *Iron Rhine* arbitration is illustrative. There, the Tribunal held that the boundary treaty at issue had an evolutive nature, in light of its object and purpose. The treaty incorporated cross-border rights regarding the operation and maintenance of a railway. The dispute concerned, inter alia, the scope of the Netherlands' obligation to maintain (and/or modernize) the railway over the long term. The treaty's object and purpose could be stated in more or less abstract forms: for example, as simply 'establishing a stable border', or as 'demarcating the border while maintaining Belgium's most efficient rail-access to Germany in order to effect a stable boundary without undermining the economic capacity of either State'. The latter could be read into the former, broadly construed. However, it only becomes clear that the treaty must be read as evolutive if its object and purpose is construed in the latter complex form. If necessary maintenance were not considered part of the treaty's object and purpose, Belgium could have lost one of its central gains—an efficient rail link to Germany—thereby undermining the future stability of the boundary settlement.[40] Important as it is, no bright line rule can realistically resolve this issue of abstraction; tribunals can

---

[39] WTO-AB, *US–Shrimp/Turtle*, [114].
[40] *Arbitration Regarding the Iron Rhine (Ijzeren Rijn) Railway (Belgium v Netherlands)* (2005) 27 RIAA 35, [80]–[84].

only try to determine the full meaning of a treaty's object(s) and purpose(s) on a case-by-case basis.

Finally, beyond its potential indeterminacy, the inquiry into object and purpose does not necessarily exhaust all fundamental considerations relevant to interpretation over time. Even where a treaty's goals are sufficiently determinate, the interpreter must still ask how far the parties were willing to go to *achieve* their goals. Given the centrality of consent to the interpretive process, it is important to distinguish between the parties' ends and their chosen means. Insofar as the inquiry into object and purpose fails to take the parties' level of commitment into account, it cannot adequately explain how much weight such object and purpose is due vis-à-vis the other factors in the Vienna rules.

Higgins is right to underscore the importance of object and purpose to questions of interpretation over time, as reflective of the parties' intentions. And as Klabbers rightly notes, the malleability of object and purpose as a consideration in interpretation 'is not necessarily a bad thing... as it opens up a space for political debate and discussion on the most desirable interpretation of a treaty'.[41] But the vagaries inherent in the concept dilute its analytical value for assessing the particularly sensitive question of whether and how interpretation can bring about treaty change over time. There are serious ambiguities about what goes into the analysis, and an over-reliance on this one facet of interpretation risks leaving fundamental considerations aside.

C. Third party rights and reliance

A very different and promising recent proposal is grounded in private law. It emphasizes a particular objective characteristic of certain treaties—the conferral of rights on third parties, including individuals or other non-state actors. Anthea Roberts has argued that the rules of interpretation should be specially tailored when applied to treaties granting directly enforceable rights to non-state actors, including a wide array of investment treaties and human rights conventions (particularly the ECHR).[42] Roberts argues for a differential approach to such treaties in light of their asymmetric nature. 'Treaties that grant rights to nonstate actors, such as human rights and investment treaties, do not share the symmetry between those who hold the rights and those who can interpret them', Roberts contends.[43] Therefore, she suggests that care be taken in the application of doctrines like subsequent practice to protect the rights and legitimate expectations of third party rights conferees: 'The treaty parties may still be the masters of the treaty, but one cannot assume no harm, no foul in accepting their interpretations of nonstate actors' rights.'[44]

---

[41] Klabbers, 'Treaties, Object and Purpose', [22].

[42] Anthea Roberts, 'Power and Persuasion in Investment Treaty Interpretation: The Dual Role of States' (2010) 104 AJIL 179, 181, 199.

[43] Roberts, 'Power and Persuasion in Investment Treaty Interpretation', 202.

[44] Roberts, 'Power and Persuasion in Investment Treaty Interpretation', 202.

Roberts confines her analysis to the propriety of relying on subsequent practice in interpreting treaties that confer directly enforceable rights upon non-state actors. She proposes that in the case of such treaties interpreters should keep in mind both the interests of the rights-conferring states parties as 'masters of the treaty', and at the same time the interests of the rights-conferees in the substance of their rights, and in legal certainty as to the stability of that substance. A key question for Roberts involves reliance—whether the third party has relied on such rights, and when such reliance can vest. As such, Roberts argues, interpreters should still give weight to subsequent party agreement and practice, but in a modified form that takes into account the asymmetry of interests inherent in these treaties.[45] Turning specifically to investment treaties, Roberts argues that it is important to distinguish between three issues: scope (whether the subsequent practice supports an interpretation that expands or narrows rights); reasonableness (whether the new interpretation appears to strain the text); and timing (whether the subsequent practice established the new interpretation before or after the investment was made, the alleged breach occurred, and any claim was filed, in order to determine and weigh reliance). Roberts highlights these issues to prod tribunals to consider subsequent practice in the interpretation of investment treaties, while paying due attention to the legitimate expectations of the investors to whom these treaties grant rights.[46]

Roberts provides an insightful picture of how subsequent practice could be tailored to take into account both state and investor interests in the interpretation of investment treaties over time. However, as a general theory for distinguishing between types of treaties for the purposes of interpretation, this rights-based explanation is potentially both over- and under-inclusive.

First, it is not clear that all rights-conferring treaties should be understood as equally insulated or autonomous from the mastery of the parties. The mere fact that a treaty grants rights to an individual does not imply, of itself, that states have given up *any* of their mastery of the treaty—including their capacity to reinterpret the treaty at will through subsequent agreement or practice. The question turns upon what *kind* of rights are conferred, or more precisely, what kind of obligations the states parties take on to confer and guarantee those rights. Roberts recognizes that treaties conferring rights to individuals are due differential treatment, while mere benefit-conferring treaties are not. And as she further acknowledges, third party rights may sometimes be little more than mere benefits, conferred on the tenuous basis of reciprocity by the other parties to the treaty. A diplomat's rights conferred by a diplomatic treaty are not easily equated with the rights of an investor under a BIT, which are distinct in turn from an individual's fundamental rights under a human rights treaty. These differences in character are highly material to the question of the continued vitality of party consent and intentions in interpretation over time. The issue is how to determine whether such rights are something more than benefits and to what extent any such difference should play

---

[45] Roberts, 'Power and Persuasion in Investment Treaty Interpretation', 209.
[46] Roberts, 'Power and Persuasion in Investment Treaty Interpretation', 209–15.

a role in interpretation. Do the states agree to grant rights to an individual solely as an aspect of their agreement inter se, or do they intend to grant rights to that individual as an end in itself and thereby give up some of their capacity to interpret those rights away?

At the same time, despite its merits, this private law approach would prove ultimately under-inclusive as a *general* account of differences in treaty type, material to the question of interpretation and change over time. In particular, we still need to explain why a treaty norm that confers no third party rights may yet be equally (or even more) insulated from subsequent party intentions and/or capable of autonomous evolution over time—for example, treaty provisions concerning the protection of the environment, the protection of civilians during armed conflict, or even the resolution of territorial disputes.

Roberts is correct that the incorporation of third party rights is crucial, and indeed it often signals something deeper. Under the more general approach proposed here, the granting of directly enforceable rights to individuals or non-state actors, with its attendant counterpart of granting a tribunal compulsory jurisdiction, should be taken as *probative evidence* that a treaty may require special treatment—that under these circumstances, '[t]he treaty parties may still be masters of the treaty, but one cannot assume no harm, no foul in accepting their interpretations of nonstate actors' rights'.[47] From a more pragmatic (or realist) perspective, such features may also raise our expectations that the treaty *will* be given special treatment—especially where such jurisdiction is conferred upon a standing judicial body like the ECtHR or the IACtHR. But the interpreter must take care to assess what kinds of rights the treaty confers, and how it confers them. I argue that it is not the rights themselves doing the work, but the type of obligation the states take on in granting and committing to ensure those rights.

II. The Nature of the Obligation

I accept the premise, shared by all the views canvassed above, that treaties are not all the same, and that it is not always appropriate to apply the same techniques of interpretation to different kinds of treaties—at least not in the same way. This is especially true in the context of interpretation over time, which, in ascertaining state 'intentions', necessarily implicates systemic issues of state consent and legal certainty. The problem is that Article 31 of the VCLT does not provide for how its component doctrines interrelate, or how they are to be weighed against one another.[48] On the one hand, the rules cannot be mechanically applied to derive

---

[47] Roberts, 'Power and Persuasion in Investment Treaty Interpretation', 202.

[48] ILC, 'Draft Articles on the Law of Treaties with Commentaries' (1966) II ILC Ybk 219–20 (indicating that in general there is no hierarchy between the elements of Article 31 VCLT, but that '[a]ll the various elements, as they were present in any given case, would be thrown into the crucible, and their interaction would give rise to the legally relevant interpretation'); Richard Gardiner, *Treaty Interpretation* (OUP 2008) 9.

a 'correct' answer to interpretive questions (nor could any rules be expected to do so). On the other hand, the rules cannot be taken as meaningless legalistic justifications for achieving desired outcomes without doing imprudent violation to the idea of international law *as law*, as well as its foundations in state consent. The difficulty of differentiating between treaties for the purposes of interpretation over time is to determine what factors are important to take into consideration in applying the Vienna rules—without either reducing everything to outcomes (the subject-matter approach), or boiling everything down to one aspect of the rules (object and purpose).

I propose that a critical piece of this interpretive puzzle is the nature of the norm under interpretation—in other words, the kind of obligation set up by the parties to achieve their goals.[49] The key question is whether a treaty provision incorporates a merely reciprocal exchange of rights and duties between states, or rather establishes a more durable kind of obligation, resilient against shifts in party intention. Integral obligations represent the archetypal counterpart to merely reciprocal obligations, while interdependent obligations lie somewhere in between. As indicative of the states parties' level of commitment, the nature of a treaty obligation as reciprocal, integral, or interdependent is as relevant to the interpretation of that norm over time as the object and purpose it seeks to achieve.

A. Types of obligation in the law of treaties

Though absent from the VCLT's general rule on interpretation, the distinction between treaty norms according to type of obligation has a pedigree in the law of treaties. The nature and extent of an obligation is a venerable, but perennially under-appreciated and under-theorized, criterion for distinguishing between treaties or treaty norms—particularly because it was not expressly included in any portion of the final VCLT.

Sir Hersch Lauterpacht already formulated the core idea as Second Rapporteur on the Law of Treaties. He called upon the International Law Commission (ILC) to distinguish between contractual and law-making treaties for the purpose of successive treaty-making. According to Lauterpacht, treaties of the law-making type, 'affecting all members of the international community or which must be deemed to have been concluded in the international interest', would take precedence over merely contractual treaties in case of temporal conflict.[50] In his view, a later-in-time contractual treaty could not trump a conflicting law-making treaty and would be invalid to whatever extent it conflicted with the prior instrument.

Succeeding Lauterpacht as Third Special Rapporteur, Sir Gerald Fitzmaurice set aside the language of contractual and law-making treaties, but extended the

---

[49] See eg Fitzmaurice, 'Dynamic (Evolutive) Interpretation of Treaties, Part I'; Malgosia Fitzmaurice, 'Interpretation of Human Rights Treaties' in Dinah Shelton (ed), *The Oxford Handbook of International Human Rights Law* (OUP 2013) 739, 742; Pauwelyn, 'A Typology of Multilateral Treaty Obligations'.

[50] See Hersch Lauterpacht, 'Report' (1954) II ILC Ybk 156, draft art 16.

idea at its root, envisioning distinctions among treaty norms meriting differential treatment. Rather than distinguishing between sweeping generalized types of treaties, Fitzmaurice took a more fine-grained approach—reorienting the focus towards the nature of particular treaty norms. He distinguished between norms establishing *reciprocal* obligations, reflecting mere exchanges of rights and duties between parties (akin to Lauterpacht's 'contractual treaties'), and those treaty norms incorporating more absolute obligations (akin to instruments of public law). Within the latter set, Fitzmaurice identified two types: those truly absolute *integral* obligations and *interdependent* obligations, representing a kind of hybrid between the integral and the reciprocal types.[51]

Fitzmaurice attached two significant legal issues to the distinction between types of treaty obligations: one concerning the consequences of breach, and the other concerning successive treaty-making. According to him, a party could appropriately suspend or terminate a treaty in response to the other party's material breach of a reciprocal norm. Further, the parties could derogate from a reciprocal treaty obligation through enacting a subsequent treaty on the same matter. By contrast, it would be impermissible to respond to the breach of integral norms with suspension or termination. Such norms as are found in the Genocide Convention, to use Fitzmaurice's example, are meant to bind all parties irrespective of the behaviour of the other parties. They are meant to withstand violation, and enforcement must occur through channels other than the mutual threat of noncompliance.[52] Similarly, unlike with reciprocal norms, any reciprocal treaty conflicting with a prior integral norm would be invalid to the extent of their contradiction.

It is important to see that the qualification of an obligation as reciprocal or integral does not depend on the number of parties to a treaty.[53] A multilateral treaty may well entail no more than a complex web of reciprocal obligations among its parties, as in Fitzmaurice's example of the Vienna Convention on Diplomatic Relations (VCDR).[54] At the same time, a bilateral treaty could easily incorporate integral obligations, as is arguably the case where a BIT accords substantive rights and access to arbitration to third party individuals and non-state actors.[55]

Beyond reciprocal and integral norms, Fitzmaurice envisaged a third category of interdependent obligations, for which the model was an arms control treaty.[56] These fall somewhere in between reciprocal and integral norms. On the one hand, because they depend on unanimous application, they are more like reciprocal

---

[51] See Gerald Fitzmaurice, 'Third Report on the Law of Treaties' (1958) UN Doc A/CN.4/115 and Corr.1, 27, arts 18–19, [2]; *Fragmentation Report*, [493(1)(d)].

[52] Fitzmaurice, 'Third Report on the Law of Treaties'. For further historical background, see Surabhi Ranganathan, 'Between Philosophy and Anxiety? The Early International Law Commission, Treaty Conflict and the Project of International Law' (2013) 83 BYBIL 82.

[53] Fitzmaurice, 'Third Report on the Law of Treaties', arts 18–19, [2].

[54] Fitzmaurice, 'Third Report on the Law of Treaties', arts 18–19, [2]. See also Pauwelyn, 'A Typology of Multilateral Treaty Obligations', 928–9 (characterizing the GATT as a web of reciprocal commitments).

[55] See Roberts, 'Power and Persuasion in Investment Treaty Interpretation'. Cf *RosInvest*, [40].

[56] Fitzmaurice, 'Third Report on the Law of Treaties', arts 18–19, [2].

obligations for purposes of determining the consequences of material breach—the parties only agree to abide by this kind of obligation insofar as the others *all* do the same. Each party understands that if any party began to violate the treaty by stockpiling the controlled weapon, no party would continue to see itself as bound. However, with respect to successive treaties, interdependent norms are more like integral obligations. Precisely because any slippage by one party would likely engender slippage by all the other parties (rendering the treaty norm a dead letter), Fitzmaurice believed that any inter se agreement between some of the parties cutting against the object of the interdependent norm would be null and void. The interdependent treaty would take absolute priority over any subsequent treaties between only some of the parties.[57]

Here at last is a distinction that gets to the heart of the issue of differential treatment in treaty interpretation over time—if not, perhaps, ascribed such a purpose by Fitzmaurice himself. By reorienting focus away from the treaty's object and purpose or subject matter, the tripartite distinction between reciprocal, integral, and interdependent obligations affords more solid ground for explaining why some treaties attain a degree of autonomy from the parties in a manner consistent with the core notion of state consent. By focusing on the modalities by which the parties agree to take on obligations giving effect to their diverse objects and purposes, it becomes easier to account for (and argue for) differences in approach to the interpretation of different kinds of treaties over time.

In stark terms, differences in type of obligation—typified in terms of the extent to which states consent to be bound—should have a strong bearing on the relative weight and appropriate contours of the component rules of Article 31 VCLT. Type of obligation, in other words, should constitute an authentic criterion in the interpretation of treaties over time.

It is important to note that Fitzmaurice's strong vision of the role of the distinction, with regard to the consequences of breach and for resolving conflicts between successive treaties, is not necessarily reflected in current law. The last Special Rapporteur on the law of treaties, Sir Humphrey Waldock, abandoned the distinction in his final reports. He considered the notion overly complicated, and insufficiently grounded in state practice.[58] The final VCLT elided any express reference to the distinction between types of obligation.[59] But Waldock's abandonment of the distinction was not the end of the story. The type of obligation has retained more subtle relevance in the VCLT, and, more recently, the ILC has returned to the distinction for the purposes of state responsibility and addressing problems of successive treaties through interpretation.[60]

First, it bears noting that the ghost of the distinction can be felt throughout the final VCLT. Most obviously, the recognition of a limited set of hierarchical norms (*jus cogens*) ensures that certain integral norms like those in Fitzmaurice's preferred

---

[57] Fitzmaurice, 'Third Report on the Law of Treaties', arts 18–19, [2].
[58] Humphrey Waldock, 'Second Report' (1963) II ILC Ybk [28]–[30].
[59] Waldock, 'Second Report', 58–60, [20]–[21], [25]–[30].
[60] Fitzmaurice, 'Dynamic (Evolutive) Interpretation of Treaties, Part I'.

example—the Genocide Convention—will get special treatment.[61] Moreover, Joost Pauwelyn finds additional traces of the idea.[62] He notes that Article 60(5) on material breach bars termination or suspension in response to breach of a wider set of integral norms than those codifying *jus cogens*—ie provisions relating to the 'protection of the human person contained in treaties of a humanitarian character'.[63] And with regard to successive treaties, Article 40(1)(b)(i) bans (without invalidating) inter se modifications among only some parties to a multilateral treaty when they 'affect the enjoyment by the other parties of their rights under the treaty or the performance of their obligations'; and Article 40(1)(b)(ii) prohibits inter se modifications that relate to 'a provision, derogation from which is incompatible with the effective execution of the object and purpose of the treaty as whole'. Thus, between these two provisions, it would be impermissible in most cases for only some parties to a multilateral treaty to contract around any norm that could properly be called integral. To do so would likely undercut the rights of others or undermine the object and purpose of the treaty as a whole, if not both. Finally, Article 58 provides similar rules regarding the inter se termination or suspension of treaties.[64]

More recently the ILC's work on state responsibility and fragmentation has breathed new life into the idea of distinguishing between abstract types of obligation. The ILC's Draft Articles on State Responsibility recognize a difference, for the purposes of standing, between bilateral (or reciprocal) obligations, and multilateral obligations owed to all the parties of a particular regime (*erga omnes partes*) or to the international community as a whole (*erga omnes*).[65]

But it was the *Fragmentation Report* that did the most to resuscitate the distinction between reciprocal, integral, and interdependent norms in the context of successive treaties. The *Report* turned to the distinction not for the purpose of determining which treaties would get 'hard' priority in the sense of invalidating conflicting instruments, but rather for the 'softer' purpose of harmonizing potentially conflicting treaties through interpretation. Most of the time, according to the *Report*, harmonization turns on interpretive canons like *lex posterior* and *lex specialis*—it is not that one treaty invalidates the other, but rather that the treaty that is later in time, or more specific, gets precedence. However, according to the *Report*, the picture changes in cases of potential conflict between reciprocal and more absolute types of treaty obligation. In such situations, the nature of the norm should be taken into consideration as a counterweight to the normal canons of *lex posterior* and *lex specialis*, because the parties' choice to establish an integral norm provides in and of itself a good reason to give interpretive priority to that norm. All else being equal, the reciprocal should be interpreted to be in line with the integral or interdependent (as much as possible), and not the other way

---

[61] Article 53 VCLT.
[62] Pauwelyn, 'A Typology of Multilateral Treaty Obligations', 912.
[63] Article 60(5) VCLT.   [64] Article 58 VCLT.
[65] ILC, 'Draft Articles on the Responsibility of States for Internationally Wrongful Acts' (2001) UN Doc A/CN.4/L.602/Rev.1, arts 42(b), 48, and commentary.

around.[66] The *Report* noted that '[n]othing has undermined Fitzmaurice's original point': that certain norms in 'human rights and humanitarian law treaties, (as well as for example environmental treaties) form a special class of non-bilateral ("integral" or "interdependent") instruments that cannot be operated through the same techniques as "ordinary" treaties creating bilateral relationships'.[67]

The point to take from all this is that states try to achieve a wide variety of goals through international treaties, and in so doing they agree to take on very different kinds of obligations—even within a single instrument. The type of obligation they decide to take on has important consequences for their continued mastery over the treaty. It seems relatively unproblematic that states retain their mastery over treaty norms incorporating reciprocal obligations, being free to modify or replace them through mutual agreement, or to suspend or terminate them in response to one another's breach. On the other hand, it is much less clear that they maintain such mastery with regard to more absolute types of treaty norms (whether interdependent or integral, *erga omnes partes* or *erga omnes*). To the contrary, it appears that by incorporating such obligations states establish norms over and above themselves that are beyond their grasp. And interdependent norms lie somewhere in between. The issue at the heart of the distinction between types of treaty obligation is the relevance of state consent to the continued vitality of a treaty norm. It is this issue also that makes the distinction relevant to problems of interpretation over time.

B. Categories of obligation and interpretation over time

For many of the same systemic reasons underlying its relevance throughout the law of treaties, Fitzmaurice's distinction between types of obligations should be an important consideration in the process of treaty interpretation—particularly with regard to whether and how such interpretation may bring about treaty change over time. The nature of a treaty obligation is germane to at least three interpretive questions that are left unresolved by the text of Article 31 of the VCLT: (1) whether one or another technique of interpretation over time is appropriate at all in a particular case; (2) how liberally and expansively such dynamic techniques should be applied; and (3) how to weigh such doctrines against the other elements of the Vienna rules. The point here is both descriptive and normative. I am suggesting that distinguishing between reciprocal, integral, and interdependent norms helps both to *explain* the instincts of international adjudicators in a wide variety of cases, and to *justify* drawing distinctions between types of treaty norms for the purposes of interpretation over time in certain circumstances.

Questions of dynamic interpretation over time on the basis of the parties' subsequent practice or the purported evolutionary character of a treaty norm strongly implicate the core notion of state consent undergirding the entire law of treaties. Here, as with questions of material breach or harmonizing successive treaties, the

---

question of the *extent* to which the parties agreed to be bound should be carefully assessed. As noted above, states can take on different kinds of obligations in establishing their joint projects. In acceding to mere reciprocal norms, states agree to a pseudo-contractual exchange of rights and duties, which may be enforced by retaliatory suspension or termination, or abrogated by successive treaty-making. With integral norms, states agree to create obligations meant to withstand violations and the changing whims of the parties. This distinction is vital to the question of whether and how the parties can exercise their interpretive authority to develop, augment, or restrict a treaty's provisions, as well as the question of whether and to what extent such provisions are amenable to autonomous change over time.

Consider the weight assigned to the subsequent practice of the parties. As regards an integral norm, the nature of the obligation would seem to weigh against an interpretation on the basis of subsequent practice that cuts against the object and purpose of a treaty. For example, it would seem uncomfortable (and unlikely) for the ECtHR to narrow an integral rights protection provision in the ECHR on the basis of the subsequent practice of the parties.[68] In the case of *Demir & Baykara v Turkey*, the Court relied on the overwhelming subsequent practice of the parties, *inter alia*, to justify expanding ECHR Article 11 (freedom of association) to include the rights of municipal civil servants to unionize, and the right of all unions to bargain collectively. But imagine the situation had been the reverse—that Article 11 had clearly included the rights of public workers in its ambit at the outset, but a majority of states had subsequently banned public worker unionization (without any protest by the minority). There would seem to be something wrong with relying on such conduct to establish a restrictive interpretation of the Convention. To the contrary, this behaviour would look more like *violations* of the freedom of association *en masse*. The mere fact that these violations occurred in a group, without protest by the other states parties, should not necessarily transform them into the grounds of a new authoritative interpretation of the law.[69]

Both the original case and my hypothetical turned on interpreting the same integral obligation to respect the freedom of association—the difference is the conformity of the subsequent practice to the object and purpose of an integral treaty norm meant to protect individual rights from encroachment by the states parties. Here the integral nature of the norm hews toward privileging object and purpose over subsequent practice.[70] On the other hand, the object and purpose

[68] See Alexander Orakhelashvili, 'Restrictive Interpretation of Human Rights Treaties in the Recent Jurisprudence of the European Court of Human Rights' (2003) 14 EJIL 529, 535–6. Cf *Mangouras v Spain* (2012) 54 EHRR 25.

[69] Such a restrictive interpretation would not be impossible in the case of integral norms. But in such cases arguments for a restrictive interpretation based on party practice should be viewed quite a bit more sceptically and subjected to more rigorous evidentiary standards than in cases of merely reciprocal obligations: Fitzmaurice, 'Interpretation of Human Rights Treaties', 742.

[70] Fitzmaurice, 'Interpretation of Human Rights Treaties', 742 (noting that the integral nature of human rights treaties seems to lead to 'reductions in the importance of the actual text of the treaty in relation to other factors relevant to interpretation—in particular enhancing the importance of the object and purpose of the treaty').

may not have proven so decisive in the case of a treaty conferring reciprocal obligations (for example, the VCDR). If the parties remain masters of the treaty, as with merely reciprocal norms, then it is not clear that a court's determination of the object and purpose of the treaty should defeat evidence of the parties mutually changing intent about the meaning of the agreement—even if that subsequent intent seems to cut against the treaty's original object. And of course the issue will not always be clear, as in the more borderline case of investor rights.[71]

The consequences of this analysis for interdependent norms lie, as always, somewhere in the middle. There is reason to be cautious in labelling restrictive party practice as breaches *en masse* rather than evidence of a narrow interpretation. By contrast to integral norms, which are meant to withstand treaty breach, interdependent norms permit suspension and termination by all parties in the case of any one party's material breach. Thus, with interdependent norms, a clearly common practice evidencing the parties' agreement would have to be given effect, as failing to do so could have the farcical consequence of vitiating the treaty entirely. But recalling that such norms are supposed to withstand later in time conflicting treaties or inter se modifications, there is reason to be especially watchful for real commonality, consistency, and concordance in the parties' practice in terms of evidence (as compared to reciprocal norms)—for example by subjecting claims based on limited practice plus acquiescence to heightened scrutiny.

Distinguishing between reciprocal, integral, and interdependent norms further helps us explain (and justify) the instincts of judges and arbitrators in singling out certain kinds of treaties as specially capable of autonomous evolution. A handful of cases expressly draw our attention to the nature of the obligations at issue. Beyond exhorting the red herring of subject matter or the incomplete explanation of object and purpose, the IACtHR and ECtHR have both at times emphasized the integral nature of the treaty norms under their charge in adopting an evolutionary approach to interpretation.[72] The former stressed that such instruments 'are not multilateral treaties of the traditional type concluded to accomplish the reciprocal exchange of rights for the mutual benefit of the contracting States',[73] concluding that 'human rights treaties are living instruments whose interpretation must consider the changes over time and present-day conditions'.[74] By contrast, the Tribunal in *RosInvest* held that the obligations entailed by the UK–Soviet BIT were not amenable to autonomous evolution over time, absent evidence of the parties' consent, by specific appeal to their merely reciprocal nature. Acknowledging the propriety of evolutive interpretation for human rights conventions like the ECHR, the *RosInvest* Tribunal strongly questioned 'whether these special kinds of *multilateral* treaty are at all analogous to bilateral engagements regulating a particular area of the relations between one Party and the other'. According to the

---

[71] See Roberts, 'Power and Persuasion in Investment Treaty Interpretation'.
[72] *Loizidou; Information on Consular Assistance*, [114].
[73] *Effect of Reservations*, [29].
[74] *Information on Consular Assistance*, [114].

Tribunal, the BIT reflected merely 'a (reciprocal) bargain and the Parties must be held to what they agreed to, but not more, or less'.[75]

We need not agree that the matter is as cut and dried as portrayed in these cases (ie that integral norms are capable of evolution but reciprocal norms are not). But what should be clear is that the nature of the obligation has an important bearing on the extent to which we can plausibly view a treaty norm as insulated from the mastery of the parties. Absolute obligations are more insulated from the changing will of the parties (reducing the weight assigned to subsequent practice that deviates from the treaty's object and purpose), and are potentially more amenable to autonomous evolution (again in light of its object and purpose). Reciprocal obligations are, by contrast, more amenable to change over time on the basis of the parties' subsequent agreement and practice, but less easily presumed capable of autonomous evolution absent party action. Whether or not we agree in particular instances, the distinction provides a helpful explanation for the tendency of international courts and tribunals to afford special treatment to certain kinds of treaties. Even more importantly, it provides a principled basis for accounting for difference going forward.

While the nature of a treaty obligation is highly material to the question of interpretation over time, it should be emphasized that it is not a panacea. It is no more than one consideration among many, and it is crucial not to give too much weight to any one factor. Real cases are complicated. Most disputes over treaty interpretation in public international law involve a great many factors weighing in different directions, which are generally not easily or mechanically resolved. Take for example the border dispute between Eritrea and Ethiopia, arbitrated in 2002.[76] One aspect of that dispute concerned a portion of the treaty delineating the border between those two countries. The Tribunal had to determine whether the border had shifted from the line envisioned in the treaty on the basis of the subsequent practice of the two states. It ultimately held that the practice of the parties had modified the treaty border, but for present purposes the result is less important than the analysis.

Were the relevant treaty provisions simply reciprocal in nature, it would have been easy to come to the Tribunal's conclusion. But a boundary treaty of this type is inherently integral, constituting an objective and stable boundary to be respected by *all* states in the international community—not just the signatories.[77] The integral nature of such obligations necessitates a measure of caution in considering the subsequent practice of the parties, in appreciation of the treaty's object and purpose.

At first glance, there appears to have been a real tension between the object and purpose of the treaty and the subsequent practice of the parties. As with any

---

[75] *RosInvest*, [40].

[76] *Decision Regarding the Delimitation of the Border between Eritrea and Ethiopia* (2002) 25 RIAA 83, [4.60].

[77] See Shaw, 'Title, Control, and Closure?', 761; Kohen, 'The Decision on the Delimitation of the Eritrea/Ethiopia Boundary', 767, 772.

border treaty, a major aspect of the agreement's object and purpose is the stability and finality of the border, in the interest of peace. And yet the practice of the parties seemed to indicate that for some time Ethiopia had treated as its own a significantly populated rural township situated on Eritrea's side of the treaty line, to no apparent protest by the latter, as well as treating the residents there as its own nationals for various administrative purposes.[78] Framed in the abstract, modifying the treaty line to take party practice into account might seem to cut against the object and purpose of stability of boundaries. However, in full view of the current situation—admittedly resulting from the parties' practices—the demands of object and purpose appear more ambivalent. By the time of arbitration, a reversion to the textual boundary would have also been highly disruptive and destabilizing, imposing an overnight change in territorial and administrative status on the residents of the disputed township, with unclear effects on their personal status.

The integral nature of the boundary provision only goes so far in resolving these thorny interpretive questions. It hews toward taking the treaty's object and purpose particularly seriously in assigning weight to the subsequent practice of the parties; but insofar as object and purpose proves ambivalent, the relevance of subsequent practice becomes an increasingly open question. The Tribunal ultimately decided that the boundary had changed, and unsurprisingly the result was controversial.[79] But more importantly, for present purposes, the example underscores the complexity of the interpretive process, in which the nature of a treaty obligation plays an important but certainly not decisive part.

The most we can say is that appreciating the type of obligation is critical to the process of treaty interpretation, just as it is for assessing the consequences of material breach or successive treaty-making. And indeed the concept helps account for the instincts of international courts and tribunals in a wide variety of cases. This consideration helps us navigate among the various doctrines comprising the Vienna rules, especially in determining their appropriate scope and weight vis-à-vis one another in particular cases. But as the *Ethiopia–Eritrea* case shows, this consideration should not be taken as a trump. It cannot provide mechanical answers to complex interpretive questions any more than the other canons codified at Article 31 of the VCLT. It is a crucial consideration, given the centrality of state consent in the interpretive process, but it is not an all-encompassing one.

Conclusion

The practice of treaty interpretation demonstrates that adjudicators occasionally feel compelled to draw critical distinctions between types of treaties. While

---

[78] *Eritrea/Ethiopia*, [4.73]–[4.78].

[79] Compare Kohen, 'The Decision on the Delimitation of the Eritrea/Ethiopia Boundary' (criticizing the Tribunal's reasoning) with Shaw, 'Title, Control, and Closure?' (taking a sympathetic view).

the basic insight at work in such cases is often compelling, the justifications and explanations proffered for such differential treatment have thus far proven unsatisfactory or incomplete from the perspective of general international law. In this chapter I have argued that the practice of differential treatment is indeed justifiable and can be accounted for *within* the law of treaties.

In accounting for difference in treaty interpretation over time, the crucial consideration ought to be the nature of the obligation under interpretation. Is the provision merely a reciprocal exchange of rights and obligations? Or is it a more absolute integral or interdependent norm? Just as the nature of a norm bears on the consequences of material breach, or the resolution of conflicts between successive treaties, I have argued that the nature of an obligation is germane to determining how to interpret a treaty over time, especially as regards the possibility and legitimate extent of interpretive change. What these questions share is a common concern with the continued vitality of state consent, or, put another way, the parties' mastery over their treaties.

One important consequence of my account is that different norms in the same treaty may be subject to different interpretive yardsticks. This certainly complicates the task of interpretation, but it is a complication worth internalizing. Integral and interdependent norms are not especially common, and it is likely they will be found packaged in large multilateral treaties along with various reciprocal obligations. If it is correct that distinguishing between these types of obligations matters in the abstract, it would be a serious mistake to pave over such differences by assuming that all provisions of a particular treaty are of the same type.

Finally, it remains to be acknowledged that drawing legally significant distinctions between types of obligations will not be completely free of problems, particularly as regards classifying norms in particular treaties. Even if one accepts the value of such distinctions in the abstract, it will often be unclear and disputable whether a treaty norm is really best classified as reciprocal, integral, or interdependent. This short chapter is not the place for a comprehensive analysis of that evidentiary question. Suffice it to say that the question should not be simply reduced to subjectivity; the nature of a treaty obligation need not be entirely in the eye of the beholder. While express language will likely be rare, interpreters should look to objective indicia of the parties' level of commitment. Does the treaty permit parties to make reservations or interpretive declarations? Does it express particular consequences for material breach (as with most GATT commitments) or successive treaty-making (as with Article 103 of the UN Charter, which declares the Charter's superiority over conflicting later-in-time treaties)? Does it envision compulsory international adjudication? Does it grant rights to third parties, along with the means to enforce them? This list is of course not exhaustive, but affirmative answers to any of the above will be probative evidence that the parties intended to create something more than merely reciprocal obligations susceptible to easy derogation or retaliatory breach.

I hope to have shown that temporal problems in the interpretation of treaties should not be decided on the basis of their object and purpose alone, any more than by recourse to abstract generalizations about their subject matter. Especially in light of the voluntaristic roots of the law of treaties, the interpreter must also take into account the extent to which the parties were willing to commit to achieving their ends. But I do not suggest that simply doing so will *resolve* such temporal problems by yielding a 'correct' interpretation. Like any canon of interpretation, thinking in terms of types of obligation can only help guide the interpreter toward a right, or at least legitimate, answer. And of course there will always be disputes about whether a norm is really reciprocal or integral, and how much weight this factor should ultimately have. In the final analysis, the application of all such rules will always require judgment.[80] Insofar as such judgment can never be fully mechanized, the art of interpretation is to determine when the rules apply, and to give them appropriate weight vis-à-vis one another in particular cases.

---

[80] See Hans Kelsen, *The Law of the United Nations: A Critical Analysis of its Fundamental Problems* (Praeger 1950) xv.

11

Interpreting Transplanted Treaty Rules

Anne-Marie Carstens

Introduction

The increasing specialization of international law not only has led to the much-observed fragmentation of international law,[1] but also has fostered the proliferation of transplanted treaty rules. Transplantation occurs when pre-existing treaty rules are incorporated into a subsequent treaty between different parties, in a different context, or even in a different legal regime. The resulting transplanted treaty rules can offer obvious benefits, including promoting uniformity in international law, reducing the need to create new legal rules from whole cloth, and eliminating reprisals of contentious legal debates. These efficiencies give transplanted treaty rules significant value in contemporary treaties and also ensure their continued proliferation.

Transplanted treaty rules nonetheless present distinct challenges for the task of interpreting international law. In this volume, Andrea Bianchi usefully lays out the metaphor of interpreting international law as a game in which 'the cards are mostly those contained in the Vienna Convention on the Law of Treaties' (VCLT).[2] Despite a consensus that the VCLT provides the relevant framework for treaty interpretation, the operative 'cards' for interpreting transplanted treaty rules under the VCLT remain uncertain. The practice of borrowing and adapting pre-existing treaty provisions complicates the downstream task of interpreting transplanted treaty rules in various ways. The most difficult questions arise in determining not only which part of the VCLT's framework allows consideration of the so-called 'source rules'—the original treaty rules from which transplanted treaty rules are derived—but also how much consideration to give to such rules. To date, the interpreters of transplanted treaty rules, or the 'players' in the game of interpretation, typically refer to source rules and their origins in ways that suggest that they consider source rules highly relevant to the interpretive analysis.

---

[1] See eg Report of the ILC, UN Doc A/61/10 (2006) 403–7, [241]–[250] (citing extensive literature on fragmentation of international law).

[2] See Chapter 2 (Andrea Bianchi), 43 (citing Vienna Convention on the Law of Treaties (adopted 23 May 1969, entered into force 27 January 1980) (1980) 1155 UNTS 331 (VCLT)).

Yet the interpreters often fail to provide clear or consistent indications as to how source rules factor into the existing framework governing treaty interpretation. Interpreters likewise sometimes refer to the origins and negotiating history of source rules without providing discernible guidance as to whether and how far that history can be imputed to the parties to the later treaty.

This chapter examines the VCLT to consider how its framework applies to the interpretation of transplanted treaty rules. This examination begins by identifying several characteristic features or risks of transplanted treaty rules: substantive negotiations that are removed from the treaty under interpretation, opaque origins of the transplanted rule, incremental revisions to the rule, incomplete borrowing, and the possibility of a fundamental dissonance between two regimes in which the rules are incorporated. With each of these features or risks, the source rule can play a critical role in the interpretive process or even operate *in pari materia* with the transplanted treaty rule.

The chapter therefore scrutinizes the general rule of interpretation under Article 31 of the VCLT, searching for avenues for interpreters to consider source rules. This analysis reveals a fundamental difficulty: despite the long-standing existence and rapid proliferation of transplanted treaty rules, none of the component parts of the general rule of interpretation provides an obvious or perfect foothold for interpreters to consider source rules. The general rule of interpretation instead steers interpreters largely toward the four corners of the text and to acts or instruments that coincided with or followed the adoption of the transplanted treaty rule.

One therefore might argue that source rules have no certain place in the interpretive process except as a supplemental means of interpretation permitted under Article 32 of the VCLT. Surely Article 32 permits recourse to source rules as a supplemental means of interpretation, as necessary to confirm the meaning provided under the general rule or where application of the general rule results in an otherwise ambiguous, absurd, or unreasonable meaning. Yet the treatment that interpreters often afford to source rules suggests that interpreters are inclined to elevate source rules to some higher relevance. The chapter presents a case study from the jurisprudence of the International Court of Justice (ICJ), *Interpretation of the Agreement of 25 March 1951 between the WHO and Egypt (WHO/Egypt)*,[3] to illustrate this point. The great variety of opinions that the *WHO/Egypt* case generated—and the different judges' contorted efforts to interpret the transplanted treaty rule at issue—expose the lack of predictable or consistent strategies for interpreting transplanted treaty rules.

Absent greater predictability and consistency in the interpretive process, the risk of divergent interpretations will increase as transplanted treaty rules are reused in treaties that are several times removed from the original treaties that contain the source rules. Transplanted treaty rules transcend different subject matters and are not limited to certain specialities, such as human rights treaties or investment treaties, for which some nuanced deviations from the interpretive framework have

---

[3] *Interpretation of the Agreement of 25 March 1951 between the WHO and Egypt* (Advisory Opinion) [1980] ICJ Rep 73.

developed.[4] Most international lawyers will be able to think reflexively of one or more examples of transplanted treaty rules from their own study or experience, no matter their areas of expertise.

The difficulties of interpreting transplanted treaty rules do not warrant a reversion away from their use, nor are interpreters unlikely to abandon the practice of foraging through earlier treaties in their efforts to interpret transplanted treaty rules. Instead, by minimizing the risk of divergent interpretations, transplanted treaty rules can serve as an effective tool to promote the systemic integration of international law.

A challenge nonetheless remains in determining how to shoehorn consideration of transplanted treaty rules into the VCLT framework. This chapter contends that the VCLT is sufficiently flexible to allow more predictable and consistent consideration of source rules, but only if interpreters and other commentators develop effective and transparent 'rules of play' for interpreting transplanted treaty rules with reference to source rules. Continuing with the game-playing metaphor, the 'rules of play' set out in the VCLT otherwise might need to undergo a more structured change to establish which 'strategies' are allowed and which 'cards' of treaty interpretation provide the best avenues toward a correct interpretation of transplanted treaty rules.

I. An Overview of Transplanted Treaty Rules

A. The practice of transplanting legal rules

The practice of transplanting existing legal rules into new legal contexts is not a phenomenon peculiar to international law. The concept of 'legal transplants' originated in comparative law, where it refers to a foreign legal regime or rule being transplanted across jurisdictions 'from one country to another, or from one people to another'.[5] For example, comparative constitutional law scholars have noted that the Constitution of the United States has been adopted wholesale by a number of countries, despite their different founding histories and institutional frameworks.[6] Transplantation also occurs within domestic regimes and even in a 'vertical' fashion from domestic to international regimes (or vice versa).[7]

---

[4] See Chapter 10 (Julian Arato).

[5] Alan Watson, *Legal Transplants: An Approach to Comparative Law* (Scottish Academic Press 1974) 21; Alan Watson, 'Legal Change: Sources of Law and Legal Culture' (1983) 131 University of Pennsylvania LR 1121.

[6] Vicki C Jackson and Mark Tushnet, *Comparative Constitutional Law* (2nd edn, Foundation Press 2006) 188–94 (quoting AE Dick Howard, 'The Indeterminacy of Constitutions' (1996) 31 Wake Forest LR 383, 402–4); Louis Henkin, 'Introduction' in Louis Henkin and Albert Rosenthal (eds), *Constitutionalism and Rights: The Influence of the US Constitution Abroad* (OUP 1990) 1, 13–14.

[7] See eg Jonathan B Wiener, 'Something Borrowed for Something Blue: Legal Transplants and the Evolution of Global Environmental Law' (2001) 27 Ecology LQ 1295.

In international treaties, the practice of transplantation takes a variety of forms. Most commonly, transplanted rules appear in different bilateral treaties within specialized fields of law. Transplanted rules of this type might have originated in a two-party or multi-party negotiation or even within a state that introduced them across its own series of bilateral treaties with different parties. Such rules begin to percolate throughout the legal regime whenever additional states transplant these rules in their own successive treaties. The greater the volume of treaties within a specialized legal regime and the number of treaty parties that enter such treaties, the greater the likelihood that some of the treaties will contain transplanted treaty rules.

Transplanted treaty rules also appear in different treaties within closely related legal regimes. Several instruments governing modern international criminal tribunals not only share parallels with each other and with the post-World War II Nuremberg Charter; they also incorporate many of the terms and expressions found in treaties on the law of armed conflict, particularly the 1899 and 1907 Hague Conventions governing land warfare and the 1949 Geneva Conventions.[8]

Less often, given the somewhat myopic focus and subject-specific expertise of treaty drafters, transplanted treaty rules are incorporated to address an analogous circumstance that arises in a rather different legal regime. Rules that are transferred across legal regimes often must be adapted, or should be adapted, to accommodate relevant distinctions between the two regimes. As just one example, several treaty rules governing the protection of cultural property during armed conflict are drawn from treaties governing the protection of civilians during armed conflict. Treaty rules that grant a role to the United Nations Educational, Scientific and Cultural Organization (UNESCO) akin to that given to the International Committee for the Red Cross (ICRC) in the civilian protection context, however, must account for the important distinctions between UNESCO as a multigovernmental organization and the ICRC as a non-governmental organization.[9]

Wherever the occurrence, the practice of transplantation often is motivated by a desire for rule-making efficiency. The practice of transplantation thus is not dissimilar to the use of model agreements, except that the source rules come not from a hypothetical instrument but from a functioning agreement.

Generally speaking, the greater the similarity in the subject matter of the treaty containing the source rule and the treaty under negotiation, the greater the compulsion to incorporate and adapt pre-existing rules because parity of the issues is presumed. Within the same or related regimes, the treaty negotiators also are

---

[8] See eg Statute of the International Criminal Court for the Former Yugoslavia, in UNSC, 'Report of the Secretary-General Pursuant to Paragraph 2 of Security Council Resolution 808 (1993)' (3 May 1993) UN Doc S/25704, 9, adopted by UNSC Res 827 (25 May 1993) UN Doc S/RES/808; Rome Statute of the International Criminal Court, UN Doc A/CONF.183/9 (1998); Charter of the International Military Tribunal, in *Trial of the Major War Criminals Before the International Military Tribunal*, vol 1 (International Military Tribunal 1947) 10.

[9] Geneva Convention Relative to the Protection of Civilian Persons in Time of War (adopted 12 August 1949, entered into force 21 October 1950) 75 UNTS 287, Articles 3, 11–12; Convention for the Protection of Cultural Property in the Event of Armed Conflict (adopted 14 May 1954, entered into force 7 Aug 1956) 249 UNTS 240, Articles 19, 22–23.

predisposed by their training and respective specialities to know of existing rules that they consider could apply *mutatis mutandis* to the issues at hand. Where one party enters into similar agreements with a variety of different parties, consistency among the treaties also facilitates consistency in that party's implementation.

The practice of transplantation also can reflect a transparent effort by the drafters to 'piggyback' on the success of the earlier treaty rules. The drafters may presuppose that the adoption of rules already negotiated and adopted will obviate some of the difficulties that might arise from creating treaty rules anew. For issues that have proven particularly controversial, incorporating the source rule can help smooth over known rifts between different parties to the treaty negotiations that otherwise might threaten to derail the treaty negotiations or adoption of the treaty.

B. Features of transplanted treaty rules

The interpretation of transplanted treaty rules must account for characteristics or factors that are more likely to complicate the task of interpretation by comparison with treaty rules generally. These features challenge, at least to a degree, the notion that the chosen treaty text best captures the intentions of the parties, consistent with Bjorge's characterization of the VCLT framework as providing a 'keyhole view' of the presumed intentions of the parties.[10]

1. Negotiations are once, twice, thrice (or more) removed

The fullest negotiation of a treaty rule generally occurs during the drafting of the source rule. When source rules subsequently are transplanted into later treaties, the transfer often is accompanied by only limited negotiation and discussion. Transplanted treaty rules sometimes are incorporated without any discussion at all, at least not one that can be ascertained from the *travaux préparatoires*.[11] Likewise, the tendency to adopt a source rule without meaningful deliberation increases as the source rule is injected into successive instruments. On the one hand, this tendency may reflect a growing consensus as to the meaning of the treaty rule or clarity as to the ordinary meaning of the text, eliminating the need for extensive discussion. Yet it also may mean that the rules are adopted without full understanding of their meaning by parties less experienced with them or less exposed to their pre-existing use.

2. Opaque origins

The origins of a transplanted treaty rule rarely are identified in the text of the treaty that contains the rule. Even recourse to the negotiating history may not

---

[10] See Chapter 9 (Eirik Bjorge), 192; Eirik Bjorge, *The Evolutionary Interpretation of Treaties* (OUP 2014) 56–141.

[11] See nn 59–66 and accompanying text.

clarify the origins, for the reasons noted above. In the absence of clear attribution of a transplanted rule's origins, inquiries into the genesis of transplanted treaty rules can become dependent on collective memory or knowledge, which may diminish over time and which can foster conflicting views. Moreover, with the proliferation of transplanted treaty rules, interpreters may have difficulty discerning which of a variety of iterations of the source rule proves to be the operative one. If the source rule is pertinent to interpretation in the given case, a failure to appreciate the full or true origins of a transplanted treaty rule can influence the correctness of the interpretation.

3. Incremental revisions

The practice of transplanting treaty rules in a succession of treaties increases the likelihood of incremental revisions to the transplanted rules. Participants in the treaty drafting process often demonstrate a particular propensity to tweak and refine legal provisions. The reasons can include a desire to clarify the meaning, to comport with the object and purpose of the treaty within the specialized field, to satisfy an internal policy goal, or to bridge differences between competing viewpoints. Moreover, the underlying reasons for the changes introduced by one party may not be clear to all the parties to the negotiation.[12] Subtle differences between the treaty containing the source rule and the treaty under interpretation do not always demand a different interpretation, though incremental changes also may reflect a substantial distinction between the treaties that might easily be overlooked. Incremental revisions can create additional pitfalls for the interpretation of transplanted treaty rules. The subsequent transplantation of these rules, with further incremental revisions to the text, can lead to a body of treaties whose rules are more heterogeneous than homogenous, despite their shared origins. The cumulative effect of successive, incremental revisions therefore can substantially alter or impair the probative value of the earlier treaties.

4. Incomplete borrowing

Transplanted legal rules also present a higher risk of 'incomplete borrowing'. Incomplete borrowing occurs where the source rule has been adopted without corresponding provisions that are necessary to its application or understanding. This may occur either because the drafters of the treaty under interpretation failed to transfer all the corresponding provisions from the source treaty or because the adapted context does not possess the necessary framework for the rule without the addition of further provisions. The appearance of incomplete borrowing raises questions for an interpreter as to how far he should fill in the gaps and what his sources should be for doing so.

---

[12] See Chapter 18 (Philip Allott), 377.

5. *Fundamental dissonance*

Finally, a more subtle but important difficulty may arise that can be difficult to discern when one's gaze is fixed on the minutiae of a treaty text or even on the *travaux préparatoires*. One of the principal lessons that can be gleaned from the comparative law scholarship on legal transplants is that some contexts are fundamentally ill-suited for transplanted rules that were conceived in a different legal context.[13]

In international law, a fundamental dissonance may exist between the subjects of the treaties that precludes a determination that the source rule applies *mutatis mutandis* in the treaty under interpretation, whatever the attraction of adopting a successful source rule from a perceived analogous setting. This risk increases where the source rule is adapted to a different legal regime or different context. This kind of dissonance may not be apparent at the micro level but, instead, only by undertaking a holistic inquiry that takes into account inherent differences between the regimes and the interests of the international community.

II. The Framework for Interpreting Transplanted Treaty Rules

Nothing distinguishes the basic process of interpreting transplanted treaty rules from the interpretive process generally applicable to treaties. Following the game-playing metaphor set out by Bianchi, the 'cards' therefore consist of the components of the VCLT's general rule of interpretation, as well as the various principles and sources to which one might refer as supplemental means of interpretation.[14] One's strategy for achieving the correct interpretation should rely on one or more of these cards, aided by the exercise of 'logic and good sense'.[15]

The need to locate consideration of source rules within the VCLT's framework stems from a need to reconcile two aspects of treaty interpretation for transplanted treaty rules: the instinctive tendency of interpreters to refer to source rules and the now-prevailing view that treaty interpretation must take place within the VCLT's apparatus. The VCLT's framework contains several integrated parts that are collectively designed to determine the meaning of a treaty provision under interpretation, and it is generally recognized as reflecting customary international law.[16] The difficulty for transplanted treaty rules resides in the fact that the VCLT carefully circumscribes the circumstances under which the players can resort to

---

[13] See eg Ann Seidman and Robert B Seidman, 'Law in Aid of Development: "Hasty Legal Transplants" and the Fatal Race' (2006) 1 J of Comp L 282, 283.

[14] See Chapter 2 (Andrea Bianchi).

[15] See eg Humphrey Waldock, Third Report on the Law of Treaties (1964) II ILC Ybk 54; Santiago Torres Bernárdez, 'Interpretation of Treaties by the International Court of Justice following the Adoption of the 1969 Vienna Convention on the Law of Treaties' in Gerhard Hafner, Gerhard Loibl, Alfred Rest, Lilly Sucharipa-Behrmann, and Karl Zemanck (eds), *Liber amicorum Professor Ignaz Seidl-Hohenveldern* (Kluwer Law International 1998) 721; Ian McTaggart Sinclair, *The Vienna Convention on the Law of Treaties* (2nd edn, Manchester University Press 1984) 117–18; Richard K Gardiner, *Treaty Interpretation* (OUP 2008) 111.

[16] *Arbitral Award of 31 July 1989* (*Guinea Bissau v Senegal*) (Judgment) [1991] ICJ Rep 70, [47]; *Territorial Dispute (Libya v Chad)* (Judgment) [1994] ICJ Rep 21–22, [41]; *Oil Platforms (Iran v*

instruments extrinsic to the treaty, which would encompass the earlier treaties containing the source rules.

A. The general rule of treaty interpretation

1. Core elements of the general rule

The thrust of the general rule of interpretation is that a treaty should be interpreted 'in good faith in accordance with the ordinary meaning to be given to the terms of the treaty in their context and in light of its object and purpose'.[17] The primary elements of 'ordinary meaning', 'context', and 'object and purpose', however, are not conclusively conducive to considering the source rules underlying transplanted treaty rules.

'Ordinary meaning' presents the most attractive avenue by which to consider source rules under the general rule. As Lauterpacht once wrote, international judges sometimes 'used the device of ascertaining the meaning of similar expressions employed in other treaties' because the parties to the later treaty 'must have had in contemplation at the time when they concluded the second instrument the meaning which had been attributed to like expressions in the earlier instruments'.[18] This reasoning holds for a pervasive source rule that has been used consistently across a body of treaties that is known and familiar to all parties to the subsequent treaty. Put another way, a transplanted treaty rule might become so ubiquitous within a particular series of treaties that an 'ordinary meaning' can be ascribed to the common terms within it by reference to the wider body of earlier treaties. Other authorities similarly have suggested that reference to an external treaty is analogous to (and theoretically indistinguishable from) reference to a dictionary to determine the meaning of a treaty term.[19]

Overreliance on 'ordinary meaning' nonetheless is misplaced because extensive reference to outside treaties in this manner potentially allows the inquiry into 'ordinary meaning' to swallow much of the remaining framework of treaty interpretation. For starters, the VCLT framework contains certain safeguards against unsupported presumptions of what the parties 'contemplated' at the time of treaty adoption. As noted earlier, the negotiating history often becomes increasingly silent as transplanted treaty rules proliferate across a swath of treaties. This

---

United States) (Merits) [2003] ICJ Rep 161, 181–2, [22]. See also Oliver Dörr, 'Article 31: General Rule of Interpretation' in Oliver Dörr and Kirsten Schmalenbach (eds), *Vienna Convention on the Law of Treaties: A Commentary* (Springer 2012) 521, 523–6 (citing ICJ practice, other international court practice, State practice, and expression in treaties); Mark E Villiger, 'The Rules on Interpretation' in Enzo Cannizzaro (ed), *The Law of Treaties Beyond the Vienna Convention* (OUP 2011) 105, 117–18 (citing sources).

[17] Article 31 VCLT.

[18] Elihu Lauterpacht, 'The Development of the Law of International Organization by the Decisions of International Tribunals' (1976) 152 Recueil des Cours 377, 396.

[19] WTO, *EC: Measures Affecting the Marketing and Approval of Biotech Products—Report of the Panel* (29 September 2006) WT/DS291, WT/DS292, and WT/DS293 341, [7.92] (*EC–Biotech*). See also Frank Berman, 'Treaty "Interpretation" in a Judicial Context' (2004) 29 Yale J Int'l L 315, 318–19 (examining similar practice of ICJ in *Oil Platforms* case).

silence might well demonstrate a shared understanding of the reasons for the transplanted rule. As the different opinions in the *WHO/Egypt* case demonstrate (examined below), however, it also might well be true that a party with less experience with or participation in the earlier treaties might remain unaware of the reasons therefor.[20] Employed too reflexively, this approach also allows interpreters to gloss over differences between the source rules and their progeny, a point of contention highlighted in the decision of the Permanent Court of International Justice and dissenting opinions in the early case of *SS Wimbledon*.[21]

This approach also appears to stand somewhat at odds with the traditional understanding of how an interpreter should determine the 'ordinary meaning'. The ICJ has suggested, for example, that either 'the relevant words in their natural and ordinary meaning make sense in their context' or else they are inconclusive or ambiguous and therefore require 'resort to other methods of interpretation' not included in the general rule of interpretation.[22] This position is perhaps too rigid if employed to foreclose consideration of widely reiterated source rules as part of the inquiry into 'ordinary meaning'. At the same time, though, interpreters must remain wary of employing 'ordinary meaning' as a vehicle to consider source rules that have not passed into common parlance, that have been adopted in subsequent treaties between different parties, or that have come to comprise a heterogeneous body.

The other primary elements of the general rule are less applicable than 'ordinary meaning'. The VCLT's definition of 'context' focuses on the text and corresponding agreements or instruments made 'in connection with the conclusion of the treaty'.[23] This element therefore precludes consideration of a prior treaty containing the source rule. A treaty's 'object and purpose' also presents a thin reed on which to base consideration of the source rule. Writers often declare that 'object and purpose' correlates to the subject *of the treaty* under interpretation (often expressed in the title) and the fundamental goal(s) that the drafters hoped to achieve. It does not extend to determinations of 'object and purpose' of a treaty's component parts, including specific terms or provisions.[24]

2. *Additional obligatory elements of the general rule*

Of the additional obligatory elements to 'take into account' under the general rule of interpretation, only two—reference to 'any relevant rules of international law

---

[20] See nn 60–64 and accompanying text.

[21] *SS Wimbledon* [1923] PCIJ Rep Series A No 1, 15; ibid 35, 39–40 (Anzilotti and Huber, dissenting op); ibid 43–4 (Schücking, dissenting op). For a brief discussion of similar and dissimilar rules borrowed from earlier treaties, see Martins Paparinskis, 'Analogies and Other Regimes of International Law' in Zachary Douglas, Joost Pauwelyn, and Jorge E Viñuales (eds), *The Foundations of International Investment Law: Bringing Theory into Practice* (OUP 2014) 73, 77–8.

[22] *Competence of Assembly regarding Admission to the United Nations* (Advisory Opinion) [1950] ICJ Rep 4, 8.

[23] Article 31(2)(a)–(b) VCLT.

[24] Jan Klabbers, 'Some Problems Regarding the Object and Purpose of Treaties' (1997) 8 FYBIL 137, 151–6.

applicable between the parties' and to the 'special meaning' given to certain terms by the parties—warrant consideration as applicable with reference to source rules. The obligation to take into account 'any relevant rules of international law applicable in the relations between the parties' appears in Article 31(3)(c) of the VCLT. The reference to 'special meaning' occurs in Article 31(4). Both these provisions nonetheless require further development in the interpretive process before they can succeed as clear and consistent avenues for considering source rules.

Until a decade ago, few scholars or judicial authorities gave Article 31(3)(c)'s reference to 'relevant rules of international law' much heed as a tool of treaty interpretation. That changed in the early 2000s, when the rule was cited by the ICJ in the *Oil Platforms* case,[25] by the Study Group of the International Law Commission (ILC) on the Fragmentation of International Law,[26] and by a WTO panel and the Appellate Body.[27] This flurry of attention has led one commentator to characterize Article 31(3)(c) as the 'neglected son of treaty interpretation until its recent ascendancy'.[28]

None of these authorities considered the specific question of using Article 31(3)(c) in the interpretation of transplanted treaty rules, nor was the provision crafted for this purpose. Instead, the drafters of the VCLT, the ILC Study Group, and the WTO dispute settlement bodies have contemplated the provision as a basis for referring generically to 'other treaty rules'.[29] The problematic feature of Article 31(3)(c) is its qualifier that the interpreter must consider relevant international law that is 'applicable in the relations between the parties'. This qualifier nearly always will preclude consideration of source rules, particularly if it means that absolute congruence must exist among the parties to the earlier treaty and the treaty under interpretation.

The ILC Study Group focused at length on this qualifier and whether it requires absolute congruence of the parties. In its preliminary report, it presented four possible scenarios. These scenarios ranged from 'a clear but very narrow standard' of absolute congruence between the parties to a standard that does not require congruence so long as 'the other rule relied upon could be said to have been implicitly

---

[25] *Oil Platforms*, [39]–[41].

[26] Report of the Study Group on Fragmentation of International Law: Difficulties arising from the Diversification and Expansion of International Law, UN Doc A/CN.4/L.676 (29 July 2005); Martti Koskeniemmi, 'Report of the Study Group of the International Law Commission: Fragmentation of International Law: Problems arising from the Diversification and Expansion of International Law', UN Doc A/CN.4/L.682 (13 April 2006) (Koskeniemmi report).

[27] WTO, *EC–Biotech*; WTO, *US: Definitive Anti-Dumping and Countervailing Duties on Certain Products from China—Report of the Appellate Body* (11 March 2011) WT/DS379/AB/R, 16–19, [36]–[41], [117]–[121], [304]–[313] (*US–AD/CVD*); WTO, *EC and Certain Member States: Measures Affecting Trade in Large Civil Aircraft—Report of the Appellate Body* (18 May 2011) WT/DS316/AB/R (*EC–Large Civil Aircraft*).

[28] Campbell McLachlan, 'The Principle of Systemic Integration and Article 31(3)(c) of the Vienna Convention' (2005) 54 ICLQ 279, 289. See also Philippe Sands and Jeffery Commission, 'Treaty, Custom and Time: Interpretation/Application?' in Malgosia Fitzmaurice, Olufemi Elias, and Panos Merkouris (eds), *Treaty Interpretation and the Vienna Convention on the Law of Treaties: 30 Years On* (Martinus Nijhoff 2010) 39.

[29] See eg Koskeniemmi Report, 212, [422]; Report of the International Law Commission covering the work of its sixteenth session, UN Doc A/CN.4/167 (1964), vol 2, 173, 199.

accepted or tolerated by all parties to the treaty under interpretation'.[30] The ILC Study Group also asserted that even if absolute congruence was required, another treaty 'may always be used as evidence of a common understanding between the parties'.[31] However, it declined to endorse any of the four approaches in its preliminary report. It stated that the 'task for determination rested upon the judge or the administrator on the basis of the nature of the treaty under interpretation and the concrete facts in each case'.[32]

The Study Group nonetheless crystallized its view in its final report. It concluded that Article 31(3)(c) did not demand absolute congruence of the parties as a prerequisite to considering 'other treaty rules':

Such other rules are of particular relevance where the parties to the treaty under interpretation are also parties to the other treaty, where the treaty rule has passed into or expresses customary international law *or* where they provide evidence of the common understanding of the parties as to the object and purpose of the treaty under interpretation or as to the meaning of a particular term.[33]

In articulating this formulation, however, the Study Group abandoned the additional proposition that another treaty rule could be relied upon if it was 'implicitly accepted or tolerated by all parties to the treaty under interpretation'. This omission eliminated a useful, if controversial, basis for considering source rules in the interpretation of transplanted treaty rules. The ILC's ultimate conclusion instead reflects an intermediate approach: that another treaty should be taken into account pursuant to the general rule of interpretation if it provides 'evidence of the common understanding of the parties' or elucidates the 'meaning of a particular term'. This conclusion opens the door to consideration of a source rule from a different treaty, though it remains unclear whether this basis allows greater consideration of source rules than can be accomplished in determining 'ordinary meaning'.

Moreover, this interpretation of Article 31(3)(c) does not necessarily reflect the contemporary consensus. As the ILC Study Group observed, a WTO panel adopted a position requiring absolute congruence of the parties in its 2006 decision in *EC—Measures Affecting the Approval and Marketing of Biotech Products*.[34] This same narrow position has been adopted by Sinclair, Villiger, and others in the academic literature.[35] In 2011, however, the WTO Appellate Body declined to endorse or reject this position in a different case, instead ruling that the particular

---

[30] Koskeniemmi Report, 15, [32].   [31] Koskeniemmi Report, 15, [32(a)].

[32] Koskeniemmi Report, 17–18, [38].

[33] Report of the Study Group of the International Law Commission, Fragmentation of International Law: Difficulties arising from the Diversification and Expansion of International Law, UN Doc A/CN.4/L.702 (18 July 2006) 15 (emphasis added). See also Richard Gardiner, 'The Vienna Convention Rules on Treaty Interpretation' in Duncan B Hollis (ed), *Oxford Guide to Treaties* (OUP 2012) 475, 499.

[34] Koskeniemmi Report, 226–8, [448]–[450] (citing *EC–Biotech*).

[35] See eg Sinclair, *The Vienna Convention*, 119; Mark E Villiger, *Commentary on the Vienna Convention on the Law of Treaties* (Martinus Nijhoff 2009) 433.

treaty rules in the given case were not 'relevant' to an interpretation of the treaty before it.[36]

Given Article 31(3)(c)'s relatively recent emergence as a meaningful tool of treaty interpretation, interpreters engaged in treaty interpretation should develop Article 31(3)(c) as a useful basis for supporting reference to source rules. Whether this will occur in a manner consistent with either the Study Group's final conclusions or with the Study Group's earlier and broader propositions, however, remains to be seen.

Finally, Article 31(4) recognizes that parties to a treaty may have given certain terms 'special meaning'. If Article 31(3)(c) has experienced a recent ascendancy, then Article 31(4) is a star yet to rise. What entails 'special meaning' and how this meaning should be determined have not been subjected to exacting scrutiny. A particular void exists with respect to applying this element to the interpretation of transplanted treaty rules. For many transplanted treaty rules, deficiencies in the negotiating history will prevent an interpreter from concluding both that the parties intended a special meaning and the substance of that meaning.

In sum, the above analysis shows that the general rule of interpretation presents possible avenues for inquiry into the source rule. Many interpreters and commentators have suggested (often implicitly) that source rules fall under the inquiry into 'ordinary meaning' of treaty terms. While source rules may well elucidate the 'ordinary meaning' in many cases, interpreters should exercise caution before shoehorning consideration of the source rule into an inquiry into 'ordinary meaning'. A more consistent basis could exist in Article 31(3)(c) and its reference to 'relevant rules of international law applicable between the parties', but only if interpreters further develop and refine the rule, particularly with reference to the question of whether absolute congruence of the parties is required. As a matter of secondary resort, interpreters might develop the 'special meaning' element of Article 31(4) as an alternate basis for considering source rules under the general rule of interpretation. In short, the flexibility of the VCLT framework should allow the development of a consistent basis for considering the source rule under the general rule of treaty interpretation.

3. *The general rule of interpretation in* WHO/Egypt

The difficulty of establishing whether, where, and how a source rule can factor into the general rule of interpretation is amply exposed by the array of opinions in the ICJ's 1980 advisory opinion in *WHO/Egypt*.[37] The variety of opinions itself suggests the difficulties that the judges encountered in interpreting the transplanted treaty rule at issue. In addition to the ICJ's advisory opinion, eight judges issued

---

[36] WTO, *EC–Large Civil Aircraft*, 360–6, [839]–[851]; see also WTO, *EC–Large Civil Aircraft*, 38–40, [80]–[82]; 131–3, [309]–[313]; 214–15, [514]–[515]; 341, [799] (arguments of the parties on the interpretation of Article 31(3)(c)); WTO, *US–AD/CVD*, 16–19, [36]–[41]; 117–21, [304]–[313].
[37] *WHO/Egypt*.

separate opinions, and one judge issued a dissenting opinion. All but three of these opinions addressed, in one way or another, the relevance of the source rule.

The ICJ was requested to determine the application of a provision in a host agreement (or a headquarters agreement) between Egypt and the World Health Organization (WHO) regarding the termination and transfer of the WHO's regional headquarters at Alexandria.[38] The VCLT would not apply expressly to the interpretation of the treaty because it was an agreement between a state and an international organization,[39] not between states, but the general rule of Article 31 nonetheless guided the interpretation as a codification of customary law.

According to the Court, the provision at issue was a second-generation transplant: it was patterned on a provision contained in a host agreement between Switzerland and the WHO regarding the organization's global headquarters, which in turn was patterned on a renegotiated provision in the host agreement between Switzerland and the International Labour Organization (ILO). The provision therefore originated in an agreement that did not involve any of the same parties as the agreement in dispute. Moreover, as with many transplanted treaty rules, the WHO/Egypt agreement did not contain any references to the earlier agreements from which its rules derived.

In its advisory opinion, the Court declined to interpret the treaty provision because it concluded that the answer to the 'true legal question under consideration' did not turn on the specific treaty provision relied upon by the parties.[40] It reached this conclusion, however, after its rather lengthy treatment of the earlier agreements. The Court cited the prior WHO and ILO agreements and stated that the corollary provisions of the earlier host agreements 'are not without significance in the present connection'.[41] The Court also surveyed other headquarters agreements, including the agreement between the United States and the United Nations. The dictum regarding the 'significance' of the earlier agreements and the ICJ's corresponding discussion of the agreements reinforced their probative value, even if the advisory opinion ultimately did not turn on them.

At the same time, however, the Court noted that its survey of headquarters agreements generally, not limited to the agreements immediately underlying the WHO/Egypt agreement, revealed a collective lack of coherency given their 'variety and imperfections'.[42] The Court determined that this heterogeneity made it difficult to extract consistent meaning from them, despite their common origins.

---

[38] Whether the agreement was, in fact, a host agreement or headquarters agreement (or, instead, merely a supplemental agreement dealing with privileges and immunities) was the source of debate among some of the judges, but that characterization is not relevant to this discussion.

[39] The 1986 Vienna Convention on the Law of Treaties between States and International Organizations or between International Organizations has not yet entered into force. At present, 31 states have joined the Convention, and the Convention requires 35 states parties to enter into force. Articles 31 and 32 of the 1986 Vienna Convention are examples of transplanted treaty rules, being nearly verbatim copies of Articles 31 and 32 in the 1969 Vienna Convention. The provisions were inserted without debate. See Dörr, 'Article 31', 525 (citations omitted).

[40] *WHO/Egypt*, 88, [35].   [41] *WHO/Egypt*, 94, [46].

[42] *WHO/Egypt*, 94, [46].

It therefore felt 'bound to observe that in future closer attention might with advantage be given to their drafting'.[43]

The separate opinions of Judges Mosler, Oda, and Ago each proceeded to interpret the treaty provision at issue and placed heavy emphasis on the earlier agreements *precisely because* they constituted the source of the transplanted rule. Their opinions also strongly suggest that they considered the source rule to determine the meaning of the provision pursuant to the general rule of interpretation, not just to confirm or clarify the meaning by using the source rule as a supplemental means of interpretation.

Judge Mosler favoured consideration of the earlier WHO/Switzerland agreement because 'the matters dealt with in it are, *mutatis mutandis*, the same as those in the 1951 Agreement with Egypt'.[44] He nonetheless noted that the practice 'of interpreting a treaty by reference to another treaty' was controversial.[45]

Judge Oda went so far as to suggest that the source rule should be considered as a starting point because the provision in issue 'is practically identical' to a provision in the earlier WHO/Switzerland agreement. He wrote that 'it is pertinent *to start* by examining the establishment in 1948 of the headquarters of the WHO in Geneva and the conclusion of the 1948 WHO/Swiss Agreement', and continued to examine the ILO/Switzerland agreement.[46]

Judge Ago also considered the origin of the provision as an integral part of the interpretive process. Though he began with a textual analysis, he went on to 'point out that the question which has been raised in this connection could not in any event be resolved without a close examination of the origins of the clause'.[47] He continued that he found it 'truly difficult to imagine that this formula acquired in what, so to speak, were derivative instruments some other meaning and scope than it possessed in the underlying model'.[48]

The combined elements of 'text', 'context', and 'object and purpose', however, were addressed expressly by only one judge, Judge Ruda, who did not discuss the prior WHO/Switzerland or ILO/Switzerland agreements.[49] Ruda evaluated the 1951 Agreement against the historical background of the establishment of the Alexandria office and found 'nothing in the text of the 1951 Agreement, in its context, or in its object and purpose to show that it dealt with the establishment of the seat of the Regional Office or its removal'.[50]

In Judge Lachs' separate opinion, he lamented the heterogeneity of the treaties that served similar functions, echoing the complaint of the majority in the advisory opinion. Judge Lachs expressed a stronger admonition than the Court did regarding the 'new category of treaties known as headquarters agreements',

---

[43] *WHO/Egypt*, 94, [46].   [44] *WHO/Egypt*, 126 (Mosler, J, sep op).

[45] *WHO/Egypt*, 126 (citing *Constitution of the Maritime Safety Committee of the Inter-Governmental Maritime Consultative Organization* (Advisory Opinion) [1960] ICJ Rep 150, 169ff).

[46] *WHO/Egypt*, 131 (Oda, J, sep op) (emphasis added).

[47] *WHO/Egypt*, 160 (Ago, J, sep op).   [48] *WHO/Egypt*, 162 (Ago, J, sep op).

[49] *WHO/Egypt*, 122 (Ruda, J, sep op).   [50] *WHO/Egypt*, 122 (Ruda, J, sep op).

but his warning also applies to types of treaty containing transplanted treaty rules more generally:

[T]hey show striking discrepancies, some well founded on the peculiarities of the specific cases, others evidently due to lack of adequate attention from the lawyer's eye. There can be little doubt that this is not conducive to the proper operation of international organizations [governed by these treaties] and may constitute a source of misunderstanding, misconstruction or even conflict, and not only in cases of proposed transfer.[51]

Judge Lachs therefore advocated for '[g]reater precision and comprehensiveness, closer attention to legal formulations, and the introduction of uniformity wherever desirable'.[52]

The comments by both the Court and by Judge Lachs highlight the problems of incremental revisions and incomplete borrowing that attended the transplanted treaty rules in the given case. They also highlight the fact that greater attention to consistency, uniformity, and good draftsmanship would be a good start. Several of the particular difficulties raised by transplanted treaty rules also could be resolved through transparent attribution to the source rules and original treaties from which the transplanted rules derived. The variations in the opinions suggest that had the Court not decided the case on alternative grounds, it would have been hard-pressed to agree on the relevance of the source rule and the avenue(s) for considering it under the general rule of interpretation.

B. Supplemental means of interpretation

1. Recourse to the travaux préparatoires of the original and subsequent treaties

The 'supplemental means of interpretation' allowed pursuant to Article 32 of the VCLT includes any extrinsic material, including the source rule, that will shed light on the meaning of a treaty under interpretation.[53] Article 32 lists the 'preparatory work of the treaty' (or *travaux préparatoires*) and the 'circumstances of [the treaty's] conclusion' as the primary, non-exclusive examples of sources that can be employed as part of this exercise. Principles or maxims of international law and canons of interpretation also can play an important part. As with all means of supplemental interpretation, however, recourse to the source rule pursuant to this catch-all provision is limited to carefully delineated circumstances: either to confirm the meaning determined pursuant to Article 31, or if application of the general rule in Article 31 produces a meaning that is ambiguous or absurd.

For transplanted treaty rules, a particular concern arises over the extent to which the *travaux préparatoires* of the source rule can be imputed to the parties to the treaty under interpretation. As noted earlier, the *travaux* of the treaty under interpretation itself often reflects a lack of discussion or negotiation of the rule

---

[51] *WHO/Egypt*, 108, 112 (Lachs, J, sep op).   [52] *WHO/Egypt*, 112 (Lachs, J, sep op).
[53] See eg Gardiner, *Treaty Interpretation*, 99–101.

that is transplanted or the reasons for borrowing the source rule. This tendency increases as the transplanted rule is introduced into successive treaties. A deficient *travaux* of the transplanted treaty rule thus invites consideration of the *travaux* of the source rule. In many cases, however, the *travaux* of the underlying source rule is not necessarily known to, used by, or available to both parties to the agreement containing the transplanted rule.

The lack of publicity, transparency, and accessibility of the *travaux* of the source rule therefore establishes a tension between considering extrinsic sources that might shed light on the meaning of the transplanted rule, on the one hand, but also excluding sources that played no part in the negotiation of the treaty under interpretation. The interpretation of transplanted treaty rules presents a heightened likelihood that an interpreter will have to resolve this tension.

Several commentators have predicated use of the *travaux* on some degree of publicity, publication, or assent. Dörr, for example, excludes confidential or unwritten sources from the *travaux* unless admitted in the negotiating process, as well as unilateral sources attributable to only one party.[54] He observes that during the drafting of the VCLT, the ILC did not condition use of the *travaux* on a party's participation in the drafting or negotiating process, but it did draw the line at confidential or inaccessible sources.[55] Villiger, too, states that 'all the parties concerned must have been aware of these supplementary means of interpretation—eg the *travaux préparatoires*—if they are to be invoked in respect of a treaty's interpretation'.[56] Villiger's articulation suggests that he considers knowledge a precondition to considering not only the *travaux* but any supplemental means of interpretation.

Dörr distinguishes the *travaux* of the treaty under interpretation from the *travaux* of related instruments, both of which are encompassed under the broader category of supplemental means. He thus expressly considers transplanted treaty rules in this regard and observes a prevailing failure of interpreters to note the distinction:

In practice, however, interpreters sometimes refer to material leading up to an identical predecessor treaty and even to similar treaties and apply that material as if it were the preparatory work to the treaty under consideration.[57]

Dörr, then, gets to the crux of the difficulty: in the absence of an adequate *travaux* for the treaty containing the transplanted treaty rule, can an interpreter consider the *travaux* of the treaty containing the source rule in its place? Dörr answers this question in the negative, but this answer does not end the debate over the relevance of the *travaux* of the source rule. Though both sets of materials can be considered pursuant to the rule on supplemental means of interpretation, the

---

[54] Oliver Dörr, 'Article 32: Supplemental Means of Interpretation' in Oliver Dörr and Kirsten Schmalenbach (eds), *Vienna Convention on the Law of Treaties: A Commentary* (Springer 2012) 571, 575–7.
[55] Dörr, 'Article 32'.
[56] Villiger, *Commentary on the Vienna Convention on the Law of Treaties*, 446.
[57] Dörr, 'Article 32', 577.

distinction between them goes to the interpretive weight of the earlier preparatory work and its attribution to the parties to the treaty under interpretation. Dörr is quite right to suggest that many authorities have collapsed their inquiries into the *travaux préparatoires* of the treaty under interpretation and of related treaties or else fail to note this important distinction.

2. Supplemental means of interpretation in WHO/Egypt

In the *WHO/Egypt* case, the majority of the Court and several judges (in their separate opinions) considered the documents related to the preparatory work of the earlier treaties. The opinions displayed disparate approaches to the treatment of the *travaux préparatoires* of the earlier treaties.

As is often the case with transplanted treaty rules, the source rule was discussed, negotiated, and vetted in the process of its inclusion in the original treaty, but the transplanted rule did not occasion much discussion in the subsequent negotiation of the WHO/Egypt treaty. A gap therefore existed in the *travaux* of the treaty under interpretation itself. During the Court proceedings, a representative to the WHO stated that 'the text in question was not the subject of thorough discussion when it was adopted, since it reproduced a clause that was already well known'.[58]

A review of the materials considered or cited by the judges, however, challenges the suggestion that the transplanted rule and its meaning were 'well known' to both parties to the agreement. Certainly the WHO introduced the rule from treaties known to it, but Egypt's knowledge and assent were far less clear.

The *travaux* of the source rule contained in the ILO/Switzerland agreement, in particular, does not appear necessarily to have been contemplated during the negotiation of the WHO/Egypt agreement. Prior to issuing the advisory opinion, the Registrar specifically requested that both the WHO and the ILO provide documentation related to the earlier agreements so that the Court 'may have available to it all material which might possibly be found to throw light on the legal questions laid before it for advisory opinion'.[59] The Court requested the documentation related to the prior Switzerland/WHO agreement of its own accord, but it requested the *travaux préparatoires* of the ILO agreement on the suggestion of the United States, which remarked that the *travaux préparatoires* was 'contained in a largely unpublished file' kept by the ILO.[60] This suggestion is striking as it called into question

---

[58] *WHO/Egypt*, 131 (Oda, J, sep op) (quoting Director of the Legal Division of the WHO, oral proceedings (23 October 1980)).

[59] Letter from the Registrar to the Legal Adviser and Assistant Director-General of the International Labour Organisation (2 September 1980), Correspondence, Annex 24, at 325; Letter from the Deputy Registrar to the Director of the Legal Division of the WHO (29 July 1980), Correspondence, Annex 12, 319–20 (in French); Letter from the Senior Legal Officer of the WHO to the Deputy Registrar (6 Aug 1980), Correspondence, Annex 13, 321; Letter from the Senior Legal Office of the WHO to the Deputy Registrar (18 August 1980), Correspondence, Annex 16, 323.

[60] Letter from the Acting Legal Adviser to the Department of State of the United States of America to the Deputy Registrar (13 August 1980), Correspondence, Annex 15, 322; Letter from the Registrar to the Deputy Legal Adviser to the Department of State of the United States of

both the common knowledge of and access to the file by the parties to the agreement under interpretation.

Several judges nonetheless appeared inclined to rely on the negotiating history of the source rule in interpreting the treaty provision at issue, despite the fact that it was 'largely unpublished' and involved entirely different parties. Judge Gros, for example, wrote that the WHO recognized that its agreement with Egypt followed a model draft agreement copied (but twice removed) from the ILO/Switzerland agreement. From there, Judge Gros refers to the twice-removed source rule, seemingly for its probative value:

[T]he Court has seen extracts from the report of the ILO delegation to the 1946 Montreal Conference, in which Mr. Wilfred Jenks, who negotiated the text of the Headquarters Agreement with Switzerland, concluded that in his view 'the arrangement is terminated by mutual agreement'.[61]

Judges Oda and Sette-Camara also each relied, in part, on 'an informal *procès-verbal de négociations*' related to the ILO/Switzerland agreement. Judge Oda cited this source despite observing that his consideration was 'based on notes taken at the time by the ILO negotiators, but which has never been seen or approved by the other party'.[62]

Judge Sette-Camara went further and stated that the relevant '*travaux préparatoires*' comes not just from the ILO/Switzerland Agreement and the WHO/Switzerland Agreement, but in fact went back to the '1926 *modus vivendi* concluded between the League of Nations and Switzerland'.[63] This comment highlights the difficulty that interpreters sometimes have in identifying the origins of a transplanted treaty rule that has been through several iterations.

Judge Lachs, however, downplayed the relevance of the earlier agreements, observing that although they all belonged 'to the family' of instruments concluded between international organizations 'and States on whose territories their offices are located', the agreements were 'a very heterogeneous collection'.[64] His comments also suggested that he might have supported reliance on earlier treaties pursuant to the maxim of interpretation *per analogiam* had they comprised a more homogenous collection. 'Whatever analogies may be drawn', Judge Lachs wrote, 'they should not be allowed to obscure the fact that the 1951 Agreement does not enshrine any decision concerning the establishment of the office at Alexandria', and 'does not have any bearing on the event of terminating the operations of the Alexandria office, whether by transfer of the functions elsewhere or otherwise'.[65]

America (4 September 1980), Correspondence, Annex 27, 327. The United States also made reference to an 'apparently unpublished' agreement between the ILO and Turkey. The ILO supplied the relevant agreements and associated *travaux préparatoires*. Documents received from the International Labour Organization, Documents, 121–36.

[61] *WHO/Egypt*, 99, 106 (Gros, J, sep op).
[62] *WHO/Egypt*, 136 (Oda, J, sep op). See also *WHO/Egypt* 178, 186 (Sette-Camara, J, sep op).
[63] *WHO/Egypt*, 178, 185 (Sette-Camara, J, sep op).
[64] *WHO/Egypt*, 108 (Lachs, J, sep op).   [65] *WHO/Egypt*, 108–9 (Oda, J, sep op).

These discussions confirm the difficulties presented by a deficient negotiating history and by the opaque origins of a transplanted treaty rule. The opinions reflect little heed to the lack of publicity, transparency, or accessibility of the preparatory work underlying the source rule. They also suggest an unequal knowledge base among the parties. In such circumstances, neither the *travaux* of the treaty under interpretation nor the *travaux* of the source rule fully illuminate the common understanding or the intentions of the parties. This lacuna raises particular questions regarding the role of the *travaux* of the source rule in the interpretive process.

Conclusion

Transplanted treaty rules present particular difficulties under international law's interpretive framework, if one assumes that interpretation must account for source rules and must do so within the construct of the VCLT. Of course, the VCLT does not require rigid or mechanical application of the various elements. The ILC and many writers have highlighted the importance of 'logic and good sense' as overarching principles, though an interpreter nonetheless must apply logic and good sense within the framework of the VCLT, as Bernárdez explains:

> The artistic aspects of treaty interpretation, as well as the exercise of logic and good sense required by any process of interpretation, are nowadays supposed to be undertaken in accordance with a set of rules seen as binding upon the interpreter, as they may be applicable in the circumstances of a given case.[66]

This composite approach can be particularly difficult to apply in interpreting transplanted legal rules. The VCLT's rules on treaty interpretation were developed based on the presumption of an original treaty. It reflects a vision of treaty drafters who assembled at the negotiating table and crafted an instrument from scratch that expresses their common intentions, carefully selecting terms appropriate to the context and to the object and purpose at hand. This vision may be idealistic for any treaty, but it is particularly idealistic in the case of transplanted treaty rules.

In some cases, the source rule presents such formidable evidence of meaning that its relevance should not be precluded by a narrow construction of the general rule of treaty interpretation. An inquiry into 'ordinary meaning' may provide a sufficient basis in the many cases where a transplanted treaty rule has been widely adopted such that knowledge of meaning can be imputed to a practised drafter in the field. Not all transplanted treaty rules, however, are so widespread.

The ILC Study Group's suggestion that 'other treaty rules' can be considered as 'relevant rules of international law' if they 'provide evidence of the common understanding of the parties' reinforces the same notion and provides an

---

[66] Bernárdez, 'Interpretation of Treaties', 721.

additional basis for considering source rules. This flexible interpretation of Article 31(3)(c) provides the strongest grounds for considering the source rule as part of the general rule of interpretation, but it is not clear that this interpretation is embraced by the general rule as presently understood and interpreted by the wider international community. Furthermore, a broader interpretation of Article 31(4) would provide an even stronger basis for considering source rules.

In cases where reference to the source rule presents less urgency, recourse to the source rule and the surrounding documents as supplemental means of interpretation might be sufficient. Nonetheless, significant questions are raised by reliance on the *travaux préparatoires* of the source rule in the event that the *travaux* of the treaty under interpretation is lacking, which often reflects that the transplanted rules were adopted without significant discussion or negotiation. An interpreter should take account of whether the *travaux* of the source rule was transparent, publicized, and available to the parties in determining its relevance in the given case.

In the course of a flexible approach to interpreting transplanted treaty rules, the given case may prompt additional inquiries, including into the relevance of textual similarities and discrepancies that have been introduced in the transplanted treaty rule and whether a fundamental dissonance exists between the treaties or their respective regimes. The interpretive process is an integrated approach that allows for consideration of these additional factors without assigning them any particular weight. At the same time, though, an interpreter must be alive to the distinct difficulties posed by rules that originated in a different instrument than the one before him.

PART V
THE STRATEGIES

12

A Genealogy of Textualism in Treaty Interpretation

Fuad Zarbiyev

Introduction: Taking Historicity Seriously

Queen Anne, the first sovereign of Great Britain, is reported to have said that the architecture of St Paul's Cathedral was 'awful, artificial, and amusing', words that are likely to be understood by modern readers as testifying to her deep disappointment with the architecture of the Cathedral. Relating this story in their recent treatise on legal interpretation, Justice Antonin Scalia and Bryan Garner caution that such a reading would be a misreading because, far from being disappointed, Queen Anne quite simply expressed her admiration of the architecture by using words equivalent to 'awe-inspiring, highly artistic, and thought-provoking' in eighteenth-century English.[1]

What this episode exemplifies is by no means unknown in international law. How international law must deal with historical variations in the meaning of terms used in legal texts is one of the long-standing puzzles of interpretation in international law. Can the phrase 'territorial status' employed in a 1931 instrument be interpreted as covering the continental shelf, although the latter concept was unknown back then? Is it permissible to read the term *'comercio'* in an 1858 treaty as encompassing tourism? Does the right to marry conferred upon 'men and women of marriageable age' in a human rights treaty adopted in 1950 enable a transsexual to marry a person of the same biological sex? All these questions have actually presented themselves in practice.[2] The issue has also generated a renewed interest since the International Law Commission (ILC) decided, in 2008, to include the topic of 'Treaties over Time' in its programme of work.[3]

---

[1] Antonin Scalia and Bryan Garner, *Reading Law: The Interpretation of Legal Texts* (West 2012) 78.

[2] See *Aegean Sea Continental Shelf (Greece v Turkey)* (Judgment) [1978] ICJ Rep 3, 32; *Dispute regarding Navigational and Related Rights (Nicaragua v Costa Rica)* (Judgment) [2009] ICJ Rep 213, 242–3; *Goodwin v United Kingdom* (2002) 35 EHRR 18.

[3] ILC, Report of the sixtieth session (2008), A/63/10, [353]. The Commission decided during its sixty-fourth session that with effect from its sixty-fifth session (2013) the topic will be pursued as 'Subsequent agreements and subsequent practice in relation to the interpretation of treaties'. See ILC, Report of the sixty-fourth session (2012), A/67/10, [227].

However, what is conspicuous by its absence in the literature is a consideration of whether interpretive regimes prevailing at any given time in international law are themselves historically contingent. To appreciate the implications of this issue, consider the following two interpretive statements separated from each other by a time interval of 87 years. The first statement issued by an arbitral tribunal in 1897 reads as follows:

[W]e are to interpret and give effect to the treaty of April 15, 1858, in the way in which it was mutually understood at the time by its makers . . . It is the meaning of the men who framed the treaty which we are to seek, rather than some possible meaning which can be forced upon isolated words or sentences.[4]

The second statement, issued by the Iran–US Special Claims Tribunal in 1984, holds that:

[T]he Vienna Convention does not require any demonstration of a 'converging will' or of a conscious acceptance by each Party of all implications of the terms to which it has agreed. It is the 'terms of the treaty in their context and in the light of its object and purpose' with which the Tribunal is to be concerned not the subjective understanding or intent of either of the Parties.[5]

It would be hard to conceive of two interpretive philosophies farther apart from each other. While the first statement focuses on the intention of the parties, marginalizing the significance of the terms of the treaty in the process, the second suggests the exact opposite and denies all legitimacy to the intentional approach as such. Yet a cursory glance at the international case law reveals that such historical variations in interpretive regimes are hardly acknowledged in the official discourse on treaty interpretation. Consider, for example, how the rules on treaty interpretation embodied in the Vienna Convention on the Law of Treaties (VCLT) are treated in international jurisprudence.[6] Set out in 1969, these rules have been applied to the interpretation of treaties dating back to the nineteenth century,[7] and a whole range of treaties concluded in the twentieth century before the entry into force of the VCLT.[8] This line of decisions is traditionally justified by the predictable, but deeply problematic, argument that the VCLT's rules on interpretation are customary rules with almost trans-historical validity. This argument

---

[4] *First Award under the Convention between Costa Rica and Nicaragua of 8 April 1896 for the Demarcation of the Boundary between the two Republics* (1897) 28 RIAA 215, 216.

[5] *Iran v United States (Case No A/18)* (1984) 5 Iran-USCTR 251, 260.

[6] Vienna Convention on the Law of Treaties concluded at Vienna on 23 May 1969, UNTS vol 1155, No 18232.

[7] See *Award in the Arbitration regarding the Iron Rhine ('Ijzeren Rijn') (Belgium v Netherlands)* (2005) 27 RIAA 35, 62; *Dispute regarding Navigational and Related Rights*, 237; *Case Concerning a Dispute between Argentina and Chile Concerning the Beagle Channel* (1977) 21 RIAA 53, 84; *Case Concerning the Delimitation of the Maritime Boundary between Guinea and Guinea-Bissau* (1985) 19 RIAA 149, 165; *Case concerning Kasikili/Sedudu Island (Botswana/Namibia)* (Judgment) [1999] ICJ Rep 1045, 1059.

[8] See eg *Territorial Dispute (Libyan Arab Jamahiriya/Chad)* (Judgment) [1994] ICJ Reports 1994, 6, 21–2; *Partial Award on the Lawfulness of the Recall of the Privately Held Shares on 8 January 2001 and the Applicable Standards for Valuation of Those Shares* (2002) 23 RIAA 183, 224.

is problematic because, however attractive it may be for practical purposes, it does not stand up to historical scrutiny. There is ample evidence that the interpretive approach set forth in the VCLT has by no means prevailed throughout the history of international law.[9]

Why the historical contingency of the VCLT rules has rarely given pause to international lawyers is somewhat puzzling. Can it be the case that any divergence between the rules of interpretation under the VCLT and the interpretive techniques applicable at the time of the conclusion of a treaty is a distinction without a difference? This seems hardly plausible because what literary theorist Jeffrey Stout stated about 'the reader's interests and purposes' is equally relevant for rules of interpretation:

They direct interpretation toward some things and away from countless others. They mobilize some categories for interpretive duty and leave others uncalled.[10]

That said, one might find it tempting to venture that the question whether and to what extent interpretive regimes have historically varied might not present much of theoretical or practical interest. If a treaty is being applied today, it is only natural—so the argument would run—to interpret it in light of the rules of interpretation prevailing in the legal system currently in force, as opposed to the rules applicable when the treaty was drafted and adopted.[11] Such an approach would accord with the general principles of intertemporal law: while the retroactive application of substantive rules tends to be regarded as something of a legal heresy, rules of interpretation seem more akin to procedural rules—a category for which retroactive application is more readily admitted.[12]

---

[9] Interestingly enough, this is sometimes openly acknowledged in practice. See *Aguas del Tunari SA v Bolivia*, ICSID Case No ARB/02/3, Decision on Jurisdiction, 21 October 2005, [91] ('[T]he Vienna Convention represents a move away from the canons of interpretation previously common in treaty interpretation and which erroneously persist in various international law decisions today. For example, the Vienna Convention does not mention the canon that treaties are to be construed narrowly, a canon that presumes States cannot have intended to restrict their range of action'); *Case concerning the re-evaluation of the German Mark* (1980) 19 RIAA 67, 92 ('The Tribunal takes the view that the habit occasionally found in earlier international practice of referring to the basic or original text as an aid to interpretation is now, as a general rule, incompatible with the principle, incorporated in Article 33 (1) of the VCLT, of the equal status of all authentic texts in plurilingual treaties'). See also the separate opinion of Judge Oda in *Kasikili/Sedudu Island*, 1118 ('It appears to me that the Judgment places excessive reliance upon the Vienna Convention on the Law of Treaties for the purpose of the Court's interpretation of the 1890 Anglo-German Treaty'). Although Judge Oda did not clearly indicate why such reliance on the Vienna Convention seemed odd to him, it is reasonable to assume that the difference between the interpretive regimes of two periods was amongst his concerns.

[10] Jeffrey Stout, 'What is the Meaning of a Text' (1982) 14 New Literary History 1, 7–8. This was recently endorsed by a WTO Panel in *EC: Measures Affecting the Approval and Marketing of Biotech Products—Reports of the Panel* WT/DS291/R WT/DS292/R WT/DS293/R (29 September 2006), [7.70] (stating that consideration of 'other applicable rules of international law [mandated by Article 31(3)(c)] may prompt a treaty interpreter to adopt one interpretation rather than another').

[11] *Legal Consequences for States of the Continued Presence of South Africa in Namibia (South West Africa) notwithstanding Security Council Resolution 276* (1970) (Advisory Opinion) [1971] ICJ Rep 16, 31 ('[A]n international instrument has to be interpreted and applied within the framework of the entire legal system prevailing at the time of the interpretation').

[12] Hans W Baade, 'Time and Meaning: Notes on the Intertemporal Law of Statutory Construction and Constitutional Interpretation' (1995) 43 Am J Comp L 319.

An objection along these lines could be met in various ways. One could point out, for instance, that the procedural nature of interpretive rules is open to discussion, to say the least. Moreover, when a treaty pre-dating the VCLT is interpreted in light of the interpretive regime embodied in the latter, the ensuing interpretation is traditionally presented not only as what that treaty means in the legal system prevailing at the time of the interpretation, but as reflecting what the treaty has always meant, including to its drafters.[13]

However, a more straightforward case can be made to demonstrate that the temporal scope of interpretive regimes is of significant theoretical and practical interest. Implicit in the assumption that the VCLT interpretive regime is applicable to treaties that pre-date the Convention is a theory of meaning according to which meaning is something 'out there', with the rules of interpretation serving as a tool for the interpreter to discover that meaning. On this view, the rules of interpretation would be no different from the laws of physics. Common sense has it that the laws of physics operate in a way that is wholly unmediated by social factors or historical circumstances. As one author nicely put it, 'Einstein's theory of gravitation replaced Newton's, but apples did not suspend themselves in mid-air pending the outcome'.[14] In the same vein, one may be tempted to say that the fact that interpretive regimes have changed throughout history does not mean that the true meaning of a treaty has not always been there despite such variations. However, if the success of the interpretive paradigm of the VCLT is a time- and context-sensitive phenomenon, as this chapter will argue, meaning can hardly be seen as a natural phenomenon.

The practical relevance of the question seems beyond doubt as well, if one bears in mind that the ways in which treaties are interpreted and the techniques and strategies employed in their drafting process are closely related. At a time when textualism was not a prominent interpretive approach, one could not have reasonably expected drafters to be as concerned by the textual completeness, clarity, and precision of treaty provisions as they would be nowadays.[15]

Working from the above premise—that properly situating an interpretive regime in history is a worthwhile enterprise—this chapter sets out to investigate how textualism has come to be accepted as the dominant interpretive paradigm in a legal

---

[13] This interpretive posture is, of course, dictated by the official image of judicial interpretation. Official discourse has it that a correct interpretation merely amounts to faithfully reproducing the content of the rule being interpreted. Thus, 'the terms [of a treaty] must be held to have always borne the meaning placed upon them by [the] interpretation'. *Access to German Minority Schools in Upper Silesia* (Advisory Opinion) PCIJ Rep Series A/B No 40, 4, 19. For instance, according to the ICJ, when it recognized the binding force of its interim measures, it 'did no more than give the provisions of the Statute the meaning and scope that they had possessed from the outset': *Case concerning Application of the Convention on the Prevention and Punishment of the Crime of Genocide (Bosnia and Herzegovina v Serbia and Montenegro)* (Judgment) [2007] ICJ Rep 43, 230.

[14] Stephen Jay Gould, *Hen's Teeth and Horse's Toes: Further Reflections in Natural History* (Norton 1994) 254.

[15] See the statement by the representative of Sweden, United Nations Conference on the Law of Treaties, First Session, Vienna, 26 March–24 May 1968, Official Records, Thirty-Third Meeting, 22 April 1968, 179 ('Whereas the textual approach [does] not entail [the dangers of the subjective approach], it [has] the drawback, or hardship, that it [requires] representatives of States drafting the text of a treaty to consider all the implications of a subsequent textual approach to interpretation in

system in which consent of states has been, and is still said to be, at the heart of legal commitments.[16] After all, intentionalism seems by definition more deferential to state consent than textualism. To take an example from practice, when the Foreign Minister of Bahrain claimed to have never contemplated the possibility that he was signing a binding agreement with Qatar, in the context of the *Maritime Delimitation and Territorial Questions between Qatar and Bahrain* case before the International Court of Justice,[17] his objection could arguably have been entitled to more weight had intentionalism been the guiding principle instead of textualism. If that is so, the official victory of textualism appears to be something of a paradox that needs to be explained.

This chapter proceeds as follows. Before engaging in discussion of the central theme of the chapter, a few words might be in order to substantiate the claim about the status of textualism in modern international law (Part I). Part II then attempts to outline some of the factors that can plausibly explain textualism's current dominant status.

I. Textualism: The Dominant Interpretive Paradigm in Modern International Law

As an interpretive philosophy, textualism mandates that a legal text must be read based upon the meaning of its terms, 'without reference to extraneous factors'.[18] The prevalence of textualism thus understood in modern interpretive discourse in international law might not appear as immediately obvious because no such thing seems to emerge 'textually' from the VCLT itself. Indeed, Article 31 of the VCLT seems to put the terms, the context, and the object and purpose of the treaty on an equal footing.[19] Such an understanding of Article 31 has received authoritative support from the ILC itself.[20] It nonetheless remains the case that the interpretive regime

---

the event of a dispute; it [calls] for energetic efforts to achieve the utmost clarity and completeness in formulating the text of a treaty'). See also Jacques Soubeyrol, '*L'interprétation internationale des traités et la considération de l'intention des parties*' (1958) JDI 686, 758.

[16] See Alan Boyle and Christine Chinkin, *The Making of International Law* (OUP 2007) 226 ('In [the] international system…the consent or acquiescence of states is still an essential precondition for the development of new law or changes to existing law').

[17] *Maritime Delimitation and Territorial Questions between Qatar and Bahrain (Qatar v Bahrain)* (Judgment) [1995] ICJ Rep 6.

[18] Gerald Fitzmaurice, 'The Law and Procedure of the International Court of Justice 1951: Treaty Interpretation and Other Treaty Points' (1957) 33 BYBIL 203, 212.

[19] According to Article 31(1) VCLT, '[a] treaty shall be interpreted in good faith in accordance with the ordinary meaning to be given to the terms of the treaty in their context and in the light of its object and purpose'.

[20] The ILC specified that the interpretive regime of the VCLT was based on a holistic approach. Reports of the International Law Commission on the Second Part of its Seventeenth Session and on its Eighteenth Session, (1966) II ILC Ybk 219–20. See also WTO, *United States: Sections 301–310 of the Trade Act of 1974—Report of the Panel* (22 December 1999) WT/DS152/R, [7.22]; *Case Concerning the Audit of Accounts between the Netherlands and France*, (2004) 25 RIAA 267, 295.

of the VCLT is traditionally understood as having elevated textualism, as narrowly defined above, to a priority status.[21] The last ILC Special Rapporteur on the law of treaties, Sir Humphrey Waldock, made no secret of the ILC's 'strong predilection for textual interpretation'.[22] His comment on one of the early incarnations of Article 31 of the VCLT specified that this provision 'takes as the basic rule of treaty interpretation the primacy of the text',[23] and described the text as 'the dominant factor in the interpretation of the treaty'.[24] Waldock even pointed out that the ILC had to take sides in the long-standing debates relating to treaty interpretation and insist on the fundamental importance of the text.[25]

The dominance of textualism is also reflected in the manner in which international law deals with the choice between textualism and intentionalism. In view of the real and symbolic importance of state consent throughout the history of international law, it is not surprising that intentionalism is not denied all legitimacy in international legal discourse as such. In fact, the World Trade Organization (WTO) Appellate Body went so far as to hold that the purpose of interpretation is to give effect to the intentions of the parties.[26] This should not, however, be mistaken for testimony of intentionalism's pre-eminence in international legal discourse. Indeed, the full story is that even though the purpose of interpretation is to give effect to parties' intentions, those intentions are best regarded as being expressed in the text.[27] Therefore, the argument goes, text must be taken as the most important element in treaty interpretation.

International jurisprudence also largely supports the proposition that textualism is the dominant interpretive approach, despite the holistic philosophy formally enunciated by the ILC. For instance, the object and purpose of a treaty is often regarded not as one of the starting points in the interpretive process but as an auxiliary and largely dispensable element that might optionally be used to confirm the ordinary meaning of the terms of the treaty, or to clarify those

---

[21] See Robert Jennings and Arthur Watts, *Oppenheim's International Law* (Longman 1992) 1271; Anthony Aust, *Modern Treaty Law and Practice* (2nd edn, CUP 2007) 235; Jean-Mark Sorel and Valérie Boré Eveno, 'Article 31' in Olivier Corten and Pierre Klein (eds), *The Vienna Convention on the Law of Treaties: A Commentary* (OUP 2011) 815, 829; James Crawford, *Brownlie's Principles of Public International Law* (OUP 2012) 379.

[22] (1964) I ILC Ybk 314. On the ILC's preference for textualism, see Richard Gardiner, *Treaty Interpretation* (OUP 2008) 144.

[23] Third Report on the law of treaties, by Sir Humphrey Waldock, Special Rapporteur, A/CN.4/167 and Add.1-3, (1964) II ILC Ybk 56.

[24] Third Report on the law of treaties.

[25] Third Report on the law of treaties, 54 ('[D]octrinal differences concerning the methods of interpretation have tended to weaken the significance of the text as the expression of the will of the parties, and it seems desirable that the Commission should take a clear position in regard to the role of the text in treaty interpretation').

[26] WTO, *EC: Customs Classification of Certain Computer Equipment—Report of the Appellate Body* (5 June 1998) WT/DS62/AB/R, WT/DS67/AB/R, WT/DS68/AB/R, [93].

[27] (1966) II ILC Ybk 219–20 ('[T]he text must be presumed to be the authentic expression of the intentions of the parties; and that, in consequence, the starting point and purpose of interpretation is to elucidate the meaning of the text, not to investigate *ab initio* the intentions of the parties').

terms when they are deemed ambiguous.²⁸ The WTO Appellate Body stated this approach in clear terms:

Where the meaning imparted by the text itself is equivocal or inconclusive, or where confirmation of the correctness of the reading of the text itself is desired, light from the object and purpose of the treaty as a whole may usefully be sought.²⁹

An ICSID tribunal likewise observed:

[The] strict textual approach, i.e., going no further than the ordinary meaning of the text of the treaty, is regarded as fundamental in international law. Even though the [ILC], in its Final Draft Articles…suggested that the 'process of interpretation is a unity and that the provisions of the article [now Article 31] form a single, closely integrated rule,' nevertheless, the article itself indicates a clear, logical interpretive order in which textual interpretation is primary…Article 31, when read in conjunction with Articles 32 and 33 of the Vienna Convention reveals an interpretive structure in which subsequent practice and the other two methods of treaty interpretation, subjective and teleological, are supplementary in nature. They are to be used to assist in the interpretation when the textual method is insufficient.³⁰

This approach is also supported in international law scholarship, undermining the supposedly holistic philosophy of the VCLT regime.³¹

II. The Official Victory of Textualism: Situating a Success Story

I propose to analyse the historical contingency of the rise of textualism as defined above by using a genealogical line of inquiry. Even though genealogy is traditionally associated with Friedrich Nietzsche, one has to turn to Michel Foucault to discern its methodological assumptions. Foucault differentiates genealogy from historical analysis on various grounds, two of which are particularly relevant for our purposes. First, historical analysis is guided by the idea of the 'solemnities of

---

²⁸ *Territorial Dispute*, 26; *Kasikili/Sedudu Island*, 1072; *Case concerning Oil Platforms (Iran v USA)* (Judgment) [1996] ICJ Rep 803, 813.

²⁹ WTO, *US: Import Prohibition of Certain Shrimp and Shrimp Products—Report of the Appellate Body* (12 October 1998) WT/DS58/AB/R, [114]. See also *Case concerning Revaluation of German Mark*, 102 ('Article 31 (1) of the [VCLT] requires, in addition to the wording and context, the "object and purpose" of the treaty to be taken into account when interpreting unclear treaty provisions'); *Prosecutor v Stanislav Galić* (Judgment) ITCY-98-29-A (30 November 2006), [103] ('Where a treaty provision is capable of sustaining more than one meaning, Article 31 (1) of the [VCLT] directs that it shall be interpreted in accordance with its ordinary meaning in light of its object and purpose and in the context of the treaty').

³⁰ *RSM Production Corporation v Grenada*, ICSID Case No ARB/05/14, Award, 13 March 2009, [383].

³¹ Ian Sinclair, *The Vienna Convention on the Law of Treaties* (2nd edn, Manchester University Press 1984) 130; Anthony Aust, *Modern Treaty Law and Practice* (2nd edn, CUP 2007) 235; Alexander Orakhelashvili, *The Interpretation of Acts and Rules in Public International Law* (OUP 2008) 310–11; Ulf Linderfalk, 'Is the Hierarchical Structure of Articles 31 and 32 of the Vienna Convention Real or Not? Interpreting the Rules of Interpretation' (2007) 54 NILR 133, 146.

the origin',[32] designed to satisfy our need to believe that our present has deeply meaningful grounds in history. Since what one finds in the course of an investigation is largely a function of the paradigm guiding that investigation, it is not surprising that official history tends to associate the origin with ideal-sounding and commonly valued motivations, and systematically neglects circumstances which do not fit in well with such motivations.

An example might help illustrate this point. Given the legendary formalism of the British legal tradition in the field of interpretation, it seems at least arguable that the fact that British international lawyers played an important part in shaping the international law of treaty interpretation, in both their personal and institutional capacities, might have something to do with the official victory of textualism. Although Vattel's famous example of an Englishman who married three wives in order to avoid breaching the law which prohibited marrying two was a caricature, it was not a completely unwarranted one in view of the way in which written contracts were construed in English law until very recently.[33] Yet such factual circumstances are rarely deemed 'solemn' enough to be dignified by scholarly attention. The reason why such a self-restraining approach is problematic is obvious: if scholarly discourse is to reproduce the official self-image of the law, it could hardly be of any analytical interest.[34]

The second ground on which genealogy differs from historical analysis is that, while history rests on the paradigm of continuity and a linear succession of events, 'genealogy does not pretend to go back in time to restore an unbroken continuity that operates beyond the dispersion of [events]'.[35] The assertion that the Vienna Convention interpretive regime was valid even in the nineteenth century is premised on a naive assumption that legal rules could remain unaltered in spite of radical changes in historical circumstances.[36] By analysing 'passing events in their proper dispersion',[37] genealogy rejects this ideal of continuity, and claims that those events do not respond to any transcendental necessity, and can only be understood in light of the contingencies of their time.

With this methodological premise clarified, the ensuing analysis attempts to account for the predominance of textualism in modern international law. Its starting point is that the preference for textualism has a long pedigree in the intellectual history of the discipline of international law. But however strong and deeply embedded it might have been, a mere intellectual preference for textualism would have hardly been sufficient in and of itself to transform textualism into the officially

---

[32] Michel Foucault, 'Nietzsche, Genealogy, History' in Donald F Bouchard (ed), *Language, Counter-Memory, Practice: Selected Essays and Interviews by Michel Foucault* (Cornell University Press 1977) 143.

[33] In English law, a literal approach to contract construction was replaced by contextualism in *Investors Compensation Scheme Ltd v West Bromwich Building Society* [1998] 1 WLR 896 (HL).

[34] Paul W Kahn, *The Cultural Study of Law* (University of Chicago Press 1999) 27 (stating that '[w]e cannot grasp the law as an object of study if the conceptual tools we bring to the inquiry are nothing but the self-replication of legal practice itself').

[35] Foucault, 'Nietzsche, Genealogy, History', 146.

[36] Such an assumption is all the more implausible in the case of rules of interpretation. See Chapter 2 (Andrea Bianchi).

[37] Foucault, 'Nietzsche, Genealogy, History', 146.

sanctioned dominant interpretive paradigm that it has become.[38] Therefore, this section also identifies a series of factors prevailing at the time when the VCLT regime came into being that could plausibly explain textualism's official victory.

A. Textualism as panacea against the structural shortcomings of international law

Due to some structural features of international law, the preference for textualism is a seldom-questioned and deeply rooted feature of the discipline of international law. Consider a stunning feature of the scholarly discussions relating to interpretation in international law: while interpretive methodologies are subject to endless debates in the domestic law scholarship, one would be hard-pressed to find something even remotely similar in range or depth in the context of international law. For instance, there seems to be virtually no scholarly writing offering a well-developed intentionalist interpretive philosophy for treaty interpretation.[39] The temptation is strong to explain this state of affairs by the fact that, unlike what happens in most domestic legal systems, there exists a set of well-defined rules on interpretation in international law. What would be the point of abstract theorizing if conclusive interpretive choices have already been made officially?

Such temptation should be resisted, however, not only because of the obvious anti-intellectualism underpinning it, but fundamentally because the predilection for textualism is not concomitant with the Vienna Convention. Even though textualism has not always been dominant in the official interpretive discourse, it has always been given a clear preference in the intellectual history of international law.

One needs to pause to consider the benefits traditionally attached to literalism in the positivist legal tradition to appreciate the full implications of such a pro-textualist preference. Literalism is usually thought to reduce interpretation's empire by limiting the need for interpretation to the greatest possible extent. Such attempts to keep the game of interpretation within manageable proportions constitute one of the basic tenets of positivist thinking. One need go no further than HLA Hart's jurisprudence to illustrate the point. As is well known, Hart's famous distinction between 'a core of settled meaning', which supposedly imposes itself naturally, and 'a penumbra of doubt', which implies an interpretive discretion, is based on the view that the very possibility of communication in law centrally depends on the existence of a core of undisputed legal meaning.[40]

---

[38] After all, the provision of international courts with compulsory jurisdiction has long been cherished by international law scholars, but the consensual basis of the jurisdiction of international tribunals has remained undisturbed to date.

[39] The Report prepared by Sir Hersch Lauterpacht for the *Institut de Droit international* is a remarkable exception. See 'De l'interprétation des traités. Rapport et projets de Résolutions présentés par M. H. Lauterpacht' (1950) 43 *Annuaire de l'Institut de droit international* 366.

[40] HLA Hart, 'Positivism and the Separation of Law and Morals' (1958) 71 Harv L Rev 593, 614 ('[T]he hard core of settled meaning is law in some centrally important sense'). For an excellent analysis of Hart's jurisprudence along these lines, see Stanley Fish, *Doing What Comes Naturally: Change, Rhetoric, and the Practice of Theory in Literary and Legal Studies* (Duke University Press 1990) 508.

Since positivism is also the language of the official international legal discourse, the foregoing is equally valid in international law. However, in the case of international law, there has always been an additional reason for constraining the game of interpretation. Owing to its decentralized nature, international society possesses no 'authoritative law-declaring machinery'.[41] By virtue of its sovereignty, each state is considered to be the interpreter of its own rights and obligations.[42] Recognized as an inherent feature of international society, this 'boundless legal relativism' has always deeply preoccupied international lawyers.[43]

Vattel's famous distinction between 'the necessary Law of Nations' and 'the voluntary Law of Nations' bears witness to such a preoccupation.[44] The former is 'that law which results from applying the natural law to Nations'.[45] Each nation must observe the prescriptions of the necessary law of nations. However, given that nations are all free and independent, 'it is for each Nation to decide what its conscience demands of it, what it can or can not do'.[46] Vattel forcefully highlights the danger involved in such relativism as follows:

> But how shall this law be made to prevail in the quarrels of the Nations and sovereigns who live together in the state of nature? They recognize no superior who shall decide between them and define the rights and obligations of each, who shall say to this one, 'You have a right to take up arms, to attack your enemy and subdue him by force,' and to that other, 'Your hostilities are unwarranted, your victories are but murder, your conquests are but the spoil of robbery and pillage'.[47]

It is here that 'the voluntary Law of Nations' comes into play in Vattel's theory:

> Let us, therefore, leave to the conscience of sovereigns the observance of the natural and necessary law in all its strictness ... But as regards the external operation of that law in human society, we must necessarily have recourse to certain rules of more certain and easy application, and this in the interest of the safety and welfare of the great society of the human race. These rules are those of the voluntary Law of Nations.[48]

This desire to avoid abandoning international law to the subjective appreciation of states has understandably been powerfully present in the realm of interpretation. It is no accident that the treatment of interpretation in the classic international law literature is replete with examples designed to show why ordinary

---

[41] James L Brierly, *The Law of Nations: An Introduction to the International Law of Peace* (Clarendon Press 1949) 76.

[42] *Lake Lanoux Arbitration* (1957) 12 RIAA 28 ('It is for each State to evaluate in a reasonable manner and in good faith the situations and rules which will involve it in controversies'); *Air Service Agreement of 27 March 1946 between the United States of America and France* (1978) 18 RIAA 417, 443 ('Under the rules of present-day international law, and unless the contrary results from special obligations arising under particular treaties, notably from mechanisms created within the framework of international organisations, each State establishes for itself its legal situation vis-à-vis other States').

[43] Paul Reuter, 'Principes de droit international public' (1961) 103 Recueil des Cours 425, 440.

[44] Emerich de Vattel, *The Law of Nations or the Principles of Natural Law Applied to the Conduct and to the Affairs of Nations and of Sovereigns* (Carnegie 1916) 4, 8.

[45] Vattel, *The Law of Nations*, 4.   [46] Vattel, *The Law of Nations*, 6.

[47] Vattel, *The Law of Nations*, 304.   [48] Vattel, *The Law of Nations*, 304.

meaning is an indispensable device to avoid perfidy.[49] Vattel pursued this trend to its logical extreme by banning interpretation altogether in standard instances of treaty application, on the basis that 'it is not permissible to interpret what has no need of interpretation'.[50] As Vattel pointed out, this maxim, among others, was expected to 'frustrate the designs of one who enters into the contract in bad faith..., to repress fraud and to prevent the effect of its tricks'.[51]

The preference for textualism seems therefore to reflect the constant concern of international lawyers to place international law upon solid foundations, incapable of being manipulated by states in pursuit of their subjective interests. There are at least two reasons for such concern. First, what is at stake is nothing less than the very existence of international law. International law cannot survive as a legal order unless it is somehow dissociated from its wholly unconstrained subjective interpretations by states.[52]

The second reason has to do with the basic mission of international law, which is generally regarded as consisting in bringing and maintaining some sort of order in an otherwise anarchical society.[53] That the power of auto-interpretation may be a source of danger for this perennial mission hardly needs elaboration. Given that the principle of equality of states implies that no state is legally bound by the interpretation put forward by another state,[54] the power of auto-interpretation has the potential to generate disputes.[55] Coupled with the fact that 'no State can, without its consent, be compelled to submit its disputes with other States either to mediation or to arbitration, or to any other kind of pacific settlement',[56] the danger of unrestrained auto-interpretive power cannot be over-estimated.

[49] Hugo Grotius, *De Jure Belli Ac Pacis* (Clarendon Press 1925) 410 ('The Locrians...availed themselves of a stupid evasion in their perfidy; for they took oath that they would keep the agreement as long as they should stand on that ground and should bear heads on their shoulders; then they threw away the earth which they had placed in their shoes, and the heads of garlic which they had laid on their shoulders, as if in that manner they could free themselves from the religious obligation'). See also Samuel Pufendorf, *De Jure Naturae et Gentium* (Clarendon Press 1934) 795.

[50] Vattel, *The Law of Nations*, 199.   [51] Vattel, *The Law of Nations*, 199.

[52] The International Military Tribunal in Nuremberg expressed the same view when holding that 'whether action taken under the claim of self-defense was in fact aggressive or defensive must ultimately be subject to investigation and adjudication if international law is ever to be enforced': Trial of the Major War Criminals, Nuremberg, 1947, vol I, 208.

[53] See eg Rein Müllerson, *Ordering Anarchy: International Law in International Society* (Kluwer Law 2000). The World Court has also emphasized the role of international law in maintaining the coexistence of independent entities. See *The Case of the SS Lotus (France v Turkey)* (Judgment) PCIJ Rep Series A No 10, 18; *Delimitation of the Maritime Boundary in the Gulf of Maine Area (Canada/ USA)* (Judgment) [1984] ICJ Rep 246, 299.

[54] Jules Basdevant, 'Règles générales du droit de la paix' (1936) 58 Recueil des Cours 471, 589.

[55] *Lake Lanoux*. See also Georges Abi-Saab, 'Interprétation et auto-interprétation. Quelques réflexions sur leur rôle dans la formation et la résolution du différend international' in Ulrich Beyerlin, Michael Bothe, Rainer Hofmann, and Ernst-Ulrich Petersmann (eds), *Festschrift für Rudolf Bernhardt* (Springer-Verlag 1995) 9, 16–18.

[56] *Status of Eastern Carelia* (Advisory Opinion) PCIJ Rep Series B No 5, 7, 27. See also *Rights of Minorities in Upper Silesia (Minority Schools) (Germany v Poland)* (Judgment) PCIJ Rep Series A No 15, 4, 22; *Corfu Channel (UK v Albania)* (Judgment) [1948] ICJ Rep 15, 27; *Anglo-Iranian Oil Co (UK v Iran)* (Judgment) [1952] ICJ Rep 93, 103; *Monetary Gold Removed from Rome in 1943 (Italy v France, UK, USA)* (Judgment) [1954] ICJ Rep 19, 32; *Continental Shelf (Libyan Arab Jamahiriya/ Malta)* (Judgment) [1984] ICJ Rep 3, 22; *Land, Island and Maritime Frontier Dispute (El Salvador/ Honduras, Nicaragua intervening)* (Judgment) [1990] ICJ Rep 92, 133; *Case concerning East Timor (Portugal v Australia)* (Judgment) [1995] ICJ Rep 90, 101.

To prevent this danger, international lawyers have devised certain strategies to contain the game of interpretation. One of them is the principle of good faith. Although it is the case that every state has the power to interpret its rights and obligations, it must do so 'honestly'.[57] Textualism is another such device to the extent that it is expected to intervene preventively by delegitimizing self-interested misreadings that do not comport with what passes for the ordinary meaning of the terms used in treaties.

B. The phenomenon of permanent international tribunals

For reasons that are not hard to explain, the marginalization of the intention of the parties in the process of treaty interpretation seems to be largely coextensive with the rise of permanent international courts and tribunals. An important feature of permanent tribunals is that they are, by definition, more distanced from the parties than an arbitral tribunal. While the former has a standing composition and does not owe its existence to the parties before it, the latter is intimately tied up with the parties, who appoint 'judges of their own choice' to settle their disputes.[58] Consequently, party-originated arbitral bodies are usually considered more as a common organ of the parties,[59] than a truly independent 'organ of international law'.[60] This explains why permanent standing tribunals conceive of their mission differently from arbitral tribunals. While arbitration was 'characterized frequently by the need for mutual accommodation, for an arrangement which would give offence to neither party',[61] permanent tribunals are ordinarily expected to settle disputes on the strict basis of the law.

Such a fundamental difference between the two proceedings could not fail to impact on their respective interpretive methodologies. While arbitral tribunals were bound to be careful in tracing their interpretations back to the intention of the parties from which they derived their legitimacy, permanent tribunals feel less constrained in this regard and more entitled to place priority on 'objective' elements. An important sign of this tendency has been the remarkable decrease in the importance attached to *travaux préparatoires* in the process of interpretation. The Permanent Court of International Justice (PCIJ) paved the way by laying down the rule that recourse to *travaux préparatoires* was unnecessary when the

---

[57] Basdevant, 'Règles générales du droit de la paix', 588.
[58] Hague Convention for the Pacific Settlement of International Disputes of 1899 and 1907, Article XV.
[59] David Caron, 'Towards a Political Theory of International Courts and Tribunals' (2006) 24 Berk J Intl L 401, 404 (noting that '[m]embers of a party-originated tribunal believe themselves to be working for the parties'). See also Dinah Shelton, 'Form, Function, and the Powers of International Courts' (2008–2009) 9 Chi J Int'l L 537, 543.
[60] That is how the PCIJ once characterized itself: see *Certain German Interests in Polish Upper Silesia* (Merits) PCIJ Rep Series A No 7, 1, 19.
[61] General Assembly, Official Records, 13th Session, 6th Committee, 65–6.

treaty language was clear.[62] The same rule was reaffirmed by the ICJ.[63] Given the authority enjoyed by these two courts, it is safe to conclude that their largely intention-free interpretive philosophy has significantly contributed to the shaping of the modern discourse on interpretation in international law.

C. Textualism as an ideological device: using the same words to mean different things

In his commentary on Max Weber, Julien Freund points out that the privilege enjoyed by written instruments is an urban phenomenon, as a matter of social history.[64] Whereas rural communities tended to rely on the virtues of oral discussions, merchants in the cities gave priority to written contracts. As Freund explains, what is at issue here is the difference between 'commercial exchanges between anonymous persons and accommodations between individuals who know each other personally'.[65] Where common experience and shared world-views are lacking, abstract generalizations tend to dominate communication.

This sociological insight seems relevant in explaining why textualism officially gained pre-eminence in the historical circumstances prevailing in the 1960s. The importance of a community of shared values, interests, and principles for the harmonious functioning of any legal system hardly needs further elaboration.[66] What makes the period of the elaboration of the VCLT somewhat special in this regard is the profound ideological schism dividing international society. Ideological confrontation between the communist bloc and the capitalist countries was so pervasive that international lawyers were deeply pessimistic as to the prospect of the development of international law under such circumstances.[67] Writing in this period, Charles de Visscher pointed out that 'the spread of new political ideologies and the sudden entry of peoples of highly diverse civilizations into international relations drastically reduced the common ethical basis of international law'.[68] Some international lawyers went so far as to suggest that a community of selected states should be set up with a view to laying down a separate law for the free world.[69]

---

[62] See eg *Lotus*, 16. On the difference between the treatments of *travaux préparatoires* in the case law of the PCIJ and arbitral jurisprudence, see Charles Rousseau, *Principes généraux du droit international public* (Pedone 1944) 749.

[63] *Conditions of Admission of a State to Membership in the United Nations (Article 4 of the Charter)* (Advisory Opinion) [1948] ICJ Rep 57, 63; *Competence of the General Assembly for the Admission of a State to the United Nations* (Advisory Opinion) [1950] ICJ Rep 4, 8.

[64] Julien Freund, *Etudes sur Max Weber* (Librairie Droz 1990) 245.

[65] Freund, *Etudes sur Max Weber*, 245.

[66] The point was eloquently made from the standpoint of international law by Charles de Visscher in his masterpiece, *Theory and Reality in Public International Law* (Princeton University Press 1968) 140–1.

[67] Kurt Wilk, 'International Law and Global Ideological Conflict: Reflections on the Universality of International Law' (1951) 45 AJIL 648; Quincy Wright, 'International Law and Ideologies' (1954) 48 AJIL 616; Joseph Kunz, 'La crise et la transformation du droit des gens' (1955) 88 Recueil des Cours 1.

[68] de Visscher, *Theory and Reality in Public International Law*, 141.

[69] Philip Jessup, *The Use of International Law* (University of Michigan 1959) 29, 153; Frederik Van Asbeck, 'Growth and Movement of International Law' (1962) 11 ICLQ 1071 ('As long as the

Intentionalism could have hardly been an attractive option under such circumstances because any search for common intentions was likely to be a largely hopeless enterprise.[70] The then US Secretary of State, John Foster Dulles, aptly described this reality:

> An agreement is a meeting of minds, and so far I do not know of any agreement that the Soviet Union has made which has reflected a real meeting of the minds. We may have agreed on the same form of words, but there has not been a meeting of the minds.[71]

Analysing the consequences of ideological conflict for international law, the leading Soviet international lawyer Grigory Tunkin made a strikingly similar point.[72] According to Tunkin, if ideological conflicts did not prevent agreement on technical aspects of international law, the same could not be said of the prospect for agreement on value-laden concepts such as 'justice', 'social progress', or 'democracy', for those concepts could not possibly have the same significance for opposing ideological blocks.[73] Such a climate of mutual distrust was bound to reflect itself in the choice of official interpretive methodology. It is therefore no accident that the amendment to the draft Vienna Convention proposed by the US delegation, which sought to deny textualism any hierarchically superior status, was regarded by the Soviet representative as 'politically dangerous'.[74]

In view of the foregoing, it becomes easier to understand why the Soviet delegation defended textualism as opposed to intentionalism, despite the indisputable political preference of the Soviet Union for the voluntarist conception of international law. The idea that the USSR could conceivably have a common intention with 'bourgeois' states was utterly unacceptable in terms of the Soviet doctrine of international law, as Tunkin explained in his *Theory of International Law*: 'The character of [the will of a state] is determined by the nature of the state: in capitalist countries, it is the will of the ruling class in the state concerned; in the Soviet state...it is the will of the entire people'.[75] Such ideological stakes plausibly

antagonism in fundamental convictions continues to divide the world, the road to an international legal order for the world as a whole lies barred...Let us then work all the more strenuously to achieve a real regional legal order').

[70] See the remarks by M Van Asbeck in (1956) 46 *Annuaire de l'Institut de Droit international* 343 ('il est normal que l'exégèse d'un texte revête une importance plus grande en droit international que dans les droits internes vu le manque d'unité de vision et de conception dans la société internationale').

[71] (1957) 37 *Department of State Bulletin* No 958, 711–12. See also Wilk, 'International Law and Global Ideological Conflict', 668.

[72] Grigory I Tunkin, 'Le conflit idéologique et le droit international contemporain' in *Recueil d'études de droit international en hommage à Paul Guggenheim* (Imprimerie de la Tribune de Genève 1968) 888–98.

[73] Tunkin, 'Le conflit idéologique et le droit international contemporain', 896.

[74] United Nations Conference on the Law of Treaties, First Session, Vienna, 26 March–24 May 1968, Official Records, Thirty-Second Meeting, 20 April 1968, 175.

[75] Grigory I Tunkin, *Theory of International Law* (Harvard University Press 1974) 211. This explains why the Soviet international legal scholars had to revise the classic voluntarist conception of international law, given the emphasis of the latter on the idea of 'common will'. See Grigory I Tunkin, 'Co-existence and International Law' (1958) 95 Recueil des Cours 35: 'This co-ordination

account for the somewhat counter-intuitive pro-textualist stance of the communist bloc countries.

D. Textualism as a sovereignty-protective device

International society underwent major transformations in the 1950s and 1960s as dozens of former colonial territories acceded to statehood through decolonization. This was more than a mere numeric change in the composition of international society, as the newly independent states levelled a systemic challenge against international law and the very way in which the latter was traditionally conceived to function.[76] As Michel Virally pointed out, the newly independent states were highly sceptical regarding an international law that had historically legitimized their colonization and that was currently of no help in resolving their development problems.[77] Such deeply rooted suspicion towards international law explains why these states were strongly attached to their sovereignty, endeavouring to rely on it in their fight to change the structure and content of classic international law, in the making of which they had been in no position to participate. In such circumstances, the newly independent states generally considered treaties as more responsive to their interests and needs.[78] Many reasons could justify such a preference. For one thing, compared to custom, treaties provided a rationally structured and much more meaningful way to participate in the making of international law. For another, given their basis in state consent, treaties were deemed more respectful of the sovereignty of the newly independent states.

What the foregoing shows is that much was at stake for the newly independent states in the choice of official methodology for treaty interpretation.[79] There are

---

of wills of the States...does not signify their merging into some kind of "common will" or "single will". To explain that these wills cannot fuse, it is sufficient to say that their class natures, expressed in the aims and tasks of the States concerned, are different and even antagonistic (the wills of socialist and capitalist States).'

[76] See eg Wilfred Jenks, *The Common Law of Mankind* (Stevens Sons 1958) 63; Bert Röling, *International Law in an Expanded World* (Djambatan 1960); JJG Syatauw, *Some Newly Established Asian States and the Development of International Law* (Martinus Nijhoff 1961); Jorge Castaneda, 'The Underdeveloped Nations and the Development of International Law' (1961) 15 Int'l Org 38; RP Anand, 'Role of the "New" Asian-African Countries in the Present International Legal Order' (1962) 56 AJIL 383; Georges Abi-Saab, 'The Newly Independent States and the Rules of International Law: An Outline' (1962) 8 How L J 95; S Prakash Sinha, 'Perspective of the Newly Independent States on the Binding Quality of International Law' (1965) 14 ICLQ 21; RP Anand, 'Attitude of the Asian-African States toward Certain Problems of International Law' (1966) 15 ICLQ 55; Angelo Piero Sereni, 'Les nouveaux Etats et le droit international' (1968) 72 RGDIP 305.

[77] Michel Virally, 'Le droit international en question' (1963) 8 *Archives de philosophie du droit* 150.

[78] Marion Mushkat, 'The African Approach to Some Basic Problems of Modern International Law' (1967) 7 IJIL 357; Patricia Buirette-Maurau, *La participation du Tiers-Monde à l'élaboration du droit international. Essai de qualification* (LGDJ 1983) 72.

[79] Their special interests in this regard were, in fact, explicitly acknowledged. See the statement made by the representative of Yugoslavia during the debates of the Sixth Committee, Official Records of the General Assembly, Twenty-First Session, Sixth Committee, Summary Records of Meetings 20 September–14 December 1966, 907th meeting, 11 October 1966, [22]: 'the interpretation of multilateral treaties [has] become a task of the first importance since the emergence of many new independent States as a result of the process of decolonization. Those rules should take account of the dynamic forces of international life and of the needs of the States that now [form] a majority'.

at least two reasons why intentionalism could not seem attractive to the newly independent states. First, references to intention could be seen by these states as involving a serious risk of manipulation of the scope of their treaty commitments, which was hardly an acceptable prospect for the newly independent states in view of their palpable sovereignty-sensitivity. Second, to the extent that intentionalism was generally regarded as referring to the common intention of the original parties, such an argument could be seen as contradicting the principle of sovereign equality to which the newly independent states were deeply attached. This second reason seems particularly plausible given that it was explicitly voiced both within the ILC,[80] and during the Vienna Conference.[81]

Conclusion

Why the historically contingent nature of the modern interpretive regime in international law has been systematically neglected in international legal scholarship is not easy to explain. One possible reason could be that the VCLT provides a workable interpretive code,[82] which, by virtue of its facially holistic and logical structure and content, tends to be taken as an instantiation of a sort of universal, trans-historical reason. One could also presume that the remarkably consistent invocation of the VCLT interpretive regime by almost all international tribunals might have given rise to its 'objectification'.[83] A further explanation might be that, despite its statement to the contrary, the ILC desired to put an end to long-standing theoretical disputes by making a set of explicit choices and that international lawyers since then have refrained from invigorating old debates in order to avoid undermining the nascent VCLT regime. This explanation is not implausible. As Albert O Hirschman stated, 'once [collectively] desired effects fail to happen and refuse to come into the world, the fact that they were originally counted on is

---

[80] See the remarks by Manfred Lachs (1964) I ILC Ybk 286: 'The burden of the operation of a treaty, in the light of the realities of international relations, fell upon all its signatories; there was therefore no reason for giving a higher standing to the intentions of the original parties in the matter of interpretation'.

[81] See the remarks by Ian Sinclair, representative of the United Kingdom, United Nations Conference on the Law of Treaties, First Session, Vienna, 26 March–24 May 1968, Official Records, Thirty-Third Meeting, 22 April 1968, 177: '[I]n the case of many important multilateral conventions, some of the parties might have joined by subsequent accession, particularly in the case of new States which had not been in a position to participate in preparing the original instruments. It was hardly possible to interpret the rights and obligations of those acceding States in the light of the supposed common intention of the original drafters.'

[82] See the statement made by the ILC Special Rapporteur at the UN Conference on the Law of Treaties, Official Records of the Conference, First Session (26 March–24 May 1968) 184. See also the remarks by S Rosenne, (1964) I ILC Ybk 289 (noting that 'interpretation should not be viewed as an academic intellectual exercise performed in the abstract but as a practical process undertaken in concrete political circumstances').

[83] As shown in a seminal sociological treatise, the historical contingency of any 'objectified' institution tends to be forgotten. See Peter L Berger and Thomas Luckmann, *The Social Construction of Reality: A Treatise in the Sociology of Knowledge* (Anchor 1967) 70.

likely to be not only forgotten but actively repressed'.[84] It is a fact that the much-praised qualities of the VCLT regime have proved vastly exaggerated in practice. Not only has the VCLT regime failed to prevent interpretive controversies, which are as vivid and frequent as before, but the VCLT rules themselves are often part of these controversies inasmuch as they can support more than one interpretive outcome.[85]

Whatever the explanation might be, it is hoped that the present chapter has made the case that the historical contingency of the treaty interpretation regime that prevails today in international law needs to be openly acknowledged and broadly investigated. Further research could well identify other possibly relevant circumstances and factors that might account for the interpretive apparatus of modern international law. However, that the latter cannot claim any trans-historical validity seems fairly certain.

[84] Albert O Hirschman, *The Passions and the Interests: Political Arguments for Capitalism before its Triumph* (Princeton University Press 1977) 131.
[85] See Chapter 18 (Philip Allott), 375.

13

Theorizing Precedent in International Law

Harlan Grant Cohen

Introduction

In February 2013, NBC News released a leaked US Department of Justice (DOJ) White Paper on the 'Lawfulness of a Lethal Operation Against a US Citizen Who Is a Senior Operational Leader of Al-Qa'ida or An Associated Force'.[1] The memo, which laid out the US Government's legal reasoning and criteria for such targeted attacks, set off a firestorm of commentary.[2] Commentators pulled apart the document to understand and critique the Government's position. One thing less noticed—unsurprisingly, given the importance of the substantive debate—was the curious citation to *Prosecutor v Tadic*, a decision of the International Criminal Tribunal for the former Yugoslavia (ICTY).[3]

The citation appears almost as a throwaway, part of an argument by 'some commentators' about the scope of an armed conflict to which the memo-writer is responding.[4] And yet, it is notable that it appears at all in a 'confidential' memo intended for internal DOJ consumption. Moreover, the framing of the paragraph suggests that the decision does stand for the proposition 'that an armed conflict exists whenever there is...protracted armed violence between governmental authorities and organized armed groups'. The memo-writer's argument is that the commentators are simply misreading that precedent to find an international law limitation on the scope of armed conflict. The implication is that the *Tadic* decision is one the US Government needs to know about and needs to be able to

---

[1] Department of Justice White Paper, 'Lawfulness of a Lethal Operation Against a US Citizen Who Is a Senior Operational Leader of Al-Qa'ida or An Associated Force' (*MSNBCMedia*) <http://www.4 <msnbcmedia.msn.com/i/msnbc/sections/news/020413_DOJ_White_Paper.pdf> accessed 22 March 2014 (hereinafter DOJ White Paper).

[2] See eg David Kaye, 'International Law Issues in the Department of Justice White Paper on Targeted Killing' (2013) 17/8 ASIL <http://www.asil.org/insights/volume/17/issue/8/international-law-issues-department-justice-white-paper-targeted-killing> accessed 23 March 2014.

[3] DOJ White Paper, 4, citing *Prosecutor v Tadic* (Decision on the Motion for Interlocutory Appeal on Jurisdiction) Case No IT-94-1-A, ICTY Appeals Chamber, 2 October 1995, [70].

[4] DOJ White Paper, 4.

distinguish. The commentators' argument about the *meaning* of *Tadic* needs to be rebutted.

None of this would be surprising if the decisions of international tribunals were, as a matter of doctrine, given precedential weight. But in fact, the opposite has always been the case. International law today, like international law a century ago, generally denies international precedents doctrinal force. Since at least the establishment of the Permanent Court of International Justice in 1922, judicial decisions have been relegated to 'subsidiary means for the determination of rules of law'.[5] This understanding, carried into Article 38 of the Statute of the International Court of Justice (ICJ),[6] and reified by casebooks and treatises as part of international law's 'doctrine of sources',[7] has meant that as a matter of international law doctrine, judicial decisions construing international law are not in and of themselves law—decisions are not binding on future parties in future cases, even before the same tribunal.[8] Precedent, as a matter of doctrine, exerts no special force. This is an understanding that states like the US have strenuously protected.[9]

And yet, as in the DOJ White Paper, the invocation of international decisions as precedent is ubiquitous. Reports from international investment arbitration,[10] international criminal law,[11] international human rights,[12] and international trade[13] all testify to precedent's apparent authority. Across international law, practitioners invoke it and tribunals apply it. This would be remarkable if courts and tribunals simply cited their own precedent as international law doctrine requires no such result. But courts and tribunals go much farther (following the lead of international advocates), citing positively or negatively even the decisions of other unrelated courts and tribunals emanating from different areas of international

[5] Statute of the Permanent Court of International Justice, Article 38(4) (16 December 1920) 6 LNTS 380.

[6] Statute of the International Court of Justice, Article 38(1)(d) (26 June 1945) 59 Stat 1055, 1060 (ICJ Statute).

[7] See eg Henry J Steiner, Detlev F Vagts, and Harold Hongju Koh, *Transnational Legal Problems: Materials and Text* (4th edn, University Casebook Series 1994) 232; Lori F Damrosch, Louis Henkin, Richard Crawford Pugh, Oscar Schachter, and Hans Smit, *International Law: Cases and Materials* (4th edn, West Group 2001) 56–7.

[8] ICJ Statute, Article 38(1)(d), Article 59 ('The decision of the Court has no binding force except between the parties and in respect of that particular case').

[9] See Brief for the United States as Amicus Curiae Supporting Respondents, *Bustillo v Johnson* [2006] 271823 WL 30 ('The United States has no obligation to accept the reasoning underlying the ICJ's judgments, however, or to apply that reasoning in other cases'). The United States has also objected to a doctrine of *stare decisis* at the WTO. See WTO, *Minutes of DSB Meeting held 20 May 2008*, WT/DSB/M/250 (1 July 2008) 9 ff.

[10] See eg *Int'l Thunderbird Gaming Corp v United Mexican States* (Final Award) (26 January 2006) 2006 WL 247692, [129] ('In international and international economic law...there may not be a formal "stare decisis" rule as in common law countries, but precedent plays an important role').

[11] See eg Alexander KA Greenawalt, 'The Pluralism of International Criminal Law' (2011) 86 Ind LJ 1063, 1073–8.

[12] See eg Christina Binder, 'The Prohibition of Amnesties by the Inter-American Court of Human Rights' (2011) 12 German LJ 1203, 1204.

[13] See eg Raj Bhala, 'The Myth about Stare Decisis and International Trade Law (Part One of a Trilogy)' (1999) 14 Am U Int'l L Rev 845, 850.

law, with different mandates. The precedents from one regional body are argued to others,[14] precedents from human rights courts are argued to investment tribunals,[15] and precedents from ad hoc criminal tribunals are applied to domestic civil judgments.[16] The widely cited *Tadic* case,[17] referenced in the DOJ White Paper, has even made appearances in the decisions of ICSID arbitration panels.[18] And citations by courts and tribunals can only begin to capture the much wider practice of invoking these decisions in arguments and discussions, formal and informal, over the law's meaning.

So why does an ICTY decision carry weight in internal US Executive Branch discussions? Or in broader terms, when and why do particular decisions become precedents? This chapter begins to answer that question. Its goal is to develop a framework for a broader account of international precedent's emergence. To use this book's metaphor, in the game of international interpretation, what are the spoken and unspoken strategies of precedent? Why will certain prior interpretations be invoked in certain contexts and with certain audiences? When will those strategies be effective, forcing other actors to respond to a prior interpretation, echoing it, building upon it, or distinguishing it?

For the most part, existing discussions of international precedent fail to deal squarely with the question asked here. Many observers have noted the emergence of precedent within particular fields;[19] some have even opined as to whether that trend is good or bad.[20] But few have gone further to ask why a system or habit of precedent has emerged in the first place, let alone to explain the varied shapes those systems or habits might take. Other accounts have dealt with the question obliquely, focusing on: (1) *delegation*, (2) *compliance*, or (3) *strategy*. Part I surveys some of these approaches. Although each captures some aspect of international precedent's story, even considered together, pages—even chapters—seem missing.

---

[14] See eg Laurence R Helfer, 'Overlegalizing Human Rights: International Relations Theory and the Commonwealth Caribbean Backlash Against Human Rights Regimes' (2002) 102 Colum L Rev 1832 (describing ECtHR *Soering* precedent's migration to other bodies).

[15] See generally Andrea K Bjorklund and Sophie Nappert, 'Beyond Fragmentation' (2010) UC Davis Legal Studies Research Paper No 243, 439 <http://papers.ssrn.com/sol3/papers.cfm?abstract_id=1739997> accessed 22 March 2014.

[16] US courts have, for example, turned to the jurisprudence of the ICTY and ICTR to ascertain the standard for aiding and abetting liability under the Alien Tort Statute, 28 USC §1350. Compare *Sarei v Rio Tinto PLC* 671 F 3d 736 (9th Cir 2011) with *Presbyterian Church of Sudan v Talisman Energy Inc* 582 F 3d 244 (2d Cir 2009).

[17] *Prosecutor v Duško Tadic* (Judgment) ICTY-94-1-A (November 1999). See also Harlan Grant Cohen, 'Lawyers and Precedent' (2013) 46 Vand J Transnat'l L 1025 (further describing *Tadic*'s wide dispersion).

[18] See eg International Centre for the Settlement of Investment Disputes *Teinver SA Transportes de Cercanias SA Autobuses Urbanos del Sur SA v Argentine Republic* (Decision on Jurisdiction and Separate Opinion of Arbitrator Kamal Hossain) ICSID Case No ARB/09/1.

[19] See nn 10–13 and accompanying text.

[20] See eg Meredith Crowley and Robert Howse, 'US–Stainless Steel (Mexico)' (2010) 9 World Trade Rev 117 (considering *stare decisis* a valuable development at the WTO); Irene M Ten-Cate, 'The Costs of Consistency: Precedent in Investment Treaty Arbitration' (2013) 51 Colum J Transnat'l L 418, 421 (arguing against precedent in investment arbitration).

Part II starts from the beginning and imagines what a full story of international precedent would need to incorporate. Each of the prevailing accounts focuses on a particular moment: a tribunal's creation, a decision whether to comply, or the choice of an advocacy strategy. In each, precedent is a choice. A fuller account of precedent needs to look at international law between those moments, to look at international law as an ongoing, dynamic practice in which precedent is as much a burden as a choice, exerting independent pressure on actors that reframes the choices available to them. (The assumption implicit in each of the prior accounts is that the choice being made has consequences, and that someone, either themselves or another, will be burdened by what they choose.) Using the metaphor of the game, existing accounts focus on individual moves international players make. But those moves only have meaning within the broader strategies players employ and respond to in a larger, longer game. They can only be understood in relation to prior moves and to the game's overall culture(s). Precedent must be understood within the *practice* of international law.

By focusing on precedent's potential role in international law practice, we can start to tease apart the factors that might contribute to a precedent's emergence. Part II continues by identifying three clusters of factors whose interaction dictate the weight accorded to a particular interpretation of the law: (1) the range of sources that might be treated as precedential in international law; (2) the list of factors that might imbue an interpretation with authority; and (3) the actors who take part in that practice (and judge a source's weight).

Part III sets those factors in motion and tells three overlapping stories about precedent—one jurisprudential, a second sociological, and a third rationalist. It then looks at two examples, official immunity and self-defence against non-state actors, to explore how these three stories interact with one another.

I. Precedent's Purpose

Although the presence of precedent in international law is now widely acknowledged, few have sought to explain its emergence, at least not directly. This is somewhat surprising, given the apparent disparity between this reality and the one described by traditional doctrine. Accounts that touch on the issue tend to focus not on precedent itself, but on other related but somewhat tangential questions.

A. Delegation

Precedent sometimes comes up in discussions concerning the creation of international courts or tribunals and their respective mandates. To what extent have states granted tribunals the power to issue binding judgments, to speak authoritatively with regard to the law they are applying, and to bind future courts that might hear the same or a similar legal issue? Some of these accounts are positivist, starting with the constitutive agreement establishing the court and asking what, if anything, those documents say about the force of that court's judgments. In these accounts, precedent is a design feature to be chosen or rejected by a tribunal's designers. Some have read these documents to suggest at least limited forms of horizontal or vertical *stare decisis*.[21] In general though, support for precedential force is hard to find in positivist readings of these agreements which, if not denying precedent force (as in the case of the ICJ statute), are silent on the matter.[22] As a result, these accounts have a hard time explaining the rampant recourse to those tribunals' decisions as precedent.

Other accounts take a more functional approach, asking less what a particular treaty or statute explicitly says than what it implies. These accounts might focus on the structure of a dispute settlement procedure, on the open-endedness of the substantive obligations the tribunal is meant to interpret, or on the presence of third party rights holders as suggestive of a broader delegation to the tribunal.[23] From a functional standpoint, the suggestion is that states creating the tribunal *must* have intended the tribunal to have a certain amount of interpretive authority. Such moves have been used to defend the authority of World Trade Organization (WTO) Appellate Body and European Court of Human Rights (ECtHR) decisions. Although these accounts do a better job justifying at least some recourse to precedent in legal argumentation, suggesting that some regimes are designed with precedent in mind, they often rely more on *ex ante* normative conclusions about precedent's desirability for a particular regime than text or explicit state consent.[24] Unsurprisingly, their suggestions are often highly contested.

B. Compliance

According to some rationalist accounts of courts and compliance, precedent might emerge simply because it is useful.[25] In some contexts, states may disagree over a particular rule, each preferring a particular interpretation, yet nonetheless prefer coordination to continued disagreement. To the extent third party adjudication can provide a mutually acceptable rule, involving sufficient benefits for each party, continuing to hew to that rule may be desirable.[26] According to this explanation, precedent is merely epiphenomenal. A precedent's force derives solely from the desirability of the rule reflected in it. Neither its status as the opinion of

---

[21] Krzysztof J Pelc, 'The Politics of Precedent in International Law: A Social Network Application' (2013) APSA Annual Meeting Paper <http://papers.ssrn.com/sol3/papers.cfm?abstract_id=2299638> accessed 22 March 2014.

[22] Crowley and Howse, 'US–Stainless Steel (Mexico)' (describing silence of the WTO Dispute Settlement Understanding and the ICTY Statute). The notable exception is the Rome Statute of the International Criminal Court, Article 21.2 (17 July 1998) 2187 UNTS 90 ('The Court may apply principles and rules of law as interpreted in its previous decisions').

[23] See eg Crowley and Howse, 'US–Stainless Steel (Mexico)' (describing functionalist argument for WTO and ICTY *stare decisis*); Karen J Alter, 'Agents or Trustees? International Courts in Their Political Context' (2008) 14 Eur J Int'l Rel 33, 38–9.

[24] See eg Anthea Roberts, 'Power and Persuasion in Investment Treaty Interpretation: The Dual Role of States' (2010) 104 AJIL 179, 206–7.

[25] See generally Eric A Posner and John C Yoo, 'Judicial Independence in International Tribunals' (2005) 93 Cal L Rev 1.

[26] Posner and Yoo, 'Judicial Independence in International Tribunals', 18.

some body nor its internal reasoning have any independent effect. Although such accounts may explain the stickiness of some international precedents, they have a hard time explaining precedent in non-coordination games like human rights, or why arguments from precedent would have any force when the underlying decision goes against state interests.[27]

C. Strategy

Still other accounts consider precedent from the standpoint of strategy. Arguing to a body from its own precedent may make it more favourably inclined to your position. This is true both for advocates to courts or tribunals and for courts or tribunals seeking the support of other courts, something empirical data regarding the European Court of Justice (ECJ), ECtHR, and national court precedent bears out.[28] Such accounts bring us closer to understanding precedent's role as advocacy, but they too fail to capture why advocates regularly cite precedents from courts other than the ones they are trying to convince. Perhaps citing other bodies lends prestige,[29] but this begs the question where such prestige would come from. Why would particular audiences view certain citations in decisions as carrying extra weight? These accounts do suggest some answers in passing, which will be taken up in greater detail below.[30]

A different strategic account treats precedent as soft law.[31] While the prior strategic accounts focus on the citation to specific decisions, this account looks at the strategic value of creating or promoting a system of precedent. States creating a regime may not be able to get full agreement from each other on rules or interpretations they might favour. Expecting that a tribunal might expand the language of a treaty in favoured directions, such states might create a tribunal as a way of legislating rules or interpretations that they could not achieve by agreement.[32] From an individual state's point of view, its legal obligations are defined by predictions of what others will consider lawful and unlawful. States reading the tribunal's views will have to take into account the possibility that that decision will be treated as binding law by other states and adjust their calculus and

---

[27] See generally Laurence R Helfer and Anne-Marie Slaughter, 'Why States Create International Tribunals: A Response to Professors Posner and Yoo' (2005) 93 Cal L Rev 899.

[28] See eg Laurence R Helfer and Anne-Marie Slaughter, 'Toward a Theory of Effective Transnational Adjudication' (1997) 107 Yale LJ 273; Erik Voeten, 'Does a Professional Judiciary Induce More Compliance?: Evidence from the European Court of Human Rights', 4–6 <http://papers.ssrn.com/sol3/papers.cfm?abstract_id=2029786> accessed 22 March 2014.

[29] Helfer and Slaughter, 'Effective Transnational Adjudication', 325–6 (suggesting that the ECJ and ECtHR enhance each other's prestige by citing each other's decisions).

[30] In examining the attributes of an effective supranational court, Helfer and Slaughter note that strong reasoning, adherence, and coherence may play a role in the perceived legitimacy of specific decisions: Helfer and Slaughter, 'Effective Transnational Adjudication', 319–21.

[31] See generally Andrew T Guzman and Timothy L Meyer, 'International Common Law: The Soft Law of International Tribunals' (2009) 9 Chi J Int'l L 515.

[32] See Pelc, 'The Politics of Precedent in International Law' (arguing WTO members bring disputes with an eye towards favourable precedents victory may establish).

actions accordingly.[33] Precedent becomes a prediction of what other states might expect a rule to require. This takes us farther towards understanding precedent's weight. What this account fails to explain is why states would expect other states to hold them to the interpretations of that tribunal. A key explanatory cog is missing.

Although each of these accounts tells part of the story of precedent's emergence within international law, even together, they cannot explain the extraordinary pervasiveness of precedent's attraction. There are two (intertwined) limitations to these accounts. First, these accounts are almost entirely and exclusively concerned with the inputs and outputs of international law. Each looks at a particular decision point in international law—the drafting of a treaty, the decision whether to comply, or the choice of arguments to make in a brief or a decision—and attempts to explain why particular actors will or will not support the precedential weight of a decision. Second, in focusing on these decisions, each account is largely rationalist in perspective. It looks at the key actors (mostly states, but sometimes courts) as strategic, rational actors who are able to see how giving a decision precedential weight might facilitate or impede their goals. It assumes that these actors can and do calibrate precedent's general impact in a regime or how much weight to give a particular potential precedent.

These focuses, however, fail to fully capture how precedent operates within the legal system. The question is not only why states may consciously create a system of precedent, but also why it emerges even when they do not.[34] The question is not simply why actors choose to invoke certain decisions as precedents, but when and why that choice is effective, when and why that choice carries weight with other actors. Answering these questions requires a broader view of precedent's role within legal argumentation.

Moreover, by focusing on particular actors—the tribunals who claim authority, the actors who decide whether to yield to it, or the actors who invoke it—the accounts are only able to capture a particular angle, a still image of precedent's role. Explaining precedent requires putting these accounts into motion and watching them interact in three dimensions and in 360 degrees. The difference is visible in these accounts' language. Rather than speaking of precedent, they speak of decisions, citations, or compliance. Each depicts a moment in time. But precedent implies a relationship between past, present, and future. An interpretation at one point is imbued with authority at another in the hopes (or fears) that it will be complied with or deemed authoritative in a third. Moreover, precedent's authority is itself dynamic. Whether for philosophical or rationalist reasons, the more a precedent is cited, the more authority it is likely to be given. The reverse is true as well.

---

[33] This description highlights the similarity between international law and more sophisticated multiplayer games in which each player must make their moves with an eye on how other players may react to it.

[34] The soft law account recognizes that this may happen and suggests that states may use this reality to their benefit. See Guzman and Meyer, 'International Common Law'. It does not, however, explain *why* it happens.

II. Precedent as Practice

What is needed then is an account not just of the inputs and outputs of the legal process, but of that process itself. What is needed is an account of the *practice* of international law.[35] Law does not simply provide rules to be followed. Law also sets norms for discerning, interpreting, advocating, and debating the contents of those rules. It provides spoken and unspoken ground-rules that structure an ongoing claim and response over the applicable law. One party argues for one interpretation of the rules; another argues for a different one. The law frames which arguments are better or worse, which arguments will be convincing, and which will fail.

It is in this sense that the law operates like a game, establishing the rules for making interpretative and argumentative moves. And it is in this game, this practice, that precedents gain their legal force and play their role. Precedent might best be understood as the burden prior interpretations of a particular rule put on future arguments about the content or meaning of the rule.[36] In its weakest form, precedent simply supplies an argument that one must respond to; one cannot make an argument about the rule's meaning without some reference to why the prior decision is right, wrong, or distinguishable.[37] In its strongest form, precedent creates a strong presumption that the prior interpretation of the rule is in fact the rule. The question is not why actors do or do not follow precedent, but instead when and why prior interpretations place these burdens on arguments about the rule.

This means that to fully understand how and why interpretations take on weight as precedents, one must understand the process of legal argumentation and the practitioners who take part in it. What sources might those practitioners look to as potential precedents? What are the features of those sources that imbue them with greater or lesser weight in legal arguments? Most of all, who makes up the 'community of practice' in a particular area of international law? It is in the interaction of these three factors that a pattern of precedent will emerge.

A. Source of precedent

Although this chapter has so far been concerned primarily with the precedential effect of the decisions of international court or tribunals, there is a wide range of potential sources that actors could invoke as precedents in their arguments. As noted above, a precedent might be thought of as a prior interpretation of a rule

---

[35] Cf Jutta Brunnée and Stephen J Toope, *Legitimacy and Legality in International Law: An Interactional Account* (CUP 2010) 25–6.

[36] Marc Jacob, 'Precedents: Lawmaking Through International Adjudication' (2011) 12 German LJ 1005, 1019.

[37] Jacob, 'Precedents', 1019 (suggesting that 'deliberately ignoring relevant prior decisions is so arbitrary and artificial a suggestion as to verge on farce').

that places some burden on current or future arguments about that rule. Those interpretations can come from a number of places.

First, any number of international court-like bodies might be a source of a precedent. At the most basic level, the prior decision of a particular tribunal might be invoked in current or future arguments before that same tribunal. An ICJ decision might be invoked in a dispute before the ICJ, a WTO Appellate Body decision before the WTO Appellate Body, and so on. As noted above, even this can be controversial. More fine-grained distinctions might be drawn based on whether the parties or facts are the same in the first and second case, whether the interpretation was part of the holding or dicta in the decision, or whether the claimed precedent came in an advisory opinion or a contentious case. At the next level, decisions by international courts or tribunals with general jurisdiction over international law broadly or an area of international law specifically might be invoked as precedential with regard to that area of law regardless of the forum for the current argument. ICJ judgments might be cited to domestic courts on questions of sovereign immunity,[38] WTO Appellate Body decisions might be cited to other tribunals on trade law,[39] ECtHR decisions might be invoked regarding human rights,[40] and ICTY decisions might be invoked with regard to international criminal law.[41] These precedents might also be extended to closely related, but different areas: ICTY decisions might be invoked as precedents for interpreting domestic statutes,[42] investment tribunals interpreting one treaty might be used as precedent regarding similar language in another, and one regional human rights body might be invoked before a different one operating under a different treaty.[43] Finally, at the farthest end of the spectrum, decisions of international tribunals dealing with one issue might be invoked as precedent on an entirely different one, as when human rights decisions are invoked in investment tribunals.[44] And if all of this extends to advocacy before particular bodies, it extends to all the day-to-day arguments between actors as they try to work out the rules that govern their actions.

In a similar vein, domestic court opinions may be invoked as precedents regarding international law. Examples might include domestic decisions on

---

[38] See Part III.

[39] See eg Sheng Li, Meng Jia Yang, and Alec Stone Sweet, 'The Institutional Evolution of the Investor-State Arbitration Regime: Judicialization and Governance' (2013) Yale Law School Roundtable Paper <http://www.law.yale.edu/.../Stone_Sweet_Lee_and_Yang_Roundtable_Paper. pdf> accessed 22 March 2014.

[40] For citations of the ECtHR's *Soering* decision, see *Kindler v Canada* (1993) UN Doc CCPR/ C/48/D/470/1991 and *Pratt v Attorney General for Jamaica* [1994] 2 AC 1.

[41] See eg *Application of the Convention on the Prevention and Punishment of the Crime of Genocide, (Bosnia & Herzegovina v Serbia & Montenegro)* (Judgment) [2007] ICJ Rep 43, [223] (hereinafter ICJ, Application of Genocide Convention).

[42] See n 16.

[43] See Research Report, References to the Inter-American Court of Human Rights in the case law of the European Court of Human Rights, Council of Europe/European Court of Human Rights (2012) <http://www.echr.coe.int/.../Research_report_inter_american_court_ENG.pdf> accessed 22 March 2014

[44] See generally Bjorklund and Nappert, 'Beyond Fragmentation'.

international criminal liability,[45] sovereign immunity,[46] or lethal targeting.[47] Invoking these decisions as precedent requires attention to whether the decision is really interpreting international law or a related but distinct question of domestic law.[48] Doctrinally, like the decisions of international bodies, nothing makes these decisions precedential outside their domestic systems. And yet, they are regularly invoked.

But courts and tribunals are not the only potential sources of precedent. Courts and tribunals exist on a spectrum of interpretive bodies, with permanent courts, ad hoc arbitral tribunals, and expert bodies under various treaties. And other international actors with interpretative authority could also be invoked as precedent. To the extent that the International Law Commission or the UN General Assembly purport to interpret an existing rule of international law, some may claim that their decisions have authority over the meaning of that rule. The UN Security Council's interpretations of 'threat to the peace, breach of the peace, or act of aggression',[49] as well as its understanding of its power to respond, have been cited in exactly this way.[50] In fact, US and UK arguments for the legality of the Iraq war relied heavily on the 'precedents' set by Security Council resolutions from the First Gulf War to that point.[51] The views of a UN Special Rapporteur might be given similar weight.[52] In some cases, the views of an NGO like the International Committee of the Red Cross (ICRC) might even be invoked.

Finally, state acts might be invoked as precedent.[53] This is perhaps the oldest source of international precedent. States are interpreting the rules they follow whenever they act. How states customarily act or react may reveal the rule's proper interpretation.[54] This form of precedent is embodied in both the ICJ Statute's definition of customary international law and in the VCLT's invocation

[45] See eg Andre Nollkaemper, 'Decisions of National Courts as Sources of International Law: An Analysis of the Practice of the ICTY' in Gideon Boas and William A Schabas (eds), *International Criminal Law Developments in the Case Law of the ICTY* (Martinus Nijhoff Publishers 2003) 277.

[46] See *Jurisdictional Immunities of the State (Germany v Italy)* (Judgment) [2012] ICJ Rep 99, [96].

[47] See eg *The Public Committee against Torture in Israel v The Government of Israel* (14 December 2006) HCJ 769/02.

[48] See generally Anthea Roberts, 'Comparative International Law? The Role of National Courts in Creating and Enforcing International Law' (2011) 60 ICLQ 57.

[49] Charter of the United Nations, Article 39.

[50] See generally Rosalyn Higgins, *The Development of International Law Through the Political Organs of the United Nations* (OUP 1963); Jose E Alvarez, *International Organizations as Law-Makers* (OUP 2005) 184–217.

[51] See eg William H Taft and Todd F Buchwald, 'Preemption, Iraq, and International Law' (2003) 97 AJIL 557.

[52] For the centrality of Philip Alston's report on the legality of targeted killings in arguments about the relationship between International Humanitarian Law (IHL) and Human Rights Law, see eg Kaye, 'International Law Issues'; Ashley S Deeks, 'Unwilling or Unable: Toward a Normative Framework for Extraterritorial Self-Defense' (2012) 52 Va J Int'l L 483, 504.

[53] See Michael Reisman, 'International Incidents: Introduction to a New Genre in the Study of International Law' (1984) 10 Yale J Int'l L 1.

[54] See Harlan Grant Cohen, 'International Law's *Erie* Moment' (2013) 34 Mich J Int'l L 249, 256–7, 270–1.

of subsequent practice as an interpretive tool for understanding treaties.[55] The most prominent example might be the invocation of the 1837 *Caroline* incident between the US and the UK as evidence of the standard for legal anticipatory self-defence.[56]

Although any of the above sources could be invoked as precedent, only some will be in any given discussion. Even fewer will actually carry the intended weight with the desired audience. Which ones will is a function of the next two factors.

B. Reasons for authority

Even within a particular set of sources, some interpretations will carry more weight than others. A variety of factors might influence whether a particular community of practitioners regards a given interpretation as authoritative.

Actors may have self-interested reasons for invoking a particular decision as a precedent. Some of these reasons will be internal to the cited precedent. They may agree with or favour a particular interpretation or may believe that that interpretation has been or will be useful. Other reasons will be external to the decision. They may have some control over the precedent's author (as in the case of arbitration) and trust her decisions. Or they may desire the predictability that hewing to a decision might produce. Alternatively, they may cite decisions that will enhance their prestige. A court might cite another high prestige court in the hope that that other court will cite them in return. They might cite their own decisions (or be open to arguments from their own decisions) in order to enhance their authority over the meaning of particular rules.

But scholars have also identified factors that might exert 'compliance pull' independent of outcomes.[57] The quality of the legal reasoning, the clarity of the interpretation, an interpretation's adherence to prior interpretations, and how well an interpretation fits within a broader legal regime may all be factors internal to a particular decision that may either attract actors to it or burden actors to respond to it.[58] External to the decision itself, the independence or prestige of the decision-maker and the frequency of citation to that particular interpretation (discussed more below) may exert force on arguments. So too might the relative availability of the source compared to others. An ICJ opinion laying out a rule of customary international law is much easier to cite than all the evidence of state practice and *opinio juris* that might support a different one.

---

[55] There is a distinction between the use of state practice as evidence of customary international law and as precedent. When used as precedent, it is invoked as authority for an interpretation, rather than an element in a test.

[56] See eg Anthony Clark Arend, 'International Law and the Preemptive Use of Military Force' (2003) 26 Wash Q 89; Abraham D Sofaer, 'On the Necessity of Pre-emption' (2003) 14 EJIL 209.

[57] See generally Thomas M Franck, 'Legitimacy in the International System' (1988) 82 AJIL 705.

[58] Franck, 'Legitimacy in the International System'.

	Internal aspects	External aspects
Outcome driven	Success or potential success, agreement with interpretation	Control over decision-maker, perceived expertise of decision-maker, ability to enhance prestige, predictability of future results
Outcome independent	Quality of legal reasoning, clarity of rule, adherence to prior interpretations, coherence within broader legal system	Independence of decision-maker, prestige of decision-maker, density or frequency of citation, availability

Clean lines cannot be drawn between these different types of reasons. Actors may adopt outcome-driven rule-utilitarian beliefs that independent judges produce 'better' decisions, or that adherence to prior interpretations is better for the success of a regime they find favourable to their interests even if it sometimes produces decisions they do not like. The complex question precedent raises is how these various factors will balance out when thrown together in real-world situations.

C. Actors and audiences

Elsewhere, I have argued that thinking about international law as the product of specific communities of practice can help explain the philosophical, theoretical, and doctrinal differences developing between different areas of international law, as well as the emergence of areas of transnational law almost completely divorced from state control like global administrative law.[59] Imagining international law as a product of these communities of practice can also help unlock the mystery of precedent.

Precedent is hard to understand as an objective fact disconnected from a particular group of actors. A prior decision by a particular legal body is a fact, but how much weight it should be given in future debates over a particular rule is dependent on how it is perceived by the actors reading it. Precedent is instead an 'institutional fact'.[60] Like a 'hit' or a 'strike' in baseball, it is only a fact within the particular rules of a particular institution or community.[61] Just as a student of baseball and a student of cricket will see two very different sets of facts in a group of people with bats and ball on a field, so too will actors biased towards the authority of courts or the bindingness of precedent perceive the value of a tribunal decision differently than actors biased towards state consent and pragmatism.

---

[59] See generally Harlan Grant Cohen, 'Finding International Law, Part II: Our Fragmenting Legal Community' (2012) 44 NYU J Int'l L & Pol 1049.

[60] Friedrich Kratochwil, *Rules, Norms and Decisions: On the Conditions of Practical and Legal Reasoning in International Relations and Domestic Affairs* (CUP 1989) 22–8.

[61] Kratochwil, *Rules, Norms and Decisions*, 91, quoting John Rawls, 'Two Concepts of Justice' (1955) 64 Phil Rev 3, 25.

Different international law regimes involve different mixes of actors—advocates, political leaders, diplomats, military personnel, scientists, economists, international lawyers, and domestic lawyers.[62] Each of these different actors brings their own professional norms and biases to the debate, and different mixes of actors will agree on different norms and operating assumptions. Understanding the relative weight different decisions by different bodies carry in different contexts requires understanding the communities of actors who might perceive them that way.[63] The key is identifying the actors who practise in a particular area of law, both at the centre of that practice, interacting regularly and intensely over the meaning of rules, and at the periphery.[64] These are the players in international law's interpretative game.[65]

The actors listed above are, of course, only archetypes. Real-world actors wear multiple hats at the same time or over time. A government lawyer may go into private practice or become a judge, a politician may be a trained lawyer, and a lawyer may be a member of the military. Nonetheless, these archetypes allow us to isolate characteristics, habits, biases, or incentives that shape the international legal practice in which they engage. Moreover, identifying specific types of actors allows us to group them in ways that help us to understand how they interact with particular potential legal sources and answer legal questions. Thus we might group actors by *professional training*, grouping together lawyers, economists, or scientists. Or we might group them within *epistemic communities*, asking who they interact with in their issue areas: military professionals, business leaders, or diplomats. Alternatively, we might group them based on their *social and political capital* or incentives. How is success in their job defined and who defines it? Even if all trained as lawyers, politicians, bureaucrats, NGO activists, judges, and military lawyers may all respond to different incentives and may look to different audiences for career or personal advancement. Finally, we might group them according to their *function* and relationship to precedent: are they advocating, judging, administering, or seeking guidance for action?

Importantly, we also need to look at these various actors as both actors and audiences. We need to understand not just why those who reference a precedent might find it weighty, authoritative, or even binding, but also why the audience that reference is aimed at might as well. In other words, we need to know why a lawyer assessing policy options or advocating a position might feel the need to cite a particular reference, as well as why her intended audience, whether policymakers, judges, or opposing lawyers, might respond favourably to it. We might think of this as first person and second person points of view on the weight of a

---

[62] Each of these groups could be divided into increasingly small subgroups. Lawyers, for example, might be divided into domestic and international lawyers, government and private practice lawyers, public interest and private lawyers, litigators and transactional attorneys, not to mention lawyers working or trained in different legal cultures and different parts of the world.
[63] See generally Chapter 2 (Andrea Bianchi); Cohen, 'Finding International Law'.
[64] For a fuller discussion of how communities of practice are structured, see Cohen, 'Finding International Law', 1065–9, 1089–90; Emanuel Adler, *Communitarian International Relations: The Epistemic Foundations of International Relations* (Routledge 2005).
[65] See Chapter 2 (Andrea Bianchi).

given precedent. Different factors may speak more to one than the other. Both the legitimacy-pull of treating like cases alike and training in legal-analogical reasoning may generate first-person reasons to cite a precedent; a belief that judges might respond favourably to citations of court opinions or that policymakers will respond favourably to anecdotes about prior state actions would generate second-person ones. In reality, because all of the actors making and responding to arguments operate within an ongoing, iterative practice, the lines between the two are impossible to draw. Conceptions of authoritative sources are constantly being constructed through the interaction of the various actors. Legal arguments are inherently relational; they are attempts by one actor to convince another actor to act in a particular way. An advocate must predict how other advocates and judges will respond to their argument; a judge must predict how lawyers and policymakers will respond to theirs. First-and second-person points of view merge.

III. Telling Precedent's Story

The ingredients discussed in Part II—sources, features, actors—can be combined to tell three intertwined stories about the emergence of international precedent, one rationalist, one jurisprudential, and one sociological.

A. A rationalist account

Under this account, interpretations should be invoked or treated as precedent when doing so helps achieve various actors' broader goals. Such an account largely tracks existing explanations for precedent described earlier. For a state actor, this may mean citing a precedent that supports a position a state wants to take or that a court might predictably favour (for example, one of that court's own prior decisions). For the judge, it might mean citing a precedent from a court it is trying to convince or citing its own decisions to solidify its control over interpretation.

But such a rationalist story could also explain why states might support a broader system of precedent, even when doing so may not always favour their desired positions. To the extent states are invested in a particular regime, predictability may be valuable enough for them to support precedent-based arguments generally. This is true whether the potential precedents are found in state actions or in judicial opinions. To the extent third party decision-making is capable of resolving difficult coordination problems, states may give a court or tribunal's decision precedential force in order to preserve that court or tribunal's authority in the regime. (Questioning that body's decisions too often might undermine that body's authority.) Moreover, treating prior decisions as precedential might add desirable clarity to the rules. To the extent states value general clarity more highly than winning the cases precedent might cost them, states should support precedent.[66]

---

[66] Cf Pelc, 'The Politics of Precedent in International Law'.

Of course, few (if any) regimes explicitly provide for precedential effect. This suggests that for the states designing those regimes, the optimal level of clarity and predictability is greater than a system of *de novo* review but less than one of *stare decisis*. Denying the force of precedent, while nonetheless arguing from it, may be a way of calibrating precedent's exact weight. Assuming that arguments from precedent will have some natural force, this strategy could allow states to take advantage of the predictability of precedent, while still retaining some room to argue against a precedent's relevance in a particular case. The danger of this strategy, as demonstrated by the precedent-creep in the WTO, ECJ, and ECtHR, is that if every state uses this strategy, precedent-based arguments are likely to predominate. Even if one state has an interest in flexibility in a given case, states in the aggregate are likely to favour predictability over flexibility, and a de facto doctrine of precedent will likely emerge. This is reinforced by the normative power of oft-cited precedent (discussed below), which may make erasing the prior interpretation nearly impossible.

B. A jurisprudential account

But all of this assumes that when an argument is made that a prior interpretation dictates a current one, that argument carries some independent additional weight and has some authority beyond the reasoning attached to it. Under the rationalist account, this extra weight may just reflect an implicit understanding of the system-value of precedents for achieving the relevant actor's goal. But from a jurisprudential standpoint, it might be that the authority of precedents inheres in legal argumentation.

Precedents carry whatever weight or authority they have *within* a legal argument. As noted above, precedent might best be seen as the burden a prior interpretation of a rule places on future arguments about that rule. In the absence of any prior interpretation, an interpreter has a lot of latitude to choose a particular interpretation of a rule. Evidence of a prior interpretation seems to change that equation. As a matter of reasoned legal argument, such an interpretation cannot be ignored. Depending on a variety of factors that might give the prior interpretation greater legal authority—the prestige of the prior interpreter, the quality of the legal reasoning behind it, its perceived adherence to other prior interpretations or coherence within the system—that decision might be brushed aside, distinguished, narrowed, adopted, or extended, but it must be dealt with. Failing to do so might be seen as arbitrary and a violation of rule of law norms.[67] This effect is compounded the more the particular prior decision is considered and cited. The greater the frequency of citation, the harder it is to ignore the decision, and the greater the burden on current interpretation.[68]

Moreover, the discursive power of precedent may have normative force. Common to many theories of law is a view that one of law's core principles or

---

[67] See Jacob, 'Precedents'.   [68] Cohen, 'International Law's *Erie* Moment', 276–80.

qualities is that it treats like situations alike. Lon Fuller describes consistency as part of the internal morality of law,[69] Ronald Dworkin's law as integrity denies the legitimacy of checkerboard laws that treat like cases differently,[70] and Tom Franck describes coherence and adherence as key factors in the perceived legitimacy of laws.[71] From this standpoint, precedent's pull can be seen as a direct articulation of rule of law norms. If like cases must be treated alike, future decisions must at least make reference to prior ones.[72]

A related jurisprudential argument often made in support of precedent is reliance, that law must protect the reasonable expectations of the governed.[73] It might seem bizarre to suggest that states have a reliance interest in the decisions of international tribunals that they have so deliberately denied precedential effect, but such arguments are sometimes made.[74] (States are more likely to argue that they relied on the precedent set by prior state acts than a prior tribunal decision.[75]) More often, the argument about reliance on prior decisions is made on behalf of individuals rather than states, either in the human rights or investment protection context. It is essentially an argument against state prerogative. Invocation of the legality principle in the international criminal context may contain a version of this argument. Some notion that individuals should be able to rely on the prior decisions of international criminal courts may explain why the International Criminal Court is the sole international court authorized by treaty to look to its prior decisions as a source of law.[76]

Whether the argument is about treating like cases alike or concerns about reasonable reliance, these jurisprudential arguments suggest that it is the most proximate and similar decisions—from the same body or actors or on the same issue—that will carry the most weight. The easier it is to distinguish the context, the less weight an interpretation will carry. It also suggests that the less clear the precedent and the more ad hoc the interpretation appears to be, the easier it will be to distinguish. This helps explain why judicial interpretations, which are usually clearer and nested within a body of jurisprudence, seem to become precedents so much more rapidly than interpretations derived from state practice, which are often purposely ambiguous.[77]

[69] See generally Lon Fuller, *The Morality of Law* (Yale University Press 1964).

[70] Ronald Dworkin, *Law's Empire* (Harvard University Press 1986) 176–224.

[71] Thomas M Franck, 'Legitimacy in the International System' (1988) 82 AJIL 705, 712.

[72] See Helfer and Slaughter, 'Effective Transnational Adjudication', 319–20.

[73] See generally Hillel Levin, 'A Reliance Approach to Precedent' (2012) 47 Ga L Rev 1035.

[74] See WTO, *Japan: Alcoholic Beverages—Report of the Appellate Body* (4 October 1996) WT/DS8/AB/R and WT/DS10/AB/R, WT/DS11/AB/R, [14]. ('Adopted panel reports...create legitimate expectations among WTO Members, and, therefore, should be taken into account where they are relevant to any dispute').

[75] This might be thought of as a version of *tu quoque*, but one used not as an excuse but as a positive legal argument. A good example might be Russia's open invocation of NATO policy to Kosovo as precedent for its actions in Georgia.

[76] Rome Statute.

[77] See Cohen, 'International Law's *Erie* Moment', 257–71 (describing the different features of gap-filling through negotiation and adjudication, including the latter's relative clarity, speed of development, and path-dependence).

C. A sociological account

But for this jurisprudential account to have force, someone must actually believe in it or have some other incentive to abide by it. Nor can the jurisprudential account on its own choose between different sources of precedent. Prior interpretations might have weight, but which ones: judicial opinions, state practice, expert reports? It is here that a sociological account of the actors who invoke and respond to arguments from precedent becomes essential. This sociological account has so far been neglected in the literature on international precedent, but it is this account that provides the key to understanding the operation and effectiveness of the other two. It explains why invoking precedent self-interestedly may get a response and why the jurisprudential account may exert some independent pull. In essence, the sociological account provides the context of the game in which precedent-based moves will either succeed or fail.

Specific actors may be trained to see certain sources as authoritative. Lawyers, particularly those trained in a common law tradition, are trained to seek out, read, and argue from judicial decisions. Members of the military may be trained to look to historical combat actions for lessons. Specific actors may also belong to professional communities that respond to those sources or expect reference to those sources. Lawyers, for example, might experience professional opprobrium or sanction for failing to cite relevant precedents. And different actors may face a range of social and political incentives to cite particular sources. Politicians, for example, will have incentives to cite precedents that will help sway voters in their favour.[78]

Take the example of lawyers very generally. Lawyers are indoctrinated with rule of law principles, principles which, in turn, are embodied in legal professional ethics. To the extent they work with other lawyers, particularly domestic lawyers, they may be expected to argue from judicial precedent. Within a legal organization, arguments that follow the professional script and reference judicial precedents will be rewarded. Arguments that seek to be overly creative or iconoclastic might not. Given their skill sets, judicial precedents may be more readily available to them than other sources.

Most of all, when working with non-lawyers, arguments from judicial precedent may enhance the lawyer's stature. Lawyers as a professional group have specific sources of political and social capital that they can use to maintain their importance and relevance in relation to other societal actors.[79] Among these is lawyers' purported expertise in interpreting and applying complex legal sources. Lawyers, seeking to maximize their own power and authority vis-à-vis other international actors, will want to emphasize the value of precedents and their unique ability to understand them.

---

[78] See generally Katerina Linos, *The Democratic Foundations of Policy Diffusion: How Health, Family, and Employment Laws Spread Across Countries* (OUP 2013).

[79] See generally Pierre Bourdieu, 'The Force of Law: Toward a Sociology of the Juridical Field' (1987) 38 Hastings L J 805; Yves Dezalay and Bryant G Garth, *Dealing in Virtue: International Commercial Arbitration and the Construction of a Transnational Legal Order* (University of Chicago Press 1998).

In other words, lawyers at the US State Department or Defense Department may argue that precedents need to be followed (a) because they believe that the rule of law requires it, (b) because they fear formal or informal professional or group sanction (ie shunning) if they fail to adhere to it, or (c) because arguing for precedent reinforces their authority within decision-making circles.[80] One need not choose between these reasons; they reinforce one another.

Of course, the actual story is much more complicated. Lawyers are not all the same. Hailing from different parts of the world, they may have been trained differently. They may belong to different organizations with different organizational cultures, priorities, and scripts. A lawyer in a foreign ministry may see the world differently from a military lawyer or a lawyer at the ICRC.[81] Or they may belong to different epistemic communities.[82] The results of these differences, including how lawyers interact with other actors in a community of practice, may go a long way towards explaining different patterns of precedent or different ways of arguing from precedent in different areas of international law.[83] Scholars have only begun to study the sociology of these actors.[84] Much more work needs to be done.

D. Three accounts in action

As a very general matter, these three stories reinforce one another, making the turn to precedent in legal argumentation somewhat over-determined. In specific cases, however, they may point in different directions. Two examples may usefully demonstrate this.

1. *Foreign official immunity*

In a search of briefs submitted on behalf of the US State Department Legal Adviser in cases before US courts, one citation stands out. The Legal Adviser regularly cites the ICJ's *Arrest Warrant* decision[85] as precedent regarding questions

---

[80] Cf Rebecca Ingber, 'Interpretation Catalysts and Executive Branch Legal Decisionmaking' (2013) 38 Yale J Int'l L 359.

[81] David Luban, 'Military Necessity and the Cultures of Military Law' (2013) 26 LJIL 315, 318: 'Organizational cultures are interpretive communities; lawyers in them develop their own lore about what the law means and how to read it'.

[82] See eg Kenneth Anderson, 'The Rise of International Criminal Law: Intended and Unintended Consequences' (2009) 20 EJIL 331 (describing divergence between epistemic communities of international criminal law and military law).

[83] The ICJ, with jurisdiction only over consenting states and staffed by judges with strong state connections, is likely to be more conservative and hew more closely to state practice than an international criminal tribunal, with its broad mandate to bring perpetrators to justice and justice to victims, a human rights court delegated responsibility under a human rights treaty, or a domestic court that may be more experienced in redressing individual rights violations than in considering the interests of the collectivity of sovereign states.

[84] See eg Dezalay and Garth, *Dealing in Virtue*; Yves Dezalay and Mikael Rask Madsen, 'The Force of Law and Lawyers: Pierre Bourdieu and the Reflexive Sociology of Law' (2012) 8 Ann Rev of L and Soc Sci 433.

[85] *Case Concerning the Arrest Warrant of 11 April 2000 (Democratic Republic of Congo v Belgium)* (Judgment) [2002] ICJ Rep 3.

of foreign official immunity.[86] Given that the US would likely object to any claim that ICJ judgments are authoritative statements of the law, the citation to an ICJ judgment as precedent by the US Government to a domestic court might need some explanation.

Citation to the *Arrest Warrant* case, however, should hardly be surprising. Every factor seems to support it. From a sociological standpoint, those authoring the brief are practising attorneys trained to look to precedent. The arguments are, in turn, being made to American judges habituated to arguments based on judicial precedent and habituated to respect other judges. Those making the arguments belong to an organizational culture (the State Department) particularly attuned to sovereign immunity and its role in avoiding friction between states. They represent the US before the ICJ and might be more likely than other parts of the government to view that Court's judgments as important. The decision is far easier to cite than the evidence of custom underlying it. From an organizational standpoint, once the decision has been made to cite the ICJ judgment, lawyers are likely encouraged to cite to it again rather than revisit the question.

From a jurisprudential standpoint, the practice before courts is relatively dense in the area of sovereign immunity, augmenting the authority of judicial decisions. Whether one can be sued in a particular court is by its nature a question courts will be forced to decide, and sovereign immunity questions make common appearances not only in US courts, but in other domestic and international courts. Moreover, as the *Arrest Warrant* case continues to get cited, its precedential force is magnified. The citation becomes more obvious and harder to ignore without violating legal or ethical norms.

Finally, from a rationalist perspective, lawyers in the Legal Adviser's office can be assumed to be channelling the rational self-interest of the US when they cite the *Arrest Warrant* case. The US has long been invested in protecting official immunity, not least because the US wants its officials protected overseas.[87] Maintaining official immunity for its own officials requires guaranteeing it to foreign ones, and doing so requires monitoring the courts to guarantee against accidental violation. In a sense, the grant of foreign official immunity might be seen as the product of an iterated prisoner's dilemma; cooperation is maintained so long as neither side cheats.[88] Moreover, the US has an interest in promoting the authority of the ICJ judgment as a coordination point with other states and a source of clarity and predictability regarding the law.

---

[86] See eg Brief for Appellees, *Yousuf v Samantar*, 2011 WL 5040507 (4th Cir 24 October 2011) (No 11-1479); Brief for Appellee, *Habyarimana v Kagame*, 2012 WL 1572450 (10th Cir 30 April 2012) (No 11-6315). The typical brief reads simply: 'Under customary international law principles accepted by the Executive Branch, a sitting head of state's immunity is based on his status as the incumbent office holder, and it extends to all of his actions, whenever performed': *Habyarimana*.

[87] In some briefs, the self-interest is obvious, particularly where *Arrest Warrant* is cited for the proposition that foreign official immunity belongs to the state rather than the official. See eg *Samantar* Brief, 6.

[88] See Robert Axelrod, *The Evolution of Cooperation* (Basic Books 1984).

2. Self-defence against non-state actors

But this consensus around a precedent or precedents breaks down when the question is the legality of the use of force by one state against non-state actors in another. Here the factors point in different directions. The three stories above (rationalist, jurisprudential, sociological) sound different when read by different actors.

Whether a state can respond with force to a terrorist or insurgent attack emanating from another state has become a contentious issue. The text of the UN Charter leaves room for interpretation. Although Article 2(4) requires all member states to 'refrain in their international relations from the threat or use of force against the territorial integrity or political independence of any state',[89] Article 51 preserves states' 'inherent right of individual or collective self-defence' if an armed attack occurs against them.[90] Does an attack by a non-state actor implicate a state's right to self-defence? Does that right allow targeted states to violate other states' sovereignty, otherwise protected by Article 2(4), to counter the threat? If so, under what conditions?

Answering these questions has become a war over precedents. For some human rights and international humanitarian law scholars,[91] the ICJ already answered these questions in its *Nicaragua, Israeli Wall*, and *Democratic Republic of Congo (DRC) v Uganda* opinions.[92] In each case, the court at least implied that self-defence is only possible against a state and that reprisals against non-state actors in a foreign state are lawful only when the non-state actors' actions are attributable to that state.[93] As far as these scholars are concerned, these decisions are authoritative precedent.

But US Government lawyers (among others) disagree.[94] For them, these ICJ interpretations are mere dicta. Instead, they look to a different source of precedent: state practice.[95] What they find there is a common standard: when a non-state actor's actions against a state rise to the level of an armed attack, a targeted state's right to self-defence attaches, and where the host state is 'unwilling

---

[89] Charter of the United Nations (24 October 1945) 1 UNTS 16 (UN Charter), Article 2(4).

[90] Charter of the United Nations, Article 51.

[91] See eg Tom Ruys, *'Armed Attack' and Article 51 of the UN Charter: Evolutions in Customary Law and Practice* (CUP 2010) 475–6; Kevin Jon Heller, 'The Law of Neutrality Does Not Apply to the Conflict with Al-Qaeda, and It's a Good Thing, Too: A Response to Chang' (2011) 47 Tex Int'l LJ 115, 140; Mary Ellen O'Connell, 'Remarks: The Resort to Drones under International Law' (2011) 39 Denv J Int'l L & Pol'y 585, 594–5.

[92] *Case Concerning Military and Paramilitary Activities in and Against Nicaragua (Nicaragua v US)* (Merits) [1986] ICJ Rep 14 (*Nicaragua*); *Legal Consequences of the Construction of a Wall in the Occupied Palestinian Territory* (Advisory Opinion) [2004] ICJ Rep 136 (*Israeli Wall*); *Case Concerning Armed Activities on the Territory of the Congo (Democratic Republic of the Congo v Uganda)* (Judgment) [2005] ICJ Rep 168 (*DRC*).

[93] *Nicaragua*, 103–4; *Israeli Wall*, 192–4; *DRC*, 222–3.

[94] See generally Deeks, 'Unwilling or Unable'; Steven R Ratner, 'Self-Defense Against Terrorists: The Meaning of Armed Attack' in Nico Schrijver and Larissa Van den Herik, *The Leiden Policy Recommendations on Counter-terrorism and International Law*, 1 <http://papers.ssrn.com/sol3/papers.cfm?abstract_id=2047778> accessed 22 March 2014.

[95] See Deeks, 'Unwilling or Unable'.

or unable' to prevent the threat, the targeted state may use force within the host state's borders to counter the non-state actor. This is, in fact, part of the argument in the DOJ White Paper on targeted killing discussed above.

We can see how, under the circumstances, the accounts above may not yield a single answer here or coalesce around the authority of a single line of precedent. Different factors cut in different directions. On the one hand, the cited decisions emanate from an independent and prestigious international court, the ICJ. And the state practice underlying the 'unwilling or unable' standard is clearly biased in favour of those states responding to such threats. On the other hand, the ICJ's views are arguably dicta and certainly are not fully explained in the opinions. One of the opinions arose out of the court's advisory jurisdiction, suggesting that its views might be less binding. Both sides argue that the other's precedents are too few and uncertain to be authoritative.[96] The ICJ decisions might predict what a future international court might hold, but the practice of the states surveyed arguably predicts what states will actually treat as lawful or unlawful. And of course, from a self-interested angle, the two sides clearly favour different answers, answers that find support in different potential precedents.

Moreover, unlike foreign official immunity, these use of force issues are not frequently before courts. There is no thick judicial practice on the issue. Instead, the real practice on this issue takes place around two separate nodes: human rights advocacy and state national security policy. Rather than a single line of precedent gaining force by repeated citation, two lines of precedent gain force as they are repeatedly cited in particular fora and among particular practitioners.

Lawyers are involved on both sides, and notably, lawyers on both sides of the debate appeal to precedent, reflecting both the expectations of a lawyerly community and precedent's normative and discursive power. But the lawyers involved on either side belong to different professional, organizational, and epistemic communities. They may have different biases about how to interpret use of force questions,[97] and are subject to very different social and professional incentives. The incentives for a human rights advocate or a professional scholar are obviously quite different than those for government and, in particular, military attorneys embedded within state agencies and the chain of command.

Conclusion

Precedent is part of the spoken and unspoken strategies of international law interpretation. Whether realizing it or not, international actors, the players in the interpretative game, invoke or respond to particular precedents as part of a broader effort to justify their positions and persuade other players to go along with them. This chapter has sought to understand how those strategies emerge

[96] Compare Ratner, 'Self-Defense Against Terrorists', 3–4 with Heller, 'The Law of Neutrality'.
[97] See Luban, 'Military Necessity and the Cultures of Military Law'.

and evolve, and when and why they succeed or fail. It lays out a framework for thinking about precedent's force in particular contexts, suggesting both factors to look to—available sources, features of authority, actors and audiences—and lenses to apply—rationalist, jurisprudential, and sociological. What the framework indicates is the need for more in-depth case studies following particular precedents in particular fields that can begin to explain how these factors and accounts intersect, overlap, and compete to produce the practice of international law. This is the next step.

14

Interpretation in International Law as a Transcultural Project

*René Provost**

Introduction

In one trial before the Special Court for Sierra Leone (SCSL), a witness testified that she was made to eat the flesh of dead fighters,[1] while in another trial the witness recounted how she saw rebels cook and eat the body of a man.[2] In both trials, the SCSL avoided any characterization of such a practice under international criminal law. How does international law operate to create a narrative of legality or illegality in relation to an act such as cannibalism? Can a legal norm be given meaning in a manner that is disconnected from the local context in which it is applied? If a practice, considered to amount to an international crime, holds deep cultural meaning in a given circumstance, must legal interpretation yield to a significant extent to the interpretation of that practice from a standpoint internal to the community concerned?

To ask questions about the nature, meaning, and purpose of interpretation in international law is to suggest that it is a process distinct, in some significant ways, from interpretation in law in general. In many respects, interpretation in any field of law (if not in many disciplines) will give rise to similar questions. As such, the import of legal doctrine, the varied sources of law, the identity of interpreters, the relation to a broader legal order, cultural contingency, and normative indeterminacy all appear as relevant to interpretation in any area of law, national or international, private or public. It can nevertheless be argued that there is a degree of distinctiveness to interpretation in public international law, at least in some significant respects, at both institutional and normative levels.

* I wish to thank Caylee Hong for her research assistance on cannibalism. This chapter forms part of the Centaur Jurisprudence Project, an interdisciplinary team exploring the interaction of law and culture, supported by the Social Sciences and Humanities Research Council of Canada.

[1] *Prosecutor v Charles Ghankay Taylor*, SCSL-03-01-T, Court Transcript (27 October 2008), 19229–19230.

[2] *Prosecutor v Moinina Fofana and Allieu Kondewa*, SCSL-04-14-T, Court Transcript (25 February 2005), 14.

At an institutional level, the decentralized structure of the international legal order means that interpretive acts are carried out by a wider array of agents—for example, governments, individuals, corporations, and international organizations—without the possibility of continuous supervision through judicial decision-making. This leads to the need for interpretation to be checked by other types of processes to avoid abuse, as well as to the greater occurrence of divergent or contradictory interpretations which remain unresolved for long periods of time. Still at an institutional level, much could be said about the distinctiveness of the judicial function in international law as opposed to municipal law, given the looser legitimating links between the judge and the wider community. This explains, for instance, the existence of ad hoc judges at the International Court of Justice (ICJ), a vision of the judicial function that would be difficult to transpose to the domestic legal order.

At a normative level, it could be argued that interpretation in international law is distinct because the legal regime is 'thinner' and less structured than a domestic legal regime, with layered regulation covering areas in much greater detail than what can be achieved through diplomatic negotiations or gleaned through a study of international practice. International norms tend to be more indeterminate than domestic ones, as a reflection of the wider spectrum of realities which international law is meant to cover. The normative indeterminacy of treaty norms is often intentional, as a strategy to manage disagreement among negotiating parties.

In this chapter, I focus on the transcultural nature of interpretation in some areas of international law, a topic which encompasses both institutional and normative dimensions. To date, much of international law remains centred on the state. While all governments are different, all states share in a culture rooted in the idea of sovereignty, such that the transcultural dimensions of international law is in many ways limited.[3] International criminal law is one area of international law that stands as radically different in that respect, reflecting the fact that it seeks to alter the behaviour of individuals who may not share a common culture of any kind. Furthermore, the culture of those individuals to whom international criminal law is applied is often markedly different from the culture of the institutions and individuals that administer international criminal responsibility. Building on previous work on the application of the doctrine of superior responsibility to a witch-doctor by the SCSL, I consider the appropriate stance of the SCSL with respect to allegations of cannibalism.[4] I proceed by first analysing how legal interpretation unfolds in the international legal order, focusing on interpretive actors and practices (Part I), before turning to consider the impact of cultural difference on the interpretive exercise (Part II). The interpretation of international law and the interpretation of local culture emerge as ineluctably interwoven, with international law acting as a tool and a justification to reinterpret local culture through

---

[3] This is insightfully explored in Christian Reus-Smit, 'International Law and the Mediation of Cultures' (2014) 28 Ethics & Int'l Aff 65, 68–70.
[4] René Provost, 'Authority, Responsibility, and Witchcraft: From *Tintin* to the SCSL' in Charles Chernor Jalloh (ed), *The Sierra Leone Special Court and its Legacy* (CUP 2014) 159.

the prism of legal norms devoid of any local rootedness. The danger is an outcome whereby international law fails to be perceived as legitimate by the agents whose behaviour it seeks to regulate and, as a result, fails to trigger the kind of normative engagement required to make law real. To evoke the metaphor at the heart of this volume, interpretation as a game must be inclusive enough to give everyone concerned the inclination to participate in it.

I. Interpretation in International Law

To interpret in law is to invoke a norm as a basis for the legitimacy of an act or an understanding. This is an iterative exercise in which a narrative is offered that will define both the object of the interpretive claim (for example, the cross-border activities of rebels are properly understood as an armed attack under Article 51 of the UN Charter), and the identity of the subject advancing the claim (for example, the state holds sovereign authority over such territory and holds the right to self-defence under international law). Interpretation is also a communicative, inter-subjective act: while it is something to which a legal actor will contribute autonomously by expressing an opinion, implicitly or explicitly, it is directed at another.

The legal norm stands as the structure for a dialogue by which one actor seeks to persuade another of the legitimacy of its interpretive stance.[5] Thus, to interpret a legal norm is at once a call for solidarity, a statement of aspirations, a claim to legitimacy, and a definition of identity. Taking this as a starting point, there is a need to specify what we refer to when we speak of the 'interpretation' of international law. This involves determining whether only certain categories of legal subjects may be said to engage in interpretive exercises, whether only certain analytical approaches may be properly characterized as legal interpretation, and the object of what can be labelled legal interpretation. This mapping exercise will underscore the essentially contested boundaries of the notion of legal interpretation as it relates to the international legal order.

A. Interpretive actors

First, who may interpret international legal norms? A survey of the current literature on interpretation in international law reveals the tenacious link between the interpretive exercise and the judicial function.[6] This is so despite the fact that judicial interpretation in international law remains a relative rarity because of the absence of any court of compulsory jurisdiction in international relations,

---

[5] See John Tobin, 'Seeking to Persuade: A Constructive Approach to Treaty Interpretation' (2010) 23 Harv Hum Rts J 1, 7.

[6] See eg Richard Gardiner, *Treaty Interpretation* (OUP 2008); Robert Kolb, *Interprétation et création du droit international* (Bruylant 2006); and Alexander Orakhelashvili, *The Interpretation of Acts and Rules in Public International Law* (OUP 2008).

the limited acceptance of the competence of courts whose jurisdiction remains at the discretion of states, and the uneven degree of judicialization among different fields of international law.[7]

If we regard the judge as the prototypical interpreter of international law, what kind of a legal agent is she? Like the process of the creation of norms in the international legal order, the structures for their interpretation remain closely tied to the state. International judges may not necessarily sit as a representative of their state of nationality, but they are appointed by a process which is directly or indirectly grounded in state consent. Most individuals whom we would describe as 'international judges' hold their office by virtue of an appointment voted on by states or their representatives, when they are not nominated directly by states in arbitral proceedings. Judicial legitimacy to interpret international law is thus rooted in state sovereignty and a rather consensual construction of the international legal order. This is translated most directly into the institution of ad hoc judges in a number of international judicial bodies, including the ICJ. While it is generally agreed that ad hoc judges do not sit as representatives of the state that nominated them, the role is usually thought to correspond to a duty on the part of that judge to ensure that all arguments advanced by 'their' state have been considered and fairly adjudicated on. The link between judicial legitimacy and legal interpretation could not be articulated more transparently.[8]

That judicial interpretive power is derivative of state sovereignty is reflected in the fact that the state itself may engage in interpretation of international legal norms, by a process that may properly be characterized as legal interpretation. Article 31(3)(b) of the Vienna Convention on the Law of Treaties (VCLT) expressly recognizes that the practice of states party to a treaty ought to be considered as an interpretive act which can inform the later interpretation of the treaty. The norm embodied in Article 31(3)(b) does not expressly require that state practice be formally justified by the concerned state in relation to the substantive treaty provision to which it relates. Rather, a presumption is created that states abide by their treaty obligations, such that the practice of a state party will be taken to be that state's interpretation of the treaty. This practice has been described as 'auto-interpretation' in some of the literature, to capture the fact that the interpretive agent in this context is, so to speak, both judge and party.[9] The legal recognition of this practice is rendered necessary because of the lack of institutions in the

---

[7] For an analytical survey, see Benedict Kingsbury, 'International Courts: Uneven Judicialisation in Global Order' in James Crawford and Martti Koskenniemi (eds), *The Cambridge Companion to International Law* (CUP 2012) 203.

[8] See Stephen Schwebel, 'National Judges and Judges Ad Hoc of the International Court of Justice' (1999) 48 ICLQ 889; *Application of the Convention on the Prevention and Punishment of the Crime of Genocide (Bosnia and Herzegovina v Serbia and Montenegro)* (Order of 13 September 1993) [1993] ICJ Rep 407, 408–9 (Separate Opinion of Judge Elihu Lauterpacht)).

[9] See Leo Gross, 'States as Organs of International Law and the Problem of Autointerpretation' in George Lipsky (ed), *Law and Politics in the World Community: Essays on Hans Kelsen's Pure Theory and Related Problems in International Law* (University of Berkeley Press 1953) 59; Bin Cheng, 'Flight From Justiciable to Auto-Interpretative International Law: From the Jay Treaty to the Shultz Letter' in *Liber Amicorum Elie van Bogaert* (Kluwer 1985) 3.

international legal order that could intervene to provide an authoritative interpretation. Auto-interpretation is recognized but not authoritative: a state may rely on its own interpretation of law and facts at its own risk, with the possibility that a court may reject that position at some future point. A state is thus legally entitled to adopt countermeasures pursuant to its own interpretation of facts and law, but such an interpretation may be rejected by a tribunal at a later date.[10] It is interesting to note that the loosening of the requirement as to interpretive process in Article 31(3)(b) is countenanced because of the identity of the interpreting agent, the states whose will the treaty sought to capture in the first place. Here, the boundary between the creation and interpretation of international law becomes blurred, in a manner that is distinct from the normative growth occurring every time a court interprets a legal standard. When a court interprets a treaty provision, it offers a new understanding of the norm. As such, interpretation does imply a creative process, but the legitimacy of the new normative variation is rooted in the validity of the interpretive process rather than in the sovereign authority of states to bind themselves under the *pacta sunt servanda* principle.

For example, if we return to the legal characterization of cannibalism before the SCSL, there is no treaty norm that deals directly with that practice. Relevant treaty provisions that may have a bearing relate to the burial of the dead, respect for human remains, and the prohibition or outrages upon personal dignity, although not all are applicable to an internal conflict like Sierra Leone.[11] No international tribunal has ever issued a conviction for the war crime of cannibalism, although it was classified as a 'conventional war crime' in the indictment at the International Military Tribunal for the Far East.[12] A number of national military tribunals sitting in the Pacific after World War II handed down convictions for acts of cannibalism.[13] Australia even adopted a rule which explicitly declared that '"war crime"...includes...cannibalism'.[14] The implication of Article 31(3)(b) of the VCLT would be that, if such state practice can be said to amount to application of the relevant Geneva Conventions and Protocols, then they should have greater influence on the interpretation of these provisions than international judicial decisions arriving at the same conclusion by way of interpreting the text of the Geneva Conventions.

A tension between these two approaches to interpretation can also be found in the opposing positions adopted by the UN Human Rights Committee (HRC) and a number of states party to the International Covenant on Civil and Political

---

[10] See Denis Alland, *Justice privée et ordre juridique international—Étude théorique des contre-mesures en droit international public* (Pedone 1994) 107–25.

[11] See Anna Petrig, 'The War Dead and Their Gravesites' (2009) 91 IRRC 341.

[12] Bernard Röling and CF Rüter (eds), *The Tokyo Judgment: The International Military Tribunal for the Far East Majority Judgment (IMTFE), 29 April 1946–12 November 1948, Volume I* (APA-University Press 1977) 409–10.

[13] The references are included in the judgment in *United States v Max Schmid*, US General Military Court at Dachau, Case no 82, 19 May 1947, available in United Nations War Crimes Commission, 'Law Reports of Trials of War Criminals', vol 13 (1949) 151.

[14] ICRC, *Study on Customary International Humanitarian Law* (ICRC, Geneva 2005) Rule 113 State Practice.

Rights (ICCPR). In a General Comment on reservations, the HRC claimed that it necessarily fell to the Committee to interpret both the ICCPR and a state's reservation to determine whether the latter was compatible with the object and purpose of the treaty.[15] Some governments, including the United States and the United Kingdom, forcefully rejected the view that the HRC had been granted such a power, given the lack of any direct language in the ICCPR or its Optional Protocol to that effect.[16] For those governments, the practice of states in protesting the reservations of other state parties ought to be the proper vehicle to interpret a reservation's compatibility with the object and purpose of a treaty like the ICCPR. In the debate concerning the legal effect of the interpretations given by the HRC, we see that the status of agents exercising powers delegated by states leaves open many questions regarding the legal nature of such an act. It is important to point out that the debate about the HRC's General Comment on reservations is not whether the HRC's interpretations of the ICCPR and reservations have any legal effect. It seems recognized that they do. The debate centres instead on the degree of bindingness attaching to this interpretive act, ie whether states fully delegated this power and thus renounced any possibility of challenging the holdings of the HRC in this respect.[17]

If we turn to actors exercising powers delegated by states but without a clear mandate to interpret international law, the question arises again as to whether the invocation of international legal norms in the exercise of their mandate ought to be considered a form of legal interpretation. Thus, a resolution of the UN General Assembly or Security Council which characterizes a situation as a belligerent occupation calling for the application of international humanitarian law seems to constitute a form of state practice pursuant to, inter alia, the Geneva Conventions. Leaving aside the issue of the process whereby such resolutions are created, the principle embodied in Article 31(3)(b) of the VCLT should apply to this type of legal act, which would thus be properly considered as relevant in the interpretation of the Geneva Conventions. While the ICJ has not explicitly considered the question in these terms, it acknowledged in the Advisory Opinion on the *Legality of the Threat or Use of Nuclear Weapons* that General Assembly resolutions could contribute to the crystallization of new customary norms: this seems consistent with a construction of resolutions applying treaty norms as international practice relevant to the interpretation of that treaty, pursuant to the VCLT.[18] The legal capacity of actors such as the General Assembly to interpret international

---

[15] Human Rights Committee, General Comment 24 (52), *General comment on issues relating to reservations made upon ratification or accession to the Covenant or the Optional Protocols thereto, or in relation to declarations under article 41 of the Covenant*, UN Doc CCPR/C/21/Rev.1/Add. 6 (1994), [18].

[16] Observations by the United States on General Comment No 24, transmitted by letter dated 28 March 1995. UN Doc A/50/40; Observations by the United Kingdom on General Comment No 24, transmitted by letter dated 21 July 1995. UN Doc A/50/40.

[17] A central argument advanced by the US and UK is that, under the Optional Protocol, the HRC is only entitled to make recommendations to states. Unlike the European Court of Human Rights, for instance, the HRC has no power to issue a decision binding on the concerned state.

[18] *Legality of the Threat or Use of Nuclear Weapons* (Advisory Opinion) [1996] ICJ Rep 226.

law can be necessarily implied by the functions which are explicitly granted to such bodies, following the logic developed by the ICJ in its Advisory Opinion on *Reparations for Injury Suffered in the Service of the United Nations*.[19]

The idea of the interpretive community developed by Stanley Fish in the context of literary interpretation, and later applied to legal interpretation by a number of scholars, lends support to the construction of the significance of interpretive acts of states and organizations presented above.[20] According to this understanding of the nature of interpretation, a text does not have a predetermined meaning imposed by its author nor does it have a shapeless content waiting to be fixed by an eventual reader. For Fish, the fact that readers never systematically agree or disagree as to the correct understanding of a text mandates the rejection of both alternatives. Instead, meaning is derived from the converging interpretations given to a text by actors who thereby become members of an interpretive community. These insights were transposed to the practice of treaty interpretation by Ian Johnstone, who suggested that state consent to a treaty covered not only the substance of the agreement but also the process of its interpretation.[21] That process could take the form of a full delegation of interpretive powers to a given body, usually a type of court or tribunal, or more frequently an informal process whereby the community of state parties would collectively construct the meaning to be given to a treaty.

We will return to process issues shortly, but it suffices for now to observe that ratification of treaties like the Geneva Conventions or the UN Charter can be taken to amount to the creation of a community which stands united by the values and assumptions written into the substance of those instruments. As such, collective pronouncements like resolutions of the General Assembly would effectively capture the converging interpretation which constitutes that community. Fish's description of interpretive communities does not investigate the definition of such a community but rather focuses on its function.[22] In the literary context, the community in question would be composed of readers who agree on the meaning of a text, excluding readers who do not share the same interpretation. In the international legal context, the issue is further complicated by the fact that

---

[19] *Reparations for Injury Suffered in the Service of the United Nations* (Advisory Opinion) [1949] ICJ Rep 174. The same approach was adopted by the International Criminal Tribunal for the former Yugoslavia in *Prosecutor v Simic*, in which it decided that the functions attributed by nearly every state to the International Committee of the Red Cross (ICRC) necessarily implied that the ICRC had the right to withhold the testimony of its delegates if it considered that such participation in the international criminal process would be inconsistent with its neutrality and impartiality: *Prosecutor v Simic* (Decision on the prosecution motion under rule 73 for a ruling concerning the testimony of a witness) ICTY-95-9 (27 July 1999). The holding was later endorsed by states in the context of the International Criminal Court (ICC), whose Rules of Procedures and Evidence codify the same legal right for the ICRC: ICC Rules of Procedure and Evidence, Rule 73(4).

[20] See Stanley Fish, *Is There a Text in this Class? The Authority of Interpretive Communities* (Harvard University Press 1982); Owen Fiss, 'Objectivity and Interpretation' (1982) 34 Stan L Rev 739; Kenneth Abraham, 'Statutory Interpretation and Literary Theory: Some Common Concerns of an Unlikely Pair' (1979) 32 Rutgers L Rev 676.

[21] Ian Johnstone, 'Treaty Interpretation: The Authority of Interpretive Communities' (1991) 12 Mich J Int'l L 371.

[22] Johnstone, 'Treaty Interpretation', 376.

community members might be determined not only by shared understanding but also by shared legal status. In other words, would the interpretive community relevant to the understanding of a treaty include only states, or could it include non-state actors? In his studies of the relevance of interpretive communities for treaty interpretation, Johnstone suggested a distinction between three concentric circles: a first circle, the *narrow interpretive community*, composed of governmental and intergovernmental officials negotiating and interpreting a treaty; a second circle, the *broader interpretive community*, which would include officials of third states and experts in international law or other fields of relevance to the treaty; and finally a third unbound circle, the *public sphere*, comprising social movements, the media, and civil society organizations interested in or affected by the treaty.[23] The picture of concentric interpretive circles suggests that, ultimately, it is states that will make the determinative interpretation of the treaty. Legal agents relegated to the third sphere, in particular, are described as 'an audience', not so much actors and even less contributing to the script.[24] This begs the question of the legal significance of interpretive acts by non-state actors which are in no way directed at or connected to state interpretation of the same norm.

Can we rethink the metaphor of interpretive circles so that the statements and practices of actors that cannot be considered to exercise powers delegated by states in any meaningful way might be regarded as meaningful acts of interpretation? This would include multinational corporations, NGOs, individuals, and groups. To begin with, the reference to 'teachings of the most highly qualified publicists of the various nations' as a 'subsidiary means for the determination of the rules of law' in Article 38(1)(d) of the ICJ Statute appears to be an express recognition that actors whose status is in no way derivative of state sovereignty do have the power to interpret international law. This is an approach which echoes civil law's construction of the role of *doctrine* as a supplementary source of the law, and more specifically as a source of interpretation of the Civil Code.[25] According to Johnstone, they are linked by expertise as an epistemic community and are included in the broader interpretive community circle.

A more challenging example of non-state actors interpreting international law concerns the positions taken by non-state armed groups during armed conflicts. Article 1(4) of the 1977 Additional Protocol I envisages that a conflict in which a people is struggling for its self-determination against colonial rule, a racist regime, or alien occupation ought to be considered as an international armed conflict.[26] It seems logical to presume that such a characterization could only occur when the non-state armed group representing the people asserts that it is indeed fighting against colonial, racist, or alien rule, on the basis of the group's interpretation of international legal

---

[23] Johnstone, 'Treaty Interpretation', 385–91; Ian Johnstone, *The Power of Deliberation: International Law, Politics and Organizations* (OUP 2011) 41–2.

[24] Johnstone, *Power of Deliberation*, 53.

[25] See Ingo Venzke, *How Interpretation Makes International Law* (OUP 2012) 65–6; Oscar Schachter, 'The Invisible College of International Lawyers' (1977) 72 North U L Rev 217.

[26] *Protocol Additional to the Geneva Conventions of 12 August 1949, and relating to the Protection of Victims of International Armed Conflicts (Protocol I)*, 8 June 1977, 1125 UNTS 3.

Interpretation in International Law as a Transcultural Project

standards on the right to self-determination. It would seem difficult to argue, for instance, that the African National Congress (ANC) was engaged in a struggle for self-determination against the racist regime in South Africa, if the ANC itself did not advance that claim. The legal recognition of the agency of the national liberation movement in this context seems reflected in the declaration required under Article 96 of Protocol I, whereby the movement binds itself to the rules of that instrument. Even beyond the limited and contested scope of the application of Article 1(4) of Protocol I, the general applicability of treaty and customary international humanitarian law to non-international armed conflicts turns to a significant extent on the insurgents' willingness to label the situation as such. It is broadly recognized that this is so de facto, but a strong argument can be made that this is so de jure as well. There is a recognized principle under the law of state responsibility that the actions of an insurgency movement that succeeds in toppling the established government are to be attributed to that state, in a manner concurrent to the action of the deposed government.[27] Clearly, then, the auto-interpretations of the insurgents are given legal recognition equivalent to that of the organs of the state. Likewise, if we move to acknowledge that corporations may directly commit an internationally wrongful act, and be held accountable on that basis, then again it seems coherent to ascribe some legal significance to interpretive acts attributable to this type of actor.[28]

In the legal characterization of the armed conflict in Sierra Leone, for instance, there could be several competing acts of auto-interpretation emanating from the organs of the state, from the various non-state armed groups involved in the hostilities, from third states, from international organizations, and even from NGOs like the International Committee of the Red Cross (ICRC). We can frame the question of the relative significance of these parallel interpretations by returning to the idea of the interpretive community: are the state, insurgents, NGOs, and other actors all putative members of a single interpretive community that can support an accepted construction of a legal norm? As we saw, the concept of such a community in literary theory remained largely undefined beyond consensus on the meaning of a text. In the international legal context, the exclusion of non-state actors from the relevant interpretive community could only rely on the special status of states in the legal order, a state-centric vision that has been significantly challenged in the last few years.[29]

It would be reasonable to suggest that individuals, armed groups, NGOs, and others may well construe norms of international law but nevertheless remain ultimately subject to more formal mechanisms tasked with interpreting the law. In the case of cannibalism in Sierra Leone, for example, it is the Prosecutor and eventually the SCSL that makes a determination as to whether cannibalism can properly

---

[27] Article 10, Responsibility of States for Internationally Wrongful Acts, GA Res 56/83 (2001) Annex. See René Provost, *International Human Rights and Humanitarian Law* (CUP 2002) 282–4; *Prosecutor v Kayishema and Ruzindana* (Judgment) ICTR-95-I-T, T Ch (21 May 1999), [157].

[28] *Presbyterian Church of the Sudan v Talisman Energy*, 244 F Supp 2d 289, 339 (SDNY 2003). The case was reversed on appeal in 2009, but the Circuit Court of Appeals refrained from deciding this specific issue: 453 F Supp 2d 663 (2d Cir 2009). See José Alvarez, 'Are Corporations Subjects of International Law?' (2011) 9 Santa Clara J Int'l L 1.

[29] See Susan Marks, 'State-Centrism, International Law, and the Anxieties of Influence' (2006) 19 LJIL 339.

be considered as a war crime. This is a compelling point, but only in relation to a legal order the ambition of which is narrowly curtailed. In other words, if we are fundamentally interested in whether an individual could be convicted for the war crime of cannibalism by an international tribunal, then the interpretive act that truly counts is that performed by an official actor, most importantly a court. In light of this, it is reasonable to conclude that the fact that acts of interpretation by non-state actors are not given any legal weight by a tribunal that is given the task to interpret the same norm suggests that such non-state behaviour does not amount to real legal interpretation. We find another example of this in international trade law, where the business practices of economic actors are not considered relevant to the interpretation of state obligations under the World Trade Organization.[30] If, however, our normative ambition extends beyond the repressive function of the law to encompass not only its prescriptive function (cannibalism taken as an abhorrent act that no one should countenance) but also its narrative function (the way in which the law construes cannibalism as a social practice contributes to shaping both the practice and the response thereto), then we are confronted with the very limited reach of the application of formal legal standards and established legal institutions. Even in relation to the episodic occurrence of cannibalism in the Sierra Leone conflict, very few people are likely to be convicted of the war crime of cannibalism. In fact, as we have seen in the case law of the SCSL, no one was convicted or even indicted for this practice. Should we conclude from this fact that the current state of affairs is unlikely to change any time soon and that there cannot be a legal norm labelling cannibalism as a war crime? Surely not.

The maxim that 'ignorance of the law is no excuse' is widely regarded as a necessary principle to make our laws operational, lest everyone plead that the law is too complex or too inaccessible to really know. The normative implications of such a foundational idea are rarely articulated: no one may ignore the law, because everyone is meant to gain knowledge of it and behave accordingly. But legal subjects are not mere conduits through which legal norms circulate without being affected by the process, nor automatons that can be programmed to execute norms without transforming them in some way. As powerfully articulated by James Boyd White, the process of interpreting the law in order to apply it is a form of translation. This is an exercise in which the individual, far from remaining neutral, affirms her own values and identity while maintaining a sense of fidelity to the original text.[31] If we wish law to be real beyond the limited reach of formal institutions, then we must concede that the terrain in which it must grow roots implicates the very subjects it seeks to regulate. Law becomes tangible only inasmuch as it is appropriated by those to whom and through whom it applies:

The obligational force of legal rules derives not from the normative status with which they are vested when ultimately wielded by officials, but from the normative status human beings afford them in their everyday lives.[32]

---

[30] See Isabelle Van Damme, *Treaty Interpretation by the WTO Appellate Body* (OUP 2009) 268.
[31] James Boyd White, *Justice as Translation* (Chicago University Press 1990) 260.
[32] Roderick Macdonald and David Sandomierski, 'Against Nomopolies' (2006) 57 NILQ 610, 615.

In that sense, cannibalism can truly become a war crime in Sierra Leone only when a range of legal actors extending widely beyond the walls of the SCSL court-room in Freetown considers it as such. The way to reach this broader range of actors in a place like Sierra Leone includes not only the *rayonnement* of legal norms but also related and connected phenomena from political pronouncements to the spreading of rumours through the grapevines.[33]

The vision of interpretation in international law advanced here covers a wide range of practices by many different kinds of actors. How these actors interpret will reflect their identity as well as their function. As noted earlier, much of the literature on interpretation in international law focuses on the judicial function, most often in relation to treaty interpretation.[34] That literature is significant for the analysis offered here in many ways. I will avoid covering that well-trodden field, and instead offer a limited argument to deny that there is a direct and necessary link between the status of an interpretive agent and the process of interpretation. In other words, all categories of actors can engage in all processes of interpret-ation, so that it is difficult to make claims as to fundamental differences which aim to delegitimize certain types of interpretive practices on that basis alone.

B. Interpretive practices

Let us turn first to actors whose status as interpreters is derived directly or indi-rectly from state sovereignty. As noted earlier, the prototypical interpreter of inter-national law is the member of a judicial body like the ICJ, the SCSL, or the European Court of Human Rights. A detailed analysis of the elements that com-prise this formal state-based interpretive process would not only risk amounting to no more than a survey of existing literature, but would also fail to contribute to the central claim of this chapter. It suffices to underscore that the process and agent largely merge in this exercise: the features of judicial treaty interpretation tend to loop back towards the state. The ordinary meaning of the words cho-sen by states, the *travaux préparatoires* largely or exclusively carried out by states, subsequent state practice, and so on, all channel interpretation back to the state. Even in cases before international criminal tribunals, to which the state is not a party, the same dynamic is evident. Thus, the central tool used by international criminal courts to expand the scope of international law through interpretation has been the consideration of general principles of domestic law, again an eman-ation of state sovereignty. Broadly speaking, the interpretation of customary law by international judges is likewise an exercise rooted in the state, its actions, and its purported sense of the normative reach of international obligations (in the guise of *opinio juris*).

---

[33] See Mariane Ferme, *The Underneath of Things: Violence, History, and the Everyday in Sierra Leone* (University of California Press 2001).
[34] See n 6.

There are marginal principles informing the international judge's interpretive process that escape this state-bound logic. One is the legitimate consideration of 'teachings of the most highly qualified publicists of the various nations', to which I alluded earlier. Article 38(1)(d) of the ICJ Statute is framed by a chapeau which suggests that the ensuing list is comprised of sources, underscoring the agency of publicists as interpreters of international law. In addition, Article 38(1)(d) identifies the writings of publicists as a 'subsidiary means for the determination of rules of law', evoking it as a part of the interpretive process by the ICJ which is (at least initially) not state-centred. More radically, the jurisprudence of the International Criminal Tribunal for the former Yugoslavia (ICTY) has invoked the practice of non-state actors as relevant to the interpretation and formation of customary international law. In the *Prosecutor v Tadic* judgment on interlocutory appeal, the Appeals Chamber held that the work of the ICRC 'ought…to be regarded as an element of actual international practice'.[35] This is a remarkable—and rare—expansion of the judicial interpretive exercise beyond the realm of what is connected to the state.

It is important to underscore the fact that states interpret international law in ways which do not necessarily adhere to a formal process like that of courts. I mentioned earlier the necessity for states to auto-interpret international law if they are ever to avail themselves of the legal right to adopt countermeasures in reaction to a prior violation of international law. On a continuous basis, states consider the relevant international legal norms in order to develop national policies and guide practice. In general, states do not usually make public the opinion of their international legal advisers or other internal interpretive processes, so all we are left with is the practice or policy itself as an interpretive act.

In some interstate institutions, however, there is a public deliberative process whereby states articulate certain interpretations of international law. Prime examples are the UN General Assembly and Security Council, in which states routinely invoke, interpret, and apply international legal standards. Should these invocations be considered acts of interpretation of international law? The ICJ in the *Admission of a State to the United Nations* advisory opinion considered the place of law in decisions of the General Assembly and Security Council. The ICJ was deeply divided on whether states could legitimately consider elements beyond the conditions for admission listed in Article 4 of the UN Charter, when deciding how to vote on a request for the admission of a new state.[36] The majority considered that the General Assembly and Security Council performed a quasi-judicial function in this context, and were legally bound to apply the legal criteria as expressed in Article 4, to the exclusion of any other factor.[37] For the dissenters, on the contrary, these were regarded as political decisions made by political bodies, and thus it was appropriate for political factors to be considered beyond

---

[35] *Prosecutor v Tadic* (Decision in the Defence Motion for Interlocutory Appeal on Jurisdiction) ICTY-94-I (2 October 1995), [109].

[36] *Admission of a State to the United Nations* (Advisory Opinion) [1947-48] ICJ Rep 57.

[37] [1947-48] ICJ Rep 64.

the legal criteria listed in Article 4.[38] In part, the division within the ICJ related to the bounded nature of the decision-making process in the General Assembly and Security Council, a question which only partially overlaps with the issue of labelling the exercise an act of interpretation. It is in this respect that the inter-subjective nature of interpretation becomes central: the United States could argue in the Security Council that the requisite conditions were met for the use of force against Iraq in 2003, but other governments failed to be persuaded.[39] This may have been an interpretation, but it was not compelling and certainly not authoritative. The reverse observation also holds: an opinion may be neither compelling nor authoritative and yet still qualify as a legal interpretation. Once interpretation moves beyond the rarefied judicial atmosphere, it becomes a way of engaging with others much more than a basis for an unassailable conclusion.

'Interpretation as conversation' begs the question of the boundaries of the potential interpretive community supporting a given understanding of a legal norm. Like any other legal regime, international law structures the conditions under which these relations of meaning and relations of power are managed, at the same time that it sets parameters for actions and understandings. International law proclaims the distinctiveness of the state as a legal subject but, as I have suggested earlier, other legal subjects nevertheless engage in interpretive acts. Like states, these other subjects interpret by way of a spectrum of processes, both formal and informal. The less structured nature of non-state actors suggests a more natural or organic association with informal interpretive processes.

To return to the example of Article 1(4) of Additional Protocol I, a national liberation movement may affirmatively assert that it is indeed 'fighting against colonial domination and alien occupation and against racist regimes in the exercise of their right to self-determination', and accordingly make a declaration pursuant to Article 96(3) that it will apply the Protocol.[40] In such an act, there is an interpretive claim that the provisions of the treaty can be read to cover the conflict in question. A national liberation movement may or may not offer a detailed analysis of the law and facts which led it to such a conclusion. Given the limited legal resources and institutional organization of most non-state armed groups, we can expect that, more often than not, the interpretation is reduced to a statement asserting a particular construction and application of a given norm.

Perhaps less intuitively, there are also instances in which non-state actors adopt formal processes for the interpretation of international law. Thus, non-state armed groups have on occasion established courts to try individuals accused of violating the code of conduct of the group, or even committing war crimes prohibited by international law. In some cases, especially where the rebels controlled a significant portion of national territory for an extended period of time, 'real' tribunals

---

[38] [1947-48] ICJ Rep 85.

[39] See Ian Johnstone, 'The Power of Interpretive Communities' in Michael Barnett and Raymond Duvall (eds), *Power in Global Governance* (CUP 2005) 185, 193–204.

[40] See Denise Plattner, 'La portée juridique des déclarations de respect du droit international humanitaire qui émanent de mouvements en lutte dans un conflit armé' (1984–5) 18 RBDI 298.

have been established which can operate in a fashion quite close to tribunals established by states. Insurgent courts have been established in countries including Sri Lanka, El Salvador, Nepal, Sierra Leone, Colombia, Kosovo, and Sudan. In Sri Lanka, where the Liberation Tigers of Tamil Elam (LTTE) insurgency controlled a large swath of the country for a very long period, a structured court system was established: the 17 different courts in that judicial structure handled more than 20,000 civil and criminal cases over the years. There was even an LTTE law school to train judges and lawyers![41] In one trial, the SCSL found that the existence of this type of system offered a tool to sanction violations of international humanitarian law, and that a commander could be found responsible if he failed to avail himself of that possibility.[42] Although insurgent courts usually function away from the public eye and do not keep formal records, it seems difficult to deny that at least some of them are engaged in what can properly be termed the interpretation of international law.

The interpretation of international law can thus be seen to involve a diverse range of legal actors, both state and non-state, operating on the basis of a range of interpretive practices, both formal and informal. Robert Cover used the image of a 'shadow of coercion' to explain the fact that although norms emerge in a wide array of social structures, the potential intervention of the state and the 'jurispathic' function of the courts means that these normative regimes are never wholly free of the state's influence and possible determinative intervention.[43] In the international legal regime, there is also a shadow of state coercion, although it appears thinner and incomplete, leaving many normative regimes largely beyond the reach of direct state influence. Viewed as such, interpretation in international law emerges as transcultural, in that it will involve an inter-subjective process which brings together actors who do not necessarily share sovereignty as a common culture.

II. The Transcultural Nature of Interpretation in International Law

Given the polycentric and polyphonic nature of the interpretive process in international law, as described in Part I above, this section considers whether is it possible to generate a coherent narrative of legality regarding a practice such as cannibalism under the relevant standards of international criminal law. I suggest that approaches relying on a concept such as the interpretive community fail to

---

[41] See Sandesh Sivakumaran, 'Courts of Armed Opposition Groups' (2009) 7 JICJ 489; Jonathan Somer, 'Jungle Justice: Passing Sentence on the Equality of Belligerents in Non-International Armed Conflicts' (2007) 89 IRRC 655, 678–90.

[42] *Prosecutor v Brima, Kamara, Kanu* (AFRC Trial) (Judgment) SCSL-04-16-T (20 June 2007), [1739]–[1741].

[43] See Robert M Cover, 'The Supreme Court, 1982 Term—Foreword: Nomos and Narrative' (1983) 97 Harv L Rev 4, 53.

support the normative claim embodied in international law. Instead, a thicker understanding of the interpretive process projects a pluralistic construction of international law that can more accurately capture the promise and limits of that regime.

At a very general level, to reflect upon the nature of the interpretive process is to offer a vision of the concept of law.[44] Much of the literature on interpretation in international law appears to be predicated on a concept of law that rests on four precepts: *monism* (the claim that international law is a unified, coherent regime); *centralism* (associating the power to validly create legal standards with state sovereignty); *positivism* (viewing law as ontologically distinguished from fact, thus allowing the systematic delineation of the frontier of legality to reflect preexisting legal standards); and *prescriptivism* (offering legal norms as external constraints descending upon legal agents to try to modify patterns of behaviour).[45] This supports a vision of the interpretive function in international law that aims to discover the single proper meaning of a legal standard, via the discovery of the intention of states whose consent lends legitimacy to that standard, so that it can be applied to facts as found by the interpreter.[46] This account of interpretation in international law is radically different from the description, offered in Part II, of the variety of ways in which diverse categories of actors give meaning to international legal norms. That vision of interpretation in turn reflects a concept of law that challenges each of the four tenets identified as the basis for a positivist understanding of international law. Instead, international law is given a pluralistic understanding, whereby law is *fragmented* (with no necessary coherence across international law as a whole), *decentralized* (where many centres and processes exist to create and interpret law), *contingent* (norms do not exist *a priori* but emerge from an engagement with the particular circumstances of their invocation, including agents and context), and *deliberative* (law is not so much a series of commands as a space in which meaning is collectively created in relation to social practices). Clearly, when international law is understood in this fashion, it makes little sense to ask whether interpretation amounts to the creation of legal norms. Instead, the creation, interpretation, and application of legal norms are interconnected processes that do not necessarily call for systematic differentiation.

Can the concept of an interpretive community, evoked earlier, provide a framework which can account for a pluralistic understanding of interpretation in international law? As discussed above, the attractiveness of the interpretive community concept lies in its ability to speak to legal interpretation as understood beyond the formal, institutionalized process carried out by courts, to encompass a variety of actors and processes. In the literature on interpretation in international law that makes use of the idea of an interpretive community, not much is said regarding

---

[44] Space constraints prevent me from fully articulating this link. For an especially lucid account, see Venzke, *How Interpretation Makes International Law*, 16–37.

[45] Macdonald and Sandomierski, 'Against Nomopolies', 615; Roderick Macdonald, 'Here, There…and Everywhere—Theorizing Legal Pluralism; Theorizing Jacques Vanderlinden' in Nicholas Kasirer (ed), *Mélanges Jacques Vanderlinden* (Yvon Blais 2006) 381.

[46] Kolb, *Interprétation et création du droit international*, 74–80.

the constitution of this type of community beyond a claim that it is constituted by concentric circles.[47] In literary theory, the argument was that the community was constituted by all those who subscribed to a particular interpretation. In other words, the interpretation *is* the community, and vice versa. Kenneth Abraham notes that what makes this consensus possible within a community are shared beliefs whose role in constructing the object of interpretation largely goes unacknowledged.[48] We can understand the trend in international legal literature that maintains a strong focus on the state as a central participant in communities of interpretation to be a reflection of the shared values embodied in sovereignty.[49] This is all the more evident when the norm to be interpreted issues from a treaty ratified by the concerned states, the treaty standing here as a consensual framework affirming a set of values.[50]

When we consider the proper legal characterization of cannibalism under international criminal law, calling for the interpretation of a set of standards that are by no means clear on the matter, to what interpretive community do we refer? It is of course possible to refer only to states which have ratified the 1949 Geneva Conventions and the 1998 Rome Statute of the ICC, but that would bring us back to a narrow understanding of interpretation which, as has been suggested, fails to account for the richness and complexity of the interpretive process. If, on the contrary, we enlarge the community to include a wide range of actors that may interact with a given norm, should we then include cannibals within the relevant interpretive community? They are, after all, undeniably significant actors in this regard. This begs the question, to go back to Abraham's insight, of whether states and cannibals share assumptions and understandings that provide a common-sense foundation to the constitution of the object to be interpreted. Perhaps they do not. In this sense, an approach inspired by the idea of interpretive communities appears to cling to a variant of monism, recognizing the possibility of competing interpretive communities but not articulating the normative relationship that may exist among them or providing a foundation for an overarching normative order. Without a broader community that would encompass many or all relevant interpretive communities, there is no law that can be meaningfully shared. Ultimately, according to this perspective, one is forced to choose whether to be an international lawyer or a cannibal. The image is of two normative universes existing side by side, but not interacting. It suggests a radical failure of the law to shape the broader construction of cannibalism.

To be a legal interpreter is to be the architect of a bridge linking the imagination of the authors of a legal norm to the aspirations of those who invoke it. In this respect, the process of interpretation is a variation of the process of translation—indeed, 'to interpret' may refer to interpretation or translation

---

[47] The most elaborate discussion in international law is Johnstone, *Power of Deliberation*.
[48] Abraham, 'Statutory Interpretation and Literary Theory', 686.
[49] Johnstone, 'Treaty Interpretation', 389.
[50] Johnstone, 'Treaty Interpretation', 383.

depending on the circumstances. As brilliantly explored by Boyd White, translation provides a metaphor that captures the very life of the law.[51] Boyd White observes that the word 'translation' is derived from the Latin *trans* (across) and *latus* (to carry), whereas the word 'metaphor' is derived from the Greek *meta* (across) and *phor* (to carry). In other words, to translate or to interpret is to invoke a metaphor. This representation of interpretation moves us away from the linking of an abstract legal standard to a concrete factual setting, to evoke instead the linking of two realms of the imagination, both of which are projections of the mind of the interpreter. On the one hand, there is the norm, whether in text, words, or patterns of practice, to which the interpreter has no direct access but only an indirect one, mediated by language. Of course, for treaty norms, there is a written text, but as has been observed so many times, no text speaks for itself, and someone must speak for it. The legitimacy of its source, or authority of its formulation, does not alter this state of affairs in any way.

On the other hand, there is the reading to be given by the interpreter to the norm, an act of creation that perhaps triggers fewer challenges to its imaginary character. The metaphor of the bridge speaks to the fact that the interpreter may inhabit an uncertain space between two realms of the imagination, but nevertheless owe fidelity to the norm as she can discover it and to the claim as she can perceive it. We may recognize in this description the process of interpretive commitments that Robert Cover found to be essential to the law's existence, a commitment made through a process he termed 'jurisgenesis',[52] but which is a form of interpretation as understood here. What is significant in Cover's representation is the centrality of the interpreter's role in the process. Like the translator for Boyd White, the legal actor for Cover does not disappear behind the norm but rather affirms his own identity in this process. As such, jurisgenesis for Cover and translation for Boyd White are necessarily rooted in culture.[53]

What is the implication of holding that interpreters affirm their own identity and, by that token, their own culture in the process of interpretation? On one understanding of interpretation, it would lead to the conclusion that the interpreter can thereby impose her own culture on the interpretive process. In the cannibalism example, it suggests that the SCSL can project its own culture, rooted in Western legalism, onto the practice of cannibalism as it occurred within some segments of Sierra Leonian society. To a large extent, that is precisely the construction of the interpretive function of courts entrenched in legal culture. As Cover evocatively observed: 'Judges are people of violence. Because of the violence they command, judges characteristically do not create law, but kill it. Theirs is the jurispathic office.'[54] What Cover describes is the mode of intervention of a court confronted with a plurality of competing interpretations offered by numerous

---

[51] White, *Justice as Translation*, 233.   [52] Cover, 'Nomos and Narrative', 11–19.

[53] Cover, 'Nomos and Narrative', 11: 'The creation of legal meaning—"jurisgenesis"—takes place always through an essentially cultural medium'; White, *Justice as Translation*, 252: 'There is no position outside of culture from which the original can be experienced'.

[54] Cover, 'Nomos and Narrative', 53.

participants, whereby the court identifies the one 'proper' interpretation of what ought to be considered *the* law, thereby deeming illegitimate, and destroying, any other interpretations. This interpretive monopoly, corresponding to a hermeneutic supremacy, is grounded in the idea of sovereignty and the state's power to ultimately arbitrate the meaning of law. In other words, the legal culture's claim to supremacy is reflective of, and thus limited by, legal culture. The law's totalizing cosmology ultimately appears as circular, like a cat chasing its tail whilst claiming to rule the world. Each community underpinning an interpretation of the law will generate its own normative universe, reflecting its own *Grundnorm*.[55] This holds true for every community, even for fighters in Sierra Leone who embrace cannibalism as a practice. I mentioned earlier the significance for Cover of the 'shadow of coercion' that exerted an influence on all interpretive commitments, even those that are individual and private as opposed to collective and public. He had in mind the dissenting views of religious groups in the United States, at odds with the constitutionalized majoritarian view enforced by the courts. That specific context explained the need to acknowledge the political ascendance and material power of courts as a feature of the broader community to which these religious groups otherwise belonged. When transplanting these ideas to the interpretation of international law generally and the laws of war in particular, the political ascendance and material power of a court like the SCSL may not correspond to reality as perceived by many of the concerned actors, including cannibals. The 'shadow of coercion' of international law stands evanescent, if not altogether vanished, in the darkness of war.

It emerges from all this that legal interpretation is not about the dominance of one culture (the interpreter's) over any other, but instead about the mediation of cultural difference. At the same time, interpretation does not demand the erasure of the interpreter's own culture; on the contrary, a legal interpretation appears as valid only to the extent that it represents a maxim one is willing to live by. Interpretation thus must be one and the other, located in the culture of the interpreter but reflective of the fact of difference. The ethical stance of the interpreter is not one of dominance but of respect, not necessarily respect of the values embraced by other cultures but rather respect for the fact of difference and the fluidity of cultures.[56] As such, legal interpretation speaks to the nature of law not merely as a system of rules but also as a system of meaning, and to the interconnections that exist between different normative universes. In this deliberative sense, the law corresponds to an episteme, understood as an inter-subjective knowledge underpinning legal narratives that aim to organize differences rather than generate uniformity.[57]

---

[55] Cover, 'Nomos and Narrative', 42–3.   [56] White, *Justice as Translation*, 257.
[57] Emanuel Adler and Steven Bernstein, 'Knowledge in Power: The Epistemic Construction of Global Governance' in Michael Barnett and Raymond Duvall (eds), *Power in Global Governance* (CUP 2005) 294, 296.

Conclusion

If legal interpretation in international law can be likened to a game, it is a complex game occurring in many interrelated sites and involving a wide array of actors. In this type of game, participants must develop diverse strategies, each adjusted to the particular context and the nature and identities of players. Central to these strategies will be the establishment of formal or informal relationships with other players, as no one can hope to win either by imposing their will through sheer power or by luck. The official rules of the game may be the same for all players, and everyone enters the fray with the same objective of winning, but each participant will bring to the game her own particular strategies. These strategies reflect both the player's understanding of the game and his or her sense of self.

Understood in light of this metaphor, legal interpretation of international law emerges as a phenomenon that is both broad (covering a wide range of processes) and ambitious (aiming to exert an influence considerably beyond the courtroom and other legal institutions). It is also an invitation to international lawyers to show humility (perhaps not their natural inclination) in accepting the limits of legal discourse and the pervasiveness of other narratives that compete and interact with the law to give meaning to our lives. Returning to cannibalism, nothing in this vision of interpretation would prevent the SCSL from concluding that cannibalism as a practice in the conflict in Sierra Leone amounted to a war crime. It would, however, proscribe an interpretive posture to the effect that cannibalism is a practice that is senseless and devoid of meaning. Instead, the SCSL ought to acknowledge that this is a social practice embedded in a specific culture, albeit arguably contrary to international criminal law. Only in this way can any interpreter hope to occupy a space in between norm and application that opens the possibility of shared understanding.

PART VI

PLAYING THE GAME OF GAME-PLAYING

15

Towards a Politics of Hermeneutics

Jens Olesen

Introduction

The question of whether or not there is such a thing as the 'politics of interpretation' has occupied students of literature and those interested in interpretation more generally for many years. Various articles and books have been written that explicitly address this question, the majority of which declare that interpretation has a political dimension.[1] Yet, despite this interest in the topic, little light has been shed on what it actually means to speak of interpretation as having a politics or being political. The aim of this chapter is to offer some orientation in the dark by elucidating the relationship between interpretation and politics, which has been obscured in at least three ways.

First, in common parlance we usually refer to textual interpretations as individual activities, while we allude to politics as a collective enterprise. However, the gulf between the two practices is not as wide as we tend to believe. To be sure, interpretation is not a collective activity, yet it is constrained by collectively constructed frameworks; that is, interpretation is invariably shaped by pre-judgements and conventions whose politics frequently escape our notice. Interpreters also draw on, speak as members of, and respond to 'interpretive communities',[2] which are comprised of all those who share methods for reading texts. Those communities exert an influence over their members, distance themselves from other groups of readers, and exercise some degree of power, particularly within the academy.

Second, we associate the interpretation of texts with an endeavour in which we are all engaged at different levels of sophistication—the sober task of construing the meaning of (more or less) complex articles, books, and the law—whereas we

---

[1] In WJ Thomas Mitchell (ed), *The Politics of Interpretation* (University of Chicago Press 1983), most of the eminent contributors claim that interpretation has a political dimension yet there is no consensus on what this dimension might entail, let alone where in the interpretive process it is to be found. See also Peter J Rabinowitz, *Before Reading: Narrative Conventions and the Politics of Interpretation* (Ohio State University Press 1987); Patrick Hogan, *The Politics of Interpretation: Ideology, Professionalism, and the Study of Literature* (OUP 1990).

[2] The term was coined in Stanley Fish, *Is There a Text in This Class? The Authority of Interpretive Communities* (Harvard University Press 1980).

tend to think that only a small number of people are 'doing' politics, usually politicians. We also associate concepts such as power and ideology with the domain of
politics, rather than textual interpretation. Yet this chapter will suggest that such
concepts do have a bearing on the interpretation of texts, thus making the latter
more overtly political. My claim is not that textual interpretations are *only* ideological and instigated by power, but that they are *also* shaped by ideology and power.

Third, we note that legal interpreters do not normally consider textual interpretation as a political act, but rather as a neutral tool with which the meaning
of texts can be unlocked.[3] That is, they bracket their political commitments from
interpretive considerations. Ronald Dworkin may be seen as an exception to this
trend. He argues that lawyers and judges 'cannot avoid politics in the broad sense
of political theory', by which he means that they need to have a sound understanding of political concepts such as justice and equality since those concepts
have a bearing on the interpretation of particular cases. Yet Dworkin hastens to
add that law is not 'a matter of personal or partisan politics'.[4] On the contrary, the
only criterion by which interpretations of legal texts should ultimately be assessed
is whether or not they convey the true meaning of the law.[5] However, such a focus
on the truth-value of interpretations comes at a price, for it means that ideological
convictions, which creep into juridical interpretations, go unnoticed.[6]

What is perhaps more surprising is that this depoliticized view of interpretation is not only pervasive among laymen and women and legal theorists, but also
among eminent scholars of hermeneutics. Even though the history of hermeneutics offers numerous examples that attest to the political consequences of textual
interpretations,[7] hermeneutics' 'ontological turn', under the aegis of Heidegger
and Gadamer, has led to a neglect of its politics. This chapter will debunk the
false dichotomy between political commitments, at one end of the spectrum, and
interpretive practice, on the other. I hope to show how certain ideological and
political commitments, related to such issues as what it means for interpreters
to give an account of a text and to interpret its meaning, both control the way
that interpretive enquiries are conducted and determine the significance of the
resulting interpretations. Accordingly, methods of interpretation are not the basis of

---

[3] For this positivist conception of legal interpretation, see Hans Kelsen, *Pure Theory of Law*
(University of California Press 1967) and HLA Hart, *The Concept of Law* (2nd edn, Clarendon
Press 1994).

[4] Ronald Dworkin, 'Law as Interpretation' in WJ Thomas Mitchell (ed), *The Politics of
Interpretation* (University of Chicago Press 1983) 249, 266.

[5] Ronald Dworkin, *A Matter of Principle* (Harvard University Press 1985) 146.

[6] Dworkin, *A Matter of Principle*, 146. More recently, Dworkin has sustained this view by arguing that there is truth to be had in textual interpretation. See *Justice for Hedgehogs* (Belknap Press of
Harvard University Press 2011) 123–56.

[7] For instance, Luther's interpretation and translation of the Bible into German contributed to
widening the circle of readers to every reasonably intelligent layman who was able to read. Only
through reading the Bible, Luther argued in the preface to the New Testament, could various
abuses of papal and churchly power, which had been justified by recourse to the Bible, be remedied.
See Martin Luther, *Die gantze Heilige Schrifft. Der komplette Originaltext von 1545 in modernem
Schriftbild* (Rogner & Bernhard 1972) and Peter J Brenner, *Das Problem der Interpretation. Eine
Einführung in die Grundlagen der Literaturwissenschaft.* (Niemeyer Verlag 1998) 63.

neutral enquiry; rather, they are more or less systematically developed decontestation devices, which serve as the building blocks of interpretive communities.[8]

The scope of my enquiry will be limited to the interpreter's 'will to power' and drive to finality, and the performative dimension and political consequences of interpretive speech acts. I will conclude by sketching out an approach that enables us to decode the ideological underpinnings of our interpretations of texts. Needless to say, any approach necessarily simplifies and imposes coherence on to messier processes, and this approach is no exception. Since it is based on my understanding of what we do when we read a text, it represents *a* politics of interpretation with all its limitations, and does not pretend to explain *the* politics of interpretation.

My operational definition of politics is that it is a set of 'assumptions or principles relating to or underlying any activity, theory, or attitude, ... when concerned with questions of power and status in a society' and 'informed by a certain ideological outlook on the world'.[9] That is to say, politics involves actions that are directed toward the 'acquisition and exercise of power, status or authority'.[10] By ideology, I mean a set of beliefs and ideas 'through which individuals and groups construct an understanding of the political world they ... inhabit, and then act on that understanding'.[11] Ideologies are mapping devices that give us a sense of orientation by interpreting, evaluating, and presenting the world in a way designed to organize, direct, mobilize, and justify 'certain modes or courses of action and to anathematise others'.[12] As it is impossible to define politics and ideology in an apolitical manner, the aforementioned attempts at definitions should be considered as tentative and inviting contestation.

I. Against a Politics of Interpretation

Before I draw on insights from Nietzsche's philosophy and speech act theory, I need to consider some objections that have been advanced against the very possibility of a politics of interpretation. The ensuing discussion will serve a dual purpose. Not only will I demonstrate that the objections are unfounded, but I will also show that the presuppositions we bring to bear on texts in the course of the interpretive process are at least, in part, ideological.

In his response to those contributors who put the case for a 'politics of interpretation' in an edited volume of the same title, Walter Benn Michaels advances what might be regarded as a very compelling counter-argument.[13] Michaels suggests

---

[8] The term 'decontestation' was coined by Michael Freeden: *Ideologies and Political Theory: A Conceptual Approach* (Clarendon Press 1996) 5.

[9] Oxford English Dictionary <http://www.oed.com/view/Entry/237575?redirectedFrom=politics#eid> accessed 28 July 2014.

[10] Oxford English Dictionary. [11] Freeden, *Ideologies and Political Theory*, 3.

[12] David Kettler, 'Politics' in David Miller, Janet Coleman, William Connolly, and Alan Ryan (eds), *The Blackwell Encyclopedia of Political Thought* (Blackwell 1991) 235.

[13] Walter Benn Michaels, 'Is there a Politics of Interpretation?' in WJ Thomas Mitchell (ed), *The Politics of Interpretation* (University of Chicago Press 1983) 335.

that those that back the hypothesis that there is a politics of interpretation believe that since texts confront us with a range of equally plausible meanings we can, and indeed must, choose among them on the basis of our own political preferences. Interpretation is thus the result of free political choice. On the contrary, Michaels claims that it does not make sense to conceive of interpretation as involving a choice at all. To be sure, he admits that we can choose to read and interpret a text in a particular way, yet he denies that we can choose to believe that the interpretation we provide is true.[14] Instead, that choice was made by the author of the text. Hence, Michaels claims that the notion that interpretation is intrinsically political rests on an 'implausible and ultimately incoherent epistemology'.[15]

Unsurprisingly, I am not convinced by Michaels' argument. First of all, I do not think that we should accept his reduction of politics to choice, for this would empty the concept of other, equally important features. But let us, for argument's sake, accept that politics is most importantly, though not exclusively, about choice. What I then need to demonstrate is that the same holds true for interpretation, or at the very least, that interpretation does in fact involve choice. To begin with, Michaels himself admits of two cases in which interpretation involves choice: the choice of the text we wish to interpret and that we can choose to interpret it in a particular way. Both cases are instances of selections among alternatives (texts and methods), whereby those selections are informed by all kinds of background assumptions and preferences, some of which are political. As Habermas has argued forcefully, knowledge cannot be separated from 'interests' and preferences, because they shape the very interpretations from which 'facts' are constituted.[16] Therefore, I am not convinced by Michaels' claim that what we consider to be right, epistemologically speaking, is ever independent from our way of thinking, because our way of thinking is not wholly independent of certain experiences or preferences (cultural, political, and others) that help us reduce complexity and make decisions. That is why decisions about the truth of a matter are never entirely unrelated to, or distinct from, political preferences and ideological beliefs.

But then we may wonder how much choice there actually is in interpretation. If political preferences and ideological beliefs constrain our way of reading texts, are we still free to choose one interpretation at the expense of another? I do think that we are because my claim does not amount to saying that (1) these preferences and beliefs single-handedly predetermine our interpretation, nor (2) that 'they come into play independent of and outside of the actual interpretive process'.[17] Rather, my claim is that experiences and preferences (both individual and societal[18]) provide interpreters with a pool of possible associations, some of which are evoked in the process of interpretation and by confrontation with the text. As players of the interpretive game, we draw on our experiences from other games, and adopt

[14] Michaels, 'Is there a Politics of Interpretation?', 336.
[15] Michaels, 'Is there a Politics of Interpretation?', 344.
[16] Jürgen Habermas, *Erkenntnis und Interesse* (Suhrkamp 1968).
[17] Michaels, 'Is there a Politics of Interpretation?', 337.
[18] By societal experiences or preferences, I mean Durkheimian 'social facts', such as conventions or ideologies, which will be discussed below.

strategies which conform to the rules of the game and which we deem appropriate in the circumstances. In other words, there is an interplay between the interpreter and a multitude of social conditions, on the one hand, and the text, on the other.[19]

In order to see that ideological presuppositions creep into our understanding of what it means to interpret, we only need to take a closer look at Michaels' own account. Michaels maintains that readers gain the text's meaning from the author. But he does not seem to recognize that this understanding of textual interpretation is already informed by certain conservative presuppositions, nor does he concede that interpretation would be political even if the author, with the choices that he or she made, was the only significant agent in the interpretive process. Michaels' view of the interpretive process is premised on the following assumptions: that readers need to subject themselves to the authority of the author, accepting that the author is the sole determiner of the text; that the author is not just single-handedly determining the meaning of their text, but is able to directly communicate that meaning to their informed readers, whose only task it is to recover meaning that was put there by the author; and that since the text's meaning is equivalent to what its author intends it to mean, texts do not permit any number of interpretations. On the contrary, there is no pluralism in interpretation, but only one correct interpretation that corresponds to what the author intended. Such views reflect a conservative outlook on matters of interpretation. As Michael Freeden has shown, the inequality of human beings (in Michaels' case, of readers and authors), 'respect for authority and its institutional manifestations' (readers' acceptance of authorial authority), and the rejection of pluralism as a threat to social order and values are three of the most important conceptual ingredients of conservatism.[20] While Michaels presents his views as facts, they are rather decisions he has made, decisions which *nolens volens* imply that he had a choice. In other words, we should consider Michaels' claims for what they are: ideologically informed decontestations of the interpretive process. (I will return to the question of how ideological presuppositions can be decoded below.)

Having cast serious doubts on some objections that have been made against the politics of interpretation, I now need to consider at greater length what the politics of interpretation consists of.

II. Nietzsche and the Interpretive 'Will to Power'

This section will demonstrate that interpretation and power are closely linked.[21] My discussion will begin with a critical analysis of Nietzsche's understanding of interpretation, as he has made a strong case for its relationship with power. While

---

[19] To be more precise, the knowledge of language, representations of the natural and social world, assumptions, beliefs, and values exert their influence on the interpreter, and thus on the process of interpretation. See Norman Fairclough, *Language and Power* (Longman 1989) 25.

[20] Freeden, *Ideologies and Political Theory*, 331.

[21] The following discussion is a substantially revised version of an earlier account. See Jens Olesen, 'Von Deutungsmacht und wie Deutung Macht macht' in Carsten Baker, Matthias Klatt, and Sabrina Zucca-Soest (eds), *Sprache-Recht-Gesellschaft* (Mohr Siebeck 2012) 38–43.

Nietzsche's notion of interpretation extends well beyond the domain of textual interpretation,[22] I will use the term interpretation in a narrower sense and focus primarily on the link between power and the interpretation of texts. Since my aim is not to make a contribution to Nietzsche scholarship but to advance our understanding of the politics of interpretation, my reading will be deliberately selective and based on those passages in Nietzsche's *On the Genealogy of Morality*, where the relationship between interpretation and power is at the forefront of the discussion.[23]

While *On the Genealogy of Morality* is principally concerned with the formation of morals, Nietzsche's reflections on moral language prompt him to spell out the fundamental assumptions behind his philosophy of language. As we shall see, the tripartite relationship between interpretation, language use, and power is constitutive of his philosophical reflections on language. Indeed, for Nietzsche, language itself originates in the exercise of power by the ruling class:

> The seigneurial privilege of giving names even allows us to conceive of the origin of language itself as a manifestation of the power of the rulers: they say 'this is so and so', they set their seal on everything and every occurrence with a sound and thereby take possession of it, as it were.[24]

That is, the naming of words and definition of their meaning already constitutes an execution of power by the rulers. This means, in turn, that when power shifts from one ruling elite to another, words are reinterpreted by the new primary definer. As Nietzsche puts it, 'anything in existence, having somehow come about, is continually interpreted anew, requisitioned anew, transformed and redirected to a new purpose by a power superior to it'.[25] Redefinitions are thus the product of processes of overpowering, in the course of which 'their former "meaning" and "purpose" must necessarily be obscured or completely obliterated'.[26] Another way of saying this is that reinterpretations do not add a further dimension of meaning to a particular term, but rather destroy the old meaning in order to replace it with a new one.[27] This bears consequences for Nietzsche's notions of interpretation and meaning.

First of all, as the meaning of words depends on what those currently in power take them to mean, there is no meaning in itself or timeless meaning. Thus meaning is rendered perspectival, purely subjective, and contingent upon the capability,

---

[22] Christoph Cox, *Nietzsche: Naturalism and Interpretation* (University of California Press 1999) 111–18.

[23] Friedrich Nietzsche, *On the Genealogy of Morality* (CUP 2006). The reason I have chosen to focus on Nietzsche rather than Foucault is that, unlike Nietzsche, Foucault does not offer any reflections on the interpretations of texts but focuses exclusively on the interpretation and genealogy of historical practices.

[24] Nietzsche, *On the Genealogy of Morality*, 12.

[25] Nietzsche, *On the Genealogy of Morality*, 51.

[26] Nietzsche, *On the Genealogy of Morality*, 51.

[27] Wulf Kellerwessel, 'Nietzsches interpretatorische Sprachphilosophie im Kontext seiner Erkenntnistheorie- unter besonder Berücksichtigung der "Genealogie der Moral": Rekonstruktion und Kritik' (2004) 17(3) Prima Philosophia 331, 339.

intention, and power potential of those in charge. The text does not seem to set tight limits to interpretation; rather, it allows for a wide spectrum of diverging accounts, involving 'forcing, adjusting, shortening, omitting, filling-out, inventing, falsifying and everything else essential to interpretation'.[28] Provided that primary definers are not obstructed by others (or their own incompetence), they may use their interpretive monopoly as they see fit, and their interpretive will to power is unimpeded.

Nietzsche's much-discussed notion of the 'will to power' has many different modalities and its precise scope is a matter of some dispute. However, for the purpose of this chapter, I take it to mean the political drive towards mastery and control, which manifests itself in claims to conclusiveness and finality in the exegesis of texts. This drive to finality reveals itself through an imposition of meaning and significance on texts.[29] Ideologies exercise power by 'imposing a pattern—some form of structure or organisation—on how we read (and misread) political facts, events, occurrences, actions, on how we see images and hear voices'.[30] They decontest the meaning of texts and concepts, 'thus injecting certainty into what is by default an indeterminate world of meaning'.[31] The will to power is therefore ideological to the extent that it handles indeterminacy by ranking and prioritizing certain passages and meanings of texts, while ignoring others. However, in the next section we will see that interpreters do not exercise their will to power in a vacuum, but in a linguistically constituted social world with conventions, which partly constrain the way in which individual interpreters can unleash their power on texts. Even though all ideologies express themselves through a will to power, the way in which they decontest interpretations of texts vis-à-vis other interpreters depends on the specific set of beliefs and outlook on the world (such as conservative, liberal, or socialist) their members have.[32]

If we return to Nietzsche's account of interpretation, we can now see why it runs into difficulties. To begin with, he appears to underrate the extent to which the linguistic manifestations of texts limit the spectrum of possible interpretations, and he imputes to interpreters, per se, the intention to use the text unscrupulously at their own discretion.[33] Yet even interpreters who actually use the text in such a way are at least bound to reference some of the words or concepts of the text in question if they want their interpretations to qualify as such; for 'interpretations' that do not even provide an account of the text are certainly not discernible as readings of this text rather than another. Provided that this is the case, the role of the text's author as a variable in interpretive analysis has to be duly considered;

---

[28] Nietzsche, *On the Genealogy of Morality*, 112.

[29] My definition broadly follows the one offered in Paul Fairfield, *The Ways of Power: Hermeneutics, Ethics, and Social Criticism* (Duquesne University Press 2002) 18.

[30] Michael Freeden, *Ideology: A Very Short Introduction* (OUP 2003) 3.

[31] Michael Freeden, 'World of Ideologies: An Interview with Michael Freeden' (2012) 4 *niin & näin* <http://www.academia.edu/4101817/Syrjamaki_Michael_Freeden_interview> accessed 28 July 2014.

[32] See nn 13–20 and accompanying text.

[33] This lapse on Nietzsche's part can, of course, be traced back to his broader notion of 'interpretation' and his intention to point out the transvaluation of our moral convictions.

authors direct readers to pay particular attention to some parts rather than others by mentioning key points at privileged positions, such as the title, the introduction, and conclusion, as well as throughout the unfolding of a narrative.[34] This does not mean that we need to adopt Michaels' understanding of the author as sole determiner of meaning (as discussed in Part II above), but what it does mean is that the interpretive power of the exegete is limited both by the text and the author's power to scaffold their narrative.

There is another reason why we do not need to accept Nietzsche's generalizations: there is, strictly speaking, no such thing as *the* text or *the* reader. Interpreters' freedom to read as they please depends on the genre of the text and the setting in which their interpretations are conducted. For example, poems allow for and arguably require that much wider associations be brought to the text than legal texts. Moreover, unlike lay readers, interpreters in academia and especially lawyers and judges can certainly be expected, based on an unwritten code of professional practice, to engage with the text in such a way as to do justice to the arguments presented therein. Hence it is exaggerated to insinuate that interpreters *en bloc* tend to treat texts as Nietzsche claims they would. Whilst there might be some for which this is the case, the majority of trained interpreters arguably construe texts to the best of their knowledge and in accordance with professional norms. This is not to deny that deliberate or unintended misinterpretations can occur, nor to downplay the role of rhetoric, polemics, and power in academic literature. Rather, it is to counter-balance Nietzsche's lopsided view on interpreters' thought-practices, and to acknowledge that the 'will to power' manifests itself differently in different contexts.

But let us assume that Nietzsche is right in arguing that power manifests itself in infinite interpretive leeway. To accept Nietzsche's views here would be a sign of weakness, for it would effectively mean subjugation to his interpretive power. Based on Nietzsche's own theory, this would not be in our interest, and we should not adopt this position, provided we are aware of that power. Put differently, if Nietzsche's remarks are to be taken seriously (and this is an assumption that even a minimally charitable interpretation has to make), they appear to be pragmatically inconsistent, because they indicate that the recipient should not be convinced by Nietzsche's claims.[35] In defence of Nietzsche, one might say that this is no argumentative dead-end: if he advanced his notion of interpretation from a meta-perspective, the adoption of his point of view could be plausible. But, as we shall see, Nietzsche himself denies that such a perspective exists.

In any case, Nietzsche is surely right to suggest that interpreters do not usually mince their words but are fairly assertive. Once doubts about their reading are

[34] Rabinowitz, *Before Reading*.

[35] Kellerwessel, 'Nietzsches', 351. Gilles Deleuze has made a similar objection, arguing that to interpret the will to power as the desire for domination over other people would undermine the power of the will, as it would always depend on the recognition by the weak and powerless: *Nietzsche and Philosophy* (Athlone Press 2006) 80. For a discussion of Deleuze's account of Nietzsche, see Andrius Bielskis, *Toward a Post-Modern Understanding of the Political: From Genealogy to Hermeneutics* (Palgrave Macmillan 2005) 33, 169.

removed or conventional readings are shattered, they unleash their interpretive will to power onto the text and at other interpreters and exclaim: 'This is what it means!' Such a claim to have proffered *the* correct or true interpretation are 'instances of power-wielding',[36] because the text has been beaten into a shape which will serve the interpretation, thereby bestowing a decontested meaning on the latter and shutting down other readings. This is what characterizes the language of politics: it aims to nail things down, to close up, and to sort out.[37] But this quest for finality is elusive given that language contains features that work in the opposite direction. The fact that language is ambiguous, inconclusive, indeterminate, and vague means that there is no final handle on what texts mean. This suggests that we should be wary of such claims, expose the interests and motivations behind them, and try to recover suppressed alternative readings.

Now, one might retort that we should distinguish between political and heuristic preferences. To prefer a certain way of reading a text is not to be confused with the normative competition over public decision-making processes which ideologies pursue, but rather an attempt to 'employ ontological and epistemological choices in the service of recommending productive or insightful ways of interpreting political thought'.[38] Yet, it does not follow that in their search for the most insightful interpretation of a text, interpreters are not influenced by their ideological convictions. It only means that we should not equate the interpreter with the ideologue. Thus, our Nietzschean claims remain in place. Having said that, scholars try to distance themselves from their motives and political convictions, and submit them to critical interrogation, which is precisely what they should do. But they will never have immediate access to texts, nor will their pre-judgements ever be entirely free of ideological presuppositions. This is not to be lamented, however, because those presuppositions help scholars to make sense of texts by alerting them to relevant passages in the text and by offering them contextual clues against which those passages may be construed. (We will return to the relationship between contexts and pre-judgements in the next section.)

Now, Nietzsche not only advocates for perspectivism in language but also in questions of epistemology. Nietzsche considers it impossible to speak of the world as it is because a perspective-free world is epistemologically inaccessible. As a result, there are no 'true' or 'truer' interpretations but only equally justified accounts of what you and I think is correct independently of each other. But this also means that there is no solid ground for inter-subjective understanding. Due to each individual's perspectivism, successful communication is by no means guaranteed, not even under optimal circumstances. Yet if this is so, we do not even know, *pace* Nietzsche, that other interpretations differ from our own.[39]

---

[36] Freeden, *Ideologies and Political Theory*, 77.

[37] As Michael Freeden asserts, 'The need for semantic control...is at the heart of the political': *The Political Theory of Political Thinking* (OUP 2013) 6.

[38] Michael Freeden, 'On the Responsibilities of the Political Theorist' in Ben Jackson and Marc Stears (eds), *Liberalism as Ideology: Essays in Honour of Michael Freeden* (OUP 2012) 269.

[39] Kellerwessel, 'Nietzsches', 353.

As Wittgenstein compellingly argued in *Philosophical Investigations*, differences of opinion (or of interpretation, in our case) already presuppose a shared understanding or a common set of language rules, otherwise one could not identify the differences in the first place:

'So you are saying that human agreement decides what is true and what is false?'—It is what human beings *say* that is true and false; and they agree in the *language* they use. That is not agreement in opinions but in form of life.[40]

Thus, Nietzsche owes us an explanation as to how inter-subjective communication is possible in the absence of, or at least without a stable basis for, shared understanding. One of the weaknesses of his philosophy of language and interpretation is that he does not seem to acknowledge the role of linguistic conventions in facilitating inter-subjective understanding and the extent to which they curtail the interpreter's will to power. In order to impose one's will onto texts or other interpreters, one must abide by certain linguistic rules, such as referring to the text's semantic content and communicating to other interpreters using a language they understand. Without a shared basis of understanding one's claims to power, there can be no point at which one interpreter rules over others, but rather a constant and altogether futile battle (unless, of course, the force of weapons rather than words are used).

The fundamental difficulty in Nietzsche's philosophy of language is that he considers language exclusively from the point of view of the individual language user. This leads him to the assumption that every use of language is an interpretation, and that every such interpretation is perspectival and subjective. He neglects the interrelation of textual phenomena, authorial agency, reader response, and rules of language, and their role in making inter-subjective communication possible. (In the next section, we will see how interpretations always rely on conventions and the consequences this has for the power of the interpreter.) Nietzsche also disregards the role of language consumption in favour of the production of words or texts. As he takes the reader to produce his own interpretation, virtually regardless of what the text actually says (for the actual meaning is inconceivable according to Nietzsche), he overlooks the extent to which the reader is engaged in a battle with the text, as it were. It follows that there is anarchy in interpretation because anything goes. Accordingly, one might conclude that Nietzsche calls on us to exercise our will to power through interpretation. Searching for the correct reading of a text would be a naive undertaking. Rather, the point would be to beat the text into shape such that it serves our aims.

However, scholars often overlook the fact that Nietzsche mitigates the radical nature of his claims by distinguishing between a 'healthy' and an 'unhealthy' will to power, and by introducing two interpretive virtues—honesty (*Redlichkeit*) and justice (*Gerechtigkeit*)—which readers are expected to cultivate.[41] Though Nietzsche still rejects the view that there is only one correct interpretation of a

---

[40] Ludwig Wittgenstein, *Philosophical Investigations* (Oxford 2001) [241].
[41] Giorgio Colli and Mario Montinari (eds), *Friedrich Nietzsche: Sämtliche Werke, Kritische Studienausgabe in 15 Bänden*, Vol 6 (de Gruyter 1980) 247. Kellerwessel, for instance, does not take these distinctions into account.

text, he nonetheless proposes an 'art of reading well'. 'Reading well' is slow and attentive reading, which not only records how the meaning of the text unfolds, but also critically discusses its content. For Nietzsche, being 'honest' and 'just' to the text lets the text speak, rather than predetermining textual meaning through the desire to solve a specific problem.[42] The 'art of reading well' therefore 'yields an apparent safeguard against the relativistic tendency of [Nietzsche's] perspectival account of knowledge', inasmuch as it 'proffers a notion of textual *autonomy*', which cautions the reader to '*respect* the text and remain open to that which the text presents'.[43] In light of those distinctions, Nietzsche is now in a position to argue that some interpretations are better than others, and to express his disapproval about interpreters who beat the text into shape, regardless of its meaning, because they ignore the interpretive limitations set by the text and thus display an 'unhealthy' will to power. But, we might wonder, is there not a contradiction in Nietzsche's seemingly non-perspectival account of the text as a 'thing-in-itself'? How does Nietzsche resolve the hermeneutic dilemma of relativism and dogmatism? And, as a corollary to the latter question, how does he reconcile his perspectivism with his will to power, which seems to presuppose what his perspectivism rejects—the notion of a correct understanding of the world?[44]

In order to understand why there is no dilemma for Nietzsche, we should reconsider our understanding of perspectivism. Perspectivism should not be treated as an ontological position,[45] but rather as a function of power. In other words, for Nietzsche, 'truth' can be justified only if it is the focus of a faculty that strengthens the will to power. Nietzsche does not deny readers' ability to interpret the meaning of a text as its author intended it, but he claims that such an interpretation is only valuable to the extent that it serves interpreters' will to power. Thus, perspectivism is not equivalent to relativism. Nietzsche navigates between relativism and dogmatism by sharing the scientific rejection of metaphysics and combining it with the irreducibility of interpretation. In order words, Nietzsche's naturalism holds perspectivism in check, and grants that the doctrine of the will to power is based on interpretations themselves.[46] This does not mean that the interpreter's will to power is a psychological impulse; rather, it is the political drive to finality and decontestation. Nietzsche does not want to arrogate to himself a privileged position, but instead proposes what I would call an agonistic conception of hermeneutics, in which contrary interpretations face one another.

Even though Nietzsche's revisions to his interpretive theory are important, he is aware that he cannot introduce terms such as 'justice' and 'honesty' in *On the Genealogy of Morality*, without being accused of contradicting himself, in light of both his account of interpretation and his notorious narrative of 'master and slave morality'. However, for Nietzsche, justice is not given but rather created by

---

[42] Friedric Nietzsche, *Will to Power* (Random House 1967) 479.
[43] Alan Schrift, *Nietzsche and the Question of Interpretation: Between Hermeneutics and Deconstruction* (Routledge 1990) 163, 165.
[44] Cox, *Nietzsche*, 3.   [45] Cox, *Nietzsche*, 243.   [46] Cox, *Nietzsche*, 3.

exceptional individuals, who establish what justice is by making impersonal laws and rules. The supreme power defines what is right and just, and prohibits arbitrary acts done by individuals.[47] Yet the supreme power only defines justice for the duration in which it is in power.

Applied to interpretation within the university and jurisprudence, this would mean that academic or juridical authorities can create frameworks of 'legitimate' interpretation, but that those frameworks would only exist as long as they are 'in power'. Indeed, proponents of a particular interpretive method constitute, at least from outside, a scholarly group or 'interpretive community'. Those interpretive communities exert their power by defending standards of reading to which they hold other readers accountable. From this position of power, they can accuse interpreters of 'misreading', shape the intellectual climate within which legal theorizing is to be conducted, and influence (directly or indirectly) how it is taught, what gets published, who gets a job, and so on. As such, there are two reasons why methods of interpretation can never be neutral. For one thing, they are inextricably tied to the epistemological and political presuppositions we have as interpreters. For another thing, they are critical elements in the 'internal social organization of fields... and the battle for the control of knowledge production in academia and, to some extent, society-at-large'.[48]

III. Enter Language Conventions

The discussion in the preceding section has shown that Nietzsche's reflections on the relationship between interpretation and power overestimate interpreters' influence and neglect the role that conventions play in the interpretive process. Nietzsche's interpretive account is premised on a view of language as a tool that interpreters can use as they see fit. However, as this section will suggest, language is '*constitutive* of political phenomena rather than... merely *about* political phenomena'.[49]

Wittgenstein and Austin have been particularly influential in spreading this view of language.[50] Wittgenstein's *Philosophical Investigations* has challenged correspondence theories of language and truth by showing that the relationship of word and object is not simply one where the former describes the latter, but where the 'use' of words determines their meaning within the relevant context or 'language

[47] Cox, *Nietzsche*, 3.

[48] Steven Ward, 'The Revenge of the Humanities: Reality, Rhetoric, and the Politics of Postmodernism' (1995) 38(2) Sociological Perspectives 109, 111.

[49] Michael Shapiro, *Language and Political Understanding: The Politics of Discursive Practices* (Yale University Press 1981) 5.

[50] Ferdinand de Saussure has also advanced a conception of language, according to which the meaning of a word depends on the word's relation to other words. Yet, unlike de Saussure, Wittgenstein and Austin have emphasized the extent to which language use is firmly anchored in conventions and they have shown that 'words are also deeds'. This is why my focus lies on their theories rather than de Saussure's. For de Saussure's theory of language, see *Course in General Linguistics* (Fontana 1974).

game'.[51] Understanding the meaning of a word requires knowledge of the rules of how the word is commonly used in different language games. It requires, in short, familiarity with the conventions of a given community.[52] Meanings are not just the products of arbitrary agreement, but of the world in which language games are being performed.[53] Like Wittgenstein, Austin has claimed that the relationship between word and object is based on conventional rules rather than correspondence. For both thinkers, language is 'an activity ... and a representation of norms for activity rather than a static, denotational tool'.[54]

In *How To Do Things With Words*, Austin initially distinguished between 'constative' and 'performative' utterances. The former are said to be descriptions of a situation, while the latter are interventions in that situation.[55] That is to say, constative utterances are descriptions or 'saying something', whereas performative utterances are actions or 'doing something'.[56] Austin argued that, for such actions to be performed, the circumstances in which the performance takes place needs to be appropriate so that others can, in principle, understand the utterance in question. In the case of constatives, by contrast, the validity of their descriptions suffice. However, in the course of his investigation, Austin noticed that the distinction between constatives and performatives evaporated, and that 'every genuine speech act is both'.[57]

Now, a critic might ask what this account of Austin's speech act theory has to do with textual interpretation. Surely interpreters do not usually couch their interpretations in the form of performative utterances. They say things like 'the author claims X' or 'the meaning of the text is Y', whereas performatives require a statement in which the verb at once offers a description of the action *and* constitutes the action to the effect that the speaker performs the action named by the verb. Consider the example 'I order you to leave the room'.[58] In uttering this statement, a speaker performs the act that she states she is performing, thus verifying her own action. And to the extent that her statement is 'true' (ie appropriate and intelligible), she orders her interlocutor to leave the room.[59] Rather than describing a situation in an attempt to mirror reality as constative utterances do, a performative utterance transforms a situation and intervenes in the world.

---

[51] Wittgenstein, *Philosophical Investigations*, [7], [23], [43].

[52] AC Grayling, *Wittgenstein: A Very Short Introduction* (OUP 2001) 96.

[53] Hanna Pitkin, *Wittgenstein and Justice: On the Significance of Ludwig Wittgenstein for Social and Political Thought* (University of California Press 1972) 122.

[54] Shapiro, *Language and Political Understanding*, 59.

[55] John Austin, *How To Do Things With Words* (OUP 1982) 3–6.

[56] Austin, *How To Do Things With Words*, 133.

[57] Austin, *How To Do Things With Words*, 147.

[58] The example is borrowed from John Searle, *Consciousness and Language* (CUP 2002) 158. Unlike Searle, I do not think that what constitutes the speech act as performative is the intention of the speaker. For compelling critical discussions of Searle's view, see Gunther Grewendorf, 'How Performatives Don't Work' and Al Martinich, 'On the Proper Treatment of Performatives' in Gunther Grewendorf and Georg Meggle (eds), *Speech Acts, Mind, and Social Reality: Discussions with John R. Searle* (Kluwer 2002) 25–40 and 93–104.

[59] Uwe Wirth, 'Der Performanzbegriff im Spannungsfeld von Illokution, Iteration and Indexikalität' in *Zwischen Sprachphilosophie und Kulturwissenschaften* (Suhrkamp 2002) 11.

However, as we have seen in the previous sections, there is no such thing as a purely descriptive account of a text. To the contrary, interpreters approach texts with certain pre-judgements, some of which are political, and decontest the meaning of texts in a manner that serves their interests. In light of those insights, we can now see that such statements as 'the meaning of the text is Y' are not purely descriptive. Rather, they also have a clandestine performative dimension. What speakers state are not 'objective' and disinterested accounts of texts, but their interpretations of them, ie their attempts to control the meaning of texts. This performative and power-driven dimension of interpretive claims becomes more explicit when we rephrase their statements as follows: 'I *conclude* that the author means to say X—and only X' or 'Unlike other interpreters, I *posit* the meaning of the text is Y, not T'. Those statements meet the aforementioned criteria of performatives because: (a) they constitute acts specified by the verb of the utterance ('I conclude, I posit' which decontest the meaning of the text); (b) they are self-referential and self-verifying statements (for the interpreter declares the act that he or she is performing, namely to 'hammer home' the interpretation, *and* performs this act); and (c) in performing the interpretive act, the interpreter provokes certain consequences by virtue of the fact that he or she has determined the meaning of the text.

Accordingly, textual interpretations contain constative *and* performative layers. First, they present the text in such a way that their presentation confirms the interpretation they provide, which means that they combine the 'saying' with the 'doing', in as much as the propositional content of the text matches their interpretation and vice versa. Second, they constitute both a commentary on the text as well as an intervention in a certain context, insofar as they have the potential to shape the way in which the text is subsequently interpreted and the way readers assess the content of the text.

In short, behind supposedly 'neutral' claims to truth frequently lie power-driven ventures to determine the meaning of a text conclusively, which sustained Austin's recognition that the transition from constatives to performatives, or vice versa, is more transient than it appears at first glance. This had profound consequences for Austin's speech act theory because it shifted his attention away from the descriptive nature of statements to their force or 'point'. Jacques Derrida rightly remarked that as soon as Austin abandoned the distinction between constatives and performatives, his theory of speech acts moved from truth to force, 'in the direction of Nietzsche',[60] for it now acknowledged that language use is also a matter of power.

While Austin emphasized the value of force in his discussion of performatives, Bonnie Honig retorts that Austin sought to domesticate it 'through the reassuring security of the "value of context"'.[61] Honig argues that Austin mitigates the force of speech acts by pointing out that circumstances have to be appropriate for speech acts to work, ie to be conceived as such by one's interlocutors. Yet Honig

[60] Jacques Derrida, *Limited Inc* (Northwestern University Press 1988) 13.
[61] Bonnie Honig, *Political Theory and the Displacement of Politics* (Cornell University Press 1993) 90.

exaggerates the extent of that domestication when she claims that the introduction of context 'denies the insights with which Austin's account of performativity began: the creative power and the differentiated force of performatives'.[62]

Far from denying those insights, Austin's account of context merely puts speech acts into perspective by acknowledging that speakers utter their statements in pre-established social settings. Unlike Nietzsche, Austin displays an awareness of those linguistic conventions and circumstances without which we could not express ourselves in the first place, let alone be understood by others. Being initiated into society qua language means that we owe our social existence in part to our ability to communicate with others. It also means that we inherit codes, values and pre-judgements from society via the language we use. Ours is a language, which we have not made but which 'consists largely of the sedimentation and institutionalisation of speech-acts performed by other persons'.[63] In other words, speech-acts must be performed by 'institutionalised means'.[64] Their success accordingly depends on their echoing of prior actions. However, Austin did not acknowledge that, in so doing, our speech:

> …*accumulates the force of authority through the repetition or citation of a prior and authoritative set of practices*. It is not simply that the speech act takes place *within* a practice, but that the act is itself a ritualised practice. What this means, then, is that a performative 'works' to the extent that *it draws on and covers over* the constitutive conventions by which it is mobilised.[65]

Translated into the language of textual interpretation, this suggests that both authors and readers invoke conventions, whose origin lie in decontestations enacted by previous interpreters or language users more generally.

To be sure, this does not suggest that speech act theory or textual interpretation is necessarily conservative, for language users and interpreters do not need to affirm all systems of authority.[66] While we necessarily draw on pre-existing power structures to launch our speech-acts and articulate our interpretations, we can act on those power structures and change them. And when such changes are understood and 'used' by our interlocutors in their own speech acts, they can gradually change the politics of our conventions. Put differently, language signifies both 'innovation and continuity', because language changes in 'predictable ways', whereby those changes 'result from the free choices of many individuals'.[67]

Now, if conventions are the products of prior decontestations and are political, then so is the very act of seeking to contextualize an utterance or a text. As Derrida puts it, 'the simple recalling of a context is never a gesture that is neutral, innocent, transparent, disinterested'.[68] To the contrary, there is always

---

[62] Honig, *Political Theory and the Displacement of Politics*, 90.

[63] JGA Pocock, 'Verbalizing A Political Act: Toward a Politics of Speech' (1973) 1(1) Pol Theory 27, 31.

[64] Pocock, 'Verbalizing A Political Act', 33.

[65] Judith Butler, *Excitable Speech: A Politics of the Performative* (Routledge 1997) 41.

[66] Shapiro, *Language and Political Understanding*, 63.

[67] Pitkin, *Wittgenstein and Justice*, 3.

[68] Derrida, *Limited Inc*, 131.

something political in the very project of attempting to fix the contexts of utterances. Contextualization is:

...always political because it implies, insofar as it involves determination, a certain type of non-'natural' relationship to others...Once this generality and this a priori structure have been recognised, the question can be raised, not whether a politics is implied (it always is), but which politics is implied in such a practice of contextualisation.[69]

This has significant repercussions for textual interpretation because it suggests that the attempt to decontest the context of a text is a political gesture and involves a mediation between the 'commitments and practices contained in language',[70] and the interpreters' background assumptions. As a result, when interpreters contextualize texts, they merge the ideologically entrenched pre-judgements that shape their initial understanding of the text and partly determine their choice of contexts with the politics of existing conventions. We therefore need to distinguish between the context in which an interpreter reads a text, which we might call the 'reader's context', and the context that the interpreter singles out in order to narrow down the meaning of the text, which we might call 'the text's context'. To be sure, the two often overlap at least in part in as much as the reader's context (pre-judgements, disciplinary training, problems he or she seeks to address and the interests he or she has) shape and constrain what the reader might single out as the text's context. Nonetheless, there is a mediation between both contexts and linguistic conventions.

While conventions have a bearing on the power of interpretation, this is not to say that such power is necessarily mitigated by them; over time, interpretations can become disjointed from their initial contexts and take on new meanings in other contexts, through which they gain new force.[71] Though most interpretations may always be conceived as 'mere' commentaries on texts, some take on a new life either by being read as a text in their own right, rather than as an interpretation of another text, or by being deployed as 'context' for the reading of another text.[72] In both cases, the performative dimension of those interpretations at once relies on and overwrites the conventions that have informed them in the first place.[73]

---

[69] Derrida, *Limited Inc*, 136.

[70] Michael Shapiro, 'Literary Production as a Politicizing Practice' (1984) 12(3) Pol Theory 387, 389.

[71] Butler, *Excitable Speech*, 145.

[72] An example of an interpretation of a text, which was initially considered as nothing but an interpretation of Marx, but over the years came to be recognized as text in its own right, is Louis Althusser and Étienne Balibar, *Reading Capital* (Pantheon Books 1971). An example of an interpretive text that came to be viewed as context for the reading of texts by Gadamer, Strauss, and others is Martin Heidegger, *Being and Time* (Blackwell 1962).

[73] Throughout this section, I have treated textual interpretation as a kind of speech act without considering the implications of this analogy. For a discussion of this analogy, see Paul Ricoeur, 'The Model of the Text: Meaningful Action Considered as a Text' in *From Text to Action: Essays in Hermeneutics, II* (Continuum 1991) 146–51.

Conclusion: On Decoding Ideology

In this chapter, we have seen that the political dimension of textual interpretation consists of pre-judgements that we bring to bear on texts, and interpreters' power-driven attempts to decontest the meaning of texts. Such attempts are constrained by conventions, which they rely on or shape, in order to performatively intervene in the world and convince other interpreters of their reading. Now I need to turn to the question of how political and, above all, ideological presuppositions might be decoded.

There is no shortage of approaches to the study of ideology, which proclaim to uncover ideological presuppositions. However, for the purposes of this chapter, what we need is an approach that focuses on the way in which ideologies manifest themselves in the language that we use, which allows us to ascribe this use of language to a particular ideology, which considers interpreters as both consumers and producers of language, and which accounts for those concepts which are an essential part of any reading ('author', 'reader', 'text', and 'context'). That interpretations rely on those concepts is trivially true. What is less obvious is that interpreters in general, and methodologists in particular, must have a certain understanding of what should count as, say, 'context' in the first place, and what significance this context should have in their exegesis, for them to be able to interpret a text and/or invent a method of interpretation. In other words, methodologists necessarily impose certain meanings on the above concepts, decontest those meanings, and rank the concepts in order of significance. In short, their methods and interpretations are the result of a certain conceptual pattern, which represents their understanding of the interpretive process. As my discussion of Michaels' claims in Part I indicated, our understanding of textual interpretation is predicated on a certain view of how those concepts factor into the interpretive process, which is partly shaped by ideological assumptions. What we need for the purpose of this chapter is thus a conceptual approach to ideology.

Quentin Skinner has offered such a conceptual analysis of ideologies. Skinner's approach places particular emphasis on the way in which political concepts and conventions are used in particular contexts and at particular historical junctures. Drawing on Max Weber's concept of legitimation, Skinner holds the view that ideologies are invoked for the purpose of legitimizing or overturning configurations of power.[74] Skinner's notion of ideology combines the investigation of explicitly political concepts with conventions, and thus broadens the scope of ideological analysis from such concepts as 'political obligation', 'authority', 'liberty', 'freedom', and 'rhetoric'. However, Skinner's approach, especially in his early work, over-emphasizes the extent to which influential individual authors more or less single-handedly 'produce' ideological innovations, which disregards

---

[74] Quentin Skinner, *Visions of Politics, Volume I: Regarding Method* (CUP 2002) 128–44 and 145–57.

the group-orientation of ideology.[75] In his later work, Skinner's focus somewhat shifted to a conception of authors, which sees them less as producers and more as consumers of an ideology and as representatives of certain discursive formations that were 'in the air' at the time of writing. Nevertheless, Skinner's approach does little to show how we can ascribe interpreters' use of concepts and conventions to a particular ideology because he does not offer us the conceptual framework that we would need, in order to see which conceptual cluster differentiates, say, a conservative interpretation from a liberal one. This is because Skinner's historical work zooms in on small-scale ideological shifts enacted by an elite minority and ignores the broader formations of mainstream ideologies. This gap can be filled by recourse to another approach.

Over the past two decades, Michael Freeden's 'morphological approach' has come to be viewed as the primary source for conceptual enquiries into political ideologies. For Freeden, ideologies are made up of a certain cluster of concepts. Within those clusters, concepts are endowed with particular meanings and arranged vis-à-vis other concepts, in a way which is specific to that ideology.[76] Liberalism, for instance, is premised on such core concepts as 'liberty, individuality, progress, rationality, sociability, a concern for the general interest, and the notion of limited and accountable power',[77] whose precise definition and allocation are pivotal in describing the ideal-type liberal outlook on the world.

While Freeden's approach provides us with the tools to decode decontestations of certain clusters of political concepts, his analysis loses sight of seemingly 'apolitical' concepts of lesser complexity that are also contested.[78] In order to be suitable for our enquiry, his approach must be applied to the core concepts of textual interpretation, that is, 'reader', 'text', and 'context'. Such an application is not without its problems, of course, because concepts like 'author' have changed drastically over the past 300 years and have meant different things in different contexts. So what might have been a 'liberal' or progressive view of the role of the author in textual analyses among theologians in the eighteenth century may be considered as a 'conservative' view in political theory today. This suggests that our approach must be attuned to conceptual variations at different times and within different contexts.

While Freeden's approach caters for such conceptual fine-tuning by analysing concepts both synchronically and diachronically, his analyses place greater emphasis on the consumption of ideologies than their production, thus reversing the focus of Skinner's early work. This emphasis on consumption is particularly apt for the purpose of this chapter, however, because I do not consider interpreters

---

[75] Freeden, *Ideologies and Political Theory*, 104–8.   [76] Freeden, *Ideology*, 51.
[77] Freeden, 'World of Ideologies', 3. See also Freeden, *Ideology*, 81, and Freeden, *Ideologies and Political Theory*, 178.
[78] As Freeden acknowledges, ideologies 'endow concepts customarily held to be apolitical with political import': *Ideology*, 100. The same observation had been made by Aletta Norval, 'Review Article: The Things We Do with Words—Contemporary Approaches to the Analysis of Ideology' (2000) 30 B J Pol S 313, 316.

as ideologues. Rather, I enquire into how their interpretations are shaped by ideological presuppositions.

In what follows, I will apply Freeden's research on mainstream ideologies to textual interpretations, in an attempt to briefly sketch out how interpreters' views on 'author', 'reader', 'text', and 'context' are shaped by their ideological outlook on the world. In so doing, I will focus specifically on conservative and liberal interpreters.

As my discussion of Michaels' views on textual interpretation in Part II indicated, conservative interpreters tend to place great emphasis on the authority of the author as the sole producer of the text. Though more often than not a figure from the past, for conservative interpreters the author is very much alive in the reading process; for he or she has intended the text to be read in a certain way, and it is the reader's task to understand how that was supposed to be done. The reader's role is thus to serve the author and to uncover the author's intention. Accordingly, conservative interpreters hold strong views on what is to count as a proper reading of the text: interpretation proper, in their eyes, allows the author to speak to the reader. Contexts are regarded as scholarly tools that allow readers to recover the meaning of the text, which was put there by the author. Biographical and particularly historical sources are believed to be especially illuminating when putting a text in context. The reader's own presuppositions, whether ideological or otherwise, are by contrast considered as unhelpful distractions from the task of interpreting the author's text, if they are considered at all.

Liberal interpreters typically regard author and reader as more or less equal partners in a conversation across time. They do not draw as sharp a distinction between consumers and producers, as do conservative interpreters. They believe that readers primarily interpret texts, in order to find answers to their own questions, thus ascribing to them a much more active role in the reading process. Liberals are much less concerned about authorial intent than conservative interpreters, even though they do not entirely disregard intentionality either. While they acknowledge that the author produced the text, liberals regard themselves as the producers of their own account of the text and they virtually see their own work as important as that of the author; for without their interpretation, the text would merely be a historical document. In other words, they consider themselves as breathing new life into the text by applying it to the present. Contexts are therefore the interpreter's research questions and interests, rather than the historical context of the author. The anachronism that might come with such a contextualization of the text is not considered as a problem but as the inevitable consequence of the reader's research demands and the temporal gap that separates him or her from the author.

What, if anything, do we gain from such a perspective on methods of interpretation? Applying the morphological approach to textual interpretation allows us to decode the ideological underpinnings of our interpretive claims and thus generates greater reflexivity in the interpretation of texts. When we read a newspaper in order to inform ourselves about a certain topic, we will find it easier to assess the information we get from the newspaper if we know where it is located on the ideological map, since this will enable us to come to an informed opinion about the way the journalist presented the information. Without this knowledge about the article's ideological stance, our judgement and critical faculties may be clouded.

The same applies to interpretive methods. Because they give interpreters the tools to read texts, interpreters should know in advance what ideological underpinnings those tools have and how this might affect the interpretations that they may ultimately conduct. This is not to imply that there is a strict logical relationship between a method and its application, as no such relationship exists. Still, there are what Wittgenstein calls 'family resemblances' between a method and its application because methods do leave certain conceptual and theoretical marks in their application to texts, which are characteristic of that method.[79] So it is possible to establish a connection between the interpretation of a text and the method that has informed it. Provided that this is the case, the enquiry proposed in this chapter will enable scholars to arrive at a more informed judgment about interpretive methods, teasing out the political presuppositions that inform the salient methods and showing how those presuppositions help us understand what a method can and cannot do when applied to texts. As we said at the outset, our claim is not that interpretations and methods are *only* political, but that they *also* have a political dimension—a dimension that has not been made the subject of sufficient scholarly analysis yet.

---

[79] Wittgenstein, *Philosophical Investigations*, [67].

16

Cognitive Frames of Interpretation in International Law

Martin Wählisch

Introduction

Succeeding in the game of interpretation requires the strategic use of language. Words need to be carefully chosen, phrases adjusted, and terminology sharpened. In order to win, players have to be aware of the linguistic posture of their counterparts, as much as their own. Advanced players are capable of playing the game on subliminal levels. Professionals have the ability to activate and change cognitive frames in the interpretation of international law. Masters are consciously aware of their subconscious limitations while 'playing the game of game playing'.[1]

International law is contingent on the standpoint of the decision-maker towards an international problem.[2] Martti Koskenniemi has argued that international legal practice as experienced by advisers, judges, activists, and academics 'enables the simultaneous justification and critique of particular normative outcomes'.[3] Indeed, interpretations and arguments can vary drastically depending on whether international law is regarded from within an international court, international legal advisory body, or governmental entity. In the so-called 'war on terror', for instance, waterboarding and other life-threatening conduct were elegantly reframed by the Bush administration in the US as 'enhanced interrogation techniques' or as an 'alternative set of procedures'.[4] The Obama administration later clarified that this counter-terrorism practice had been nothing less than 'torture'.[5]

---

[1] See Chapter 2 (Andrea Bianchi).

[2] Tai-Heng Cheng, *When International Law Works: Realistic Idealism After 9/11 and the Global Recession* (OUP 2012) 4.

[3] Martti Koskenniemi, 'Between Commitment and Cynicism: Outline for a Theory of International Law as Practice' in *Collection of Essays by Legal Advisers of States, Legal Advisers of International Organizations and Practitioners in the Field of International Law* (United Nations 1999) 511.

[4] Speech on Terrorism, President George W Bush, Transcript, *NY Times*, 6 September 2006, <http://www.nytimes.com/2006/09/06/washington/06bush_transcript.html> accessed 29 July 2014.

[5] News Conference by the President, The White House, Office of the Press Secretary, 30 April 2009, <http://www.whitehouse.gov/the-press-office/news-conference-president-4292009> accessed

Commenting on the armed conflict in Syria in 2013, US President Obama recognized the Syrian Opposition Coalition as 'the legitimate representative of the
Syrian people'.[6] Other labels for the Coalition have included 'terrorists', 'freedom
fighters', a 'resistance movement', and 'non-state actors'.[7] These examples indicate
that interpretations differ depending on the interpreter's perspective, which is frequently oriented by strategic policy aims that impact on the use of vocabulary and
the direction of interpretation.

This chapter explores the relationship between cognitive frames of interpretation and the objectivity of the law. Individual and institutional frames shape the
interpretation of international law. They can help to build coalitions and mobilize
international consensus. At the same time, they can hinder the development of
universal principles and relativize the application of norms in the struggle for
'semantic authority'.[8] The chapter argues that, despite their subjective nature, the
existence of different frames does not necessarily affect the objectivity of the law.
The 'biased lexicon', or the choice of vocabulary by interpreters, is a reflection of
the fact that international law is a dialogue of competing ideas and a constantly
evolving process that can hold contradicting interpretations simultaneously.

The first part of the analysis gives an overview of the concept and evolution
of cognitive frames theory. The second part assesses in three case studies how
linguistic nuances and distinctions have reflected colliding concepts and values.
Particular attention is given to the 'wall' dispute in the context of the Israel–
Palestine conflict, the US 'enhanced interrogation' counter-terrorism practice,
and the different interpretations deployed to justify 'liberation movements'. The
conclusion concentrates on the challenges and opportunities in applying international law from multiple perspectives. The chapter ends with general observations
and practical guidance for legal interpreters, advisers, and decision-makers.

I. Cognitive Frame Theory and the Sociology of Law

As an introduction to the concept of cognitive frames, natural scientists regularly use the following experiment as an example. The scientist asks their subject
not to think of an elephant.[9] It is likely that most subjects would nonetheless

---

29 July 2014. See generally Jeremy Waldron, *Torture, Terror, and Trade-Offs: Philosophy for the White House* (OUP 2012).

  [6] Statement by the President, The White House, Office of the Press Secretary, 29 January 2013, <http://www.whitehouse.gov/the-press-office/2013/01/29/statement-president-announcing-155-million-additional-humanitarian-assis> accessed 29 July 2014.

  [7] 'Syria Urges UN Action Against Terrorists', *Press TV*, 28 July 2013, <http://www.presstv.com/detail/2013/07/28/315980/syria-urges-un-action-against-terrorists/> accessed 29 July 2014; John J Metzler, 'Syria "Descends Into the Inferno"', *China Post*, 20 July 2013, <http://www.chinapost.com.tw/commentary/the-china-post/john-metzler/2013/07/20/384254/p2/Syria-descends.htm> accessed 29 July 2014.

  [8] Ingo Venzke, *How Interpretation Makes International Law: On Semantic Change and Normative Twists* (OUP 2012) 224.

  [9] George Lakoff, *Don't Think of an Elephant!: Know Your Values and Frame the Debate* (Chelsea Green 2004).

immediately visualize an elephant in their mind. What occurs in that moment is a subconscious access of *cognitive frames*, containing images, emotions, and shapes that are stored in our memory. They are ready to be displayed whenever their titles are mentioned, initiating a 'mind cinema' of assumptions, expectations, and beliefs.[10] Besides tangible objects, cognitive frames also pertain to abstract terminology.[11] For example, the words 'illegal' and 'legal' trigger associations with what one thinks is right or wrong. The term 'national security' results in vastly different responses and interpretations, although it frequently makes one think about danger and the objective of curtailing it. Michael Reisman gives the example of the word 'crusade', which 'may have a powerful authorizing force for some audiences of Christians, evoking at deep levels of consciousness images of heroism and self-sacrifice', while having 'exactly the opposite effect for an audience of Moslems'.[12] Similarly, the word 'Jihad' may 'evoke a powerful positive emotion for many Moslems and the converse effect for Christians'.[13] Avoiding the activation of those cognitive frames is often impossible, as they inevitably influence thinking and decision-making.

A. Definition of 'cognitive frames'

Historically, the concept of *frames* has been developed in cognitive sciences since the 1970s.[14] Nowadays, the study of frames spans over a multitude of disciplines, including sociology, computer science, psychology, linguistics, politics, and also law.[15] The focus of the cognitive-linguistic perspective is on the interaction of language, interpretation, abstraction, categorization, and our cognitive system.[16] Initially, cognitive scholars tried to understand how our brain works in order to recreate neural structures for artificial intelligence. Marvin Minsky, for instance, observed that our memory and perceptions are structured in 'chunks'.[17] This collection of knowledge fragments influences our mode of reasoning and our perceptions. In establishing the concept of cognitive frames, Minsky noted that:

When one encounters a new situation (or makes a substantial change in one's view of the present problem) one selects from memory a structure called a *Frame*. This is a remembered framework to be adapted to fit reality by changing details as necessary.[18]

[10] For an introductory overview, see Alan Cienki, 'Cognitive Models, and Domains' in Dirk Geeraerts and Hubert Cuycken (eds), *The Oxford Handbook of Cognitive Linguistics* (OUP 2007) 170.
[11] William Croft and D Alan Cruse, *Cognitive Linguistics* (CUP 2004) 24.
[12] W Michael Reisman, *The Quest for World Order and Human Dignity in the Twenty-first Century: Constitutive Process and Individual Commitment* (Brill 2013) 82.
[13] Reisman, *The Quest for World Order*, 82.
[14] José Luis Bermúdez, *Cognitive Science: An Introduction to the Science of the Mind* (CUP 2010) 5.
[15] Bermúdez, *Cognitive Science*, 86.
[16] René Dirven and Marjolijn Verspoor, *Cognitive Exploration of Language and Linguistics* (John Benjamins 2004) ix.
[17] Marvin Minsky, 'A Framework for Representing Knowledge' in John Haugeland (ed), *Mind Design II: Philosophy, Psychology, Artificial Intelligence* (MIT Press 1997) 111.
[18] Minsky, 'A Framework for Representing Knowledge', 111.

Minsky explains how common-sense thought is established within a society. For Minsky, frames are cognitive boxes for capturing and preserving stereotypic descriptions. Collections of related frames are linked together into frame-systems of prejudices and hopes. Minsky summarized:

A *frame* is a data-structure for representing a stereotyped situation...Attached to each frame are several kinds of information. Some of this information is about how to use the frame. Some is about what one can expect to happen next. Some is about what to do if these expectations are not confirmed.[19]

Parallel to Minsky, the American sociologist Erving Goffman explored the existence of multiple realities. He studied institutional settings, such as hospitals and casinos, as well as conventionalized social behaviour, such as behaviour during shopping or dating. Founding the social science research method of 'frame analysis', he observed that when individuals recognize a certain event they respond by employing a certain interpretive scheme.[20] Goffman emphasized that social life is reflexive as society impacts on how we think and act. Frames organize our experience. As cognitive short cuts they help us to make sense of current circumstances.

The linguist Charles Fillmore subsequently examined how the human mind combines knowledge with words. He stressed that the meaning associated with a particular word is always connected with a specific frame. Fillmore concluded that people associate certain scenes with certain linguistic frames. As he puts it, 'a person, in interpreting a text, mentally creates a partially specific world', where 'expectations get set up which later on are fulfilled or thwarted'.[21]

B. Subconscious and subjective nature of frames

Whether the concept of cognitive frames is sufficient to explain divergent interpretations between societies has been widely debated. Some scholars have tackled the question of frames as a matter of 'political culture'.[22] Others prefer the notion of 'mental models', 'narratives', 'schema', or 'scripts'.[23] All of those efforts have the common aim of explaining that there are patterns to the underlying cognitive process of thinking, understanding, and decision-making.

A key feature of the contemporary conception of cognitive frames is that they are mostly subconsciously evoked. Frames underlie thought processes, maintaining archetypes of interpretations that help construct meaning. The linguists

[19] Minsky, 'A Framework for Representing Knowledge', 111–12.
[20] Erving Goffman, *Frame Analysis: An Essay on the Organization of Experience* (Harper 1974) 21.
[21] Charles Fillmore, 'An Alternative to Checklist Theories of Meaning' *Proceedings of the First Annual Meeting of the Berkeley Linguistics Society* (Berkeley Linguistic Society 1975) 125.
[22] David Elkins and Richard Simeon, 'A Cause in Search of Its Effect, or What Does Political Culture Explain?' (1979) 11 Comp Pol 127.
[23] Charles Fillmore and Collin Baker, 'A Frames Approach to Semantic Analysis' in Bernd Heine and Heiko Narrog (eds), *The Oxford Handbook of Linguistic Analysis* (OUP 2009) 313.

George Lakoff and Mark Johnson have called this 'the hidden hand that shapes conscious thought':

Our unconscious conceptual system functions like a 'hidden hand' that shapes how we conceptualize all aspects of our experience...It thus shapes how we automatically and unconsciously comprehend what we experience. It constitutes our unreflective common sense.[24]

Lakoff and Johnson suggest that frames are not universal.[25] They reject objectivist theories of reasoning and, instead, they argue that reason is largely 'imaginative' and subjective, subconsciously arising from our individual and collective experience.[26] For them the activation of meaning is dependent on the interpreter and one's 'mental lexicon'.[27]

C. Creation and types of frames

The creation of frames relies on repetition, anchoring, and time. Constant repetition embeds frames in the brain. Repeating the same words with the same explanation and interpretation leaves cognitive traces. Each time a cognitive frame is activated, neural connections are strengthened and become more pronounced in shaping our thoughts. Strategic advertisement uses these techniques quite profoundly by showing the same message again and again in shorter and longer frequencies in order to be remembered well.

The expression of the same idea again and again helps create 'deep frames', which are those that shape our worldviews.[28] Deep frames transcend particular thematic issues, and contain values, principles, and moral fundamentals. They define one's overall common sense and are often embedded in the public mind. 'Surface frames' on the other hand create cognitive orientation for certain issues, providing assumptions for specific thematic debates and interpretations. Surface frames are themselves composed of 'lexical frames', which give meaning to words. At an intermediate depth between surface and deep frames are 'issue-defining frames', which function as conceptual filters for information. They block relevant concerns if those concerns are outside of the overall frame.[29] The more abstract an idea, the more layers of frames are required to absorb the topic.

One example Lakoff gives is the mental perception associated with the slogan 'war on terror', which constitutes the individual and collective ordinary sense of the lexical frames 'war' and 'terror'.[30] Both terms combined build a surface

[24] George Lakoff and Mark Johnson, *Philosophy in the Flesh: The Embodied Mind and Its Challenge to Western Thought* (Basic Books 1999) 12–13.
[25] Lakoff and Johnson, *Philosophy in the Flesh*, 45.
[26] Lakoff and Johnson, *Philosophy in the Flesh*, 4.
[27] Lakoff and Johnson, *Philosophy in the Flesh*, 11. For an introduction on cognitive psychology and the concept of 'mental lexicon', see Robert Sternberg, *Cognitive Psychology* (Wadsworth 2009) 363.
[28] George Lakoff, *Thinking Points* (Farrar, Straus and Giroux 2006) 10.
[29] Lakoff, *Thinking Points*, 12.
[30] Lakoff, *Thinking Points*, 12.

frame, which relates here to the '9/11' context, helping orient the justification for the 'fight with the enemy'.[31] Issue-defining frames help us decide whether or not we perceive the post-9/11 era as a global 'war', whether it is to be seen as just and which action should result. This interpretation is linked to deep frames, which enshrine our perception of security and freedom. Complex topics such as this can prompt a network of frames, which also include links to the frames 'international crime', 'fear', and 'safety', and also other slogans such as 'axis of the evil' and 'coalition of the willing'.

D. Functions and risks of frames

Cognitive frames affect actions and choices. They influence received information and impact on subsequent judgement. They are 'thought organizers', and 'devices for packaging complex issues' in persuasive ways by focusing on certain interpretations over others, which activate value predispositions.[32] At the same time, frames confer authority and power on actors who initiate, support, or identify with them.[33] On a positive note, frames provide stable and coherent meanings that enable us to make sense of long-term memories, formulate hypotheses, and prevent chaos in our minds. Without frames, thoughts would need to be exhaustively tested until they could be verified. Frames can enhance the speed of decision-making. Instead of lengthy evaluations, they can help to recognize situations, classify them, and cognitively suggest directions for typical interpretations. As David Elkins and Richard Simeon put it:

Those assumptions about the political world focus attention on certain features of events, institutions, and behaviour, define the realm of the possible, identify the problems deemed pertinent, and set the range of alternatives among which members of the population make decisions.[34]

The fact that frames impact on how a problem is perceived entails challenges for legal interpretation. Because frames result in the interpreter considering certain features and ignoring others, blind spots can appear and help generate a limited view.[35] Once established in the mind of the interpreter, frames can lead to conclusions that block consideration of other possible facts and interpretations. If the facts do not fit into the pre-existing frame, the frame stays while the facts are ignored. If a scenario is activated in the mind, other options are downplayed

[31] Christopher Daase and Oliver Kessler, 'Knowns and Unknowns in the "War on Terror": Uncertainty and the Political Construction of Danger' (2007) 38(4) Security Dialogue 411.
[32] Morgan Meyer, 'Increasing the Frame: Interdisciplinarity, Transdisciplinarity and Representativity' (2007) 32(3) Interdiscipl Sci Rev 204.
[33] Yves Surel, 'The Role of Cognitive and Normative Frames in Policy-Making' (2011) 7(4) JEPP 495.
[34] Elkins and Simeon, 'A Cause in Search of Its Effect', 128.
[35] As David Kennedy put it, we can 'betray our best intentions by our unconscious desires and hidden ambivalence, by bad faith and hypocrisy, or by blind spots and biases in our institutional practices and professional vocabularies': *The Dark Sides of Virtue: Reassessing International Humanitarianism* (Princeton University Press 2004) xxi.

due to the suspicion that they are incompatible. Eventually, alternative ways of thinking are suppressed, which can create 'tunnel vision'. The cultivation of new deep frames requires going on the offensive with one's own values and principles. Cognitively, the activation of surface frames strengthens deep frames and inhibits opposing, uncommon interpretations. Attempts to negate the frames of one's opponent only reinforces them. Lakoff has observed that arguing simply in terms of facts can fall on deaf ears. He stresses that the 'facts alone will not set you free', as 'facts can be assimilated into the brain only if there is an [appropriate] frame to make sense out of them'.[36] In this regard, frames can override rational and critical thinking. The interpreter might prefer to conform to a familiar pattern, instead of distancing him or herself from the issue at stake.

E. Difference between frames and strategic choice of language

A word of caution must be raised in relation to the difference between frames and the strategic choice of language. In many cases, if not most, policymakers, diplomats, and international legal advisers may favour a distinct interpretation after a thorough policy assessment, disregarding the 'invisible hand' of their accompanying frames. 'Strategic choice' in this context means that a conscious decision has been made to utilize certain terms pursuant to a policy interest.[37] This could be done in order to serve and accommodate existing frames, or in order to create frames for mobilizing unified support.[38] Instead of a cognitive bias, there might be a 'selective advantage' in engaging particular frames that resonate widely and are able to justify action in favour of the interpreter.[39] Indeed, even in those moments, frames shape strategic choices. However, strategic decision-making emphasizes the intentional selection of an interpretation after having considered alternatives, implications, desirability, and feasibility.[40] Strategic choices are determined by the way in which the strategist conceptualizes the approach.[41] Strategic decision-making objectifies the subjective preference. Following a heuristic, or a technique of problem solving, the strategic choice of language and interpretation aims to induce an effect and achieve a result.

One of those choices might be to deliberately reframe a context through the strategic choice of language. For example, governments might argue there has been 'collateral damage' in order to avoid or defer responsibility, instead of frankly speaking of 'innocent civilian victims' in a war.[42] 'Killing' during military action

[36] Lakoff, *Thinking Points*, 38.
[37] Ray Loveridge, 'Institutional Theory' in David Faulkner and Andrew Campbell (eds), *The Oxford Handbook of Strategy* (OUP 2006) 128.
[38] Michael Kelly, 'Genocide: The Power of a Label' (2008) 40 Case W Res J Int'l L 147.
[39] Sarah Kaplan, 'Framing Contests: Strategy Making Under Uncertainty' (2008) 19(5) Org Sci 729.
[40] Charles R Schwenk, 'The Cognitive Perspective on Strategic Decision Making' (1988) 25(1) J Manag Stud 41.
[41] Schwenk, 'The Cognitive Perspective on Strategic Decision Making', 46.
[42] Ma Regina E Estuar, Nico A Canoy, Divya Japa, Janice Jones, Sherri McCarthy, Ellora Puri, Megan Reif, Haslina Muhamed, Nisha Raj, and Jas Jafaar, 'Perspectives on Invasion in South and Southeast Asia' in Kathleen Malley-Morrison, Andrea Mercurio, and Gabriel Twose (eds), *International Handbook of War, Torture, and Terrorism* (Springer 2013) 469.

is often relabelled as a necessary 'act of protecting one's country to pursue peace'.[43] The 'invasion of Iraq' was euphemistically reframed by the interveners in terms of 'the defence of democracy' or 'liberation'.[44] While some downplayed the conflict in Rwanda as a case of 'ancient ethnic hatred', others talked about it as a 'civil war', 'a crisis', or 'humanitarian suffering', and warned of 'genocide', 'atrocities', or raised concerns about a 'human rights emergency'.[45] The Rwanda example in particular shows that the strategic choice of language is frequently predicated on whether the interpreter wants certain legal norms to be applicable or not. The strategic choice of language can help to mobilize opinions and support for a cause by arguing that certain rights are violated or that state obligations need to be fulfilled.

F. The sociology of law and the interpretation of law

Sociologists have intensively explored the application of cognitive frame theory in the context of law and legal interpretation.[46] Among others, Niklas Luhmann elaborated on cognitive and normative expectations in order to explain the 'select-ivity' of lawyers in legal interpretation.[47] He highlights that in communication processes people choose pieces of information from a multitude of possibilities and base other kinds of choices on the outcome of this pre-selection, which 'largely relieves the individual of independent testing of alternatives'.[48] The start-ing point is often 'common assumptions', whose own selectivity 'remains latent'.[49] This unconscious 'structural selection' has simply become a way of living, helping to avoid the 'possibility of disappointments' of expectations. Luhmann concludes that, although there can be errors of interpretation and occasional experiences of disappointment, cognitive pre-selection regulates fear:

> Structures fix a rather narrow section of the possible as expectable... In this way they transform the *permanent* stress arising from complexity into the problem of *occasional* experiences of disappointment about which something can be done in a concrete fashion. As seen from the psychological system, we can therefore say: they regulate fear.[50]

For Luhmann, norms are 'counterfactually stabilised behavioural expectations' and their meaning 'implies unconditional validity'.[51] Luhmann suggests that jurists must have an 'operative flexibility' to convincingly substantiate decisions.[52]

---

[43] 'Perspectives on Invasion in South and Southeast Asia', 469.

[44] Robert M Entman, *Projections of Power: Framing News, Public Opinion, and US Foreign Policy* (Chicago University Press 2004) 112.

[45] Melissa Labonte, *Human Rights and Humanitarian Norms, Strategic Framing, and Intervention: Lessons for the Responsibility to Protect* (Routledge 2013) 99.

[46] Piet Strydom, 'Contemporary European Cognitive Social Theory' in Gerald Delanty (ed), *Handbook of Contemporary European Social Theory* (Routledge 2006) 218.

[47] Niklas Luhmann, *A Sociological Theory of Law* (Routledge 1985) 31.

[48] Luhmann, *A Sociological Theory of Law*, 31.

[49] Luhmann, *A Sociological Theory of Law*, 31.

[50] Luhmann, *A Sociological Theory of Law*, 32.

[51] Luhmann, *A Sociological Theory of Law*, 33.

[52] Luhmann, *A Sociological Theory of Law*, 140.

However, while fulfilling their role of interpreting the law, they need 'to see other possibilities and give consideration to them'.[53] Under certain circumstances, there might be 'tactical considerations' which challenge the objectivity of the interpreter.[54] At the same time, Luhmann reminds that 'law is [deliberately] kept elastic by abstraction', in order to allow an adaptation to gradual changes in societal needs by different interpretations.[55] His work maintains that there is no contradiction between the subjectivity of meanings of law offered by interpreters and the normativity of the law itself.[56]

II. Case Studies and Examples

The list of potential examples of cognitive frames in international legal disputes and the interpretation of law is extensive. Language can be reshuffled and terminology can be recomposed creatively, nearly without limits, and on demand. Talking about 'neighbourhoods' instead of 'illegal settlements' is an example of one of those strategic choices.[57] A common linguistic trope, repeatedly appearing in the media, is the description of a conflict as 'sectarian violence' or 'riots' rather than a 'civil war', or vice versa, which is contingent on the needs of the interpreter.[58] In June 2012, the Assad Government in Syria still claimed that:

Syria has not descended into civil war, but is witnessing a struggle to eradicate the scourge of terrorism and revenge killing, kidnappings and ransom, bombings and attacks on state institutions and the destruction of public and private property and other brutal crimes...[59]

Those grades of language choice influence the perception about whether or not an 'internal armed conflict' is factually present, introducing a 'battle for the minds' instead of a 'contest of the facts'.[60]

In this section, three case studies aim to exemplify the challenge of cognitive frames in the interpretation of international law. The debates about talking of a 'separation wall' versus a 'security fence' in the Israel–Palestine conflict, the legitimization of 'enhanced interrogation techniques' vis-à-vis the interpretation of such conduct as 'torture', and the ambiguity of speaking of 'terrorism' or 'liberation' will be analysed. All three cases remain an object of heated debate in international law and international relations.

---

[53] Luhmann, *A Sociological Theory of Law*, 140.
[54] Luhmann, *A Sociological Theory of Law*, 140.
[55] Luhmann, *A Sociological Theory of Law*, 142.
[56] Christina Boswell, *The Political Uses of Expert Knowledge: Immigration Policy and Social Research* (CUP 2009) 45.
[57] Mona Baker, *Translation, Power and Conflict: A Narrative Account* (Routledge 2006) 127.
[58] Roger W Shuy, *The Language of Defamation Cases* (OUP 2010) 58.
[59] 'Syria Not in Civil War: Foreign Ministry', *Reuters*, 13 June 2012.
[60] On the 'battle of semantics', see Ralph Christensen and Michael Sokolowski, 'Recht als Einsatz im Semantischen Kampf' in Ekkehard Felder (ed), *Semantische Kämpfe: Macht und Sprache in den Wissenschaften* (de Gruyter 2006) 353.

A. 'Separation wall' versus 'security fence'

An example of the strategic use of frames and anchored cognitive mindsets can be found in the Advisory Opinion of the International Court of Justice (ICJ) on the *Legal Consequences of the Construction of a Wall in the Occupied Palestinian Territory*.[61] In 2003, the UN Special Rapporteur on the Situation of Human Rights in the Occupied Territories, John Dugard, remarked on the power of language and cognitive mindsets in relation to the Israel–Palestine conflict:

Language is a powerful instrument. This explains why words that accurately describe a particular situation are often avoided out of fear that they will too vividly portray the situation which they seek to depict. In politics euphemism is often preferred to accuracy in language. So it is with the Wall that Israel is presently constructing within the territory of the West Bank. It goes by the name of 'Seam Zone', 'Security Fence' or 'Separation Wall'. The word 'annexation' is avoided as it is too accurate a description and too unconcerned about the need to obfuscate the truth in the interests of anti-terrorism measures.[62]

Initially, the Report of the UN Secretary General used the general term 'barrier'.[63] The Report clarified that the Palestinian authorities often call this system the 'separation wall', while the Israeli Government use the term 'security fence'.[64] Subsequently, the UN General Assembly mentioned the term 'wall' in its resolution on the ICJ Advisory Opinion.[65] The Israeli Government contested the terminology in its written submissions, arguing that the word 'wall' could provoke negative associations:

The use of the term 'wall' in the resolution requesting an opinion is neither happenstance nor oversight. It reflects a calculated media campaign to raise pejorative connotations in the mind of the Court of great concrete constructions of separation such as the Berlin Wall, intended to stop people escaping from tyranny.[66]

The Israeli Government stated that the use of the term 'wall' would be 'intentionally pejorative', whereas the term 'barrier' would be neutral.[67] The 'acute sensitivity about terminology in this matter' was stressed in a subsequent letter to the Court, and alleged that the language used by the ICJ 'suggest[s] that the Court has already formed a view of the barrier which is supportive of the Palestinian position'.[68] The Palestinian National Authority included a list of definitions for

---

[61] *Legal Consequences of the Construction of a Wall in the Occupied Palestinian Territory* (Advisory Opinion) [2004] ICJ Rep 136.

[62] Report of the Special Rapporteur of the Commission on Human Rights, John Dugard, on the Situation of Human Rights in the Palestinian territories, UN Doc E/CN.4/2004/6, 8 September 2003, [6].

[63] Report of the Secretary-General prepared pursuant to General Assembly resolution ES-10/13, UN Doc A/ES-10/248, 24 November 2003.

[64] UN Doc A/ES-10/248, [2].   [65] UN Doc A/ES-10/248.

[66] Letter dated 29 January 2004 from the Deputy Director General and Legal Advisor of the Ministry of Foreign Affairs, together with the Written Statement of the Government of Israel, 30 January 2004, [2.7].

[67] Letter dated 29 January 2004 from the Deputy Director General and Legal Advisor of the Ministry of Foreign Affairs, [2.8].

[68] Letter dated 29 January 2004 from the Deputy Director General and Legal Advisor of the Ministry of Foreign Affairs, Annex 2.

commonly used terminology in their statement and highlighted that the term 'wall' is understood as:

[An] integrated system of concrete walls, fences (including electric fences), barriers, barbed wire zones, ditches, trenches, trace paths, patrol roads, and fortified guard towers being built by Israel...[69]

States that submitted written statements to the Court showed diplomatic caution in order not to be trapped on one side or the other. Germany, for instance, stressed that it 'will use the term "wall", as used in the request for an Advisory Opinion, without implying that it is a more accurate or appropriate term than "security fence", "barrier" or such other term as may be employed'.[70] Some states, such as Russia, only mentioned the term 'wall' in parentheses, treating the word like a contaminated term.[71] Other states, such as Saudi Arabia, wrote the word 'the Wall' in capital letters, highlighting the importance of the issue by giving it a 'personal name'.[72]

In its Advisory Opinion, the Court followed the terminology of the General Assembly. The ICJ argued that technically 'the other terms used, either by Israel ("fence") or by the Secretary-General ("barrier"), are no more accurate if understood in the physical sense'.[73] On the merits, the Court was 'not convinced that the specific course Israel has chosen for the wall was necessary to attain its security objectives'.[74] By 14 votes to one, the ICJ found that the 'construction of such a wall accordingly constitutes breaches by Israel of various of its obligations under the applicable international humanitarian law and human rights instruments'.[75] In dissent, Judge Buergenthal agreed with the General Assembly wording 'wall' instead of using the Israeli term 'security fence'.[76]

The ICJ Advisory Opinion illustrates how difficult it is to find wording that pleases all parties in a dispute yet is specific enough to capture a highly political matter with precision. It is one of the rare cases where the ICJ openly addressed strategic language preferences, while indicating awareness about cognitive frames. Some commentators tried to frame the issue in the most neutral way by speaking about the 'structure between Israel and the Palestinian Territories'.[77] And

---

[69] International Court of Justice Advisory Opinion Proceedings on Legal Consequences of the Construction of a Wall in the Occupied Palestinian Territory, Palestine Written Statement, 30 January 2004, and Oral Pleading, 23 February 2004, <http://palestineun.org/wp-content/uploads/2013/08/ICJ-writtenstatementenglish.pdf> accessed 29 July 2014.

[70] Letter dated 29 January 2004 from the Ambassador of the Federal Republic of Germany to the Netherlands, together with the Statement of the Government of the Federal Republic of Germany, 30 January 2004.

[71] Written Statement of the Russian Federation, 29 January 2004.

[72] Written Statement of the Kingdom of Saudi Arabia, 27 January 2004.

[73] *Legal Consequences of the Construction of a Wall in the Occupied Palestinian Territory*, [67].

[74] *Legal Consequences of the Construction of a Wall in the Occupied Palestinian Territory*, [137].

[75] *Legal Consequences of the Construction of a Wall in the Occupied Palestinian Territory*, [137].

[76] *Legal Consequences of the Construction of a Wall in the Occupied Palestinian Territory*, Declaration of Judge Buergenthal.

[77] Richard Rogers and Anat Ben-David, 'Coming to Terms: A Conflict Analysis of the Usage, in Official and Unofficial Sources, of "Security Fence", "Apartheid Wall", and other Terms for the Structure between Israel and the Palestinian Territories' (2010) 3(2) Media, War & Conflict 202.

indeed, the ICJ could have tried to reframe the wording of the General Assembly in order to appear unprejudiced and non-aligned. Still, the rhetoric in the General Assembly resolution eventually set the tone. As the judges agreed on the merits with the underlying arguments by Palestine, and condemned the construction of the 'wall', there was no need for reframing. This goes to show that interpretation in international law is inherently political. As Hersch Lauterpacht put it: 'There is no escape from the fact that all international disputes are "political" to a larger or smaller degree.'[78] Evidently, courts take sides in an international legal dispute through their judgment, which is reflected in the substance of their reasoning but also through the lexicon or vocabulary they use.

B. 'Enhanced interrogation techniques' versus 'torture'

An example at the edge of legal interpretation, framing, and argumentation is the justification of counter-terrorism measures by the US in the so-called 'war on terror'. In the aftermath of the 9/11 attacks, the Bush administration created a 'salient and resilient theme, the war on terror, which resonated with the American public'.[79] As one commentator summarized: 'Without rhetorical framing, it would be impossible for any policy maker to present a case for war.'[80] Critical in this context was the framing of certain interrogation methods as 'enhanced interrogation techniques', rather than 'torture'.[81] The techniques applied involved physical and psychological means of coercion, including stress positions, extreme temperature changes, sleep deprivation, and waterboarding, which is the technique of simulated drowning.[82]

In her memoir, the former US Secretary of State Condoleezza Rice recalls that the US Central Intelligence Agency (CIA) initially referred to 'enhanced interrogation techniques', requesting the authorization of the President to 'use particular procedures'.[83] Rice stresses that CIA Director George Tenet had affirmed that the 'techniques were safe and effective and had been used in the military training of thousands of U.S. soldiers'.[84] President George W Bush maintained that the US Department of Justice had carried out a 'careful legal review', concluding that 'enhanced interrogation techniques' complied with the US Constitution and

---

[78] Hersch Lauterpacht, *The Function of Law in the International Community* (OUP 2011) 163.
[79] Wojtek Mackiewicz Wolfe, *Winning the War of Words: Selling the War on Terror from Afghanistan to Iraq* (Praeger Security International 2008) 2.
[80] Wolfe, *Winning the War of Words*, 2.
[81] Yuval Ginbar, *Why Not Torture Terrorists?: Moral, Practical, and Legal Aspects of the 'Ticking Bomb' Justification for Torture* (OUP 2010) 242.
[82] Jason Ralph, *America's War on Terror: The State of the 9/11 Exception from Bush to Obama* (OUP 2013) 117.
[83] Condoleezza Rice, *No Higher Honor: A Memoir of My Years in Washington* (Random House 2011) 117.
[84] Rice, *No Higher Honor*, 117.

all applicable laws, including those banning torture.[85] On the legitimacy of the 'enhanced interrogation techniques', President Bush highlighted:

I knew that an interrogation program this sensitive and controversial would one day become public. When it did, we would open ourselves up to criticism that America had compromised our moral values...But the choice between security and values was real...My most solemn responsibility as president was to protect the country...[And] the new techniques proved highly effective.[86]

Under international law, the UN Convention against Torture and Other Cruel, Inhuman or Degrading Treatment or Punishment prohibits 'torture', defining it as:

Any act by which severe pain or suffering, whether physical or mental, is intentionally inflicted on a person...when such pain or suffering is inflicted by or at the instigation of or with the consent or acquiescence of a public official or other person acting in an official capacity.[87]

The Office of the Legal Counsel (OLC) of the Department of Justice concluded in its legal assessment that 'certain acts may be cruel, inhuman, or degrading, but still not produce pain and suffering of the requisite intensity to fall within [the] proscription against torture'.[88] The OLC argued that the term 'severe' regarding pain or suffering is not defined. In its understanding, 'the term encompasses only extreme acts' and 'only the most heinous acts', while 'damage must rise to the level of death, organ failure, or the permanent impairment of a significant body function'.[89] The OLC concluded that 'only the worst forms of cruel, inhuman, or degrading treatment or punishment' are prohibited, which leaves one wondering whether interrogations can involve more heinous techniques than waterboarding. Most importantly, the OLC stressed that one had to discuss the question of permissible interrogation techniques 'in the context of the current war against the al Qaeda terrorist network'.[90]

The Bush administration's policy approach, and consequently the interpretation of the law, changed under the Obama administration. In 2009, President Obama restricted the use of enhanced interrogation techniques. In his perspective, they undermined the 'moral authority' of the US without making the country safer.[91] The Obama administration argued that enhanced interrogation techniques might not be the most effective means of interrogation, given that they contradict the rule of law and 'alienate' the US in the world.[92]

[85] George W Bush, *Decision Points* (Random House 2010) 169.
[86] Bush, *Decision Points*, 169.
[87] Convention against Torture and Other Cruel, Inhuman or Degrading Treatment or Punishment, 10 December 1984, Article 1.
[88] US Justice Department, Office of Legal Counsel, Memorandum for Alberto Gonzales, Counsel to the President, Re: Standards of Conduct for Interrogation under 18 USC [2340]–[2340A], 1 August 2002.
[89] US Justice Department, Office of Legal Counsel, Memorandum for Alberto Gonzales.
[90] US Justice Department, Office of Legal Counsel, Memorandum for Alberto Gonzales.
[91] Statement of President Barack Obama on Release of OLC Memos, The White House, Office of the Press Secretary, 16 April 2009.
[92] Remarks by the President on National Security, The White House, Office of the Press Secretary, 21 May 2009.

Cassandra Burke Robertson has remarked that it would be 'difficult to prove that the [OLC torture memos] were written in bad faith'.[93] Although the memos 'represent bad legal advice', the 'existence of perceptual filters and deep partisan identification may have shaped the lawyers' views of the situation in ways that appear unfathomable to outsiders'.[94] Burke Robertson argues that the perceptual filters of the OLC leadership, who had been recruited from Republican Party circles, created a type of 'echo chamber' where 'dissenting views were not just unaired, but were actually unseen and unknown'.[95] As a consequence, 'political sympathizer[s] would be less likely to see those weaknesses, and would therefore be more likely to give legal advice that the administration viewed favorably, even without any deliberate attempt to subvert the law'.[96]

This case study reveals that the strategic use of language is not just an instrument for camouflaging problematic policy decisions through semantics, but that it can also lead to cognitive traps. Lexical and deep frames are particularly engaged in the formulation of the 'ordinary meaning' of legal terms, as stipulated in the Vienna Convention on the Law of Treaties (VCLT).[97] This might explain why waterboarding was perceived of less gravity when the OLC was tasked with interpreting the severity of the pain or suffering it caused, pursuant to the UN Convention against Torture.[98] During the drafting of the VCLT in 1968, the US representative Myres McDougal observed that the criterion of ordinary meaning can open 'the door to arbitrary interpretations' and can 'create greater uncertainties'.[99] And indeed, the challenge of the ordinary meaning principle is that the undefined term 'ordinary' allows multiple ordinary meanings while aiming for a common one.[100] It is a 'rule of thumb', which can result in disputes at the concrete application stage and depends on the group of interpreters.[101] As the example of 'enhanced interrogation techniques' versus 'torture' demonstrates, rules of interpretation can become a gateway for cognitive frames being prone to perceptual bias.

[93] Cassandra Burke Robertson, 'Beyond the Torture Memos: Perceptual Filters, Cultural Commitments, and Partisan Identity' (2009) 42 Case W Res J Int'l L 389.
[94] Robertson, 'Beyond the Torture Memos', 389.
[95] Robertson, 'Beyond the Torture Memos', 390.
[96] Robertson, 'Beyond the Torture Memos', 390.   [97] Article 31(1) VCLT.
[98] Memorandum for John A Rizzo, Senior Deputy General Counsel, Central Intelligence Agency, Re: Application of United States Obligations Under Article 16 of the Convention Against Torture to Certain Techniques that May Be Used in the Interrogation of High Value al Qaeda Detainees, US Department of Justice, Office of Legal Counsel, 30 May 2005, III.B.1, 14 <http://www.justice.gov/olc/docs/memo-bradbury2005.pdf> accessed 29 July 2014. See also Rebecca Sanders, '(Im)plausible Legality: The Rationalisation of Human Rights Abuses in the American "Global War on Terror"' (2011) 15(4) IJHR 605.
[99] UN Doc A/CONF.39/11, 26 March–24 May 1968, [48].
[100] See Ulf Linderfalk, *On the Interpretation of Treaties: The Modern International Law as Expressed in the 1969 Vienna Convention on the Law of Treaties* (Springer 2007) 66.
[101] Lawrence Solan, *The Language of Statutes: Laws and Their Interpretation* (University of Chicago Press 2010) 69.

C. 'Terrorism' versus 'liberation'

In his novel *Harry's Game*, Gerald Seymour tells the story of the assassination of a British Government minister by a member of the Irish Republican Army (IRA).[102] The incident occurs in the 1970s during the time of 'the Troubles', as the intra-state conflict in Northern Ireland was called. An undercover agent, Harry Brown, is sent to Belfast to track down the assassin before he kills again. At one point in the story, a member of the Red Cross makes a significant comment, which has become an often quoted paragraph in describing the twofold cognitive mindset in interpreting terrorism:

He'd said to the colonel something like, 'One man's terrorist is another man's freedom fighter.' The colonel hadn't liked that. Pretty heady stuff, they all thought in the mess. Such rubbish. Terrorist they were then, wog terrorists at that...[103]

The frames 'terrorism' versus 'liberation' endure in present contexts, exemplifying a split perception predicated on which side of a political contest one stands on. In 2004, the UN Special Rapporteur on Human Rights and Terrorism Kalliopi Koufa remarked:

This is an issue of great international controversy, in need of careful review due to the 'your freedom fighter is my terrorist' problem and the increase in the rhetorical use of the expression 'war on terrorism', labelling wars as terrorism, and combatants in wars as terrorists, and it has an extremely undesirable effect of nullifying application of and compliance with humanitarian law in those situations, while at the same time providing no positive results in combating actual terrorism.[104]

As Koufa noted, a number of UN member states 'clearly differentiate between terrorism and the struggle for self-determination', yet definitional controversies remain.[105] Problems in delimiting the definition of terrorist acts has kept the terrorism versus liberation frame in limbo. In international humanitarian law, a legal distinction is made between 'armed forces', 'dissident armed forces', and 'other organised armed groups'.[106] However, a comprehensive and coherent international definition of the term 'terrorist' is still under development.[107]

The repertoire of terminology in this context is endless, ranging from 'guerrilla fighters', 'rebel groups', 'insurgent forces', 'liberation fronts', 'revolutionary guards', 'patriotic movements', or 'people's revolutionary armies' to 'homeland

---

[102] Gerald Seymour, *Harry's Game* (Random House 1975).

[103] Seymour, *Harry's Game*, 91. See also Michael V Bhatia, 'Fighting Words: Naming Terrorists, Bandits, Rebels and Other Violent Actors' (2005) 26(1) Third World Quarterly 5; Mark R Dixon, Simon Dymond, Ruth Anne Rehfeldt, Bryan Roche, and Kimberly R Zlomke, 'Terrorism and Relational Frame Theory' (2003) 13(1) Behavior & Social Issues 129; Pippa Norris, Montague Kern, and Marion Just, 'Framing Terrorism' in Pippa Norris, Montague Kern, and Marion Just, *Framing Terrorism: The News Media, the Government and the Public* (Routledge 2003) 3.

[104] UN Doc E/CN.4/Sub.2/2004/40, 25 June 2004, [72].

[105] UN Doc E/CN.4/Sub.2/2004/40, [13].

[106] Protocol Additional to the Geneva Conventions of 12 August 1949, and relating to the Protection of Victims of Non-International Armed Conflicts (Protocol II), 8 June 1977, Article 1(1).

[107] Ben Saul, *Terrorism* (Hart 2012) lxvii.

and freedom forces', 'partisans', 'national retrieval groups', 'martyrs' brigades', 'democratic armies', or 'justice and equality movements'.[108] An eminent example is Hezbollah, which literally means the 'Party of God' (Party of Allah). While the group is classified by some states as a 'terrorist organization' and is criticized by its political national opponents in Lebanon for being an 'armed militia', it considers itself as a 'resistance movement'.[109] What is at stake in this terminological debate is whether the use of force can be justified. The use of force is partly accepted under international law as a means for resistance by liberation movements under certain conditions in order to enforce the right of self-determination through civil disobedience and armed defence.[110]

Interestingly, some international media outlets voluntarily created rules for how the issue of terrorism should be framed and interpreted. For instance, the British Broadcasting Corporation (BBC) noted in its editorial guidelines:

> Terrorism is a difficult and emotive subject with significant political overtones and care is required in the use of language that carries value judgements. We try to avoid the use of the term 'terrorist' without attribution.[111]

The BBC underlines that those who comment on sensitive political situations must exercise responsibility with respect to the language they use. As the BBC notes, the term 'terrorist' can create a cognitive barrier that potentially excludes consideration of other facts and circumstances:

> The word 'terrorist' itself can be a barrier rather than an aid to understanding. We should convey to our audience the full consequences of the act by describing what happened. We should use words which specifically describe the perpetrator such as 'bomber', 'attacker', 'gunman', 'kidnapper', 'insurgent', and 'militant'. We should not adopt other people's language as our own; our responsibility is to remain objective and report in ways that enable our audiences to make their own assessments about who is doing what to whom.[112]

This final example reveals that interpreters bear a responsibility for how they evaluate and present arguments. Michael Rosenfeld wrote that 'just interpretations' are required for a legal system to qualify as legitimate.[113] He draws attention to the fact that 'pragmatic interpretations', where interpretation is a means to a desired end, bear 'limits and dangers'.[114] Similarly, Susanna Lindroos-Hovinheimo argues that interpreters not only have the unwritten responsibility to read legal texts carefully, but they must have an eye on the effects of the interpretation in a particular

---

[108] Kenneth Watkin, '21st Century Conflict and International Humanitarian Law: Status Quo or Change?' in Michael Schmitt and Jelena Pejic (eds), *International Law and Armed Conflict: Exploring the Faultlines* (Martinus Nijhoff 2007) 268.

[109] Augustus Norton, *Hezbollah: A Short History* (Princeton University Press 2009) 83.

[110] Judith Palmer Harik, *Hezbollah: The Changing Face of Terrorism* (IB Tauris 2004) 165.

[111] BBC Guidelines, Section 11: War, Terror and Emergencies, [11.4.5].

[112] BBC Guidelines, Section 11: War, Terror and Emergencies, [11.4.5].

[113] Michel Rosenfeld, *Just Interpretations: Law Between Ethics and Politics* (University of California Press 1998) 2.

[114] Rosenfeld, *Just Interpretations*, 190.

situation.[115] She rightly argues that interpretation is 'not arbitrary choice'.[116] If the interpretation of the law sometimes resembles a 'legal language game', it requires self-awareness, sensitivity, and at least a shade of responsibility on the part of those playing it.[117]

Conclusion

Speaking about the rule of (international) law in his General Course at the Hague Academy, James Crawford made the following telling comment:

International law is a means of communication as well as of limitation, a language in which disputes can be carried on as well as a vehicle for resolving them.[118]

Crawford's words hint that law and its interpretation is never one-sided. The inherent purpose of international law and legal interpretation is to absorb disagreement while trying to transform differences into consensus. At its best, this results in a joint vocabulary while hopefully also creating a common understanding of international rights and rules.

Ronald Dworkin wrote that law is 'deeply and thoroughly political'.[119] This observation equally pertains to the interpretation of law. As Dworkin elaborates, our political beliefs influence how we read texts and form judgements. They lead to both genuine 'reactions' and inarticulate 'tactics'.[120] Commenting on the subjectivity and objectivity of literary interpretation, Dworkin concluded that interpretation is 'a matter of discovering' how various actors conceive of the law.[121] His thinking reveals that legal interpretation is a puzzle, where the enshrined intrinsic value of the law highly depends on the interpreter.[122]

As demonstrated in this chapter, the delicate practice of legal interpretation is challenged by cognitive frames or strategic choices of language. Cognitive frames impose a subconscious layer of interpretation of terminology, which makes it difficult for judges, legal advisers, or advocacy groups to distance themselves from their predefined assumptions in order to be self-reflexive about their own blind spots and the perceptions of others about the law.

---

[115] Susanna Lindroos-Hovinheimo, *Justice and the Ethics of Legal Interpretation* (Routledge 2012) 160.

[116] Lindroos-Hovinheimo, *Justice and the Ethics of Legal Interpretation*, 160.

[117] Lindroos-Hovinheimo, *Justice and the Ethics of Legal Interpretation*, 29. See also Martti Koskenniemi, *From Apology to Utopia: The Structure of International Legal Argument* (CUP 2006) 54; Christine Parker and Adrian Evans, *Inside Lawyers' Ethics* (CUP 2007) 229.

[118] James Crawford, *Chance, Order, Change: The Course of International Law* (Brill 2014) 320.

[119] Ronald Dworkin, 'Law as Interpretation' (1982) 60 Tex Law Rev 527.

[120] Dworkin, 'Law as Interpretation', 533.

[121] Dworkin, 'Law as Interpretation', 564.

[122] See Joseph Raz, *Between Authority and Interpretation: On the Theory of Law and Practical Reason* (OUP 2010) 103.

A. Challenges for the objectivity of the law?

The existence of cognitive frames in the interpretation of international law might be thought to reduce the objectivity of the law. Legal philosophers remain divided about whether or not there can be a reality that is true and absolute. The issue of the objectivity of law rotates around the question of whether or not law can be independent (objective) of the individual opinions and views of interpreters (subjective).[123] Objectivity, in the epistemological sense, requires that law and its interpretations be free of 'factors that distort cognition'.[124] Circumstances such as 'bias for or against one party' and 'ignorance of pertinent rules or facts' present obstacles to objectivity as they influence 'the selection and evaluation of evidence', which impacts on the direction of arguments and legal interpretation.[125] In this regard, one could indeed argue that objectivity and the interpretation of international law is hampered by the existence of cognitive subconscious structures.

Yet, the supposition of the objectivity of the law is itself a frame, based on the belief that there can be objectivity.[126] Some scholars, such as Andrei Marmor, argue that the whole 'objective-subjective dichotomy is a philosophical invention'.[127] Brian Leiter highlights that it is society that often expects 'legal decisions to be objective in the sense of reaching the result that law really requires without letting bias or prejudice intervene'.[128] As Neil MacCormick exposes, objectivity is particularly expected from judges, who present themselves as 'impartial determiners of disputes'.[129] They are appointed to do 'justice according to law' and act as 'the watchdogs of the public interest'.[130] Without aiming for objectivity, the 'Rule of Law' turns into the 'Rule of Men'. On the other hand, it is the official duty and mandate of legal advisers and advocacy groups to argue for one party or the other. In these practice contexts, international law is contingent on the standpoint of the decision-maker towards an international problem, which enables the simultaneous justification and critique of particular outcomes.[131] Here, the professional role of the interpreter impacts on their perceptions. This phenomenon does not necessarily undermine the objectivity of the law, but certainly influences their interpretation of legal norms.

---

[123] For the debate, see eg Jaakko Husa and Mark van Hoecke (eds), *Objectivity in Law and Legal Reasoning* (Hart 2013); Matthew Kramer, *Objectivity and the Rule of Law* (CUP 2007); Kent Greenawalt, *Law and Objectivity* (OUP 1995).

[124] Brian Leiter, 'Law and Objectivity' in Jules Coleman and Scott Shapiro (eds), *The Oxford Handbook of Jurisprudence and Philosophy of Law* (OUP 2002) 973.

[125] Leiter, 'Law and Objectivity', 973.

[126] The American realism movement runs counter to this frame. See Charles E Clark, 'The Limits of Judicial Objectivity' (1963) 12(1) Am U L Rev 1; Owen Fiss, 'Objectivity and Interpretation' (1982) 34(3) Stan L Rev 739; Steven L Winter, 'The Cognitive Dimension of the Agon Between Legal Power and Narrative Meaning' (1989) 87(8) Mich L Rev 2225.

[127] Andrei Marmor, *Positive Law and Objective Values* (OUP 2001) 112.

[128] Brian Leiter, 'Introduction' in Brian Leiter (ed), *Objectivity in Law and Morals* (CUP 2001) 3.

[129] Neil MacCormick, *Legal Reasoning and Legal Theory* (Clarendon Press 1994) 17.

[130] MacCormick, *Legal Reasoning and Legal Theory*, 17.

[131] Cheng, *When International Law Works*; Koskenniemi, 'Between Commitment and Cynicism'.

B. Self-awareness and responsibility of interpreters

Over the last decades, legal scholarship has been increasingly informed and inspired by psychological research and neuroscience. This development has led to what is nowadays known as 'neurolaw' or 'behavioural law'.[132] Respectively, the conception of objectivity regarding the interpretation of law and normative judgement appears to have become more modest than it used to be.[133] Cognitive research has been particularly relevant in the field of criminal responsibility and understanding free will.[134] Some scholarly voices have even advocated a 'cognitive science of legal interpretation'.[135] However, much cognitive research is still in the process of being thoroughly considered by legal scholars and practitioners.[136] The full integration of neuroscience insights with theories of legal interpretation will probably take further time.

The case study on the cognitive frames implicated in the 'enhanced interrogation techniques' versus 'torture' debate reveals that legal interpretation engages the professional responsibility of those involved in delivering legal advice. Interpretations can be involuntary entry points for subconscious presuppositions, political agendas or stereotypes, which arrive in legal judgments and decisions like 'Trojan horses'. Michael Reisman differentiated between the 'task' and 'outcome responsibility' of international lawyers: the first involves the responsibility attendant on discharging a given task, while the second involves carrying the responsibility for the result of legal interpretation.[137] He argued that 'international professional responsibility to the international community as a whole' is critical to achieve.[138]

However, *individual* responsibility is possible to achieve. As James Nafziger argued, the responsibility of international lawyers 'extends beyond the role of technicians' or 'wordsmith[s]'.[139] Others have stressed, in the context of legal advice in armed conflict, that ethics require international jurists and legal advisers to serve 'the spirit of the law, even if this means interpreting the law progressively, boldly or freely'.[140] As Koskenniemi emphasized, the interpretation of international law requires the 'enlightened responsibility' of judges, lawyers, and

---

[132] See eg Nicole A Vincent, *Neuroscience and Legal Responsibility* (OUP 2013); Tade Matthias Spranger, *International Neurolaw: A Comparative Analysis* (Springer 2012); Brent Garland (ed), *Neuroscience and the Law: Brain, Mind, and the Scales of Justice* (Dana Press 2004).

[133] See also Michael S Pardo and Dennis Patterson, *Minds, Brains, and Law: The Conceptual Foundations of Law and Neuroscience* (OUP 2013) 15; Oliver R Goodenough and Micaela Tucker, 'Law and Cognitive Neuroscience' (2010) 6 Ann Rev Law & Soc Sci 61.

[134] Thomas Nadelhoffer, Dena Gromet, Geoffrey Goodwin, Eddy Nahmias, Chandra Sripada, and Walter Sinnott-Armstrong, 'The Mind, the Brain, and the Law' in Thomas Nadelhoffer (ed), *The Future of Punishment* (OUP 2013) 193.

[135] Benjamin Shaer, 'Toward a Cognitive Science of Legal Interpretation' in Michael Freeman and Fiona Smith (eds), *Law and Language: Current Legal Issues* (OUP 2013) 259.

[136] Michael Freeman, 'Introduction: Law and the Brain' in Michael Freeman (ed), *Law and Neuroscience: Current Legal Issues* (OUP 2011) 1.

[137] Reisman, *The Quest for World Order*, 467.

[138] Reisman, *The Quest for World Order*, 468.

[139] James AR Nafziger, 'The Development of International Law: Obstacles and Hopes' (1984) 38(1) Aust J Int'l Aff 33, 35.

[140] Michel Veuthey, 'Remedies to Promote the Respect of Fundamental Human Values in Non-International Armed Conflicts' (2001) 30 Israel YB Hum Rts 60.

advisers.[141] They need to be aware of their subconscious cognitive frames when applying the law. Interpreters may not always be conscious of the often undetectable substance of subliminal frames when making decisions, but they can act responsibly by being attentive to their possible existence.

C. Law as dialogue

Domestic legal codes on professional responsibility entail explicit rules for legal practice that try to remind practitioners of their professional commitments. Most ethical codes dictate that lawyers should avoid bias,[142] and should not appear in a professional capacity before a tribunal while 'manifesting bias or prejudice'.[143] In the international context, judges at the ICJ solemnly swear that they are exercising their powers 'impartially and conscientiously'.[144] The International Criminal Court has a Code of Professional Conduct for Counsel whereby counsel declare to perform their duty with 'integrity and diligence, honourably, freely, independently, expeditiously and conscientiously'.[145] Other ethics rules for international courts and tribunals and international legal advisory practice have been debated, but are still rare in practice.[146]

A recent empirical study on policy preferences and legal interpretation concludes that 'it is difficult to separate judgements about the linguistic meaning of a statute from policy preferences'.[147] This conclusion was similar to the outcome of earlier behavioural studies on legal decision-making.[148] Some scholars have coined this phenomenon 'the ideology of legal interpretation'.[149] Adrian Vermeule regards this 'inescapable problem' of bias in the decision-procedure of legal interpreters as an 'institutional dilemma'.[150] He argues that, besides individual

---

[141] Martti Koskenniemi, *The Gentle Civilizer of Nations: The Rise and Fall of International Law 1870–1960* (CUP 2002) 404.

[142] See eg New York Lawyer's Code of Professional Responsibility, 28 December 2007, EC 1–7.

[143] See eg Massachusetts Rules of Professional Conduct, 1 January 2013, 3.4(i).

[144] Statute of the International Court of Justice, 18 April 1946, Article 20.

[145] Code of Professional Conduct for Counsel, Article 5, ICC-ASP/4/Res.1, 2 December 2005.

[146] See eg The Hague Principles on Ethical Standards for Counsel Appearing before International Courts and Tribunals, The Study Group of the International Law Association on the Practice and Procedure of International Courts and Tribunals, 27 September 2010. See also Arman Sarvarian, *Professional Ethics at the International Bar* (OUP 2013) 17; Catherine Gibson, 'Representing the United States Abroad: Proper Conduct of US Government Attorneys in International Tribunals' (2013) 44 Geo J Int'l L 1167; Rosemary Byrne, 'The New Public International Lawyer and the Hidden Art of International Trial Practice' (2010) 25(2) Conn J Int'l L 243; Detlev Vagts, 'The International Legal Profession: A Need for More Governance?' (1996) 90(2) AJIL 250.

[147] Ward Farnsworth, Dustin Guzior, and Anup Malani, 'Policy Preferences and Legal Interpretation' (2013) 1(1) J L & Courts 115.

[148] See eg Howard Gillman, 'What's Law Got to Do with It?: Judicial Behavioralists Test the "Legal Model" of Judicial Decision Making' (2001) 26(2) Law & Soc Inq 465; Martin van Hees and Bernard Steunenberg, 'The Choices Judges Make: Court Rulings, Personal Values, and Legal Constraints' (2000) 12(3) J Theor Polit 305.

[149] Sara C Benesh and Jason J Czarnezki, 'The Ideology of Legal Interpretation' (2009) 29 Wash UJL & Pol'y 113; Marcelo Dascal and Jerzy Wróblewski, 'The Rational Law-maker and the Pragmatics of Legal Interpretation' (1991) 15(5) J Pragmat 421.

[150] Adrian Vermeule, *Judging Under Uncertainty: An Institutional Theory of Legal Interpretation* (Harvard University Press 2006) 1–3.

frames, institutional affiliation has systemic effects on legal conclusions. Indeed, as explored throughout this chapter, non-partisanship and 'objectivity' is hard to achieve, especially for those interpreters who serve strategic policy interests while applying international law. In any event, involuntary cognitive frames that narrow or widen legal interpretation are unavoidable.

Conceiving of interpretation as a game is itself an attempt to anchor or activate a cognitive frame. This is done under the metaphorical proposition that interpretation involves players, rules, and an overarching object. As this chapter has shown, legal interpretation is not just a text-driven exercise, but a test for one's subconscious. This chapter demonstrated that strategic legal interpretation correlates with the choice of language. At this intersection, frames are established, re-emphasized, or dissolved.[151] Although rules of interpretation in international law do not touch on cognitive issues yet, legal practitioners should be mindful of the fact that assumptions, communication, and the interpretation of law are closely interlinked. Finally, cognitive frames are constantly modified by the interplay of actors.[152] Law involves persuasion, deliberation, and dialogue.[153] Understood as a process, interpretation is a product of exchanges between individuals, groups, and states. In that endeavour, the interpretation of international law is a conversation, carried out with others and with oneself.

---

[151] Andrei Marmor, 'Can the Law Imply More Than It Says?: On Some Pragmatic Aspects of Strategic Speech' in Andrei Marmor and Scott Soames (eds), *Philosophical Foundations of Language in the Law* (OUP 2011) 83.
[152] Surel, 'The Role of Cognitive and Normative Frames in Policy-Making', 9.
[153] Guyora Binder and Robert Weisberg, *Literary Criticisms of Law* (Princeton University Press 2000) 23.

17

Is Interpretation in International Law a Game?

*Ingo Venzke**

Introduction

International lawyers of contrasting colours converge in thinking of international law as a language. The United Nations, in its 1995 Congress on Public International Law, already chose *International Law as a Language for International Relations* as its overarching theme.[1] Depending on their specific outlook, international lawyers perceive the language of international law as doing a whole range of things. It offers a steadfast vocabulary of progress and resistance, it brings opponents together through a pacifying grammar, or it provides a battleground on which to carry out conflicts. Some note with a sense of sober nonchalance that international law is nothing more than rhetoric. Others show an upbeat attitude against ages of realist critique, arguing that international law is a pervasive language after all.

The present chapter explores what it means to play with that language of international law. It takes the metaphor of the language of international law seriously and combines it with the analogy between interpretation and the playing of games.[2] This overall outlook resonates with images such as that drawn by Marc Weller, who notes that 'to some, the practice of international law is akin to an exciting game of chess. Expert players, or litigators move the pieces on the board, seeking to convert tactical dominance into strategic victory in the case they argue'.[3] The chapter will discuss three common ways of using the metaphor of the language of international law. It highlights the linguistic assumptions nested in each usage, thereby elucidating precisely what it means to play the interpretative game from each perspective. It then draws attention to the limits connected to this analogy

* Thanks to Valerio Priuli, Tim Staal, and Matthew Windsor for valuable comments and suggestions.
[1] United Nations, *International Law as a Language for International Relations* (Kluwer Law International 1996).
[2] See Chapter 1 (Daniel Peat and Matthew Windsor).
[3] Marc Weller, 'Modesty Can Be a Virtue: Judicial Economy in the ICJ Kosovo Opinion?' (2011) 24 LJIL 127, 127.

between interpretation in international law and the playing of games. Finally, it points out ways to overcome them.

First, the metaphor of the language of international law is used in the sense that it functions as a defence against the powerful for the benefit of the right and virtuous. It stands firm and unyielding against forces that corrupt. In just one instance of such a view, Dino Kritsiotis argues that '[t]he rhetoric and reality of might, power, force, and war are thus gradually being displaced by a new rhetoric—or, more accurately—a new language of law, principle, precedent, and procedure'.[4] The language of the law is at least sufficiently stable so as not to be easily corrupted. From a linguistic perspective, language relates to speaking like a background scheme relates to its execution (Part I).

A similar view is nested in a second approach, according to which the language of international law bridges troubled waters and allows conflicting sides to converse in a common idiom. Especially where issues are sensitive and divisive, international law offers, as Georg Nolte put it, 'a language in which states and other relevant actors exchange views on the specific problems of difficult cases'.[5] The idiom of international law brings opponents together in a pacifying grammar. To play the game of interpretation requires a competence or technique shared by other professionals that allows them to speak to one another when others have stopped speaking. On this account, professional competence decides what counts as a good performance in the game (Part II).

A third variation breaks with the first two approaches by rejecting a dualism between a background scheme, or grammar, and its execution. Instead, it emphasizes how participants in international legal discourse try to use and bend the rules of the game in a struggle for the law.[6] As Martti Koskenniemi observes, 'international actors routinely challenge each other by invoking legal rules and principles on which they have projected meanings that support their preferences and counteract those of their opponents'.[7] Here, the language of international law provides a battleground to carry out conflicts and interpretation involves a potential exercise of power (Part III(A)).

While the first two understandings portray language as providing the rules of the game and as clarifying which moves are possible and correct, the third opens up towards a view in which success in the interpretative game decides what the law is and how the game should be played. The nature of the game accordingly changes. The dualism between rules of the game and their performance, I will argue, should indeed be rejected. The focus should instead fall on the side of concrete performances and the forces that shape them (Part III(B)). The continuing challenge is to make sense of interpretation in international law without

---

[4] Dino Kritsiotis, 'The Power of International Law as Language' (1998) 34 Cal W L Rev 397, 409.
[5] Georg Nolte, 'Multipurpose Self-Defence, Proportionality Disoriented: A Response to David Kretzmer' (2013) 24 EJIL 283, 290.
[6] For such a view in further detail see Ingo Venzke, *How Interpretation Makes International Law: On Semantic Change and Normative Twists* (OUP 2012) 37–64.
[7] Martti Koskenniemi, 'International Law and Hegemony: A Reconfiguration' (2004) 17 Cam Rev Int'l Aff 197, 199.

(re-)introducing such a dualism (Part III(C)). It ultimately transpires that interpretation may in fact not be well understood by analogy to a game, not if that game is anything like chess. In law, as in language, we make up the rules 'as we go along'.[8]

I argue that the continuing challenge may be met by understanding interpretation as a practice that is stabilized by tradition (Part IV). A powerful and radical alternative, finally, is to suggest that there is no language to play with. Interpretation, on this account, is not viewed as participating in the linguistic practice of international law at all. Such a view instead allows for a better appreciation of the interpreter and draws out what she takes to be true in international law (Part V).

By investigating these ways of understanding international law as a language and interpretation as a game, I pursue three aims. First and foremost, my inquiry aspires to contribute to a better view of the practice of interpretation. Second, I will critically discuss the different ideas about the relationship between language and interpretation. How much water do they hold? This comes, finally, with programmatic ambitions of informing views of interpretation in international law more thoroughly with theories of language. The aim is to irritate and to possibly provoke adjustments in our conceptions of interpretation. Put simply, I want to see what traction the analogy between interpretation and playing games has and to thereby contribute to mapping the game of game-playing.[9] I will place my bets on the third approach, which presents the language of international law as a battleground and interpretation as a struggle for the law. To make good sense of that approach, interpretation should either be seen as a practice that shapes the rules of the game or, alternatively, it should be seen as an attempt at better understanding what the interpreter takes to be true in international law. The choice between the latter two views depends on strategy and the specific interests of inquiry.

I. Like a Game of Chess

In the words of former UN Secretary-General Boutros Boutros-Ghali, 'next to the society of states, there is an international scientific community that desires to establish law as a language of international relations'.[10] The UN supports such desires, as Rosalyn Higgins explained, in order 'to promote a common language of international law among the peoples of the United Nations and a universal culture shared by all nations that is conducive to peace, justice, and the rule of law'.[11]

---

[8] Ludwig Wittgenstein, *Philosophical Investigations* (Basil Blackwell 1958) [83]; see also Donald Davidson, 'Communication and Convention (1982)' in *Truth, Language and History* (Clarendon Press 2005) 265, 267–8.

[9] See Chapter 2 (Andrea Bianchi).

[10] Boutros Boutros-Ghali, 'Foreword' in United Nations, *International Law as a Language for International Relations*, xiv.

[11] Rosalyn Higgins, 'Teaching and Practicing International Law in a Global Environment: Toward a Common Language of International Law' (2010) 104 ASIL Proceedings 196, 200.

The language of international law offers a vocabulary of virtue. Playing the game of interpretation puts it to use.

Further examples in this vein abound. For Dino Kritsiotis, international law provides 'a new communicative medium which professes to be: more peaceful in its outlook… [and] more secure in terms of the answers and solutions it provides'.[12] It would be easy to belittle this view as rosy naivety; it would be unfair as well. Arguments that law is as much an expression of power as its antidote prompt Kritsiotis to ask: 'Is international law a meaningful and real counter-language to power, or are its credentials skin-deep and ephemeral?'[13] His answer first reverts to well-known accounts of power politics in which the language of the law prevailed.[14] But whatever the critique, the language of international law is pervasive and that bodes well. According to Kritsiotis, we should not be 'distract[ed] from the increasing influence that international law has as a language for inter-state and even intra-state intercourse'.[15] On balance, that language functions as a bulwark against power.

This view of the language of international law boils down to the postulation of a language that instructs and supports its speakers. Interpretations tap into the resources that the language of international law provides for its speakers in order to fight the rival language of power and to aim at peace, justice, and the rule of law. Interpretations are structured and supported by the language they use.

This view of the practice of legal interpretation finds support in the classic work of Ferdinand de Saussure, who famously distinguished between a language (*langue*) and speaking (*parole*).[16] The former orders the latter. Saussure influentially paved the way for modern linguistics by developing a theory of language that overcame modes of thinking which tied language all too closely to the world. Previously, the meaning of words in one way or another was linked to what they represented in reality. Through its representation of reality, language was thought to gain stability.[17] Saussure freed himself from this spell. On his approach, the meaning of 'combatant', for instance, is not stable because it represents a combatant. Instead it gains its meaning through its distinction from other expressions such as 'civilian'. Saussure's core proposition was that '[l]anguage is a system of signs'.[18] Such a system is markedly different from any act of speaking. The two are

---

[12] Kritsiotis, 'The Power of International Law as Language', 398. See also Christian Tomuschat, 'International Law: Ensuring the Survival of Mankind on the Eve of a New Century' (2001) 281 Recueil des Cours 13, 28.

[13] Kritsiotis, 'The Power of International Law as Language', 400.

[14] Kritsiotis, 'The Power of International Law as Language', 400–1 with reference to Abram Chayes, *The Cuban Missile Crisis* (OUP 1974) 13–14.

[15] Kritsiotis, 'The Power of International Law as Language', 401.

[16] Ferdinand de Saussure, *Course in General Linguistics* (Philosophical Library 1965) 13.

[17] Foucault bitingly described how this way of thinking has endured in the human sciences: Michel Foucault, *The Order of Things: An Archeology of the Human Sciences* (Random House 1994) 57–63.

[18] Saussure, *Course in General Linguistics*, 16. I am leaving aside the strand of critique that focuses on the relationship between signs and sounds in Saussure's work: see Jacques Derrida, *Of Grammatology* (Johns Hopkins University Press 1997) 30–44.

related, but 'their interdependence does not prevent their being two absolutely distinct things'.[19] On this account, language orders the facts of speech and constitutes 'the norm of all other manifestations of speech'.[20]

Saussure offers an illustrative and evocative comparison in this regard. '[O]f all comparisons that might be imagined', he writes, 'the most fruitful is the one that might be drawn between the functioning of language and a game of chess...A game of chess is like an artificial form of what language presents in a natural form'.[21] Certainly each move on the chessboard changes the state of the game and it affects later moves. But it does not affect the rules of the game. For present purposes, this would mean that speaking the language of international law does not change the law. Language not only exists independently of its operation, but it also forms the basis for deciding which operations are correct, and which are mistakes. Accordingly, the language of international law is something like a sweet symphony in which interpreters play by the score and the score ensures that every individual interpretation contributes to something beautiful in the broader scheme of things.[22] Mistakes are not only easy to hear, at least to the trained ear. They also leave the score unblemished.

II. The Grammar of the Game

A second and related way of thinking about the language of international law does not imply a similar degree of faith in the virtues of a given vocabulary. Yet it sees certain benefits in using its grammar. If not a bulwark against power, the language of international law nonetheless builds bridges. Participants in contentious political disputes speak the language of law if, or especially when, waters are rough. One commentator argues that:

[t]he desire to test the objectivity of international law vis-à-vis the alleged subjectivity of politics obscures the most universal claim that international law makes—that of a constructive, problem-solving communicative device for the speech community of diplomats.[23]

For example, James Crawford notes that the discourse on the divisive issue of Palestinian statehood does not give up the pretence of the legal game itself. Instead, 'the obstinate fact remains that the actors, most of the time, continue to

---

[19] Derrida, *Of Grammatology*, 19. For a discussion of the reasons that might have driven Saussure to such a view, see Sybille Krämer, *Sprache, Sprechakt, Kommunikation* (Suhrkamp 2001) 22.

[20] Saussure, *Course in General Linguistics*, 9.

[21] Saussure, *Course in General Linguistics*, 88.

[22] The comparison with a symphony, too, stems from Saussure's treatise. He asserts that 'what the symphony actually is stands completely apart from how it is performed; the mistakes that musicians make in playing the symphony do not compromise this fact': Saussure, *Course in General Linguistics*, 18.

[23] Jared Wessel, 'International Law as Language—Towards a "Neo" New Haven School' (2010) 23 IJSL 123, 123–4.

use the language of law in making and assessing claims'.[24] This game is meaningful because it provides the participants with yardsticks for critique. For Crawford:

International law scholars are not like critics in an empty theatre...[the fact that] the language of law is used implies that these claims can be assessed, on the basis of values which extend beyond allegiance to a particular party, country, bloc or religion.[25]

In this vein, Ian Johnstone has traced the prevailing legal discourse in Security Council deliberations, concluding that 'international law is at once the language of international society and an important determinant of who has a voice'.[26] While it excludes those who do not know its technique or lack access to venues of authoritative discourse, it also brings actors together. Johnstone notes that 'the specialized discourse of international law provides an additional layer of cohesiveness', and that 'governmental, inter-governmental, and nongovernmental actors...speak the language of law'.[27] The game is characterized by a distinct grammar. It isolates the speaker from other contexts and reconstitutes her as a player in a different game. Oscar Schachter embraced this idea when he pointed to lawyers' capacity to speak to one another while other disciplines are divided through specializations.[28]

Much international legal scholarship has converged on the view that international law is, above all, a technique—a technique that allows for meaningful engagement with one another as lawyers and a technique that constitutes law as a distinct discipline. It is this idea of potentially unifying rules of the game that partly underpins the recent calls to defend a 'culture of formalism' and to safeguard international law's autonomy against the intrusion of other language games of morality and politics.[29] The common grammar can unite a variety of actors with different roles and different world-views.[30] What interpreters do as they speak the language of international law is to employ their technical competence and demonstrate their craft as legal professionals. What accounts for their competence?

Noam Chomsky might have an answer when he suggests that language is indeed best studied as a competence. It is easiest to unfold his argument against

---

[24] James Crawford, 'The Creation of the State of Palestine: Too Much Too Soon ?' (1990) 1 EJIL 307, 307.

[25] Crawford, 'The Creation of the State of Palestine', 307.

[26] Ian Johnstone, 'The Power of Interpretive Communities' in Michael Barnett and Raymond Duvall (eds), *Power in Global Governance* (CUP 2005) 185, 192.

[27] Ian Johnstone, *The Power of Deliberation: International Law, Politics and Organizations* (OUP 2011) 181.

[28] Oscar Schachter, 'The Invisible College of International Lawyers' (1977) 72 North U L Rev 217, 222. See also James Crawford, 'International Law as Discipline and Profession' (2012) ASIL Proceedings 471, 480.

[29] See Martti Koskenniemi, *The Gentle Civiliser of Nations: The Rise and Fall of International Law 1870–1960* (CUP 2001) 494; Martti Koskenniemi, 'The Fate of Public International Law: Between Technique and Politics' (2007) 70 MLR 1; Jan Klabbers, 'The Relative Autonomy of International Law or The Forgotten Politics of Interdisciplinarity' (2004) 1 JILIR 35; Jochen von Bernstorff, *The Public International Law Theory of Hans Kelsen: Believing in Universal Law* (CUP 2010) 271.

[30] Such actors may even be different national courts. See Francesco Francioni, 'International Law as a Common Language for National Courts' (2001) 36 Tex Int'l L J 587.

the backdrop of an apparent puzzle: children learn the correct use of a language in spite of the fact that the input to which they are exposed mostly consists of grammatically truncated sentences ('poverty of stimulus').[31] Moreover, the input certainly falls short of the unlimited possibilities for using any language:

A record of natural speech will show numerous false starts, deviations from rules, changes of plan in mid-course, and so on. The problem for the linguist, as well as for the child learning the language, is to determine from the data of performance the underlying system of rules that has been mastered by the speaker-hearer and that he puts to use in actual performance.[32]

The poverty of stimulus prompts Chomsky and others to argue that language is really best explained in terms of the innate competence of every speaker. This innate competence enables speakers who are faced with the mixed record of actual performance to identify grammatically correct uses of language. Martti Koskenniemi likewise noted that '[a] grammar is not a description of what native language-speakers say in fact—it is an account of *what it is possible to say* in that language'.[33]

Chomsky argues that it is not feasible to approach language through observation of what speakers actually say or through studying language as a system of signs, as Saussure would have it.[34] Deep structures (language/competence) cannot be identified by looking at surface structures (speaking/performance), he notes, simply because there are an infinite set of potential deep structures that could explain any act of speaking.[35] The choice between different possible deep structures thus requires intuition. Speakers of native language(s) have a feeling for what is right even when they cannot articulate the grammatical rule.[36]

While Chomsky rejects Saussure's juxtaposition of language and speech, he introduces a new dichotomy between linguistic competence and actual performance. Echoing Saussure's comparison of speaking a language and playing a game of chess, Chomsky makes 'a fundamental distinction between competence (the speaker-hearer's knowledge of his language) and performance (the actual use of language in concrete situations)'.[37] Innate linguistic competence enables every speaker to separate the correct uses of a language from its deformations.[38] This theoretical distinction reminds us that performance does not feed back into what

---

[31] Noam Chomsky, *Language and Mind* (CUP 2006) xi.

[32] Noam Chomsky, *Aspects of the Theory of Syntax* (MIT Press 1965) 4.

[33] Martti Koskenniemi, *From Apology to Utopia: The Structure of International Legal Argument* (CUP 2005) 589 (emphasis added).

[34] Chomsky, *Aspects of the Theory of Syntax*, 4.

[35] Chomsky, *Language and Mind*, 27; Noam Chomsky, *Topics in the Theory of Generative Grammar* (Mouton 1966) 17.

[36] Over time, Chomsky switched from speaking about *rules* that are followed to *parameters* and *principles*: *Language and Mind*, 23–4.

[37] Chomsky, *Aspects of the Theory of Syntax*, 4.

[38] One may even follow Chomsky and distinguish between internal and external languages, where the former offers the scheme against which to judge the latter: *Language and Mind*, 175; Neil Smith, 'Chomsky's Science of Language' in James McGilvray (ed), *The Cambridge Companion to Chomsky* (CUP 2005) 21, 35–6.

it means to speak a language correctly. It does not affect the rules of the game. In other words, the symphony's score remains unblemished by mistakes in its performance.

On this account, interpreters in the game of international law are tied together by a deep structure of syntactic rules and principles. This grammar draws the contours of what it means to speak the language of international law and what it means to speak it correctly. The language of international law is less a model against which specific interpretations could be termed right and wrong. Instead, knowing the grammar of the language allows an infinite variety of things to be said and done with that language. In this way, Chomsky differs from Saussure. The role of international law changes from constituting a bulwark against power to a shared competence that brings opponents together. But like Saussure, who privileged language over speaking, Chomsky regards linguistic competence as ordering actual performance. Transposed to the language of international law, it is this language that stabilizes interpretation.

III. The Nature of the Game Reconsidered

A. The game as a struggle for the law

In a third approach the stabilizing ground of a given language is lost.[39] Instead, that language is shaped in the process of playing the game. With their interpretations, actors struggle for the law and thereby make the law. They try every trick in the book in order to pull the law onto their side. The emphasis here does not fall on a background language but on the act of speaking, less on competence and more on performance. This third approach to interpretation may be captured as a semantic struggle in which actors try to find acceptance for the claims they make about the law as they try to influence what is considered (il)legal.[40] The language of international law above all provides a battleground to carry out conflicts.

This understanding is well reflected in Jean Combacau's and Serge Sur's general treatise on international law, where they write lucidly that '[t]he controversies pertaining to interpretation would not be so animated were they not a translation of a struggle for the mastery of the legal system'.[41] The understanding is also reflected in Koskenniemi's aphorism that 'international law is what lawyers do and how they think'.[42] If actors want to play the game of international law, then

---

[39] A helpful early overview is offered by Deborah Cass, 'Navigating the Newstream: Recent Critical Scholarship in International Law' (1996) 65 Nord J Int'l L 341.

[40] I have sketched such a perspective of semantic struggles in the practice of legal interpretation in detail in Venzke, *How Interpretation Makes International Law*, 37–64.

[41] Jean Combacau and Sergio Sur, *Droit international public* (Montchrestien 2010) 172 (translation by the author).

[42] Martti Koskenniemi, 'Between Commitment and Cynicism: Outline for a Theory of International Law as Practice' in United Nations (ed), *Collection of Essays by Legal Advisers of States, Legal Advisers of International Organisations and Practitioners in the Field of International Law* (United Nations 1999) 495, 523.

they need to compete on its terms. But these terms are incapable of telling us who is right and who is wrong. Such an essence remains elusive. Each interpretative claim remains particular and its aspiration to universality doomed to fall flat. According to Koskenniemi, if an interpretation of international law succeeds, it is hegemonic in the sense that it portrays as universal what is really particular.[43] In his view, '[t]he task for international lawyers is not to learn new managerial vocabularies but to use the language of international law to articulate the politics of critical universalism'.[44] International lawyers emulate Sisyphus in their quest for objectivity only to realize that it escapes them every time they think they have laid their hands on it.[45] Interpretation is a game without end.[46]

A number of studies have embraced a similar understanding of the language of international law to show its emancipatory potential as well as the factors that hold it back.[47] Others, with a bleaker outlook, have suggested that the language of international law offers little more than a lullaby that lures its speakers into mantras of objectivity and progress while catastrophes pile up.[48] Even worse, it could lift burdens of responsibility from the shoulders of those who should feel them heavily. David Kennedy notably argues that in war, the language of international law ultimately camouflages political decisions and stifles second thoughts.[49] In international criminal law, it has been argued that legal language might, above all, offer comfort for practitioners, academics, and politicians alike.[50]

Several things have happened to the game of interpretation in this variation of the theme when compared to the first two approaches. It seems that there is no longer a model that could offer guidance. With a shift in focus from competence to performance, the distinction between the law and its interpretation is questioned. The dualism between a linguistic model and its execution collapses.

[43] Koskenniemi, 'International Law and Hegemony'. See also Ingo Venzke, 'Legal Contestation about "Enemy Combatants": On the Exercise of Power in Legal Interpretation' (2009) 5 JILIR 155.
[44] Koskenniemi, *The Gentle Civiliser of Nations*, 1.
[45] Jochen von Bernstorff, 'Sisyphus was an International Lawyer: On Martti Koskenniemi's "From Apology to Utopia" and the Place of Law in International Politics' (2006) 7 German LJ 1015.
[46] See Anthony Carty, 'Language Games of International Law: Koskenniemi as the Discipline's Wittgenstein' (2012) 13 Melb J Int'l L 1.
[47] Anthony Anghie, *Imperialism, Sovereignty, and the Making of International Law* (CUP 2005) 31; Arnulf Lorca, 'International Law in Latin America or Latin American International Law? Rise, Fall, and Retrieval of a Tradition of Legal Thinking and Political Imagination' (2006) 47 HILJ 283; Michelle Burgis, 'Discourses of Division: Law, Politics and the ICJ Advisory Opinion on the Legal Consequences of the Construction of a Wall in the Occupied Palestinian Territory' (2008) 7 Chinese JIL 33.
[48] David Kennedy, 'The International Human Rights Movement: Part of the Problem?' (2002) 15 Harv Hum Rts J 101; David Kennedy, 'The Politics of the Invisible College: International Governance and the Politics of Expertise' (2001) 5 EHRLR 463, 478; James Dawes, 'Language, Violence, and Human Rights Law' (1999) 11 Yale J L & Human 215.
[49] David Kennedy, *Of War and Law* (Princeton University Press 2006). See also Martti Koskenniemi, 'The Lady Doth Protest Too Much: Kosovo, and the Turn to Ethics in International Law' (2002) 65 MLR 159.
[50] Christine Schwöbel, 'The Comfort of International Criminal Law' (2013) 24 Law & Crit 169.

B. Why reject the dualism?

The linguistic assumptions nested in attempts at making sense of the language of international law by analogy to a game of chess, where a move in the game leaves the rules unaffected (speech ordered by language), or where its stable grammar transcends geographical and professional boundaries (performance ordered by competence), have come under criticism from a variety of angles. Critics question the decision to privilege the model over its application, the abstract and idealized over the concrete and perceptible. For them, speech and performance should be the primary object of study. In other words, interpretation in international law should be the object of study in its own right, rather than the proxy of an underlying scheme of rules. Wittgenstein already suggested as much when he pushed the notion of language games into the limelight:

[I]n philosophy we often compare the use of words with games and calculi which have fixed rules... But if you say that our languages only approximate to such calculi you are standing on the very brink of a misunderstanding. For then it may look as if what we were talking about were an ideal language. As if our logic were, so to speak, a logic for a vacuum.[51]

Dell Hymes, in his contribution to the counter-current of sociolinguistics, thus described Chomsky's work as offering a 'garden of Eden view'.[52] For Hymes, the focus of study should really fall on the *sociocultural* features that permeate language acquisition and usage. It is not that the rules of the game remain unmoved by the practice of playing. Rather, they are the product of the game as it is played in specific situations. In order to capture context-specific differences, Hymes presents the notion of a *speech community*, which he defines as 'a community sharing rules for the conduct and interpretation of speech, and rules for the interpretation of at least one linguistic variety'.[53] The concept of *communicative* rather than *linguistic* competence reflects the shift from background language to surface communication.[54]

In international legal communication, the spotlight would fall on differences between ways of speaking in human rights and trade law, for instance.[55] They

---

[51] Wittgenstein, *Philosophical Investigations*, [81].

[52] Dell Hymes, 'On Communicative Competence' in JB Pride and Janet Holmes (eds), *Sociolinguistics* (Penguin 1979) 269, 272. For a more recent articulation of the critique, see Dell Hymes, 'Speech and Language: On the Origins and Foundations of Inequality among Speakers' in *Ethnography, Linguistics, Narrative Inequality: Toward and Understanding of Voice* (Taylor & Francis 1996) 25. See also Kanti Lal Das, *Philosophical Relevance of Language: A Methodological Reflection* (Northern Book Centre 2006) 207.

[53] Dell Hymes, 'Models of the Interaction of Language and Social Life' in John J Gumperz and Dell Hymes (eds), *Directions in Sociolinguistics: The Ethnography of Communication* (Wiley-Blackwell 1991) 35, 54. See also Dell Hymes, 'Speech and Language', 30–4.

[54] Dell Hymes, 'Two Types of Linguistic Relativity' in William Bright (ed), *Sociolinguistics* (Mouton 1966) 114.

[55] On those differences, see Armin von Bogdandy and Ingo Venzke, 'On the Functions of International Courts: An Appraisal in Light of Their Burgeoning Public Authority' (2013) 26 LJIL 49; Joost Pauwelyn and Manfred Elsig, 'The Politics of Treaty Interpretation: Variations and Explanations Across International Tribunals' in Jeffrey Dunoff and Mark Pollock (eds), *Interdisciplinary Perspectives on International Law and International Relations: The State of the Art* (CUP 2013) 445.

would not be brushed aside as variations of the same language.[56] From the angle of sociolinguistics, it could be seen how 'people act out the social structure, affirming their own statuses and roles and establishing and transmitting the shared systems of value and of knowledge'.[57] This would easily get lost if the analogy between the practice of interpretation and the playing of a game were to suggest a dualism between an ideal set of rules in the background, on the one hand, and acts of interpretation as their manifestation.

In a sweeping blow against idealizations aiming at objectivity, Pierre Bourdieu further adds to the critique of linguistics à la Saussure and Chomsky. His argument first supports the view of international law as a battlefield on which actors struggle for the law when he notes that '[t]he practical content of the law ... is the product of a symbolic struggle between professionals possessing unequal technical skills and social influence'.[58] He decidedly rejects forms of objectivism that fall for:

the illusion of linguistic communism ... the illusion that everyone participates in language as they enjoy sun, the air, or water ... [But] access to legitimate language is quite unequal, and the theoretically universal competence liberally granted to all by linguists is in reality monopolised by some.[59]

In a broader methodological critique, Bourdieu argues that there is a profound problem with presenting language 'as an objective reality that exists independent of the individuals who live and act in that reality'.[60] It matters what speakers want to do with language, how they act with it, and what they practically can do with it. Bourdieu argues that abstracting from these contexts and constraints is a 'scholastic fallacy', with reference to the work of linguist John Austin.[61]

Austin himself presented two main arguments for rejecting the dualism between language and speech or between competence and performance.[62] The first one is crucial and programmatic: speaking is a creative activity. '[T]here can hardly be any longer a possibility of not seeing that stating is performing an act', he writes prominently.[63] Austin develops his argument with dramatic tension.

[56] For an account of how that can be done with good reasons in international law, see Bruno Simma, 'Universality of International Law from the Perspective of a Practitioner' (2009) 20 EJIL 265.
[57] Michael Halliday, *Language as a Social Semiotic: The Social Interpretation of Language and Meaning* (University Park Press 1978) 2. See also Michael Halliday and Ruqaiya Hasan, *Language, Context, and Text: Aspects of Language in a Social-Semiotic Perspective* (OUP 1989) 16–24.
[58] Pierre Bourdieu, 'The Force of Law: Toward a Sociology of the Juridical Field' (1987) 38 Hastings L J 814, 827.
[59] Pierre Bourdieu and Loïc Wacquant, *An Invitation to Reflexive Sociology* (University of Chicago Press 1992) 146.
[60] Bourdieu and Wacquant, *An Invitation to Reflexive Sociology*, 141.
[61] Bourdieu and Wacquant, *An Invitation to Reflexive Sociology*, 141. In further detail, see Pierre Bourdieu, 'The Scholastic Point of View' (1990) 5 Cult Anthropol 380.
[62] See Sybille Krämer, 'Sprache und Sprechen oder: Wie sinnvoll ist die Unterscheidung zwischen einem Schema und seinem Gebrauch?' in Sybille Krämer and Ekkehard König (eds), *Gibt es eine Sprache hinter dem Sprechen?* (Suhrkamp 2002) 265.
[63] John Austin, *How to Do Things with Words* (OUP 1979).

At the outset he suggests distinguishing *constative* from *performative* speech acts, where the former are of a descriptive nature such as 'this is a combatant' in the laws of war, and the latter do things with words, such as baptizing a child or christening a ship.[64] Then the inexorable conclusion slowly transpires. Any attempt at distinguishing constative and performative speech acts ultimately fails. All speech acts are performative. It is impossible not to interpret and to partake in the creation of the world and of the language in it.[65]

The second complementary reason for rejecting the dualism observes that not all speech acts succeed in performing what they want to achieve.[66] Clearly, not anybody can christen a ship in passing. Whether speech acts succeed is subject to a series of contextual constraints. The standard against which they need to be assessed, according to Austin, is not any background scheme that could identify them as true or false. They are measured by their success. By way of illustration, a statement such as 'this is a combatant' would fail not because there really was a civilian and not a combatant. Saussure already cut those ties between words and what they represent.[67] For Austin, social conventions and context are the only standard against which it is possible to say whether a speech act succeeds. Does social convention support that the person with army insignia and a rifle is called a combatant? The standard of success sits nowhere other than in the contextualized practice of speaking.

In sum, Austin argues that any distinction between constative and performative speech acts collapses and that speech acts cannot be assessed on any basis sitting behind or beyond the context of performance. Instead, the context of speaking and the conventions to which it gives rise offer the only test for the success of speech acts.[68] Austin, who was a contemporary of HLA Hart in Oxford, wrote with a sideswipe to lawyers: '[o]f all people, jurists should be best aware of the true sense of affairs... Yet they succumb to their own timorous fiction, that a statement of "the law" is a statement of fact.'[69] Quite to the contrary, a statement of the law contributes to the making of law.[70] Austin himself concludes:

We have discussed the performative utterance and its infelicities. That equips us, we may suppose, with two shining new tools to crack the crib of reality maybe. It also equips us— it always does—with two shining new skids under our metaphysical feet. The question is how we use them.[71]

---

[64] Austin, *How to Do Things with Words*, 140–1.

[65] Austin, *How to Do Things with Words*, 141.

[66] They can be 'infelicitous', as Austin would say: 'Performative Utterances' in *Philosophical Papers* (OUP 1961) 220, 235, 244.

[67] See Saussure, *Course in General Linguistics*, 13.

[68] On these three main conclusions from Austin's work, see Gilles Deleuze and Félix Guattari, *A Thousand Plateaus: Capitalism and Schizophrenia* (University of Minnesota Press 1987) 78.

[69] Austin, *How to Do Things with Words*, 4.

[70] See also Niklas Luhmann, *Law as a Social System* (OUP 2004) 243.

[71] Austin, *Philosophical Papers*, 228.

C. How interpretation is unlike playing a game

One way of using the 'shining new skids' further develops Austin's inchoate theory concerning the contextual conditions that account for the success of speech acts. When does a claim in the language of international law succeed? John Searle continues in Austin's tracks when he argues that the success of a speech act depends on whether it conforms to background conventions. What Searle purports to add is an exhaustive taxonomy of speech acts which are based on background conventions, ensuring that speakers can do the things with words that they want.[72] Background conventions tie speakers and hearers together and permit others to understand what the speaker means. Accordingly, Searle's main argument is that '[s]peaking a language is engaging in a (highly complex) rule-governed form of behaviour'.[73] Speaking is constituted by rules and would not be possible otherwise.

Like Saussure, Searle draws an analogy with chess. The rules for both language and chess are constitutive in the sense that they render the activity possible in the first place.[74] Background conventions are constitutive rules establishing that a sentence x counts as y in a given context c. This can be illustrated by a straightforward example from the language of international law. If the UN Security Council decides that a situation amounts to a threat or breach of international peace and security, then this opens up options under Chapter VII of the UN Charter. Searle supports his argument by suggesting that:

> [t]he semantic structure of a language may be regarded as a conventional realisation of a series of sets of underlying constitutive rules, and that speech acts are acts characteristically performed by uttering expressions in accordance with these sets of constitutive rules.[75]

In this way, Searle notably re-introduces the dualism of a background scheme and its execution. He turns around midway on the 'shining new skids' with which Austin had equipped him.

Searle's work has inspired a number of international law and international relations scholars, especially in their quest to offer a definition of international law.[76] Nicholas Onuf, for example, framed the international legal order as a set of interconnected speech acts in order to argue that it is the defining feature of legal claims that they are able to achieve what they want without the assent of the hearer.[77] Probing what Onuf and others have to offer for an understanding of

---

[72] That the notion of background is important in Searle's grander theoretical set-up suggests that speakers do not need to be aware of the rules they follow. See John Searle, *Making the Social World* (OUP 2010) 155–60.

[73] John Searle, *Speech Acts: An Essay in the Philosophy of Language* (CUP 1969) 12.

[74] Searle, *Speech Acts*, 33–4.   [75] Searle, *Speech Acts*, 37.

[76] See eg Dick Ruiter and Ramses Wessel, 'The Legal Nature of Informal International Law: A Legal Theoretical Exercise' in Joost Pauwelyn, Ramses Wessel, and Jan Wouters (eds), *Informal International Lawmaking* (OUP 2012) 162, 167–70; Ulrich Fastenrath, 'Relative Normativity in International Law' (1993) 4 EJIL 305, 309; Jean d'Aspremont, 'Wording in International Law' (2012) 25 LJIL 575, 579.

[77] Nicholas Onuf, 'Do Rules Say What They Do? From Ordinary Language to International Law' (1985) 26 HILJ 385, 408.

interpretation starts to reveal some of the main problems that come with understanding the language of international law in light of speech act theory à la Searle (that is, by analogy to a game of chess).

I see three main problems. First, Searle pursues a strategy of deliberate idealization when he argues that background conventions provide the conditions for speech acts to be successful. Conventions in fact ensure that speakers' intentions can be revealed.[78] Generally, such a view can be critiqued on methodological grounds. Again there is a stabilizing background that structures performance. The more specific point of critique becomes clearer in light of a related second problem. It was Searle's aim to provide an account of how understanding is possible. That is typically not the issue in any interpretative dispute in (international) law. It is not that opponents do not understand one another, although that can happen. Usually they do understand and disagree. The third problem is that constitutive rules are troubled by indeterminacy. It is unconvincing to simply take any given context *c* as a given. Speaking is not like playing chess because the world is not chequered in black and white, because speaking typically has an ulterior purpose, and because in speaking we make the rules 'as we go along'.[79]

There is one way in which the analogy between interpretation and playing a game can be rescued from the pitfalls of an easy dualism between rules and moves. That is to understand speaking the language of international law as a practice (Part IV). The more radical alternative would be to suggest that there is no language to play with (Part V).

IV. International Law as a Practice

How could it be possible to make sense of interpretative games in international law without a background scheme that serves as a standard against which interpretations can be assessed as right or wrong moves? What could stabilize the language of international law if it is not some kind of guiding background structure? Saussure already hinted at an answer when he argued that nothing outside language secures the meaning of words. He argued instead that meaning is only created through arbitrary distinctions, and that the sole thing that can stabilize those distinctions is tradition. 'Because the sign is arbitrary', he wrote, 'it follows no law other than that of tradition, and because it is based on tradition, it is arbitrary.'[80]

This idea has now caught on. A truly ubiquitous way of rearticulating the stabilizing role of tradition is to say that meaning is conventional in the way I have just discussed. Indeed, for Wittgenstein, meaning cannot possibly be found anywhere but in the conventions about how words are used.[81] This is precisely how he

---

[78] Following Searle, they even allow thinking of interpretation as an act of cognition: Krämer, *Sprache, Sprechakt, Kommunikation*, 70.

[79] Wittgenstein, *Philosophical Investigations*, [83].

[80] Saussure, *Course in General Linguistics*, 74.

[81] Wittgenstein, *Philosophical Investigations*, [43]; Ludwig Wittgenstein, *Philosophical Grammar* (Basil Blackwell 1974) [32] ('[A]n explanation of meaning is…a rule, a convention').

thought of language games. But the way Searle refined this position re-introduces a dualism not between language and speaking but between conventions and their application. The main problem is that any rule—generally, *x* counts as *y* in context *c*—will be troubled by indeterminacy. What, for instance, counts as context *c*? Following Wittgenstein, the articulation of a rule that explains meaning is subject to the same fate of only gaining meaning through another rule of conventional use. The result is an infinite regress: 'Any interpretation ... hangs in the air along with what it interprets, and cannot give it any support'.[82] In a similar vein, HLA Hart observed that:

the canons of interpretation ... are themselves general rules for the use of language, and make use of general terms which themselves require interpretation. They cannot, any more than other rules, provide for their own interpretation.[83]

The way to get out of this conundrum leads via practice, for Wittgenstein as well as for Hart.[84] Wittgenstein's idea is that actors learn and internalize in a process of socialization what signposts mean or, arguably, what the words of treaty norms mean.[85] How then is it at all possible to tell that a rule can be said to be applied (in)correctly? What orders interpretation if it is not that which is being interpreted? The law itself does not give away the answer because it gains its meaning only through the practice of how it is used. Interpretation substitutes one expression of the rule for another.[86] Together with the interpretation, the law hangs in the air and cannot offer support for what are regarded as (in)correct interpretations.

The question of what is a wrong interpretation can only be answered by other participants in an interpretative community. Other participants need to say what an interpreter can get away with. There are many factors that influence the likely success of an interpretation. The most important one in the language of (international) law is how any legal claim connects to tradition. Robert Brandom, speaking on strands of semantic pragmatism in the philosophy of language, has expressed this thought with profound insight when he wrote that '[t]he current judge is held accountable to the tradition she inherits by the judges yet to come'.[87]

---

[82] Wittgenstein, *Philosophical Investigations*, [198]. See also Immanuel Kant, *Critique of Pure Reason* (CUP 1998) 263.

[83] HLA Hart, *The Concept of Law* (2nd edn, Clarendon Press 1994) 126.

[84] Wittgenstein, *Philosophical Investigations*, [202]; Ludwig Wittgenstein, *On Certainty* (Basil Blackwell 1969) [501]. HLA Hart, on his part, showed the way out as part of his 'social thesis'. See Jean d'Aspremont, *Formalism and the Sources of International Law: A Theory of the Ascertainment of Legal Rules* (OUP 2011) 55 and 201.

[85] Wittgenstein, *Philosophical Investigations*, [219].

[86] Wittgenstein, *Philosophical Investigations*, [201]; Dennis Patterson, 'Interpretation in Law' (2005) 42 San Diego L Rev 685, 692.

[87] Robert Brandom, 'Some Pragmatist Themes in Hegel's Idealism: Negotiation and Administration in Hegel's Account of the Structure and Content of Conceptual Norms' (1999) 7 Eur J Philos 164, 181. For a concise introduction and summary, see Jasper Liptow, *Regel und Interpretation: Eine Untersuchung zur sozialen Struktur sprachlicher Praxis* (Velbrück 2004) 220–6; Ralph Christensen, 'Neo-Pragmatismus: Brandom' in Sonja Buckel, Ralph Christensen, and Andreas Fischer-Lescano (eds), *Neue Theorien des Rechts* (Lucius und Lucius 2009) 239.

It is a characteristic feature of the language of (international) law that it compels its speakers to connect to the past, to prior instances of speaking.[88]

Interpretative games in international law, on this account, present themselves as a practice that is both creative and constrained. Actors struggle for the law. Language offers a battleground.[89] It may look like a game but it is not well understood by analogy to something like chess. It is a game like those of children when they make up the rules as they go along.[90] The trick is to see interpretation as a rule-guided activity without stipulating the rules as a background scheme that sits on the outside. Only later interpretations will tell what is right and wrong. Stability in this practice flows from tradition and from historical practices.[91] Wittgenstein sums this up with typical eloquence: 'Grammar is the account books of language. They must show the actual transactions of language.'[92] David Lewis picked up this idea in his seminal paper 'Scorekeeping in a Language Game' and Brandom develops it further, showing how scorekeeping tracks the correct use of words.[93] The imagery of playing games sneaks back in, but Brandom is quick to note how it misleads and should thus be treated with caution.[94]

V. And if There Was No Language to Play With?

Lewis not only developed the idea of scorekeeping in language games. He also opined that '[i]t is a platitude that language is ruled by convention'.[95] In addition, he noted that it is the profession of philosophers to question platitudes.[96] Sure enough, the platitude that language is ruled by convention has also been questioned. Donald Davidson has probably set out the most refined argument in this regard, causing a stir when he concluded that 'there is no such thing as a language, not if a language is anything like what many philosophers and linguists

---

[88] Johnstone, *The Power of Deliberation*, 25; Martti Koskenniemi, 'The Place of Law in Collective Security' (1996) 17 Mich J Int'l L 455, 478 (the language of international law 'compels a move away from one's idiosyncratic interests and preferences *by insisting on their justification in terms of the historical practices*') (emphasis added); Friedrich Kratochwil, 'How do Norms Matter?' in Michael Byers (ed), *The Role of Law in International Politics: Essays in International Relations and International Law* (OUP 2000) 35, 47. See Chapter 13 (Harlan Grant Cohen).

[89] Ralph Christensen and Michael Sokolowski, 'Recht als Einsatz im Semantischen Kampf' in Ekkehard Felder (ed), *Semantische Kämpfe. Macht und Sprache in den Wissenschaften* (de Gruyter 2006).

[90] Wittgenstein in fact uses the concept of 'game' to show how the things referred to as a game do not share a common core but a family resemblance: *Philosophical Investigations*, [67]–[70].

[91] These factors underpin what counts as 'competent performance'. For the understanding of practice as competent performance, see Emanuel Adler and Vincent Pouliot, 'International Practices' (2011) 3 Int Theory 1, 4–5.

[92] Wittgenstein, *Philosophical Investigations*, [44].

[93] Robert Brandom, *Making it Explicit: Reasoning, Representing and Discursive Commitment* (Harvard University Press 1988) 181–2 with reference to David Lewis, 'Scorekeeping in a Language Game' (1979) 8 J Phil Logic 339.

[94] Brandom, *Making it Explicit*, 184–5.

[95] David Lewis, *Convention: A Philosophical Study* (Blackwell 2002) 1.

[96] Lewis, *Convention*, 1.

have supposed'.[97] The core of his argument is that conventions or anything like a shared language—a shared vocabulary and a shared sense of how words ought to be used—are not at all necessary for communication to be successful. Communication, he argues, can and should be understood without reference to such a thing as a language.

In order to show how that might be possible, Davidson suggests shifting the perspective from the speaker to the hearer.[98] The paradigmatic focus of his argument is not the capacity of the speaker to make herself understood, but the role of the interpreter who has to make sense of the world, the text and the noise around her. His focus rests on radical interpretations, namely moments in which an interpreter enters a completely new context such as a hypothetical field linguist in some forgotten place of the earth.[99] What does that radical interpreter need to do in order to make sense of the linguistic practice of any person? She needs to observe social and linguistic behaviour and, gradually, build up a theory on what the speaker takes to be true when she says certain things.[100]

Over time, we get so good at it that understanding becomes effortless and even automatic, according to Davidson.[101] Most international legal arguments are immediately accessible to us whether we agree with them or not. But the fact of rather effortless understanding is prone to mislead, he notes. It makes us think all too readily that we are indeed speaking the same language. For Davidson:

[w]hat is conventional about language, if anything is, is that people tend to speak much as their neighbours do. But in indicating this element of the conventional, or of the conditioning process that makes speakers rough linguistic facsimiles of their friends and parents, we explain no more than the convergence; we throw no light on the essential nature of the skills that are thus made to converge.[102]

Since understanding frequently proceeds effortlessly, it is easy to think that there is a language that brings interlocutors together. But that assumption is not necessary. It *can* be done away with, according to Davidson, and it also *should* be rejected.[103] There are two main reasons. First, from the perspective of the interpreter, any theory that she will come up with about what a speaker

---

[97] Donald Davidson, 'A Nice Derangement of Epitaphs' in *Truth, Language and History* (OUP 2005) 89, 107. For a nicely accessible introduction to the work of Davidson that is geared to the context of law, see Jochen Bung, 'Theorie der Interpretation: Davidson' in Sonja Buckel, Ralph Christensen, and Andreas Fischer-Lescano (eds), *Neue Theorien des Rechts* (Lucius und Lucius 2009) 271.

[98] Krämer, *Sprache, Sprechakt, Kommunikation*, 175–7.

[99] Donald Davidson, 'Thought and Talk (1975)' in *Inquiries into Truth and Interpretation* (Clarendon Press 1984) 155, building on Willard Quine, *Word and Object* (MIT Press 1960) 26–31.

[100] The concept of truth employed in Davidson's line of argument is markedly not an epistemological one. Language offers no window onto the world. See Donald Davidson, 'Seeing Through Language (1997)' in *Truth, Language and History* (OUP 2005) 127.

[101] Donald Davidson, 'The Social Aspect of Language (1994)' in *Truth, Language and History* (OUP 2005) 112.

[102] Davidson, 'Communication and Convention (1982)', 278.

[103] Krämer, *Sprache, Sprechakt, Kommunikation*, 190.

takes to be true is bound to be indeterminate.[104] There is the indeterminacy of what a sentence refers to. When a speaker says 'this is a combatant', does she do so because the person she points to holds a rifle or because that person wears insignia of an army? Interpreters can reasonably come up with different theories about what a single speaker takes to be true. Second, there are no grounds for choosing only one out of the many possibilities. Whether the same sentence 'this is a combatant' is taken to be true depends on the specific speaker—one speaker could take it to be true whenever she sees an individual with a rifle, another when she sees army insignia. The sentence can be true under different conditions (if the person has a rifle, if the person has army insignia). Once again: how could the interpreter choose *the* language of international law that counts? It is for these two reasons that Davidson suggests '[w]e must give up the idea of a clearly defined shared structure which language-users acquire and then apply to cases'.[105] There is 'no learnable common core of consistent behaviour, no shared grammar or rules, no portable interpreting machine set to grind out the meaning of an arbitrary utterance'.[106] What interpreters must develop is the ability to arrive at theories on what others take to be true. In Davidson's view then, knowing a language amounts to the same thing as 'knowing our way around in the world generally'.[107] Doing so well is like setting up new theories in any field and is 'derived by wit, luck, and wisdom'.[108]

With the curt statement that 'there is no such thing as language', Davidson concludes an argument focused on the necessary conditions for people to understand one another. A shared language is not part of those conditions. When it comes to the semantic struggle for international law, to be sure, actors not only want to understand and to be understood. They also want to find recognition and endorsements for their claims so that their language becomes *the* language of international law. Davidson's theory has the effect of alerting us that there might well not be any such language, at least as long as it is thought of as a background scheme that can be learned with a shared grammar and a stable vocabulary.[109] The

---

[104] See Kathrin Glüer, *Sprache und Regeln: Zur Normativität von Bedeutung* (Akademie Verlag 1999) 89.

[105] Davidson, 'A Nice Derangement of Epitaphs', 107.

[106] Davidson, 'A Nice Derangement of Epitaphs', 107.

[107] Davidson, 'A Nice Derangement of Epitaphs', 100 and 107. In a similar vein, Ian Johnstone has remarked that participants in the field of legal practice 'have learned its purpose and conventions not as a set of abstract rules but through the acquisition of "know-how", a mastering of discipline or technique': Johnstone, 'The Power of Interpretive Communities', with reference to Gerald Postema, 'Protestant Interpretation and Social Practices' (1987) 6 Law & Phil 283, 304.

[108] Davidson, 'A Nice Derangement of Epitaphs', 107.

[109] But note that Davidson's theory leaves room for a stock of autonomous meaning that is invariant between different theories of truth. See Donald Davidson, 'Reality without Reference' in *Inquiries into Truth and Interpretation* (Clarendon Press 1984) 215, 225. Davidson is adamant about the 'autonomy of meaning', precisely because the pitch of his argument pulls in the opposite direction. See Donald Davidson, 'Communication and Convention', 274–5.

upshot of this perspective is that it studies interpretation in its own right, not as an application of a model. Thinking that way draws attention to the beliefs of the interpreter. It offers an alienating view that might just help to better understand the familiar: the practice of interpretation.[110]

---

[110] See Bertolt Brecht, 'Short Description of a New Technique of Acting which Produces an Alienation Effect' in John Willett, *Brecht on Theatre: The Development of an Aesthetic* (Eyre Methuen 1977) 136, 143–4 ('The alienation-effect consists in turning the object of which one is to be made aware, to which one's attention is to be drawn, from something ordinary, familiar, immediately accessible, into something peculiar, striking and unexpected. What is obvious is in a certain sense made incomprehensible, but this is only in order that it may then be made all the easier to comprehend'). I was referred to this passage in presenting Davidson's theory by Bung, 'Theorie der Interpretation: Davidson', 271–2.

PART VII

CONCLUSION

18

Interpretation—An Exact Art

Philip Allott

Introduction

The chapters in the present volume show the surprisingly significant, creative, dynamic, and disparate roles that interpretation plays in a wide range of areas within International Law. They encourage us to attempt to form a synoptic view of interpretation in International Law, its relation to interpretation in law in general, and its relation to the general phenomenon of interpretation in fields outside the law.

I. What is Interpretation?

Interpretation is an act of violence against a text. We wring its neck—*lui tordre le cou* (echoing Paul Verlaine, 'Art poétique' (1874/1884)). We disrespect the text for not saying what it means, not meaning what it says, concealing obscurity in delusive clarity.

Interpretation is a threefold act of power.

(1) Interpretation *dis-integrates* the *linguistic* structure and substance of the text, in order to *re-word* it. Interpretation is a subspecies of translation. 'Intralingual translation or *rewording* is an interpretation of verbal signs by means of other signs of the same language', according to Roman Jakobson, the Russian-American linguist, in his much-discussed essay 'On Linguistic Aspects of Translation' (1959).

Our interpretation is a new act of the imagination set alongside, and claiming precedence over, the interpreted text. But a particular interpretation is intrinsically provisional and contestable and vulnerable, given that there can be any number of other ad hoc interpretations of the original text by the same or another interpreter.

The original text loses its universal and independent authenticity by becoming the focal point of a boundless and timeless constellation of penumbral and parasitical texts, actual and potential, all of them speculations unilaterally asserted by someone other than the author of the text. *Obscurum per obscurius*—the more obscure from the obscure.

(2) Interpretation *re-forms* the *semantic* substance of the text. We purport to discover what is not said in what is said. We make the text say something that it does not say—the hermeneutic voice.

The hermeneutic tradition is as old as philosophy, perhaps even as old as mythology and religion, priests and shamans. It finds hidden meaning in the open texture of written matter in particular, but also hidden iconographic meaning in visual matter. The interpreter is our guide in a forest of symbols (echoing Charles Baudelaire, 'Correspondances' (1861)).

Interpretation is an act of power across time and space. We interpret in the present, here and now, something created elsewhere in the past. Alienation in time—the text speaks to us from the past. Alienation in culture—the text speaks to us from a previous state of our own culture or from a different culture. In interpreting a text, we make choices about reconciling the past and the present, the close and the remote, as we launch our interpretation into an unknowable and uncontrollable future.

At its philosophical extreme, hermeneutics sees existence itself as a construction of meaning (Martin Heidegger and existentialism). At its religious extreme, it sees sacred texts as containing the silent voice of God, a practice developed with intense sophistication in the Judaic and Christian religious traditions. In its literary form, it sees words as containing unlimited potential allusions and associations which may be ignited in the mind of a reader. In its legal form, interpretation sees the text as mere potentiality, offering an unlimited range of possible applications, to respond to the infinite profusion of everyday particularities with which the universalism of the law is confronted. But the pragmatic lawyer (especially the judge) may stifle the hermeneutic voice: 'If the drafters had meant to say that, they would have said it.'

(3) Interpretation *imposes the will* of the interpreter on the long-suffering text. An interpreter may claim to find '*the* meaning' of the text, when everyone knows full well that a text has countless possible meanings.

The first authoritative translator of the Bible from Hebrew and Greek into Latin—Jerome (347–420 CE)—described a previous translator as having freed himself from literalness and 'like a conqueror (*iure victoris*), he has led away captive into his own tongue the meaning of his originals' (*Letter LVII to Pammachius on the Best Method of Translating* (395 CE)). A traditional Italian saying is *traduttore traditore* (translator traitor). The interpreter exercises a no less insidious power.

> 'When *I* use a word,' Humpty Dumpty said, in rather a scornful tone, 'it means just what I choose it to mean—neither more nor less.'
> 'The question is,' said Alice, 'whether you *can* make words mean so many different things.'
> 'The question is,' said Humpty Dumpty, 'which is to be master—that's all.'
>
> Lewis Carroll, *Through the Looking-Glass* (1871)

This passage has been cited as authority in countless legal proceedings, not least by Lord Atkin, who dissented in the leading case of *Liversidge v Anderson* (1942) before the House of Lords in Britain, and in over 250 judicial decisions in the United States, including two US Supreme Court cases.

II. The Illusion of Meaning

The provisions in the Vienna Convention on the Law of Treaties concerning the 'Interpretation of Treaties' are constructed around a central concept of 'the meaning'.

To anyone who knows anything about the branch of general philosophy called epistemology, such a thing may seem comical in its naivety. From the beginning of philosophy, at least in the Western tradition, it has always been noticed that *language*, as a mirror of thought, is not merely a reflecting mirror. Language also refracts and distorts. Between the mind of the speaker and the mind of the listener is an area of turbulence out of which a thought may emerge transformed into any number of new forms, each of them masquerading as a 'meaning'.

It is a source of special intellectual pleasure to note that, from the moment they were put on paper, the Vienna Convention provisions on the interpretation of treaties have themselves been subjected to interpretation of an exceptionally intense and contentious kind. The Vienna Convention text on 'meaning' certainly has no 'meaning'.

Philosophy, which has not established many things in the course of its history—that not being its function—has established beyond doubt something that we may call *linguistic indeterminacy*. In the twentieth century, that idea became a central obsession of professional philosophy, which came to regard itself as nothing but the study of linguistic indeterminacy. Philosophy pronounced itself incapable of telling us anything *true* about anything.

To followers of this philosophical fashion, *meaning* came to be seen as nothing but an arc of potentiality, a cause of potential effects in the mind of a potential listener, effects whose range may be arbitrarily determined (say, by a dictionary) but is, in principle, unlimited. Words might be seen as tools for performing tasks, or counters for playing the game of communication (Ludwig Wittgenstein). But, of course, there are an infinite variety of tasks that language performs. And every language-game (whether in religion, natural science, morality, or law) has its own rules, so that there can be no universal theory of language and, hence, no universal theory of meaning—and, hence, no transcendental philosophy speaking authoritatively about everything, or even about anything!

A closely related view suggests that language is nothing but a collection of *symbols*. 'France' as a word has no physical connection with a place, a nation, a state, a culture, or a state of mind, or anything else that it might be thought to symbolize. On this view, language is a psychological phenomenon, allowing one mind to produce an infinite number of possible mental events in other minds.

Our Interpretation of any sign is our psychological reaction to it, as determined by our past experience in similar situations, and by our present experience.

CK Ogden and IA Richards, *The Meaning of Meaning* (1923)

In *Spectacles and Predicaments* (1991), Ernest Gellner, a determined opponent of the new philosophy, recalled something that John Wisdom, a Cambridge philosopher, had said to him: 'He knew people who thought there was no philosophy after Hegel, and others who thought there was none before Wittgenstein; and he saw no reason for excluding the possibility that both were right.'

There are those of us who are not prepared to accept that linguistic unphilosophy was anything more than a useful prolegomenon to the resumption and continuation of the general philosophical tradition. We may concede that such ideas have contributed to some further clearing of the ground on the problem of language. Plato had set himself to that task, especially in the dialogues known as *Cratylus* and *Gorgias*, as had Aristotle in the book of the *Organon* known as *De Interpretatione*, in which he tried to find formal rules for determining the validity of linguistic propositions. His relative unsuccess in that enterprise has inspired a rich tradition of exploration of language as a wonderfully creative function of the human mind, and as a wonderful achievement of evolution in making the human brain.

III. Legal Interpretation

Legal interpretation is a special case of interpretation in general. Interpretation in International Law is a special case of legal interpretation, with differences arising from: (a) the *inter-lingual* character of International Law, especially in treaty texts that are equally authentic in several languages; (b) the extreme diversity of cultural backgrounds, especially in legal culture, of those participating in the drafting and interpreting processes; and (c) the primitive crudity of intergovernmental relations in general, from which an intergovernmental self-legislating process cannot be immune.

A text is a *living process*, not merely a thing. A text is a becoming, not merely a being (to borrow an Aristotelianism), with an interesting past and an uncertain future. An interpretation is a moment in the colourful life of a text, an event in its ongoing biography.

Car le mot, qu'on le sache, est un être vivant... Les mots sont les passants mystérieux de l'âme. [For the word, we should know, is a living being... Words are mysterious passers-by of the soul.]

Victor Hugo, *Les contemplations* (1856)

In a *legal* context, interpretation is applied to a remarkable variety of texts—treaty, written constitution, legislation, resolution, judicial decision, contract, canonical scholarly text, religious text, historical document, parliamentary debate, political speech, newspaper, journal.

In an *international legal* context, there is a particular case—the treaty—that raises especially interesting problems. The life-history of a treaty is exceptionally eventful—discussing, proposing, convening, negotiating, drafting, adopting, ratifying, implementing, interpreting, applying, interpreting the applications, interpreting the interpretations, modifying by subsequent agreement, amendment.

A treaty is a disagreement reduced to writing: Philip Allott, *The Health of Nations: Society and Law Beyond the State* (2002). This is more or less true of all formal legal agreements. In the case of a treaty, it is not merely an incidental characteristic. It is of the essence of a treaty. The negotiation of a treaty—as a form of rudimentary self-ruling by governments—is diplomacy by other means, at least in the present state of development of international society. Given the primitive crudity of inter-governmental relations, the diplomatic negotiation of a treaty is a rough-and-ready process. As in all diplomacy, each potential party to a treaty seeks to implement an elementary programme, with something to achieve and something to protect.

Well-prepared negotiators have 'instructions' from their government which identify those things. Their job is then to find a form of words—any form, any words—that satisfies those instructions, as far as practically possible. *Ad quidquid* (whatever), rather than *ad idem* (of one mind). Negotiation is collusive diplomatic alchemy. Treaties turn conflicts of power into little gems of literature. Treaty texts are hieroglyphs of an altered world. Often it is difficult to say, after the event, how and why and when the language emerged and took on its independent existence. It follows that treaty *interpretation* is an especially interesting game, a secondary collusive alchemy, applied now to the long-suffering text in order to transform it into something other than that which it was and is. It follows also that the general nature of interpretation as an *act of power*, discussed above, takes on a special character in treaty interpretation, where interpretation may be the continuation of power-governed diplomacy by still other means.

A. International legal interpretation: some notorious examples

(a) 'A treaty shall be interpreted in good faith in accordance with the *ordinary meaning* to be given to the terms of the treaty in their context and *in the light of its object and purpose.*'

Vienna Convention on the Law of Treaties (1969),
Article 31 (emphasis added)

A bolting-together of conflicting (italicized) ideas. 'Object and purpose' is a trans-muted form of 'policy'—the watchword of an approach to interpretation favoured by the US delegation at the United Nations Conference on the Law of Treaties and promoted by a school of thought associated with the name of Myres S McDougal of Yale Law School, who was a member of the US delegation. That approach had been rejected by a majority of states at the Conference, especially by the govern-ments of developing and smaller countries which saw open-ended interpretation as favouring governments with dominating political power and cleverer lawyers. A legal ship containing a bolted-together contradiction is not a seaworthy legal ship. Article 31 is accordingly worthless as a general *rule* of interpretation. It is a poem about interpretation.

(b) 'For the purposes of this Convention, the term "torture" means any act by which severe pain or suffering, whether physical or mental, is intentionally inflicted on a person...It does not include pain or suffering arising only from, inherent in or incidental to *lawful* sanctions.'

Convention against Torture and Other Cruel,
Inhuman or Degrading Treatment or Punishment (1984),
Article 1(1) (emphasis added)

'Lawful' by whose law? The law of the torturing government? Another bolting-together of a contradiction, making the provision worse than useless.

(c) 'Freedom of the high seas…comprises, *inter alia*…' ('*Elle comporte notamment*')

UN Law of the Sea Convention (1982), Article 87

'Comprises' and '*comporte*' are exhaustive, used to list all contents. '*Inter alia*' and '*notamment*' are non-exhaustive, leaving some contents unlisted. A contradiction—completeness versus incompleteness—that leaves the text crudely uncertain as a *rule* of law, even if it was presumably designed to conceal some serious negotiating purpose that the hermeneutic voice may consider it impolitic ever to reveal.

(d) 'The delimitation of [the exclusive economic zone and the continental shelf] between States with opposite or adjacent coasts shall be effected by *agreement* on the basis of *international law*, as referred to in Article 38 of the Statute of the International Court of Justice, in order to achieve an *equitable solution*.'

UN Law of the Sea Convention (1982), Articles 74 and 83 (emphasis added)

Another bolting-together of several contradictory approaches to the problem, produced in desperate circumstances at the UN Conference on the Law of the Sea, but with the result that the provision is worse than useless as a *rule* of law. The meaningless reference to Article 38 of the Statute of the International Court compounds the misery, that provision being one of the most notorious examples of dire treaty-drafting.

(e) 'Nothing in the present Charter shall impair the inherent right of individual or collective self-defence *if an armed attack occurs* against a Member of the United Nations' ('*Aucune disposition de la présente Charte ne porte atteinte au droit naturel de légitime défense, individuelle ou collective, dans le cas où un Membre des Nations Unies est l'objet d'une agression armée*').

Charter of the United Nations (1945), Article 51 (emphasis added)

Do the italicized words in the English text merely mean an 'armed' attack as opposed to a 'non-armed' attack? Does 'occurs' mean that the armed attack must be underway? But that contradicts the idea of an 'inherent right' (*droit naturel*) of self-defence which has always, not surprisingly, included the right to prevent an armed attack before it happens, if the defending state is *l'objet d'une agression armée* ('object' implying a wider eventuality than 'occurs').

Another radical confusion that makes the text as a legal rule worse than no text at all. The hermeneutic voice has said a very great deal about this text, but it is still nothing more than a rhetorical resource.

(f) 'The Security Council…[a]ffirms…the following principles: (i) Withdrawal of Israel armed forces *from territories* occupied in [the Six Day War of 1967]' ('*Retrait des forces armées israéliennes des territoires occupés au cours du récent conflit*').

United Nations Security Council Resolution 242, 22 November 1967 (emphasis added)

The hermeneutic voice spoke out rather volubly on this occasion, especially through three of those mainly responsible for the drafting of the English text—George Brown (British Foreign Secretary); Lord Caradon (British Permanent Representative to the UN); and Lawrence Hargrove (legal adviser to the US Permanent Representative to the UN)—telling us that the omission of the word 'the' before the word 'territories' in the English text was intended to make clear that the withdrawal was not to be from *all* the territories occupied and that the French text should be ignored. The French text can only mean 'all the territories'.

From various sources, we may learn that there were important reasons for the omission of the word 'the', including at least three 'hidden' meanings: (i) any withdrawal was to be a matter of detailed further negotiation; (ii) the resolution should not be taken as saying anything about the law on the acquisition of territory by conquest; and (iii) withdrawal from all the territories would leave a boundary which no one wanted. Legal drafting as diplomacy by other, ingenious but obscure, means!

(g) 'Every internationally wrongful act of a State entails the international responsibility of that State.'

International Law Commission, *Draft Articles on Responsibility of States for Internationally Wrongful Acts* (2001) Article 1

The bolting-together of two distinct concepts—*liability* and *responsibility*. The confusion becomes clear if the text is reworded as: 'A State may be liable for an unlawful act or omission attributable to that State.' *Liability* and *attribution* are legal devices for linking unlawful behaviour to legal consequences. *Responsibility* is a theoretical concept describing the effect of those devices: Philip Allott, 'State Responsibility and the Unmaking of International Law' (1988).

Given the existing state of development of International Law, it is not possible to have a universal treaty containing universal law on *treaties*, or a universal treaty containing universal law on *legal liability*. Nationally, such a thing may be made possible by a hierarchical distinction between law at the constitutional level, which may apply to all law, and law made under the constitution. Internationally, it is possible to have higher law *within* an international constitutional structure, such as the United Nations or the European Union. And it is possible to have a universal treaty on, say, the law of the sea, because such a treaty creates substantive law, not law about law.

(h) 'All such rights, powers, liabilities, obligations and restrictions [under EU law]...[are] to be given legal effect or used in the United Kingdom shall be recognised and available in law.'
'[A]ny enactment passed *or to be passed*...shall be construed and have effect subject to the foregoing provisions of this section...'

European Communities Act 1972, s 2(1) and (4) (emphasis added)

Hermeneutic heaven. Things not said, but contained, in the European Community Treaties are not said, but are contained, in the Treaty of Accession, and are not said, but are contained, in the 1972 Act of Parliament. Two of these unsaid things are important: EU law is law in the UK legal system in addition to the two other forms of UK law (Acts of Parliament and the Common Law); and EU law overrides the other forms of law in case of conflict.

These things had been found hermeneutically in the European Treaties by the Court of Justice of the European Union (as it is now called), had been transmitted in the Accession Treaty under the French code-name of *acquis communautaire* (the collective term for the hermeneutic supplementation of the European Treaties), and are incorporated in UK law in the minimalist, but wonderfully ingenious, drafting of section 2 of the European Communities Act 1972.

This interesting state of affairs has generated its own hermeneutic mountain of judicial decisions, parliamentary debates, polemical writing, and academic literature. And there is an incidental irony. There is no such thing as the 'sovereignty' of the British Parliament allegedly threatened by the provision. See Philip Allott, 'The courts and Parliament—Who whom?' (1979). And the last word on the legal effect of the situation rests with the courts, in accordance with the fundamental principle of liberal democracy known as the Rule of Law. But supreme courts in several of the member states, especially constitutional courts, have been willing to genuflect before, but not finally to surrender their constitutional authority to, the European Court of Justice. We are left with an interesting and familiar meta-hermeneutic question: 'Which is to be master—that's all.'

IV. The Moments of Interpretation

We tend to think of legal interpretation especially in relation to authoritative interpretation by courts and tribunals, or other public authorities exercising a decision-making power under the law. And so we also tend to think of legal interpretation as a specific event at a specific time. But interpretation is carried out by many people in different circumstances and for different purposes, at every stage in the continuing life-history of a text, and its unique 'becoming'.

We may refer to these differential acts of interpretation as *moments*, not merely in the temporal sense of the word (in German, *der Moment*), but in a sense taken metaphorically from physics and mechanics: a turning effect produced by a force acting on an object (*das Moment*). This metaphorical usage was favoured by Hegel for whom, for example, universality and particularity and individuality are dialectical 'moments' of any concept (*Begriff*)—an analysis which could prove surprisingly useful in legal interpretation, given that law can be seen as being precisely a manifestation of three analogous 'moments'.

The three moments of legal interpretation are heuristically separable but, needless to say, they are vigorously interdependent, each acting upon the others.

A. Programmatic moment

Interpretation in *making* the text. The drafters, knowing that the text will be interpreted by others, are seeking to influence their interpretation in advance, to programme it so far as possible. They have to imagine the effect that interpreters may give to the words that they choose to construct the text. They must do proto-hermeneutics on the text they are making. It is their opportunity to insert creative ambiguity and deception in the text. It is also the opportunity to make mistakes, grammatical or semantic or structural (failure of coherence within the provision or with other provisions), or what turn out to be mistakes of substantive public policy. In the case of a treaty, so-called *travaux préparatoires* may be evidence of proto-hermeneutic interpretation. Accordingly, experienced negotiators know how to make 'good record' surrounding a text, such as explanation of votes, and public statements. At the First Conference for the Codification of International Law in the Hague in 1930, the Italian delegate is recorded as saying that he supported the text of Article 2 of the draft convention on state responsibility only because he believed it to be meaningless.

B. Prevenient moment

Interpreting an existing text in order to exercise *influence* over its future interpretation. Political, religious, or academic actors (and others) analysing, explicating, commenting, arguing, advising, preaching, teaching, or selling. Prevenient interpreters—in all forms of interpretation, not only legal interpretation—act as self-appointed mediators between the author of the text and eventual audiences. Their interpretative efforts may be particularly designed to influence interpretation by those who have an exceptional legal power (or other form of social power) to make interpretations and decisions.

C. Pragmatic moment

Interpreting the text in order to *apply* it authoritatively (in ancient Greek, *pragma* means 'act' or 'deed'). Judiciary, priesthood, government, or the general public voting in an election or a referendum or an opinion poll. Such an interpretation can, of course, be challenged by others, thereby serving as a stimulus for programmatic interpretation and prevenient interpretation of an endless series of potential new texts.

Thus interpretation, not merely legal interpretation but interpretation of all kinds, is a dense involution of ideas adding themselves like coral to a text, with an unlimited number of people mediating between the text and its audiences. The accretion of new ideas attaches itself to the original text—the *Urtext*, as we may call it—which changes protean-like under their influence to take on a new form—a *Retext*, as we may call it. The *Urtext* is the original text before it is interpreted, or with all subsequent interpretations set aside.

Urtext + Interpretation = *Retext*. (*Ur* is a German prefix, conveying the idea of 'original'. Goethe devoted premature Darwinian effort to searching for the *Urpflanze*, the plant from which, he supposed, all other plants had evolved. In German, *der Urtext* is the original version of a literary or musical or other work, before it is revised by the author or composer or editor, or otherwise.)

V. Deontology of Interpretation

Is the freedom of the interpreter an absolute freedom (Humpty Dumptyism)? Is there anything that can limit the arc of potential meaning? Is the hermeneutic voice best seen as a rhetorical voice, governed only by the duty to persuade? Is interpretation a collusive game, given that games are freedom within established rules? Is interpretation an art, given that art is a creative freedom within the conventional constraints of a genre?

Modernism was an intentional transgression of the conventional constraints of a genre (literary, artistic, musical).

J'ai disloqué ce grand niais d'alexandrin. (I have dislocated that great idiot of the *alexandrin* [the classical French verse form]).

Victor Hugo, *Les contemplations* (1856)

But the transgressive forms, ironically, became civilized as modified forms of traditional art genres. Logical positivism and 'ordinary language' philosophy and structuralism and postmodernism were transgressive forms of philosophy in the twentieth century. Ironically, they too became part of the 'establishment' of academic general philosophy. Legal realism and analytical jurisprudence and legal postmodernism were transgressive forms of legal philosophy that, unfortunately, became part of the 'establishment' of academic legal philosophy.

The New Haven School of International Law, proposed by Myres S McDougal and others in the spirit of the social philosopher Harold Lasswell, is transgressive International Law. The present writer's Social Idealism is transgressive in relation to the present state of the international system and International Law. These two transgressions stand as dialectical challenges to the intellectual inadequacy and the spiritual aridity and the inhumanity of International Law in its present condition.

Textual interpretation in all its forms, including interpretation in International Law, is also a freedom within constraints. The constraints are so numerous and so subtle that we may rather think of interpretation not as an exact science, but as an *exact art*, to borrow a term used by George Steiner in *After Babel* (1975), his monumental study of interlingual translation, in which he says that intralingual interpretation may raise the same issues as translation. *Exact scientific methods* produce a form of provisional certainty. *Art* is a work of the imagination.

It is possible to identify here only the most significant of the actual constraints on freedom of interpretation, which are as wide and deep as the phenomenon of language itself.

A. Context

Context is the *negation* of text (all that is not said in the text). Context is a *content* of text (all that gives meaning to the text). The opposition of *text* and *context* is the efficient secret at the heart of all interpretation. An act of interpretation is a resolution of the dialectical tension of text and context—an *Aufhebung*, using the Hegelian word in its strict sense. The interpretation *contains* the text and the context, *overcomes* the opposition between them, and *produces* a third thing—an *untext*, as we may call it, that is a new, but virtual, text. Text + Context = Untext. Untext is an *unwritten* text spoken by the *silent* hermeneutic voice. *Urtext* + Untext = *Retext*.

> ... if an armed attack occurs [*or is imminent*].
>
> Charter of the United Nations (1945), Article 51

> Withdrawal... from territories occupied [as determined hereafter under the authority of the Security Council].
>
> United Nations Security Council Resolution 242, 22 November 1967

> Any enactment [*even an Act of Parliament*] ... shall be construed and have effect subject...
>
> European Communities Act 1972, s 2(4)

However, re-texting is always subject to the stifling of the hermeneutic voice. 'If they had meant to say that, they would have said it in the Urtext.'

Especially in France and the United States, in the latter half of the twentieth century, the question of the interpretation of literary texts came to be dominated by struggles focused on theories referred to as Contextualism and New Criticism, for and against the incorporation of exterior contexts in the interpretation of texts respectively.

Jacques Derrida, a high priest of poststructuralism and postmodernism, said '*il n'y a pas de hors-texte*' ('there is no such thing as [context] outside [*hors*] the text'): *De La Grammatologie* (1967). He called this 'the axial proposition of this essay' and it came to be seen as an axiom of postmodernism. When objection was raised to this formula as being merely perverse, he said that he was also willing to say that '*l'hors-texte est dans le texte*' ('context is inside the text'), a more ingenious and interesting formula. (The original formula has a respectable heritage as an axiom of Jewish biblical hermeneutics. A new form of biblical hermeneutics emerged in the nineteenth century studying the historical origins of the biblical texts and their subsequent history (a rich *hors-texte*), and interpreting the interpretations that they had generated.)

Legislation, treaties, and contracts often contain explicit provisions on interpretation, that is to say, internal rules of interpretation for use in interpreting the text in question, in an effort to stifle or limit the hermeneutic voice. But those provisions are themselves subject to interpretation, of which the 128 words in the definition of 'torture' above is a striking and tragic case.

The provisions on interpretation in the Vienna Convention use 'context' as a structural concept, opening the interpretative process as wide as the imagination of interpreters—another illustration of the fatuity of a legal text which supposedly contains universal rules for the interpretation of legal texts, including interpretation of that text itself.

Is this an exotic instance of a violation of the mathematical principle of 'incompleteness' or 'indeterminacy' proposed by Kurt Gödel in 1931, a principle that has profound, more-than-metaphorical, resonances throughout human thought?

A theorem cannot be proved by something that the theorem is intended to prove. A set of ideas cannot be proved by ideas taken from within that set of ideas. A religion's own justification of its truth may not convince those who are not believers in that religion. A philosophy's explanation of its own validity may not convince those who do not accept that philosophy. In the *Prior Analytics*, Aristotle identified an analogous logical fallacy generally known by its Latin name—*petitio principii* (begging the question)—where an argument relies implicitly on the conclusion that the argument is intended to prove.

We may also be reminded of the poet Byron, commenting on the philosophically inclined poet Coleridge 'explaining metaphysics to the nation': 'I wish he would explain his Explanation' (*Don Juan* (1819)).

B. General rationality

Rationality is a semantic structuring of language that makes effective communication possible, at least language that is not merely the expression of emotion. But rationality, as conceived in the Western philosophical tradition stemming from Aristotle, has been contested, especially in its relentless 'two-value' form: true-false; good-evil; self-other; right-duty; public-private; male-female; lawful-unlawful; theism-atheism; time-space; and so on. It must be said, however, that much of the most valuable human thought has stemmed from efforts to explore and correct such dialectical oppositions in countless different ways. The central place of rationality in the Western tradition is also contested on *cultural* grounds. Other cultures have different conceptions of the elementary functioning of the human mind. This fact is relevant to the problem of interpretation in International Law, which must presumably aim to be universal in character, encompassing all cultural traditions.

C. Legal rationality

Lawyers underestimate the extent to which law is a language of its own. It even makes use of its own categories of rationality, especially *truth* and *cause* and *motivation* and *attribution* and *justification*. Also, as exposed by Jeremy Bentham (his ideas being developed further by Hans Vaihinger), law is constructed out of *fictions*, which are not symbolic references (CK Ogden and IA Richards) to anything in outside reality but names of metaphysical entities invented for the purposes of the law (*property*, *right*, *power*, *obligation*, *offence*, *contract*, *tort (delict)*, *negligence*, *infant*, *life*, *death*, and so on). Law is a vast imagined structure of language creating its own esoteric legal reality. Needless to say, International Law is no different in principle. It takes an imagined legal reality as it finds it, adding some of its own fictional entities (*state*, *government*, *treaty*, *war*, and so on).

D. Unwritten law

Unwritten law presents a special problem of interpretation, especially in International Law. There is no text. There is no Urtext. And yet unwritten law is regularly interpreted. Local custom. Custom. Customary law. Customary International Law. Common Law. Equity. Precedent. *Stare decisis. La jurisprudence. La doctrine juridique. Acquis communautaire.*

It is important to distinguish between two kinds of unwritten law. *Unwritten law Mark 1* is law, but law without a legislator. *Unwritten law Mark 2* is an adjunct to law, produced by many different kinds of author. The Romans, who invented law in its modern form, and the Byzantines, who enriched the Roman tradition, distinguished *ius scriptum* from *ius non scriptum*, but they included in the former many forms of *writing about law*, especially extra-judicial opinions and commentaries. In Roman law, and modern legal systems influenced by Roman law, legal interpretation came to include interpretation of these Mark 2 supplementary forms of unwritten law. Hence Article 38 of the Statute of the International Court of Justice and hence the *acquis communautaire* of the EU.

The Court, whose function is to decide in accordance with international law such disputes as are submitted to it, shall apply: a. international conventions, whether general or particular, establishing rules expressly recognised by the contesting states; b. international custom, as evidence of a general practice accepted as law; c. the general principles of law recognised by civilised nations; d. ... judicial decisions and the teachings of the most highly qualified publicists of the various nations, as subsidiary means for the determination of rules of law.

Statute of the International Court of Justice, Article 38

This text has regularly misled interpreters into supposing that such a rag-bag of things identifies the *sources* of International Law. Nothing could be more incorrect. Even Article 38, in its Romano-Byzantinism, does not use the word 'sources'. Customary International Law and Treaties are not the *sources* of International Law. They *are* International Law. To this extent, Article 38 is right in using the word 'apply', even if everything else in the article is deplorable. In a legal system, especially a liberal democratic legal system, it is essential that the citizen should be able to know precisely the only forms that the law may take. That is a fundamental implication of the principle of the Rule of Law. Law-makers in making law are strictly confined and controlled by law that regulates the making of law, that is to say, higher law contained in written and unwritten constitutions. The citizen is, rather optimistically, deemed to know the law, not a miscellany of lawish things.

In the UK, for example, there are three forms of law: EU law, Acts of Parliament, and the Common Law. Customary International Law is the product of an age-old and worldwide and highly efficient system of law-making in which the subjects of the law make the law unconsciously and in which the *common interest* of society is secreted silently and organically. In Britain, *legislation*—instant law, as it were, as opposed to the putting-into-writing of existing customary law—dates from the fourteenth century, at a time when the country was in a state of dramatic economic and social and legal development. The Common Law is a splendid quasi-customary survival from the earlier period.

In the present under-developed condition of international society and its unwritten constitution, and of International Law itself, *treaties* are a very special kind of law. In the absence of a general international legislator, the treaty-parties are a virtual legislator, the subjects of the law that they make. In the case of general multilateral treaties, especially if the parties are very numerous, the law may seem to be made by a virtual universal legislator, distantly approaching the legislating of a global *common interest*, a primitive version of the legislated law of national legal systems.

For the purpose of interpreting unwritten law, the Untext is treated as if it were an Urtext. But constructing this virtual Urtext is itself, of course, a special form of interpretation, subject (*mutatis mutandis*) to the considerations and constraints discussed in the present chapter. We may borrow the Vattelian word *imperfect* and say that unwritten law is *imperfect law*, until it is perfected by being applied as law by a law-deciding authority. At all times, it is liable to interpretation within the 'moments' of interpretation identified above.

But it is vitally important to say that *unwritten law Mark 1 is law*. This includes Customary International Law, whatever mistaken publicists may teach, even publicists of the most highly qualified kind, and whatever hypocritical and self-serving governments and their sycophantic intellectual camp-followers may say. There is little enough public order in the intergovernmental world without despising the modicum of intelligent self-ordering that, over long centuries, it has been able to find within itself.

E. Psychic context

Human beings are instinctive poets. They use words to make themselves human and to make the mind-world that is their second habitat: Giambattista Vico, *Scienza Nuova* (New Science) (1725). Ideas are molecules of thought that may be expressed as words. The human species has evolved many forms of language—gestural and symbolic and verbal and visual—to exchange ideas in every kind of human situation. Language is psychic power exercised by one human mind over another, and an instrument of collective social power.

In Greece and Rome and early modern Europe, *rhetoric* was an important intellectual discipline. Aristotle's *De Interpretatione*, mentioned above, is mostly concerned with the persuasive power of language. It discusses *logic* as an effective form of language, if it enables the speaker and the hearer to share standards of incontrovertible speech. Cicero, politician and lawyer and orator, wrote busily on the theory and practice of effective speech.

Legal language is designed par excellence to change states of mind, through the public mind of society speaking to the private minds of citizens and to holders of public power. Legal ideas are a striking example of Alfred Fouillée's *idées-forces* at their most forceful, designed to be life-changing and world-changing. And the spoken language of the law has a shadowy hinterland in which it speaks silently of its impassive authority and its ultimate threat of violence. It plays subliminally on human passions of desire and fear and selfishness and altruism, among many others, conscripting them into its service.

Legal language is constantly evolving, seeking to maximize its functional effect. Paradoxically but characteristically, the law seeks to enhance its authority by way of communicative exclusion, speaking a coded legal language or legal dialect, more or less understood by lawyers, more or less incomprehensible for everyone else. The dialectical conjunction of William Blackstone and Jeremy Bentham and the unsparing pen of Charles Dickens revealed this to the citizen, who was already painfully familiar with the scandals and the mysteries of English law before its reformation in the nineteenth century. And, in its imposing rituals, the law speaks its authority with overwhelming non-verbal eloquence.

A court of law is theatre, temple and battlefield. A court enacts social process as drama, sacrament and contest.

Philip Allott, 'The International Court and the Voice of Justice' (1995)

Legal language reflects different cultures and societies and social situations at different times. But the language of International Law, a legal system applying to all peoples everywhere, should be universal. Discussion of International Law has traditionally taken place in a collusive conversation among the holders of ultimate power in their so-called 'states' and those who advise them, with interventions from those who practise International Law professionally, as lawyers or in universities.

This has given a uniquely problematic character to the interpretation of International Law. At least until recently, with the rise of a more effective international public opinion, the self-centred intransigence of the holders of supreme public power, based on the ancient idea that diplomacy is a dark art not accessible to the uninitiated, has meant that the context in which interpretation takes place is unnaturally constricted. In international legal interpretation, there is the presence of a double psychic absence—the absence of the limitless diversity of the voices of International Law's long-suffering subject peoples, and the absence of ruling ideas and ruling high values dominating the search for the all-human public interest, the context of all contexts, the public policy of all public policies. And governments may avoid the risks of collective interpretation by using non-ratification of a treaty to defy a tentative international General Will to which they may have contributed much in the making of the treaty, a General Will to which they are willing to subject others in their absence.

F. Metaphysical context

The phenomenology of law. Law is ideas, present only in the human mind, a work of the human imagination, a fiction among fictions—metaphysical not physical, not present in the natural world, whatever the all-too-physical manifestations that the law generates.

In the early twentieth century, *phenomenology* took up a theme from Kant and Hegel and Schopenhauer. If, as Kant suggests, the human mind cannot know the reality of the real world except through the phenomena that present themselves to the human mind, then it is a proper function of philosophy to consider the way in which the mind organizes that mind-made reality. Linguistics (Ferdinand de Saussure) and logical positivism (Gottlob Frege and the Vienna Circle) took a step further. Mind-made reality, including that constructed by the natural sciences, is expressed in mathematics and in language. The nature and functioning of mathematics and language are thus a proper focus of philosophy.

This left open the tempting idea that the study of mathematics and language is the *only possible* function of philosophy, since philosophy must always, in the end, dissolve into language-about-language. It was a temptation to which some of those in 'ordinary language' philosophy and structuralism and postmodernism cheerfully succumbed. A necessary inference from this view was thought to be that there cannot be a metaphysical realm beyond language that language can re-present to us—a realm which contains, for example, transcendental values.

In this way universal 'qualities' [truth, beauty, goodness etc.] arise, phantoms due to the refractive power of the linguistic medium; these must not be treated as part of the furniture of the universe, but are useful as symbolic accessories enabling us to economise our speech material.

> CK Ogden and IA Richards, *The Meaning of Meaning* (1923)

I define postmodernism as incredulity towards metanarratives [*métarécits*].

> Jean-François Lyotard, *The Postmodern Condition: Report on Knowledge* (1979)

Such self-denying ideas present a serious challenge to the philosophy of law. Legal language creates its own legal reality within the general mind-made reality studied by philosophy. But law is a massive imposition of public power on human beings. It needs a great deal of explanation and justification in terms of values and, especially, of *high values*, values that transcend societies and their law. And that explanation and justification must be regarded as actual and practical and convincing, not merely a linguistic hypothesis. This is an especially serious challenge for International Law, which needs all the help that it can get from philosophy in order to increase its authority and effectiveness over a chaotic intergovernmental and transnational world, much inclined to believe in the idea of the supremacy of power over law.

We may want to console ourselves with the thought that terminal scepticism about metanarratives may be a disease that affects only a small number of Western intellectuals. Most people across the world still live by universals and metanarratives and the ideals contained in high values.

> We live and die for words; we create and kill for words; we build and destroy for words.
> Philip Allott, *Eunomia: New Order for a New World* (1990)

> Words, words, words.
> William Shakespeare, *Hamlet* (Hamlet speaking, and longing for something beyond words)

> Words without thoughts never to heaven go.
> William Shakespeare, *Hamlet* (Claudius speaking, with forked tongue)

From the leading phenomenologists, Edmund Husserl and Paul Ricœur, comes a particular idea which is especially useful in relation to the contextual aspects of legal interpretation—*Horizon*. When we apply our mind to phenomena presented by something that we suppose is present in the 'real' world, we bring to those phenomena an *internal* horizon of expectations that together construct something which causes us to recognize the collection of phenomena as, say, a chair. And we then apply an *external* horizon of expectations to place that object in relation to other phenomena constructed by the mind in the same way—the room where the chair is located, the idea of *owner*, and then, perhaps, the idea of *property*, and, perhaps, some affective or aesthetic category. Such a process is surely at the heart of all knowledge. We have ready-made templates of meaning with which we give meaning to reality in thought and language. By way of an example, consider Vincent Van Gogh, *La chaise et la pipe* (1888).

These *models-of-meaning*, as we may call them, may be inherent in our minds or socially acquired. They determine our thinking and our behaviour. Legal systems are constructed from them, also using the categories and fictions discussed in terms of legal rationality above. They condition every form of interpretation. In interpreting law, including International Law, they may be a matter of life and death, of war and peace. In pre-processed thought, interpreters see what they expect to see, what their culture prepares them to see, what public interest encourages them to see, what national interest inspires them to see, what self-interest inclines them to see, what they are conditioned to want to see.

G. Cultural context

Law is the physiology of a society. Without law a society could not continue to exist as an organic living thing. This means that the law of a society is utterly integrated into the culture of its society and vice versa—'culture' in the widest sense of the word.

Countless social philosophers, from Plato to the present day, have devoted much effort to determining the degree of mental cohesion necessary to enable a society to survive and prosper. That determination is contentious in every society and requires compromises to be made, compromises that may be enacted as law.

Everyone has the right to freedom of expression. This right shall include [particular freedoms]... The exercise of these freedoms, since it carries with it duties and responsibilities, may be subject to such formalities, conditions, restrictions or penalties as are prescribed by law and are necessary in a democratic society...

European Convention on Human Rights (1950), Article 10

Émile Durkheim speaks of the *conscience collective* (collective consciousness) of a society. Gilbert Murray speaks of a society's *inherited conglomerate* of beliefs and taboos. And from these comes a *collective world-view* that must condition every act of interpretation. Lucien Lévy-Bruhl calls it *représentation collective*, the way in which a society presents reality to itself. Benjamin Lee Whorf speaks of a society's *thought-world*. Jürgen Habermas speaks of a *language community*. And, of course, all the players in one of Ludwig Wittgenstein's *language-games* must talk the same language while they are playing that game. Throughout human history, religion has been the foundation-in-consciousness of organized societies.

In Europe, a collective mental crisis occurred in the nineteenth century when it became clear that religion was ceasing to perform that function. In many other countries, religions still dominate the collective mind.

These facts make cross-cultural interpretation exceptionally difficult. Relativism is a central and permanent feature of philosophical scepticism—from Xenophanes (if oxen or horses made a religion, their God would be an ox or a horse) to Karl Marx (ruling ideas are the ideas of the ruling class); from Thrasymachus (justice is the self-interest of the stronger) to Vladimir Lenin (the only constitutional question is 'who whom?'); from Protagoras (morality is a set of ideas required to make good citizens) to all those who have tediously told us that cannibalism has been good social practice in some places at some times.

Good, and evil, are names that signify our appetites, and aversions; which in different tempers, customs, and doctrines of men, are different.

Thomas Hobbes, *Leviathan* (1651)

However, the wonderfully dialectical nature of the working of the human mind means that a central and permanent feature of philosophy has been an unceasing struggle between scepticism and relativism, on the one hand, and universalism and transcendentalism, on the other. Interpretation, even legal interpretation, cannot avoid that struggle.

The problem of cultural context is at its most acute when social philosophy and social systems must establish themselves at the level of the whole of humanity, where the diversity of cultures is a wonderful fact and an overwhelming challenge. It is an overwhelming challenge for the *making* of International Law, articulating in legal language a universal legal system. It is a serious challenge in the *interpretation* of International Law. The extreme diversity of cultural contexts across the world haunts the interpretation of legal texts designed to be cross-cultural, or even universal, in their application.

It is significant that, in the European Union and in the European system of human rights, we have found that, within what may seem to be a coherent European culture, there are sub-cultures, national and cross-national, whose values are liable to be cherished and defended in the face of 'European' values enforced by European-level institutions.

The present writer has specialized in the problem of creating social consciousness at the universal level, with universal ideas of *society* and *law*, without which a true International Law cannot emerge as the physiology of a true international society.

H. Historical context

The hermeneutic voice is heard in the present but it may speak from the past. What shall be the authority of the author in the interpreting of an author's text? Wilhelm Dilthey, philosopher of hermeneutics, speaks of a form of deep understanding (*Verstehen*) that the interpreter must apply to the mind of the author contained in the text. Thomas Hobbes, in *Leviathan*, makes use of the author/

authority play-on-words in a crucial context. The people are the *author* of a constitution in which they transfer their *authority* as 'sovereignty' to the commonwealth. John Locke then tells us, in *Two Treatises of Government* (1689), that the people transfer their authority subject to rather important terms and conditions, which we have come to interpret as principles of 'liberal democracy'.

Do the authors of texts lose all their rights over the interpretation of their texts? Is the interpreter sovereign? Should we listen to the author's voice? These are especially important questions in legal interpretation, above all in interpreting written constitutions, including international constitutional texts.

The American 'founding fathers' haunt every moment of American constitutional interpretation. The San Francisco Conference haunts the interpretation of the UN Charter, but may be discounted by interpreters from member states which joined the UN thereafter. The treaties establishing the European Union have been re-engineered so roughly for so many years that reference is rarely made to the states of mind of those who first wrote them.

The historical school of jurisprudence in Germany in the nineteenth century saw the past, especially the Roman past and the Teutonic past, in every manifestation of law in the present. Marxian historicism sees the power of the past as the dominant source of social power in the present, including legal power and legal ideas. There is a form of historiography which seeks to understand texts and ideas in the light of the states of mind of those who originated them, and the social and cultural circumstances in which they originated. In the UK, it is represented by a group of scholars referred to as the Cambridge School of historical contextualism, associated particularly with the name of JGA Pocock.

International Law is grievously burdened by an inheritance of outdated categories of social organization and out-dated conceptions of human flourishing. The hermeneutic voice of International Law is a ghostly presence from a dead human past.

I. Social milieu

The meaning of a text is in the eye of the interpreter. Interpretation varies, and properly varies, not only in the different 'moments' of interpretation discussed above, but also in the social circumstances in which it occurs, and as a function of the social status of the interpreter. Interpretation speaks in many different voices.

Judge, counsel, cleric, theologian, philosopher, academic, historian, artist, composer, writer, critic, politician in a liberal democracy, politician in a tyranny, diplomat, public official, public intellectual, journalist, advertiser, salesman, entertainer, humble citizen.

There are winners and losers in the game of legal interpretation, a game not decided by some abstract standard of rightness. Inequality of social power among all the potential interpretative actors means that some are more equal than others in gaining acceptance for their own interpretation. And nowhere is this more evident than in all the 'moments' of interpretation in International Law, where gross inequality of 'state-power' is matched by inequalities of resources, especially diplomatic and legal and technical resources, and by the possibility of a mind-bending threat or use of force, political or military or economic.

Interpretation in International Law is an art and a game and a field of battle. It is an ultimate art of the possible, and the possible includes a better kind of law for a better kind of international society.

Summary

The role of interpretation in International Law is a particular instance of the role of interpretation in the making and application of law in general, which is itself a particular instance of the role of interpretation in countless other fields.

Interpretation is dynamic and creative and transformative, not merely mechanical, and not merely an incidental or ancillary aspect of the real-world effect of a text. Interpretation is a permanent life-changing force acting on the text, constantly modifying its effect throughout its life-history.

Legal interpretation, including interpretation in International Law, is a bridge between the inherent universalism of legal rules and the infinite particularity of the everyday situations and events to which the law must be applied.

Interpretation in all fields, including in the legal field, has no inherent limits to its reliance on external contexts and references and associations. But its effectiveness in changing minds and causing social change depends on pragmatic respect for conventionally determined expectations limiting its inherent freedom, expectations that are indeterminate but numerous and powerful.

However, interpretation in International Law has a particular negative characteristic. It can readily contribute to the uncertainty and weakness of the law. So long as governments see International Law as little more than mild intergovernmental self-limiting, international law-making will be closer to an exercise of diplomacy-by-other-means than to legislation in a sophisticated sense, that is to say, the making of universal law in the general public interest. And, for so long also, interpretation in International Law will be seen as an agonistic ritual within the age-old intergovernmental game of competitive political power.

Index

Abraham, Kenneth 305
Academics 40–3, 141–2, 153, 156, 159, 162, 331
Ackerman, Bruce 53
Actors—*see* Players
Adhesion 64, 70–1, 73
Adjudication 24. *See also* Judges
African National Congress 298
Aggression 277
Alexis, Robert 76
Allott, Philip 32, 373–92
Amicus curiae briefs 138–9
Analogical reasoning 72, 281. *See also* Reasoning
Antarctic Treaty 89
Anzilotti, Dionisio 213
Arato, Julian 30, 205–28
Arbitrariness 112, 129
Arendt, Hannah 25, 27
Argumentation 62, 64, 72, 73, 74–5, 111. *See also* Rhetoric
Aristotle 65, 69, 376, 384, 386
Armed conflict 268, 297, 349
Atiyah, Patrick 7
Atkin, Lord 374
Audience 36–8, 50, 68–77, 102, 113, 162, 175, 180, 273, 279–81, 297
Austin, John 322–5, 362–4
Author (of object of interpretation) 9, 10, 13, 14, 16, 314–15, 318, 328, 373
Authorial intent—*see* Intention of the parties
Authority 36, 37, 41, 43, 54, 87–90, 107–8, 110, 114–15, 118–19, 121, 129
Auto-interpretation 27, 89, 293–4, 298, 301

Background schemes 32, 353, 363–4, 367, 369
Baxter, Richard 94
Beckett, Eric 197
Beckett, Jason 179
Bentham, Jeremy 384
Bernárdez, Santiago Torres 247
Bianchi, Andrea 13, 20, 28, 34–57, 122, 168
Bias 32, 54, 140, 170, 204, 279, 280, 288, 332, 344, 348, 350
Bjorge, Eirik 30, 189–204
Blackstone, William 387
Bourdieu, Pierre 56, 362
Boutros-Ghali, Boutros 354
Brandom, Robert 366–7
Brest, Paul 161
Brierly, James 48, 195
Brown, George 379

Brownlie, Ian 41
Bush, George 342–3

Cambridge School of historical contextualism 391
Cannibalism 291, 294, 298–300, 303, 305–8
Capital (political and social) 284
Carstens, Anne Marie 30, 192, 229–48
Central Intelligence Agency 342
Certainty 3, 12. *See also* Determinacy
Chess 22, 23, 24, 26, 33, 352, 354–6, 364–5
Choice 72–3, 314
Chomsky, Noam 357–9, 361–2
Cicero 386
Clapham, Andrew 140
Cognitive frames 13, 32, 331–51
    creation and types of frames 335–6
    deep frames 335–6, 344
    functions and risks 336–7
    lexical frames 335, 344
    subconscious nature 334–5
Cognitive linguistics 20
Cohen, Harlan Grant 31, 268–89
Coherence 56, 71, 152, 166–84, 279, 282–3
Combacau, Jean 359
Communication 10, 21, 65, 124, 126, 144, 259, 263, 320, 338, 347, 361, 368
Communitarian dimension of meaning 13. *See also* Interpretive community and Convention
Community of practice 275, 279–81, 285, 305
Compliance 99, 270, 272–3, 278
Conaglen, Matthew 152
Conference for the Codification of International Law 381
Confrontation 115–16, 119
Conservatism 315, 329
Constitutional interpretation 4, 8, 11, 391
Constitutive function 12, 20
Constraint(s) 4, 25, 26, 27, 29, 32, 73, 111–12, 121–7, 145, 180, 363, 382
Construction 11, 12
Content determination 29, 112–14, 116–21, 124, 126–8
Context 3, 5, 12, 13, 16, 75, 105, 114, 149–51, 231–7, 280, 283, 284, 325–6, 329, 382–3
Contingency 9, 14, 16, 24, 27, 31, 290, 304
Convention 10, 24, 32, 317, 320, 322–6
Conversation (interpretation as) 302, 351
Corporation 298
Council of Europe 11

Countermeasures 294, 301
Cover, Robert 13, 172, 303, 306–7
Crawford, James 19, 147–8, 158, 199–200, 347, 356–7
Cricket 23, 279
Critical legal studies 12, 13
Culture 17, 19, 31, 290–308, 374, 376, 389–90
Culture of formalism 357. *See also* Formalism
Customary international law 5, 79, 90–2, 94, 98, 118, 135, 277–8, 300–1, 385–6

D'Aspremont, Jean 29, 111–29
Darnton, Robert 154–5
Davidson, Donald 367–70
Decoding (of ideology) 327–30
Decontestation devices 313–5, 321, 325
De Visscher, Charles 199, 263
Decentralisation 304
Delegation 270–2, 295–6
Deleuze, Gilles 25–6, 27
Deontology (of interpretation) 382–91
Derrida, Jacques 324–5, 383
Determinacy 11, 12, 13, 83, 112, 120, 168–73, 291, 317, 365–6, 375, 383
Dialogue 292, 350–1
Differential treatment 30
Dilthey, Wilhelm 390
Diplomacy 376–7
Disciplining rules 122–3, 127
Discourse 20, 28, 43, 70, 80, 101–3, 108, 308, 353, 356–7
Doctrine 80, 101, 103–4
Dörr, Oliver 244
Dualism 353–4, 360–6
Dugard, John 340
Dunn, Frederick 158
Dunoff, Jeffrey 19
Dupuy, Pierre-Marie 180
Dupuy, René-Jean 92
Durkheim, Émile 389
Dworkin, Ronald 15–16, 86, 110, 121, 169–70, 172, 178, 181, 283, 312, 347
Dynamic interpretation—*see* Evolutionary Interpretation

Easterbrook, Frank 152
Effet utile 46
Elkins, David 336
Enhanced interrogation techniques 342–4
Epistemic community 29, 115, 149–65, 181, 280, 285, 288, 297. *See also* Interpretive community
Epistemology 319
Ethics 349–50
European Communities Act 1972 (UK) 379–80, 383
European Convention on Human Rights
    Article 3 205
    Article 6 205

Article 8 11, 137
Article 10 389
Article 11 223
Article 34 45
European Court of Human Rights 11, 38, 43, 50, 137, 198, 205, 272, 276, 282, 300
European Court of Justice 50, 97, 152, 273, 282, 380
Evidence 90–1, 104, 108
Evolutionary interpretation 11, 30, 189–204, 205–28
Existential function of interpretation 28–9, 79, 84–7, 90, 91–2, 95–8, 101–3, 108, 374

Family resemblance concept 21–2, 330. *See also* Wittgenstein, Ludwig
Fillmore, Charles 334
Fish, Stanley 10, 34, 121, 123, 125, 127, 150, 296
Fiss, Owen 121, 123, 125–7, 152, 171, 173
Fitzmaurice, Gerald 38, 39, 46–7, 195–6, 198, 218–19
Fitzmaurice, Malgosia 201
Foreign official immunity—*see* Official immunity
Formalism 3, 5, 12, 13, 33
Formalization 118, 120
Foucault, Michel 25, 27, 257–8
Fouillée, Alfred 386
Fragmentation 5, 56, 83, 109, 154–60, 164–5, 221–2, 238–9, 304
Franck, Thomas 283
Freeden, Michael 315, 328–9
Frege, Gottlob 387
Freund, Julian 263
Fuller, Lon 29, 145–6, 283

Gadamer, Hans-Georg 14–15, 312
Gaja, Giorgio 191
Game (of interpretation) 4, 16–28, 32–3, 35, 36, 38–40, 42, 49, 108, 112–13, 116, 128, 275, 284, 292, 308, 314, 351, 352–70
    feel for 56
    object 112–13
    stakes 54
    winning 55
    worth the candle 54, 56
Games (Board) 34, 35, 43, 52
Gellner, Ernest 375
General rule/exception (paradigm) 51
Generalists (international law) 43, 56
Geneva Conventions 294–6, 305
Global administrative law 100, 279
Gödel, Kurt 383
Goffman, Erving 334
Good faith 4
Grammar 32, 356–9

Gross, Leo 89
Guattari, Félix 25–7

Haas, Peter 149
Habermas, Jürgen 314, 389
Habitus 37, 52
Hargrove, Lawrence 379
Harper, Tauel 26
Hart, HLA 12, 24, 97, 169, 172, 259, 363, 366
Harvard Draft Convention on the Law of Treaties 175–6
Hegel, Georg Wilhelm Friedrich 376, 380, 383, 387
Heidegger, Martin 312, 374
Hermeneutics 4, 13, 14, 15, 16, 183, 307, 311–30, 374, 383, 390–1
Hernández, Gleider 29, 166–85
Hezbollah 346
Higgins, Rosalyn 212, 215, 354
Historical context 390–1
Historical contingency 251–67
Hobbes, Thomas 390
Hollis, Duncan 28–9, 78–110, 118, 121
Honig, Bonnie 324–5
Huizinga, Johan 17
Human Rights Committee 88–9, 103, 106
Husserl, Edmund 388
Hutchinson, Alan 24
Hymes, Dell 361

Ideology 12, 32, 311–30, 350
Implied powers 50, 104
Incompletely theorized agreements 106
Indeterminacy 11, 12, 13, 83, 112, 120, 170–3, 291, 317, 366, 375, 383
Inner morality of law 145–6
Institut de Droit international 40, 46–7, 115, 196, 201
Insurgents 303
Integrity 15, 283
Intentionalism 114, 122
Intention of the parties 5, 9, 10, 13, 15, 16, 30, 46–8, 105, 167, 169, 173, 178–9, 189–204, 207–8, 212, 216–18, 233, 247, 252, 255–6, 262–6, 329, 365
Inter-American Court of Human Rights 45, 205
International Center for the Settlement of International Disputes (ICSID) 270
International Civil Aviation Organization (ICAO) 98
International Committee of the Red Cross (ICRC) 90–91, 103, 277, 298, 301
International Court of Justice (ICJ) 5, 37, 41, 43, 49, 51, 79, 88, 92, 95, 97–8, 105, 107, 124, 167, 192–4, 201–2, 240–3, 269, 272, 276–8, 285–6, 288, 291, 295–6, 300–2, 340–2, 350, 385

International criminal law 31, 269, 276–7, 290–308, 360
International Covenant on Civil and Political Rights (ICCPR) 88–9, 106, 294–5
International Criminal Court (ICC) 283, 305, 350
International Criminal Tribunal for the Former Yugoslavia (ICTY) 49, 95, 268, 270, 276, 301
International humanitarian law 90–1, 345
International human rights law 269, 276
International investment law 6, 159–60, 211, 216, 224–5, 269
International judiciary 29, 139–41, 166–85. *See also* Judges
International Law Association (ILA) 40
International Law Commission (ILC) 7, 46–7, 81–2, 84, 98, 121, 123, 191, 194–8, 202–4, 218–22, 255–6, 277, 379
International Monetary Fund (IMF) 163–4
International relations 18, 19, 23
International trade law 269, 276, 299. *See also* World Trade Organization
Interpretation
  authentic 134, 173
  authoritative 174–5
  performative and constitutive 113
  broad or restrictive 113
  evaluative and normative 114
Interpretive community 13, 28, 29, 39, 40, 43, 86, 110, 123, 125, 127, 133, 147–65, 173, 296–8, 302–5, 311, 322, 366. *See also* Epistemic community
Inter-subjectivity 292, 302–3, 307, 319–20
Intertemporal rule 210
Iran-US Claims Tribunal 45, 252
Iraq War 277, 302
Israel-Palestine conflict 18, 340–2

Jakobson, Roman 373
Jennings, Robert 41, 142, 162
Johns, Fleur 119
Johnson, Mark 20–1, 335
Johnstone, Ian 172–3, 296–7, 357
Judge(s) 41–2, 139–41, 157–8, 166–85, 293
Judicial interpretation 41, 139–41, 152–4, 156–8, 164, 166–85, 291–3, 300. See also Judges
Jurisdictional Immunities 37, 38
Jurisgenerative interpretations 102, 181–3
Jurispathic interpretations 102
Jurisprudence 7, 22, 31
Jus cogens 85

Kant, Immanuel 387
Kelsen, Hans 134, 168–9
Kennedy, David 360
Kennedy, Duncan 12
Klabbers, Jan 6, 81, 100, 213

Knowledge 111, 120, 125, 129
Kolb, Robert 180
Korhonen, Outi 14, 15
Koskenniemi, Martti 12–13, 19, 83, 162, 179,
    204, 211, 331, 349–50, 353, 358–60
Kosovo 108
Koufa, Kalliopi 345
Kritsiotis, Dino 353, 355

Lakoff, George 20–1, 335, 337
Language 64, 80, 352–70
Language game 323, 347, 361, 366, 375, 389.
    See also Wittgenstein, Ludwig
Laswell, Harold 159, 382
Lauterpacht, Elihu 236
Lauterpacht, Hersch 46–8, 93, 141, 167,
    177–8, 195–8, 218, 342
Law ascertainment 16, 29, 112–14, 116–121,
    124, 126–8
League of Nations 190
Legal Advisers 135–7, 156, 285–6, 301
Legal argumentation—see Argumentation
Legal construction—see Construction
Legal reasoning—see Reasoning
Legality 290, 303
Legitimacy 12, 45, 162, 173–4, 281, 283,
    292–4
Lévy-Bruhl, Lucien 389
Lewis, David 367
Lex specialis 51, 85
Liberalism 328
Liberation 345–7
Linderfalk, Ulf 176
Lindroos-Hovinheimo, Susanna 346–7
Linguistics 387
Linguistic turn 13
Literary theory 4, 13, 15, 296, 298, 305
Litigation 64, 143–4
Litigators 143–4
Living instrument 206. See also Evolutionary
    interpretation and European Court of
    Human Rights
Locke, John 391
Logic 65, 67
Luhmann, Niklas 338–9
Lyotard, Jean-François 388

MacCormick, Neil 348
MacIntyre, Alasdair 23, 126
Marmor, Andrei 10–11, 12, 24, 348
Marx, Karl 390–1
McDougal, Myres 48, 344, 377, 382
McNair, Arnold 190
Meaning 3, 4, 5, 9–16, 23, 28–9, 33, 41, 43,
    46, 48, 62–4, 80–1, 84–6, 101–5, 114,
    118, 120, 149, 170–3, 183, 191, 201–3,
    241–2, 247, 254, 275, 296, 311–12,
    316–17, 323, 335, 365, 375–6
Mendelson, Maurice 85

Metaphor 17–28, 32–3, 34, 69, 297, 306,
    352–70
Metaphysical context 387–9
Method (interpretive) 330
Michaels, Walter Benn 313–15, 327, 329
Mills, Alex 158
Minsky, Marvin 333–4
Mitchell, Mark 126
Moglen, Eben 151
Monism 304–5
Morality of aspiration 29, 145–6
Morality of duty 29, 145–6
Morgenthau, Hans 18
Morphological approach (to interpretation)
    328–9
Mortenson, Julian 197
Murray, Gilbert 389

North American Free Trade Agreement
    (NAFTA) 88–9
Nafziger, James 349
Narrative 299, 307
Natural language 10, 63, 67, 72
Naturalist theories 106
Negotiation 377
Neuroscience 349
New Haven School 105, 382
Nietzsche, Friedrich 257, 313, 315–22,
    324–5
Nolte, Georg 353
Non-governmental Organisations (NGOs)
    137–9, 277, 297–8
Non-state actors 287–8, 297–9, 301–3, 332
Normative universe 111–12, 115

Object and purpose 3, 5, 9, 30, 50, 82, 207,
    212–15, 224–6. See also Teleological
    interpretation
Objective meaning 3, 5, 12, 14, 32, 332,
    348 *See also* Ordinary meaning *and*
    Determinacy
Object (of interpretation) 9, 13, 28–9, 199
Objectivized intent 191–204
Obligations
    Types of 218–28, 299
    integral 219, 223
    interdependent 219–20, 224
    reciprocal 219, 224
Official immunity 271, 285–6
Ogden, CK 375, 384, 388
Olbrechts-Tyteca, Lucie 63, 66
Olesen, Jens 31–2, 311–30
Onuf, Nicholas 364
Opinio juris 91–2, 300
Ordinary meaning 3, 5, 9, 12, 14, 16, 21,
    47, 105, 236–7, 344. *See also* Objective
    meaning
Originalism 8
Ost, François 23

Pacta Sunt Servanda 294
Palchetti, Paolo 194
Pauwelyn, Joost 221
Peat, Daniel 3–33
Perelman, Chaïm 28, 35, 36, 62–4, 66–76
Permanent Court of International Justice
    (PCIJ) 213, 262, 269
Persuasion 66. *See also* Rhetoric
Phenomenology 387–8
Philosophical hermeneutics—*see* Hermeneutics
Philosophy of language 4, 11, 13, 32, 316,
    320, 366
Pierce, Richard 151
Plato 65, 376, 389
Players 23, 28, 29, 39–40, 49, 52, 54, 279–81,
    288, 292–300, 308, 314, 331
Playing the game of game playing 28, 31, 35,
    52–3, 311–30, 331, 352–70
Pluralism 304, 315
Pocock, JGA 391
Polanyi, Michael 126
Politics 12, 31, 311–330
Positivism 13, 15, 24, 271, 304, 387
Power 118–19, 311–30, 374
Practice (argumentative and
    interpretative) 61, 113
Practice (of international law) 271, 275–81,
    289, 354, 365–7, 370
Pragmatism 7–8
Precautionary principle 95
Precedent 31, 83, 268–89
    actors and audiences 279–81
    jurisprudential account 271, 282–3
    rationalist account 271, 281–2
    reasons for authority 278–9
    sociological account 271, 284–5
    source of 275–8
Predictability 50
Preparatory works 5, 46–7, 105, 196–7,
    243–8, 262–3, 300, 381
Prescriptivism 304
Prestige 273, 278
Primary norms 116
Principal-agent theory 106
Prisoner's Dilemma 18
Professional responsibility 350
Professional roles 43, 133–46, 279–81
Prost, Mario 110
Provost, René 31, 290–308
Pulkowski, Dirk 149, 163
Purpose (of interpretation) 4, 5, 12, 28
Purposeful interpretation 35, 53
Purposive interpretation 10, 11
Purposivism 114, 122

Rational choice 18
Rationalist account (of interpretation) 31
Rationality 384
Reasoning 73–74

Reflexivity 16, 33
Reisman, Michael 333, 349
Relational potential 85
Relativism 321
Reliance 283
Reservations 295
Resistance movement 332
Responsibility of the interpreter 184, 349–50
Responsibility to protect 78, 79, 84, 86, 95,
    103–4, 106–7, 109
Retext 381, 383
Retrieval view of interpretation 9, 11, 15, 16.
    See also Meaning
Reuter, Paul 200
Rhetoric 28, 61–77, 111
    art, as 61, 77
    rhetorical argument(s) 65–6, 71
    rhetorical choices 77
    rhetorical skills 36–7
    rhetorical syllogisms 65
    rhetorical tools 51
    types of 66
Richards, Ivor A 62, 64, 375, 384, 388
Ricoeur, Paul 388
Roberts, Anthea 158, 215–17
Robertson, Cassandra Burke 344
Rosenfeld, Michael 12, 16, 346
Rosene, Shabtai 19
Ruggie, John 149
Rule of law 282–3, 285, 348, 380, 385
Rules (of interpretation) 5, 7, 8, 15, 17, 19, 24,
    25, 28, 29, 30, 32, 33, 81, 112–13, 123,
    125, 308, 354, 357, 361. *See also* Vienna
    Convention on the Law of Treaties
    existence 47
    historical contingent nature 35. *See also*
        Zarbiyev, Fuad
    social agreement 48
Rules of discourse production 119
Rules of play 35, 43, 49, 53–5
Rules of recognition 116
Rule-based approaches 34, 55, 126, 128

Saussure, Ferdinand de 355–9, 362–5, 387
Schachter, Oscar 150, 159, 357
Schlag, Pierre 32, 42, 122, 127
Schopenhauer, Arthur 387
Schwarzenberger, Georg 176
Scobbie, Iain 28, 61–77
Searle, John 364–6
Secondary rules 97, 112, 124
Security Council—*see* United Nations
    Security Council
Self-defence 278, 292, 378
Self-defence against non-state
    actors 271, 287–8
Self-determination 297–8
Semantic authority 115, 168, 183, 332
Semantic meaning 10, 11, 374

Seymour, Gerald 345
Shared understanding 24, 27, 29, 147–8, 160, 237, 297, 308, 320. *See also* Interpretive community
Shelton, Dinah 100
Simeon, Richard 336
Sinclair, Ian 213
Situatedness 14–15
Skinner, Quentin 327–8
Smith, Adam 61–2
Social consensus 49, 55. *See also* Convention *and* Interpretive community
Social milieu 391–2
Social practice 23–4, 27, 124
Sociolinguistics 361–2
Socialization 52, 56
Sociology (of interpretation) 13, 31, 338–9
Socrates 65
Soft law 99–100, 273
Sources 79, 97, 101, 105, 108, 110, 114, 124, 269, 271, 281, 385
Sovereign immunity 276–7, 286
Sovereignty 291–2, 300, 305, 307
Special Court for Sierra Leone (SCSL) 290, 294, 298–300, 303, 306–8
Special meaning 240
Specialization 158–60
Speech acts 32, 313, 323–5, 363
Speech community 361. See also Epistemic community *and* Interpretive community
Stare decisis 272, 282, 385. *See also* Precedent
State acts 277
State immunity 37–8, 46, 51
State practice 79, 91–2, 104, 106, 283, 287, 300
State responsibility 298, 379
States 17–18, 23, 291, 298
Statutory interpretation 4
Steiner, George 382
Strategic choice of language 337–8
Strategy (of interpretation) 4, 12, 13, 28, 30, 32, 49, 52–3, 161–4, 261–2, 270–1, 273–4, 282, 290–308, 315, 354
Stone, Julius 178, 184
Subsequent practice 5, 223, 278
Sunstein, Cass 106, 153
Supplementary means of interpretation 142, 243–7
Sur, Serge 359
Systemic integration 5

Tammelo, Ilmar 70
Tams, Christian 182
Targeted killing 277, 288
Teleological interpretation 5, 10, 11, 81. *See also* Object and purpose
Tenet, George 342

Terrorism 332, 345–7
Textualism 12, 31, 47–8, 96, 114, 122, 129, 197, 251–67
Third-party rights 215–17
Topics/Topoi 66, 69–70, 75–7
Torture 331, 342–4, 383
Toulmin, Stephen 63, 66
Tradition 41, 111–12, 127, 354
Transcultural project (interpretation as) 290–308
Translation 299, 305–6, 373
Transnational law 279
Transplanted treaty rules 30, 229–48
Travaux préparatoires 5, 105, 196–7, 243–8, 262–3, 300, 381. *See also* Preparatory works
Tribe, Laurence 53
TRIPS Doha Declaration 99
Tunkin, Grigory 264–5
Tzanakopoulos, Antonios 182

United Nations 353, 354
United Nations Charter 11, 50, 86, 102, 287, 292, 296, 364, 378, 383
United Nations Convention against Torture 343–4, 377
United Nations General Assembly 92, 106, 277, 295–6, 301–2
United Nations Human Rights Committee 294–5
United Nations Law of the Sea Convention 378
United Nations Security Council 11, 50, 277, 301–2, 357, 364, 378, 383
Universal Declaration of Human Rights 71, 98, 100, 104–5, 107
Universalism 374
Urtext 381, 383–4, 386
US Department of Defence 285
US Department of Justice 342
US Department of Justice White Paper 268, 288
US Department of State 90, 285
US Office of Legal Counsel (Department of Justice) 343–4
Use of force 40, 287–8
Utterances
  constantive 323–4
  performative 323–4

Vagueness 11. See also Indeterminacy
Vaihinger, Hans 384
Vattel, Emer de 260–1
Venzke, Ingo 32, 122, 183, 352–70
Verdross, Alfred 123
Verlaine, Paul 373
Vermeule, Adrian 350
Vico, Giambattista 386
Vienna Circle 387

Vienna Convention on the Law of Treaties
  Article 3(1) 4–5, 9, 45, 48, 81, 85, 104, 189,
    194, 198–200, 212, 217, 220, 236, 255–7,
    377
  Article 31(3)(a) 237
  Article 31(3)(b) 192, 207, 237, 293–5
  Article 31(3)(c) 45, 46, 56, 85, 104,
    238–40, 248
  Article 31(4) 198, 238, 240, 248
  Article 32 30, 81, 93, 203, 230, 243–4
  Article 33 5, 253
Viehweg, Theodor 63, 66
Villiger, Mark 244
Virally, Michel 265

Wählisch, Martin 32, 331–51
Waibel, Michael 29, 147–65
Waldock, Sir Humphrey 7, 47–8, 123, 195–7,
    199–202, 220, 256
Waldron, Jeremy 22
War 17, 21, 27
War crime 299–300, 308

War on Terror 331, 335
Weber, Max 327
Weiler, Joseph 7
Weller, Marc 352
White, James Boyd 64, 299, 306
Whorf, Benjamin Lee 389
Will (of interpreter) 374
Will to power 31, 313, 315–22
Windsor, Matthew 3–33
Wittgenstein, Ludwig 21–2, 320, 322–3, 330,
    361, 365–7, 375–6, 389
World Health Organization Code
    on Marketing of Breast-Milk
    Substitutes 99
World Trade Organization 49–50, 98, 107,
    153, 160, 161, 164, 213–14, 256–7, 272,
    276, 282, 299

Yasseen, Mustafa 200, 202

Zarbiyev, Fuad 31, 251–67
Zidar, Andraž 29, 133–46

Printed and bound by CPI Group (UK) Ltd, Croydon, CR0 4YY